Contents

W9-AZV-825

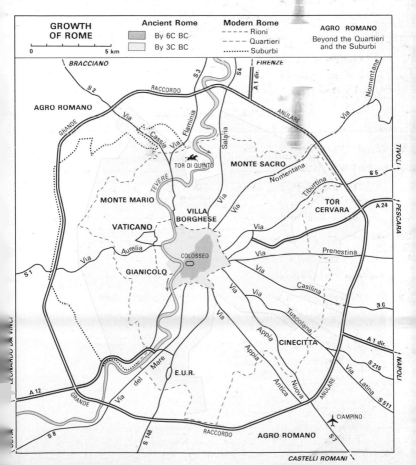

GROWTH OF ROME

0 — 5 km

Ancient Rome
By 6C BC
By 3C BC

Modern Rome
---- Rioni
---- Quartieri
.... Suburbi

AGRO ROMANO
Beyond the Quartieri and the Suburbi

BRACCIANO

AGRO ROMANO

MONTE SACRO

MONTE MARIO

VILLA BORGHESE

VATICANO

TOR CERVARA

COLOSSEO

GIANICOLO

CINECITTÀ

E.U.R.

AGRO ROMANO

CASTELLI ROMANI

R. An. 1

1

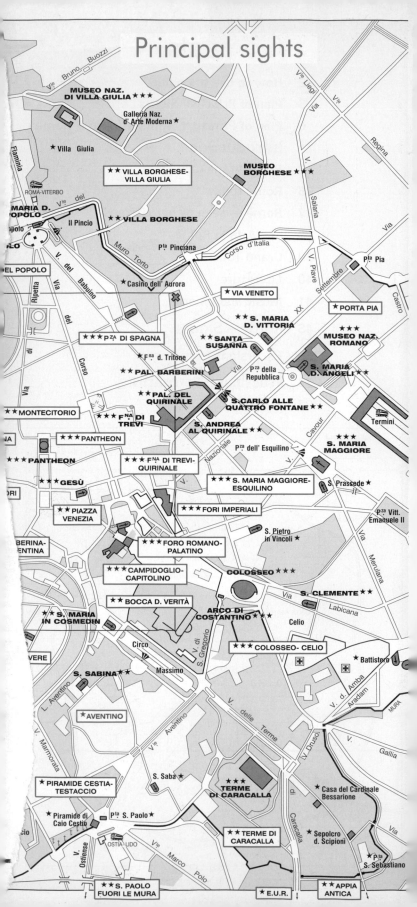

Principal sights

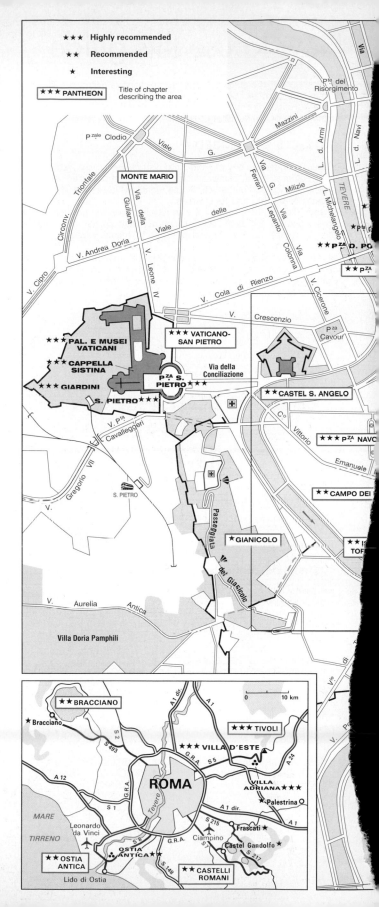

How to use this guide

The first part of the guide contains several chapters giving details about various aspects of the city of Rome. They provide the sort of practical and background information which visitors find it useful to read before leaving home or while visiting the city.

DISTRICTS DESCRIBED

The guide divides the city of Rome into districts which are identified by their traditional Italian names and listed in alphabetical order.
In each district the guide selects the sights which reveal the varied character of the city and its environs.
For each district there is a local plan which shows the position of the sights identified by their Italian names as they appear on the local signs; there are also recommended routes to follow, except in certain cases.
The text is supplemented by detailed plans of monuments, museums and archeological sites. At the end of each chapter there is a list of the neighbouring districts so that readers can see if there are other interesting sights within walking distance.

Districts described in the sights sections

★★ APPIA ANTICA
★ AVENTINO
★★ BOCCA DELLA VERITÀ
★★★ CAMPIDOGLIO – CAPITOLINO
★★ CAMPO DEI FIORI
★★ CASTEL SANT'ANGELO
★ CATACOMBE DI PRISCILLA
★★★ COLOSSEO – CELIO
★ EUR
★★★ FONTANA DI TREVI – QUIRINALE
★★★ FORI IMPERIALI
★★★ FORO ROMANO – PALATINO
★ GIANICOLO
★★ ISOLA TIBERINA – TORRE ARGENTINA
★★ MONTECITORIO MONTE MARIO
★★★ PANTHEON

★★★ PIAZZA NAVONA
★★ PIAZZA DEL POPOLO
★★★ PIAZZA DI SPAGNA
★★ PIAZZA VENEZIA
★ PIRAMIDE CESTIA – TESTACCIO
★ PORTA PIA
★★★ SAN GIOVANNI IN LATERANO
★ SAN LORENZO FUORI LE MURA
★★ SAN PAOLO FUORI LE MURA
★★★ SANTA MARIA MAGGIORE – ESQUILINO
★★ TERME DI CARACALLA
★★ TRASTEVERE
★★★ VATICANO – SAN PIETRO
★ VIA VENETO
★★ VILLA BORGHESE – VILLA GIULIA

Excursions from Rome

★★ BRACCIANO
★★ CASTELLI ROMANI

★★ OSTIA ANTICA
★★★ TIVOLI

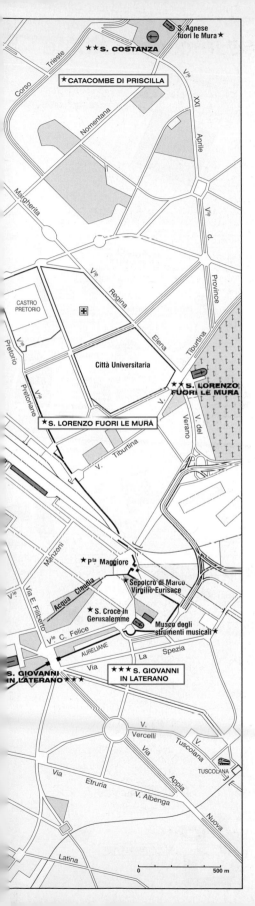

THOSE INTERESTED IN...

Ancient Rome   *should VISIT...*

- Roman Forum and the Palatine
- Colosseum and Constantine's Arch
- Castel Sant'Angelo
- Pantheon
- Imperial Fora
- Old Appian Way
- Baths of Caracalla
- Hadrian's Villa at Tivoli
- Ostia
- Masterpieces of Classical art in the museums:
    Palazzo dei Conservatori
    Capitoline
    National Roman
    Vatican
    Villa Giulia
See "Classical Rome" itinerary

Early Christian Rome:

- Santa Maria Maggiore
- Lateran District
- Caelian Hill churches
- Church of St Paul Without the Walls
- Catacombs
- Christian mosaics in churches:
    Santa Maria Maggiore
    Santa Costanza
    St Cosmas and St Damian
    Santa Maria in Dominica
    Santa Maria in Trastevere
    St Clement's Basilica
See "Early Christian Rome" itinerary

Renaissance Rome:

- Architectural masterpieces in:
    Piazza del Campidoglio
    Palazzo Farnese
    Palazzo della Cancelleria
    Villa d'Este, Tivoli
- Interior décor:
    Sistine Chapel
    Raphael's Rooms
    Borgia Apartment
    Nicholas V's Chapel
    Villa Farnesina
- Sculptural masterpieces:
    Michelangelo's *Pietà*
    Michelangelo's *Moses*
- Museum church:
    Santa Maria del Popolo
See "Renaissance and Mannerist Rome"

Baroque Rome:

- Bernini's work:
    St Peter's Square
    St Peter's Chair and Baldaquin
    Ecstasy of St Teresa in Santa Maria della Vittoria
    Sculpture in the Borghese Museum
    Sant'Andrea al Quirinale
    Fiumi Fountain
- Borromini's work:
    San Carlo alle Quattro Fontane
    St Ivo's Church
- Trevi Fountain
- Caravaggio's work:
    Santa Maria del Popolo
    San Luigi dei Francesi
    Borghese Museum
    Vatican Picture Galleries
    St Augustine's Church
- Brother Andrea Pozzo's work:
    Ceiling frescoes in St Ignatius' Church
    St Ignatius' Chapel in the Gesù Church
See "Baroque Rome" itinerary

Panoramic viewpoints:

- Janiculum Hill
- Pincian Hill
- Dome of St Peter's Basilica
- Castel Sant'Angelo terrace

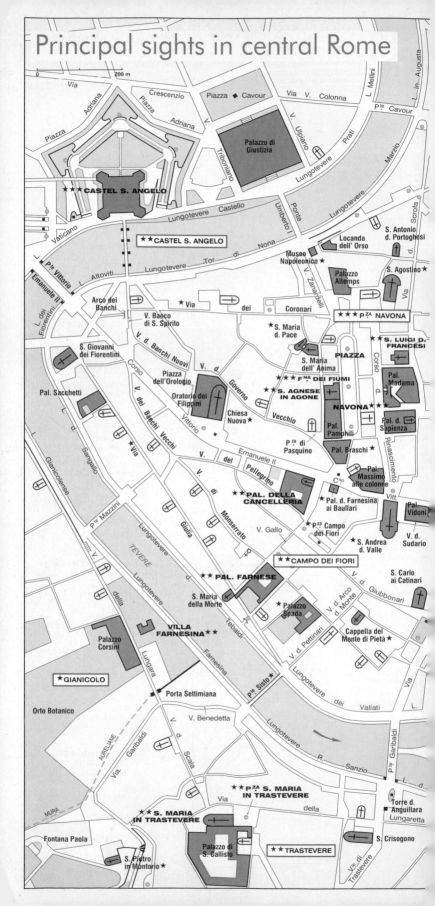
Principal sights in central Rome

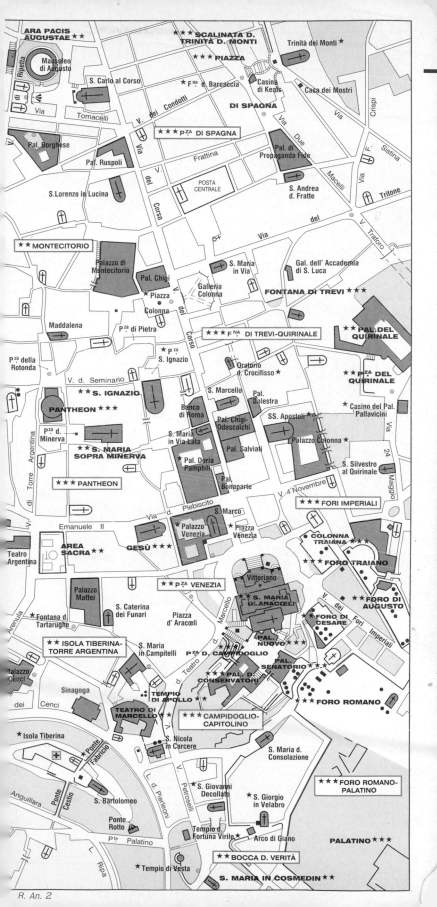

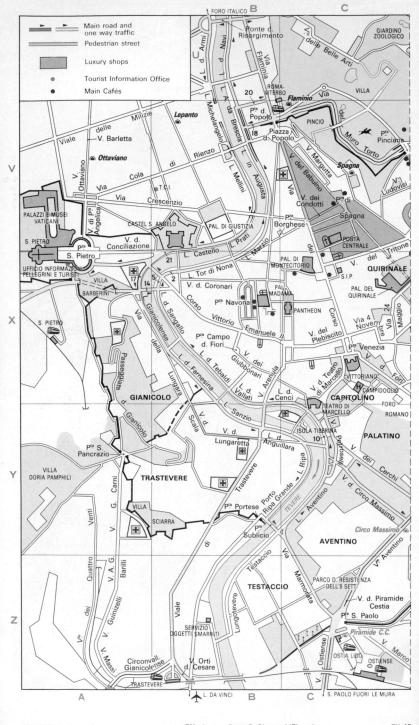

PUBLIC SERVICES

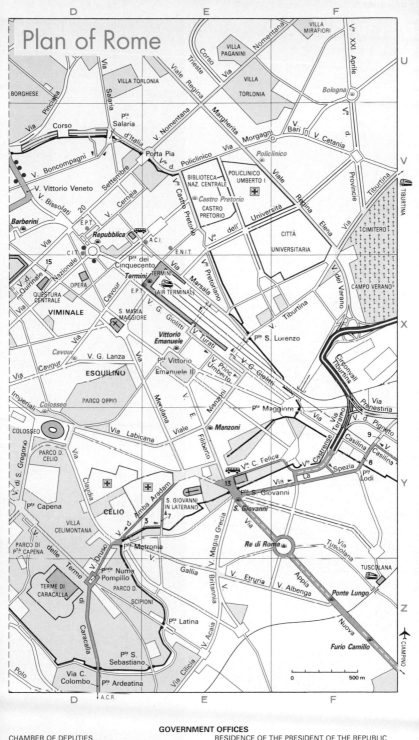

Plan of Rome

The Swiss Guards, who have been in the service of the Pope since 1506, form the armed corps of the Vatican State. They wear a distinctive and picturesque uniform, consisting of pantaloons gathered below the knee and a full-sleeved jacket, both in broad yellow, red and blue stripes, said to have been designed by Michelangelo. They are armed with a halbard and a sword.

Swiss Guard

Introduction

Rome in the past

MONARCHY (7523-509 BC)

753	Legendary foundation of Rome by **Romulus** on the Palatine Hill.
c8C BC	Union of the Latin and Sabine settlements on the hills **(Septimontium)**.
715-672	Reigns of three Sabine kings – Numa Pompilius, Tullus Hostilius, Ancus Martius.
616-509	Etruscan hegemony – Tarquin the Elder who laid out the Forum, Servius Tullius and Tarquin the Proud.
509	Etruscan yoke thrown off by Rome. Fall of the monarchy. Beginning of the Republic under patrician rule.

ROMAN REPUBLIC (509-27 BC)

The Republican era is marked by the struggle between the patricians and the plebeians. The secession of the plebeians in 493, which deprived the city of their labour and the army of their manpower, was provoked by the resistance of the patrician families *(gentes)* who were linked by religious ties and owned the greater part of the land most suitable for cultivation and stock rearing. This period saw the Roman conquest of the Italian peninsula and the Mediterranean basin. The increasing importance of the army promoted the generals who imposed their personality to the detriment of the Senate.

450	Nomination from among the plebeians of 10 tribunes, inviolable magistrates with the right of veto over all decisions.
440	Codification of the law in Twelve Tables.
395	Veia, the Estuscan capital, captured by the Romans.
390	Invasions of Rome by the Gauls.
366	Plebeians granted access to the consulship.
321	Romans defeated at the Claudine Forks by the Samnites from the southern Apennines.
312	Appius Claudius Caecus, censor and consul, after whom was named the Appian Way linking Rome and Capua.
295	Samnites defeated at Sentinum; central Italy under Roman control.
282-272	War against Tarentum and its ally, Pyrrhus, King of Epiros; Roman victory at Beneventum ensuring Roman domination of southern Italy.
264-241	**First Punic War** between Rome and Carthage for the possession of Sicily.
218-201	**Second Punic War** in the western Mediterranean.
218	March by Hannibal, a Carthaginian general, from Spain, over the Pyrenees and the Alps, to engage the Romans in battle.
217	Battle of Lake Trasimene in which Hannibal was victorious.
216	Romans crushed at Cannae near Bari.
210	Capture of Carthage and conquest of Spain (the first province to be annexed by Rome) by **Scipio Africanus.**
202	**Scipio Africanus** victorious at Zama, near Carthage; the western section of the Mediterranean basin under Roman control.
148-146	**Third Punic War** against Carthage.
146	Capture and destruction of Carthage.
133-121	Increasing dispute between the patricians and the plebeians; promulgation by the Gracchi, tribunes of the plebeians, of agrarian laws to distribute common land to the plebeians; assassination of the Gracchi brothers – Tiberius in 133 and Caius in 121 – ordered by the discontented Senate.

Caesar

Augustus

Tiberius

Museo Nazionale, Napoli-GIRAUDON

Museo Capitolino, Roma-S. Chirol

Musée du Louvre, Paris-Nimatallah/ARTEPHOT

121-109	Authoritarian government established by the senators.
107	**Marius,** military general who defeated Jugurtha of Numidia, the Cimbri and the Teutons, elected consul by the popular party against the Senate party.
92-89	First Civil War; rivalry between Marius and Sulla for command of the war against Mithridates.
88	**Sulla,** general, elected consul; height of power of the nobility and the Senate party.
82	Sulla as dictator.
79	Abdication of Sulla under pressure from the Senate.
73-71	Slave Revolt led by Spartacus put down by Crassus (6 000 prisoners crucified).
70	**Crassus** elected consul with **Pompey,** who defeated Mithridates in Asia Minor.
60	**First triumvirate** composed of Pompey, Caesar and Crassus.
59	**Caesar** as consul.
58-52	Defeat of the Gauls.
49-55	Second Civil War between the supporters of Caesar and Pompey.
49	Caesar as dictator.
48	Assassination of Pompey.
44	Assassination of Caesar on the Ides of March (15 March).
43	**Second triumvirate** composed of Octavian (in the west), Antony (in the east) and Lepidus (in Africa); assassination of Cicero.
31	Battle of **Actium** between the troops of Antony (married to Cleopatra) and the troops of Octavian, upholder of Roman tradition.
30	Capture of Egypt by Octavian; suicide of Antony and Cleopatra.
27	Octavian received the title **Augustus** and promoted a new political system which led to the Empire.

The historians of ancient Rome usually dated events as so many years from the founding of Rome - Ab Urbe Condita (AUC).
It was Dionysius Exiguus, a 6C Scythian monk living in Rome, who introduced a chronology based on the birth of Christ - Anno Domini (AD).

THE EARLY EMPIRE (27 BC-3C AD)

Julio-Claudian Emperors

Augustus (27-14 BC)	Augustus, Pontifex Maximus as Emperor and religious chief. **Livy** (59 BC-AD 17), historian; **Propertius** (47-15 BC), poet of despair; **Ovid** (43 BC-AD 17), writer of light verse, author of the *Metamorphoses,* a poem based on Greek fables. Roman victories in Germany (12-9 BC) under **Drusus** (38-9 BC), adopted son of Augustus and military chief, the first Roman to reach the Elbe.
Tiberius (14 BC-37)	Good administrator. Roman army at war in Germany under the generalship of **Germanicus** (15 BC-19), son of Drusus.
27	Tiberius settled in Capri.
29	**Jesus** condemned to death.
Caligula (37-41)	Assassination of **Caligula,** a violent madman.
Claudius (41-54)	Definition of the role of his wives, Messalina and Agrippina.
Nero (54-68)	**Nero,** adopted by Claudius in 50, initially a good governor under the influence of **Seneca** (c4 BC-65), philosopher and politician, whom he later forced to commit suicide.
64	Violent repression of Christians after the destruction of much of Rome by fire; martyrdom of St Peter and St Paul.
68-69	Succession disputed: reigns of Galba, Otho and Vitellius.

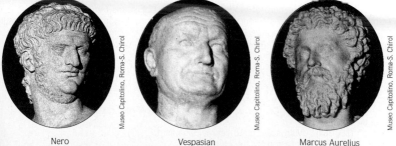

Nero   Vespasian   Marcus Aurelius

Flavian Emperors

Vespasian (69-79)	Order re-established in the Empire; great works in Rome including the Colosseum.
Titus (79-81)	Son of Vespasian.
79	Eruption of **Vesuvius**; destruction of Pompei, Herculaneum, Stabia and Oplontis. **Pliny the Elder** (23-79), author of a Natural History in 37 volumes, described the eruption of Vesuvius and was killed by venturing too close.
Domitian (81-96)	Son of Vespasian. Pontificate of Clement I (88-97).
95	Persecution of Christians.

Antonine Emperors, high point of the Empire

Nerva (96-98)	**Martial** (*c*40-*c*104), satirical poet.
Trajan (98-117)	First provincial Emperor; repression of the Dacians recorded on Trajan's Column; the Roman Empire reached it greatest extent. **Tacitus** (*c*55-*c*150), politician and writer. **Pliny the Younger** (62-*c*114), politician and writer. **Apollodorus of Damascus** (677-*c*129), architect to Trajan and Hadrian.
Hadrian (117-138)	Promotion of peace and construction of fortifications to defend the boundaries *(limes)* of the Empire. **Juvenal** (*c*60-*c*140), poet who pilloried society.
Antoninus Pius (138-161)	**Suetonius** (c69-c125), historian who recorded the lives of the Emperors.
Marcus Aurelius (161-180)	Stoic philosopher and statesman. **Apuleius** (125-*c*180), philosopher, famous for writing the *Golden Ass,* a Latin romance.
Commodus (180-192)	

Severan Emperors

Septimius-Severus (193-211)	Pontificate of Zephyrinus (199-217).
202	Edict forbidding conversion to Christianity.
Caracalla (211-217)	Reasonable ruler.
212	Edict granting Roman citizenship to all free men in the Empire. **Tertullian** (*c*155-*c*220), a model of eloquence, wrote in defence of Christianity and attacked luke-warm adherents.
Elagabalus (218-222)	**Origen** (*c*182-*c*253), a Christian writer.
Alexander Severus (222-235)	Following his death a period of **anarchy,** during which most emperors were proclaimed by their soldiers and died by assassination. Fragmentation of the Empire under invasion by German tribes in the north and other tribes in the east.
Decius (249-251)	Pontificate of Fabian (236-250).
250	Persecution of Christians.
Valerian (253-260)	Christian worship forbidden; sacrifice to the gods made obligatory. Valerian died a prisoner of the Persians.
Aurelian (270-275)	Re-unification of the Empire and construction of a new wall of enclosure round Rome.

LATER EMPIRE (3C - 4C)

Diocletian (284-305)	Institution of the **tetrarchy,** rule by four: in the east Diocletian, who
293	transferred the capital to Nicomedia where he lived, assisted by Galerius (293-311), who transferred the capital to Mitrovizza; in the west Maximian (286-305), who lived in Milan, assisted by Constantius-Chlorus (293-306), who lived in Trier in Germany.
303	Systematic and ruthless persecution of Christians by Diocletian. Pontificate of Marcellinus (296-304).
311	Freedom of worship granted to Christians by Galerius.
Constantine (306-337)	Chlorus's son, Constantine, defeated Maximian's son, Maxentius,
312	and became **Emperor in the west.**
313	**Edict of Milan** granting freedom of worship to all and official recognition to Christianity.
324	Re-unification of the Empire.
330	Transfer of the capital to Byzantium, which was renamed Constantinople. Following Constantine's death, re-division of the Empire among his three sons.
325	First Council of the church held in Nicea.
Julian the Apostate (360-363)	Vain attempt to revive paganism.
375	Invasion by the Huns.

| Theodosius (379-395) 391 | Edict against paganism issued under the influence of St Ambrose, Bishop of Milan; following the Emperor's death, division of the Empire between his two sons – Arcadius in the east and Honorius in the west in Ravenna. |
| 386 | Conversion to Christianity of **St Augustine** (354-430), the most authoritarian of the fathers of the Church, author of the *City of God* and of *Confessions*. |

INVASIONS (5C-6C)

410	Rome sacked by Alaric, King of the Visigoths.
455	Rome sacked by Genseric, King of the Vandals, who landed in Ostia.
476	Romulus Augustolus deposed by Odoacer, King of the Heruli: **end of the Roman Empire in the west.**
493	Ostrogoths settled in Italy.
Justinian (527-565)	Emperor of Byzantium, expulsion of the Ostrogoths from Rome.
568	Lombard invasion.

PAPAL CENTURIES (6C-19C)

Gregory I (590-604)	End of western Empire; Rome officially subject to the Emperor in Byzantium, who was represented in Ravenna by an exarch; Rome in fact defended and sustained by the Pope, who was resident in the city.
Stephen II (752-757) 752	Rome threatened by the Lombards; Stephen II appealed for help to Pepin the Short.
756	Donation of Quiersy-sur-Oise *(see Index)*; **birth of the Papal States.**
800	**Charlemagne,** conqueror and then King of the Lombards, crowned Emperor of Rome by Leo III.
9C	Disintegration of the Carolingian Empire; transfer of the papacy into the hands of powerful families: Theophylacti, Crescenzi (10C) and the Counts of Tuscany (early 11C).
John XII (955-964) 962	Appeal by John XII to Otho I, King of the Saxons, who became King of the Lombards. As Emperor of the Holy Roman Empire, Otho controlled the church in Germany and Italy through Earl-Bishops and established that a pope could not be elected without the consent of the Emperor.
Stephen IX (1057-58) 1057	Stephen IX elected Pope without the Emperor's approval.
Gregory VII (1073-85) 1075	Declaration by Gregory VII that laymen could not make ecclesiastical appointments; beginning of the **Investiture Controversy,** a conflict between the papacy and the Emperor. Invasion of Rome by Henry IV (1084).
Calixtus II (1119-24) 1122	**Concordat of Worms;** renunciation of the power of investiture by the emperor.
Innocent II (1130-43) 1130-1155	Attempt by Arnaldo da Brescia to institute a republic in Rome in defiance of the Pope.
Eugenius III (1145-53) 1153	Pope protected by Frederick Barbarossa under the Treaty of Constance; Arnaldo da Brescia captured and hanged; new conflict between the Pope and the Emperor; Rome fortified with towers *(Roma turrita)* built by powerful families, some supporters of the Pope and some of the Emperor.
Adrian IV (1154-59) Innocent III (1198-1216)	
1309-1377	Popes resident in Avignon.
1347	Rome dominated by Cola di Rienzo.
1378-1417	**Great Schism of the West** – Two popes reigned simultaneously, one in Rome and one in Avignon in France; in 1409 there was a third in Pisa.
Martin V (1417-31) 1417	The papacy returned to Rome.
Nicholas V (1447-55) 1453	Constantinople captured by the Turks; **end of the eastern Empire.**
Alexander VI (1492-1503) 1494	Charles VIII, en route for Naples, entered Rome but was expelled from Italy by a coalition which included Alexander VI.

1498-1502	Papacy at war with the Italian states; conquest of the Romagna by Caesar Borgia, son of Alexander VI, with the assistance of Louis XII installed in the Milan area.
Julius II (1503-13) **1508-1512**	Julius II at war in order to retain Romagna, with the assistance of Louis XII, and to expel Louis XII.
Leo X (1513-21) **1517**	Publication of the Lutheran thesis, the basis of the **Reformation.**
Clement VII (1523-34) **6 May 1527**	Rome sacked by the troops of Charles V.

Julius II by Raphael (Uffizi, Florence)

Galleria degli Uffizi, Firenze/GIRAUDON

Paul III (1534-49) **1545-1563**	**Council of Trent;** birth of the **Counter-Reformation.**
Julius III (1550-55) **Marcellus II (1555)** **Paul IV (1555-59)** **Pius IV (1559-65)** **Pius V (1566-72)** **1571**	Battle of **Lepanto** in which the Turks were defeated by the Christians; Pius V foresaw the result in a vision before the news reached Rome.
Paul V (1605-21) **1618-1648**	Thirty Years War caused by political and religious questions.
Gregory XV (1621-23) **Urban VIII (1623-44)** **Innocent X (1644-55)** **Pius VI (1775-99)** **1791**	Renunciation by the Papacy of Avignon and the Comtat-Venaissin which are annexed to France.
1797	**Treaty of Tolentino** between the Pope and Napoleon Bonaparte.
1798	Rome occupied by French troops; Roman republic proclaimed. Pius VI driven from Rome; died in exile in Valence.
Pius VII (1800-23) **1800**	Pius VII elected in Venice; returned to Rome.
1801	Concordat between Pius VII and Napoleon.
1805-1806	Disagreement between Pius VII and Napoleon over the annulment of the marriage of Jerome Bonaparte; Pius VII refused to apply the continental blockade.
1808	Rome occupied by the French; Pius VII confined in Savona (1809) and then at Fontainebleau.
1814	Pius VII returned to Rome.

CAPITAL OF ITALY

1820-1861	Struggle for the unification of the Italian states. Kingdom of Italy proclaimed with Turin as its capital and Victor Emmanuel II as its king; Papal State reduced to the suburbs of Rome.
1846-78	Pontificate of **Pius IX.**
1869	First Vatican Council convenes.
1870	Rome proclaimed capital of the kingdom; Law of Guarantees proposed to the Holy See but refused by the Pope who retired into the Vatican.
1914-22	Pontificate of **Benedict XV.**
28-29 October 1922	Fascist march on Rome.
1922-39	Pontificate of **Pius XI.**
1926	Mussolini head of the government.
1929	Lateran Treaty.
1939-1958	Pontificate of **Pius XII.**

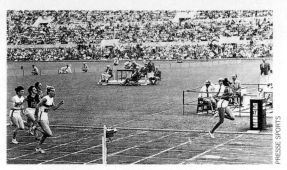

1960 Olympic Games: Wilma Rudolph wins the 200m

PRESSE SPORTS

19 July 1943	Rome under bombardment.
4 June 1944	Rome liberated.
June 1946	Republic established after a referendum; Italy divided into 20 regions; Rome nominated as the capital of Lazio (ancient Latium).
1957	Treaty of Rome setting up the Common Market (now the European Union).
1958-63	Pontificate of **John XXIII**.
1960	Olympic Games held in Rome.
1962-1965	Second Vatican Council.
1963-78	Pontificate of **Paul VI**.
1978-present	Pontificate of **John Paul II**, first foreign Pope for centuries, formerly Cardinal Karol Wojtyla, bishop of Cracow in Poland.
1994	Second Republic.

Rome in Antiquity

FOUNDING OF ROME

Legendary origins: Venus and Mars – According to the Roman historians and poets (Livy in his Roman History, Virgil in the Aeneid), Aeneas, son of the goddess Venus and the mortal Anchises, fled from Troy when it was captured, landed at the mouth of the Tiber and married Lavinia, the King of Latium's daughter. He defeated Turnus, the chief of the Rutules, with the aid of Evander, the founder of Pallantea on the Palatine, and founded Lavinium (now Pratica di Mare). On Aeneas' death, his son Ascanius (or Iulus) left Lavinia in charge of Lavinium and went off to found Alba Longa *(see Index)*. The last king of this Alban dynasty was Amulius who deposed his brother Numitor and placed the latter's daughter, Rhea Silvia with the Vestals. Her union with the god Mars gave birth to the twins Romulus and Remus whom Amulius tried to eliminate by abandoning them on the Tiber. The river however was in flood and the twins came to rest at the foot of the Palatine where they were nursed by a wolf and brought up by a couple of shepherds, Faustulus and Larentia. When they reached adolescence they reinstated their grandfather Numitor on the throne of Alba and left to found a new town where they had spent their childhood. There they consulted the birds to discover the omens and Romulus marked a furrow around the sacred area on which the new city was to be built. Jesting, Remus stepped over the line; Romulus killed him for violating the sacred precinct *(pomerium)*. These events took place on the Palatine in about 753 BC. Romulus populated his village with outlaws who settled on the Capitol and he provided them with Sabine wives. An alliance grew between the two peoples who were ruled by a succession of kings, alternately Sabine and Latin, until the Etruscans arrived.

Historical origins – Livy and Virgil, who chronicled the earliest days of Rome, and Cicero and Dionysius of Halicarnassus, who commented on the period of the monarchy, were writing in the Augustan age, some seven centuries after the events which they described. Modern historians have therefore been obliged to turn to archeology and epigraphy to retrace the birth of Rome and identify the legendary aspects of the

The Wolf suckling Romulus and Remus

Da una foto Gab. Fot. Naz.

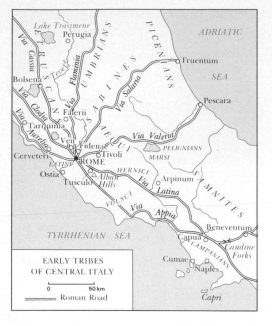

EARLY TRIBES OF CENTRAL ITALY

0   50 km

═══ Roman Road

city's early years. They have distinguished the true facts from the picturesque embellishments inspired by excessive patriotism. They also take into considera- tion the theory that Livy's account may be based on Indo-European myths which reflect a conception of society being divided into three classes: priests, soldiers and workers.

A favourable site – The lower Tiber valley was occupied by the Etruscans to the northwest (on the right bank) and by the Latins and Sabines to the south and northeast (on the left bank). The hills on the left bank, shaped by erosion of the volcanic lava-flows from the Alban hills (Monti Albani), made excellent defensive posi- tions: particularly the Pala- tine, its steep sides rising from the surrounding marshy ground and its twin peaks giving a clear view of the Tiber. This site was moreover an ideal staging-post on the salt road (Via Salaria) between the salt pans at the mouth of the Tiber and the Sabine country. These favourable features no doubt led to the development of Sabine and Latin settlements around the Palatine.

In the 6C BC the Etruscans embarked on a campaign to conquer Campania; they crossed the Tiber by the bridge provided by the Latin and Sabine settlements, already established as a 'fortress' at the point where the marshy and alluvial plain is relatively easy to cross. It was then that Rome began to develop into a city.

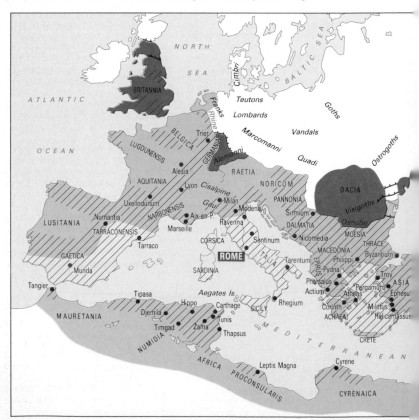

CAPITAL OF THE EMPIRE

It was, no doubt, desire for extra territory and fear of other peoples strong enough to constitute a threat, that drove the Romans out of their village on the Palatine to found an empire. The newly acquired territory had to be defended so the Romans were continually at war. They were also attracted by the desire for gain (booty for the soldiers, new lands to be exploited, taxes to be paid by the subject people) and by the desire for the glory of victory.

Exceptional men – **Julius Caesar** (101-44 BC), soldier and statesman, orator and writer, is a remarkable example of a determined character. His policies and actions were instrumental in the establishment of the Roman Empire.

He proved his amazing capacity for taking decisions while he was still very young; he was captured by pirates near Miletus in the Aegean; on regaining his liberty he raised a fleet against them and wiped them out. According to a speech he made from the Rostra on the occasion of his aunt Julia's funeral he was descended from Venus. While consul in 59 he showed his desire to have his own way by reducing the second consul Bibulus to silence; this was so marked that "certain facetious people... wrote... not of the consulate of Caesar and Bibulus – but – of the consulate of Julius and Caesar" (Suetonius). In 58 he became Governor of Cisalpine Gaul and of Provincia (later Narbonese Gaul); by 51 he had conquered the whole of Gaul, although the Gauls were thought to be invincible. In January 49 he crossed the Rubicon and marched on Rome against the official powers; Pompey, who had been sole consul since 52, and the Senate fled. Civil war followed. Pompey's army was defeated at Pharsalus in Greece; Pompey was murdered in Egypt.

Early in 44 Caesar was appointed consul and dictator for life; he minted money bearing his effigy, gave his name to the month of his birth (July), pardoned his enemies and weakened the power of the senators by reducing their number to 900. The Republic disintegrated. On 15 March 44 BC (the Ides of March) when the Senate was expected to grant Caesar the title of King of the Orient he was stabbed to death by a group of senators.

His death was followed by the rise of **Octavian**, the son of Caesar's niece, whom he had adopted as his heir in his will. This young man of 29, who had delicate health and had won no military glory, was to demonstrate great self-control, tenacity of purpose and political genius.

Opposing him was Marc-Antony, consul with Caesar and pretender to the succession. Octavian first weakened his adversary and then became his ally and together with Lepidus, Caesar's cavalry general, they formed the second triumvirate (43 BC). In 13 BC Lepidus died; there remained Antony who was discredited in the eyes of the Romans for repudiating Octavia, Octavian's sister, and marrying Queen Cleopatra of Egypt. Octavian attacked Cleopatra. His victory at Actium in Greece in 31 BC led to Antony's suicide and then to Cleopatra's when she realised that Octavian intended to parade her with the war booty in his victory procession.

In 27 BC the Senate granted Octavian the title Augustus which invested him with an aura of holiness. A new regime was thus born, the Principate. While maintaining the appearance of Republican government, **Octavian-Augustus** gradually transferred to his own person the political, religious and judicial powers and became the first Roman Emperor. His achievements were considerable: he restored peace to the known world, re-organised society which had broken down and divided Rome into 14 districts *(see map Rome during the Empire)*. The end of his life was saddened by the conduct of his daughter and grand-daughter, both called Julia, whom he banned from the family tomb. Suetonius records that on his death bed he asked his friends whether "he had played the farce of life well to the very end". "If the play has pleased you, applaud it and all together show your joy."

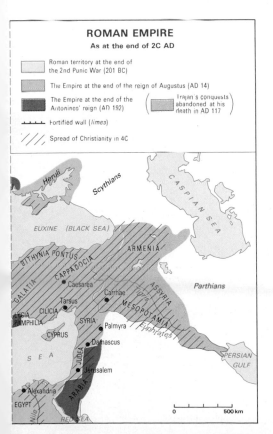

ROMAN EMPIRE
As at the end of 2C AD

Roman territory at the end of the 2nd Punic War (201 BC)

The Empire at the end of the reign of Augustus (AD 14)

The Empire at the end of the Antoninos' reign (AD 192)

Trajan's conquests abandoned at his death in AD 117

Fortified wall (*limes*)

Spread of Christianity in 4C

19

ROME
DURING THE EMPIRE

(from 1C BC to 4C AD)

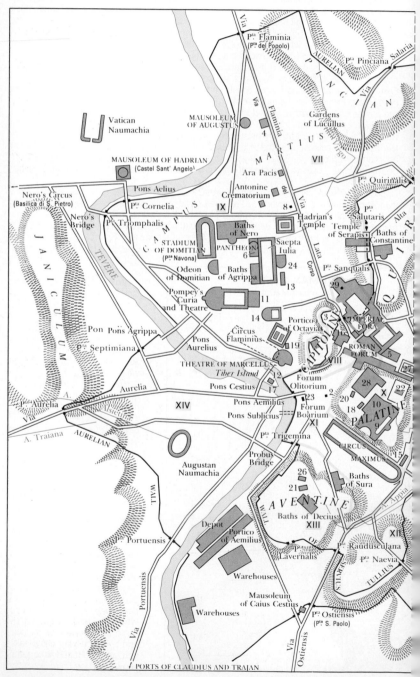

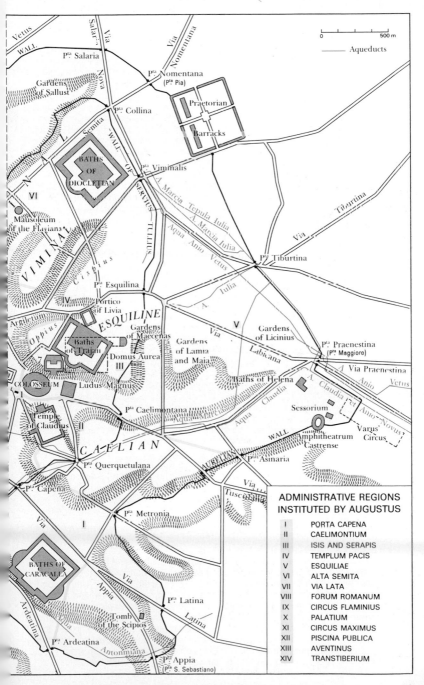

ADMINISTRATIVE REGIONS
INSTITUTED BY AUGUSTUS

I	PORTA CAPENA
II	CAELIMONTIUM
III	ISIS AND SERAPIS
IV	TEMPLUM PACIS
V	ESQUILIAE
VI	ALTA SEMITA
VII	VIA LATA
VIII	FORUM ROMANUM
IX	CIRCUS FLAMINIUS
X	PALATIUM
XI	CIRCUS MAXIMUS
XII	PISCINA PUBLICA
XIII	AVENTINUS
XIV	TRANSTIBERIUM

DAILY LIFE IN ANCIENT ROME

Political and social life – From the earliest times Roman society was traditionally divided into two main classes. The class to which a person belonged was determined by birth. The **patricians** were the privileged class participating in the government of the state; the **plebeians**, who had no rights at all, were excluded from public office. The patricians owned a great many slaves, who were the lowest order in the population, but they could be granted their freedom by their masters. At the time of the Roman Republic, when the division of the classes was based on wealth, plebeians who grew rich began to enter the world of politics. Power was invested in two **consuls**, who held office for one year. The **Senate**, composed of members who were appointed for life and who, from the 4C BC, were also drawn from the plebeian class, established itself as a consultative assembly with the authority to make laws. The provinces conquered by the Roman legions were administered by praetors, propraetors and proconsuls. During the Empire, the powers exercised by the consuls were united in the person of the **Emperor**, who was responsible for appointing senators and, as head of the army, for declaring peace or war. During the late Empire, these powers became absolute.

Religion – Rome drew on all mythological sources for her deities; the 12 main gods and goddesses were the same in number, if not always in name, as their Greek counterparts on Mount Olympus. **Jupiter** *(Zeus in Greek)*, senior god and ruler of the heavens, the elements and light, is often shown with an eagle, holding a thunderbolt and wearing a crown. **Juno** *(Hera)*, his wife, protectress of womanhood and marriage, is shown with a peacock and a pomegranate. **Minerva** *(Athena)*, goddess of wisdom, is represented by an owl. She is the third member of the Capitoline Triad together with Juno and Jupiter, her father, from whose head she sprang fully armed, and is often shown with a shield and a helmet. **Apollo**, god of beauty, the sun and the arts, sings to a lyre accompaniment and carries a bow like his sister **Diana** *(Artemis)*, goddess of hunting, chastity and the moon (she wears a crescent moon on her head). The animal representing Diana is the doe. **Mercury** *(Hermes)*, protector of commerce and travel, wears winged sandals and carries a staff (caduceus) in his hand. **Vulcan** *(Hephaistos)*, god of fire, works in a forge with an anvil and hammer. **Vesta**, goddess of the hearth, carries a simple flame as a symbol of fire in the home. **Mars** *(Aries)*, god of war, is identified by his weapons and his helmet. **Venus** *(Aphrodite)*, goddess of love and goodness, is represented by a dove. Born out of the foam of the sea, she is often represented standing in a shell or surrounded by sea deities such as **Neptune** *(Poseidon)*, god of the sea armed with a trident. **Ceres** *(Demeter)*, protectress of the earth, tillage and corn and fecundity, is represented with a sheaf of corn and a scythe.

Public worship was held in the temples but people also worshipped the various household gods *(lares et penates)* in their own homes. Many houses had a sort of shrine **(lararium)** where offerings were made to the souls of ancestors.

Cult of the dead – Burial sites in Rome were located outside the city walls; the roads leading into the city were often lined with tombs.

Romans practised both burial and cremation. The oldest inhumations were, in the case of burial, in a **pit tomb** *(fossa)* dug to accommodate a full-length sarcophagus possibly carved from a tree-trunk and, in the case of cremation, in a **shaft tomb** *(pozzo)*, a small hole in the ground in which the amphora or urn containing the ashes was placed; the container was often in the shape of a small house. Etruscan influence brought about an increase in the practice of burial – during the Republic tombs with several chambers were built where the sarcophagi were placed. The most common and elementary way of indicating a tomb was to erect a **memorial tablet** *(cippus)*, a simple block of stone bearing an inscription. More elaborately worked memorials with a greater level of decoration, made of stone or marble were called **steles** *(steli)*. Mausoleums were the prerogative of wealthy families.

Much later, large underground communal chambers **(colombarium)** became the popular form of burial for the poor and for slaves. The walls were lined with small recesses in which the urns were placed. The dead person was often "accompanied" on his journey to the other world with clothing, weapons, tools, jewellery (for a woman) and playthings (for a child) to be used in the new existence.

Housing – Houses built by the Romans were of three types: multi-storey buildings **(insula)** containing several dwellings; small houses for the middle classes; the large-scale residential house **(domus)** for the upper classes. Although in the luxury bracket, these patrician houses were modest as the walls were simple and lacked windows. These early houses contained a large rectangular room *(atrium)* with an open roof in the centre which allowed rain water *(pluvial)* to be collected in a basin *(impluvium)*. This atrium contained the room where the head of the family worked and received visitors, as well as other smaller rooms. Top-ranking officials, wealthy farmers and prosperous merchants had a second house, built in a more elegant Greek style, which was reserved for the family. It was used only at certain times of the year and consisted of rooms built round various atria and a colonnaded courtyard *(peristylium)* with a garden or sometimes a fishpond in the centre. In the dining room *(triclinium)*, guests sat in a semi-reclining position on couches arranged around the table.

After his death he was deified by the Senate and his cult was associated with the cult of Rome and propagated throughout the Empire. In time his reign came to be called the "Augustan era".

Among Augustus' successors there were those who were motivated by cruelty and by hatred of the human race. Such a one was **Tiberius,** son-in-law to Augustus who chose him as his successor against his better judgment following the premature death of his two grandsons Caius and Lucius Caesar. **Caligula** was a psychiatric case: he liked to flatten mountains and raise valleys and hoped for a massacre, a famine or a cataclysm to make his reign memorable in posterity; when the news of his assassination first broke, no one dared rejoice for fear of a trap. After suffering a stroke **Claudius** became very slow-witted: "on seeing his funeral, he realised that he was dead" said Seneca. **Nero** was a monster who saw himself as a man of the theatre; "what an artist will perish with me!" he said as he committed suicide.

This succession of disasters came to an end with **Vespasian** who was a good Emperor, concerned for the security of the Empire. His sense of economy led to the installation of public urinals for which the user paid, thus cleansing the streets and providing funds to the exchequer. His son Titus was offended that the State should receive revenue from such a source but the Emperor replied that funds raised in this way had no smell. Titus, who was known as the love and delight of the human race, reigned only two years while his brother **Domitian** was responsible for 15 years of misery.

The reign of the **Antonines** earned the title "golden age" and marked the apogee of the Empire. The Antonines included **Trajan,** the "best of Emperors". He was a Spaniard, the first Emperor to come from the provinces, intelligent and energetic. He carried out great public works: building a forum, enlarging the port of Ostia, laying the Via Trajana from Beneventum to Brindisi, constructing a bridge in Alcantara and an aqueduct in Segovia. These projects were largely financed by the gold he amassed from his conquests in Dacia. He also led campaigns against the Parthians and penetrated as far as the Persian Gulf so that the Empire should profit from the trade between the Far East and the Mediterranean. In 117 he died of exhaustion while returning to Rome. He was succeeded by **Hadrian,** an indefatigable traveller and passionate Hellenist, who toured the Empire from 121 to 125, visited Africa in 128 and journeyed in the Orient from 128 to 134. He was almost always away from Rome but he set up a remarkable administrative system which was capable of working in his absence.

CHRISTIAN ROME

As the old order passed away, under attack by barbarians from without and undermined from within by the combined effects of a powerful army, the concentration of authority in the hands of one man, economic misery and moral collapse, a new force – Christianity – emerged.

It had first reached Rome in the reign of Augustus. When Paul arrived in about AD 60 there was already a Christian community in existence, although its founder is unknown. There had probably been Christians in Rome since the reign of Claudius (41-54). Suetonius tells how Claudius expelled the Jews who had revolted at the instigation of one Chrestos; Christianity had its roots in Judaism and at first Jews and Christians were confused with one another.

As the Empire crumbled and the world fell into disarray, Christianity preached a new doctrine of brotherly love and the hope of happiness after death. During the last years of the 1C and the early years of the 2C the Christian church became organised. A collection of texts written at this period by the Apostolic Fathers explains that the Church consisted of deacons who were responsible for providing for the material needs of the community and presbyters whose responsibilities were spiritual and liturgical, with a bishop at the head of each community. Christians met and celebrated the Eucharist in the private house of a convert which was known as a **titulus.**

From the beginning Christians found themselves outside the law because the Emperor was also the chief priest (Pontifex Maximus); to show his loyalty to the State every citizen had to worship the pagan gods. The first violent persecution in Rome was started by Nero *(see SAN-PAOLO-FUORI-LE-MURA)* in 64. Trajan recommended that the Christians should not be hounded systematically but that only the most obstinate should be punished. Decius (249-51) and Valerian (253-60), whose reigns were periods of pure anarchy, tried to restore a semblance of unity to the Empire by forcing the Christians to sacrifice to the gods. Under Diocletian (284-305) the repression was extended and reinforced, particularly against the upper classes in society.

It was not until the **Edict of Milan** (313) and the conversion of Constantine (314) that the Church could come out into the open and that Christianity emerged victorious over all attempts to bring back paganism. Theodosius (379-95) was the first Emperor to refuse the title of Pontifex Maximus and in his reign under the influence of Ambrose, Bishop of Milan, Christianity appeared as the state religion. St Jerome (347?-420), Father of the Church and adviser to Pope Damasus, translated the Bible into Latin (the "Vulgate").

As the organisation of the Church evolved, there was soon one bishop at the head of several communities and the idea arose that the first bishop of each community had been appointed by an apostle. The Bishop of Rome *(see VATICANO-SAN PIETRO)* claimed primacy. For 19 centuries the popes at the head of the Roman Church have influenced the history of Christianity.

A reforming pope – At the end of a period when several popes died of poison if they had not already succumbed to the blows of a cuckolded husband, when the papal tiara was quite shamelessly bought and sold and when Rome had an appalling reputation, **Gregory VII** (1073-85) addressed himself to two scourges which were undermining the Church: the buying and selling of church property and the marriage of the clergy. During the declining years of Charlemagne's Empire it had become current practice for a local lord to expropriate an archbishopric, a see, an abbey or a parish so as to protect them and for the clergy to buy them. Once in possession the clergy took wives so as to pass on their property to their children or transformed their houses into virtual courts.

In February 1075 Gregory VII issued a series of decrees against these abuses which started the Investiture Controversy. Outnumbered by the Emperor Henry IV's German soldiery, the Pope retreated to the Castel Sant'Angelo and called on the mercenary Robert Guiscard for assistance. Rome suffered terribly from pillaging and massacre and many of the inhabitants were sold into slavery.

A nepotic pope – **Sixtus IV** (1471-84) was a learned and energetic pope; he wrote a thesis on the blood of Christ and a study of the Immaculate Conception; he made an important contribution to the architectural beauty of Rome: the Sistine Chapel, Santa Maria della Pace, Santa Maria del Popolo.

In order to obtain the bishopric and archbishopric of Imola for his nephews, Jerome and Raphael Riario, he entered into conflict with Lorenzo de' Medici and joined the Pazzi conspiracy which ended in the assassination of Giulio de' Medici, Lorenzo's brother, in Florence cathedral and in the massacre of the conspirators by the furious crowd.

Raphael Riario came to possess two archbishoprics, five bishoprics and two abbeys. He was a warrior pope, almost as much as his nephew Giulio della Rovere (future Pope Julius II); he fought against the other Italian states and defeated Mahomet II, who had landed at Otranto and massacred the population.

INFLUENTIAL FAMILIES IN THE HISTORY OF ROME

Barberini – This Roman family, originally from Tuscany, produced Pope **Urban VIII** (1623-44). He commissioned the Barberini Palace on the Quirinal on which both the young Bernini and Borromini worked; it contains a magnificent picture gallery. He commissioned the Triton Fountain and the Fountain of the Bees in Piazza Barberini. He was a friend of Galileo and the first to engage Bernini from whom he commissioned a bust of himself and the baldaquin above the high altar in St Peter's Basilica.

Borghese – This noble family from Siena settled in Rome when one of its members was elected Pope **Paul V** (1605-21). The family has left its mark in the Palazzo Borghese, in the city centre, and in the Villa Borghese to the north of Rome. During his pontificate the Villa became a museum and houses many important works of art collected over the years by generations of the family. Paul V also commissioned the Pauline Fountain (Fontana Paolina) on the Janiculum. He is buried in the Pauline Chapel in the Church of Santa Maria Maggiore.

Borgia – Originally from Spain, this family produced two popes: **Calixtus III** (1455-1458) and **Alexander VI** (1492-1503). It was during Alexander's reign that America was discovered and he used gold from Peru to decorate the ceiling of Santa Maria Maggiore; his coat of arms is shown there *(see SANTA MARIA MAGGIORE)*. He was also responsible for the decoration of the Borgia Apartments in the Vatican. His son, **Cesare,** is remembered for his uncontrollable lust for power which inspired Machiavelli to write *The Prince;* his daughter, **Lucrezia,** was the victim of political intrigue between her father and her brother.

Chigi – This family of Roman bankers originally came from Siena. They became more important from the 15C through **Agostino Chigi,** who commissioned the young Raphael to decorate his residence, the Villa Farnesina. The Chigi Palace, official residence of the president of the Council of Ministers, owes its name to **Alexander VII** (1655-67), a member of the illustrious family who acquired it in the 17C. The Pope commissioned Bernini to build the colonnades of St Peter's. The Chigi coat of arms also appears on the fountain in Piazza d'Aracoeli.

Colonna – This ancient noble Roman family was very powerful in Rome from the 13C to the 17C. The election of one of its members **Martin V** (1417-1431) as pope during the Council of Constance ended the great schism of the west which followed the 68 years of captivity in Avignon. When the papacy returned to Rome, Martin concentrated totally, right up to his death, on re-instating the primacy of the Vatican.

A worldly pope – Julius II was succeeded by Giovanni de' Medici, son of Lorenzo the Magnificent, a cultured man. Archbishop at age seven and Cardinal at 14, he became pope at 39 taking the name of **Leo X** (1513-21). He was immensely rich and inaugurated his reign by a procession from the Vatican to the Lateran more sumptuous than ever before. Then he made his cousin Giulio de' Medici (future Clement VII) archbishop of Florence and presented him with a cardinal's hat.

During his reign "the court of Rome was the most brilliant in the world". Stendhal remarked that this pope "had a horror of anything which might upset his pleasant carefree life of self indulgence".

Nonetheless Leo X had to face the Lutheran storm. Had not the Holy See suggested to a German archbishop who was in debt that he should preach indulgences, keeping half the proceeds to reimburse his creditors and giving the other half to the rebuilding of St Peter's? On 15 June 1520 Leo X published a bull against Luther, condemning his ideas and ordering his books to be burned.

A builder pope – Felix Peretti was born in 1521, the son of poor village folk. He had the face of "a sly old peasant, quite capable of doing someone a bad turn" and was elected pope in 1585.

As Pope **Sixtus V** (1585-90) he accomplished an astonishing number of projects in his five years on the throne.

With the assistance of Domenico Fontana he set up obelisks in Piazza dell' Esquilino, Piazza del Popolo, outside St John Lateran and in St Peter's Square; he built a chapel in the basilica of Santa Maria Maggiore to contain his tomb, replaced the statue of the Emperor on Trajan's column with one of St Peter, opened up Via Sistina and set out the crossroads with the Four Fountains, and partially achieved his intention of creating broad streets to link the major basilicas and the different districts of Rome.

He built an aqueduct *(acqua Felice – see VIA VENETO)* which terminated in a fountain in Piazza di San Bernardo, rebuilt the Lateran palace, constructed a building to house the Scala sancta, and left his mark on countless churches.

Della Rovere – Two great popes were born into this family from Savona: **Sixtus IV** (1471-1484) and **Julius II** (1503-1513). Sixtus was responsible for major works including the construction of the Sistine chapel and its decoration by the greatest artists of the day such as Botticelli, Ghirlandaio and Perugino. Julius II was blessed with great gifts both as a politician and as a generous patron; implementation of Bramante's design for St Peter's, the painting of the Vatican Rooms by Raphael, the designing of his mausoleum, which remained unfinished, by Michelangelo (in the church of San Pietro in Vincoli), and the collection of antique sculptures in the Vatican. He was also responsible for the building of Via Giulia, a long straight thoroughfare between the bend in the Tiber and the island downstream.

Farnese – This aristocratic family from Umbria, which was already famous by the 12C, came to Rome through **Paul III** (1534-1549), the Pope who called the Council of Trent (1545-63). He was the driving force behing major projects and, while still a cardinal, commissioned Sangallo to build the Farnese Palace which was finished by Michelangelo. When he became pope, he turned once again to the Florentine master for the *Last Judgement* in the Sistine Chapel and put him in charge of work on St Peter's Basilica. The family also held dukedoms in Parma and Piacenza from 1545 to 1731.

Medici – This Florentine merchant and banking family ruled Florence and the whole of Tuscany from the 15C to the 18C. It produced several popes: **Leo X** (1513-1521), son of Lorenzo the Magnificent, a man of letters and patron of the arts, who put Raphael and Giulio Romano in charge of the Loggias in the Vatican; **Clement VII** (1523-1534), an ally of François I, who was not able to prevent the Sack of Rome by the troops of Charles V nor to comprehend the significance of the Lutheran reforms which erupted during his pontificate; **Pius IV** (1559-1565) who presided over the closure of the Council of Trent (1545-63); **Leo XI**, who died a few days after he was elected in 1605, but who, while still a cardinal, had acquired the Villa Medici, which later became the French Academy in Rome.

Pamphili – Originally from Umbria, the family settled in Rome during the 15C. In 1461 its members were honoured with the title of Counts of the Holy Roman Empire. In the 16C Giovanni Battista became Pope **Innocent X** (1644-55). He was responsible for many changes in Piazza Navona: the rebuilding of the Pamphili Palace, the transformation into a family chapel of the church of Sant'Agnese in Agore for which the façade and dome were built by Borromini; the building of the Fountain of the Four Rivers (Fontana dei Fiumi) which he commissioned from Bernini. He turned, however, to Borromini, a rival of Bernini, for the Palace for the Propagation of the Faith and the rebuilding of St John Lateran. The Villa Doria Pamphili was built for the pope's nephew, Camillo Pamphili, whose wife inherited the palace known as the Palazzo Doria Pamphili.

Rome today

From the belvedere on the Janiculum hill there is a wide view over the roofs of the city above which rise countless domes. In the streets, statues of the Virgin adorned with little cherubs watch over the life of every narrow alley. Rome is the **city of churches**; there are said to be about 300 in all. Since the 7C Christians from all over the world have been making pilgrimages to the tombs of St Peter and St Paul, the catacombs and the Vatican state.

Fountains and obelisks – The streets with their churches and palaces all emerge eventually into a square with a cooling fountain or commanding obelisk as its focal point. The water pours forth in a variety of forms – the Baroque torrents of the Trevi fountain, the modest trickle from the Facchino's barrel, the delicate tracery of the Turtle fountain – from a multitude of orifices – the depths of a basin, from the mouth of an Egyptian lion, from a dolphin or a monster, or a Triton's shell. As for obelisks – Egyptian, imperial and papal – they seem to grow in Rome like trees: curiously perched on an elephant's back, contrasting starkly with the façade of the Pantheon, boldly mounted on the fountain of the Four Rivers.

Ruins – They are usually hemmed in by the modern town and are rarely very extensive but their attraction lies in the role they played in ancient history.
Rome may still operate under the emblem of the wolf and use the old republican formula S P Q R. (Senatus Populusque Romanus), the ancient city may still be visible beneath the new street plan, whole districts may still be dressed in their Renaissance or Baroque décor, but it is no longer the marble capital left by Augustus and the emperors nor the ostentatious city of the popes.
To fulfil its modern role as capital of a united Italy since 1870, the city has had to double in size, to use concrete, metal and glass to house its new population, to construct administrative buildings and to improve its public transport and traffic flow. A city with more than 2500 years of heritage is bound to contain contrasting elements, which make it all the more fascinating and "eternal".

Urban development

For its first 20 years as the capital of Italy Rome was a building site. The town plans of 1871 and 1883 provided for the construction of housing for the new civil servants around Piazza Vittorio Emanuele, Piazza dell'Independenza, at Castro Pretorio and in the Prati; for the demolition of the slum districts of the inner city; for the construction of administrative buildings; for the establishment of banks and newspapers; for the provision of arterial roads: Via del Corso and Via Nazionale, which were opened soon after the inclusion of Rome in the kingdom of Italy, were followed by Corso Vittorio Emanuele II and Via XX Settembre.

First Quarter of 20C – More public works were undertaken. In 1902 the Humbert I tunnel was built linking the Quirinal and the business centre. Extensive parks, formerly the private property of the great families, were opened to the public or, like the Villa Ludovisi, sold as building lots for residential development. The Tiber embankment was constructed and the Capitol was cut away to make room for the monument to Victor Emmanuel II. The International Exhibition in 1911 was responsible for the development of the district around Piazza Mazzini and a huge museum of modern art in a garden setting was bestowed on the capital. 1920 brought the beginning of the garden suburbs: near to Monte Sacro in the north and at Garbatella in the south.

Mussolini's Rome – The arrival of Mussolini in 1922 ushered in a policy of grandiose town planning linked to the fascist ideology which favoured a return to ancient grandeur.
Three new streets – Corso del Rinascimento, Via della Botteghe Oscure and Via del Teatro di Marcello – were opened up to allow traffic to penetrate the Campus Martius. Via dei Fori Imperiali was opened in 1932 to give a clear view of the Colosseum from Piazza Venezia. The reconciliation of the Church and State, sealed in the Lateran Treaty in 1929, was marked by the opening of Via della Conciliazione (1936) to the detriment of the medieval district of the Borgo. As it had been decided that Rome should expand towards the sea, construction began on the new district known as E U R.

All the dreams of my youth have come to life; the first engravings I remember – my father hung views of Rome in the hall – I now see in reality, and everything I have known for so long through paintings, drawings, etchings, woodcuts, plaster casts and cork models is now assembled before me. Wherever I walk, I come upon familiar objects in an unfamiliar world; everything is just as I imagined it, yet everything is new.
Goethe: Italian Journey. Rome, 1 November 1786

Rome as seen by her citizens

Rome is unusual among capital cities in that it receives double diplomatic missions: one to the Italian government and one to the Holy See. This means that a visiting head of state who has just been received at the Quirinal and wishes to go on and call on the Pope must first return to his own embassy before being collected by the diplomats from the Vatican. In addition many countries maintain permanent representation at the FAO (Food and Agriculture Organisation – a UN agency).

When Rome became the capital of Italy in 1870, the population barely exceeded 200 000. By 1979 it had risen to 2 911 671. The Commune of Rome (about 1 500 km^2 – c580sq miles) is divided into **Rioni** which have replaced the subdivisions of antiquity and are comparable to the wards of other large cities; they cover the area contained within the Aurelian wall (Mura Aureliane) and extend on to the right (west) bank of the Tiber *(maps Growth of Rome and Plan of Rome)*.

Between the Aurelian wall and the Orbital Road (Grande Raccordo Anulare) are the **Quartieri** (suburbs) where three quarters of the population live: residential to the north, cheaper and more densely developed to the east, southeast and south, cheaper and less densely developed to the west.

Beyond the western suburbs *(quartieri)* are the **Suburbi**, undeveloped districts, which become quartieri as they are provided with metalled roads and public services.

Within and beyond the Orbital Road is the **Agro Romano** (the Roman plain), a sparsely populated area which was devastated by malaria until the marshes were drained under Fascism.

Romans at work – About 70 % of the working population is employed in the **services sector** national or local government, transport, tourism, banking, insurance and commerce.

Agriculture is confined to the Agro Romano and employs about 2 % of manpower either in family-run small holdings or in larger enterprises owned by companies or mixed-economy operations: the land to the north of Rome is given over to dairy farming and the processing of dairy products, while to the south and west, where the land has been improved, sheep and cows are grazed and cereals are grown.

It was not until 1962 that a plan was drawn up for the provision of industrial estates around Rome. The major sites are to the north of the city, along the Tiber, at San Palomba to the southeast, beside Via Pontina to the south, near Acilia and Fiumicino airport to the west.

The industrialisation project was followed in 1965 by the formation of an association between the Commune of Rome and a part of the province of Latina. At the head of this Rome-Latina partnership is the building industry, followed by machine tools, publishing, textiles, food processing, carpentry, chemicals and the cinema.

The output of the building, food processing, timber and textile industries is mostly absorbed by the local and regional market, whereas the other products are exported to the rest of Italy (35 %) and abroad (20 %).

Entertainment in Rome – Like all cities on high days and holidays, Rome puts on her own particular party appearance. People pour into the historic centre, stroll along the picturesque steets and flock into the cafés. There are countless restaurants (trattorie) serving typical Roman dishes and whole families meet to spend several happy hours together over a meal. Young people go to discotheques, as well as to other places, to hear good live music and sip a drink.

Rome is not immune to the Italian passion for football and every Sunday the fans flock into the Olympic stadium.

Near the basilica of St Paul without the Walls, the faithful punters go to the dogs at the Ponte Marconi greyhound track; amateurs of horse racing are attracted to the Hippodromo delle Capannelle in via Appia Nuova.

S. Chirol

27

The arts in Rome

In the early days Rome was built of very simple materials: **tufa**, a soft brownish stone, volcanic or calcareous in origin; **peperine**, also of volcanic origin, which owes its name to its greyish hue and its granular texture suggestive of grains of pepper (*pepe* in Italian). **Travertine**, a whitish limestone, mostly quarried near Tivoli, is a superior material to the earlier ones and was used only sparingly in the early centuries. **Marble** made rare appearances as a decorative material from the 2C BC but became very popular under the Empire. **Brick** was first used in the 1C BC; it is usually seen today stripped of its marble facing.

ANTIQUITY (1C BC-4C)

Etruscan Art

Pottery – The *impasto* technique used for rudimentary clay pots was succeeded in the 7C BC by *bucchero* (black terracotta). At first the vases were simply decorated with a stippled design but the shapes grew ever more ornate up to the 5C when they were fashioned in the form of human beings or fantastic animals. Many vases were imported from Greece – fine pieces are displayed in the Vatican Museum and at the Villa Giulia.

Ornamentation – The work is exquisitely rich: engraved on bronze, in gold filigree or granulation, in finely carved ivory.

Sculpture – The Etruscans never used marble; they worked in bronze and clay. Their statues are distinguished by an enigmatic smile and large staring eyes.

Architecture – An Etruscan temple was approached by a flight of steps at the front which led up to a columned portico. The sanctuary itself was a rectangular building, standing on a high podium and containing three shrines *(cellae)* at the rear.

Roman Art

The remains of only a few public works have survived from the period of the kings and the early Republic, such as the channel of the **Cloaca Maxima** (a sewer dug in the 6C BC), the **town wall** built by **Servius Tullius** (578-534 BC), the **Appian Way** and the **Acqua Appia**, both the work of **Appius Claudius Caecus**, censor in 312 BC. The Acqua Appia, the oldest aqueduct in Rome, ran almost totally underground for over 16km - 12 miles.

The major artistic influences on the Romans came from the Etruscans, whose works they pillaged, and from the East, whence their victorious generals returned, dazzled by the splendours they had seen and accompanied by the artists they had engaged in cities such as Athens or Alexandria.

Architecture – The principles of Classical Roman architecture were undoubtedly modelled upon those used in Ancient Greece. The mastery of three distinctive feats of civil engineering, however, heralded new building practices in Rome.

Firstly, as distinct from their Greek counterparts, the Romans discovered how to make and use concrete, allowing them to build more quickly and therefore more prolifically.

Secondly they learnt how to apply marble (and any other finely finished stone like granite, porphyry and alabaster) as surface decoration rather than having to use large (and expensive) quantities as building blocks: hence the reason for Roman ruins surviving today as sad reddish or greying husks of brick or concrete, stripped of their marble facing and friezes which have long been reappropriated.

Thirdly, the Romans learnt from their campaigns in the Eastern Mediterranean (modern-day Turkey and Syria) the use of the arch, vaulting, squinches and consequently, the art of constructing domes. At last they were able to break the linearity of the Hellenistic style with round arcs.

Structural detail of the Baths of Caracalla

Concrete – The liquid mixture of sand and cement was usually poured between simple brick parapets to make a solid wall or over a brick layer to anchor the voussoirs of an archway, vault or dome: indeed the Romans seem to have avoided using wooden coffering because of its expense. One particular feature of Roman concrete is its ability to harden with time through the centuries: the honeycomb appearance of ruins that survive is largely caused by the erosion of the brickwork leaving a lattice of now bare mortar.

Several distinctive bricklaying techniques were adopted through time: square bricks or tiles could be split diagonally and laid with the right angle facing inwards so as to provide a broader area wedged in the concrete; cubes of terracotta were laid obliquely making a decorative trellis pattern; in some instances different methods are used in the same wall.

Vaulting – In their constructions the Romans used the semicircular arch. The one built over the Cloaca Maxima in about the 2C BC is a true masterpiece. Circular rooms were covered by hemispherical domes, niches set in walls were covered by half-domes and the lintel over an opening was surmounted by a rounded arch. There are some impressive examples of vaulting in the Domus Augustana on the Palatine, in the Pantheon, in Hadrian's Villa at Tivoli, in the Baths of Caracalla and in the Colosseum.

The Romans were masters of the technique of building theatres on level ground rather than set into a hillside as was the Greek practice. This involved the construction of vaults to support the terraces, as in the Theatre of Marcellus.

Classical orders – They used the Greek architectural **orders** with modifications: In the Tuscan or Roman Doric order the column rests on a base rather than directly on the ground; the Ionic order was seldom used in Rome; the Corinthian order, however, was very popular – the Romans sometimes replaced the curling acanthus leaves on the capital with smooth overhanging leaves and for the flower in the centre of the curved side they substituted various motifs: animals, gods, human figures.

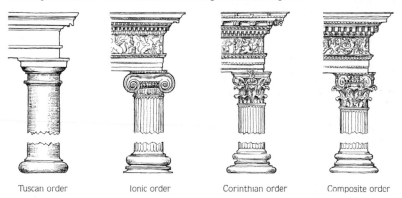

| Tuscan order | Ionic order | Corinthian order | Composite order |

To the three Classical orders they added a fourth, called composite, which was distinguished by a capital in which the four scrolls of the Ionic order surmounted the acanthus leaves. The entablature (comprising the architrave, frieze and cornice) was very ornate, richly decorated with pearls, ovoli and ornamental foliage.

The names of two architects have survived: Rabirius, active under Domitian (81-95), and Apollodorus of Damascus who worked for Trajan (98-117) and Hadrian (117-138).

Monuments – It requires a powerful effort of imagination to envisage the original construction.

Temples – Temples were places devoted to the worship of the gods and of the Emperor, who, since the time of Caesar, had risen to the status of a god. Their design was inspired by Etruscan and Greek models and varied from the elemental simplicity of the Temple of Fortuna Virilis to the more complex design of the Temple of Venus and Rome. Each temple had a place **(cella)** reserved for the statue of the divinity to whom the temple was dedicated. In front of the cella was a **pronaos** set behind a colonnade. The whole structure stood on a podium.

Theatres – The first permanent theatre was built by Pompey. Previously, mobile wooden stages had been used. Theatres were designed for the staging of comedies and tragedies; they were also used for political, literary and musical events as well as for competitions and lotteries and the distribution of bread or money.

Unlike the Greeks, the Romans built a certain number of theatres on flat sites, using vaults to support the rows of seats which often ended in a colonnade. The space in front of the stage (orchestra) was reserved for actors and later people of rank, who came to watch the play. The leading actors came on the stage, which was raised above the orchestra, through three doors in the wall at the back of the stage. Animals and chariots came in from the sides.

Theatrical masks

The rear wall, the most beautiful part of the theatre, was decorated with many columns, statues set in recesses, and facings of marble and mosaic. Behind the rear wall of the stage were the dressing rooms, store rooms and a portico overlooking a garden. The stage hands were responsible for special effects: smoke, lights, thunder, apparitions and grand finales, gods and heroes who descended from heaven or disappeared into the clouds. The actors wore masks to enable the audience to identify the different characters. The acoustics were influenced by the canvas awning slanting down over the stage, which concentrated the sound so that it penetrated to the top row of the terraces, and also, perhaps, by resonant vessels strategically placed to act as loud speakers. It has been suggested that, when the actors sang, they stood in front of the rear wall of the stage so that the doors acted as sounding boards.

Amphitheatres – Amphitheatres, such as the magnificent Colosseum, were invented by the Romans for holding displays of gymnastics and horse-drawn chariot races. Their main use, however, was for combats between gladiators, who were mostly slaves or prisoners and faced death if they lost, or between wild beasts, which were specially kept for the major spectacles held either in Rome or in the provinces and which were attended by the Emperor.

These bloody spectacles, which were offered to the people, were considered so important by the Romans that candidates for public office treated them as an element of entertainment in their electoral campaigns.

Baths – Going to the baths occupied an important place in the Roman day, particularly during the Empire. These were free public clubs providing thermal baths, gymnasia and places to stroll, read or converse. These were built on a large scale and decorated with columns, capitals, mosaics, coloured marbles, statues and frescoes (Caracalla Baths).

During the spectacle, slaves burned or sprayed perfume to neutralise the smell of the animals, covered the sand in the arena with red dust to hide the bloodstains and used lead-weighted whips to coerce human contestants or animals into the fray. Loud music played throughout the spectacle.

Amphitheatres were more or less oval in shape. The outer wall consisted of three storeys of arcades, surmounted by a wall in which were fixed the poles which supported the huge awnings shading the spectators from the sun. The many doors under the arcades, the three circular galleries which formed the balconies for spectators and the stairs and corridors *(vomitoria)* where the spectators congregated, allowed access to the seats without any intermixing of the classes and without the danger of people being crushed. The most important spectators sat on a podium, protected by a balustrade; it was raised above the arena and positioned in the centre of one of the longer sides at the foot of the terraced area *(cavea)* which surrounded the arena on all sides.

Basilicas – Originally, basilicas were built to accommodate law courts and stall holders: located in the forum, it was where people might congregate out of the sun or rain, it had no religious function as such. The term, which literally means royal portico referred to it being a covered area; the roof was supported by rows of free-standing columns, dividing the internal rectangular space into a "nave" flanked by two side aisles. The first basilica to be built in Rome was the Basilica Porcia; this was erected at the foot of the Capitolino in 185BC. Unfortunately nothing of the building remains. Their use for religious functions was assumed with the rise of the early Christian church.

Triumphal arches – These arches were built to commemorate the triumph of a victorious general or to raise the statue of a prominent person into prominent view. Some had only one arched opening (Arch of Titus); others had three arched openings (Arch of Septimus Severus, Arch of Constantine). It is thought that the original designs of these monuments was linked to the belief that a defeated army lost its powers of destruction on passing under the arch.

Circuses – The huge oblong arenas were built to host popular chariot races; these include the Circus Maximus and Maxentius' Circus off the Old Appian Way. The layout of the arena can be likened to a quadrangle with rounded corners: at one end was the **oppidum** which opened out on to the concourse; the internal perimeter would have been lined with rows of steps for the spectators. In the centre of the concourse was the **spina,** a long divided track around which the chariots ran.

Stadiums – These too were oblong in shape but were used rather for athletic competitions. The site of Domitian's Stadium is now occupied by Piazza Navona.

Aquaducts – The impressive engineering of these great constructions has probably contributed more than anything else to the Roman reputation for building. The Acqua Appia, the oldest aqueduct is some 100m long and was built in 312BC by Appius Claudius the Blind.

Roads – In some places, considerable stretches of the original paving are still intact. The word *civus* alludes to a street going up or down hill; a *vicus* is a side street.

For tombs and housing see Rome in Antiquity: Daily Life in Ancient Rome – Cult of the dead.

Sculpture – It was in this discipline that the Romans were most imitative of Greek art. Such was the enthusiasm for statues that they were erected all over Rome. They were mass produced: bodies were supplied (dressed in togas) ready to receive suitable heads. There were workshops in Rome employing Greeks and local artists but figures were also imported from Greece: a ship loaded with statues, which was wrecked in about the 1C BC and found near Madhia in Tunisia, was probably on its way to Rome.

The originality of Roman sculpture is to be found in the **portraits.** The taste for likenesses was fostered by the practice in aristocratic families of preserving death masks made of wax. Caesar's portraits always show a calm, reflective and energetic character whereas Augustus, with his prominent ears, displays serenity and coldness. There is malice in Vespasian's face set on his thick neck. Trajan must in reality have had a very broad face and his hair style curiously accentuates this peculiarity. The equestrian statue of Marcus Aurelius (see Index) is the sole survivor of a tradition established by Julius Caesar which portrays the emperor as an all-powerful conqueror.

The Romans also excelled in **historical low relief sculptures.** The scenes on a sarcophagus or on Trajan's column are models of composition and precision.

Decorative sculpture, which was exceptionally rare in the Republican era as the sarcophagus of Scipio Barbatus (see VATICAN – Museo Pio-Clementino) shows, reached its apogee in the Augustan era with the Ara Pacis (see Index). There was also a current which gave expression to **popular taste** in depicting various crafts and scenes from everyday life on the tombstones of the working people.

Decadence in sculpture became apparent in the 3C: the folds of garments were scored too deep making the figures rigid, the expressions became fixed owing to excessive hollowing out of the pupil of the eye, the hair was carelessly treated.

Materials – The Romans liked white and coloured marble, dark red spotted porphyry and alabaster. They also worked in bronze (Marcus Aurelius' statue).

Painting – A study of the frescoes in Pompeii has identified four periods in Roman painting. The "first style" consists of simple panels imitating marble facing; the "second style" is marked by architectural features in *trompe-l'œil* to which small illustrated panels were added in the "third style"; with the "fourth style" the *trompe-l'œil* became excessive and the decoration overloaded. Examples of Roman painting can be seen in Livia's House and the Griffin House on the Palatine and in the National Roman Museum.

Mosaic in Santa Maria in Trastevere

Mosaic – This technique developed from an attempt to strengthen the floor surface, which was made of a mixture of broken tiles and chalk, by inserting pebbles and then small pieces of marble which could be cut to a uniform size and arranged to form a design.

The simplest method, which was used for floors, consisted of inserting small cubes of marble all cut to the same size into a bed of cement. Larger surfaces (baths) were covered with black figures on a white ground.

Sometimes the cubes were cut in different sizes so as to form curved lines; very small cubes could produce the effect of light and shade. This method was less durable and was reserved for wall panels or for the centre piece of a floor.

Roman workshops also copied the **opus sectile** technique which originated in the East: a stencil of a decorative motif was cut out and applied to a marble base; the outline was traced on to the marble which was then hollowed out within the outline; the hollow itself was filled with small pieces of coloured marble. Examples of this technique can be seen on display at the entrance to the Picture Gallery in the Conservators' Palace (see Index) and in the Ostia museum.

Christian Art

The pagan cult of idols and the commandment in the Bible against "graven images" inhibited the spontaneous development of a new style of art among the early Christian communities.

At first Christian art borrowed from the pagan repertoire those subjects which could be used as symbols of Christianity: the vine, the dove, the anchor, etc.

Painting – The earliest Christian paintings appeared on the walls of the catacombs as a result of people following the pagan tradition and decorating the tombs of their relatives. The oldest date from the 2C.

Sculpture – The evolution of Roman sculpture, both in the round and in relief, can be traced in the Christian Museum in the Vatican from the use of symbols to the representation of the leading figures in Christianity (Jesus, St Peter, St Paul) and scenes from the Bible.

Architecture – The chief Christian building was the **basilica** (not to be confused with the pagan basilicas which had nothing to do with religion). The first buildings of this type were erected by Constantine over the tombs of Peter and Paul the Apostles (St Peter's in the Vatican; St Paul Without the Walls) and next to the Imperial Palace (St John Lateran).

MEDIEVAL PERIOD (5C-14C)

Supplanted by Constantinople as the capital of the Empire and invaded by barbarians, by the 6C Rome was a ruined city with barely 20 000 inhabitants. In the 10C it became the battleground in the struggle between the Pope and the German Emperor. Until the 15C only simple constructions were built.

Architecture – Civil architecture consisted mainly of fortresses built by the noble families on strategic sites (Crescenzi House; Militia Tower).

Churches – They were constructed of material taken from ancient monuments which provided a great choice of capitals, friezes and columns such as can be seen in Santa Maria Maggiore, Santa Sabina etc. As such material grew scarcer, items from different sources were combined in one church (columns in San Giorgio in Velabro, Santa Maria in Cosmedin etc.).

The **basilical plan** of the early churches was retained during the medieval period *(see plans of Santa Maria d'Aracoeli; Santa Maria in Cosmedin; San Clemente).* It consisted of a rectangular building divided down its length into a nave flanked by two or four aisles separated by rows of columns; one of the shorter sides contained the entrance, the other the apse (with quarter-sphere vault). Between the apse and the nave and at right angles to them ran the transept. The nave extended above the side aisles and was lit by clerestoreys. It was covered by a pitched roof, left open or masked by a flat ceiling in the interior. The main entrance was sometimes preceded by a square court surrounded by a portico *(quadriporticus)* or by a simple portico supported on columns which served as a narthex (the area reserved for those who had not yet been baptised).

The façade was often flanked by a bell tower *(campanile).* In Rome these towers are decorated with horizontal cornices dividing them into several storeys, with white mini columns standing out against the brick work and ceramic insets in brilliant colours.

By the 6C a rail had been introduced separating the congregation from the clergy and creating the chancel **(presbyterium)** on either side of the bishop's throne **(cathedra)** which stood in the apse. In front were the choristers in the **schola cantorum.** Beneath the high altar there was often a crypt containing the relics of a martyr **(martyrium);** the **confessio** also contained the relics of a martyr but could only be seen through a small window. The high altar was covered by a baldaquin or canopy **(ciborium).**

Sculpture, painting and mosaic – The period from the 12C to 14C is dominated by the **Cosmati,** who were descended from one Cosma and formed a guild of marble workers to which the Vasselletto family was related. The Cosmati workshops used fragments of ancient materials to create beautiful floors with decorative motifs of multicoloured marble and the furniture of a medieval church: episcopal throne, *ambones* (lecterns), paschal candlesticks. The early works, composed entirely of white marble, are very simple. Later they added porphyry and serpentine marble (green) cut in geometric shapes (roundels, lozenges etc.); they produced very lively effects with incrustations of enamels – blue, red and gold – on the friezes and wreathed columns of cloisters.

Arnolfo di Cambio moved to Rome from Florence in about 1276 (baldaquins in St Paul Without the Walls, and in Santa Cecilia; statue of Charles of Anjou in the Museo del Palazzo dei Conservatori).

Frescoes and mosaics were the chief forms of medieval decoration. The Romans had a taste for anecdotes and bright colours.

In the latter half of the 5C but particularly in the 6C the influence of Byzantine mosaics was introduced to Rome by the entourage of Justinian's general, Narses, who occupied Rome in 552, and also by Eastern monks who took refuge in Rome in the 7C (St Sabas). The mosaics of this period show figures with enigmatic expressions, often richly dressed, in conventional poses, which express the mysticism of the Eastern church through symbolism.

ARTISTS WHO WORKED IN ROME FROM THE 15C TO 18C

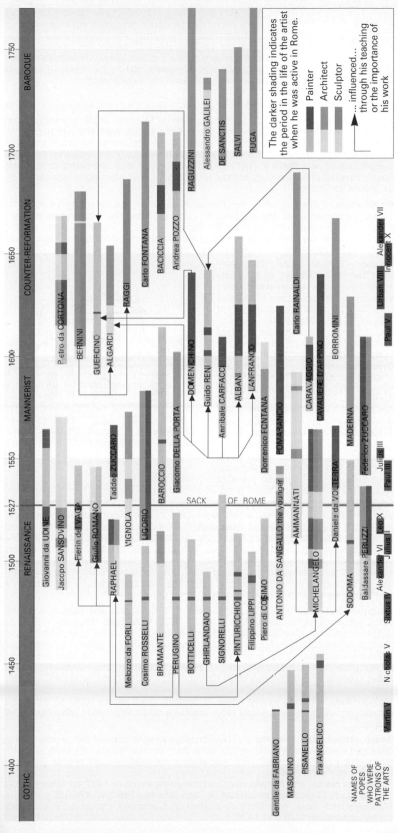

The darker shading indicates the period in the life of the artist when he was active in Rome.

Painter
Architect
Sculptor

...influenced... through his teaching or the importance of his work

GOTHIC · RENAISSANCE · MANNERIST · COUNTER-REFORMATION · BAROQUE

1400 · 1450 · 1500 · 1527 · 1550 · 1600 · 1650 · 1700 · 1750

SACK OF ROME

Gentile da FABRIANO
MASOLINO
PISANELLO
Fra ANGELICO

Melozzo da FORLI
Cosimo ROSSELLI
BRAMANTE
PERUGINO
BOTTICELLI
GHIRLANDAIO
SIGNORELLI
PINTURICCHIO
Filippino LIPPI
Piero di COSIMO
ANTONIO DA SANGALLO the younger
RAPHAEL
VIGNOLA
LIGORIO
BAROCCIO
Giacomo DELLA PORTA
MICHELANGELO
SODOMA
Baldassare PERUZZI
Daniela da VOLTERRA
AMMANNATI
Domenico FONTANA
POMARANCIO
Federico ZUCCARO
MADERNA
CAVALIERE D'ARPINO
CARAVAGGIO
BORROMINI
Carlo RAINALDI
Anibale CARRACCI
Guido RENI
DOMENICHINO
ALBANI
LANFRANCO
Giovanni da UDINE
Jaccpo SANSOVINO
Pierin del VAGA
Giulio ROMANO
Taddeo ZUCCARO
Pietro da CORTONA
BERNINI
GUERCINO
ALGARDI
RAGGI
Carlo FONTANA
BACICCIA
Andrea POZZO
RAGUZZINI
Alessandro GALILEI
DE SANCTIS
SALVI
FUGA

NAMES OF POPES WHO WERE PATRONS OF THE ARTS

Martin V
Nicolas V
Sixtus IV
Alexander VI
Julius II
Leo X
Paul III
Julius III
Paul V
Urban VIII
Innocent X
Alexander VII

33

Through the good relations enjoyed by the papacy with Pepin the Short and then Charlemagne, Carolingian art brought a less rigid style to Roman mosaics, e.g. works dating from the reign of Paschal I (817-24) (Santa Prassede; Santa Maria in Domnica). From the 11C to 13C the Roman workshops produced sumptuous work (apse in San Clemente). **Pietro Cavallini**, the greatest artist in this period, must have worked in Rome at the end of the 13C and early in the 14C. He was both painter and mosaicist and a master of the different influences; his very pure art is best known through the mosaic of the life of the Virgin in Santa Maria in Trastevere and by the fresco of the Last Judgement in Santa Cecilia. **Jacopo Torriti** and **Rusuti** were disciples of his.

RENAISSANCE ART (15C-16C)

The Renaissance made less impact on Rome than on Florence. At the beginning of the 15C Rome was exhausted by the struggles of the Middle Ages and had nothing to show of artistic merit. By the end of the century the city was an important archeological centre and was famous for its abundant artistic activity commissioned by popes and prelates. It was **Martin V** (1417-31) the first pope after the Great Schism who inaugurated this brilliant period. It came to an end in 1527 when Rome was sacked by the troops of Charles V.

Architecture – The inspiration for Roman Renaissance buildings is to be found in Classical monuments: in the Colosseum – its superimposed orders and engaged columns are imitated in the court of the Farnese Palace; in Maxentius' Basilica – the vaulting inspired the dome of St Peter's in the Vatican; in the Pantheon – the curved and triangular pediments in the interior have been reproduced many times.

Churches – They are austere in appearance. The nave is covered by rib vaulting and flanked by apsidal side chapels; the arms of the transept end in rounded chapels. The first domes began to appear (Santa Maria del Popolo, Sant'Agostino). The screen-like façade is composed of two stages one above the other linked by scrolls. Broad flat surfaces predominate; shallow pilasters are preferred to columns. The first hints of the Counter-Reformation and the Baroque can be seen in the use of broken lines, of recesses and columns progressively more and more accentuated.

Sixtus IV (1471-84) was responsible for the majority of the Renaissance churches: Sant'Agostino, Santa Maria del Popolo and San Pietro in Montorio were built in his reign; he founded

Santa Maria del Popolo

Santa Maria della Pace and made great alterations to the Church of the Holy Apostles.

Palaces – The *palazzi* were large private houses built in the district between Via del Corso and the Tiber, in the streets which were used by the pilgrims and by the papal processions which proceeded on feast days from the Vatican to the Lateran: Via del Governo Vecchio, Via dei Banchi Nuovi, Via dei Banchi Vecchi, Via di Monserrato, Via Giulia etc. They supplanted the medieval fortresses; the Palazzo Venezia which was begun in 1452 has retained its crenellations. From the outside the *palazzi* are gaunt and austere (barred windows on the ground floor). The inside was designed to accommodate an elegant and cultivated life style, associated with men of letters and artists in a setting of ancient sculptures and paintings.

Sculpture and painting – The personalities of Michelangelo and Raphael predominated. After working in Rome from 1496 to 1501 **Michelangelo** returned in 1505 to design a tomb for Julius II. **Raphael** had lived in Urbino, his home town, Perugia and Florence before coming to Rome in 1508; he was presented to Julius II by Bramante. In **decorative sculpture** delicate ornamental foliage and floral motifs are often picked out in gold (door frames, balustrades etc.). Funeral art flourished under **Andrea Bregno** and **Andrea Sansovino** who combined a taste for decoration with a taste for ancient architecture.

Mino da Fiesole, who was usually based in Tuscany, made several visits to Rome; he became famous for his very simple representations of the Virgin and Child in low relief sculpture.

Rome attracts the masters – The Renaissance style reached Rome after being developed elsewhere and all the artists came from outside the city: the Umbrians with their gentle touch, the Tuscans with their elegant and intellectual art and the Lombards with their rich decoration.

- **Gentile da Fabriano** and **Pisanello** were summoned to Rome in 1427 by Martin V and Eugenius IV to decorate the nave of St John Lateran (destroyed 17C-18C).
- **Masolino** who came from Florence painted St Catherine's Chapel in St Clement's Basilica between 1428 and 1430.

- From 1447 to 1451 **Fra Angelico**, also from Florence, decorated Nicholas V's Chapel in the Vatican.
- For the painting of the Sistine Chapel walls Sixtus IV called on **Pinturicchio, Perugino** and **Signorelli** from Umbria and on **Botticelli, Ghirlandaio, Cosimo Rosselli** and his son **Piero di Cosimo** from Florence. He also commissioned **Melozzo da Forli** to paint the Ascension in the apse of the Church of the Holy Apostles (fine fragments in the Vatican Picture Gallery and in the Quirinal Palace).
- In about 1485 **Pinturicchio** painted the life of St Bernard in Santa d'Aracoeli and a Nativity in Santa Maria del Popolo; between 1492 and 1494 he decorated the Borgia Apartment in the Vatican for Alexander VI.
- From 1489 to 1493 **Filippino Lippi** was at work on the Carafa Chapel in Santa Maria Sopra Minerva.
- **Bramante** who arrived in 1499 designed the *tempietto* (1502), built the cloisters at Santa Maria della Pace (1504) and extended the choir of Santa Maria del Popolo (1505-09).
- From 1508 to 1512 **Michelangelo** was at work painting the ceiling of the Sistine Chapel for Julius II. In 1513 he began the pope's tomb. The Last Judgement was painted between 1535 and 1541 and he worked on the dome of St Peter's from 1547 until his death in 1564. His last work was the Porta Pia (1561-64).
- From 1508 to 1511 **Baldassarre Peruzzi** built the Villa Farnesina for Agostino Chigi.
- In 1508 **Raphael** began to paint the *Stanze* in the Vatican. In 1510 he designed the plan for the Chigi Chapel in Santa Maria del Popolo. From 1511 he worked on the decoration of the Villa Farnesina for Agostino Chigi. In 1512 he painted Isaiah in Sant'Agostino and the Sibyls in Santa Maria della Pace in 1514.
- **Sodoma** arrived in Rome from Milan in 1508 to paint the ceiling of the Signature Room in the Vatican for Julius II; he worked on the Farnesina in about 1509.
- Early in the 16C **Jacopo Sansovino** built San Giovanni dei Fiorentini for Leo X.
- In 1515 **Antonio da Sangallo the Younger** began to build the Farnese Palace; Michelangelo took over in 1546.

COUNTER-REFORMATION (16C-17C)

The Counter-Reformation, which covered the period from the reign of Paul III (1534-49) to the reign of Urban VIII (1623-44), was marked by the sack of Rome in 1527 and by the rise of Protestantism. The Counter-Reformation movement sought to put down the heretics, restore the primacy of Rome and to rally the faithful to the church. The Society of Jesus, which was formed in 1540, proved to be a most efficacious instrument in the struggle. Henceforward the influential power of art was put at the service of the Faith.

The initial period of struggle was followed by several successes – the battle of Lepanto (1571), the conversion of Henri IV of France (1593) and the Jubilee (1600) – all expressed in an artistic style which presaged the Baroque.

Architecture

Churches – The style is sometimes called 'Jesuit' owing to the comprehensive contribution made by the Society of Jesus. The architecture combines an austere solemnity with a rich marble décor: the Church was to appear majestic and powerful. Since they were designed to assemble the faithful together, the churches of the Counter-Reformation are vast. The *Gesù Church* is a typical example. The nave is broad and uncluttered so that every member of the congregation could see the altar and hear the preaching. On the façade, the plain surfaces of the Renaissance are replaced with recesses and projections and engaged columns are gradually substituted for the flat pilasters.

Civil architecture – The most flourishing period was the early years of the Counter-Reformation during the reigns of Paul III, Julius III, Paul IV and Pius IV who continued to live like Renaissance princes.

The Borghese family illustrates the era of the Church triumphant: Paul V acquired the Borghese Palace and built the Pauline fountain; his nephew, Cardinal Scipione Borghese led a cultivated life as is evident from the splendours of the Palazzo Pallavicini and the "Palazzina" Borghese, which now houses the Borghese Gallery.

The Gesù Church

Sculpture and painting

In the spirit of the Counter-Reformation painting had to exalt the themes rejected by the Protestants: the Virgin, the primacy of St Peter, the doctrine of the Eucharist, the cult of the saints and their intercession for the souls in Purgatory.

The work of the Counter-Reformation artists followed in the wake of Michelangelo and Raphael and continued to be in the attenuated 'manner' of these two giants; hence the term **Mannerist** which is applied to 16C sculpture and painting.

In sculpture there is the work of two of Michelangelo's close followers: **Ammanati** (1511-92) and **Guglielmo della Porta** (1500?-77). The end of the period is marked by the presence in Rome of **Pietro Bernini** (1562-1629), the father of Gian Lorenzo Bernini.

Among the painters are **Daniele da Volterra**, who worked with Michelangelo, **Giovanni da Udine, Sermoneta, Francesco Penni, Giulio Romano**, who formed part of the 'Roman School' around Raphael. The style of the next generation – **Federico** and **Taddeo Zuccari, Pomarancio, Cesare Nebbia, Cavaliere d'Arpino** etc – is a direct development of Raphael's art. **Barocci**, whose soft and emotional style never lapsed into affectation, deserves a special place.

In their attempts to imitate, the Mannerist painters were often guilty of excess. Their colours are pallid as if faded by the light; fresco paintings are framed with stucco and gilding or elaborate combinations of marble; large areas are often divided into smaller panels which are easier to paint.

Reaction – Reaction was introduced by Caravaggio, who heralded the first signs of the Baroque, and the **Bologna group**, led by the **Carracci** who ran an academy in Bologna from 1585 to 1595: Ludovico (1555-1619), founder of the academy, his cousins Agostino (1557-1602) and Annibale (1560-1609) who were brothers. Guido Reni (1575-1642), Domenichino (1581-1641) and Guercino (1591-1666) tried to achieve more verity of expression without abandoning idealism.

Michelangelo Merisi (1573-1610), known as **Caravaggio** after the name of his home village near Bergamo, began to work in Rome with Cavaliere d'Arpino in 1588 but he was quarrelsome and had to flee from the city in 1605. His painting was quite unconventional; his powerful figures are illuminated by a harsh light which causes contrasting heavy shadow. His influence had repercussions throughout Europe and many artists were said to paint in the style of Caravaggio.

BAROQUE ART (17C-18C)

The Baroque style evolved in the 17C and 18C. Several theories expound the origin of the term Baroque: in Portuguese *barroco* alludes to an uneven or irregular pearl (from which the French derived the term *baroque* meaning bizarre, eccentric, profusely decorative). In both cases, however, the attributed meaning tends to be pejorative, deriding the intentions of Baroque artists to create their own values rather than follow the established Classical rules and cannons of harmony and beauty. It was a long time before the style was re-evaluated and appreciated thus losing its pejorative connotations.

Baroque, meanwhile, enjoyed a great vogue in the papal city during the reign of Urban VIII (1623-44) becoming synonymous with the triumph of the Roman Church over heresy.

Leading artists

Gian Lorenzo Bernini (1598-1680) was born in Naples. From the very first his talent was recognised by Cardinal Scipione Borghese who commissioned him to do the sculptures for his villa (now in the Borghese Gallery). At the age of 17, Bernini produced his first work *Jupiter and the goat Amalthea*. On the election of Urban VIII, he was appointed official artist to the papal court and to the Barberini family. After Maderna's death in 1629, the Pope put him in charge of the rebuilding of St Peter's Basilica.

During the reign of Innocent X (1644-1655) Bernini sculpted his extraordinary *Ecstasy of St Theresa* and the *Fountain of the Four Rivers (see PIAZZA NAVONA)*. In the reign of Alexander VII (1655-1667) he built the church of St Andrew on the Quirinal, the colonnade enclosing St Peter's Square, re-designed St Peter's Chair and built the Royal Stair (Scala Regia) in the Vatican Palace.

In 1665 he was summoned to Paris by Louis XIV and his minister, Colbert, to design the façade of the Cour Carrée in the Louvre but as the King turned his attention to Versailles, Bernini's design was never carried out.

Bernini was not only an architect and sculptor but also a theatrical scene designer, poet and painter. He probably painted some hundred pictures of which only a few have survived. He produced a great deal of work, rose rapidly and was very successful.

His genius was recognised in his lifetime and he received many decorations; his contemporaries saw in him another Michelangelo. He was welcome in the most brilliant circles; he put on plays for his friends, designing the stage sets, writing the words and playing a role. He was fleetingly eclipsed by Borromini when Innocent X succeeded Urban VIII but soon returned to favour with his Fountain of the Four Rivers.

Francesco Borromini (1599-1667) was the son of Giovanni Domenico Castelli, an architect to the Visconti family in Milan. He trained as a stone mason and acquired great technical experience. In 1621 he was in Rome where he worked as Carlo Maderno's assistant on St Peter's, Sant'Andrea della Valle and the Barberini Palace. In 1625 he

S. Chirol

Ecstasy of St Theresa by Bernini in Santa Maria della Vittoria

received the title of *maestro* and in 1628 he took his mother's name of Borromini. He based his art on rigour and sobriety excluding marble decorations and paintings. In Borromini's art the Baroque style is expressed by the lines of the architecture which he cut and curved with a sure hand.

San Carlo alle Quattro Fontane, which was his first full-scale work (1638), probably shows his genius at its best. At the same period he designed the façade of the Oratory of St Philip Neri which is typical of his original and balanced style. These projects earned him the protection of Fr Spada who became Innocent X's adviser. The Pope raised him to the first rank and appointed him to renovate St John Lateran. The façade of San Carlo alle Quattro Fontane was designed in the year in which he died.

Da una foto Gab. Fot. Naz.

San Carlo alle Quatro Fontane

Borromini, an introvert who shunned the world, lived in constant anxiety and never knew the fame enjoyed by his rival. One night in a fit of anguish and anger against his servant he took his own life.

There were other architects working in Rome at that period. **Carlo Maderno,** the designer of the façades of St Peter's and Santa Susanna, and **Giacomo della Porta,** probably the most active architect around 1580, were both great admirers of Michelangelo and are often included among the Mannerists. **Flaminio Ponzio** worked for the Borghese (façade of the Borghese Palace, Pauline Fountain). **Giovanni Battista Soria** designed the façades of Santa Maria della Vittoria and St Gregory the Great. The well-proportioned architecture of **Pietro da Cortona** is most attractive (St Luke and St Martina, the façades of Santa Maria della Pace and Santa Maria in Via Lata, the dome of San Carlo al Corso). The name of **Carlo Rainaldi** deserves to be remembered for his work in Santa Maria in Campitelli (1655-65) and for his arrangement of the 'twin' churches in the Piazza del Popolo.

Roman Baroque

An inherent quality of Baroque art is its restlessness, its sense of movement and contrast. Water, with its undulations and powers of reflection, was an essential element. Dazzling effects were created with expensive materials such as marble and precious stones. Stucco (chalk, plaster and marble dust mixed with water) was often used for its plastic qualities. Allegories were taken from Cesare Ripa's dictionary which appeared in 1594 and explained how to express an abstract idea.

ALINARI-GIRAUDON

Ceiling by Andrea Pozzo in Sant'Ignazio

Architecture – Even the plan of the buildings was contrived so as to express movement (San Carlo alle Quattro Fontane, Sant'Andrea al Quirinale). Façades are embellished with disengaged columns, bold projections, curved contours and recesses.

Sculpture – Sculpture is dominated by flowing garments and figures expressing abstract qualities. The altarpieces are decorated with pictures of sculpted marble and wreathed columns; the latter, a feature of ancient Roman art, were very popular with Bernini (baldaquin in St Peter's). Church interiors are full of cherubs perched on pediments and cornices.
In addition to the sculptors associated as pupils with Bernini (Antonio Raggi, Ercole Ferrata, Francesco Mochi etc.) mention must be made of **Alessandro Algardi** (1592-1654), who produced some remarkable portraits and marble pictures.

Painting – Baroque painters sought to achieve effects of perspective and *trompe-l'œil* with spiralling or diagonal compositions. They included **Pietro da Cortona**, architect but also interior decorator, Giovanni Battista Gaulli, known as **Baciccia** and protégé of Bernini, and **Lanfranco** (1582-1647). **Andrea Pozzo**, a Jesuit, who was a painter, studied the theory of architecture and had a passion for *trompe-l'œil*. His book *Prospettiva de' pittori e architetti* appeared in 1693 and circulated throughout Europe.
Rome attracted artists of all nationalities. Nicolas Poussin died there in 1665, Claude Lorrain in 1682. Rubens made several visits; he admired Michelangelo, the Carracci and Caravaggio and completed the paintings in the apse of the New Church. During his long stay in Rome, Velazquez painted a fine portrait of Innocent X *(now in the Galleria Doria Pamphili)*.

FROM THE 18C TO THE PRESENT

Neo-Classicism – This trend developed from the middle of the 18C until the early 19C and was marked by a return to Greek and Roman architecture which had recently been discovered during the excavations of Herculaneum, Pompeii and Paestum. Following Baroque exuberance, neo-Classicism was characterised by simplicity and symmetry, even a touch of frigidity. This was the period when Winckelmann, who was Librarian at the Vatican and in charge of Roman antiquities, published his works on Classical art, when Francesco Milizia launched his violent criticism of the Baroque style and superfluous decoration, and praised the simplicity and nobility of ancient monuments.
Piranesi (1720-78), engraver and architect, took up permanent residence in Rome in 1754. He produced some 2 000 engravings including the series "Views of Rome" which was published in 1750 and constitutes an incomparable collection full of charm and melancholy. It was he who designed the attractive Piazza dei Cavalieri di Malta.
Antonio Canova (1757-1821) was the dominant talent at this time and Napoleon's favourite sculptor. The calm regularity of his work enchanted his contemporaries.
In architecture mention should be made of **Giuseppe Valadier** who laid out Piazza del Popolo (1816-20). In painting it is the foreigners, such as the German Mengs and the French at the Villa Medici who stand out. David in particular came to Rome twice.
The end of the 19C saw artists such as C Maccari (frescoes in the Palazzo Madama) and G A Sartorio (frieze in the chamber of the Parliament building) working in Rome.

Modern artists and contemporary art movements – An exponent of Roman futurism, G Balla (1861-1958) moved to Rome in 1895; with Depero he signed the 1914 manifesto of the "Futurist Reconstruction of the Universe"; after 1930 his painting reverted to pre-Futurist themes. Other important artists were M Mafai (1902-1965) and G Bonichi (also known as Scipione) (1904-33), members of the Roman School which R Guttuso joined in 1931. The major developments in both painting and sculpture can be seen in the National Gallery of Modern Art *(see VILLA BORGHESE – VILLA GIULIA)*.

Architecture and town planning – Immediately after 1870 art produced in Rome was a simple reproduction of artistic styles from the past. Sometimes this was even carried to excess as can be seen from the Victor Emanuel II monument. During the Fascist period repairs were carried out to the Theatre of Marcellus and excavations were conducted in the ruins in the Sacred Precinct in the Largo Argentina (Area Sacra del Largo Argentina). The opening of Via dei Fori, however, resulted in the disappearance of a large part of the Fora. Work began on the main railway station (Stazione Termini), the Foro Italico sports complex and the EUR district.

The Holy Year in 1950, when masses of pilgrims were expected, saw the completion of both Via Cristoforo Colombo and the railway station (Stazione Termini). The Flaminia Stadium, the small Sports Palace in Via Flaminia and the Sports Palace in EUR were built for the 1960 Olympic Games. The Olympic Village in Via Flaminia was built on a site cleared of old run-down housing. Corso di Francia, a wide elevated highway, is also a daring piece of architectural design. In the west, Via Olimpica connects the Foro Italico to EUR. In 1961 the international airport at Fiumicino (Leonardo da Vinci) was built to complement the existing one at Ciampino. In 1970 the main orbital road round the city (Grande Raccordo Anulare – 70km - 44 miles) was finished.

Among Rome's modern buildings, mention should be made of the RAI block *(see MONTE MARIO)*, the British Embassy *(see PORTA PIA)*, some of the buildings in EUR, the Chamber for papal audiences built by Pier Luigi Nervi in 1971 and the Profane and Christian Museum which dates from 1970 (both in the Vatican), some large hotels, including The Jolly with its glass walls which reflect the trees in the park of the Villa Borghese, and the Hilton which stands on Monte Mario and caused great controversy when it was built.

The grand tour

A continental tour of one or two years, culminating in a visit to Rome, was a peculiarly British custom which lasted 300 years, reaching its height in the 18C when the Grand Tour formed part of a gentleman's education. A young man would set out with a tutor, known as a 'bear leader', to superintend his studies, protect him from bad company and show him the sights. On arriving in Rome, preferably at Easter time, these early tourists would set out "equipped with all things needful to measure the dimensions of the antiquities they would be shown". It was important to engage a good guide such as Winckelmann, a German archeologist, who was superintendent of antiquities in Rome, or Gavin Hamilton who became well known as a dealer and antiquary. The tour had great influence at home on manners and architectural style and the formation of art collections. **Lord Burlington,** the arbiter of good taste in the early 18C, made two tours which led to his patronage of **William Kent** and the introduction of the **Palladian** style into England.

Many English artists studied in Rome: **Richard Wilson** (1752-56); **Sir Joshua Reynolds** (1750-52); **Sir George Romney** (1773-75) whose portraits show the influence of the Classical style in their backgrounds and draperies; **John Flaxman,** the sculptor (1787-94), nicknamed the English Michelangelo, who encouraged **John Gibson** to become a pupil of Canova. **Benjamin West** (1760-63) and **John Copley** (1774) from America visited Rome before settling in London.

In the 19C instead of the established tour of the most famous cities, works of art and monuments, with its accent on antiquities, visitors preferred to settle in less well-known towns, taking an interest in Italian life and customs and even in the nationalist movement. **Charles Dickens** visited Rome in 1845 while writing a travel book *Pictures of Italy.*

Rome provided poetic inspiration: in May 1817 **Byron** toured the ruins gathering material for the Fourth Canto of *Childe Harold;* **Shelley** composed *Prometheus Unbound* and *The Cenci* while lodging in the Corso in 1819; in 1860 **Robert** and **Elizabeth Barrett Browning** made a visit to Rome which inspired his greatest work *The Ring and the Book,* a poem based on a 17C Roman murder trial.

Rome still attracted many artists: **Eastlake** made invaluable purchases of early Italian art for the National Gallery in London; **Turner** visited Rome twice (1819, 1828) and used quotations from *Childe Harold* as titles for his paintings. From America came **William Page** (1849-60) who painted portraits of Robert and Elizabeth Browning; he had trained under **Samuel Morse,** an artist who studied in Europe in 1832 and invented the electric telegraph.

Many American writers visited Rome: **Washington Irving** (1804-06), **Fenimore Cooper** (1820-27), **Longfellow** (1828), **Hermann Melville** (1856-57), **Nathaniel Hawthorne** (1858-59) and **Mark Twain** (1867) while collecting material for *Innocents Abroad.* Most famous of all was **Henry James** who first visited Italy in 1869; his first important novel was set in Rome.

Literature

Ever since the poet **Naevius** wrote his epic poem on the First Punic War, Rome has been a source of inspiration for writers. **Cicero** (106-43 BC), prince of the Forum, denounced profiteers and sedition-mongers *(The Verrines, Pro Murena, Pro Milone, The Catilines, The Philippics)*. **Caesar** (101-44 BC) wrote about his own contribution to the might of Rome *(The Gallic Wars and The Civil War)*. In the calm of his villa which stood where Via Veneto runs today, **Sallust** (86-35 BC) wrote about many important events in the history of Rome. **Livy** (d 17 AD) devoted 140 scrolls of papyrus to a vivid description of events between the founding of the city and 9 BC. **Tacitus** (*c*55-*c*120), lawyer and imperial civil servant, wrote a history of the periods from Tiberius to Nero and from Galba to Domitian. In his writing **Pliny the Younger** (62?-114), top-ranking civil servant during the reigns of Domitian and Trajan, and governor of Bythinia, gave a picturesque account of Roman high society. **Suetonius** (*c*69-*c*125), one of the imperial secretaries under Hadrian, left a fascinating work on the lives of the 12 Caesars, filled with details of the public and private lives of the Emperors from Julius Caesar to Domitian. In contrast to the official histories there is the *Satyricon*, attributed to **Petronius**, which describes some of the more depraved aspects of Roman life.

> *As we move about the Rome of to-day, we may*
> *find it hard to believe in her old magnificence*
> Mark Twain

From the Middle Ages Rome gradually lost her supremacy in the literary arts to Tuscany, where poetry and prose were flourishing. It was in the Humanist period that the city began to express itself again with particular authority, as is borne out by the development of the Roman Academy which grew to prominence not only in Rome but also in Florence and Naples.

The year 1690 saw the foundation of the **Arcadia Society** which established ideals for literature at the beginning of the 18C. The "shepherds", as the society's members were appropriately called, championed a style reminiscent of Petrarch as opposed to the 17C "Reign of Bad Taste". The founders, much appreciated for their literary salons, were two lyric poets, **Giambattista Felice Zappi** and his wife **Faustina Maratti.** Texts of songs and plays were written by **Pietro Metastasio** and **Paolo Rolli.** The former met with notable success both in Italy and abroad; his libretto for *Dido Abandoned* and his frenzied activity as officially-appointed poet at the Imperial Court in Vienna guaranteed his fame throughout Europe.

For many decades to follow, a taste for the Classical remained a fundamental element in Roman culture as can be seen from the Classical romances of **Alessandro Verri** who was resident in Rome at the time.

Like the other arts, literature too was influenced by the Church. The pre-Romantic creative ideas, which were spreading across Europe, were regarded with suspicion in ecclesiastical circles which condemned the works of Rousseau.

The same scholars seemed to regard Rome as unique so that she became separated from other centres of culture not only abroad but also in Italy itself. This separation gave rise to extremes of high praise or fierce condemnation.

Thus, although **Goethe** hurled abuse at the racket going on in Via del Corso during Carnival, he confessed that he felt as if he had been reborn the day he arrived in Rome *(Italianische Reise – Italian Journey)*. **Mark Twain**, champion of the right to freedom, equality and happiness – divine gifts according to the Declaration of Independence – did not look favourably on the papacy or the superstitious trappings which he saw as indications that Rome was still living in the Dark Ages *(The Innocents Abroad)*. **Leopardi** had a deeply disturbing impression of the city at the beginning of the 19C; he saw it as somehow shut in, lacking in imagination, full of women whom he did not hesitate to describe as "quite repulsive", and suffering from the deep dichotomy of being unable to distinguish reality from fantasy, an irredeemable predicament unless people recognise the vanity of their ways.

Among other famous "guests" in the city was **Massimo D'Azeglio** from Turin who wrote historical romances and took up painting both in Rome and Castelli Romani. Among the various romantic themes, a prominent position was reserved for regional literature written in local dialect. The Milanese writer Porta is coupled with Giuseppe Gioachino **Belli** (1791-1863), although the "raw materials" at their disposal differed greatly. Lombardy culture, which had spread to France (l'école de Milan) and the rest of Europe through Verri, Beccaria and Parini, increased its store of works written in dialect. The fine gradations of tone in the language began to contain even more nuance, which lent greater psychological depth to the characters in the stories. Literature in Roman dialect, which lacked a tradition comparable to the one in Lombardy, had to compromise in a society divided between the aristocracy and clerics on the one hand, and uncouth and unsophisticated citizens on the other. Belli composed sonnets in dialect "not to create a model but to record a faithful image of something still in existence but abandoned without any attempt at improvement." It was not until **Giosuè Carducci** (1835-1907) (*Odi Barbare*, 1877) and **Cesare Pascarella** (1858-1940), both of whom wrote in dialect, that Rome could once again hold her head high.

Between the 19C and the 20C Rome was a recurring theme in the works of Gabriele d'Annunzio (1863-1938) (Il Piacere) and Pascoli (Carmina). Two other leading lights were **Vincenzo Cardarelli** and **Antonio Baldini** who between 1919 and 1923 produced the magazine La Ronda.

Among contemporary writers, **Alberto Moravia** described the apathy and inadequacy of Rome's bourgeoisie in Gli Indifferenti and he put forward a clear perception of Italian society in La romana, Raconti romani and La Ciociara. From **Elsa Morante's** work it is clear that there is an element of psychological introspection in the people. Although **Pier Paolo Pasolini** was not a Roman and his books and films have given rise to widely differing opinions, he portrayed a sad picture of the Roman underclass in Ragazzi di vita and Una vita violenta.

While stands the Coliseum, Rome shall stand;
When falls the Coliseum, Rome shall fall;
And when Rome falls – the World.
            Lord Byron: Childe Harold's Pilgrimage

Music and cinema

2000 years of musical creativity – Music in Rome in ancient times was influenced mainly by Greek and Etruscan sources and consisted largely of music for wind instruments.

It was from the Middle Ages onwards that Rome began to refine the art of music for use in church. Chanting, which inevitably reflected the varied origins of the early Christians, achieved a certain unity in the 4C Latin rite and in the later reforms of Gregory the Great (590-604), after whom the well-known **Gregorian chant** is named. In the 14C Rome resounded with Flemish contrapuntal music, introduced by foreign musicians who were in attendance at the various Italian courts.

The master of polyphonic music was **Giovanni Pierluigi da Palestrina**, composer of the Missa Papae Marcelli. He was associated with many of the churches in Rome: Santa Maria Maggiore where he was a boy chorister and later *maestro di cappella*; the Julian Chapel where he was also *maestro di cappella*; the Sistine Chapel where he sang in the choir; St John Lateran where he was *maestro di cappella*. He was buried in St Peter's. He is particularly famous for his **a cappella** compositions for unaccompanied voices, typical of polyphonic music without any instrumental accompaniment.

Philip Neri (1515-1595), a native of Florence but active in Rome, inaugurated the practice of inserting a popular hymn *(laude)* both before and after the sermon to increase the participation of the congregation in the service. It was from this practice that the oratorio developed with its separate solo parts for the various characters in the story and the narrator. The leading composer of this type of music was **Giacomo Carissimi** (1605-74).

As the focal point of Christian belief, Rome continued to produce religious music and developed the **sacred cantata** in which the voices are accompanied by organ, theorbo (a large lute) and violins.

A century later one of the major composers of instrumental music was **Muzio Clementi** (1752-1823). He concentrated on writing mainly for the pianoforte and his works demonstrate the potential of this instrument.

A later composer was **Ottorino Respighi** (1879-1936), a native of Bologna, who was for many years connected with the St Cecilia music conservatory; he "described" the city of Rome in his symphonic poems The Fountains of Rome, the Pines of Rome and Feste romane.

Rome: film studio and inspiration – Cinema in Rome is synonymous with Cinecittà. The studios (140 000m^2) in Via Tuscolano were built in 1937; there were 16 film sets, offices, restaurants and a huge pool for shooting water scenes. These facilities contributed to an increase in domestic film production which did not diminish even at the beginning of the war. It was in Cinecittà that neo-realism was born. Although films of this type are usually shot out of doors, far from any studio, famous film makers, like **Vittorio De Sica** and **Roberto Rossellini**, did make some of their earliest films in the studios. To bridge the gap between life and its imaginary portrayal on the screen, a development of the Fascist period, these directors tried to return to realism, to the detailed observation of daily life; the main theme of the neo-realists was the war and all its tragic consequences. In Roma città aperta (1945), Paisà (1946) and Germania anno zero (1948) Rossellini portrayed Nazi-Fascist oppression. De Sica, in Sciuscià (1946) and Ladri di Biciclette (1948), drew a portrait of Italy after the war with its unemployment and misery. In Riso amaro (1949) and Pasqua di Sangue (1950) **De Santis** described a working-class divided between submission to the dominant ideology and revolutionary aspirations.

At the beginning of the 1950s neo-realism faded out – it no longer met the need of a people keen to forget the hardship of that time. It was during those years that the big-budget American films were shot at Cinnecittà. The Italian Hollywood made films which have earned a place in history of cinema: *Quo vadis* (1950), *Roman Holiday* (1953), *War and Peace* (1956), *Ben Hur* (1959) and *Cleopatra* (1963).

For Italian cinema, the 1960s were a golden age. Supported by the powerful industrial infrastructure of the studios, very many films were made – more than 200 a year – and of the best quality. The major directors included **Federico Fellini** and **Luchino Visconti.** In 1960 Fellini directed *La dolce vita,* a mirror of those infamous nights in Rome. He included some fantastic, dream-like shots in some of his films like *Amarcord,* la *Città delle donne, E la nave va* and *Ginger e Fred.* Among Visconti's masterpieces were *Notti bianche* and *Ludwig.*

The 1960s also brought a new generation of directors keen to record their political and social commitment: **Pasolini, Rosi** and **Bertolucci.** Since the end of the 1970s, however, hit by competition from television and a declining market, the cinema has been going through a period of crisis both in terms of production and creativity, which only a very few *films d'auteur* have managed to resist. Among the most recent is *La Famiglia* by **Ettore Scola.**

Sophia Loren and Marcello Mastroianni in *Una giornata particolare* by Ettore Scola (1977)

At last I can break my silence and send my friends a joyful greeting... Even to myself, I hardly dared admit where I was going and all the way I was still afraid I might be dreaming; it was not till I had passed through the Porta del Popolo that I was certain it was true, that I was really in Rome.
Goethe: Italian Journey. Rome, 1 November 1786

Places and monuments of major interest

Refer to Index at the end of the guide to find individual sights in the text.

★★★

ARCH OF CONSTANTINE
BATHS OF CARACALLA
BORGHESE MUSEUM
CAMPIDOGLIO
CASTEL SANT'ANGELO
CHIESA DEL GESÙ
COLOSSEUM
FONTANA DEI FIUMI
IMPERIAL FORA
NATIONAL ROMAN MUSEUM
PALATINE
PANTHEON
PIAZZA NAVONA

ROMAN FORUM
ST JOHN LATERAN
ST PETER'S BASILICA
ST PETER'S SQUARE
SANTA MARIA MAGGIORE
PIAZZA DI SPAGNA
TRAJAN'S COLUMN
TRAJAN'S FORUM
TREVI FOUNTAIN
VATICAN CITY
VATICAN PALACE AND MUSEUMS
VIA APPIA ANTICA CATACOMBS
VILLA GIULIA NATIONAL MUSEUM

★★

ARA PACI AUGUSTAE
CATACOMBS OF PRISCILLA
GALLERIA DORIA PAMPHILI
MUSEUM OF ROMAN CIVILISATION
LARGO ARGENTINA SACRED PRECINCT
PALAZZO BARBERINI
PALAZZO DEL QUIRINALE
PALAZZO DELLA CANCELLERIA
PALAZZO FARNESE
PIAZZA DEL POPOLO
PIAZZA DEL QUIRINALE
SAN CARLO ALLE QUATTRO FONTANE
SAN CLEMENTE
SAN LORENZO FUORI LE MURA
SAN LUIGI DEI FRANCESI
SAN PAOLO FUORI LE MURA
SANT'AGNESE IN AGONE

SANT'ANDREA AL QUIRINALE
SANT'IGNAZIO
SANTA COSTANZA
SANTA MARIA D'ARACOELI
SANTA MARIA DEGLI ANGELI
SANTA MARIA DEL POPOLO
SANTA MARIA DELLA VITTORIA
SANTA MARIA IN COSMEDIN
SANTA MARIA IN TRASTEVERE
SANTA MARIA SOPRA MINERVA
SANTA SABINA
SANTA SUSANNA
THEATRE OF MARCELLUS
VIA APPIA ANTICA
VILLA FARNESINA

Colosseum

Rome, a city for all times, has much to offer to those prepared to explore its many faces. Every corner of the city has something of interest: a church, a fountain, a palace, a legend which hovers in the air and echoes in the streets, and quiet places, away from the traffic, concealing memories of bygone times.

The city has a rich heritage from every century and constantly mixes past and present, art and life, great historical events and humdrum daily routine. The Rome of antiquity, the Renaissance and the Baroque periods coexists with the vibrant Rome of today – colourful local markets, throngs of people in Spanish Square and on the Spanish Steps where the young congregate, the loud and exuberant activity of the locals, lively or romantic evening outings in a horse-drawn carriage.

Rome

The part of the Old Appian Way (Via Appia Antica) which holds most interest for the tourist is the stretch which passes the catacombs and the nearby ancient monuments (Romulus' Tomb, Maxentius' Circus and the tomb of Cecilia Metella).
Buses for the Catacombs of St Callistus, St Sebastian and Domitilla depart from Piazza di Porta S Giovanni.
Tour: half a day. Follow the itinerary shown on the plan below. Allow 1 hour for each set of catacombs (at least 4 hours in all). On Fridays and Saturdays all the monuments and catacombs are open. From the tomb of Cecilia Metella to Casal Rotondo the Old Appian Way is accessible only by car.

The Via Appia is named after Appius Claudius Caecus, under whose magistracy the road was opened in 312 BC. Before the construction of the Aurelian Wall in the 3C, the Via Appia left Rome through the Porta Capena *(see TERME DI CARACALLA)*, and more or less followed the line of Via delle Terme di Caracalla and Via di Porta San Sebastiano and then continued to Capua, Beneventum and Brindisi.

In the early stages it was lined by tombs owing to a law, which was already in force in the 5C BC, forbidding burials within the city. In the Middle Ages the Appian Way became unsafe; the Caetani converted the tomb of Cecilia Metella into a fortress and plundered the passing travellers. This led to the opening of the New Appian Way. Late in the 17C the Old and New Appian Ways were linked by the Via Appia Pignatelli. Nowadays, with its Catacombs and the Quo Vadis Church, the Old Appian Way is an important part of Christian Rome.

Via Appia Antica

The "**Domine, quo vadis?**" **Church** recalls a famous legend. While fleeing from persecution in Rome, Peter is supposed to have met Christ on the road and asked him "Domine, quo vadis? (Lord, whither goest thou?)". "To Rome, to be crucified a second time", replied Christ and disappeared leaving his footprints in the road. Ashamed of his weakness Peter returned to Rome and met his death.

CATACOMBS

In medieval Rome the Latin expression *ad catacumbas* referred to St Sebastian's cemetery which lay in a hollow beside the Appian Way. When other similar cemeteries were discovered in the 16C they were referred to by the same name. 'Catacomb' now means an underground Christian cemetery composed of several storeys of galleries which generally extended downwards. When there was no more room in an upper gallery, excavation began on a lower one, so that the galleries nearest to the surface are usually the oldest.
Catacombs have been found not only elsewhere on the outskirts of Rome but also around Naples, and in Sicily, North Africa and Asia Minor.

Christians in the Catacombs – Until the middle of the 2C there were no formal Christian cemeteries. Very often a private burial ground belonging to a family, some of whom were pro-Christian, would be made available to Christians of their acquaintance for burying their dead. The situation changed early in the 3C when Pope Zephyrinus put Callistus in charge of the cemetery on the Appian Way. This was the first step in formalising Christian burials and creating cemeteries for Christians only on land belonging to the church.
For a long time the catacombs were simply graveyards where Christians came to pray at the tomb of a loved one. Visits became more frequent in the 3C when the persecutions (by Septimius Severus in 202, Decius in 250, Valerian in 257 and Diocletian in 295) created many martyrs; the popes strongly urged the faithful to pray at the martyrs' tombs. The catacombs however were never a place of refuge where Christians lived in hiding; they were known to the imperial authorities who closed them at the height of a persecution. It was only rarely, when they had broken the closure rule, that Christians were killed in the catacombs.

After a period of great popularity in the 4C, when Christianity experienced a great expansion, the catacombs were abandoned (except for St Sebastian's which was always a place of pilgrimage). In the 5C and 6C the Roman countryside was ravaged by Barbarians; gradually the martyrs' relics were transferred to the town where churches were built to house them. It was not until the 16C, when an underground cemetery was discovered in Via Salaria by Antonio Bosio, an Italian archeologist, that interest in the catacombs started up again. Their systematic investigation is primarily due to another archeologist Giovanni Battista de Rossi (1822-94).

Special terms used – A **hypogeum** is an underground tomb belonging to a noble Roman family.
From the *hypogeum* a network of galleries developed; each gallery was about 1metre – 3ft wide and 2 or 3 metres – 7ft or 10ft high. Opening off the galleries were small rooms, **cubicula**, where the sarcophagi were placed; sometimes there was a **lucernarium**, an opening in the roof through which air and light could enter.
When lack of space became acute, recesses **(loculi)** were hollowed out one above another in the gallery walls; the corpse was wrapped in a shroud and laid in the recess which was sealed off with a marble slab or a row of terracotta tiles inscribed with the name of the dead person and a sign to show his religion. An **arcosolium** consists of a boxed tomb, closed with a marble slab, set into an arched opening which is often frescoed.
As the cult of the martyrs developed so did the custom, borrowed from the pagans, of holding a funeral feast, called **refrigerium** by the Christians. The faithful would gather round a martyr's tomb to ask him to intercede on their behalf and to share a meal.
Near to the catacombs there is often a **columbarium**; this is a communal burial chamber, containing niches where the urns holding the ashes were placed, usually reserved for pagans of modest means.

Decorative motifs – Originally, Christians decorated their tombs with motifs found on pagan tombs (garlands of flowers, birds and cherubs). Then various other motifs began to appear, illustrating the metaphors of the Holy Scriptures, depicting scenes from the Bible and symbolizing manifestations of spiritual life. The meaning of the paintings and symbols found in the catacombs is still a subject of much controversy.
The **dove** holding a twig in its beak is a symbol of reconciliation between God and man. The **anchor** signifies hope; sometimes the horizontal bar is stressed to form a cross. The **fish** is a symbol for Christ: the Greek word for 'fish' is composed of the initial letter of each word in the Greek phrase meaning "Jesus Christ, God's son, Saviour".
The **dolphin** which comes to the rescue of shipwrecked sailors indicates Jesus the Saviour.
The **fisherman** means a preacher because of Jesus' words to his disciples "I will make you to become fishers of men."
Jonah and the whale foretells the Resurrection.
The **Good Shepherd** or Jesus searching for the lost sheep was one of the most popular ways of representing Christ among early Christians.
Other favourite scenes were the miracle of the feeding of the 5 000, the healing of the man sick of the palsy and the Baptism of Jesus, or the institution of baptism.

★★★TOUR OF THE CATACOMBS

Visitors are shown round in guided parties.
The speed of the tours, imposed by the large numbers of visitors, and the gloom in the passages mean that visitors must follow the guide closely.

★★★Catacombe di San Callisto (St Calixtus Catacombs) ⊘

The catacombs extend over an area bounded by the Appian Way, Via Ardeatina and Via delle Sette Chiese. This cemetery where almost all the 3C popes were buried is also famous for its exceptional collection of paintings. In G B de Rossi's opinion, the Christian cemetery could have grown out of the family tomb of the Caecilii who were patricians. By the 2C the property belonged to the Church and was developed as a huge burial ground for Christians. The remains of about 500 000 people have been interred here.
It was probably **Calixtus** who was chiefly responsible for the Church becoming the legal owner of the cemeteries. This change in circumstances occurred at the very end of the 2C during the reign of the Emperor Commodus (180-92) which was a peaceful period for Christians: it was said that Commodus' concubine, Marcia, was a Christian.

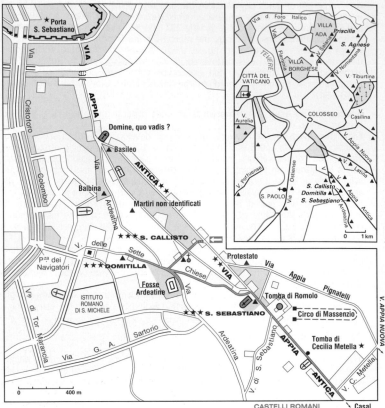

Calixtus, who may have been a native of Trastevere, was a slave whose Christian master entrusted him with his money matters. Financial failure caused Calixtus to flee. He was caught, denounced as a Christian by some Jews and sentenced to hard labour in the Sardinian quarries. He was released under an amnesty but excluded from Rome by the Pope, Victor I, who regarded him as an adventurer.

Calixtus returned to favour under Zephyrinus, Victor's successor, was made a deacon and appointed administrator of the cemetery which bears his name. In 217 he succeeded Zephyrinus as pope: five years later he died. He was not however buried in his cemetery on the Appian Way but in Calepodius' cemetery on the Aurelian Way near the Janiculum where his tomb was found in 1962.

Cripta dei papi (Papal Crypt) – Calixtus decided that his cemetery should be the popes' official burial place and the remains of the 3C popes were placed in the *loculi* hollowed out of the walls of this chamber. Among them was Sixtus II who was put to death on 6 August 258 together with four of his deacons; they had been surprised while holding a meeting in the cemetery, an act which contravened an edict issued by the Emperor Valerian forbidding Christian assemblies and closing the catacombs.

The marble plaques sealing the *loculi* bear the names and titles of the dead popes. The Greek letters M T P, which are the main consonants (MTR) in the Greek word 'martyr' meaning witness, have been added to the names of Pontianus and Fabian; the former was deported to Sardinia where he died in 235; the latter was a victim of the Emperor Decius who organised one of the worst persecutions ever suffered by the Christians.

The wreathed columns and the *lucernarium* date from the 4C.

The inscription to the glory of all the saints who lie buried in this place also dates from the 4C, put up by Pope Damasus to commemorate the martyrs with a few verses in their honour.

Cripta di Santa Cecilia (St Cecilia's Crypt) – This chamber was already being venerated by pilgrims as St Cecilia's tomb in the 7C. Her sarcophagus was found by Paschal I in the 9C in the *loculus* which now contains a copy of the statue of the saint sculpted by Maderno *(see TRASTEVERE: Santa Cecilia).*

Sala dei Sacramenti (Sacraments' Crypt) – This group of chambers contains an extraordinary collection of paintings dating from the late 2C or early 3C. The majority of the subjects generally found elsewhere in the catacombs appear here. There are no purely decorative motifs, except in a simple band framing the scenes. Calixtus' cemetery also contains the crypt in which Pope **Eusebius** (309-10) is buried (he was deported to Sicily where he died but his body was recovered by his successor); the crypt where Pope **Caius** (283-96) is buried; the crypt where, in the opinion of G B de Rossi, Pope **Melchiades** (also Miltiades) (311-14) was buried.

Lucina's precinct, which is named after a noble Roman lady, and the Papal Crypt are the oldest part of the cemetery; Lucina is thought to have recovered the remains of Pope Cornelius (251-53) and to have buried them in a chamber decorated with paintings showing Cornelius with his friend Cyprian, Bishop of Carthage. In another chamber in Lucina's precinct, also decorated with paintings, are two very faint illustrations of the mystery of the Eucharist: two fish together with two baskets of bread and glasses of wine. These paintings, which are on the left wall of the chamber, date from the 2C.

Near the entrance to the underground is a **chapel with three apses,** probably built in the 4C, which may have contained the remains of Pope Zephyrinus.

★★★Catacombe di Domitilla (Domitilla Catacombs) ⊘

Entrance at no 282 Via delle Sette Chiese.

This extensive network of galleries began in the private cemetery of Domitilla, whose uncle, the Emperor Domitian (81-96), belonged to the rich Flavian family. In 95 Domitilla's husband, Flavius Clemens was denounced as a Christian and executed on Domitian's orders. Domitilla was exiled to the Isle of Pandataria (now called Ventotene).

Domitilla's catacombs became famous in the 4C when a basilica was built over the graves of St Nereus and St Achilleus. According to legend they were two of Domitilla's servants who like their mistress converted to Christianity. In fact they were two soldiers martyred under Diocletian (284-305). Not far from their tomb lay St Petronilla whose sarcophagus was transferred to the Vatican in the 8C.

Domitilla's cemetery was discovered in the 16C by Antonio Bosio; in the 19C it was excavated by G B de Rossi and then by the Papal Commission for Sacred Archeology.

Basilica dei Santi Nereo e Achilleo – The **basilica of St Nereus and St Achilleus,** which consisted of a nave and two side aisles preceded by a narthex, was built between 390 and 395 to the detriment of the upper galleries which belonged to one of the oldest parts of the cemetery. The sarcophagi of the two saints must have been placed in the apse near Petronilla's. Pieces of the original structure, in particular of the *schola cantorum* which separated the chancel from the rest of the church, have been put back in place. In front of the chancel on the right one of the small columns which supported the canopy now bears a sculpture of Achilleus the martyr. In this basilica in the late 6C Gregory the Great preached one of his homilies deploring the misery being suffered by Rome under the barbarian menace. By the end of the 8C the basilica was deserted; in future the saints were venerated within the city walls in the new church dedicated to Nereus and Achilleus *(see TERME DI CARACALLA – Santi Nereo e Achilleo)* which was built by Leo III.

Domitilla Catacombs: The Good Shepherd

49

Cubicolo di Veneranda – This chamber behind the apse testifies to the popular enthusiasm for the cemetery in the 4C. The faithful were keen to be buried near to the tomb of a saint, hence Veneranda's wish to be buried next to St Petronilla. A painting on the *arcosolium* shows them both entering Paradise.

"Vestibolo dei Flavi" – This is the name given to the *hypogeum (see above)* on the right of the basilica. It is one of the oldest parts of the cemetery and dates from the 2C. It consists of a long wide gallery decorated with vine tendrils, birds and cupids; branching off it are *cubicula* to contain the sarcophagi; when there was no more room, *loculi* were created. Late in the 3C a room for the funeral meal was created on the right of the entrance. Linked to it is a *cubiculum* named after Love and Psyche on account of its decorations which date from the 3C but have been partially damaged by the creation of *loculi*.

Ipogeo dei Flavi Aureli (closed to the public) – To the left of the basilica is another *hypogeum* containing the names of the freedmen employed by the Flavians and the Aurelians. It is contemporary with the Flavian Vestibule. There are examples of the simple symbols such as the anchor or a monogram used by the early Christians.

Domitilla's Catacombs contain a multitude of galleries and *cubicula* such as the *cubiculum* of Diogenes, a grave digger and the *cubiculum* of Ampliatus.

Turn right out of Via della Sette Chiese into Via Ardeatina.

The **Fosse Ardeatine** ⊙ commemorate a particularly painful episode during the Second World War. Here on 24 March 1944 the Nazis killed 335 Italians as a reprisal for an attack by the Resistance in Rome in Via Rasella in which 32 German soldiers were killed. The tombs *(fosse)* of the victims are sheltered by a sanctuary; a museum gives information on the period.

Continue along Via delle Sette Chiese.

***Catacombe di San Sebastiano (St Sebastian Catacombs) ⊙

Near the catacombs, the Appian Way passes through a valley. On its slopes houses and columbarii were built. In the valley bottom were erected three mausoleums which probably marked the beginning of the cemetery.

When the Church became the owner of the site in the 3C the mausoleums were covered by a platform arranged as a covered courtyard called a *triclia (see below)*.

In the 4C a basilica with a nave and two aisles was built above the earlier structures and surrounded by mausoleums (those round the apse and on the south side have been preserved). It was here, near where the Apostles Peter and Paul were venerated, that St Sebastian was buried; he was a soldier martyred during the persecution in Diocletian's reign (284-305). His cult became so popular that in the 5C a crypt was excavated around his tomb. The basilica was altered in the 13C and then rebuilt in the 17C for Cardinal Scipio Borghese; the new church was built above the nave of the previous building.

The tour of St Sebastian's Catacombs includes a *colombarium (see INTRODUCTION – Daily life in ancient Rome)*; there are other graves of the same type parallel with the one that is visited.

Mausoleums – These three structures with their brick façades, pediments and travertine door frames probably date from the early 1C. At first they were used by pagans and then by Christians. The lefthand and central mausoleums have some beautiful stucco decorations. From these and the inscriptions found within, it seems that the structures belonged to religious sects which developed alongside Christianity; the central mausoleum contains the Greek symbol for the Son of God, Saviour left by the Christians. The righthand mausoleum is decorated with paintings and bears the name of its owner, Clodius Hermes.

'Triclia' – This section of the catacombs has proved the most controversial among archeologists. The graffiti on the walls invoking the Apostles Peter and Paul suggest that from 258 onwards Christians used to meet here to celebrate their memory; they may have met here because the relics of the two saints had been lodged here temporarily while the basilicas of St Peter in the Vatican and St Paul Without-the-Walls were being built. The participants sat on the stone benches for the meal *(refrigerium)*.

Catacombe e cripta di San Sebastiano – The network of galleries (catacombs and crypts) which began to develop in the 4C round St Sebastian's tomb was badly damaged in the Middle Ages by a ceaseless procession of pilgrims who came to invoke the martyr's name against the plague, since the searing pain of bubonic boils was thought to equal the agony of his multiple arrow wounds.

Mausoleo di Quirino e "Domus Petri" ⊙ – These two chambers are supposed to have housed the relics of Peter and Paul. One contains the graffito *Domus Petri* (Peter's house) which may indicate that Peter's remains rested there. The other, built in the 5C, was the **mausoleum of St Quirinus** who was martyred in Pannonia (western Hungary).

Present Basilica – The atmosphere in the single nave with its white walls and beautiful 17C painted wooden ceiling is fairly solemn and chill. In the relics chapel *(right)* is exhibited the stone in which Christ is said to have left his foot prints *(see Domine Quo Vadis? above)*. It may in fact be an old votive offering. St Sebastian's Chapel *(left)*, which was built in the 17C over his tomb, contains a statue of the saint by one of Bernini's pupils (17C).

In the Sacristy *(right of St Sebastian's Chapel)* there is a beautiful 14C wooden crucifix.

CIRCO DI MASSENZIO E TOMBA DI ROMOLO
(Maxentius' Circus and Romulus' Tomb) ⊙

Emperor Maxentius (306-312) built his imperial residence beside the Appian Way. He had a handsome tomb erected nearby when his young son died in 309 and also a hippodrome for chariot races. The oblong shape of the circus is well preserved as are the stables and the remains of the two towers which stood at the western end flanking the stalls and the magistrates' box where the starting signal was given.

Tomba di Romolo – The **tomb of Romulus,** which is surrounded by a wall punctuated by a quadriporticus, is a domed rotunda preceded by a *pronaos* in a style reminiscent of the Pantheon on a smaller scale. It is partly hidden by a house built on to the front.

★TOMBA DI CECILIA METELLA ⊙

This handsome tomb dates from the late Republic. The crenellations were added in the 14C when the Caetani family turned it into a keep and incorporated it into the adjacent 11C fortress which extended across the road. Its bulky silhouette is one of the best known in the Roman countryside. The cylindrical mausoleum standing on a square base was the tomb of the wife of Crassus, son of the Crassus who was a member of the first triumvirate with Caesar and Pompey in 60 BC. The decorative frieze of ox heads has caused the locality to be known as 'Capo di Bove'. Fragments of tombs from the Appian Way can be seen within the ruins of the medieval fortress *(right of the entrance)*.

On the left of the entrance is the way in to the conical funeral chamber of the original tomb.

From Tomba di Cecilia Metella to Casal Rotondo *5 km – 3 miles*

800m – 875yds beyond Cecilia Metella's Tomb the Old Appian Way becomes a one-way road.

Although the road surface is poor, this stretch of the Old Appian Way provides a pleasant view of the Roman countryside where the reddish tones of the tombs and the ruined aqueducts blend with the dark green of the cypresses and umbrella pines.

The tombs on the Appian Way were some of the finest in Rome; shaped like pyramids or tumuli and topped by a mound covered in undergrowth; sometimes only an inscription or a few carvings remain.

The tomb on the right just after the junction with Via Erode Attico was long thought to be the **tomb of one of the Curiatii** *(see Index)*, who took part in the famous combat with the Horatii.

The **Quintilian Villa** (villa dei Quintili) was a huge property going back to the time of Hadrian (117-38); part of it was turned into a fortress in the 15C.

The **Casal Rotondo** was a cylindrical mausoleum dating from the Republican era; it is now topped by a farmhouse.

From this point there is a fine view *(left)* of aqueduct ruins.

The itinerary can be combined with an excursion to the CASTELLI ROMANI by turning left into Via Casal Rotondo and taking Appia Nuova (no 7) in the direction of the Grande Raccordo Anulare (GRA) - Albano.

AVENTINO ★

Tour 1 ½ hours – Departure point – Piazzale Ugo la Malfa

The **Aventine** is the southernmost of the seven hills of Rome (about 40m – 131ft high); it has two peaks separated by a gully down which runs Viale Aventino. Throughout the ancient Roman Republican period it was a popular district, inhabited particularly by merchants who traded among the quays and warehouses on the banks of the Tiber. Many religious shrines were built; among the oldest are the Temples to Diana, Ceres and Minerva, situated between Via di S Melania and Via di S Domenico.

During the Empire the Aventine became a residential area. Trajan lived there before becoming Emperor and his friend Lucinius Sura built his own private baths there *(northwest of Santa Prisca church);* Decius also built a bath house there in 242. So much luxury aroused the envy of the Visigoths. In 410 under their leader Alaric they sacked Rome for three days, leaving the Aventine utterly devastated.

Nowadays it is a residential district, quiet and green, with many religious houses.

A plebeian stronghold –
After the expulsion of the
last king (509 BC) the institution of the Republic was
marked by a struggle be-
tween the patricians and the
plebeians. In the 5C BC the
plebeians, weary of fighting,
which brought them only misery, withdrew to the Aven-

tine as a protest. Menenius Agrippa, who was sent to reason with them, told
them the parable of the human body and its limbs: since their effort benefited
only the body, the limbs decided to stop work; the result was the death of the
whole body including the limbs. As a result of the crisis two tribunes were
elected from among the plebeians to protect them against the
consuls.

Death of a tribune – The plebeian tribune Caius Gracchus and his brother Tiberius
(the Gracchi) were among the group of Roman citizens who shaped the history of the
Republic. Continuing the work begun by Tiberius (assassinated in 133 BC), Caius
proposed reforms in the ownership of land confiscated by Rome from neighbouring
peoples, which was administered by the Senate and exploited by the wealthiest. He
took refuge on the Aventine from soldiers recruited by one of the Consuls until forced
to flee over the Sublician bridge to the foot of the Janiculum where he was finally
murdered in 121 BC.

TOUR

From the Piazzale Ugo la Malfa there is a fine **view★** of the ruins of the semi-
circular façade of the Domus Augustana on the Palatine Hill.
In the square stands a monument to **Giuseppe Mazzini** (**A**) (1805-72), a writer and
politician. In 1849 he proclaimed the Republic of Rome but papal power was
restored by the French *(see GIANICOLO)* under General Oudinot.

"Circus Maximus" – The Great Circus, laid out in the Murcia Valley between
the Palatine and the Aventine and now transformed into a long esplanade, was
the largest in Rome. It was used exclusively for two-, three- and four-horse
chariot *(biga, triga or quadriga)* races which drew larger crowds than any other
spectacle.

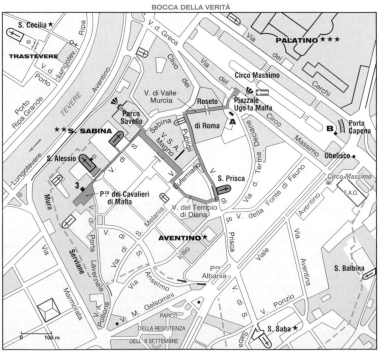

BOCCA DELLA VERITÀ

PIRAMIDE CESTIA - TESTACCIO

The track (over 500m – 550yds long), was bordered by banks of seats; the stand at the northwest end was reserved for the magistrates in charge of the spectacle; beneath it were the stalls; at the southeast end stood an archway.

From the 4C BC the arena was divided down its length by a central reservation, called the *spina*, which linked the two conical turning-posts *(metae)* around which the chariots raced.

In the Augustan era the Circus Maximus became truly grandiose. In 10 BC an obelisk (now in the Piazza del Popolo) more than 23m – 75ft high, was erected on the *spina* and a splendid stand was built below Flavian's Palace for the Emperor and his family. The Circus Maximus could accommodate 150 000 spectators.

The emperors continued to make improvements: Claudius (41-54) replaced the wooden turning-posts with new ones in gilded bronze and substituted marble for tufa in the stables; after the fire in 64 his successor Nero extended the circus to 600m – 656yds long and 200m – 219yds wide; Domitian (81-96) and Trajan (98-117) increased the number of stands and the capacity of the circus grew to 300 000 places.

The major events took place during the September games which originated in the 6C BC. In the Imperial era the games became pure entertainment, offered by the Emperor to the people, and a passion for racing often led the emperors to the worst excesses: Vitellius (68-69) who championed the 'Blues' (there were four stables each distinguished by a different colour) quite simply had his favourite charioteer's rivals put to death; Caracalla (211-217) dealt out the same fate to the 'Greens'.

The circus was still in use in the 4C and Constantinus II set up a second obelisk (now in the Piazza di San Giovanni in Laterano).

The few remains which can be seen near the Porta Capena belong to Trajan's period. The little tower (**B**) at this end dates from the Middle Ages; it was part of a fortress built by the noble Frangipani family.

Take Via di Valle Murcia on the right of the Mazzini monument.

The road is bordered by the **Rome Rose Garden** (Roseto di Roma) *(in flower in May)*.

Turn left into Clivo dei Publicii.

Santa Prisca – The church was reconstructed in the 17C and 18C but its origin goes back to the 2C; it is one of the very first places of Christian worship in Rome. Various touching legends are connected with the name of the holy woman venerated here. Prisca is said to be the first woman to have suffered martyrdom in Rome: she was baptised by Peter himself but denounced to the Imperial authorities and martyred by execution on the road to Ostia. In the 13C a Classical capital was set up as a font *(south aisle)* and inscribed with the 'fact' that Peter had used it.

According to another legend Prisca was the wife of Aquila whose memory is recalled by St Paul in his Epistle to the Romans: "Greet Prisca and Aquila, my helpers in Christ Jesus, who have for my life laid down their own necks..."

Excavations have uncovered a late 2C **Mithraeum** ⊙ *(access from the south aisle of the church)*. Contemporary with it is a neighbouring twin-nave building which may have been an earlier place of Christian worship on which the present church was built.

Traces of even older buildings, dating from the late 1C and early 2C have been found nearby; they may belong to Trajan's residence (98-117) or to the house of his friend, Licinius Sura, next to the baths he had built.

Take Via del Tempio di Diana, Via Eufemiano and then Via S A Magno.

Parco Savello – Better known as the **Giardino degli Aranci,** this park hugs the apse of Santa Sabina. In the 10C fortifications were built to defend the hill; in the 13C they became the stronghold of the Savelli family. From the northwest side high up above the river there is a pleasant **view★** of Rome: from the Janiculum, St Peter's dome and the Monte Mario with its TV mast round to the monument to Victor Emmanuel II and the Militia Tower.

★★Santa Sabina – The church was built in the 5C by Bishop Peter of Illyria who had officiated as priest to a *titulus* on this site. From the first it was dedicated to Sabina; the legend about this saint, which arose in the 6C, does not say clearly whether she lived and died on the Aventine or whether her remains were brought back here after her martyrdom in Umbria under Hadrian (117-138). The building has undergone many alterations: a campanile was added in the 10C; the crenellations were removed in the 17C. In the 13C Pope Honorius III, a member of the Savelli family, gave the church to St Dominic who built the cloisters and convent to house the members of his order.

In the 16C the enterprising Sixtus V (1585-90) and his architect Domenico Fontana transformed the interior into a typical example of the Counter-Reformation style; this together with subsequent Baroque additions completely effaced the medieval character of the church.

Extensive restoration work has revived its earlier appearance in all its glory.

Santa Sabina

D. Dorval/EXPLORER

Exterior – In the 15C a portico was added to the door in the side wall. The narthex on the west front was one side of a four-sided portico surrounding an atrium which disappeared in the 13C when the convent was built.

Opening into the nave is a very beautiful **door**★★ made of cypress wood; it belonged to the original church and dates from the 5C. The two leaves are divided into panels, 18 of which are decorated with the original low relief carvings illustrating scenes from the Old and New Testaments. High up on the left is a representation of the Crucifixion, the oldest example of a representation of this scene in a public place.

★★**Interior** – The well-proportioned interior with light streaming through the clerestory windows reflects the vigorous expansion of the flourishing early Christian church.

The basilical plan (the two side chapels added in the 16C and 17C have been retained) consists of a nave and two aisles separated by two rows of columns with Corinthian capitals directly supporting a very light arcade (no architrave). The overhead windows have been restored to their original appearance.

The mosaic above the entrance, the only one left of many which extended along both sides of the nave between the arches and the windows, bears an inscription in gold lettering commemorating the construction of the church by Peter of Illyria during the reign of Pope Celestine I (422-32); the female figures on either side are allegories of the church of the Jews ('Ecclesia ex circumcisione') converted by St Peter and the church of the Gentiles ('Ecclesia ex gentibus') converted by St Paul.

Nave: the frieze of tessellated marble above and between the arches dates from the 5C; the mosaic tomb on the floor in front of the *schola cantorum* (the space reserved for the choristers in front of the chancel) belongs to a Master General of the Dominican Order who died in 1300.

Chancel: the rich marble décor *(schola cantorum, presbyterium, ambones)* dating from the 9C and destroyed by Sixtus V has been reconstructed from fragments of the original; the ambones (Early Christian pulpits) and the Paschal candlestick are reconstructions. The Mannerist mosaic in the apse by Taddeo Zuccari (retouched in the 19C and 20C) replaced the original 16C mosaic which depicted the saints who were venerated in the church.

South aisle: the upper part of a Classical column, discovered during excavations underneath the church, may have belonged to the 3C-4C house, the *titulus* of the early church.

At the east end of the aisle is a chapel dedicated to the Virgin in the 15C by Cardinal Poggio del Monte di Auxia; his attractive tomb recalls the funeral art of Lombardy at the time of the Renaissance which was introduced to Rome by Andrea Bregno.

North aisle: the 17C Baroque chapel dedicated to St Catherine of Siena has been preserved; its multi-coloured marbles, frescoes and painted dome clash with the serenity of the rest of the church.

In the monks' garden *(apply to the sacristan)*, perfumed by jasmine and geraniums and shaded by orange and lemon trees, is a sculpture of the *Last Supper* (1974) by Gismondi.

Sant'Alessio (St Alexis) – This is a church for those who are interested in legends. On the left immediately inside the door is St Alexis' staircase: the son of a patrician family, St Alexis set out for the Holy Land as a mendicant, returning to Rome to die, but his family did not recognise him and he spent his last days beneath the staircase of his father's house. The legend of the 'Beggar beneath the stairs' was one of the main subjects of mystery plays in the 15C.

Continue along the road to Piazza dei Cavalieri di Malta.

This charming **square** was designed by Piranesi in the 18C.
The door into the Priory of the Knights of Malta (Villa del Priorato di Malta, no 3) is famous for the view through the keyhole which reveals the dome of St Peter's at the end of a well-clipped avenue of trees.

Neighbouring sights are described in the following chapters: BOCCA DELLA VERITÀ; PIRAMIDE CESTIA – TESTACCIO.

BOCCA DELLA VERITA ★★

Tour 1 $\frac{1}{2}$ hours

To visualise the unity of this part of the town, hemmed in by the Capitoline, the Palatine and the Tiber, one must go back 2 500 years to the time of the Etruscan kings and the Republic. As early as 6C BC crowds thronged the vegetable market (Forum Holitorium) at the foot of the Capitoline and the cattle market (Forum Boarium) at the foot of the Palatine. This area was also a religious centre, containing several temples, some of which were thought to have been founded by King Servius Tullius (578-34 BC).

At the end of the Republican period Caesar began the construction of the magnificent Theatre of Marcellus. Nearby was the Circus Flaminius, a vast oblong arena, built in 221 BC, where chariot races, hunting events and processions took place.

When Rome declined, these buildings fell into ruins. In the Middle Ages the area was heavily populated, particularly by artisans. Small businesses abounded, owned in particular by Jews who congregated there from 13C. The removal of the Ghetto in 1888, the clearances undertaken in 1926 to reveal the ancient monuments and the opening of new roads, have all destroyed a proportion of the narrow lanes and old houses.

Forum Holitorium and Forum Boarium – From the earliest days not far from the Roman Forum, the administrative and political centre, there were other fora devoted to trade.

One of them, the vegetable market **(Forum Holitorium)** extended from the Porticus of Octavia along the riverbank to Vicus Jugarius. Another, the cattle market **(Forum Boarium)** extended further south to the foot of the Aventine and reached as far east as the Arch of Janus (Arco di Giano) and the Arch of the Money-changers (Arco degli Argentari). These two markets were next to the Port of Rome; the boats sailed up the Tiber which was then navigable and moored by the left bank level with the Pons Aemilius (Ponte Rotto).

From the beginning this district had contained altars for the worship of the gods. Hercules, who was thought to have driven Geryon's cattle through the Forum Boarium, was honoured near to Santa Maria in Cosmedin, in recognition of his victory over Cacus *(see FORO ROMANO – Scala di Caco)*, the blind cattle thief. Parallel to the Temple of Apollo, traces have been found of another temple attributed to the Roman goddess of war, Bellona. Three temples stood side by side on the site of the Church of San Nicola in Carcere. Not far from the Church of St Omobono, beside the Vicus Jugarius, a group of sanctuaries has been uncovered; further south stands the Temple of Fortune which Servius Tullius, the slave who became king, dedicated to the god who changes man's destiny. Naturally Portumnus, the protector of harbours, had a place of worship near the port; this has sometimes been identified as the very old sanctuary known as the Temple of Fortuna Virilis *(see below)*.

Upstream from the Forum Boarium and its quays, must have been the military port, known as 'Navalia inferiora' (later on another port 'Navalia superiora' was built on the Campus Martius). In 338 BC when Rome embarked on the conquest of the Mediterranean, her citizens came to the port to admire the ships captured at Antium; the prows were displayed on the Rostra in the Forum. It was here too that Cato of Utica disembarked in 58 BC laden with treasures from King Ptolemy Auletes after an expedition to Cyprus.

★**Piazza della Bocca della Verità** – This open space more or less covers the site of the Forum Boarium. The combination of ancient, medieval and Baroque buildings, framed by umbrella pines and pink and white oleanders, makes a typical Roman scene.

Santa Maria in Cosmedin

Opposite the medieval façade of Santa Maria in Cosmedin stands an 18C fountain supported by two tritons.

★★**Santa Maria in Cosmedin** ⊙ – The soaring **belltower**★ with its bold arcading was built early in the 12C and is one of the most elegant in Rome.

Foundation – In the 6C the district between the Aventine and Tiber was inhabited by Greeks, who like other foreign colonies in Rome, formed themselves into a fighting force *(schola)* to protect Rome from the threat of the Lombards. In order to feed these soldiers, the Church was obliged to form **deaconries** *(diaconiae)*, composed of religious and lay people who inherited the duties performed by similar bodies under the Roman Empire. Their duty was to fix the price of wheat and to distribute the grain, sometimes free of charge. The Imperial organisation was administered by the *praefectus annonae* from the *Statio Annonae*. It was on the site of this building that the Church set up one of its deaconries, with an oratory in one of the store rooms. It was enlarged in the 8C by Pope Hadrian I and became the Greek church under the name of Santa Maria in Schola Greca, which later became Santa Maria in Cosmedin after the name of a district of Constantinople.

Early in the 12C the church was restored; the porch and campanile were added by Popes Gelasius II and Callistus II. The church was restored to its medieval appearance in the 19C.

Tour – In the porch is the **Bocca della Verità** (Mouth of Truth) (**1**). According to popular legend the mouth would snap shut on the hand of anyone with a guilty conscience. The name was also attributed to the fact that the mouth had never spoken. The face is that of a marine divinity, perhaps the Ocean, with two bull's horns symbolizing the surging power of the sea. The plaque is in fact a drain cover, possibly from the nearby Temple of Hercules.

In the north aisle, on either side of the entrance door and in the sacristy, now incorporated into the construction of the church, are the huge Corinthian columns which belonged to the *Statio Annonae* which extended from left to right across the back half of the church.

The three parallel apses, inspired by the plan of oriental churches, date from the period of Pope Hadrian I (8C) and the columns dividing the nave and aisles come from ancient monuments.

The beautiful floor and the marble furnishings (ambones, Paschal candlesticks, canopy above the high altar and the episcopal throne) are all Cosmati work. The *schola cantorum* ( ) for the choristers and the presbytery ( ) for the priests are 19C reconstructions. The presbytery has been screened off by a *pergula*, a colonnade hung with curtains which are drawn at certain moments in the Eastern liturgy.

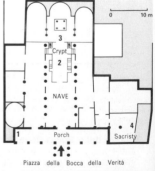

Piazza della Bocca della Verità

• Columns of the "Statio Annonae"

The 8C crypt *(accessible by appointment only)*, with its nave and aisles separated by small columns, is an original design for this period when it was usual to follow the semi-circular plan designed by Gregory the Great (590-604) for the confessio in St Peter's in the Vatican.

The beautiful 8C mosaic (**4**) in the sacristy comes from St Peter's Basilica.

From Piazza Bocca della Verità go east into Via del Velabro.

The valley of the **Velabro** (Velabrum), between the Palatine and the Capitoline Hills, used to be a very marshy place.

Arco di Giano (Arch of Janus) – This massive 4C construction with four faces, each one being pierced by an arch, was a *janus,* i.e. a public gateway spanning a busy crossroads. It marked the northern edge of the Forum Boarium. The name reflects the power of the god Janus to protect road junctions.

Arco degli Argentari (Arch of the Money Changers) – This construction is more like a monumental gate against the west wall of San Giorgio in Velabro. It was built in 204 by the Guild of Money Changers in honour of the Emperor Septimius Severus and his wife, Giulia Domna, who both appear on the arch *(inside right panel)* making an offering before a tripod. The sharp relief and the abundance of decoration are characteristic of 3C art.

★**San Giorgio in Velabro** – Founded originally as a deaconry *(see above)* in the 7C, the church was rebuilt and enlarged by Pope Gregory IV (827-44). Since its restoration in 1926 San Giorgio in Velabro has recaptured the charm of the Roman churches of the Middle Ages. The façade, the porch and the bell tower date from the 12C. The interior has a monumental simplicity. In the Middle Ages Rome was poor: builders used existing foundations resulting in asymetrical designs; columns and capitals were re-employed in a random manner.

The apsidal fresco of Christ flanked by the Virgin and St George, St Peter and St Sebastian is attributed to Pietro Cavallini (1295).

At the west end of Via del Velabro turn right into Via di S Giovanni Decollato.

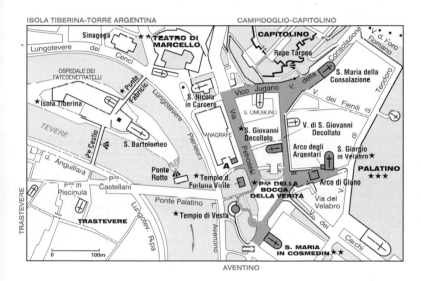

★**Oratorio di San Giovanni Decollato** ⊘ – The Oratory of the Confraternity of St John the Beheaded was built at the end of the 15C to assist people who had been condemned to death; those who died in a state of grace were buried beneath the cloisters.

The Oratory was used for the meetings of the members of the brotherhood. The decoration is by a group of Mannerist artists drawing inspiration from Michelangelo and Raphael without, however, following the style of the two masters too slavishly. Starting from the right-hand wall, near the altar, are:

The Angel Gabriel appears to Zacharias (Jacopino del Conte); on the left of the painting is a portrait of Michelangelo who was, himself, a member of the brotherhood; *The Visitation* (Salviati); *Birth of St John the Baptist* (Salviati); Above the entrance: *St John the Baptist preaching* (Jacopino del Conte); *Baptism of Christ* (Jacopino del Conte);

On the left-hand wall, near the entrance: *Arrest of St John the Baptist* (Battista Franco); *Dance of Salome* (Pirro Ligorio); *Beheading of St John the Baptist;*

On either side of the altar: *St Andrew and St Bartholomew* (Salviati);

Above the altar: *Deposition* (Jacopino del Conte).

The church adjacent to the oratory is decorated with stuccoes and paintings (late 16C) *(open 24 June)*.

Continue north and east into Via della Consolazione.

Santa Maria della Consolazione – Before the broad white façade of the church at the top of the steps is a good place to pause. A 14C chronicler recounts how a prisoner condemned to death asked for an image of the Virgin to be placed near the place of execution on the Capitol. As she brought comfort to poor wretches about to die, she was called the Virgin of Consolation.

The first church was built in 1470. In the 16C a hospital was added; it was constructed between 1583 and 1600 according to plans by Martino Longhi the Elder. He also began the façade of the church which was eventually completed in the 19C in a style inspired by the Counter-Reformation.

Take Vico Jugario and Via Petroselli to return to Piazza Bocca della Verità.

Casa dei Crescenzi (A) – This curious building is one of the rare remains of 'Roma Turrita' when Rome was bristling with fortresses. It was built in the 12C to defend the bridge (Ponte Rotto) on which the Crescenzi family had the right to collect tolls. The random use of antique elements (in the cornices and in the arch over the main door) shows how insensitively the Roman monuments were despoiled in the Middle Ages.

★**Tempio della Fortuna Virile** – The attribution of this temple to Human Fortune is without foundation. Some archeologists think it is a sanctuary dedicated to Portumnus, the god of rivers and harbours. It dates from the late 2C BC and is one of the best preserved temples in Rome. It has an air of austere solemnity typical of the rigour of the Republican era. At this period the Romans were still greatly influenced by the Etruscans and built rectangular temples, set on a high podium. The temple was used as a church probably from the 9C and dedicated to St Mary the Egyptian in the 15C.

★**Tempio di Vesta** – It is not known to which god this temple was dedicated but it has acquired its name because of its circular shape; there was in fact only one temple dedicated to Vesta, the one in the Roman Forum.

With its well proportioned fluted columns and its Corinthian capitals it is an elegant building which dates from the reign of Augustus. A church was established in the *cella* in the Middle Ages; in 16C it was dedicated to St Mary of the Sun after an image of the Virgin which had been found in the Tiber was placed there: when the coffer containing the image was opened a ray of light shone out.

Neighbouring sights are described in the following chapters: AVENTINO; CAMPIDOGLIO – CAPITOLINO; ISOLA TIBERINA – TORRE ARGENTINA; TRASTEVERE.

CAMPIDOGLIO – CAPITOLINO★★★

Tour 2 hours

Nowadays it is the seat of the local authority which administers Rome.

It was in 1764, as Edward Gibbon later wrote, "on the fifteenth of October in the gloom of the evening, as I sat musing on the Capitol, while the barefoot fryars were chanting their litanies in the temple of Jupiter, that I conceived the first thought of my history... the decline and fall of the Roman Empire."

This section of Rome borrows its name from one of the smallest but most prestigious hills in Rome, the Campidoglio. There are two summits: the **Capitolino** and the **Arx** – the citadel. The dip between them is now occupied by a fine Michelangelo-esque piazza.

In the days of Ancient Rome, this area was particularly important stretching as it did before the Forum, indeed providing access to it, and because of its two temples dedicated to Jupiter Capitolinus and Juno Moneta (the giver of council) perched on the citadel.

Jupiter Capitolinus – By 6C BC the Etruscan King, Tarquin the Proud, had already built a temple on the Capitol to Jupiter, the Best and Greatest. This was considered second only to the Heavens as the god's abode. During triumphal ceremonies the generals, dressed in gold and purple, made their way to the temple bearing an ivory sceptre surmounted by an eagle, the symbol of Jupiter.

The temple was built on the Etruscan plan and divided into three sanctuaries, the central one being dedicated to Jupiter and those on either side to Juno and Minerva. These three deities comprised the Capitoline Triad. The city treasure was kept beneath Jupiter's statue. In the sanctuary dedicated to Juno, the Romans placed a silver goose in memory of the "**geese of the Capitol**" as it was the cries of these geese which alerted the Romans, entrenched in their citadel, when the Gauls attacked Rome (390-388 BC).

Having been destroyed by fire, the temple was rebuilt twice, first by Augustus and then by Domitian.

The Rape of the Sabines and Tarpeia

The origins of this legend are lost with those of Rome's foundation in the mists of time. With his brother dead and the new city established, Romulus was anxious to increase Rome's populus apace. Having declared the Campidoglio a safe haven for outlaws seeking refuge, the area soon became crowded with a band of men. To counter-effect this imbalance of the sexes Romulus decided to draw the young Sabine women from a neighbouring tribe and organise a series of games for the occasion that involved the rape of all the young girls of marriageable age.

Outraged, Titus Tatius, King of the Sabines, set out to rescue his womenfolk and marched on Rome. According to legend as soon as Tarpeia, the daughter of the keeper of the Roman citadel, set eyes upon the Sabine king she fell hopelessly in love with him; she offered him and his men access to the citadel in exchange for his love. Tatius quickly accepted but once he was through the city gates, the poor girl was crushed by his soldiers.

The inevitable bloody confrontation of Sabine pitched against Roman that may have ensued, it is said, was prevented by the Sabine women who threw themselves between their fathers and new husbands: and so a new alliance was formed between Romulus and Titus Tatius.

Rupe Tarpea – On the southwest edge of the Capitoline Hill, just by the Temple of Jupiter, above Via della Consolazione, is the bluff where, it is said, the legendary **Tarpeian Rock** was situated – from where traitors were hurled to their death during the Republic.

Scalinata d'Aracoeli (Aracoeli Steps) – In 1348 the plague ravaged Italy; Rome miraculously was spared and built the steps as a thanks offering. The first person to climb them was **Cola di Rienzo**. At this time the Pope was in Avignon; Rome was in a state of anarchy at the hands of the noble families. Cola gave himself the task of restoring the grandeur of Rome. He stood at the top of the steps dressed like an Emperor and roused the people with his speeches. **Petrarch** himself had begged the Pope to restore the capital to its former splendour. In 1354 he set out to lend his support to Cola di Rienzo but before reaching the Capitol he learned that the 'tribune of Rome' had been killed in a riot by a servant of the Colonna family.

From the top of the steps there is a fine view of the dome of St Peter's in the background, of the Synagogue *(left)* and of Sant'Andrea della Valle and the Gesù Church.

★★SANTA MARIA D'ARACOELI ⊙

The broad plain façade of the church standing at the top of the steps is one of the famous sights of tourist Rome.

Here from the earliest days of the city's existence stood the citadel *(arx)* to defend the northern flank of the Palatine which was naturally protected by the Tiber to the west. During the Republic a temple was built here to Juno Moneta (Counsellor). According to the legend it was here that the Virgin and Child appeared to the Emperor Augustus after he had asked the Tiburtine Sibyl whether there would one day be a greater man than himself.

Following the arrival in 552 of General Narses from Greece, several Greek monasteries were established in Rome. One of them occupied an oratory which was turned into the Church of Santa Maria d'Aracoeli in 1250 by Franciscan monks. The name comes from an altar *(ara)* dedicated to the goddess of the sky or from the citadel *(arx) (see above)*.

The severity of the brick façade is relieved by the Renaissance doorway and two Gothic rose windows. The shallow concave band at the top was originally covered with mosaic.

The interior is built on the basilical plan and contains several works of art. The side chapels and the aisle ceilings were added in the 16C and 17C when the chancel and the upper part of the nave were remodelled according to contemporary taste.

Ceiling and Floor – The ceiling was an ex-voto offering by Marcantonio Colonna who fought with the troops of the Holy League at Lepanto in Greece on 7 October 1571 when the Christians scored a victory against the Turks. The floor is one of the best preserved examples of the work of the Cosmati *(see ARTS IN ROME: Medieval Period)*, Romans who worked in marble from the 12C to the 14C.

Cardinal d'Albret's tomb (1) – This is one of Andrea Bregno's best works. The fine working of motifs, particularly on the sarcophagus, and the use of architectural elements (pilasters, arcades) are characteristic of his style.

Giovanni Crivelli's tombstone (2) – It is attributed to Donatello whose signature used to be legible, so it is said, but was worn away when the stone lay on the ground.

Chapel of St Bernardino of Siena (**3**) – The decorative **frescoes**★ were painted by **Pinturicchio** in about 1485 and illustrate the life and death of Bernardino. The funeral scene *(left wall)* shows some well-composed portraits against an accomplished landscape.

The huge statue of Gregory XIII (**4**) complements that of Paul III (**5**); both are Counter-Reformation works.

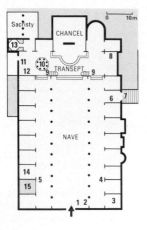

In the passage leading to the side door there is a tomb (**6**) designed by Michelangelo of a young man, Cecchino Bracci.

Step outside to admire the doorway.

Mosaic of the Virgin and Child (**7**) – This mosaic is over the side door on the outside of the church.

It comes from the Cosmati workshop and reveals the influence of Pietro Cavallini, the greatest Roman artist in the Middle Ages; his style is characterised by balanced composition, rich in Byzantine influence and knowledge of Classical art.

Although Piazza del Campidoglio can be reached from the side door of the church (down the steps), it is best approached up the "Cordonata" from the bottom of the hill to appreciate the full effect of the architecture.

Go back into the church.

Tomba della famiglia Savelli (**8**) – The Savelli family tomb contains an ancient sarcophagus re-used for the burial of Luca Savelli. The mosaic decoration and the tiny *Virgin and Child* are the work of Arnolfo di Cambio (14C).

Ambones (**9**) – Like the floor they are Cosmati work. They are signed by Lorenzo di Cosma and his son Giacomo and belong to the very elaborate Cosmati work typical of the late 12C. Earlier Cosmati work usually comprises only white marble.

St Helen's Chapel (**10**) – This is an elegant 17C domed construction. Beneath the porphyry urn is a 12C altar decorated with Romanesque sculptures and mosaic insets commemorating the appearance of the Virgin to Augustus *(see FONTANA DI TREVI)*.

Cardinal Matteo d'Acquasparta's Monument (**11**) – This is a typical Italian Gothic tomb (vertical composition with angels drawing curtains round the death bed). The painting of the Virgin and Child is related to the art of Pietro Cavallini. Cardinal d'Acquasparta, Vicar General of the Franciscans who died in 1302, is mentioned by Dante in his Divine Comedy as a man who relaxed the severity of the rule.

In the left transept is an enormous statue (**12**) of Leo X (16C).

Holy Child Chapel (**13**) – The chapel took its name from a statuette which, according to legend, had miraculous curative powers; many letters were addressed to it from all over the world. Unfortunately it was stolen on 1 February 1994.

North aisle side chapels – One of the **chapels** (**14**) was decorated in the 15C with frescoes by Benozzo Gozzoli, Fra Angelico's assistant; only St Antony of Padua remains above the altar.

In the pre-Christmas period young children gather in the adjoining **chapel** (**15**) to recite or improvise verses *(sermoni)* before the Santo Bambino.

Go down the Aracoeli steps and turn left into the 'Cordonata'.

La 'Cordonata' – Michelangelo's design for this ramp was not faithfully executed. The two lions guarding the entrance are Egyptian (restored in 1955); they were found on the Campus Martius and placed here in 1582; in 1588 Giacomo della Porta converted them into fountains which at one time on feast days flowed with red and white wine.

A **statue** (**A**) of Cola di Rienzo was put up in 19C on the spot where he was killed.

★★★PIAZZA DEL CAMPIDOGLIO

The visitor who is only passing through Rome should pause a moment in **Capitol Square**, a haven of peace where charm and majesty mingle in harmony. To see it as it was in Antiquity one must envisage the monuments and temples facing the Forum.

In the Middle Ages Capitol Square was known simply as 'Monte Caprino' (Goat Hill) where goats grazed among the ruins. Change came in the 16C. On the occasion of Charles V's visit in 1536, Pope Paul III decided that Rome, which had been sacked

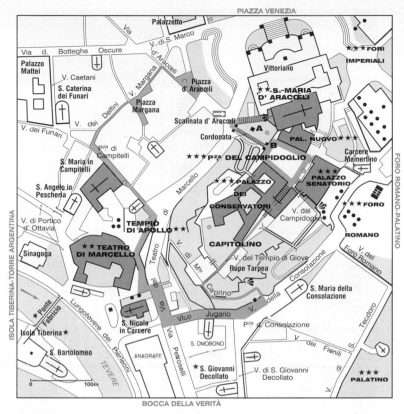

nine years earlier by the same Charles V, should be restored to its former elegance and he commissioned **Michelangelo** to draw up plans for the Capitol. The design was executed over the next 100 years or so and altered in certain respects. The square is lined by three buildings (the Senatorial Palace, the New Palace and the Conservators' Palace) and is shaped like a trapezium to accommodate the position of the Conservators' Palace which had already been built. Michelangelo turned the square round to face the modern city rather than the ancient Forum. The balustrade with its overlarge statues was not part of Michelangelo's design.

On Saturdays the square is particularly busy; after the wedding ceremonies in the registry office of the Conservators' Palace, dozens of newly-weds pose for photographs in front of the statue of the Tiber and the wolf's head or on the Cordonata steps.

At the centre of a beautiful geometric design, conceived by Michelangelo but executed only recently, is the plinth on which stood the equestrian statue of Marcus Aurelius. The statue which graced the square for many years has been removed to the Capitoline Museum after extensive restoration *(see FORO ROMANO: Tempio di Castore e Polluce)*. The piazza façade overlooking the Cordonata is ornamented with a balustrade topped with free-standing figurative sculpture *(see below)*.

***Statue dei Dioscuri** (**B**) – The two knights, the Dioscuri, are shown standing beside their horses. The statues are Roman and date from the late Empire; they were found in the 16C on the Campus Martius and restored (the head of one of them is modern).

"**Trofei di Mario**" – Marius' Trophies is the name given to the sculptures (1C BC) which commemorate Domitian's conquest of the German people. Until the 16C they adorned a fountain in Piazza Vittorio Emanuele II.

The Roman custom of piling up the arms of the vanquished goes back to earliest times when at the end of a battle they would stack up breastplates, helmets and shields against a tree.

Milestones – *Next to the statues of Constantine and Constantine II.* One was the first and the other the seventh milestone on the Appian Way.

*****Palazzo Senatorio (Senate House)** – *Closed to the public; occupied by the offices of the local authority.* In 1143 under the influence of Arnold of Brescia who inveighed against the corruption of the clergy in his speeches, the Roman people deprived the

Palazzo Senatorio

Pope of his temporal power and set up the Roman Commune. Senators were created to lead the government; the palace was constructed like a castle on the ruins of the Tabularium *(see Index)* to house the meetings of the magistrates.

Michelangelo kept the walls of this old building but designed a new façade. His plans were carried out from 1582 to 1605 by Giacomo della Porta and then by Girolamo Rainaldi.

The municipal tower was built by Martino Longhi the Elder from 1578 to 1582.

The double staircase is the only part of the building to be completed during Michelangelo's lifetime. The fountain which was added in 1588 on Sixtus V's initiative was not part of the original design. The goddess of Rome, in porphyry and marble, seems lost in her recess, perched on a pedestal which is disproportionately high. The flanking statues come from Constantine's baths on the Quirinal and represent the Nile and the Tiber. The latter statue *(right)* originally represented the Tigris but the tiger's head was replaced with a wolf's head to indicate the Tiber.

Some blocks of stone from the old **Arx Capitolina** (citadel) can be seen in a little garden on the left of the Senate House.

★★★**Palazzo dei Conservatori e Palazzo Nuovo** – The Conservators' Palace, which was built in the 15C to house the meetings of the Conservators, magistrates who governed the town with the Senators, was altered in 1568 by Giacomo della Porta according to Michelangelo's designs.

Although not built until 1654 the New Palace, which was the work of Girolamo and Carlo Rainaldi, was identical to the Conservators' Palace as Michelangelo had intended. At this time Via delle Tre Pile was opened and the development of the Capitol was complete. The two flanking palaces with their porticos at ground level and façades decorated with a single order of flat pilasters form an elegant pair.

They house two museums; the collections on display were started by Sixtus IV in 1471, enlarged by Pius V in 1566 and opened to the public in 1734 by Clement XII; they rank among the most important in Rome.

***MUSEO DEL PALAZZO DEI CONSERVATORI ⊘ *Tour 1 hour.*

In the internal courtyard are the Gothic arches of the 15C palace *(right)* and a few pieces of a colossal statue of Constantine which used to be in Constantine's Basilica in the Forum. The statue of a seated figure (10m - 33ft high) was probably an acrolith statue where only the parts of the body uncovered by clothing were made of stone and the rest was of wood covered in bronze. On the left are low relief sculptures of figures representing the Roman provinces which come from the Temple of Hadrian in Piazza di Pietra.

From the entrance hall take the stairs to the upper floor.

On the first landing are some **low relief sculptures:** three of them belonged to an arch erected in 176 to commemorate Marcus Aurelius' victories over the Germans and the Sarmatians. They show Victory (**1**), Clemency (**2**) and Imperial Piety (**3**). The place beside Marcus Aurelius in the triumphal chariot is empty; it may have been occupied by his son Commodus, whose figure was then effaced when the Senate condemned this terrible emperor. The low relief of Marcus Aurelius at a sacrificial ceremony is in traditional style: the solemnity of the scene is stressed by the definite lines of the background; the crowd seems to be contained in an enclosure. This work is also remarkable for containing a reproduction of the Temple of Jupiter Capitolinus *(back left)* of which almost nothing remains.

Statue of Charles of Anjou (**4**) – The seated figure is attributed to **Arnolfo di Cambio** who came to Rome in the late 13C, entered the service of the King of Sicily and sculpted this effigy. Both austere and majestic, it is a rare example of Gothic sculpture in the round at a period when the arts of mosaic and painting were dominant.

Horatii and Curatii Room (**1**) – The marble statue of Urban VIII (**5**) was sculpted by Bernini and his pupils. The Romans criticised the Pope for his expenses and were very indignant when he wanted to set up a statue of himself on the Capitol during his lifetime. The statue of Innocent X (**6**) which is in bronze is a masterly piece on which Algardi worked from 1645 to 1650; he was one of the greatest Baroque sculptors.

The wall frescoes which give the room its name are by Cavaliere d'Arpino *(see THE ARTS IN ROME: Counter-Reformation);* treated like tapestries in pastel shades they belong to the style which Caravaggio confronted with his 'luminism'.

Courtyard of the Palazzo dei Conservatori

J.-P. Langeland/DIAF

The Spinario in the Palazzo dei Conservatori

Captains' Room (2) – It is named after the 16C-17C statues of papal generals (Marcantonio Colonna, Alessandro Farnese etc) which are displayed there. The coffered ceiling★ with historical scenes painted in the panels comes from a 16C palace, now demolished.

The late 16C pictures hanging on the walls illustrate legendary episodes in the history of Republican Rome: *Brutus condemning his sons to death* (**7**); *The Battle of Lake Regillus* (**8**); *Horatius Cocles defending the bridge* (**9**); *Mucius Scaevola and Porsenna* (**10**).

Triumph Room (3) – Fine 16C gilded wooden ceiling. Painted 15C frieze illustrating the triumph of Emilius Paulus over Perseus, King of Macedon in 168 BC.

In the centre of the room is the famous **'Spinario'★★★** (**11**), an original Greek work or a very good 1C BC copy. In the Hellenistic period the child became a favourite subject among artists. The frailty and spontaneous grace of youth were refreshing after the Classical period with its admiration of solidity and reason. The charming pose of this boy who is removing a thorn from his foot and the studied treatment of his hair and face make this an admirable work.

The bronze vase (**12**) comes from the spoils of war taken from Mithradates, King of Pontus, who was finally defeated by Pompey in 63 BC.

The bust of **Junius Brutus★★** (**13**): the head which dates from the 3C BC was placed on a bust during the Renaissance. It was thought to be a portrait of the founder of the ancient republic whose legendary severity and integrity seemed to find expression in this head. In fact it probably belonged to an equestrian statue.

The *camillus* (**14**): this was the name given to the young servers who assisted the priests in the religious ceremonies. Work of Roman art from the Augustan era (1C).

Wolf Room (4) – Here is the famous bronze statue of the **She-wolf★★★** (**15**), the emblem of Rome. The twins were added at the Renaissance by Antonio del Pollaiuolo. It is said that in antiquity the wolf stood on the Capitol and was struck by lightening in 65 BC. Sometimes one is shown the marks of lightning on the rear paws. The statue dates from the 6C or 5C BC and could be the work of a Greek or Etruscan artist. The anatomical accuracy is treated in a remarkably stylised manner. On the walls are fragments of the 'Fasti Consulares' and the 'Fasti Triumphales': they come from the Arch of Augustus in the Forum and are lists of the successive consuls down to AD 13 and of triumphant generals from Romulus to AD 12.

Goose Room (5) – Two small bronze geese (**16**) give this room its name. The handsome mastiff in flecked green marble (**17**) derives from a 4C BC Greek original. The head of Medusa (**18**) is by Bernini. Both the ceiling and the frieze, which is illustrated with views of Rome prior to 1550, are 16C work.

Room 18 – The room contains a tomb-stone showing a **young girl with a dove★** (**19**): this is a Hellenistic work (early 5C BC), probably by an artist from southern Italy. The lion's head (**20**), also Hellenistic from the early 5C BC, shows considerable Orientalising influence.

Room 17 – The torso of an amazon (**21**) is a Greek work from 510 BC, an example from the 'severe' period of transition between Archaic and Classical art and characterised by the disappearance of rigid forms in favour of a certain naturalism.

Magistrates' Room (16) – Two magistrates (**22**) are portrayed giving the starting signal for the races (late 4C AD). The fairly heavy treatment is characteristic of the late Empire.

Return to Room 6 which leads into Room 8.

Tapestry Room (8) – The fine 16C coffered ceiling is painted and gilded. The huge tapestries were woven in a Roman workshop in 18C; one of them (**23**) shows the wolf and the twins, the subject of a picture by Rubens hanging in the picture gallery *(see below)* upstairs.

Following the Punic Wars Room (**9**) and the former chapel (**10**), there is a corridor (**11**), once occupied by the archives and now hung with several small works by **Vanvitelli** *(see Index)* showing 18C views of Rome. The Tiber near to Castel Sant'Angelo has not yet been channelled between embankments and Rome has a countrified appearance.

Three rooms of Fasti Moderni – The first (**12**) contains the list of Roman magistrates from 1640. In the second (**13**) is a bust of the Empress Faustina (**24**) (2C), wife of Antoninus Pius; together they shared a temple in the Forum.

★★**Lamiani Gardens Gallery** (**15**) – The sculptures were found in the gardens of Elius Lamia, 3C Consul, on the Esquiline. The young girl seated (**25**) is a very sophisticated Greek work from the Hellenistic period (late 2C BC). The headless statue of an old countrywoman (**26**) is a remarkably realistic Hellenistic work.

The Centaur's head (**27**) is either an original Greek work from the Pergamum school or at least a good copy probably made in Pergamum, a city in Asia Minor and one of the centres of Hellenistic art.

The Esquiline Venus (**28**): this is the name given to the statue of a young girl attending to her hair (a fragment of her hand can be seen in her hair). The work is attributed to the school of Paxiteles (1C BC), a Greek sculptor from southern Italy who mostly produced imitations of Hellenistic works from the Classical era.

The bust of Commodus as Hercules (**29**): Commodus' father, Marcus Aurelius had included him in the government of the Empire but was apprehensive of his tendency to excess. The bust of the Emperor himself as Hercules is a late 2C work. At this period Roman art had attained such technical skill that it could fashion marble as if the stone were a plastic medium.

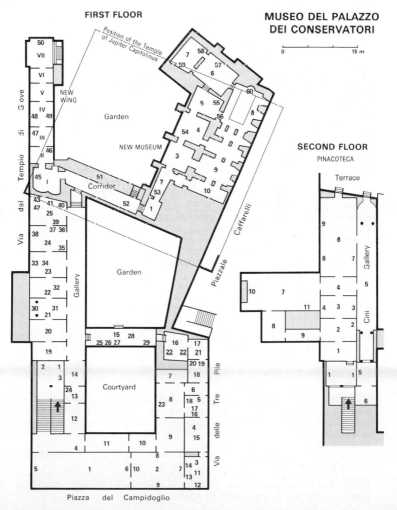

Sala Egizia (Egyptian Room) (**19**) – The works created in Rome or imported in Roman times belonged to buildings constructed in the capital and dedicated to the Alexandrine deities. The most noticeable group amongst the finds comes from the sanctuary of Isis and Serapis in the Campo Marzio.

Room of Christian Monuments (**20**) – Fragments of inscriptions, 3C and 4C sarcophagi and various fragments of Christian sculpture are to be found here.

Chimney Room (**21**) – It contains the remains of a chimney (**30**) made of Antique fragments from the Conservators' Palace. There is also a fine **collection of antefixa**★ (**31**), which, sometimes richly painted, ornamented the ridge of the Etruscan temples in Capua in the 6C and 5C BC. They demonstrate the Etruscan taste for the fantastical.

First Castellani Room (**22**) – It is named after the donor of the collection of 7C and 6C BC vases which it contains: Italic vases influenced by Greek geometric art; Etruscan vases inspired by the Corinthian workshop; black *bucchero* vases, a great Etruscan speciality. A 4C chariot (**32**), for carrying the effigies of the gods in procession, has been reconstructed.

Second Castellani Room (**23**) – The peperine low reliefs (**33**) belonged to a 6C BC Etruscan funeral couch. The display case contains a fine vase (**34**): on one side Ulysses and his companions blinding Polyphemus who is collapsing; on the other are two galleys about to engage in battle. The artist (an Etruscan or Greek of 7C BC) has signed it 'Aristonothos' (above Polyphemus' head).

Bronze Room (**24**) – The huge head (**35**) and hand (**36**) belonged to a standing figure of the Emperor Constantine (4C). The dancing god (**37**) holding a horn *(rhyton)* and a cup, is an elegant statue of Lares, protector of the domestic hearth (1C).
Here too is the sphere (**38**) which topped the Vatican obelisk until it was moved to the centre of St Peter's Square (1585). It is scored by the bullets fired by French soldiers in the sack of Rome in 1527.

Maecenas' Gardens Room (**25**) – Here are displayed the items found in the gardens which Maecenas laid out on the Esquiline in 25 BC. Hercules in combat (**39**) is a Roman work inspired by a statue sculpted by a colleague of Lysippus.
'Marsyas' (**40**) is interesting: he had dared to challenge Apollo in a musical competition and was bound to a tree before being flayed. The sculpture is a good 2C-1C BC Roman copy of a Hellenistic work.
The low relief of **maenad dancing**★ (**41**) is a Roman copy of a Greek work by Callimachus who was one of the most brilliant exponents of Greek art in the late 5C BC. The serenity of the first Classical period has passed. In his tragedies Euripides has described the extreme violence of which the Maenads (Bacchantes of Furies) were capable: in a bacchic trance they tore to pieces Pentheus, King of Thebes, because he opposed the introduction into his kingdom of the cult of Dionysus.
The statue of a **charioteer** about to climb into his chariot (**42**) is a Roman copy of a Greek bronze of the Classical period (470-460 BC).
The head of an Amazon (**43**) is a very fine replica of a statue by Kresilas (5C BC) who had been in competition with Phidias and Polyclitus for the Amazon of Ephesus.
In Rome many artists copied the neo-Attic style in vogue in Athens where the Classicism of the 5C BC was much admired.

"Braccio nuovo" (New Wing) ⊘

Room I – The low relief shows Curtius (**45**) plunging into the lake in the Forum *(see FORO ROMANO – Curtian Lake)*.

Rooms II and III – A plan of the Temple of Jupiter Capitolinus (**46**) is on display and the southern limit of the sanctuary is shown on the ground; a few traces of the foundations are also visible.
The figure holding the busts of his ancestors (**47**) in the series of 1C portraits shows the great mastery of the Roman artists in portraiture.

Room IV – The statue of Apollo (**48**) is an original Greek work dating from the first half of the 5C BC. The sculptor may have been Pythagoras of Samos, a Greek who established himself in Rhegium (Reggio di Calabria) in about 470 BC. Probably brought to Rome as the spoils of war, it was altered and set up in the Temple of Apollo Sosianus.
The statue of Aristogiton (**49**) is the best extant replica of one of the statues in the bronze group of the Tyrannicides sculpted in 477-476 BC.

Room VII – The **frieze**★ (**50**) showing a triumphal procession decorated the interior of the *cella* of the Temple of Apollo Sosianus.

Museo nuovo (New Museum) ⊘ – The New Museum was laid out in 1925 in the Caffarelli Palace.

In the passage there is part of a wall (**51**) from the Temple of Jupiter (6C BC). The urn (**52**) which contained the ashes of Agrippina the Elder, was used in the Middle Ages as a measuring instrument for grain.

Room 2 – In a cabinet (**53**) displaying many heads is one of a child, a Greek work in the 'severe' style (early 5C BC), and one of a goddess, the work of an artist in Magna Graecia (southern Italy) in the late 5C BC.

Room 4 – Polyhymnia★ (**54**), the muse of lyric poetry, is a good Roman replica of a 2C BC Hellenistic work.

Room 5 – The headless statue of Venus (**55**) is a copy of a statue by Praxiteles, the Venus of Arles in the Louvre in Paris. The low relief sculpture of Aesculapius (**56**), god of medicine, is a Greek work from the first Hellenistic period (4C BC).

Rooms 6 and 7 – In room 6 is the stele of a Roman shoemaker (**57**), identifiable by the shoes surmounting the bust of the dead man; an example of popular sculpture.

In room 7 is a fine portrait of Domitian (**58**) and some beautiful decorative sculptures: pieces of friezes and a basin decorated with acanthus leaves (**59**).

Room 8 – The huge statue of Athena (**60**) may be a copy of a Greek work by Kresilas (*c* 430 BC). In the centre of the room are traces of the Temple of Jupiter Capitolinus.

★Pinacoteca (Picture Gallery) *second floor*

On the entrance landing are two fine panels (**1**) of marble intarsia work depicting tigresses attacking cattle; these are 4C Roman. The technique, known as *opus sectile (see THE ARTS IN ROME — Mosaic)*, was developed particularly in Egypt where panels were often created in the local workshops and then brought to Rome. These two come from the Basilica of Junius Bassus which stood on the Esquiline until 17C.

Room 2 – Here are *The Baptism of Jesus* (**2**), a youthful work by Titian, and several works by Tintoretto's son Domenico.

Room 3 – *Romulus, Remus and the wolf* (**3**) was painted in 1618 by Rubens, the master of Flemish Baroque; perhaps in memory of his stay in Rome ten years earlier, he kept it till his death.

The *Allegory of Vanity* (**4**) is an early 17C work by Simon Vouet, fairly academic before he came under the influence of Caravaggio.

Galleria Cini (Cini Gallery) – This room contains 18C porcelain from Saxony and Capodimonte. The *Holy Family* (**5**) by Pompeo Batoni is an 18C work noteworthy for its delicate colours and elegant line; *St John the Baptist* (**6**) is by the young Caravaggio.

Room 6 – Here are the *Rape of the Sabine Women* (**7**), the *Sacrifice of Polixena* (**8**), large-scale compositions by the Baroque artist Pietro da Cortona, and *Mary Magdalen* (**9**), a small canvas by Guido Reni.

Room 7 – It is dominated by the huge painting by Guercino (**10**) in honour of St Petronella (1621), particularly splendid for its harmony of blue and brown hues. Its tortuous vertical lines presage the Baroque style in art.

This room contains other works by the Bologna group of artists (Domenichino, Guido Reni, Annibale Carracci) and the *Gipsy Fortune-teller* (**11**) (1589) attributed to Caravaggio.

★★MUSEO CAPITOLINO (CAPITOLINE MUSEUM) ⊘

Housed in the New Palace.

★★**Equestrian statue of Marcus Aurelius** – *On the right in the courtyard.* Michelangelo transferred it from the square outside St John Lateran to Capitol Square in 1538. He greatly admired the statue and restored it himself. Cast in bronze and once gilded, it is a fine example of late 2C Roman Realism. It has survived intact because it was thought to represent Constantine. Had they known the facts, the medieval Christians would never have tolerated the survival of an effigy of the Emperor who persecuted St Blandina, St Pothinus and St Justin.

Ground floor rooms – The rooms on the left of the entrance are devoted to the oriental cults of Mithras and Cybele.

There are several representations of the god Mithras
killing the bull while the
forces of evil (dog, scorpion
and serpent) try to prevent
the sacrifice taking place.

An altar bears a dedication
by the Vestal Claudia who
used her girdle to refloat a
ship which had gone
aground in the Tiber; the
ship was carrying the
"black stone" representing
the goddess Cybele from
Pessinus; the vestal had
been judged immoral and
the Augurs declared that
only a young virgin could
bring the ship to shore.

Talking Statues – The fountain in the courtyard
is dominated by the recumbent statue of an
antique god christened '**Marforio**'. The huge
peaceful figure seems a little bored with
watching the water in the basin. In the Middle Ages the statue was one of the group of
'talking statues' and received satirical comments directed against the people in power.
For a long time Marforio was to be found
next to the Church of St Luke and St Martina
and the cost of moving him (1595) was so
great that the government raised the price of
wine. Marforio thereupon 'wrote' to Pasquino, another talking statue, that the
Romans were having to do without wine so
that he could preside over a fountain.

In the rooms on the right of the entrance: a Roman sarcophagus showing the
battle between the Greeks and Galatians (2C). The decoration derives from models
copied from the artists of the Hellenistic period of the Pergamum school who
generally represented barbarians as Galatians (Gauls who occupied Galatia in Asia
Minor).

The next room contains a fine sarcophagus decorated with low reliefs of the life of
Achilles, surmounted by figures portraying the dead husband and wife (3C).

Atrium – The huge statue of Mars is a reproduction of the one which stood in the
Temple of Mars Ultor in Augustus' Forum.

Take the stairs to the first floor.

Sala delle Colombe (I) –
The Dove Room takes its
name from the **mosaic★★**
(**1**), an extremely fine
work, which decorated the
floor of a room in
Hadrian's Villa at Tivoli. It
is probably a copy of a 2C
BC Greek mosaic from Per-
gamum.

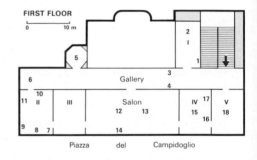

The statue of a young girl
holding a dove in her arms
and warding off a serpent
(**2**) is a Roman copy of a
2C BC Hellenistic sculpture.
During restoration the serpent was substituted for the original animal (a dog or a
cat).

Galleria – The old woman in her cups (**3**) may be a replica of a Hellenistic work
from 3C BC when artists often portrayed human nature with great realism.
Roman woman as Venus (**4**) from the Augustan period when a taste for disguise
developed. The face of the statue is the portrait of a woman from the Flavian
period (second half of 1C), her body is a copy of a 4C BC Greek model.

★★**Capitoline Venus** (**5**) – The Greek original which inspired the Roman copy of this Venus
was a Hellenistic work derived from the Venus of Cnidus sculpted by Praxiteles, the
master of feminine divinities in the Classical period. The Capitoline Venus, who is
shown leaving her bath, is distinguished from the Classical style by the double
gesture of modesty.
The stone well surround (2C) supporting a great bowl (**6**) is decorated with a
procession of the 12 Di Consentes who had a portico in the Forum.

★★**Sala degli Imperatori** (II) – It is rare to find so many portraits of famous
people assembled in one place. Every emperor is represented. Particularly noteworthy are:
Two portraits of Octavian Augustus: one (**7**) shows him at the time of the battle of
Actium (upper row), the other (**8**) (facing the window) crowned with myrtle. Both
portraits show the cold, detached determination of the Emperor.
The bust of the youthful Commodus (**9**) reveals the sculptor's great
skill in working marble alongside his search to exploit the delicacy of light and
shade.
Plotina (**10** (upper row), wife of Trajan, wears a sober and sad expression in this
portrait. When Trajan died, it was she who told the Senators that, just before
dying, her husband had named Hadrian as his successor.

The portrait of a young woman with her hair piled high in curls (**11** on a column) dates from the late 1C and is one of the most beautiful works in the collection.

Sala dei Filosofi (III) – The Philosopher's Room contains over 80 busts.

Salone – Here are two statues of Centaurs, one laughing because he is young (**12**) and the other weeping because he is old (**13**). They are Roman works from Hadrian's reign (117-138), reproductions in sombre marble of Hellenistic originals in bronze. The **wounded Amazon**★ (**14**) is a fine Roman copy of a statue sculpted by Kresilas for the Amazon of Ephesus in competition with Phidias and Polyclitus.

Sala del Fauno (IV) – In the Faun Room is a 'Satyr' (**15**) from the same period as the two Centaurs.

– Among the Roman inscriptions is the *Lex de imperio Vespasiani* (**16**) engraved on bronze. With this decree the Senate conferred full powers on Vespasian on 22 December 69. Cola di Rienzo commented on the text to the assembled crowds.

– The statue of a child wringing a goose's neck (**17**) is a 2C Roman sculpture inspired by a bronze by the Greek Boethos; in the Hellenistic period a child and an animal were often sculpted together in spontaneous poses.

Sala del Gladiatore (V) – The Gladiator Room is so called because the magnificent sculpture (**18**) in the middle of the room was long thought to be a gladiator. It is in fact a Gaul from Galatia, a Roman imitation of a work in bronze from the Pergamum school (late 3C, early 2C BC). It was probably part of a group of sculptures commemorating the victory of Attalus I, King of Pergamum, against the invading Gauls. All the nobility and suffering of the body in its agony are sensitively expressed; the **Dying Gaul**★★★ ranks among the most beautiful pieces of Antique art.

From Piazza del Campidoglio take Via del Campidoglio on the right of Palazzo Senatorio.

From the corner of the Palace one has the best **view**★★ of the Roman Forum and in particular the Tabularium, the Portico of the Di Consentes, the Temple of Vespasian and the Temple of Concord.

Return to Piazza del Campidoglio and take the steps on the left of the Conservators' Palace and then Via del Tempio di Giove.

Below Via del Tempio di Giove there are several stone blocks which formed a corner of the Temple of Jupiter *(see above)*. Beyond is a pleasant garden overlooking the area identified as the Tarpeian Rock *(see below)* which gives a good **view** of the Roman Forum, the Palatine, and the Caelian and Aventine hills.

AT THE FOOT OF THE CAPITOLINE HILL

Take Via di Monte Caprino and go down to the left to Piazza della Consolazione.

Rupe Tarpea – Via della Consolazione, an extension of Vico Jugario, is dominated on the left by the southern slope of the Capitol, where, after some considerable hesitation, scholars have sited the **Tarpeian Rock**. In antiquity it was the rock face which took its name from the traitress Tarpeia.

In ancient times the Vicus Jugarius (now called Vico Jugario) was lined with the shops of craftsmen making yokes. It wound along under the Capitol and connected the Forum Holitorium to the Roman Forum. At the entrance to the street, on the left, can be seen vestiges of porticos built at the base of the Capitol during the Republican era.

Cross Via del Teatro di Marcello.

San Nicola in Carcere – The little church of St Nicholas by the Gaol was built in 11C on the ruins of three temples which stood side by side overlooking the **Forum Holitorium** *(see BOCCA DELLA VERITÀ)*.

The church has been restored several times: the façade was designed by Giacomo della Porta in 1599. The nave is built on the site of the *cella* and *pronaos* of the middle temple and is flanked by aisles so that the side walls of the church incorporate columns belonging to the side walls of the two outer temples. The left-hand temple was the oldest; it was built in the Doric style in the 2C BC and probably dedicated to Janus. The right-hand temple was in the Ionic style – two columns from its right-hand side stand on their own to the right of the church – it was probably dedicated to Hope and has been dated to the 1C BC. The middle temple is the most recent and was probably dedicated to Juno. The tower, originally defensive, dates from the 12C when the district belonged to the Perleoni family. The words *in carcere* in the title refer to a Byzantine gaol which occupied the lefthand temple in the 7C and 8C.

Excavations ⊘ – The crypt contains the foundations of ancient temples; fragments of a frieze are visible from the roof of the church.

★★**Teatro di Marcello** – The **Theatre of Marcellus** was begun by Caesar and completed between the 13 and 11 BC by Augustus who dedicated it to Marcellus, his sister Octavia's son.

The two tiers of arches which remain were probably topped by a third row of Corinthian pilasters. They form the semi-circular part of the building which contained the tiers of seats; the stage, of which nothing is left, backed on to the riverbank. It was the second largest theatre in Rome after Pompey's Theatre in the Campus Martius; it could hold about 15 000 spectators. Its severe and sober style, with the three architectural orders – Doric, Ionic and Corinthian – one above the other, served as a model for the Coliseum which was built of the same stone, travertine from the Tivoli quarry. On the day of the inauguration Augustus suffered a slight mishap which Suetonius recorded: "the official chair *(sella curulis)* gave way beneath him and he fell backwards".

The theatre was damaged both in the fire in AD 64 and during the struggle between Vespasian and Vitellius and was finally abandoned early in the 4C. It was soon being used as a quarry; some of the stone went to repair the Ponte Cestio in the 4C. Houses were built against the walls and in 1150 it was transformed into a fortress and thus saved from further depredations.

In the 16C the noble family of Savelli turned it into a palace. It is the remains of this house, which was built by Baldassarre Peruzzi, which are visible today above the old arches. The palace later passed to the Orsini. The ancient theatre was cleared of its accretions and excavated from 1926 to 1929.

Temple of Apollo Sosianus

★★Tempio di Apollo – The Greek god Apollo was venerated by the Romans chiefly for his power to ward off disease (Apollo medicus). The first temple dedicated to him was raised on this site in the 5C BC. In 34 BC Caius Sosius, governor of Cilicia and Syria, rebuilt the sanctuary in marble and it became known as the Temple of Apollo Sosianus. The three elegant fluted **columns★★** with Corinthian capitals belonged to the porch *(pronaos)* of the temple and were re-erected in 1940.

Turn left into Piazza di Campitelli.

Santa Maria in Campitelli ⊙ – When Rome was struck by the plague in 1656 the Romans prayed ceaselessly in front of an image of the Virgin in the Church of Santa Maria in Portico; now demolished, this church stood on the site of the present Anagrafe on the riverbank. When the epidemic ceased it was decided to build a new sanctuary to house the holy image. The first stone of Santa Maria in Campitelli was laid in September 1661. The building was entrusted to Carlo Rainaldi (1611-91) who drew up his own design and executed it himself.

The exterior, like the interior, is a forest of columns. Those on the façade are clearly detached and form a pleasant harmony. Variety and movement are provided by the broken and curved pediments, the jutting cornices and multiple recessing.

The **interior★** space is defined by the advanced columns. The variation on the Greek cross plan which is extended and constricted towards the apse, the grandiose elevation of the vault and the dome and the alternating projections and recesses create a bold effect of perspective.

The church contains a few fine 17C paintings including a canvas of *St Anne, St Joachim and Mary (second chapel on the right)* by Luca Giordano (1632-1705), an exponent of the Baroque style. The picture frame is supported by two kneeling angels. Another Baroque painting *(left of the choir)* is by Giovanni Battista Gaulli, called Baciccia (1639-1709), who painted the vault of the Gesù Church. Below the painting is the tomb of Cardinal Massimi, designed by Verroi and sculpted by Qualieri (1975). Above the high altar is a Baroque glory surrounding the 11C enamel of the Virgin which came from the Church of Santa Maria in Portico.

Turn right into Via dei Delfini which leads to Piazza Margana.

In this typical little square the chaos of everyday traffic seems remote. The **Margana Tower** *(part of no 40 Via Margana)* was constructed on the remains of a Roman portico of which a column with an Ionic capital is still extant.

Fountain in Piazza d'Aracoeli – It is a modest work by Giacomo della Porta (1589), the great designer of the fountains of Rome; at least he produced the design. In the 17C the arms of the Chigi family were added and 100 years later the base with two flights of steps designed by della Porta was replaced by the present circular basin.

Neighbouring sights are described in the following chapters: BOCCA DELLA VERITÀ; FORO ROMANO – PALATINO; ISOLA TIBERINA – TORRE ARGENTINA; PIAZZA VENEZIA.

CAMPO DEI FIORI★★

Tour 2 $\frac{1}{2}$ hours

The walk follows the narrow streets of the district lying between the Tiber, Corso Vittorio Emanuele II and the Capitol. In antiquity the district was just to the south of the Campus Martius and was chosen by Pompey for the construction of several important buildings in 55 BC: a huge theatre, the first in Rome to be built of stone, a temple to Venus and a curia to house occasional meetings of the Senate. It was in Pompey's curia that a decisive event in Roman history occurred: on the Ides of March 44 BC Julius Caesar was assassinated at the foot of Pompey's statue. Almost nothing remains of this building. Archeologists working on a nearby site in 1926 uncovered a religious enclave dating from the Republican era *(Largo Argentina Sacred Precinct).*

The first Christian sanctuary in the district was San Lorenzo in Damaso, founded in 380 in the reign of Pope Damasus.

In the Middle Ages churches and castles grew in number. The churches were quite simple buildings serving the needs of the tradesmen, who in their various guilds gave a certain character to the district: there were many leather curriers *(vaccinari)* and also boiler makers *(calderari)*, and rope makers *(funari)* whose trades are recalled in many of the street names near the Cenci Hill (Monte Cenci).

After Charles V's troops had sacked Rome in 1527, civil architecture revived. Cardinal Riario spent the money he had won at the gaming tables in building the Palazzo della Cancelleria thus countering the scruples of his relative, Sixtus IV.

Cardinal Farnese, later Pope Paul III, built the Farnese Palace in line with the status of his family which he led to the heights of glory.

The narrow streets around the Campo dei Fiori contain simple houses and austerely noble palaces standing side by side in quiet harmony in the unassuming lanes *(vicoli).*

Statue of Giordano Bruno in Campo dei Fiori

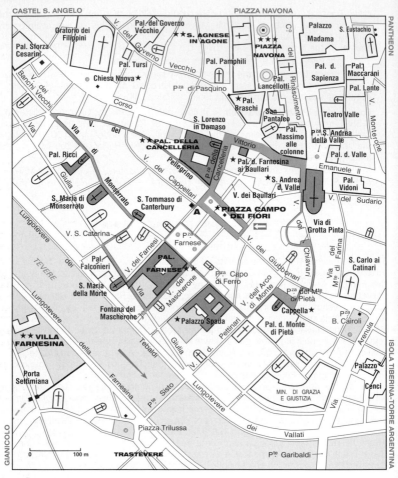

*PIAZZA CAMPO DEI FIORI

The origin of the name (which means Square of the Field of Flowers) probably goes back to the Middle Ages when the area was one vast meadow dominated by the fortress of the powerful Orsini family who were lords of the manor. By the 16C the area had become the centre of Rome, a meeting place for people of all ranks, crowded with inns. The "**Hostaria della Vacca**" (**A**) belonged to **Vanozza Caetani** (1442-1518), famous for her liaison with Rodrigo Borgia, who became Pope Alexander VI. She bore him several children including Cesare and Lucretia. The façade of her hostelry still bears an escutcheon showing the Borgia arms alongside those of Vanozza and those of one of her husbands.

The Campo was the site of all sorts of festivals as well as a place of execution. At the centre stands a statue of Giordano Bruno, a monk who was burned for heresy on 17 February 1600 during the Counter-Reformation. The statue has replaced the 'Terrina' fountain *(see CASTEL SANT'ANGELO)* which is now in Piazza della Chiesa Nuova.

Every morning the Campo dei Fiori is filled with the bustle of an extensive food market.

Campo dei Fiori Market

Cheese and cream, cured meats, meat and poultry, seasonal fruit and vegetables, colourful arrays of flowers, accented voices trading local gossip and exchanging ills for miraculous cures, the square bustles with action under the tacit eye of the astronomer and philosopher Giordano Bruno. A regular visitor amongst the housewives is the knife-sharpener with his pedal-powered grindstone.

In the streets around, bric-a-brac, sicilian ex-votos, furniture and elaborate copies of old masters are all traded...

PALAZZO DELLA CANCELLERIA (CHANCERY PALACE) ⊙

The Chancery Palace was built between 1483 and 1513 for Cardinal Raffaele Riario, upon whom "honours and riches were heaped" by his great-uncle Pope Sixtus IV. The architect has not been identified for certain. He may have been Andrea Bregno, nicknamed Antonio da Montecavallo, or his brother assisted by Bramante. The inscripton above the balcony states that the building housed the "Imperial Court", the law courts dur-

---

A fifteen hundred year old Cupid

Cardinal Riario moved into the palace in 1496. His well-known taste for antiquities gave Michelangelo the idea of sculpting a magnificent Cupid, skilfully applying an artificial patina of age and selling it to the Cardinal for 200 ducats as a genuine antique. The collector got wind of the deceit and decided to recover his money and return the statue to the artist but Michelangelo never saw his Cupid again; it was transferred to France and disappeared no one knows where.

---

ing the Napoleonic occupation (1809-14). Strengthened and restored between 1937 and 1945, the Palace is now occupied by the Papal Chancery, which is responsible for drafting pontifical acts, and therefore enjoys the privilege of extra-territoriality granted to Vatican property under the terms of the Lateran Treaty.

Façade and courtyard – These two features make the building the most elegant product of the Renaissance in Rome. The broad smooth surfaces, the straight lines and the shallow pilasters of the travertine façade give it a majestic quality. A light and delicate touch is added by the roses of Riario which decorate the second floor windows.

The central doorway was added in 1589 by Cardinal Alessandro Peretti, great nephew of Sixtus V.

The granite columns which support the two storeys of the arcading surrounding the courtyard – a harmonious composition – come from the early building of the Church of San Lorenzo in Damaso.

It was the Chapter of this church which received the rents from the ground floor shops behind the arcades in Via del Pellegrino; the upper floors are decorated with fine corner balconies overlooking this street.

The coats of arms on the corners of the palace are those of Sixtus IV and Julius II (the oak of the della Rovere family) whose reigns marked the beginning and the end of the construction.

Interior – On the main floor of the palace are the Aula Magna (the Great Hall) and the so-called Sala dei "Cento Giorni" (Room of the Hundred Days). The latter is decorated by a fresco painted by Giorgio Vasari which depicts the meeting of Paul III, Charles V and François I which took place in 1538 in Nice (now in France). The name of the room may derive from the fact that the fresco was completed in 100 days.

San Lorenzo in Damaso – *Within Palazzo della Cancelleria.*

The church, which was founded by Pope Damasus in the 4C, was later rebuilt as part of the palace. It was used as a stable during the first French occupation in 1798, restored at various times during the 19C and became an annexe to the Imperial Court during the second French occupation (1809-14). The ceiling, which was damaged by fire in 1939, has been entirely renewed.

The church consists of a nave and side aisles preceded by a vestibule. The first chapel on the right contains a 14C wooden crucifix; the last chapel on the left in the nave contains a 12C painting of the Virgin inspired by Byzantine icons.

Turn right into Corso Vittorio Emanuele II.

*PALAZZO DELLA FARNESINA AI BAULLARI

This little Renaissance building was begun in 1523 for Thomas le Roy, a French diplomat accredited to the Holy See. Raised to the peerage by François I of France he added the lily of France to the ermine of Brittany, his country of origin. The lily was mistaken for the iris of the Farnese and the building was called the "Piccola Farnesina". As it overlooks **Via dei Baullari** (luggage makers: *baule* means trunk) it acquired the name of Farnesina ai Baullari. The façade giving on to Corso Vittorio Emanuele II was erected from 1898 to 1904.

The interior, which was radically restored in 19C, houses the collection of antique sculpture left by Baron Giovanni Barraco.

Museo Barracco (Barracco Museum) ⊙ – *The numbers are the same as those in the gallery catalogue.* The collections range over Egyptian, Assyrian, Greek and Roman sculpture from their origins to the end of Antiquity.

From the elegant internal courtyard stairs lead up to the first floor where the arch is decorated with admirable 17C frescoes. **Room I** contains Egyptian sculptures dating from the 3rd millenium including the head hewn in black granite of the young Pharaoh Ramses II (**21**) and two low relief sculptures taken from the tombs of wealthy private citizens dating from the Old Kingdom, IV Dynasty (**2** and **3**). **Room II** contains a series of Assyrian low reliefs one of which shows a group of women in a palm grove (late 8C BC) (**48**); a very beautiful woman's funeral mask in gilded pasteboard from the period of Ptolemy (**22**) and an interesting head in painted stucco (**33**) of a mummy from Ermopoli and Egyptian art from the Roman period (2C). **Room III and IV** house a group of Etruscan and Cypriot works: Etruscan antefixes and memorial stones; a woman's head (**205**) (2C BC) found near Bolsena; a little statute of the god Bes (**60**), a minor Egyptian deity also venerated by other races; interesting Cypriot statues such as the quadriga (**68**) (6C BC) and the man's head with beard (**64**) (5C BC).

On the second floor are Greek, Roman and Medieval works of art. **Room V** also has a series of Greek sculpture from the Classical period (5C BC) and copies from the Roman era: head of an ephebe (**80**), an original work; a head of Marsyas (**97**, a rare copy of the work by Myron who brought together the goddess Athena and the Satyr Marsyas in the same composition; a head of Apollo (**92**), a fine copy of a work by Phidias; a head of Diadumenos (victorious athlete), a copy of the original by Polyclitus. **Room VI** contains works from the ancient Greek period and original pieces (5C and 4C BC). **Rooms VI and VIII** contain work from the Hellenistic period: a very beautiful spiral crater (**233**); **Room IX** (access from the end of the loggia) contains works of Roman and Medieval art: a fine 1C Roman bust of a young boy (**190**) and a portrait of a youth (**194**).

Continue along Corso Vittorio Emanuele II.

★SANT'ANDREA DELLA VALLE ⊙

Piazza Sant'Andrea della Valle – The fountain is attributed to Carlo Maderno: it bears the eagle and dragon of the Borghese family and was probably put up for Pope Paul V.

Church exterior – Construction of the church began in 1591 under the direction of Giacomo della Porta: it was completed between 1608 and 1623 by Carlo Maderno. The **façade★★** (1661-67), one of the most elegant of the Baroque style, was built by Carlo Rainaldi. The two storey elevation ripples with columns and projections; the original scrolls intended to unite the two levels have been replaced by angels with a spread wing – although only the left-hand statue was executed.

Interior – The Latin-cross plan with a single nave flanked by intercommunicating side chapels, as in the Gesù Church, is typical of the Counter-Reformation. The severity typical of the art of this period is to be found in the extremely sober architecture of the second chapel on the right and of the altar in the right transept. Conversely, the nave vaulting and left transept were decorated early in the 20C.

★★Dome – This is the work of Carlo Maderno; it is one of the loveliest domes in the city and second only to St Peter's in size. It was painted between 1624 and 1627 by **Lanfranco**, the first artist to implement the technique of painting a curved surface successfully. The *Glory of Paradise,* with its rich colouring, is an imitation of the fresco painted by Correggio on the dome of Parma cathedral. The Evangelists on the pendentives were painted by Domenichino. The vigour and expressiveness of the painting are reminiscent of Michelangelo's art.

★Apse – The upper section, which was frescoed by Domenichino (1624-28), is in late Renaissance style: *St Andrew is led to his death (right); the Calling of St Andrew and St Peter (centre); the Flagellation of St Andrew (left); St Andrew being received into heaven (above); St Peter and St Andrew are shown the Saviour by St John the Baptist (arcade centre).*
The large painted panels (1650-51) round the main altar depicting the death of St Andrew are by Mattia Preti inspired by Caravaggio and Lanfranco.

Piccolomini popes' tombs – *Above the last bay in the nave before the transept.* The monuments to Pius II *(left)* and Pius III *(right)* are typical of late 15C funeral art.

Take Via dei Chiavari beside the church.

Via dei Giubbonari runs very close to the site of Pompey's great theatre of which nothing remains except the semi-circular line followed by the houses in Via di Grotta Pinta. By tradition it is the street where doublet makers (*giubbone* = doublet), silk merchants and garment repairers were to be found. It has remained very commercial. Behind the theatre the great crowned portico of Pompey's Curia is where Julius Caesar was fatally stabbed in 44 BC. The remains of the Curia can be seen in the Largo Argentina Sacred Precinct *(see ISOLA TIBERTINA).*

Turn right into Via dei Giubbonari and left into a side street leading into Piazza del Monte di Pietà.

★**Capella del Monte di Pietà** ⊙ – This small oval chapel within the Monte di Pietà palace is a gem of Baroque art. Originally the work of Maderno, it was then redesigned by the architects Giovanni Antonio de' Rossi (who worked with Bernini) and Carlo Bizzaccheri (a pupil of Carlo Fontana) who took over on his death in 1695 and was responsible for the entrance hall and the dome.

The theme of the décor reinforces the aim of the institution: to put down usury. The chapel was consecrated in 1641. The work of decoration went on until 1725. Starting from the entrance and moving anti-clockwise: the allegorical statue of Faith is by Francesco Moderati; the low relief of *Tobias lending money to Gabelus* is an exuberant work by Pierre Legros, a student at the French Academy in Rome; the allegory of Charity is by Bernardino Cametti whose figures seem about to leap from their recess; the low relief of *Mercy* by Domenico Guido, who collaborated with Bernini, was finished in 1676; the statue of *Charity* by Giuseppe Mazzuoli is followed by a low relief of Joseph giving corn to the Egyptians by Jean-Baptiste Théodon, also a student at the French Academy; the last statue is an elegant expression of *Hope* by Agostino Cornacchini.

Take Via dell'Arco di Monte; turn right into Piazza Capo di Ferro.

★PALAZZO SPADA

It was built in about 1540 for Cardinal Gerolamo Capo di Ferro probably by an architect in Sangallo's circle. In 1632 it was acquired by Cardinal Bernardino Spada and in 1927 it became the property of the Italian Government for the Council of State.

Althought it was built only a few years after the Farnese Palace, the Spada Palace is quite different in conception. The noble austerity of Renaissance architecture has been replaced by fantastic decorations in the Mannerist style. The façade is almost smothered in statues, stucco garlands, medallions and scrolls bearing Latin inscriptions about the famous Classical figures which appear in the niches on the first floor. On the second floor, which is dominated by the Spada coat of arms, the decoration becomes overwhelming.

The delicate execution of the three friezes in the courtyard★ is quite admirable. On the wall facing the entrance is the French coat of arms flanked by the arms of Julius III, a souvenir of Cardinal Capo di Ferro who was papal legate to France and a friend of Julius III.

Borromini "Perspective" – *On the ground floor, behind the library and visible from the courtyard. For access ask the porter.*

★**Galleria Spada** ⊙ – The gallery presents the works of art collected by Cardinal Spada in their original setting and is typical of the private collection of a wealthy Roman in the 17C. The Cardinal was the patron of Guercino and Guido Reni, whose noble manner pleased him, while at the same time he was interested in *bambocciate*, realistic paintings which appeared in Rome in about 1630 in the circle of the painter Pieter Van Laer, a Dutchman nicknamed *Il Bamboccio* because of his deformity.

Room I – Two canvases by Guido Reni (1575-1642): *Portrait of Cardinal Bernardino Spada* (**32**), a good example of the artist's use of pure delicate line, and the *Slave of Ripa Grande* (**38**) hang beside a second portrait of Cardinal Spada (**34**) by Guercino (1591-1666).

Room II – The two console tables (**4**) are 17C. The carved walnut tabernacle (**1**) is from the late 16C. Among the paintings are: the *Visitation* (**56**) by Andrea del Sarto and the *Portrait of a Musician* (**60**), an early work by Titian (c1515). Three fine portraits by Bartolomeo Passarotti (1529-92): the *Astrologer* (**63**), the *Botanist* (**65**) and the *Surgeon* (**66**) show the figures as natural and relaxed. The *Portrait of Pope Paul III* (**86**) is a copy of a 16C portrait (Naples Capodimonte Museum) painted by Titian.

Room III – The console tables in gilded wood are by late 17C Roman craftsmen. In the allegory of the *Massacre of the Innocents* (**144**) Pietro Testa (c1606-50) painted his masterpiece; the violent contrast between light and dark accentuates the dramatic aspect of this work. The *Triumph of the Name of Jesus* (**133**) by Baciccia is a sketch for the fresco which decorates the nave of the Gesù Church. The *Death of Dido* (**132**) by Guercino, assisted by his pupils, shows the artist's lyrical style *(the Winged Cupid)*. The *Landscape with Windmills* (**102**) is a masterly work by 'Velvet' Bruegel, painted in 1607.

Room IV – These works are by artists influenced by Caravaggio. The small octagonal painting of the *Halt at the Inn* (**151**) is by Peter Van Laer. Michelangelo Cerquozzi (1602-60) was one of the chief exponents of this trend; the *Revolt of Masaniello* (**161**) is a later work; the subject taken from Neapolitan history allows the painter to give full reign to his narrative passion. Among the French artists who followed the style of Caravaggio is Valentin (1594-1632) who arrived in Rome in about 1612: *Holy Family with St John* (1841).

Continue to Piazza Farnese.

★★PALAZZO FARNESE *Not open to the public.*

At either end of Piazza Farnese are two huge granite basins found in the Baths of Caracalla and converted into fountains in 1626. On the far side stands one of the most beautiful of Roman palaces, which bears the name of the family for whom it was built. The fame of the Farnese began when Cardinal Alessandro was elected pope in 1534 taking the name of **Paul III.** As the first pope of the Counter-Reformation he set up the Council of Trent, yet conducted his reign like a Renaissance monarch: he had four children whose mother has not been identified, made three of them legitimate and loaded them with riches. He was a patron of the arts, continuing the work on St Peter's and the Sistine Chapel and building the Farnese Palace. He and his descendants amassed a magnificent collection of works of art. One of his grandchildren, Ranuccio (1530-65), commissioned Salviati to celebrate the glory of the Farnese in a series of frescoes. Another, Odoardo (1573-1626), invited the Carracci to paint the gallery on the first floor. The last of the Farnese was Elizabeth (1692-1766) who married Philip V of Spain. Their son, Don Carlos of Bourbon, who became King of Naples in 1735, inherited the Farnese family riches; almost all the works of art from the Farnese Palace are now in the Naples Archeological Museum or in the Royal Palace at Capodimonte.

Since 1635 the Farnese Palace has been occupied by the French Embassy, where Queen Christina of Sweden was a guest from 27 December 1655 to July 1656. In 1911 the palace was purchased by the French government but in 1936 it was bought back by the Italian government and then leased to France for 99 years in exchange for the building occupied by the Italian Embassy in Paris. Since 1875 the palace has also housed the Ecole Française de Rome for historians, archeologists and art historians.

Façade of the Palazzo Farnese by Sangallo and Michelangelo

Façade – The absence of pilasters and the clear horizontal lines contribute to a masterpiece of balance and proportion. Construction began in 1515 on Cardinal Alessandro Farnese's orders, to the designs of his favourite architect, Antonio da Sangallo, the Younger. When Sangallo died in 1546, Michelangelo took over. He retained the first floor windows, framed by columns with alternate pediments, curved or triangular like the recesses in the Pantheon. He added the impressive upper cornice and over the central balcony he carved the irises of the Farnese coat of arms (not to be confused with the French lily).

The **courtyard** *(not open)* is a model of Renaissance elegance. It was designed by three great architects – Sangallo, Vignola and Michelangelo. The **rear façade** overlooking Via Giulia *(see below)* is the best example of the building's elegant architecture.

The palace treasures include remarkable **frescoes** (1595-1603) painted by Annibale Carraci (in the Farnese Gallery) with the assistance of his brother Agostino and his pupils Domenichino and Lanfranco.

On the south side of the palace take Via del Mascherone; turn right into Via Giulia.

Fontana del Mascherone (Gargoyle Fountain) — It was built in 1626. The marble mask and the huge granite basin probably come from an ancient building.

Via Giulia then runs past the Farnese Palace's **rear façade**. It was designed by Vignola who took over from Michelangelo as architect. In 1573 he was succeeded by Giacomo della Porta who built the loggia. Last to be built in 1603 was the bridge over Via Giulia, linking the palace to the convent of Santa Maria della Morte and to several rooms where the Farnese kept their collection of antiquities.

Santa Maria della Morte — The façade of this church is by Ferdinando Fuga (18C) with Baroque touches.

Further on turn right into Via di S Caterina and left into Via de Monserrato.

Under the kindly eye of its many beautiful madonnas (on the corner of Via dei Farnesi) **Via di Monserrato** is lined by craft and antique shops, by palaces where the many Spanish prelates, who came to Rome in the suite of the Borgia popes (Calixtus III and Alexander VI), used to live. Many of the courtyards are worth a glance: the beauties of the Renaissance have not all disappeared.

San Tommaso di Canterbury (St Thomas of Canterbury) ⊘ — The present church was begun in 1869 by Camporese the Younger and finished on his death by Poletti and Vespignani; it contains a fine recumbent white marble effigy of Cardinal Christopher Bainbridge, Archbishop of York and Henry VIII's first Ambassador to the Holy See (d 1514). The original church was founded in 775 by Offa, King of the East Saxons; it was destroyed by fire in 817, rebuilt in 1159 and dedicated to St Thomas à Becket, who had stayed in the adjoining hospice which is now the Venerable English College. The hospice was started in 1362 by John and Alice Shepherd as a hostel for English pilgrims and is said to have survived owing to "national pride, national piety and a national distaste for being fleeced by foreigners". It was converted into a college in 1579 by Gregory XIII. Those who have stayed there include Thomas Cromwell, Milton, John Evelyn and Cardinal Manning. The church of **Santa Maria di Monserrato** is the Spanish national church.

The **Palazzo Ricci**, tucked at the back of its little square, has great charm; the façade bears traces of decorations by P da Caravaggio and M da Firenze *(see Index)*.

Via del Pellegrino was created by Sixtus IV in 1483; where it merges with Via di Monserrato the corner house, which otherwise follows the line of the streets, has been cut back to open up the crossroads; this was an innovation in town planning for those days.

Neighbouring sights are described in the following chapters: CASTEL S ANGELO; GIANICOLO; ISOLA TIBERINA — TORRE ARGENTINA; PANTHEON; PIAZZA NAVONA.

CASTEL SANT'ANGELO ★★

Tour 2 $\frac{1}{2}$ hours

This district, which was densely populated in the Middle Ages, was gradually cleared and redeveloped to become a centre for commerce and business; it was Sixtus IV (1471-84) who initiated the transformation. As the district lay on the route of religious processions passing between the Vatican and the Basilica of St John Lateran magnificent mansions were built along the Holy Pontiff's route, lining Via Banco di Santo Spirito and Via dei Banchi Nuovi — which formed the **Papal Way** (Via Papalis) — and Via del Governo Vecchio.

A quick distraction from sightseeing...

Wander off to **Ornamentum** *(via del Coronari 227)*: a treasure chest of exotic silks, opulent velvet brocades, sumptuous fabrics and princely materials borrowed from the Renaissance Age. Dressmakers, tailors, interior designers, poets and dreamers should certainly consider making a detour!

★★★CASTEL SANT'ANGELO ⊙

Hadrian's Mausoleum – This fortress-like building was intended as a sepulchre for Hadrian and his family. Begun by the Emperor in AD 135 it was finished four years later by his adopted son and successor to the Imperial throne, Antoninus Pius.

The base (84m - 276ft square) is surmounted by a drum (20m - 66ft high), on which was heaped a small mound of earth *(tumulus)*. It was crowned by a statue of the Emperor and a bronze *quadriga* (four-horse chariot). The mausoleum contained the cinerary urns of all the emperors from Hadrian to Septimius Severus (AD 211). When Aurelian surrounded the city with a wall in 270 he incorporated the mausoleum within the precinct and turned it into a fortress.

Fortress – During the medieval struggle between the papacy and the noble Roman families, the building became a fortified stronghold. Nicholas V (1447-55) built a brick storey on top of the original construction and added turrets at the corners.

The octagonal bastions were the work of Alexander VI (1492-1503). In 1527 Clement VII took

The Angel's Castle

In 590 Pope Gregory the Great led a procession against the plague which was decimating the city. Suddenly there appeared on top of the mausoleum an angel sheathing his sword. The gesture was interpreted as a sign that the plague would abate and in gratitude the Pope had a chapel built on the mausoleum.

refuge there from the troops of Charles V and made several rooms habitable. These were later improved by Paul III who already knew the castle, as he had been imprisoned there by Innocent VIII when he was only Cardinal Alexander Farnese. In his autobiography Benvenuto Cellini, the sculptor and metalworker, admits that he too had been in the castle gaol, as had Cagliostro, so it is said. After the unification of Italy the Castel Sant'Angelo became a barracks and military prison but today, surrounded by a public garden, it knows only the assaults of tourists.

A high defensive wall, the **Passetto**, built by Leo IV (847-55) links the castle to the Vatican Palace. Alexander VI created a passage along the top of the wall so that the pope could reach the fortress from the palace in case of siege.

Castel Sant'Angelo

TOUR *1 hour*

From the outside the Castel Sant'Angelo presents a somewhat squat structure; its ancient sections can be recognised from the large blocks of peperine and travertine stone. The statue of the Angel dominates the whole complex.

The entrance is through the old entrance to the mausoleum raised higher (some 3m - 10 ft) than its original position.

Spiral Ramp – *The entrance to the spiral ramp is below on the right, next to the entrance to the Tiber embankment.* When the castle was a mausoleum, the ramp (125m - 410ft) led up to the chamber where the funeral urns were kept. The walls were originally covered in marble, the floor was paved with mosaic, of which some traces still remain, and the vault was decorated with stucco. The holes in the vault were air vents except one (on the left at the back of the entrance hall) which was made to house a lift built in the 18C. At the top of the ramp is a transverse stairway. Originally it led to the Roman cinerary chamber but Boniface IX had it transformed into a passage leading from one side of the castle to the other following the north-south diameter of the drum. The part of the ramp which goes down towards the drawbridge leads to an area *(right)* where the guardroom has been reconstructed as it would have been in the 16C. At the other end of the ramp is a 19C bridge built above the funeral chamber to link the first section of the ramp to the second which emerges on to the main courtyard.

Main courtyard – This is also known as the Angel Courtyard from the 16C statue which graced the top of the castle until the 18C. There are piles of cannon balls which in the 15C to 17C were used as ammunition for the catapults, bombards and cannons.

On the right is a series of rooms from the medieval period which were reconstructed in the 17C and now make up the lower armoury. The end of the courtyard is closed by a shrine designed by Michelangelo which forms the side wall of the chapel built for Leo X; it probably stands on the site of Gregory the Great's cell *(see above).*

On the left are the Papal rooms.

Clement VII's Rooms – *Open for temporary exhibitions.* These rooms in Leo X's apartments were first rearranged by Paul III and later by Clement VIII – their names can be seen above the doors. Note in the first room the fine 17C fireplace.

Sala della Giustizia – *Open for temporary exhibitions.* Located above the Cinerary Chamber and immediately below the great circular room probably intended as Hadrian's mausoleum, this room was used throughout the 16C and 17C for legal hearings.

Sala dell'Apollo – *Access from Sala della Giustizia or from the main courtyard.* Over the doorways and fireplace is the name of Pope Paul III and the date 1547. The room takes its name from the painted scenes framed with grotesques, attributed to Perin del Vaga. The fine panels decorating the walls and ceiling illustrate figures, grotesques and racemes drawn from Roman mythology.

Sala di Clemente VII – The wooden ceilings bear the name of Pope Clement VII and 15C and 16C paintings.

From Sala dell'Apollo take the small corridor which leads to the semicircular courtyard.

Cortile di Alessandro VI – In the courtyard is a handsome well dating from the reign of this Pope (1492-1503). The alternative name – Theatre Court – recalls the theatrical performances given here by Leo X and Pius IV, both men of letters.

★**Bagno di Clemente VII** – *Access from the corridor separating Cortile di Alessandro VI from Cortile Leone X and the stairs up on the left.* The beautiful décor by Giovanni da Udine, a pupil of Raphael, is evidence of the civilised lifestyle of the Pope in 16C.

Prigioni (Prisons) – *Access by steps leading down from Alexander VI's Court.* Beatrice Cenci *(see ISOLA TIBERINA – TORRE ARGENTINA: Palazzo Cenci),* Giordano Bruno the heretic monk and Benvenuto Cellini are supposed to have been imprisoned here.

Oil and grain store – The jars could hold 22 000 litres of oil and the capacity of the five large silos was about 3 700 cwt - 100kg of grain. It was Alexander VI who made these provisions in case of siege.

Return to Alexander VI's Court and take the steps up from the centre of the semi-circle which lead to the Loggias of Pius IV, Paul III and Julius II (walking anti-clockwise).

Loggia di Pio IV (Pius IV's Loggia) – The rooms which open on to the loggia were used as living quarters for the castle staff, before becoming prisons. The loggia was rebuilt in the 19C to house political prisoners. It was here that for many years the gun was fired to tell Romans that it was midday.

Bear left.

Loggia di Paolo III (Paul III's Loggia) – The pope commissioned Antonio da Sangallo (the Younger) to design the loggia *(which faces north)* in 1543 and had it decorated with stucco work and grotesques. There is a view of the bastions and the defensive wall.

Continue beyond the restaurant-bar.

On the left is the **upper armoury** *(armeria superiore)*, containing a collection of arms and uniforms belonging to the Italian and Papal armies.

Loggia di Giulio II (Julius II's Loggia) – It faces south with a fine view of St Angelo Bridge (Ponte S Angelo) and of the city of Rome. It was probably built by Giuliano da Sangallo for Julius II.

From here steps lead up to the Papal apartments.

★**Appartamento papale (Papal Apartments)** – After the siege of 1527 when Clement VII was forced to take refuge in Castel Sant'Angelo, Paul III had a suite of rooms constructed on top of the castle which was well protected by the succession of ramps and steps.

Sala del Consiglio (Sala Paolina) – Visitors waited in this room before seeing the Pope. Its floor is marble and the frescoes are by a group of artists instructed by Perin del Vaga, a Florentine artist who was a follower of Raphael, from whom the Papal court commissioned a number of important works.

Camera del Perseo (Perseus' Room) – The name is derived from the subject of the frieze painted by Perin del Vaga.

Camera di Amore e Psiche (Cupid and Psyche's Room) – The frieze beneath the ceiling illustrates the story of the beautiful young woman who was loved by Venus' son.

Return to the Sala del Consiglio and, after the steps, turn into the corridor decorated with frescoes.

Two sets of steps linked by a passage lead up to the **Library** and two series of rooms *(one above the other)* named after their decorations: **Hadrian's Mausoleum Room**, the **Festoon Room**, which opens into a smaller apartment where Cagliostro was imprisoned, now comprising the **Dolphin Room** and the **Salamander Room**.

Return to the Library.

Sala del Tesoro e dell' Archivio Segreto – The Treasure and Secret Archive Room, at the centre of the fortress, is a circular chamber, lined with walnut presses containing the papal records which were transferred here from the Vatican in 1870. The cupboards (probably 14C) originally held the precious objects, relics and silver belonging to Julius II, Leo X and Sixtus V.

Beside the Sala del Tesoro.

Scala romana (Roman Staircase) – The staircase, part of Hadrian's mausoleum, leads to the Hall of Flags and Columns (Sala Rotonda) and the terrace.

Terrace – The bronze statue of the angel (repaired in 18C) presides over a **panorama**★★★ of Rome, one of the most famous that there is. From left to right: the Prati district and the green patch of the Villa Borghese; close to the castle, the great white mass of the Law Courts, then the Quirinal Palace, the Militia Tower and the shallow dome of the Pantheon; further right, the monument to Victor Emmanuel II and the domes and turrets of the city: the Gesù Church, St Ivo's corkscrew tower, the belfry of Santa Maria dell'Anima with its ceramic tiles, Sant'Andrea delle Valle, San Carlo ai Catinari, the Synagogue. On the extreme right is the Janiculum Hill, San Giovanni dei Fiorentini, Via della Conciliazione, St Peter's and the Vatican Palace linked to Castel Sant'Angelo by the "Passetto", Monte Mario.

It is also possible to take the parapet walk linking the four bastions: St John's, St Matthew's, St Mark's (which gives access to the "Passetto", *see above*) and St Luke's.

South of the Tiber

★**Ponte Sant'Angelo** – This is one of the most elegant bridges in Rome. It goes back to the time of Hadrian who built a fine bridge (AD 136) linking the Campus Martius with his mausoleum; its three central arches have survived. The other arches date from the 17C and were altered when the Tiber embankments were built in 1892-94. The statues of St Peter and St Paul *(south bank)* were erected by Clement VII in 1530; the ten Baroque angels are the work of Bernini commissioned by Clement IX (1667-69).

Cross the Sant'Angelo Bridge and bear right into Via Paola.

S Giovanni dei Fiorentini – It was Pope Leo X, a Medici from Florence, who decided to build a 'national' church for his fellow countrymen in Rome. The most famous Renaissance artists were invited to compete for the commission: Peruzzi, Michelangelo, Raphael. The artist chosen was Jacopo Sansovino. Work began early in the 16C; it was continued by Antonio da Sangallo and Giacomo della Porta and completed in 1614 by Carlo Maderno. The façade which dates from the 18C is in

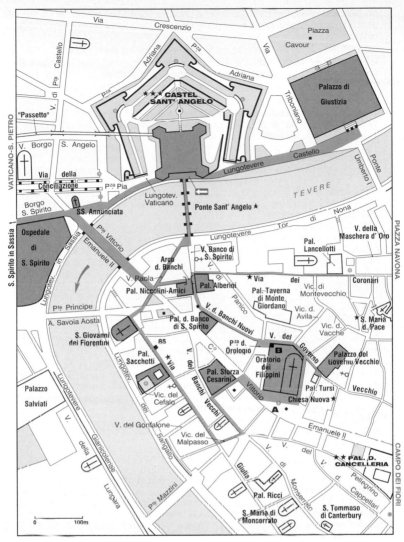

the style of the late Counter-Reformation. The decoration of the chancel is Baroque: in the centre is the *Baptism of Jesus*, a marble group by Antonio Raggi, a pupil of Bernini. The tombs on either side were designed by Borromini who is buried in the church near his teacher Carlo Maderno (tombs in the paving under the dome). There is no inscription on Borromini's tomb, as he committed suicide.

★Via Giulia – The street gained its notoriety in the 16C. It was named after Pope Julius II, its creator, and is one of the few straight streets in Rome. It had a good reputation during the Renaissance but lost favour in the 17C when Innocent X had the State prisons transferred there. Owing to recent restoration work and the arrival of antique shops and modern art galleries, it has regained some of its former standing.

Continue along Via Giulia.

No 85 is one of the houses where Raphael is said to have lived.

Palazzo Sacchetti – *No 66 Via Giulia.* It may have been designed by Sangallo the Younger, architect of the Farnese Palace or by Annibale Lippi, the architect of the Villa Medici; both buildings were commissioned in the 16C by Cardinal Ricci di Montepulciano.

Between the next two side turnings on the right, Vicolo del Cefalo and Via del Gonfalone, are huge blocks of masonry which were the foundations for Julius II's law courts designed by Bramante but never built. The Romans have christened them 'the Via Giulia sofas'.

81

No 52 is the prison which Innocent X had built in 1655. The inscription on the face of the building speaks of a model institution designed for a more humane type of detention.

Turn left into Vicolo del Malpasso and left again into Via dei Banchi Vecchi.

It was in **Via dei Banchi Vecchi**, the street of bankers in the 15C, that the **Palazzo Sforza Cesarini**, was built by Pope Alexander VI, then only a cardinal.

Turn right into Via Sforza Cesarini and cross Corso Vittorio Emanuele II to reach Piazza della Chiesa Nuova.

★**Chiesa Nuova (New Church)** – The church was founded in the 12C as Santa Maria in Vallicella; the name is probably an allusion to the little valley *(vallicella)*, the Tarentum, which lay near the Tiber in Antiquity.

The history of the church is linked to the memory of **St Philip Neri**, the Florentine founder of the Oratorians who were promoted into a Congregation in 1575 by Gregory XIII, who also offered the Church of Santa Maria in Vallicella to Neri as a base for his Order. Reconstruction was set in hand and the new building, which was finished in 1605, was called the New Church. It was restored in the 19C.

The façade is decorated with the shallow pilasters and recessed columns typical of the Counter-Reformation.

Philip Neri wanted the interior to be plain but during the Counter-Reformation it was given a more elaborate Baroque format inspired by Pietro da Cortona. On the coffered stucco ceiling, he painted *St Philip's Vision* (1664-1665): during the building of the church, Neri had a vision of the Virgin holding up a piece of the ceiling of the old building which threatened to collapse on to the altar where mass was being celebrated.

Pietro da Cortona, who had become the acknowledged master among decorative painters, enjoyed equal celebrity in Rome with Bernini. Between 1648 and 1651 he had already painted the dome which depicts Christ presenting the instruments of the Passion to God, thus abolishing punishment for mankind. In the pendentives he placed the prophets Isaiah, Jeremiah, Ezekiel and Daniel (1659-1660). Meanwhile he began painting an *Assumption* on the vault of the apse.

The three paintings in the chancel are youthful works by Rubens (1608).

The chapel *(left of the chancel)* contains the remains of St Philip Neri and is decorated in grandiose style with gold, bronze and marble encrusted with mother-of-pearl.

The chapel *(left transept)* contains a picture by the Mannerist painter Barocci, in a style very typical of the second half of the 16C.

On the altar in the sacristy *(entrance via the chapel in the left transept)* stands a beautiful marble sculpture of St Philip with an angel, executed in 1640 by Alessandro Algardi.

Oratorio dei Filippini ⊘ – The building adjoining the New Church was built between 1637 and 1662 to house the assemblies of the Congregation of the Oratory where laity and clergy met under the spiritual direction of St Philip Neri.

Nowadays the Oratory is also known as Borromini Hall and is used for conferences and various cultural activities. In addition to the Oratorian priests the vast palace also houses the Vallicelliana Library, the Roman Library, the archives of the city of Rome, which include a collection of Roman newspapers dating back to the 18C, and various cultural institutes.

The façade★ overlooking Piazza della Chiesa Nuova is in fact the side elevation of the Oratory. It was designed by Borromini so as to form a unit with the church. It is monumental: yet subtle, being an interaction of calm and frenzied movement in line and detail so characteristic of this great Baroque architect.

The façade is composed of two orders; the central section undulates with contrasting curves; convex on the lower floor and concave on the upper. The complex design combines recessed windows at ground floor level and a slightly concave pediment in the upper section.

Fontana della "Terrina"(A) – The **fountain** was transferred here in 1925 after standing in the Campo dei Fiori until 1899. The basin was carved in 1590 but a few years later was covered with a travertine lid bearing the inscription: "love God, do good and let others talk".

Take Via della Chiesa Nuova beside the church and turn right into Vicolo del Governo Vecchio.

Via del Governo Vecchio – This was one of the main streets of the district, continuing the Papal Way as Via di Parione. It is lined with craft shops, junk shops and antique dealers occupying the ground floor premises of the Renaissance palaces, some of which still bear the coat of arms of the noble families which once lived there.

Palazzo del Governo Vecchio – The building at no 39 was completed in 1478. In 1624 it became the residence of the Governor of Rome. When the Government was transferred to the Palazzo Madama under Benedict XIV (1740-58), the building became known as the Old Government Palace. It has an attractive doorway decorated with friezes and diaperwork.

Return to Piazza dell' Orologio.

From Via dei Coronari to the Palazzo di Giustizia

Piazza dell'Orologio – The plain front which the Oratory presents in Via dei Filippini ends unexpectedly on the corner of Via del Governo Vecchio in a graceful clock tower. The wrought-iron scroll work on the bell cage is recognisable as Borromini's work (1647-49). Beneath the clock is a mosaic of the Virgin of Vallicella.

On the corner of the building is a beautiful **Madonna** (**B**) surrounded by a 'glory' of cherubs, in typical Baroque taste.

Madonna in Piazza dell'Orologio

In Rome such madonnas are to be found in almost every street. The little lanterns which sometimes still burn in front of them were for many years the only illumination after sunset. It was not until January 1854 that street lighting by gas was introduced to Rome in Via del Corso by James Shepherd, an Englishman, who is buried in the Testaccio Cemetery. Foreigners have never understood the Roman aversion to bright lights. When they walked abroad at night carrying a lantern they would hear the locals cry *Volti la luce* (Dim the light).

In December the street madonnas were the object of a particular cult: peasants from the Abruzzi mountains, dressed in sheep skins, would come and give performances on their bagpipes before their favourite shrine in return for a small payment. These bagpipers who would begin to play at four in the morning exasperated the French writer and diplomat Stendhal. "To gain your neighbours' approval and avoid denunciation by the parish priest, anyone who is afraid of being thought liberal subscribes for two novennas." Their devotions accomplished, the "pipers" returned to their homes with their earnings.

Take Via dei Banchi Nuovi.

Via dei Banchi Nuovi and Via Banco di Santo Spirito – These streets gave the district the air of a commercial centre. By the 15C bankers from Florence, Siena and Genoa had set up in business. Their fortunes were immense. Under the supervision of the Cardinal Camerlengo the Chigi family administered the finances of the Holy See for over twenty years; later the Strozzi, relatives of the Medici, took over. The Papal State also granted the bankers concessions on mining and customs dues. They controlled the Pope's personal finances and those of the great Roman families.

Together with money changing, which was conducted freely in the streets, there was betting: people bet on the election of the Pope, on the sex of unborn babies... Until 1541 there was a working mint in the **Palazzo del Banco di Santo Spirito.**

From the end of the Via Banco di Santo Spirito there is a pleasant view of Castel Sant'Angelo and the bridge leading to it.

Early in the 16C the **Palazzo Niccolini-Amici** was built by Jacopo Sansovino for the Strozzi. The **Palazzo Alberini** opposite was rented in 1515 to bankers from Florence.

★ **Via dei Coronari** – This is one of the most attractive streets in Rome with its antique shops and its palaces glowing in ochre and stone.

In antiquity it was part of the Via Recta which led from the Piazza Colonna to the river. Overall it has retained the form it acquired under Sixtus IV (1471-84). It is named after the vendors of rosaries *(corone)* and other pious objects who set up their shops in the path of the pilgrims, who entered the City by the Porta del Popolo and made their way to the Vatican over St Angelo Bridge.

Arco dei Banchi – The Bankers' Arch leads to the Chigi bank. On the left under the arch is a stone with a Latin inscription which comes from the nearby Church of St Celsus and St Julian: it shows the height reached by the Tiber when it flooded in 1277.

Turn left under Arco dei Banchi.

Ponte Vittorio Emanuele II (Victor Emmanuel II Bridge) – There was a bridge here in AD 60, built by Nero, which collapsed in the 4C. The present construction, which is decorated with allegorical groups and winged Victories, was begun soon after the unification of the Italian State and completed in 1911, thus linking Rome and the Vatican.

Cross the bridge to the right (north) bank and turn right.

On the left is the imposing **Santo Spirito hospital** which was founded by Innocent III and rebuilt in 15C by Sixtus IV. The **Church of the Santissima Annunciata** (Most Holy Annunciation), although small, is graced by an attractive façade full of movement (18C).

Santo Spirito in Sassia – The church was built in the 8C for Anglo-Saxon pilgrims and rebuilt in the 16C after being sacked in 1527. The architect was Sangallo the Younger who died before it was finished. The façade, which bears the arms of Sixtus V (1585-90), in whose reign the building was completed, is in the Renaissance style with flat pilasters and an oculus, according to Sangallo's design.
The interior, beneath a beautiful coffered ceiling, is richly decorated with paintings in the Mannerist style (divided into small panels, overworked). Fine 16C organ.

Palazzo di Giustizia – The **Law Courts** were built from 1889 to 1911 by Guglielmo Calderini and are among the most conspicuous modern buildings in Rome. With a bronze quadriga by Ximenes (1855-1926) and the colossal statuary, the Law Courts can claim both Classical and Baroque inspiration.

Neighbouring sights are described in the following chapters: CAMPO DEI FIORI; PIAZZA NAVONA; VATICANO – S PIETRO.

CATACOMBE DI PRISCILLA ★

The sights are described in alphabetical order and located on the plan below

This district lies outside the walls between the Via Salaria and the Via Nomentana. It is called "African" because many of the streets are named after the countries which made up the Italian Empire and it was developed during the Fascist era (1926).
The monotonous streets, lined with large blocks of comfortable flats, give way in the **Piazza Mincio** to extravagantly decorated buildings in a mixture of Renaissance, Baroque and Egyptian styles, which were designed between 1922 and 1926 by the architect, Gino Coppede.

For a quick bite on the hoof

Romoli *(viale Etruria 140/144)* is located at the heart of the African quarter. Open until 2am, this informal establishment proffers a vast range of sweet and savoury snacks: warm stuffed parcels of deliciousness and melt-in-the-mouth biscuits...

★SANT'AGNESE FUORI LE MURA E MAUSOLEO DI SANTA COSTANZA

The history of these two buildings begins with the death of Agnes, a young girl of 12 who was martyred under Diocletian (284-305).

Early church – In the 4C (after 337) Constantia erected a huge basilica near St Agnes' tomb. Traces of the apse still exist, clearly visible from Via Bressanone and Piazza Annibaliano. Subsequently, to the south-west of the basilica, she built a circular construction which was to be her mausoleum and has become the Church of Santa Costanza. Constantia's basilica fell into ruin but a small chapel was built on the site of St Agnes' tomb. This chapel was rebuilt and enlarged by Pope Honorius (625-38). It is now known as St Agnes' Church and has been much restored, particularly in the 19C.

★**Sant'Agnese fuori le Mura** ⊙ – The church of St Agnes-Without-the-Walls can be reached from below from Via Sant'Agnese or from above from Via Nomentana through the convent court-yard and down a long flight of steps

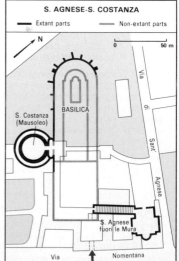

S. AGNESE-S. COSTANZA
▬ Extant parts ▬ Non-extant parts
N 0   50 m
Via di Sant' Agnese
S. Costanza (Mausoleo)
BASILICA
S. Agnese fuori le Mura
Via Nomentana

into the narthex; the steps which were restored in the 16C, were already part of the 7C construction. The walls are covered with fragments from the catacombs, in particular *(almost at the bottom on the right going down)* a low relief of St Agnes praying, which decorated her tomb, and an inscription to the glory of her martyrdom, which was commissioned by Pope Damasus (366-84) and runs to 10 lines, the first of which is:
FAMA REFERT SANCTOS DUDUM RETULISSE PARENTES.
Despite the addition of 19C painting above the chancel arch, between the clerestories and over the arcades in the nave, the interior still gives some idea of its 7C appearance; it was designed like a basilica with a nave and two aisles and galleries. The ceiling and baldaquin

Legend of St Agnes – Both St Ambrose and Damasus, writing at a period soon after the Diocletian persecution, mention the martyrdom of Agnes. The 6C legend was therefore founded on a basis of truth. Agnes refused to marry the son of the Praetor declaring that she had vowed her soul to God. She was condemned to stand naked in a place of ill-repute, possibly below the steps to Domitian's stadium, the church of Sant'Agnese in Agone nearby; her nakedness was miraculously covered by her long hair and a dazzling cloak; she was then condemned to the stake but escaped unscathed, the flames turning on her executioners; finally she was beheaded with a sword and buried in the cemetery in the Via Nomentana.

Legend of St Constantia – The saint's name is derived from that of Constantia, the Emperor Constantine's daughter or grand-daughter. Such great benefactions were attributed to Agnes that Constantia, who was suffering from leprosy, spent a night by the saint's tomb; the young martyr appeared to her in a dream, urging her to convert to Christianity; when Constantia awoke the leprosy had gone.

are 17C. It was during the restoration undertaken by Paul V (1605-21) that the bones of St Agnes were discovered next to another body, probably that of Emerentiana, who continued to pray by St Agnes' body when the other Christians fled from the stones thrown by pagans. Paul V arranged for her bones to be placed in a shrine beneath the altar.

The statue of St Agnes on the altar is a curious work by the French sculptor Nicolas Cordier (1567-1612) who used the torso of an old alabaster statue of Isis. On the left of the altar is a very fine antique candelabra made of marble.

The **mosaic★** in the apse was part of the 7C building; it shows St Agnes with Pope Symmachus (498-514) who restored the early chapel and Pope Honorius who is offering the church he built. The work is typical of Roman art with Byzantine influences: Agnes is dressed like a Byzantine empress; the colours are muted and repetitive (same for all three robes); the vertical lines are very clear, in perfect accord with the lines of the vault.

Catacombs ⊙ – A cemetery was already in existence when St Agnes' remains were buried here. The oldest part on the north side of the church dates back to the 2C. After St Agnes' burial the graves spread round behind the apse and down between the church and the mausoleum.

★★**Mausoleo di Santa Costanza** ⊙ – The Emperor Constantine's daughters, Helen and Constantia, were buried in this circular mausoleum which dates from the 4C. It was probably converted into a church in the 13C. The outline of an oval vestibule can still be traced in front of the entrance. The rotunda itself is covered by a dome resting on a drum which is supported on a ring of twinned columns linked by elegant arches. The surrounding barrel-vaulted gallery is still adorned with its original 4C **mosaic★**, which is an example of the artistic renewal which followed in the wake of Constantine's reign; the vault is divided into panels and covered with a variety of motifs against a light background: floral and geometric details, portraits in medallions, vine tendrils entwined with harvest scenes. The mosaics in the side recesses have Christian themes: God handing down the Law to Moses (or according to another interpretation, St Peter receiving the keys) and Christ giving the New Law (the Gospel) to St Peter and St Paul.

In the recess opposite the entrance is a copy of Constantia's sarcophagus.

★★CATACOMBE DI PRISCILLA (PRISCILLA CATACOMBS) ⊙ 430 Via Salaria.

The catacombs developed out of a private underground chamber *(hypogeum)* beneath the house of the Acilii, a noble family to which Priscilla belonged. Excavations in this chamber have uncovered inscriptions mentioning Priscilla and a certain Acilius Glabrio, who was mentioned by Suetonius; he was condemned to death in AD 91 by Domitian for the same offence as Domitilla's husband, Flavius Clemens *(see APPIA ANTICA – Catacombe di Domitilla)*. The family was converted to Christianity and allowed the Christian community to create underground galleries in which to bury their dead. During the 3C two storeys of galleries developed round the *hypogeum*. In the 4C St Sylvester's Basilica, in which several popes are buried, was built by Pope Sylvester (314-35) over the Christian graves.

The **Chapel of the Taking of the Veil** (Capella della Velata) is named after a scene painted on the far wall and originally interpreted as showing a young virgin taking the veil in the presence of the Virgin Mary; nowadays it is thought to represent three episodes in the dead woman's life: marriage, worship, motherhood.

The **Chapel of the Virgin and Child★** (Capella della Vergine col Bambino) contains the earliest representation of the Virgin *(on the ceiling)* who is holding the Christ child on her knees while another figure points to a star. The scene is thought to be an illustration of a passage from Isaiah, Chapter 7 ("Behold, a virgin shall conceive, and bear a son...").

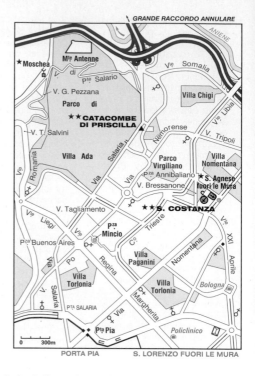

The **Greek Chapel★** (Cappella Greca), in which there are Greek inscriptions, consists of two chambers separated by an arch. Over the arch in the inner room is a painting of a banquet at which one of the figures *(left)* at the table is breaking bread; on the table are a chalice and a plate of fish; at the sides are seven baskets of bread which could be an allusion to the miracle of the feeding of the multitude. The presence of all these items has led to the painting being interpreted as a representation of the Eucharist. Archeologists date it as 2C on account of the hairstyle of one of the women seated at the table, a style made fashionable by Faustina, the wife of the Emperor Antoninus Pius (138-61).

ADDITIONAL SIGHTS

Parco di Villa Ada – This vast public park contains the site of the Monte Antenne which is closely connected with the founding of Rome; here stood the Sabine city of the Antennates who, according to Livy, were conquered by Romulus after attacking the Romans in retaliation for the rape of the Sabine women.

★Moschea – The mosque, set in the green surroundings of Mount Antenne, forms part of the largest group of monuments built in Rome within the last few decades. The mosque is not in fact the only building in the new Islamic Centre, having been built next to a library, an auditorium for 300 people, and several rooms for meetings and lectures. The design of Rome's Islamic Centre is the result of the joint efforts of three architects – P Portoghesi, V Gigliotti and S Moussawi. Building began in 1984 and ended in 1992. The other buildings in the complex will be finished in due course.

To underline the Islamic Centre's links with the city, typical Roman materials have been used in the construction, such as straw-coloured brick and travertine stone. The result is that, despite being Islamic, this building does not seem very different from the city's own traditional architecture. The interior is the real masterpiece of the mosque; the prayer hall (capacity 3000) is surmounted by a large stepped dome and 16 other small side domes, supported on 32 sunken pillars made of white cement and marble dust. The exterior walls which constitute the base of the domes, are suspended from and supported by the same sunken pillars. Indeed the domes do not actually rest on the rectangular base of the building, this allows a band (80cm) of light to run around the base (170m), creating an amazing effect. Light is the main feature of the interior. Every "step" of the domes has a series of little openings which, together with the band at the base, help to diffuse light and create a surreal atmosphere. The interlacing arches which rise from the pillars are also very beautiful and suggest an impression of continual movement reminiscent of the sinuous lines of the Italian Baroque.

Neighbouring sights are described in the following chapters:
PORTA PIA; S LORENZO FUORI LE MURA.

COLOSSEO – CELIO ★★★

The walk traverses several centuries. The first part, dedicated to the time of the Emperors, includes the Colosseum and the Arch of Constantine: the second centres on one of the greenest of the seven hills of Rome, the Caelian Hill, and the precious medieval relics which it harbours.

★★★COLOSSEO (COLOSSEUM) ⊘

Construction – Vespasian, the first of the Flavian Emperors, decided to devote a part of the huge area occupied by Nero's Domus Aurea to public entertainment. It was on the site of the lake in the grounds of Nero's house that Vespasian built the largest Roman amphitheatre in the world as a venue for the great spectacles which acquired a legendary reputation.

The Flavian amphitheatre, begun in AD 72, took the name of the Colosseum either because it stood near the huge statue of Nero, the *Colosseum*, or because of its own colossal dimensions (527m - 576yds in circumference and 57m - 187ft high). It is one of the

> ### To end the evening on a high note...
>
> Why not wander off for an ice-cream from one of Rome's best gelaterie **San Crispino** at 55/56 Via Acaia. Worthy choices for those presented with a dilemma include the honey, meringue or chocolate flavoured specialities.
>
> ### ... followed by a little jazz
>
> Check out **Saint Louis Music City** at Via del Cardello 13 (Metro A: Colosseo).

most memorable reminders of Roman grandeur of that time.

The position of the **statue of Nero** (**A**) is marked by a few slabs of travertine stone lying on the ground. The Emperor's head was surrounded by rays like a sun. According to Suetonius, the statue was 36m - 120ft high.

The last days of the Colosseum – Gladiatorial duels were banned in 404 by the Emperor Honorius. Wild animal fights disappeared in the 6C. In the 13C the Frangipani family turned the Colosseum into a fortress which then passed to the Annibaldi. It was, however, in the 15C that the building suffered its greatest damage: it literally became a quarry and the huge blocks of travertine were taken for the construction of the Palazzo Venezia, the Palazzo della Cancelleria and St Peter's Basilica. Benedict XIV put an end to the quarrying in the 18C by consecrating the building to the Christian martyrs who were thought to have perished there. The Stations of the Cross were set up round the arena. Stendhal wrote of his embarrassment at the "pious murmuring of the faithful who observe the Stations of the Cross in groups of 15 or 20". Today a cross still stands at the eastern entrance in memory of those Christians who may have met their deaths here, condemned like other criminals to fight unarmed against wild animals or armed men.

According to custom one should stand before the Colosseum, massive in its unperturbability, and in Byron's well-known words quote the prophecy made early in the 8C by the Venerable Bede, an English monk and historian:

> "While stands the Colosseum, Rome shall stand;
> When falls the Colosseum, Rome shall fall;
> And when Rome falls, also the world."

Circuses

Originally they held a religious significance for the Romans and constituted a rite intended to maintain good relations between the City and the gods. For many years the spectators attended bare-headed, as at a sacrifice. Caesar was reproved for reading his post in the amphitheatre and Suetonius, the Emperors' biographer, reproached Tiberius strongly for disliking the spectacle.

The Colosseum, though still incomplete, was inaugurated in AD 80 by Titus, Vespasian's son. The spectacle which he organised on this occasion lasted 100 days. The racing and the duels between gladiators were followed by bouts between men and wild animals: 5 000 animals died. Even naval engagements were re-enacted in the flooded arena. In 249 to celebrate the millennium of the founding of Rome 1 000 pairs of gladiators met in combat; 32 elephants, a dozen tigers and over 50 lions, brought from the Imperial provinces, were killed.

The spectacle usually lasted from dawn to dusk. Some were very cruel and caused the arena to be covered in blood. Others, such as the presentation of wild animals, were like modern circus acts.

Colosseum

Tour

The whole construction consists of three tiers of arcades supported on engaged columns, Doric on the ground floor, Ionic on the first and Corinthian on the second, surmounted by a wall divided into sections by regularly spaced engaged pilasters which alternate with small recesses. In Domitian's time the flat wall spaces were decorated with bronze shields. The projections supported wooden poles, inserted through holes in the upper cornice; the poles carried a linen awning which could be extended over the amphitheatre to protect the spectators from sun or rain. The job of putting up the awning, which was made more difficult by the wind, was entrusted to the sailors of Misenus' fleet.

The huge blocks of travertine, which were never covered in marble, were originally held together with metal tenons which were removed in the Middle Ages although the sockets are still visible. The blocks of stone were brought from the quarries at Albulae, near Tivoli, along specially built roads, 6m - 20ft wide.

The spectators entered the amphitheatre according to the entrance number which appeared on their ticket *(tessera)* and made their way to their seats through vaulted passages and stairways decorated with stuccowork.

Terraces – The construction is a rounded oval (188m - 617ft and 156m - 512ft on the axes). In the middle of the longer sides were the seats reserved for the Emperor and his suite (north) and for the Prefect of Rome and the magistrates (south).

The *cavea*, the terraces for the spectators, began 4m - 13ft above the arena. First came the *podium*, a terrace protected by a balustrade and reserved for the marble seats of the important spectators. Then came three series of terraces, separated from one another by passages and divided by sloping corridors *(vomitaria)* down which the multitude poured out after the show. Places were allotted according to social station. At the top under a colonnade sat the women while the slaves stood on the terrace supported by the colonnade. In all there were probably about 45 000 seats and space for 5 000 standing.

The gladiators, dressed in purple and gold, entered through doors at either end of the longer axis. Marching in ranks they toured the arena and then halted before the Emperor. With right arm raised they pronounced the formula: *Ave, Imperator, morituri te salutant* (Hail, Emperor, those who are about to die salute thee).

During excavations the floor of the arena where the spectacle took place disappeared, revealing the underground warren where the wild animals waited before being brought to the surface by a system of ramps and lifts for the pleasure of the assembled crowd. "This degraded people clamours with covetous anxiety for only two things in the world, bread and circuses" said Juvenal at the end of the 1C.

***ARCO DI TRIONFO DI CONSTANTINO (ARCH OF CONSTANTINE)

At the height of the tourist season it is sometimes difficult to come close to the arch. Such is its fame that anyone merely passing through Rome comes to see it. This magnificent construction with its three arches was built in 315 by the Senate and the Roman People three years after Constantine's victory over his rival Maxentius at the Milvian bridge *(see MONTE MARIO)*. Like the Colosseum it was incorpor-

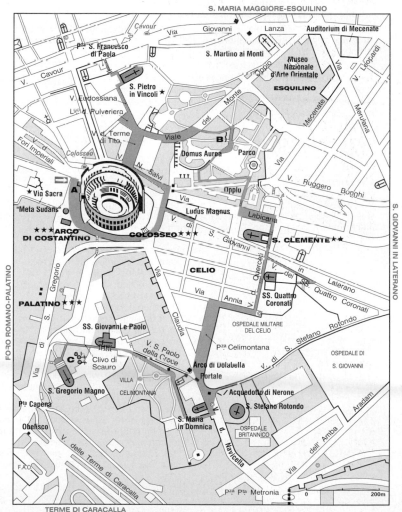

ated into the Medieval fortifications. It was first restored in the 18C and put into its present state in 1804. The proportions are harmonious. The abundant decoration was not all 4C work. Many of the sculptures were taken from 2C monuments (by Trajan, Hadrian and Marcus Aurelius) and re-employed.

North face – The statues of four Dacian prisoners on the upper storey belonged to a monument erected in honour of Trajan (98-117). The way in which they are set up on a huge base above the entablature is characteristic of 4C taste. The four low reliefs between the statues date from the 2C; together with those displayed in the museum in the Conservators' Palace, they belonged to monuments set up in honour of the Emperor Marcus Aurelius (although his head has been replaced by a head of Constantine). From left to right they represent: Marcus Aurelius being greeted by a personification of Via Flaminia on his return to Rome in 174 after fighting in Germany; his triumph; distribution of bread and money to the people; interrogation of a royal prisoner.

The four medallions come from a monument to Hadrian (117-138). The subjects are hunting, a sport of oriental origin to which Hadrian was particularly partial, and sacrifices: *(from left to right)* wild boar hunting and a sacrifice to Apollo; lion hunting and a sacrifice to Hercules, who is wearing a lion skin.

The other sculptures, which date from the 4C, illustrate the reign of Constantine.

South Face *(Facing down Via S Gregorio)* – The design is identical to that on the north face. At the top are four low reliefs belonging to the same series as those in the museum in the Conservators' Palace and on the other side of the arch; on the left, two incidents in the wars of Marcus Aurelius; on the right, the Emperor addresses his army beside a sacrificial ceremony (below are the animals being led to the sacrifice).

The four medallions (which are damaged) show *(from left to right)* the hunt moving off and a sacrifice to Silvanus, god of the forest; bear hunting and a sacrifice to Diana, goddess and huntress par excellence.

"Meta Sudans" – Only the site now remains of this fountain which was built by Titus and repaired by Constantine. It took the form of a cone of porous stone oozing water. What remained of it was demolished in 1936.

Go to Via di S Giovanni on the east side of the Colosseum.

The ruins on the north side of the street may have belonged to the **Ludus Magnus**, a gymnasium built by Domitian for training gladiators.

Proceed north up Via N Salvi and Via di Terme di Tito. Turn left into Via Eudossiana to reach Piazza San Pietro in Vincoli.

★SAN PIETRO IN VINCOLI (ST PETER IN CHAINS) ⊘

The church was consecrated in the 5C by Sixtus III (432-40) although it was probably built on a much older construction. During the Renaissance the

Cardinals of the Della Rovere family were the incumbents: Francesco, who became Pope Sixtus IV (1471-84), and then Giuliano, who became Julius II (1503-13) had it restored.

The church is one of the chief tourist attractions in Rome, as it contains the famous *Moses* by Michelangelo. It also attracts pilgrims who come to venerate the chains which bound St Peter.

In 1475 Cardinal Giuliano Della Rovere added the porch which would be quite elegant if an upper storey had not been added in the 16C.

The broad interior is divided into a nave and two aisles by two rows of Doric marble columns, beautiful in their solemn austerity. The medieval décor was altered in the 17C and 18C: the nave was vaulted and painted with frescoes.

On the left of the main door is the tomb of Antonio and Piero Pollaiuolo, famous Renaissance artists from Florence.

Da una foto Gab. Fot. Naz.

Moses by Michelangelo

Julius II's Mausoleum – This monument occasioned the meeting of two of the most powerful personalities of the Renaissance: Julius II and Michelangelo. The Pope, with his unquenchable appetite for grandeur, conceived the idea of a tomb of such splendour that it would reflect the glory of his pontificate forever. In 1505 he summoned Michelangelo from Florence to assist in the project. The tomb was to be placed in the centre of St Peter's Basilica, three storeys high, with 40 huge statues, bronze low reliefs, surmounted by the sarcophagus. Michelangelo left for Carrara where he spent eight months choosing the blocks of marble from which this superhuman work was to be created. While in Carrara he dreamed of sculpting a single gigantic figure out of the mountain of marble. He returned to Rome to the indifference of the Pope who now swore only by Bramante. Michelangelo returned to Florence hurt. After Julius II's death in 1513 the project for his tomb declined steadily; Michelangelo sculpted only the Slaves (in Florence and Paris) and the Moses; he began the statues of the daughters of Laban, Leah and Rachel, but left the mausoleum itself to his pupils.

★★★**Moses**   Pope Paul III grew tired of seeing Michelangelo working on the tomb of Julius II and, being anxious for him to start as soon as possible on the *Last Judgement* in the Sistine Chapel, he went one day to see the sculptor at work. There in front of the Moses one of his Cardinals remarked with great diplomacy that the statue was so beautiful that it alone would suffice to honour the Pope's grave.
The authoritative attitude of the huge seated figure is enhanced by the steady gaze of the eyes.

Crypta – *Not open to the public.* The crypt is visible through the grill in the confessio (beneath the high altar). A fine 4C sarcophagus conserves the relics of the Maccabees, seven brothers whose martyrdom is recounted in the Old Testament.

From San Pietro in Vincoli to Monte Celio (Caelian Hill)

On leaving the church take the covered passage (right) which leads to Piazza San Francesco di Paola.

The steps are dominated by what used to be the Borgia Palace (attractive 16C loggia); it was the residence of Vannozza Caetani, mother of Caesar and Lucretia Borgia, the children of Pope Alexander VI.

The sad end of an Etruscan king – The modern flight of steps leading up to Piazza San Francesco di Paola covers a site linked with the legendary history of early Rome when the city was administered by Etruscan kings. King Servius Tullius' daughter, Tullia, was married to Tarquin. Devoured by ambition she incited her husband to unseat her father, who, wounded in a struggle in the old Curia fomented by his son-in-law, died in the street linking Suburra to the Esquiline which followed the line of the present steps. Seven centuries later Livy tells in his Roman History how Tullia, led astray by her husband's fury, "drove her chariot over her father's body", the street was then called Vicus Scelaratus (Crime Street).

Return via Piazza San Pietro in Vincoli to Via Eudossiana which leads into Viale del Monte Oppio.

Parco Oppio takes its name from the Oppius *(qv)* and contains the relics of Trajan's Baths; there is a plan of the baths on the external wall of the apse (**B**).

Domus Aurea ⊘ – The **Golden House** is the palace built by Nero after the fire in AD 64. The vestibule was on the Velia (where the Arch of Titus stands) and contained the famous statue of Nero while the rooms were on the Oppian Hill. In the hollow between, now occupied by the Colosseum, was a lake and all around were gardens and vineyards creating a truly rural environment. Inside the house 'the dining room ceilings were composed of movable ivory tiles pierced with holes

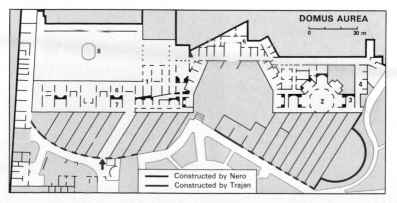

DOMUS AUREA
0   30 m

Constructed by Nero
Constructed by Trajan

so that flowers or perfume could be sprinkled on the guests below; the main dining room was circular and turned continually on its axis, day and night, like the world'. Nero committed suicide in AD 68; the Senate condemned him. The lake was drained and the Colosseum was erected on the site. Then the upper part of the house was razed and what remained was used as foundations for the Baths of Titus and Trajan. The Golden House was not discovered until the Renaissance. Raphael and some of his fellow artists were very enthusiastic about the paintings which they found: geometric designs, foliated scrolls, decorations with faces and animals. As the rooms decorated in this way were underground like caves or grottoes, the decorative motifs were called **grotesques.**

Tour – The fine brick façade belongs to Trajan's Baths. The tour begins in one of the slanting passages built in front of Nero's house as foundations for Trajan's Baths and continues through a series of fairly obscure rooms.

In the first room (**1**) are traces of the houses destroyed by the fire in 64. The next (**2**), which is octagonal and lit by a dome, leads into five other rooms and shows the daring design of the house. In a third room (**3**) the statue of *Laocoon* now in the Vatican, was found in 1506. Another room (**4**) contains rare and attractive remnants of painting including landscapes. On the ceiling of the corridor (**5**) are scratched the names of artists who entered the ruins through the ceiling. Two other rooms (**6** and **7**) exemplify the ingenious design of the house: one overlooks an internal garden (**8**) where the base of a pool is visible, the other looks out on the external garden, now filled with the slanting passages of Trajan's Baths.

MONTE CELIO (CAELIAN HILL)

The Caelian is the greenest and pleasantest of the seven hills of Rome. It was incorporated into the city in the 7C BC: when the city of Alba broke the peace treaty which had united it with Rome since the combat between the Horatii and Curiatii, King Tullus Hostilius captured the rebellious city and transferred its population to the Caelian Hill. It was continuously inhabited until the 11C when the Investiture Controversy brought war to Rome. In 1084 the army of Robert Guiscard 'liberated' the papal capital from the German troops but caused terrible devastation. Since then there has been little re-building on the Caelian Hill.

Walk south along Via Labicana and then turn right towards San Clemente.

★★San Clemente (St Clement's Basilica) *(plan below)*

The church was founded in the 4C in a private house belonging to a Christian *(titulus)* and was immediately dedicated to St Clement, the fourth Pope. It is therefore one of the oldest Roman basilicas. It was ruined in 1084 but rebuilt on the same site by Paschal II in 1108.

Upper basilica – The main entrance through an atrium shows the simple austerity of Medieval buildings *(usual entrance into south aisle from Via di S Giovanni in Laterano)*. The interior has preserved its 12C basilica plan with a nave and two aisles divided by ancient columns taken from a variety of sources. The unity of style however has been broken by the addition of Baroque stucco decorations and 18C alterations (ceiling and wall frescoes). The marble furnishings are particularly remarkable: in the *schola cantorum* (**1**) where the choristers sang, the sober *ambones* where the Epistle and Gospel were read and the Paschal candlestick are very fine 12C work; the screen separating the *schola cantorum* from the chancel belonged to the early church and dates from the 6C. The Cosmati floor (12C) is one of the best preserved in Rome.

MICHELIN

San Clemente apse mosaic

★★★**Apse Mosaic** – This composition with its dazzling colours dates from the 12C. The richness of the symbolism is enhanced by the diversity and beauty of the style. At the top of the apse, against a background of ornamental foliage interspersed with small decorative objects in the manner of the mosaicists of the early centuries, is an illustration of the Crucifixion: on the cross itself are 12 doves symbolizing the Apostles, flanked by the Virgin and St John. Above is Paradise shown in irridescent colours *(fan-shaped)* with the hand of God the Father holding out the crown to his Son. Below the cross are stags coming to quench their thirst (symbolizing candidates for baptism) while Humanity gets on with its work.

Lower down in the apse is a frieze of sheep leaving the cities of Jerusalem and Bethlehem, symbols for the Old and New Testaments, and heading towards a distant prospect to adore the Lamb. Above the chancel arch the style is influenced by Byzantine art. The prophets, Jeremiah and Isaiah (above the two towns), proclaim the triumph of God, shown as Christ surrounded by the symbols of the Evangelists. Between Christ and the Prophets are the martyrs: St Clement with his boat is accompanied by St Peter *(right)*; St Lawrence with his grill is accompanied by St Paul *(left)*.

St Catherine's Chapel (2) – The decorative **frescoes★** by Masolino da Panicale (1383-1447) combine a taste for the attitudes, thin faces and subtle colours of the Primitives with the early Renaissance search for well defined space: consider the architectural décor in the Annunciation scene above the entrance arcade.

The scene to the left of the arcade shows St Christopher carrying Jesus; in the chapel are scenes from the life of St Catherine of Alexandria *(left wall)*, the Crucifixion *(end wall)* and scenes from the life of St Ambrose *(right wall - damaged)*.

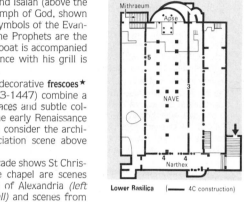

Lower Basilica ⊙ – From the north aisle steps lead down to the lower basilica (4C). This basilica consists of a narthex, a nave and two aisles and an apse. The upper basilica is built over the nave and south aisle of the lower one; a wall supporting the upper construction (**3**) divides the lower church into four.

Frescoes – Some of these (**4**) date from the 11C and 12C; others are older (9C). Those in the nave (**5**) which are notable for their good state of preservation and their lively scenes illustrate the legend of Sisinius, Prefect of Rome: he went to arrest his wife who was attending a clandestine mass celebrated by Pope Clement but was struck blind in the presence of the holy man; above this scene his servants, also blinded, are carrying off a column thinking it to be his wife.

The figures are accompanied by sentences spoken by the people depicted in the frescoes. They are perhaps the first example in history of the comic strip! Even more important is the fact that this is an extremely rare example in writing of the linguistic transition from classical to vulgar Latin.

Mithraeum – Beneath the 4C basilica are the remains of two houses built in Republican times. The house beneath the apse was converted in the 3C into a *mithraeum*, a small temple for the cult of the god Mithras. Ancient steps lead down to the mithraeum, which is well preserved with two parallel stone benches, where the initiates sat. A statue of the god was placed at the far end; in the centre is the altar showing the god cutting the throat of the bull while the dog, the serpent and the scorpion, symbols of evil, try to prevent the sacrifice which releases life-giving forces.

Take Via de SS Quattro Coronati.

Santi Quattro Coronati

In the Middle Ages the church of the **Four Crowned Saints** was part of a fortress which protected the papal Lateran Palace against attack, a constant threat, from the strongholds of the noble families on the Palatine and in the Colosseum.

The Early Christian church (4C) erected by Leo IV (847-55) lasted until 1084 when it was sacked and left in ruins by Robert Guiscard's troops. Paschal II (1099-1118) built a much smaller church, shorter and without side aisles. From the 12C to 15C it belonged to Benedictine monks but in the 16C the whole building passed to a community of Augustinian nuns.

Neither archeologists nor historians have been able to identify the four saints to whom the church is dedicated.

The story of four martyred soldiers is mixed up with the story of five sculptors martyred in Pannonia (western Hungary). According to a list of martyrs drawn up by Leo IV their remains were all placed in the crypt of this church.

Tour – The door beneath the tower, which served as a belfry in the 9C, leads into an outer courtyard. The wall opposite the entrance was the eastern façade of the early church. In the inner courtyard on the right are the columns which separated the nave and north aisle now incorporated into a wall.

Interior – The church is as Paschal II built it. The space taken up by the nave and aisles corresponds to the width of the nave only in the early church. This makes the apse seem abnormally large. In the walls of the side aisles, as in the inner courtyard, the columns which separated the nave and aisles in the early church are incorporated in Paschal II's building. The wooden ceiling and the women's galleries *(matronea)* date from the 16C. In the 17C the apse was decorated with paintings and stuccoes depicting the history of the two groups of saints venerated in the church with a glory of saints in the vault.

Against the pillar on the left of the chancel arch is a 15C tabernacle, its fine carving picked out in gold. The surrounding paintings were added in the 17C.

The crypt goes back to the time of Leo IV. The sarcophagi of four martyrs were found in it together with the silver reliquary containing St Sebastian's head.

★**Chiostro** – These delightful **cloisters** were added in the 13C by the Benedictines. The Augustinian nuns replaced the simple roof with vaulting. The ornamental basin placed at the centre of the garden dates from the time of Paschal II. The charming simplicity of the small columns is offset by the capitals which are decorated with waterlily leaves. In the eastern walk is St Barbara's Chapel, with three small apses, added by Leo IV (9C).

★**Capella di San Silvestro** – *Entrance beneath the portico in the inner courtyard. Key available in the convent entrance on the north side of the inner court.* The **chapel of St Sylvester** was built in the 13C and is decorated with a curious collection of frescoes, very naive in execution. Beneath the figure of Christ who is flanked by Mary, John the Baptist and the Apostles, is an illustration of the legend of Pope Sylvester (314-35): the leprosy of the Emperor Constantine (lying down and covered in sores), his being cured by the Pope, his baptism, the offering of his power to the Pope and the Pope's entry into Rome preceded by the Emperor.

From Arco di Dolabella to San Gregorio Magno

From Via dei SS Quattro Coronati, walk south to Piazza Celimontana.

Arco di Dolabella – The **Arch of Dolabella** (1C), which stands at the narrow entrance to Via S Paolo della Croce, carries the remains of **Nero's Aqueduct** which supplied water to the Palatine Hill from the Porta Maggiore; further traces of the aqueduct are visible in Via di S Stefano Rotondo and Via della Navicella, where one of the pillars is still standing.

Next to Dolabella's arch is an attractive **doorway;** it was decorated by Roman marble workers in the 13C with a mosaic showing Christ flanked by two figures, one black and one white, representing the Trinitarians who devoted themselves to ransoming captives. There used to be a Trinitarian hospice next to the Church of San Tomaso in Formis.

San Stefano Rotondo ⊘ – The plan of this unusual round church was inspired by the Church of the Holy Sepulchre in Jerusalem. It was built on the Caelian Hill in the late 4C to early 5C and dedicated to St Stephen (Stefano) by the Pope at the end of the 5C. The church with its concentric aisle and two naves articulated by columns with Ionic capitals, and its marble and mosaic decoration, was originally one of the most opulent in Rome. By 1450 the church had lost its roof and for conservation purposes the outer aisle was demolished and walls were built along the line of columns of the second circle. The diameter of the basilica was thus reduced from 65m - 213ft to 40m - 131ft. In the 16C Pomarancio (1530-92) painted the walls with 34 frescoes depicting scenes of martyrdom.

Santa Maria in Domnica ⊘ – The **Navicella Fountain,** in front of the church porch, was created in 1931 out of a 16C sculpture in imitation of an ancient boat. This church, a favourite with the Romans for weddings, has retained the charm of a country church. It was founded in the 9C and was greatly altered during the Renaissance. The elegant porch was added for Pope Leo X (1513-21) by Andrea Sansovino; the Pope's name is echoed by the lions on the key-stones. The interior has retained certain 9C features: the basilica plan with a nave and two aisles, the columns with antique capitals and the beautiful apsidal **mosaic★**, an example of the artistic renewal which took place in the reign of Paschal I (817-24). The artist has abandoned the Byzantine rigidity for a more life-like representation: a current of air seems to stir the raiment of the angels, attractively grouped round the Virgin; similarly the apostles above the arch are shown as men rather than in the symbolic form of lambs joyfully approaching Christ and his two angels. The green meadows of the background are dotted with brightly coloured flowers. Enthroned at the centre of the vault is the Virgin: Pope Paschal kneels at her feet, identified by the square nimbus of the living.

Walk through the Villa Celimontana Park to Piazza dei Santi Giovanni e Paolo.

Santi Giovanni e Paolo ⊘ – The quiet square is dominated by the porch and the bold campanile both dating from the 12C. The campanile rests on the foundations of the Temple of Claudius, which are visible beneath the porch of the convent of the Passionist Fathers. Its history is similar to that of other buildings on the Caelian Hill: in the 4C a certain Pammachius established a church in a private house; it was sacked by Robert Guiscard's Normans in 1084 but rebuilt in the 12C.

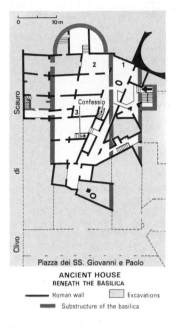

ANCIENT HOUSE
BENEATH THE BASILICA

The five arches above the porch and the gallery, which comprise the upper stage of the façade, belong to the original building.

Two handsome Medieval marble lions guard the entrance. The interior dates almost entirely from the 18C. The main interest lies underground in the rooms of the **ancient house★** ⊘ where excavations have revealed traces of beautiful paintings: *Access by steps at the west end of the north aisle*. At the foot of the stairs is a *nymphaeum* decorated with a marine fresco (**1**) dating from the 2C; its fine state of preservation is due to a coat of whitewash applied to cover up the pagan décor when the house became a Christian place of worship. There follows a suite of parallel rooms beneath the nave and the south aisle; one (**2**) contains traces of sophisticated paintings of adolescents and spirits among garlands of flowers, vine tendrils and birds. The introduction of Christianity is evoked in a vaulted room; one wall (**3**) shows a woman at prayer, her arms extended as if on the cross, surrounded by a décor of scrolls and animals. Two stairways lead to a small chapel, a confessio, built by Pammachius' family; the 4C frescoes depict the martyrdom of two oriental saints whose relics, placed in the confessio, had led to the construction of the basilica.

Take Clivo di Scauro on the left of the church.

The apse of the basilica is the only one of its kind in Rome. With its small columns it is reminiscent of the Romanesque churches in Lombardy.

San Gregorio Magno (St Gregory the Great) ⊘ – Its imposing 17C façade rises at the top of a steep flight of steps framed by cypresses and umbrella pines. It was begun in 1633 by G B Soria for Cardinal Scipione Borghese (the eagle and dragon of his arms appear above the lower arches). Legend tells how in the 6C Gregory converted his house into a church and convent. It was from here that he sent a group of monks to evangelise England; among them were St Augustine, the first Archbishop of Canterbury, St Lawrence, St Melitas, St Justus and St Honorius who all succeeded him to the See of Canterbury. In the 12C the church was rebuilt and dedicated to the saintly Pope. The present building was restored in the 17C and 18C.

In the chapel at the head of the south aisle stands Gregory's altar (15C), decorated with low reliefs depicting his legend. To the right of this chapel is a little cell containing an ancient throne which passes for the one used by the saint. At the head of the north aisle is a chapel decorated with 17C paintings; it contains a curious Virgin painted on the wall (13C) and, opposite, a 15C tabernacle.

Cross the atrium to enter the small square to the left of the church.

In the small square there are three **chapels** ⊘ (**C**), linked by a portico of antique columns. Two were built in the 17C and the third, which is older, was restored at the same time. In St Sylvia's chapel *(right)*, dedicated to St Gregory's mother, the apse is painted with a concert of angels (1608) by Guido Reni. St Andrew's Chapel *(centre)* has the *Flagellation of St Andrew* (1608) painted by Domenichino and the saint going to his martyrdom by Guido Reni. St Barbara's Chapel *(left)* was first restored in the 17C. According to legend the table in the centre was used by St Gregory to offer a meal to the poor; one day an angel came to sit with them, an event recorded in fresco.

Neighbouring sights are described in the following chapters: FORO ROMANO – PALATINO; S GIOVANNI IN LATERANO; S MARIA MAGGIORE – ESQUILINO; TERME DI CARACALLA.

EUR★

Tour about 3 ½ hours

Access: by bus or underground – consult the Plan of Rome; by car – take Via Cristoforo Colombo; see plan in the Michelin Red Guide Italia (hotels and restaurants)

The three letters EUR, which stand for *Esposizione Universale di Roma*, are the name of a new district to the south of Rome. Its origins go back to 1937 when the Government conceived a grandiose project for a universal exhibition to be held in 1942 (the district was also called E42). The idea was to develop Rome along the motorway built in 1928 to link Rome and Ostia. The contract was given to the architect Marcello Piacentini. Building began in 1939; on 10 June 1940 Italy entered the war allied to Germany and in 1941 work stopped. Following the bombing of Rome on 19 July 1943 and the fall of the Fascist government, the scheme was abandoned.

Now for a major decision...

Tucked away amongst the greenery which encloses the man-made lakes is the reputed **Giolitti** *(Passeggiata del Giapone)* which makes, tempts with and sells its famous ice-creams.

Two events – Holy Year in 1950 and the Olympic Games in 1960 – brought it to the fore once again: in 1950 Via Cristoforo Colombo was opened linking Rome and the EUR. The underground, which runs from Stazione Termini to the new district in less than a quarter of an hour, stimulated the building of an administrative and cultural centre, a business forum and residential accommodation.

The **Sports Palace**, by Marcello Piacentini and Pier Luigi Nervi, and the cycle racetrack were built for the Olympic Games.

Inspired by an obsession with size, the colossal white buildings of the actual EUR mean that it looks very much like the scheme proposed by the Fascists.

There are several museums in the EUR; apart from the Museum of Roman Civilization *(see below)*, it is worth mentioning the **Luigi Pigorini Museum** of Ethnography and Prehistory ⊘ and the **Museo dell' Alto Medioevo** ⊘ (Medieval Museum) which contains exhibits covering the 5C to 11C as well as plans of Classical and Christian Rome.

★★MUSEO DELLA CIVILTÀ ROMANA
(MUSEUM OF ROMAN CIVILISATION) ⊘

This huge museum is housed in two buildings linked by a portico and illustrates, by means of reproductions, the history of Ancient Rome from the origins of the city to the end of the Empire. It traces the development of a peasant people who founded an empire which has influenced the history of the whole world for more than a thousand years.

Room 5 – Origins: model of a temple dedicated to Jupiter on the Capitol, originally constructed in the 6C BC and maintained until the end of the Empire; example of a dwelling from Romulus' village on the Palatine.

Palazzo della Civiltà del Lavoro

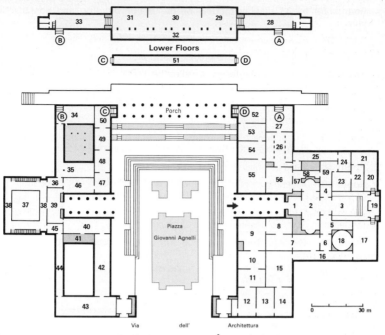

MUSEO DELLA CIVILTÀ ROMANA

Room 7 – Roman conquest of the Mediterranean: column decorated with ships' prows *(rostra)* which was erected in the Forum in honour of the Consul Duilius; he won the first Roman naval victory by defeating the Carthaginians at Mylae in 260 BC.

Model of the siege of Numantia by Scipio Aemilianus (134-33 BC).

Room 8 – Caesar: reconstructions of the two most significant episodes in the war against the Gauls: the siege of Alesia and the taking of Avaricum (Bourges) in 52BC.

Room 9 – Augustus: several monuments raised in his honour including the Trophy at La Turbie in the south of France commemorating the union of Gaul and Italy achieved by Augustus, the Ara Pacis *(see Index)*, etc.

The entrance to the next room is a reconstruction of the porch *(pronaos)* of a temple built by the inhabitants of Ankara in honour of Rome and Augustus, on which a copy of Augustus' will was inscribed.

Room 10 – Genealogical tree and portrait gallery of the family of Augustus and of the Julio-Claudian Emperors (Tiberius, Caligula, Claudius, Nero).

Room 11 – The Flavian Emperors: reproduction of the low relief sculptures on the Arch of Titus.

Rooms 12 and 13 – The Antonines to the Severans (AD 96-235).

Room 14 – Macrinus to Justinian (217-565): period of decadence and megalomania.

The following rooms are closed except for 37, 38 and 39.

Room 15 – Christianity.

Subsequent rooms illustrate Roman life in all its aspects: institutions, monuments erected throughout the Empire, economy, society, etc.

Rooms 16 to 19 – The army: engines of war *(balista* – a sort of crossbow and *onager* – a mechanical catapult).

Reconstruction of a military camp accommodating two legions.

Rooms 20 and 21 – The navy: models of war galleys.

Room 22 – Two panels outlining a naval career and Roman naval tactics.

Room 25 – Reconstruction of a triumph: the victorious general, robed like Jupiter and riding in a chariot, proceeding to the Capitol, accompanied by his soldiers and his booty.

Rooms 26 and 27 – The major monuments in the Imperial provinces and in Italy which Augustus divided into 11 regions.

Rooms 28 to 33 display models of the major building and construction works.

Room 29 – Architecture of baths, aqueducts, nymphaea and cisterns.

Room 30 – Leisure: theatres, amphitheatres, circuses, gymnasia.

Room 31 – Public life: the forum, temples, basilicas.

Room 32 – Several large-scale exhibits: the amphitheatre in Nîmes, Domitian's stadium (now the Piazza Navona), the acropolis at Baalbek, etc.

Room 33 – Roads and means of communication.

Room 37 – Huge **model**★★ of Rome at the time of Constantine (306-37) constructed by the architect Italo Gismondi in 1937 on the scale 1/250.

Room 38 – Plans of Imperial Rome.

Room 39 – Funerary monuments – models of the mausolea of Diocletian in Split, of Munatius Plancus in Gaeta and the tomb of Theodoric in Ravenna.

Room 40 – Housing: from Imperial palaces (built by Hadrian at Tivoli and by Diocletian in Split) to private houses and apartments.

Room 43 – Religion: from the early days of Rome's existence to the introduction of oriental cults.

Reconstruction of part of a temple in Rome and of a temple to Augustus in Athens. Reconstruction of a Roman calendar.

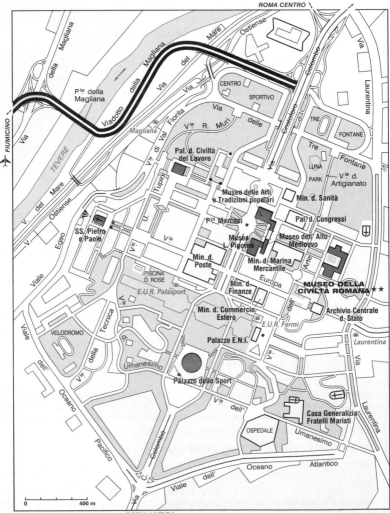

Room 46 – Law: legislative texts (the Twelve Tables published in 451 BC containing the principles of law, knowledge of which was a patrician privilege).

Room 47 – Reconstruction of a small library.

Rooms 48 to 50 – Music, literature, science and medicine.

Room 51 – Reconstruction of the low relief sculpture from Trajan's Column.

Room 59 – Reconstruction of several low relief sculptures from Marcus Aurelius' Column.

ADDITIONAL SIGHTS

Piazza Marconi – A huge obelisk in marble (sculpture finished in 1950) has been raised to the glory of the Italian physicist Guglielmo Marconi (1874-1937), inventor of wireless telegraphy.

Museo delle Arti e Tradizioni Popolari (Folk Museum) ⊙ – A modern building houses the museum which records the folklore of the regions of Italy: furniture, marionettes, costumes and farm implements etc. The ground floor is dedicated to tools and equipment for working the land, including carts and sleighs. On the first floor there is a magnificent gondola especially attired for feast days and religious festivals. Additional rooms display a **collection**★ of traditional clothes, costumes, jewellery and amulets; aspects of daily life in the different regions of Italy; musical instruments; Carnival attire; domestic utensils and country furniture.

Palazzo della Civiltà del Lavoro – The building, which is one of the most characteristic of EUR, was designed in 1938 by three architects: Guerrini, La Padula and Romano. Devoid of capital or cornice to delight the eye, its stark mass is accentuated by the rows of superimposed arches.
The ground floor arcade contains allegorical statues representing the various arts, symbols of the grandeur of Rome. The building houses several organisations connected with the improvement of working conditions.

Santi Pietro e Paolo – This spectacular travertine church, dedicated to **St Peter and St Paul**, was built between 1937 and 1941 on the highest point in the EUR. Set among shrubs and flowers its white mass dominates the whole district. The principal architect was Arnaldo Foschini. At the top of the steps stand two large statues of St Peter and St Paul. The Greek cross plan is stressed by the clean angles and sober lines. The dome, covered in little tiles overlapping like fish scales, rests on a drum pierced by oculi.
The main door, designed by Giovanni Prini (1877-1958), is made of bronze, ornamented with low reliefs illustrating the lives of St Peter and St Paul.
From the surrounding terrace, flanked by two porticos, there is a view of the suburbs of Rome.

The itinerary can be combined with a visit to OSTIA ANTICA by taking Via Cristoforo Colombo (SS 8).

FONTANA DI TREVI – QUIRINALE★★★

Tour 2 ½ hours

The walk starts at one of the most famous monuments in Rome, the Trevi Fountain, and continues to explore some of the major places of interest on the Quirinal Hill, the highest (61m - 200ft) of the seven hills of Rome.
The name Quirinal is now synonymous with Italian politics since the Quirinal Palace is the official residence of the President of the Republic.
The hill was the traditional home of the Sabines and took its name from one of their gods, Quirinus who, with Mars and Jupiter, formed the basis of Roman religion. Until the end of the 19C only the fringes of the city reached the Quirinal; the Flavian Mausoleum was built there by Domitian (81-96); Carcalla built a temple to Serapis of which the ruins survived until the Middle Ages; Constantine built a bath house which diasappeared in the 17C.

It is said that Nicola Salvi, the architect charged with overseeing the installation of the Trevi Fountain, got his revenge following a major altercation with the local resident barber of the day. Slightly to the right of the fountain, he had built a giant lather basin that blocked the view from the barber's shop opposite: today it is a glovemaker that suffers!

★★★FONTANA DI TREVI (TREVI FOUNTAIN)

This late Baroque creation is one of the most famous sights of Rome. The key to the work is given in two low relief carvings: in 19 BC Agrippa decided to build a long canal (20km - 13miles) to bring water to Rome *(left);* the canal was called Acqua Vergine after a young virgin who revealed the spring to the Roman soldiers *(right).*

Repairs were made under Pope Nicholas V and Urban VIII. It was Clement XII who commissioned Nicolà Salvi (1732) to adorn the end of the canal with a fountain. Salvi's fountain fills the whole width of the façade which forms a backdrop to it and gives the impression of a commemorative arch. The fountain was completed 30 years later during the reign of Clement XIII. Salubrity and Abundance stand in the wings flanking the central figure, the Ocean, which rides in a chariot drawn by two sea horses and two tritons and provides a photogenic spectacle for the faithful tourists, who continue to play their traditional role by throwing two coins over their shoulders into the fountain – one coin to return to Rome and the other for the fulfilment of a wish.

The façade of the church dedicated to St Vincent and St Anastasius **(Santi Vincenzo e Anastasio)** was built in 1650 by Martino Longhi the Younger for Cardinal Mazarin. Detached columns, pediments, projections and recesses create an interplay of light and shade typical of Baroque Art.

Palazzo Scanderberg – *Vicolo Modelli to the side of the church leads to Piazza Scanderberg.* The National Pasta Museum **(Museo Nazionale delle Paste Alimentari)** ⊙ charts the history of this staple Italian ingredient starting with the raw materials and their nutritious components, and finishing with amusing portrayals of famous people enjoying the end product. Displays are both imaginative and informative.

South of the church turn left into Via della Dataria which leads to Piazza del Quirinale.

S. Chirol, Paris

Trevi Fountain

Quirinal Palace

S. Chirol

★★PIAZZA DEL QUIRINALE (QUIRINALE SQUARE)

Lined by handsome palaces, adorned with an obelisk and ancient statues and refreshed by a fountain, the square typifies Roman elegance.

Its embellishment was begun by Sixtus V (1585-90) who transferred the statues of the Dioscuri from Contantine's Baths nearby; they are fine Roman copies of original Greek works. Some two centuries later, Pius VI moved them slightly apart to make room for one of the obelisks which had stood at the entrance to Augustus' mausoleum.

Finally Pius VII (1800-23) completed the group with a handsome antique basin which had served as a water trough when the Forum was known as Campo Vaccino and used for grazing cows.

★★ **Palazzo del Quirinale (Quirinal Palace)** ⊘ – This building is the work of some of the finest architects of the Counter-Reformation and the Baroque period. It was commissioned in 1573 by Gregory XIII from Martino Longhi the Elder as a summer residence for the popes. Sixtus V commissioned Ottaviano Mascherino, Domenico Fontana and Flaminio Ponzio. Under Paul V Carlo Maderno added the monumental door with its two half reclining statues of St Peter and St Paul. Bernini was brought in by Alexander VII. The palace was completed by Ferdinando Fuga for Clement XII.

Interior – The courtyard of the presidential palace, guarded by sentries who must be of a certain height (1.82m - 6ft 3in), leads to the grand staircase. The fresco of Christ *(above the arch)* by Melozzo da Forlì (1438-1494) was originally part of the *Ascension* painted on the apse of the Church of the Holy Apostles. The tour includes a succession of rooms, all sumptuously decorated, the chapel painted by Guido Reni (Annunciation on the altar piece) and the Pauline chapel which is decorated with 17C stucco.

Napoleonic Storm

In 1808 Napoleon was declared King of Italy and his brother Joseph King of Naples but Pius VII, as head of the Papal States, refused to apply an economic blockade or to recognise any king other than Ferdinand IV of Naples. On 2 February General Miollis was ordered to enter Rome with 8 000 French soldiers to bring His Holiness to reason. Pius VII shut himself up in the Quirinal Palace.

In Vienna, on the evening of 17 May 1809, Napoleon wiped the Papal States off the map of Europe. Pius VII issued a Bull of excommunication: "Let sovereigns learn once and for all that they are subject by the law of Christ to our throne and our commands." At dawn several French soldiers were found dead in the streets of Rome. On 7 July 1809 French troops broke down the door of the palace. The Pope, in cape and stole, awaited them. Despite their great respect for the Pope the soldiers took him away to spend the rest of the Napoleonic era at Fontainebleau. Thus Napoleon rendered "unto Caesar the things which are Caesar's and unto God the things that are God's".

Palazzo della Consultà – The façade★ is by Ferdinando Fuga (18C) who often used Baroque motifs. The three doorways, their pediments crowded with statues and sculptures, and the coat of arms of Clement XII, supported by a swarm of cherubs, make a lively contrast with the bare façade of the Quirinal Palace. This is now the seat of the Constitutional Court.

Take Via del Quirinale beside the Palace.

The east wing of the Palace, overlooking Via del Quirinale, was built in the 17C and 18C.

★★SANT'ANDREA AL QUIRINALE ⊘

The Church of St Andrew on the Quirinal by Bernini and the Church of St Charles by the Four Fountains (San Carlo alle Quattro Fontane) by Borromini, point up with unusual clarity the genius of two artists whose styles were diametrically opposed. The façade, which opens in to a semi-circular atrium, bears a crown showing the arms of Cardinal Camillo Pamphili, Innocent X's nephew, who commissioned the church in 1658. It was completed in 1678.

★★**Interior** – The interior, as in San Carlo, is elliptical but oriented on the shorter axis and defined by the entrance and the magnificent choir stalls. To some extent the smaller dimensions of the building are cunningly masked. The deep rectangular side chapels and the impression of depth created by the false portico in front of the high altar, give a feeling of spaciousness which helps to disguise the true proportions of the church. Bernini's skilful use of coloured marbles, gilding and stucco figures has created a rich and beautiful décor. The chapels contain three paintings by Baciccia (**1**) (1639-1709) and the *Crucifixion of St Andrew* (**2**) by Jacques Courtois (1621-

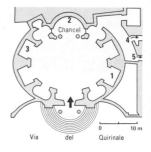

1676), known as the Burgundian. The gilt Glory over the high altar, which is lit from above, is a reminder that Bernini had a great liking for theatricality. On the left is a chapel (**3**) dedicated to the glory of St Stanislas Kostka, a young Pole who came to Rome to become a novice with the Jesuits to whom the church of St Andrew belonged. The painting by Carlo Maratta (1625-1713) shows the Virgin appearing to St Stanislas.

St Stanislas' Rooms (Camere di San Stanislao) (**4**) *(to visit apply to the sacristan)* contain a recumbent statue of the saint by Pierre Legros (1629-1714) in polychrome marble.

In the **Sacristy** (**5**) there is a beautiful vault in *trompe-l'œil.*

Continue along Via del Quirinale.

★★SAN CARLO ALLE QUATTRO FONTANE

(ST CHARLES AT THE FOUR FOUNTAINS) ⊘

The Church of St Charles at the Four Fountains, which is also known as San Carlino, is probably the best expression of Borromini's creative genius. Commissioned in 1638, it was his first known work. The façade, which was added some 30 years later, was his last; it was unfinished when he committed suicide in 1667. It reveals the torment of a man whose art was full of contradictory statements: every curve is followed by a counter curve (in particular the façade and the cornices). Against the central concave section of the upper storey is set a convex shrine (below the medallion).

Ceiling of San Carlo alle Quattro Fontane

The concave surfaces of the belfry and the lantern on the dome also express Borromini's contrary spirit in architectural terms.

★★**Interior** – The form is that of an ellipse oriented on the longer axis. The movement is supplied by the alternating concave and convex surfaces of the walls themselves. The confined space – no larger, it is said, than one of the pillars supporting the dome of St Peter's – is perfectly suited to the architect's distinctive style. It is affected and austere, bizarre and elegant and quite out of sympathy with the Baroque taste for sheer size. The intricately-designed coffering in the dome is surmounted by a lantern harbouring the Holy Ghost.

★**Cloisters** – Borromini's cloisters – two orders of Doric columns and slightly convex canted corners – are perfectly proportioned.

Continue to the crossroads.

★★**Incrocio delle Quattro Fontane** – The **Four Fountains crossroads** was created by Sixtus V (1585-90) whose efforts at town planning introduced more alterations to Rome than the city had known since the end of the Roman Empire. His aim was to link the main basilicas and the main districts by means of broad straight roads. The creation of these four straight streets opened up **views★** of the obelisks in front of the Trinità dei Monti *(west)*, the Porta Pia *(north)*, the west end of Santa Maria Maggiore in Piazza dell'Esquilino *(east)* and in Piazza del Quirinale *(south)*. The corners of the crossroads are canted to make room for four fountains decorated with statues (16C).

To get to the Palazzo delle Esposizioni follow Via Milano as far as the crossroads with Via Nazionale.

Palazzo delle Esposizioni (Exhibition Hall) ⊙ – *Temporary exhibitions, cinema and theatre productions. Entrances at 194 Via Nazionale and 9a Via Milano.* The Palace, which was opened in 1883, was designed by the architect Pio Piancentini. The main prospect is neo-Classical and its large central arch and two side entrances are reminiscent of a commemorative arch. It was the first complex in Rome built to house art and other exhibitions.

The palace was re-structured by the architect C Dardi who, while not exactly destroying the original design, installed new technical and lighting systems and new facilities: conference room and cinema for 200 people, a 130-seat theatre, cafeteria, bookshop and a restaurant on the top floor. As well as being the venue for the various exhibitions, film shows and plays that are held there, the palace has become a popular meeting-place.

Return to Piazza del Quirinale and take Via 24 Maggio.

THE NEIGHBOURHOOD

Palazzo Pallavicini – The courtyard with its palm trees, laurels, pines and holm oaks is lined on two sides by the palace which was built in 1603 by Cardinal Scipio Borghese, Paul V's nephew, more or less on the site of Constantine's Baths.

Just inside the main gates stands the **Casino★** ⊙ opening on to a terrace. This charming 17C pavilion is famous for the **Aurora fresco** painted on the ceiling by Guido Reni, a pupil of the Carracci. This is a fine example of the academic Classical style. The goddess is shown opening the gates of heaven to the sun's chariot.

On the right of the street (Via 24 Maggio) the impressive doorway approached by a flight of steps is the entrance to the **garden of the Palazzo Colonna** *(see below)*.

San Silvestro al Quirinale ⊙ – *Entrance to the left of the façade.* The façade of the Church of **St Sylvester on the Quirinal** is purely decorative; it was constructed in the 19C to disguise the difference of level between the church and the street; the latter had been widened and lowered, while the church itself was truncated.

The interior décor is suprisingly rich. The coffered ceiling which dates from the 16C was restored in the 19C. Among the Mannerist decorations are some paintings in the **first chapel** on the left by Polidoro da Caravaggio and Maturino da Firenze *(see PIAZZA NAVONA: Via della Maschera d'Oro)*. The floor has been paved with fragments of ceramic floor tiles which used to decorate the Raphael Loggia in the Vatican.

In the left arm of the transept is a beautiful octagonal domed **chapel★**: Domenichino painted the medallions in the pendentives (1628) while the stucco statues of Mary Magdalene *(left of the entrance)* and St John *(left of the chancel)* were sculpted at the same time by Alessandro Algardi.

The **chancel** vault is decorated with a late 16C fresco on a beautiful grey base.

To the left of the chancel is a door opening on to a quiet terrace where Vittoria Colonna, who had composed poems to the glory of her dead husband, spent many hours in the company of scholars and holy men. Sometimes Michelangelo came to join them. He developed a great affection for this noble and cultivated lady and was present at her death.

Turn right into Via della Cordonata and right again into Via 4 Novembre.

★**Galleria di Palazzo Colonna** – *Entrance at no17 Via della Pilotta. The numbers given below are the same as those in the gallery.* The palace dates from the 15C but was rebuilt in 1730. It is linked to its gardens *(see above)* by four arches spanning the Via Pilotta. Pope Martin V (1417-31), a member of the Colonna family, took up residence here when he returned to Rome after the Great Western Schism.

The **picture gallery**, which consists of a suite of richly furnished rooms, contains many 15C-18C paintings.

Sala della Colonna Bellica (Column Room) – The name of the room is a reference to the red column which was the family emblem. *Narcissus at the fountain* (**189**) by Tintoretto (1518-94). A portrait, which may be of Vittoria Colonna *(see above)* (**37**), long attributed to G Muziano but more recently to B Cancellieri.

In the middle of the half-dozen steps leading down into the Salon is lodged a cannon ball which was fired by the French troops who besieged Rome in 1849 in an attempt to re-establish Pius IX on the papal throne.

★★**Salone** (Salon) – A very handsome perspective, resplendent with gilt, mirrors, crystal chandeliers, yellow marble and paintings. The vault is painted with a 17C fresco depicting the triumph of Marcantonio Colonna who led Pius V's troops at the Battle of Lepanto (1571).

Sala degli Scrigni (Casket Room) – Two **caskets**★, small 17C chests: one in ebony decorated with ivory low relief carvings (in the centre, copy of Michelangelo's *Last Judgement*); the other in sandalwood, inset with precious stones and bronze gilt. A dozen paintings by Gaspard Dughet (1613-75).

Sala dell'apoteosi di Martino V (Apotheosis of Martin V Room) – The name of the room comes from the subject of the ceiling decoration. *Fine portrait of a gentleman* (**197**) by Paul Veronese (1528-88). The painting *Peasant eating beans* (**43**), which is attributed to Annibale Carracci (1560-1609), is a fine example of Naturalism.

Sala del Trono (Throne Room) – This room was intended for the reception of the Pope.

Take Via 4 Novembre west; turn left into Piazza Santi Apostoli.

In the square at no 67 is the **Museo delle Cere** (Waxworks Museum).

★**Basilica dei Santi Dodici Apostoli (Basilica of the Holy Apostles)** ◷ – The church goes back to the 6C when a basilica on the site was dedicated by Popes Pelagius I and John III to the Apostles Philip and James the Less whose relics they had received.

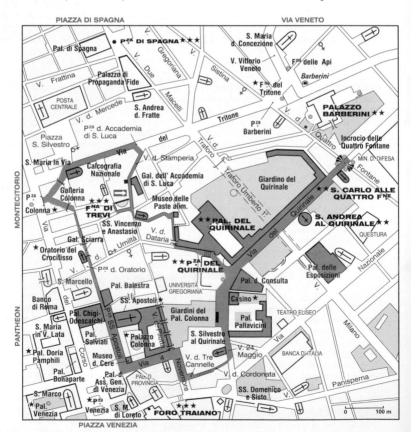

The greatest alterations were carried out by Sixtus IV (1471-84), of which only the lower part of the porch remains. The loggia above the porch was closed with rectangular windows in the Baroque era and topped with a balustrade and statues. The upper section is a 19C neo-Classical composition.

In the porch, guarding the entrance, are three lions from the medieval building.

On the nave vault Baciccia painted the Triumph of the Franciscan Order (1706). A few years earlier this artist had painted his masterpiece on the ceiling of the Gesù Church.

The chancel contains the Renaissance tombs of the two Riario cardinals, Pietro and Raffaele, who helped their uncle, Sixtus IV, to reconstruct the church: **Cardinal Pietro Riario's tomb★** *(left)* is the result of three masters of funerary art working in collaboration: Andrea Bregno, Mino da Fiesole and Giovanni Dalmata; Raffaele's tomb *(right)* is inspired by Michelangelo's favourite designs. On the chancel ceiling Giovanni Odazzi (18C) has achieved a fine *trompe-l'œil* effect with the Fallen Angels. The **monument to Clement XIV** at the top of the left aisle is the first work executed in Rome by the neo-Classical sculptor Antonio Canova (1787).

Palazzo Chigi-Odescalchi (Chigi-Odescalchi Palace) – The palace, which stands in front of the Basilica of the Holy Apostles, was redesigned by Bernini when the Chigi family acquired it in 1664. The master's involvement in the project laid down rules which were to have a great influence on the architecture of central and northern Europe.

Palazzo Balestra – At the end of the square stands a Baroque palace (now occupied by the Banco di Roma) where the Stuarts, the royal family of Scotland and England, lived in exile. Originally known as Palazzo Muti since it was built in 1644 for the Muti-Papazzuri family, it was given by Clement XI to James Stuart, the Old Pretender, in 1719 when he married Maria Clementina Sobieska of Poland. His two sons, Charles Edward, the Young Pretender, and Henry, Cardinal of York, were born in the palace and 'Bonnie Prince Charlie' returned to die there in 1788.

★**Oratorio del Crocifisso (Oratory of the Crucifix)** ⊙ – The building's construction was entrusted to Tommaso dei Cavalieri, a young Roman noble, who inspired a warm affection in Michelangelo yet chose as his adviser one of Michelangelo's bitterest enemies, Nanni di Baccio Bigio. The façade was designed by Giacomo della Porta in 1561. It marked the beginning of a brilliant career which led to his being in charge of work on the Capitol and at St Peter's (1573). The façade, which was finished in 1568 and which harmonises so well with the square it overlooks, bears traces of Michelangelo's teaching (the pediments over the recesses flanking the door). The interior is decorated with a series of frescoes by Mannerist artists. On the reverse side of the façade is the history of the Confraternity of the Crucifix of St Marcellus. The wall paintings, which are reminiscent of a theatre décor, are by Giovanni de' Vecchi, Pomarancio and Cesare Nebbia and illustrate the story of the Cross.

Take the alley on the right of the Oratory.

The **Galleria Sciarra★**, with its metal framework, its glass canopy and its fine paintings, is a highly original late 19C arcade.

Continue north along Via Santa Maria in Via.

Galleria Colonna – This arcade was built in 1923 linking Via di Santa Maria in Via with Via del Corso and Piazza Colonna.

Santa Maria in Via – A miracle led to the foundation of St Mary's Church: an image of the Virgin, painted on a tile, fell into a well; the well overflowed and the image re-appeared. Many pilgrims still come to drink the water of the famous well and to venerate the 'Madonna of the Well' *(Madonna del Pozzo)*. The late 17C Baroque façade is by Francesco da Volterra and Carlo Rainaldi.

Turn right into Via del Tritone and right into Piazza dell'Accademia di San Luca.

Via del Tritone – This street is full of shops and is one of the busiest in Rome; it links the city centre with the north-eastern suburbs.

Take Via della Stamperia.

Galleria dell'Accademia di San Luca (St Luke's Academy Gallery) ⊙ – Room I: *Portrait of Clement IX* by Baciccia (1639-1709); **Room II:** fine fragment of a fresco by Raphael; *Judith and Holophernes* by the Venetian Piazzetta (1682-1754). **Room III:** self-portrait by Mme Vigée-Lebrun (1755-1842) and another by Angelika Kauff-mann the Swiss painter, who was a friend of Goethe in Rome. **Room V:** *Virgin and Angels* by Sir Anthony van Dyck.

The **Calcographia** *(no 6 Via della Stamperia)* houses over 20 000 engravings, including some by Piranesi (1720-78) who produced some remarkable views of Rome. The collection belongs to the Istituto Nazionale per la Grafica *(Temporary exhibitions are not open to the public)*.

Neighbouring sights are described in the following chapters: MONTECITORIO; PAN-THEON; PIAZZA DI SPAGNA; PIAZZA VENEZIA; VIA VENETO.

FORI IMPERIALI ★★★

Tour 2 hours

These are the fora built by the emperors when the old forum, the Roman forum, had become too small to hold the Assemblies of the People, the judicial hearings, the conduct of public affairs and of commercial matters. Caesar was the first to build a new forum to the north of the old one; he was followed by Augustus, Vespasian, Nerva and Trajan. The Imperial fora extended approximately from Piazza Venezia to the Basilica of Maxentius and formed a monumental expression of Imperial prestige with their porticoes, their temples, their libraries, their basilicas. The old forum was not in any way abandoned. Octavius erected a temple to the divinity of Caesar; as the Emperor Augustus he was himself honoured with a commemorative arch in 19 BC; the temple to Vespasian stood at the foot of the Capitol.

The fora were excavated in the 19C and the medieval buildings which had been put up on the site were removed from 1924 to 1932 when **Via dei Fori Imperiali** was being constructed.

This road (30m - 98ft wide and 85m - 930yds long) was opened in 1932 as Via dell'Impero and drives straight through the middle of the Imperial fora in a straight line from Piazza Venezia opening up a clear view of the Colosseum, a solid reminder of Roman grandeur.

★★FORO DI CESARE (CAESAR'S FORUM)

It is usually closed but it can be clearly seen over the railings.

For his forum Caesar chose a central position at the foot of the Capitol, near the old Roman forum. In order to clear the site he had to re-locate the Curia Hostilia and the Comitium and purchase and demolish the elegant houses already in situ. This exercise cost him the exorbitant sum of 60 million sesterci according to Cicero (then consul and a friend of Caesar's) although Suetonius, the Emperors' biographer, puts the figure at 100 million. Negotiations began in 54 BC when Caesar was rich with the booty gained in the conquest of Gaul (58-51 BC); work began three years later in 51 BC.

Caesar's forum was rectangular and extended from the Curia *(east)* to Via di San Pietro in Carcere *(west)*, the long sides running more or less parallel with the Clivus Argentarius. Domitian undertook restoration work (81-96) following the fire which destroyed part of the Capitol in 80. Trajan completed the work. About two-thirds of Caesar's forum has been uncovered; the rest is beneath Via dei Fori Imperiali.

The ruins – First to catch the eye are three beautiful standing columns, richly sculpted, which belonged to the **Temple of Venus Genitrix** and date from the time of Domitian and Trajan. Caesar claimed that his family (the Julii) were descended from

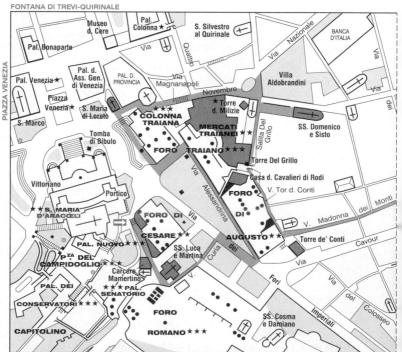

FONTANA DI TREVI-QUIRINALE

FORO ROMANO-PALATINO   COLOSSEO-CELIO

Venus through her son, Aeneas, and Aeneas' son, Iulus. He decided to dedicate a temple to her after his victory at Pharsalus in 48 BC against Pompey who was killed by Ptolemy, Cleopatra's brother.

This temple, to the north of the forum, was a veritable museum: besides the statue of Venus in the *cella*, there was a golden statue of Cleopatra, some Greek paintings and, in front of the temple, a statue of Caesar's horse: this extraordinary animal had curiously split hooves, which resembled human feet; according to the sooth-sayers this abnormality was a sign of divine intervention and meant that his master would be ruler of the world.

The edge of the forum was lined with shops, still visible beneath the Clivus Argentarius. During Trajan's reign (2C) a portico was added down the long side nearest the Clivus Argentarius; its two long rows of granite columns still remain. It has been identified as the Basilica Argentaria where the money-changers *(argentari)* plied their trade.

From the Foro di Cesare to the Foro di Augusto

Carcere Mamertino (Mamertine Prison) ⊘ – This is the name given to two rooms, one above the other, hollowed out of the Capitoline Hill beneath the Church of San Giuseppe dei Falegnami (St Joseph of the Carpenters).

The Mamertine was used as a prison where many enemies of the Roman State were incarcerated. On the right of the entrance is a list of names of well-known people who perished here. In 104 BC Jugurtha died of starvation while his conqueror Marius led his victory parade through the forum. Vercingetorix was beheaded here in 46 BC after Caesar's triumph. However, after the victory of Aemilius Paullus against Perseus of Macedonia at Pydna in 168 BC, worthy enemy chiefs often escaped death; Jugurtha and Vercingetorix had not been considered worthy of such clemency. It was here on 5 December 65 BC that Catiline's fellow conspirators were strangled after Cicero had given his fourth Catiline speech.

In the Middle Ages a legend arose that St Peter had been imprisoned here; hence the name San Pietro in Carcere (St Peter in prison). On the left of the entrance is a list of Christian martyrs who died in the prison. At the head of the staircase linking the two rooms is a hollowed-out stone said to bear the imprint of the Apostle's head as he was jostled by his gaolers.

The lower chamber *(tullianum)* was built at the end of the 4C BC out of huge blocks of tufa arranged in a vault and was used as a cistern or a tomb. Legend tells how Peter and Paul made water miraculously spring from the earth so that they could baptize their gaolers. The spring and the pillar to which the prisoners were chained can still be seen.

SS Luca e Martina (Church of St Luke and St Martina) – On the site of the Senate archive (Secretarium Senatus, an annex of the Curia) a church was built in about the 7C and dedicated to Martina who had been martyred under Septimius Severus. From 1588 it was also associated with St Luke since in that year Pope Sixtus V gave the church to the members of St Luke's Academy, a guild of painters who recognised the Evangelist as their patron saint; according to a 6C legend he had painted a portrait of the Virgin Mary.

In 1634 a terracotta sarcophagus was found containing the remains of St Martina. Cardinal Francesco Barberini commissioned Pietro da Cortona to build a new shrine above the old one. Da Cortona, who was a contemporary of Bernini and Borromini, leading exponents of the Baroque style, designed a beautiful façade★. Its shallow convex curve is reminiscent of the style of Borromini; so too is the interior, which is designed on the Greek cross plan and decorated all over with pale stuccoes in beige and grey revealing a search for complicated forms.

After crossing Via dei Fori Imperiali, it is worth walking along Via Alessandrina from the junction of Via Cavour and Via dei Fori Imperiali for an overall view of the fora.

This road junction stands more or less on the point where the Fora of Nerva *(west)* and Vespasian *(east)* met. There are very few remains.

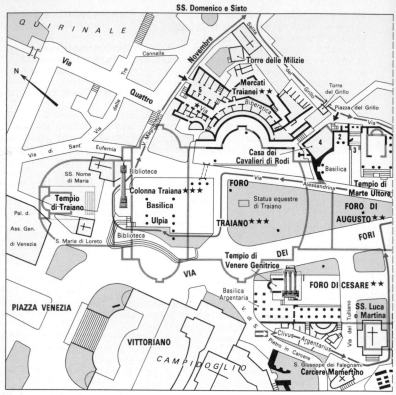

Foro di Vespasiano (Vespasiano's Forum) – It was built by Vespasian from 71 to 75 and formed a square adjoining the old Forum and extending approximately from the Basilica of Maxentius in the south to the Conti Tower (Torre dei Conti) in the north. In the south corner there was a library which is now occupied by the Church of St Cosmas and St Damian. It was also called the Peace Forum. To commemorate his conquest of the Jews in 71, Vespasian erected a Temple of Peace which contained the treasures looted from the Jewish Temple in Jerusalem: the golden seven-branched candlestick, the tablets of the Law of Moses and the silver trumpets.

Foro di Nerva (Nerva's Forum) – Although begun by Domitian, it was completed and inaugurated by Nerva in 98. It was long and narrow in shape and traversed by the Argiletum, a street linking the old Roman forum with the Suburra district; for this reason it was also known as the Forum Transitorium. Here stood the Temple of Minerva; its fine ruins were still visible early in the 17C until Pope Paul V had them demolished; the columns and cornices were used in the construction of the Pauline fountain on the Janiculum. Against the east wall stand two beautiful **columns★** (**1**) and some fragments of a frieze which adorned the wall enclosing the forum.

★★ FORO DI AUGUSTO (AUGUSTUS' FORUM)

There is an overall view from Via Alessandrina.

Octavian, who took the name Augustus when he became Emperor, wanted to avenge the murder of his adopted father Caesar. When he finally defeated the murderers, Cassius and Brutus, at Philippi (a town in northern Greece) in 42 BC, he vowed to dedicate a temple to Mars Ultor (the Avenger) to be sited in a new forum, which would be added to the two which already existed (the Roman forum and Caesar's forum) and would be particularly devoted to the administration of justice. Building began in 31 BC after a considerable amount of demolition work. The site extended from the old forum to the edge of the unsavoury Suburra district; a high wall, forming the back of the new forum, was built to isolate it from the hovels and frequent fires of Suburra; its irregular line reveals the difficulties the builders had to overcome. The two sides facing southeast and northwest bowed out in two semicircles which are still visible. In the recesses in the walls stood bronze statues of the most famous Romans "who had brought Rome from insignificance to greatness" (Suetonius): Aeneas, the kings of Alba, the founding fathers of the Julian family, Romulus, Marius, Sulla and other great generals of the Republican era.

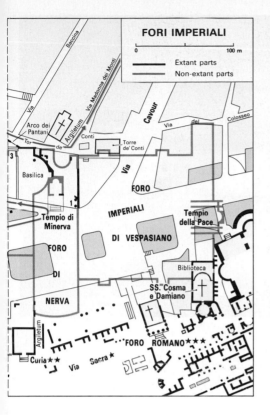

Against the centre of the back wall stood the **Temple of Mars Ultor** which was approached by a majestic flight of steps. A few columns to the front and side still stand.

This temple played an important role in public life; it served as a reliquary for Caesar's sword. It was here that members of the Imperial family came for the ceremony of the *toga virilis* which they received on passing from adolescence to manhood (at about 17). It was here too that magistrates appointed to the provinces were invested with their authority *(imperium)* and here that they deposited the trophies of their victories on their return.

The basilicas – These were formed by two porticoes, one on each side of the temple, in front of the semicircular recesses. Marble statues stood between the columns.

Two columns have been re-erected in front of a room (**2**), which housed a colossal statue of Mars or Augustus. Two flights of steps flanking the temple linked Augustus' forum with Suburra. At the top of the steps near the three re-erected columns is a fine arch, known as Arco del Pantani. There is a better view of it from Via Tor de' Conti.

Augustus' successors made further embellishments: Tiberius (14-37) erected two commemorative arches (**3**), one on each side of the temple, in honour of Drusus and Germanicus, who pacified Germany and Pannonia (western Hungary). The Emperor Claudius (41-54) continued to dispense justice there as, according to Suetonius... "one day when he was hearing a case in Augustus' Forum he was attracted by the cooking smells coming from the Temple of Mars next door: leaving his court, he went to join the Salian priests at their table."

***FORO DI TRAIANO** (TRAJAN'S FORUM)

High above the northeast corner of the forum is a charming roof-top loggia, part of a 15C building (**4**) belonging to the Knights of Rhodes.

Trajan's Forum consisted of a covered market with a concave façade and the forum itself which comprised a public place, the Basilica Ulpia, Trajan's Column, two libraries and the Temple of Trajan.

The forum was inaugurated by Trajan, the best of the Antonine emperors, in 113. Its construction had involved work on a huge scale including the cutting back and levelling of a spur of the Quirinal which extended towards the Capitol. Just as Caesar had financed the construction of his forum with booty taken from the Gauls, so Trajan used the spoils of war won from the Dacians, a redoutable people who lived in what is now Romania. Even after Trajan's death the prestige of his forum did not fade; it was the setting for official demonstrations: here Hadrian publicly burned the records of debts owed by certain of his citizens; here Marcus Aurelius (161-80) held an auction of his personal treasures to finance his wars against the Marcomanni, a German tribe, who were threatening the Empire.

Trajan's Forum which extended from Caesar's Forum to beyond the two domed churches of St Mary of Loreto and the Holy Name of Mary, was the largest of the Imperial Fora and certainly the most beautiful, if one is to believe the historian Ammianus Marcellinus (*c*330-400); he gives an account of a visit made by Constantinus II (356), Emperor in the East, to the superseded Imperial capital; already on seeing the old Forum, "the sanctuary of the old power" he had been speechless, "but on arriving in Trajan's Forum... he was stupefied." Even today, few Roman ruins so nobly evoke the ancient civilization.

Trajan's Forum

Forum – It extended from Caesar's Forum to the edge of the market. The entrance was set in a slightly curved wall facing southeast. The northeast and southwest walls were relieved by two apses, one of which is still visible, running parallel with the concave façade of the market and marked by two columns (one of which is standing). To the left of this column are a few traces of a small medieval church.

The wall on the far left of the apse is the outer wall of the forum and is composed of huge blocks of peperine and travertine.

At the centre of the forum stood an equestrian statue in gilded bronze of the Emperor Trajan which Constantinus II dreamed of imitating. Ammianus Marcellinus recounts that a prince in the Imperial suite made a subtle suggestion: "Begin, Sir, by building a stable in this style... so that the horse you envisage will be as well housed as this one." Down the sides of the forum were porticoes ornamented with statues of illustrious men as in Augustus' Forum.

Basilica Ulpia and Libraries – The basilica was named after Trajan's family. The ends open into two semicircles, one of which is beneath the building at the corner of Via Magnanapoli. The basilica was opulent with five aisles, a marble floor and two storeys of marble and granite columns (some standing, some marked by their bases).

Beyond the basilica were two public libraries *(biblioteca)* one contained Greek works, the other Latin works together with Trajan's personal records. Between the two libraries was a courtyard at the centre of which stood Trajan's Column, a master-piece of Classical art which is beyond compare.

★★★**Colonna Traiana (Trajan's Column)** – Originally there were roof-top terraces on the libraries which made it easier than it is today to view this extraordinary work. It was invented by Apollodorus of Damascus; no earlier model has been found. It stands about 38m - 125ft high and consists of 17 marble drums sculpted in a spiral of panels showing episodes in Trajan's wars against the Dacians. If the spiral of panels were laid out in a straight line it would be 200m - 656ft long.

No other Imperial victories have ever been celebrated with so much talent and genius. Both wars (101-02 and 105-06) are illustrated; their respective incidents are separated by the winged figure of Victory inscribing the Imperial victories on a shield *(visible from the terrace in front of the churches).*

There are over 100 scenes. The artistic ability of the sculptor and the technical skill required to achieve a perfect fit between two parts of a panel at the junction of two drums are matched by such precision of detail that the column serves as a faithful historical record of the Dacian campaigns and of Roman military technique. The diameter of the shaft is not uniform from top to bottom; two thirds of the way up it increases slightly to prevent the illusion of concavity which would otherwise result from the effect of the height. The size of the panels and of the figures increases towards the top of the column which was originally brilliantly coloured.

A bronze statue of Trajan was placed on top of the column probably after his death. In 1587 Pope Sixtus V had it replaced with the statue of St Peter that one sees today. Although a pagan monument Trajan's Column was never maltreated by the Christians who believed that Trajan's soul had been saved by the prayers of St Gregory. A golden urn containing the Emperor's ashes was placed in a funerary chamber within the column; the urn was stolen in the Middle Ages. Trajan's successor, Hadrian, erected a temple to the deified Emperor after his death but nothing remains to be seen.

The base of the column, which is sculpted with war trophies, bears a Latin inscription (on the side facing the Basilica Ulpia) which has given rise to lively polemics; does the height of the column indicate the height of the Quirinal Hill before it was levelled to make room for Trajan's forum?

Inside the column is a spiral staircase *(not open)* leading to the top which is lit by windows in the decorative panels; part of the designer's skill lies in the fact that these windows are scarcely visible from the outside.

From the Forum **Santa Maria di Loreto** is visible. The church was begun by Antonio da Sangallo the Younger in 1507 to a square design and completed in 1577 by Giacomo del Duca, from Sicily, who added the great octagonal drum surmounted by the cupola.

★★Mercati Traianei (Trajan's Market) ⊙ – *Entrance in Via Quattro Novembre. Time: 30min.* There were about 150 shops arranged in terraces against the Quirinal Hill above the forum. The market was not simply a retail market like the Forum Boarium and the Forum Holitorium but a centre for the acquisition, division and redistribution of supplies, administered by the Imperial authorities, under the Prefect of Rome and the Prefect of the Annona.

First comes a magnificent vaulted room (**5**) where the civil servants may have worked. The buttresses which support the pillars on which the vaulting rests are of interest; no equivalent structure has been found among the monuments of Ancient Rome.

Trajan's Column: detail

★**Via Biberatica** – This street serves the upper part of the semicircle which forms the façade of the market, the shops which lined it dealt in exotic commodities. It is still covered with its original paving and runs in a curve from the Torre del Grillo to the present Via Quattro Novembre.

From Via Biberatica the visitor walks down through the market. The shops on the first floor, which are long and vaulted, were probably used for the sale of wine and oil; they open on to a vaulted arcade.

Façade – The semicircular façade and the arrangement of the shops in tiers demonstrate the genius of Appollodorus of Damascus who gave a monumental appearance to this utilitarian complex.

The shallow shops on the ground floor opened directly on to the curving street which still has its original paving; they may have sold fruit and flowers; one has been reconstructed.

The elegance of the first floor arcades is enhanced by the curved and triangular pediments.

From Torre delle Milizie to the Viminale

★**Torre delle Milizie (Militia Tower)** – *Closed for restoration*. This is one of the best preserved buildings of Medieval Rome. It was the keep of a castle built by Pope Gregory IX (1227-41) at a time when the Pope often had to use force to establish the faith in the Empire. The tower leans slightly owing to an earthquake in the 14C; it has lost its top storey and crenellations. It has been known as "Nero's Tower": according to the legend it was from the top of this tower that the mad Emperor, dressed in theatrical costume, watched the fire that he himself had caused, "charmed by the beauty of the flames", in Suetonius' account, and reciting one of his poems.

From Via Quattro Novembre there is a view of the beautiful trees in the terraced public gardens of the **Villa Aldobrandini** and of the Baroque façade of the **Church of St Dominic and St Sixtus** (completed in 1655).

Turn right into Salita del Grillo.

This street takes its name from the Marquess del Grillo, known for his jokes and jibes at the expense of the disinherited. Beside the arcade stands the **tower** of his mansion.

Casa di Cavalieri di Rodi (House of the Knights of Rhodes) ⊘ – Marco Bembo, Bishop of Vicenza and Cardinal of St Mark's Basilica, was appointed Grand Master of the Order of the Knight Hospitallers of St John by his uncle Pope Paul II (1464-71). He reconstructed this building in the 15C in part of a medieval convent constructed around the remains of the Temple of Mars Ultor. Some of the windows show that Venetian craftsmen were employed. The beautiful 15C loggia overlooking Trajan's Forum is supported on Roman columns, their capitals carved with leaves and rosettes; the walls are decorated with frescoes.

Continue along Via Tor de' Conti.

The Via **Tor de'Conti** skirts the imposing wall built of large blocks of tufa and travertine which separated Augustus' Forum from the Suburra district. Note the fine arch (Arco dei Pentani) which marked the entrance to the Forum. At the end of the street can be seen the imposing mass of what remains of the tower from which the street takes its name. Pope Innocent III had it built around 1238 with material taken from Nerva's Forum. The tower was inhabited until reduced to its present state by an earthquake in 1348.

Turn left into Via Madonna dei Monti and left again into Via del Boschetto to reach Via Panisperna.

Slums

Via Madonna dei Monti leads to what was the **Suburra** district, the most disreputable in Ancient Rome. This zone, which harboured thieves and hired assassins, bequeathed its name to a nearby square. The narrow alleys still seem haunted by the ghost of the outrageous Empress Messalina who frequented the local brothels in secret.

Via Panisperna crosses the **Viminale**, one of the seven hills of Rome, which probably takes its name from the very large number of willow trees or from the temple dedicated to Jupiter Vimineus which stood there. The tree-lined courtyard of the Church of San **Lorenzo in Panisperna** (St Lawrence in Panisperna) ⊘ is a tiny oasis from another era separating this place of worship from the chaos of the city. On 10th August, the feast of St Lawrence, the nuns carry on an age-old tradition of offering blessed bread.

Neighbouring sights are described in the following chapters: COLOSSEO – CELIO; FONTANA DI TREVI – QUIRINALE; FORO ROMANO – PALATINO; PIAZZA VENEZIA; SANTA MARIA MAGGIORE – ESQUILINO.

FORO ROMANO – PALATINO ★★★

Tour ½ day

Allow 3 hours to visit the whole of the Forum and the Palatine. The best places for a view of the ruins are the Capitol terrace and the Farnese Gardens on the Palatine Hill. Certain parts of the ruins may be closed owing to lack of staff or to restoration work.

★★★FORO ROMANO (ROMAN FORUM) ⊙

This site, where a few columns stand among ruined walls and crumbling foundations, bears traces of the twelve centuries of history which forged the Roman civilisation.

Historical Notes

In about 750 BC the site of the Forum was a marshy valley, subject to flooding by the Tiber and by streams from the seven surrounding hills: the Palatine, the Caelian, the Esquiline, the Velia which linked the Palatine to the Esquiline, the Viminal, the Quirinal and the Capitoline *(map Rome during the Empire)*. Small villages composed of rough shacks grew up on the hillsides. Their inhabitants, the Latins and the Sabines *(map Foundation of Rome)*, were principally engaged in agriculture but would take up arms in defence of their homesteads when threatened with invasion by their neighbours. The valley, which lay roughly at the centre of the circle of hills and which later became the Forum, was used as a burial ground and as a meeting place where their leaders made decisions affecting the community and where the people exchanged goods and gathered for worship.

Two centuries later the marshy valley had completely changed in appearance and become a real square at the centre of a town: the cemetery had been abandoned and covered with houses; the west side of the Forum had been paved. The people responsible for this transformation were the **Etruscans**. Originally from the right bank of the Tiber, they extended their dominion as far as Cumae on the borders of Magna Graecia (southern Italy). They settled on the site of Rome, built a citadel on the Capitol, unified the villages and organised the social life of the community. From 616 to 509 BC Rome was governed by kings of Etruscan origin. The city was enclosed by fortifications; the stagnant water in the Forum was drained into the Tiber through a channel which was to become the Great Sewer *(Cloaca maxima)*.

The Forum during the Republic – The last Etruscan King, Tarquin the Proud, was thrown out in 509 BC and the Consulate was instituted. The Republican era had begun: from being a rural town Rome began to develop into the capital of an Empire. The Forum, barely 2 ha - 5 acres in extent was the focal point of events which ushered in the new era.

Roman Forum

D. Hée/MICHELIN

The Republican period was first and foremost a time of territorial expansion: from early in the 5C BC Rome was at war with her neighbours. Victories were celebrated in the Forum: a temple was built in honour of the Dioscuri *(see below: Temple of Castor and Pollux)* who came to the assistance of the Romans at Lake Regillus. In 260 during the first Punic war a column was raised to Caius Duilius who gained the first Roman naval victory at Milazzo in Sicily. All victorious generals processed in triumph through the Forum.

Commercial centre – The Roman conquests brought with them immense riches: the contents of confiscated enemy treasuries, indemnities paid by the conquered nations and the tribute paid by the provinces. By the 3C BC Rome was an important financial centre. Money-changing, loans and credit were arranged in the Forum. The shops which had formerly housed small traders were taken over by bankers.

Political centre – The five centuries of the Roman Republic which preceded the Empire were full of activity. The men who decided the destiny of Rome met in the **Comitium**, an area in the northwest corner of the Forum where the popular assemblies *(comices)* were held.

Right in the corner stood the Senate House *(Curia)*. It was also called the 'Hostilia' because, so it was said, it had been created by Tullius Hostilius, a Sabine king who ruled from 672 to 640 BC. The Curia was the seat of the highest level of Republican government, the Senate; 200 Senators, appointed for life, decided foreign policy, directed military operations, drew up peace treaties and enacted measures for public safety. Opposite the Curia were the Rostra where the tribunes held forth. People came to listen to the pitiless logic and measured accents of Tiberius and Gaius Gracchus. Next to it stood the *Graeco-stasis*, a platform where foreign ambassadors waited. In 185 BC the **Basilica Porcia**, the first building of this sort in Rome, was erected on one side of the Comitium by Porcius Cato, thus enabling the citizens to assemble under cover.

Religious centre – In 497 BC the Temple of Saturn was built in the Forum; other religious buildings already existed from the Regal period. Troubled times were approaching and religious belief was waning. The practice of offering the spirits of the dead a combat which ended in the death of one of the participants degenerated into an entertainment: by 264 BC gladiatorial combats were being held in the Forum.

Troubled times – For a hundred years the Republican regime tore itself to pieces in civil war. In 52 BC the tribune Clodius was killed by Milo, his body being carried to the Comitium and cremated; the fire spread, destroying the Curia and the Basilica Porcia.

Caesar had already decided that the Forum was too small and intended to enlarge it. In 44 BC he moved the Rostra and realigned the Curia.

Scarcely anything of the Republican Forum survives. The early buildings were of tufa, peperine or wood. The emperors faced them with marble, then built others larger and more magnificent. Augustus could boast that he had inherited a town built of brick and left a city built of marble.

The Forum during the Empire – On 16 January 27 BC the Senate granted Octavian the title Augustus (protected by the gods in every act); a new regime was born under the sign of grandeur. Taking up Caesar's project, Augustus, and then Vespasian, Domitian and Trajan, enlarged the old Forum and built the Imperial Fora. In the Augustan era the original Forum lost some of its uses: the huge popular assemblies and the reviews of the troops were moved to the Campus Martius.

The Forum became the chosen site for erecting monuments: commemorative arches, basilicas and temples dedicated to emperors deified after their death. Even in the 2C BC confusion reigned according to Plautus, a satirist who died in 184 BC. Every sort of citizen could be found there: "vicious or virtuous, honest or dishonest. If you want to meet a perjurer, go to the Comitium; for a liar and a braggart, try the Temple of Venus Cloacina; for wealthy married wasters, near the Basilica. There too you will find well perfumed prostitutes and men ready to do a deal, while the fish market is frequented by members of the eating clubs. Wealthy and reputable citizens stroll in the lower Forum; the middle Forum near the Canal is favoured by the merely showy set... Behind the Temple of Castor are those whom you would do well not to trust too lightly; in the Tuscan district those who are willing to sell themselves."

In the 3C building came to a halt: not only for lack of space but also because of the spread of a new religion which entailed the worship of one god. At first it was preached by a handful of nobodies and then from AD 60 by a certain Paul of Tarsus. The emperors resisted but in AD 391 Theodosius finally closed the pagan temples.

The Forum's downfall began in 410 when Alaric the Goth swept in from the Danube with his savage hordes and set fire to the Curia and the Basilica Aemilia. There followed an earthquake in 442, the depredations of Genseric's Vandals in 455, the armies of Theodoric in 500 and of Belisarius in 537, after which the

Forum was dead. Rome's prestige no longer lay in grandiose monuments but, as the resting-place of St Peter the Apostle, the city was celebrated throughout the Christian world.

The Forum from the Middle Ages to the Renaissance – Once the church became organised, the Bishop of Rome, the Pope, was recognised as the head of Christianity. Gradually the Imperial buildings were converted into places of Christian worship. Some still survive, a curious juxtaposition of traditions; many have disappeared – such as the two oratories in the portico of the Basilica Aemilia or the Church of Sts Sergius and Bacchus which existed between the Temples of Saturn and Concord until the 16C, or the Church of Santa Maria in Cannapara in the Basilica Julia. In the 9C the buildings began to crumble away; the earth built up around them and the ruins were buried.

In the 12C the quarrel between the Pope and the Holy Roman Emperor brought civil war between the noble Roman families. The ancient structures were turned into fortresses; towers rose between the Temple of Antoninus and Faustina and Caesar's Forum. The old buildings were stripped of their decoration which was used to embellish churches and palaces; the statues and columns were baked in lime kilns to produce chalk.

The deserted Forum became a sewage farm. By the 15C the pillars of the Temple of Vespasian were half underground and the podium of the Temple of the Dioscuri was completely buried; both were surrounded by fields. The Forum had become a cows' field *(campo vaccino)*. Near the Temple of the Dioscuri the marble basin of a fountain was being used as a drinking trough for animals; it is now in the Piazza del Quirinale. When Charles V visited Rome in 1536, Pope Paul III laid out a broad avenue from the Arch of Titus to the Arch of Septimius Severus.

Excavations
The names of many famous archeologists, both Italians and foreigners, are connected with the history of the excavation of the Roman Forum: Carlo Fea who began investigations in 1803, Antonio Nibby, Bunsen and Canina, Pietro Rosa after 1870, Giuseppe Fiorelli, Rodolfo Lanciani, H Jordan, C Hülsen and particularly Giacomo Boni who carried out methodical excavations from 1898 onwards, reaching the oldest levels which were essential to an understanding of early Rome.

Tour

Descend into the Forum; immediately on the right are the remains of the Basilica Emilia.

Basilica Emilia (Basilica Aemilia) – This was the second basilica to be built in Rome (in 179 BC) after the Basilica Porcia *(see above)* had been built not far away in 185 BC. Like all the monuments in the Forum it was frequently restored and reconstructed. The present remains are those of the 1C rebuilding. It was named after the Aemilia family *(gens Aemilia)* who were responsible for its maintenance. Like all the ancient basilicas it served no religious purpose. The huge covered hall was used for business transactions and for sheltering from the heat or cold; judges and litigants retreated here to hold their hearings out of the hubbub of the more public places.

Along the south side of the basilica there was a line of shops opening into a portico; the party-walls can still be seen (some have been reconstructed). The shops sold jewellery and perfume. Behind the shops was the main hall divided into three by two rows of coloured marble columns with a finely carved entablature of white marble; fragments of the architrave and columns are displayed against the rear wall.

In the southeast corner of the Basilica Aemilia stands a Latin **inscription** (**1**) dedicated to Augustus' adopted grandsons, Caius and Lucius, who died before reaching manhood.

★**Via Sacra (Sacred Way)** – This was the most famous street in ancient Rome. From the earliest days of the Forum, the Temple of Vesta and the Regia flanked the Sacred Way along which victorious generals rode in triumphal procession; dressed like Jupiter and standing in a four-horse chariot, they proceeded to the Capitoline Hill to give thanks to Jupiter, the Best and Greatest, for his protection during the campaign.

Santuario di Venere Cloacina (Sanctuary of Venus Cloacina) (**2**) – A travertine circle on the ground marks the site of the sanctuary dedicated to the goddess who protected the main sewer *(cloaca);* traces of the steps leading down to it are still visible. Here in the 5C BC Verginius, a humble plebeian officer, took his daughter's life to save her from the lust of Appius Claudius, a decemvir; Livy tells how the latter was prepared to abuse his power in his desire to make Virginia his slave; he provoked a riot among the people and the abdication of the decemvirs.

Go to the northwest corner of the Basilica Aemilia.

Beneath a protective roof are the bases of three columns and other fragments belonging to the Basilica built in the Republican period (**3**).

Argiletum – This street, one of the busiest in Rome, separated the Basilica Aemilia from the Curia and led to Suburra, a slum district. There remain some fine sections of travertine paving. During the reign of the kings there was said to be an arch over the Argiletum, flanked by a shrine containing the two-faced statue of the god Janus. Legend tells how during the war against the Sabines Janus had produced a jet of hot water from the ground which stopped the enemy dead in their attack on the Capitol. The shrine was always left open in time of war so that Janus could come to the aid of the Romans.

★★**Curia** – *May close at 1pm for administrative reasons.* The brick building visible today is not the one in which the Senate met in the Republican period when it was in charge of Roman policy. The first Curia was more or less on the site of the chancel and left transept of St Luke's Church but facing in a different direction. In the 1C BC Caesar moved it and enlarged it and Diocletian rebuilt it in the 3C.

Diocletian's Curia was restored in 1937 after the removal of St Adrian's Church which had occupied the building since the 7C. It was less austere than it is today: the façade, faced with marble and stucco, was surmounted by a tympanum covered in travertine; the bronze door was removed to St John Lateran by Alexander VII in the 17C.

The Curia was a *templum*, a consecrated place where an augur could communicate to the people the wishes of the gods as they had been revealed to him by certain signs: the flight of birds, the manner of feeding of the sacred chickens and any unusual events. Every sitting of the Senate began with the president taking the auguries to see whether they were favourable or not. The senators did not have fixed seats. Once the agenda had been read each senator in turn – according to the order fixed by the list in the *album* – was called upon to give his opinion.

For a considerable period the Senate had immense power but once Imperial government had been introduced it became practically impossible for the senators to oppose the decisions of the emperor who appointed them to office. At the very most, after an emperor's death, they could condemn him and thus oppose his deification.

The mystery of the Statue of Victory

At the far end of the Curia there are traces of a pedestal on which stood the statue of Victory: it was a golden statue placed there in 29 BC by Octavian who defeated the armies of Antony and Cleopatra at Actium in Greece in 31 BC and became the ruler of the Roman Empire. For over three centuries the emperors worshipped the statue, burning incense on the altar. At their funerals the statue was carried at the head of the cortège which culminated in the apotheosis and deification of the emperor. In his Epistle to the Romans St Paul had asserted that the one God of the Christians should have dominion over the living and the dead. In AD 380 the Edict of Thessalonica was issued stipulating that all people "should rally to the faith transmitted to the Romans by the Apostle Peter..." From then on the statue of Victory constituted an offence to Christianity, the new State religion; in 382 the Emperor Gratian had the statue removed. Symmachus, Prefect of Rome, protested but the statue never reappeared.

★★**Bassorilievi di Traiano** (Trajan's Plutei) – The Curia houses two sculpted panels found in the Forum and probably commissioned by Trajan or his successor Hadrian to decorate the Rostra. On the back of the two panels are represented the three animals which were sacrificed during the purification ceremony: a pig, a sheep and a bull; in Latin: *sus, ovis* and *taurus,* hence the name of the sacrifice: *suovetaurilia.* The anatomy of the animals is represented in a very realistic manner; each detail has been carefully executed, particularly the fleeces of the sheep. The sculptures on the other side illustrate Imperial beneficence.

The righthand panel shows two scenes:
– Trajan, standing on the Rostra with his lictors, has just announced that the interest due on loans made to smallholders will be used to assist poor children. This is the institution of the *Alimenta* which Hadrian continued to implement.
– The Emperor seated receiving a woman and child, symbolizing Italy.

On the lefthand panel:
– The Emperor is watching a group of men piling up documents. He is about to give the order for the destruction of these records which contain details of overdue taxes, thus freeing a number of citizens from their debts.

The sculptor has set these scenes against a local background showing several of the Forum buildings. The edges of the panels are decorated with the sacred fig tree *(see below)* and a statue of Marsyas, his flayed skin about his shoulders.

Behind the Curia *(walk round the building by the Argiletum)* is a small brick altar (**4**) with a recess for relics proving that the place was used for Christian worship in the 7C to 8C. *(Area closed for restoration work.)*

Lapis Niger (Black Stone) (**5**) – In 1899 Giacomo Boni, who was in charge of the excavation of the Forum, discovered an area paved with black marble slabs (currently protected by a low fence). Beneath the slabs among some piled-up blocks of tufa the archeologists found a stele bearing an inscription whose meaning is obscure. They concluded they had uncovered a monument dating from the 6C BC. When Caesar re-arranged the Forum he had protected this area because it was sacred; the Romans believed it was the tomb of Romulus or Faustulus (the shepherd who had seen the wolf suckling the twins) or Hostus Hostilius, the father of Tullus Hostilius, the third king after Romulus and Numa Pompilius.

Comitium – *See above:* Historical Notes. It extended from the Curia to the Lapis Niger and contained a fountain with a circular base of which the remains are still visible.

Decennalia Caesarum (**6**) – In 286 Diocletian decentralised the government of the Empire; he himself took charge of the affairs of the Eastern Empire and Maximian of the Western. Both were known by the title Augustus. Seven years later Maximian entrusted the administration of Gaul and Britain to Constantius and Diocletian put Galerius in charge of the Balkan peninsula. Constantius and Galerius bore the title of Caesar.

The first ten years' reign *(decennalia)* of the two Caesars and the 20 years of the Augusti were celebrated with the erection of a column of which only the base remains. The carving shows the animals of the *suovetaurilia* and certain events in the religious ceremonies. The quality of the sculpture is inferior to that of Trajan's period *(see above);* the background figures are flattened and simply indicated by a deep line; the costumes are stiff, the fold lines being too deeply chiselled.

★**Rostra** – After 338 BC the orators' platform was always called the Rostra. In that year the Romans had attacked Antium (modern Anzio), then notorious for its pirates, and captured the prows *(rostra)* of the enemy ships which they fixed to the orators' platform. In the Republican period the Rostra resounded with the speeches of all the great exponents of the oratorical art. In those days the platform stood between the Lapis Niger and the present Curia. The remains which can be seen today are those of the Rostra moved in 44 BC by Julius Caesar. After his assassination, Octavian, Antony and Lepidus formed the second triumvirate (late October 43 BC). The period of proscriptions began; Cicero was one of the most famous victims. A declared enemy of Antony, whose illegal acts and Imperial ambitions he had denounced in his Philippics, he was sacrificed for reasons of State by Octavian and murdered in his house in Gaeta in December 43 BC by agents of the triumvirate. His hands and head were exposed on the Rostra.

The construction known as the Rostra was a raised platform reached by a curving staircase at the rear (Capitoline side). When the emperors were all-powerful, the great assemblies of the people, roused by the speeches of their tribunes, had no power of decision. The platform therefore was used only for dignified official ceremonies. Before the erection of the two commemorative columns, the crowd could congregate in front of the Rostra. It became very noisy on the days when food was distributed; the numbers of the poor grew incessantly and when Caesar came to power there were about 300 000 citizens on the lists for the distribution of free corn.

★★**Arco di Settimio Severo (Arch of Septimius Severus)** – It was built in 203 and is surmounted by statues of Septimius Severus, his two sons (Caracalla and Geta) and the figure of Victory. The Emperor had just won a series of victories over the Parthians (197 to 202) and had organised a new province, Mesopotamia *(see* INTRODUCTION – Map of the Roman Empire). The heroes' names appeared in the dedicatory text; Geta's was obliterated after Caracalla had him murdered so as to be the sole successor.

In the 3C architecture became more complicated: four detached Corinthian columns stand before the façade forming a false portico. Decoration is abundant. At the base of the columns are prisoners in chains.

The panels on the façade are divided by thick ribs into horizontal bands. The figures are too small and although this style of presentation serves well for triumphal columns *(see Colonna Traiana and Colonna di Marco Aurelio)* here it only causes confusion.

Umbilicus Urbis (**7**) – The remains of a 3C circular temple which marked the symbolic centre of the city.

Altare di Vulcano (**8**) – The Altar of Vulcan, a venerable hollow in the tufa, goes back to the time of the kings. Under the Republic the day of 23 August was devoted to the Volcanalia festival: little fishes or other animals symbolising human lives that people wished to preserve were offered to the god of Fire.

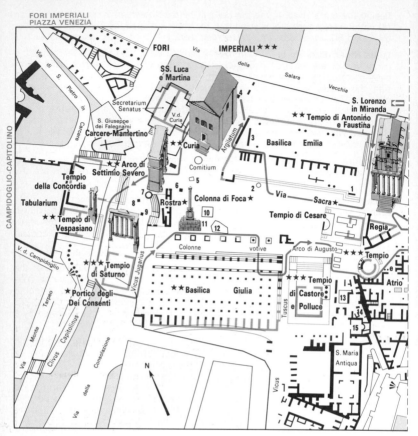

Colonna miliare d'Oro (**9**) – The **Golden Milestone** marble column covered with gilded bronze was set up by Augustus to mark the point from which mileages were measured. The distances between the capital and the major cities of the Empire were written on it.

At the foot of the Capitol a group of splendid monuments flanked the **Clivus Capitolinus**, the road used by religious processions and military triumphs proceeding from the Forum to the Temple of Jupiter on the Capitol.

Tabularium – The podium and a few extant pillars form the base of the Senatorial Palace. The tabularium filled the depression between the Citadel and the Capitol, the two peaks of the Capitoline Hill. Its façade formed the west side of the Forum. It was built in 78 BC to house the State records, including some bronze tablets on which were inscribed the old Roman laws, hence the name Tabularium. The use of peperine, a very simple building material, and of the Doric order, a plain architectural style, typify the austerity of Republican architecture.

Tempio della Concordia (Temple of Concord) – The Romans always attributed a divine character to the mysterious forces which influenced events; thus they worshipped as gods such abstract ideas as concord, justice, liberty and abundance. Most of these divinities were represented by the statue of a female figure: the attributes of Concord were two linked hands and a dove.

There had been a Temple of Concord in the Forum since 367 BC; it commemorated the re-establishment of peace between the patricians and the plebeians who had been at odds since the beginning of the 5C BC. Some two-and-a-half centuries later, when the assassination of the people's tribune, Caius Gracchus, had restored peace at home, Concord was again held in honour and the temple rebuilt.

The plan of the building is quite unusual: the *cella* extends laterally beyond the width of the *pronaos* which was reached by steps from the Clivus Capitolinus.

★★**Tempio di Vespasiano** (Temple of Vespasian) – Three very elegant columns, excavated by Valadier in 1811, are still standing; they formed a corner of the earlier part of the temple. Above the architrave is a detailed decorative frieze: a cornice with dentil, ovolo and palm leaf moulding above a band decorated with bucranes and sacrificial instruments. The temple was approached by steps from the Clivus Capitolinus.

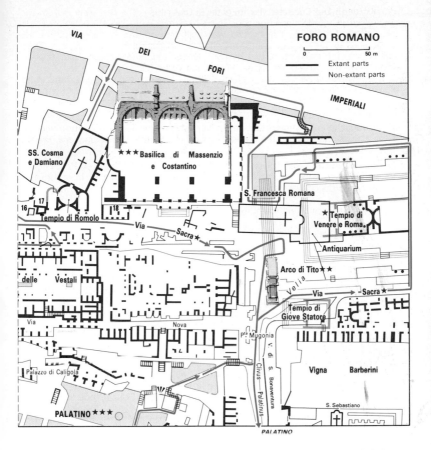

Vespasian became Emperor in AD 69 following the struggles which arose among the pretenders to Nero's succession. He therefore established the principle of a hereditary monarchy founded on primogeniture. He announced to the Senate that "his sons would succeed him or there would be no successor". His elder son Titus therefore succeeded him and began to build a temple in honour of his father who had been deified on his death; in practice, if an emperor had ruled well the Senate would issue a decree raising him to the rank of the gods; all that was needed was a witness who had seen an eagle carry off the dead man's soul during the cremation ceremony.

Titus died before the temple was finished; it was Domitian, his brother and successor as Emperor, who completed the building and dedicated it to Vespasian and Titus. Their two statues stood on a pedestal in the *cella*.

★★★ Tempio di Saturno (Temple of Saturn)

– From 497 onwards a temple dedicated to Saturn stood on this site. This god was supposed to have taught the Romans to cultivate the earth; hence his prestige with this peasant people. The temple was restored several times under the Republic and then rebuilt in the 4C after a fire. The eight columns of

---

Saturnalia

This celebrated festival took place in December in the Temple of Saturn. The general licence which accompanied it was intended to help the sun rise again in the sky. During the Saturnalia all distinctions between masters and slaves were suspended; the latter in particular were entitled to free speech.

---

the *pronaos* which remain date from this period, whereas the travertine podium goes back to the 1C BC.

State Treasury – The treasure was lodged in the temple basement. This place may have been chosen because the cult of Saturn was associated with that of Ops the goddess of Abundance. The Senate administered the treasure, assisted by the Censors and the Quaestors. Late in 49 during the civil war Caesar did not hesitate to draw on the funds.

★**Portico degli Dei Consenti (Portico of the Di Consentes)** – *The best view is from the Capitoline Hill Via del Foro Romano.* The 12 columns with Corinthian capitals were reconstructed in 1858. The portico was built by Domitian in honour of the 12 great gods in the Roman pantheon who met in council to assist Jupiter. Their statues stood in the portico, two by two: Jupiter and Juno, Neptune and Minerva, Mars and Venus, Apollo and Diana, Vulcan and Vesta, Mercury and Ceres.

It was restored in 367 by the Prefect of Rome, Vettius Agorius Praetextatus, who had been a friend of **Julian the Apostate** and shared his great sympathy for the pagan religions; it was certainly the last gesture made to paganism in Rome where 37 popes had already acceded to the throne of St Peter.

Vicus Jugarius – This important street ran between the Temple of Saturn and the Basilica Julia and led to the vegetable market (Forum Holitorium: *see BOCCA DELLA VERITÀ*).

★**Colonna di Foca (Phocas' Column)** – In AD 608 the Eastern Emperor Phocas gave the Pantheon to Pope Boniface IV and it was turned into a church. In gratitude a statue of the donor was set up on a column in the Forum. The column had to be taken from an already-existing building because by then there were no artists capable of producing fine sculpture. This was the last monument to be erected on the old public place.

The sacred **fig tree**, symbol of the tree beneath which the cradle of Romulus and Remus had been found, the **vine** and the **olive tree** (**10**), symbols of the prosperity which Rome owed to agriculture, have been replanted. Here also stood the very popular statue of Marsyas, brought from Greece in the 2C BC. It represented a Silenus looking, as they all did, like an old satyr, very ugly and often drunk, wearing a skin over his shoulders. He wore a Phrygian cap, symbol of liberty, so that newly-freed slaves would come and touch the statue.

The large **inscription** (**11**), reconstructed in bronze letters, bears the name of Naevius and commemorates the relaying of the paving carried out by this magistrate in 15 BC.

Lago di Curzio (**12**) – The **Curtian Lake** refers to a circular area paved with stone within a shallow surround, protected by a roof and a railing. During the early Republic it was a cleft full of water that could not be drained away. The oracle was consulted and pronounced that the opening would close when Rome threw her dearest treasure into it. A valuable young soldier called Curtius rode into it fully armed and the abyss closed up leaving a small pool of water. The adjacent low relief sculpture illustrating the legend was executed in the 1C BC *(now housed in the Museo del Palazzo dei Conservatori)*; it does not reveal whether this legend should be given more credit than another which says that Curtius was a Sabine soldier who was nearly sucked down into the marshy ground of the Forum during the legendary war between Romulus and Tatius.

Colonne votive (Votive columns) – There were seven, probably erected during Diocletian's reign (AD 284-305) to commemorate army generals. Two have been partly reconstructed.

★★**Basilica Giulia (Basilica Julia)** – In 170 BC the Censor Sempronius Gracchus, father of the tribunes Tiberius and Caius, built a basilica on this site which was called "Sempronia". In 55 BC Julius Caesar, who was Consul, replaced it with another basilica, larger and more elegant, which started the trend for gigantic buildings in the Forum: 109m - 358ft long, 40m - 131ft wide and divided into five aisles, it was paved with precious marble in the centre and white marble in the side aisles. Close observation of some of the paving stones will reveal geometric designs which were marked out by idlers for their games.

There was a portico on the northeast side and shops on the opposite side.

Julius Caesar was murdered in 44 BC before the basilica was finished; it bears his name nonetheless, although it was Augustus who completed it.

In about the 8C the Church of Santa Maria in Cannapara was established in the west corner (traces of brick walls).

Vicus Tuscus – This street curved round the foot of the Palatine to join the cattle market near the Tiber (Forum Boarium: *see BOCCA DELLA VERITÀ*). Many Etruscan merchants had shops there, hence its name (the Romans called the Etruscans *Tusci*).

Tempio di Cesare (Temple of Caesar) – Almost nothing is left of this building which started the cult of Emperor worship. On the evening of the Ides of March 44 BC the body of Caesar, who had been stabbed to death in the Curia of Pompey, was carried to the Forum and cremated before the Rostra. A column and altar were set up nearby but were immediately pulled down by Caesar's enemies. They were replaced by a temple consecrated by Octavian in 29 BC to the 'god' Julius Caesar.

The podium was extended forward to form a raised terrace containing a semi-circular recess at ground level in which stood a round altar (traces visible). In the *cella* stood a statue of Caesar, a star on his head. Suetonius explains why he was always represented in this way: "after his apotheosis, during the first days of the games given in his honour by his successor Augustus, a comet appeared at about the eleventh hour and burned for seven days; it was thought to be Caesar's soul being admitted to heaven..."

When Octavian defeated the fleets of Antony and Cleopatra at Actium in Greece on 2 September 31 BC, he took the prows *(rostra)* of the enemy ships and fixed them to the terrace of Caesar's Temple; the terrace became known as the Caesar's Rostra and later Emperors often spoke from there.

Arco di Augusto (Arch of Augustus) – Two commemorative arches were erected by Augustus between the Temples of Caesar and Castor: the first was built in 29 BC after his victory at Actium in Greece; ten years later as the first became dilapidated, a second was built to celebrate Augustus' recovery of the Roman standards which had been captured by the Parthians at the battle of Carrhae in Mesopotamia in 53 BC.

Only the foundations have been discovered (the bases of two pillars are visible).

***Tempio di Castore e Polluce (Temple of Castor and Pollux)** – The temple was dedicated to Castor and Pollux, known as the Dioscuri. The chief remains are three columns supporting an architrave fragment, which form one of the most famous sights of the Roman Forum. The founding of the temple goes back to the beginning of the 5C BC; it has remained on its original site.

Its whole history is surrounded by legends. Early in the 5C BC Rome took the offensive against her poorer envious neighbours: the conflict came to a head on the shores of Lake Regillus in about 496 BC. During the battle the Romans saw two divine knights fighting on their side; these were Castor and Pollux, sons of Jupiter and Leda. They subsequently made their way to Rome to announce the victory to the people gathered in the Forum; their thirsty horses drank at Juturna's spring. A temple dedicated to the Dioscuri, Castor and Pollux, was built on the site of this apparition by the son of the dictator Postumius who had directed the battle against the Latins.

The three beautiful columns, which had been pulled down in 1811, date from a reconstruction undertaken in the Augustan era and belong to the long lefthand side of the sanctuary. The very high podium which raises the columns high into the sky, the magnitude of the Corinthian capitals and the use of very white marble combine to make a most majestic effect. The remains of the temple of Castor and Pollux show what magnificence Augustus sought to bestow on the city to replace the damage caused in the civil war.

It is said that the Emperor Caligula (AD 37-41), whose excesses led to his being presumed insane, built a bridge from the Temple of Castor and Pollux (the ante-chamber to his palace on the Palatine) to the Temple of Jupiter on the Capitol so that he could go and converse with the god whom he considered his equal, or even sometimes take his place.

Cinta sacra di Giuturna (Sacred Precinct of Juturna) (13) – Juturna was a nymph who reigned over all the springs in Latium and was made immortal by Jupiter who loved her. Her shrine contained a spring which played a part in the legend of the Dioscuri. In the basin stands an altar, probably 2C, with low relief sculptures representing Castor and Pollux and a woman bearing a long torch *(on the front and back)* and Leda and the swan, and Jupiter *(on the sides)*. The adjacent **aedicule** (14), partially reconstructed, the round well and the altar were also part of the sacred precinct. The well is inscribed with the name of Barbatius Pollio who put up a dedication to Juturna probably in the reign of Augustus; low relief figures on the altar.

Santa Maria Antiqua – *Open for specialist study only* ⊙.

Oratorio dei Martiri (Oratory of the Forty Martyrs) (15) – The original purpose of the building is unknown; in the 7C it was decorated with paintings and dedicated to the 40 martyrs of Sebastea in Armenia who were exposed in chains on a frozen pond.

***Tempio e Atrio delle Vestali (Temple and Atrium of the Vestal Virgins)** – In the days when fire was still a precious commodity, the village on the Palatine where Romulus lived must have included a round hut, similar to all the other huts, where the communal fire was kept alight. This process was organised around Vesta, the goddess of Fire.

The institution of the cult in Rome goes back to Romulus or to Numa Pompilius (715-672 BC). A group of priestesses, known as the Vestal Virgins, at first four in number but later increased to six, officiated in the cult of Vesta.

When the first temple was built, probably late in the 6C BC, it conserved the circular form of the earlier hut. It was destroyed by fire and rebuilt several times, always in circular form, until the time of Septimius Severus. Only the central foundation and a few marble fragments survived to be used in the 1930 reconstruction. It was an enclosed shrine, surrounded by a portico supported on 20 fluted Corinthian columns; the frieze showed the instruments of sacrifice in low relief. The *cella* housed an altar where the fire was kept burning constantly. There

House of the Vestal Virgins

S. Chirol

was also a secret place where certain objects which were supposed to have made Rome's fortune, were jealously guarded; they included the famous Palladium, a statuette in wood or bone of the goddess Pallas, which was able to protect the city which possessed it. It had fallen from the sky on the city of Troy, possibly thrown by Zeus on Olympus. The Romans thought it had come into their possession through Aeneas who had stolen it from Troy and brought it to Italy.

Next to the temple was the house of the Vestal Virgins: the **Atrium Vestae**. It was a large two-storey building enclosing a rectangular courtyard with a portico, containing two pools of water and a garden. The Vestal Virgins were chosen from the patrician families and entered into service at the age of ten and stayed for at least 30 years: ten as pupils, ten performing their duties and ten teaching. Most of the Vestals spent their whole lives in the house. Discipline was strict: a virgin who let the fire go out, a portent of disaster for Rome, was severely punished and one who broke her vow of chastity was buried alive. From the 3C statues were erected to the Vestals in recognition of their service. Some of these statues with an inscription on the base have been placed in the courtyard of the house.

Regia – Religious observance in Rome centred on the Regia and the Temple of Vesta. The Regia was held to have been the residence of King Numa Pompilius, who succeeded Romulus and organised the State religion. Later it was the residence of the Pontifex Maximus, the head of the college of priests. During the Regal period it was the Pontifex Maximus who kept the religious records. Under the Republic he took charge of the national religion and became so influential that the Emperors appointed themselves to the position.

The legend of the shields

One day King Numa received a shield *(ancile)* from heaven which was thought to foretell victory for the Romans. He entrusted it for safekeeping to the priests of the cult of Mars, and to prevent it from being stolen he had 11 copies made; all were kept in the Regia. The workman who made the shields asked as his reward to be remembered in the chanting that accompanied the procession of the shields.

The Regia and the House of the Vestals mark the limit of the Forum at the time of the kings and the Republic. The section extending to the Arch of Titus was added later.

★★Tempio di Antonino e Faustina (Temple of Antoninus and Faustina) – The Emperor Antoninus Pius who succeeded Hadrian in 138 AD belonged to a rich family originally from Nîmes in France. He was well known for his kindness and reigned for 23 years in peace and moderation. On the death of his wife, Faustina, in 141 AD, he raised her to the ranks of the goddesses in spite of her scandalous behaviour. A huge temple to her was erected in the Forum.

When Antoninus himself died in 161 AD the Senate decided to dedicate the temple to both husband and wife.

The beautiful monolithic columns of the *pronaos* still stand on their high podium. The frieze of griffins and candelabra on the entablature is a masterpiece of fine craftsmanship.

In the 11C the Church of San Lorenzo in Miranda was established in the ruins. When Charles V visited Rome in 1536 the façade of the church was set back to reveal the colonnade. In 1602 the church was rebuilt.

Excavations beside the Temple of Antoninus and Faustina have uncovered a **cemetery (16)** dating from the time of Romulus (8C - 7C BC).

Tempio di Romolo (Temple of Romulus) – The Romulus to whom the temple is thought to be dedicated was not the founder of Rome but the son of the Emperor Maxentius who died in 307.

Dating from the early 4C the construction is circular and flanked by two rooms with apses: it may have been built in honour of Constantine

Temple of Antoninus and Faustina

to celebrate his victory over Maxentius in 312 or in honour of the divine city of Rome. In 6C when the room behind the temple became the Church of St Cosmas and St Damian the temple itself became a vestibule to the church.

The doorway between two porphyry columns in the concave façade is closed by the original 4C bronze doors; the lock still works.

On the left of the Temple of Romulus are traces of six small **rooms (17)** on either side of a corridor: they may have belonged to a brothel in the Republican era.

The remains of a medieval arcaded building **(18)** high above the Sacred Way indicate how much the ground level in the Forum had risen by the Middle Ages.

Higher up the slope quite in harmony with the ancient monuments below is the Church of Santa Francesca Romana with its Romanesque belfry and three parapet statues.

★★★**Basilica di Massenzio e Costantino (Basilica of Maxentius and Constantine)** – *This building is well known for its summer symphony concerts.* Maxentius was proclaimed Emperor by the people after the abdication of Maximian, his father, and Diocletian in 305. Almost immediately he began to build a basilica, the last to be erected in Rome. Built of brick beneath a groined vault, it was different from the other two basilicas, Aemilia and Julia. It was rectangular and divided into three by huge pillars flanked by columns; one long side ran parallel to the Sacred Way while the other followed the line of the present Via dei Fori Imperiali, one of the short sides constituted the main façade (facing east towards the Coliseum) while the other projected in an apse.

The Imperial throne, however, was coveted by Constantine, son of the Emperor Constantius, who had reigned jointly with Maximian and Diocletian. He defeated Maxentius at the battle of the Milvian Bridge in 312 and completed the basilica with modifications. He moved the entrance to the façade overlooking the Sacred Way and graced it with a portico of four porphyry columns *(still visible)*; an apse was added to the opposite façade.

This grandiose building housed some colossal statues; fragments of the statue of Constantine, which stood in the west apse, can still be seen in the courtyard of the Palazzo dei Conservatori. The gilded bronze tiles were used in the 7C to roof St Peter's Basilica.

Antiquarium – The exhibits in this museum, which is housed in a former convent attached to the Church of Santa Francesca Romana, are mostly connected with the Roman Forum: the earliest traces of Ancient Rome taken from tombs dating from 1 000 to 600 BC or found in the Forum or on the Palatine (hut-shaped urns and hollow tree trunks used as coffins).

★★**Arco di Tito (Arch of Titus)** – The arch stands on the Velia, a spur of the Palatine jutting out towards the Esquiline, and appears in all the views of the Forum.

Titus, the eldest son of Vespasian, succeeded his father as Emperor but his reign was brief – from AD 79 to 81. In 70 he had captured Jerusalem, thus bringing to a successful conclusion a campaign his father had been pursuing since 66. After his death an arch was erected to commemorate his success. The fall of Jerusalem was among the most tragic events in Jewish history. The city was destroyed and the temple, the spiritual bond between Jews of the diaspora, was burned down. In its place Hadrian built a sanctuary to Jupiter and the city was called Aelia Capitolina (Hadrian's family name was Aelius). The single archway of the Arch of Titus was restored by Luigi Valadier in 1821.

At the centre of the panelled vault is a sculpture depicting the apotheosis of Titus: his soul is carried up to heaven by an eagle; this event made him eligible for deification.

The frieze *(above the arch on the side facing the Colosseum)* is indistinct: in a sacrificial procession a recumbent figure represents the Jordan, symbolizing the defeat of Palestine.

The two low reliefs under the vault are among the masterpieces of Roman sculpture: on one side, Titus rides in his chariot in triumph, crowned with victory; on the other, the triumphal procession exhibiting the booty pillaged from the temple in Jerusalem: the seven-branch candlestick which Moses had made and placed in the Tabernacle as commanded by God on Mount Sinai, the table for the shewbread which was placed in the temple each week in the name of the 12 tribes of Israel, the silver trumpets which announced the festivals.

It was on the Velia that Nero built the vestibule to his Golden House.

Tempio di Giove Statore (Temple of Jupiter Stator) – On 8 November 63 BC Cicero delivered his first Catiline oration here before the Senate. Feeling ran high among his audience who were impressed by the security measures which had been thought necessary to protect the State.

Bear right up the hill (Clivus Palatinus) to the Palatine.

★★★ PALATINO (PALATINE HILL)

Of the seven hills of Rome, it is the Palatine which captures the visitor's imagination. As the cradle of the Eternal City it is a prime archeological site. Since the Renaissance it has offered pleasant walks among flower beds and shady trees.

Byron wrote of the beauty of the Palatine and its overgrown ruins:

> *"Cypress and ivy, weed and wallflower grown*
> *Matted and mass'd together, hillocks heap'd*
> *On what were chambers, arch crush'd, column strown*
> *In fragments, choked up vaults, and frescos steep'd*
> *In subterranean damps,..."*

Roman Forum from the Palatine Hill

History and Legend

It was inconvenient for political reasons that Romulus and Remus (*see* INTRO-DUCTION), twin sons of the Vestal Rhea Silvia and the god Mars, should survive. They were therefore abandoned on the banks of the Tiber but the river was in spate and their cradle came to rest on the Palatine. They survived thanks to a she-wolf which suckled them in the Lupercal cave. The shepherd Faustulus who witnessed this unusual event took charge of the twins and brought them up.

In the middle of the 8C BC Romulus ploughed a deep furrow around the Palatine lifting his ploughshare in three places: this was the beginning of Rome, a symbolic enclosure with three gateways: the Porta Mugonia, the Porta Romana and the Porta Scalae Caci. This is obviously a legendary account... but in 1949 traces of huts thought to date from the 8C and 7C BC were excavated on the legendary site of Romulus' house.

During the Republic the Palatine was a quiet residential area. Cicero lived on the hill as did Antony, the Triumvir, and Agrippa – Octavian's friend before becoming his son-in-law. Foreigners came to visit the shepherd's hut and the wolf's cave in the southwest face of the hill.

In 63 BC "on the ninth day before the Kalends of October, a little before day-break" Octavian was born. When he became the Emperor Augustus, the Palatine began to alter. He enlarged his house and then rebuilt it after it was destroyed by fire in the 3 BC. Tiberius, who succeeded him, Caligula, Claudius and Nero all lived on the Palatine but it was **Domitian**, the last Flavian emperor (81-96 AD), who transformed the hill by turning it into the Imperial Palace and giving it the appearance that has now been revealed by archeologists. The hollow which divided it into two peaks (Germalus and Palatium) was filled with new buildings, the ruins of which now occupy the central section of the plateau; they are the **Domus Flavia** and the **Domus Augustana**; the **Stadium** also dates from this period. In 191 the buildings on the Palatine were seriously damaged by fire. The Emperor Septimius Severus was not content with simply undertaking repairs. He enlarged the Imperial Palace to the south and built a monumental façade, the Septizonium, parallel with the Old Appian Way so that travellers arriving in Rome by this route would be immediately impressed by the grandeur of the capital. This section of the palace remained standing until Pope Sixtus V demolished it to provide building materials at the end of the 16C.

The Palatine began to go into decline in the 3C when Diocletian, Galerius, Maximian and Constantius deserted Rome and built new Imperial residences in Nicomedia, Sirmium, Milan and Trier respectively. In 330 Constantine moved the Imperial capital to Constantinople, formerly Byzantium, and the Palatine was abandoned.

The Christians generally ignored the Palatine plateau and built only on the slopes: in the 4C a sanctuary was dedicated to St Anastasia on the south side; on the north face the Church of St Sebastian was established in what had been a temple to the Sun; it had been built by the Emperor Elagabalus (218-222), a native of Emesa (modern Homs) in Syria, who dreamed of a religion which would combine the various oriental cults and appointed himself high priest to the Sun god.

In the 11C and 12C Rome became the prize in the struggles between the Pope and the Emperor and was studded with fortresses and towers; hence the description *Roma turrita*. The Frangipani family, who supported the Emperor, fortified the whole of the southeast face of the Palatine. When the Renaissance came the buildings on the Palatine (from which the word 'palace' is derived) were in ruins. The wealthy Roman families built villas on the site, surrounding them with vineyards and gardens: the Barberini near to St Sebastian, the Farnese on the northwest part of the hill between Tiberius' and Caligula's palaces. In the 16C the Mattei had built a villa on the site of the Domus Augustana; three centuries later an Englishman, Charles Mills, converted it into a sort of Romantic Gothic castle. This extraordinary building was demolished at the end of the 19C at the instigation of P Rosa, the archeologist in charge of the excavations.

Excavations – Investigative digging began in 1724 at the suggestion of Francis I of Parma, who had inherited the Farnese Villa. The Domus Flavia was the first building to see the light of day. About 50 years later a Frenchman, the Abbé Rancoureuil, excavated the Domus Augustana and the buildings overlooking the Circus Maximus. In 1860, under Napoleon III, archeologists discovered Tiberius' palace, Livia's house and the Temple of Apollo which was first attributed to Jupiter. The identification of the buildings on the Palatine has provoked passionate argument between archeologists and historians. Many of the constructions have never been discovered but excavations on the Palatine continue, particularly in the area of the Temple of Apollo.

Very little of the ruined buildings remains standing and it requires a big effort of the imagination to evoke the splendour of the ancient palaces on the Palatine.

Tour

Clivus Palatinus – This road approximately follows the hollow between the two peaks: the Palatium to the left, the Germalus to the right.

Walk straight up the path (south) leaving on the right the steps which go up to the Farnese Gardens.

The rectangular ditch (**1**) marks the site of Domitian's arch. The sections of high brick wall facing down the hill belonged to the portico of the Domus Flavia. The path emerges at the top of the hill in the centre of the artificial plateau which was created when Domitian filled in the hollow between the Palatium and the Germalus.

★**Domus Flavia** – This was the centre of official Imperial activity. Although the buildings have been razed to the ground, it is still possible to envisage them. There were three rooms behind the portico:

– the **Lararium** – the shrine of the household gods, the Lares – was the Emperor's private chapel;

– the Throne Room **(Sala del Trono)** was enormous (over 30m - 98ft wide by 40m - 131ft long) with huge statues standing in the recesses in the walls;

– the **Basilica**, where the Emperor dispensed justice, had an apse at one end and a row of columns down each of the long sides. Outside the west wall are traces of the west portico of the Domus.

Behind these three rooms is a courtyard **(Peristilium)** originally surrounded by a portico (traces of the columns remain). Suetonius wrote that Domitian was so hated by everyone for his injustice and cruelty that he had the walls of the portico faced with phengite (a very shiny stone) so that he could "see by reflection what was going on behind his back".

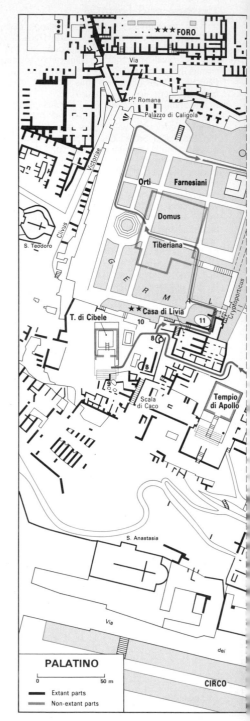

The octagonal basin at the centre of the court, which is now planted with flowers, was probably a fountain.

Beyond the peristyle is the **Triclinium**, the dining room, which was certainly the most beautiful room in the palace; part of the coloured marble floor has been preserved. It was supported on little brick pillars to allow the passage of warm air produced by an underground stove to heat the room.

The *triclinium* was flanked to right and left by two small leisure rooms, known in Latin as the *nymphaea*.

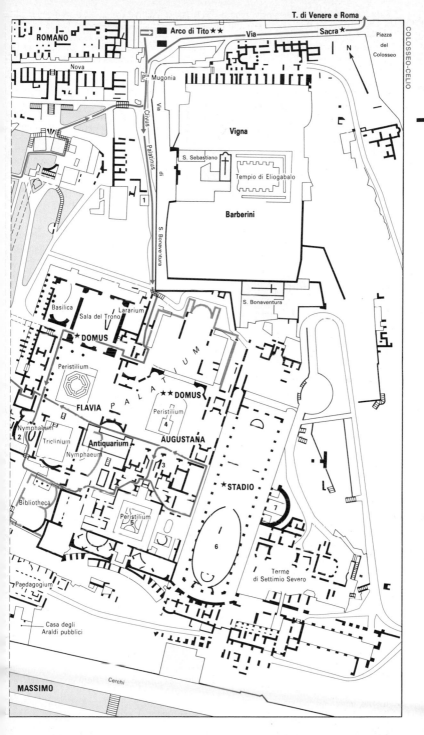

The one on the right is well preserved. Beneath it to the right are the remains (**2**) of a beautiful coloured marble floor which belonged to one of the rooms in Nero's Domus Transitoria which he built on the Palatine before embarking on his stunning Golden House.

The extant building in the far corner of the *nymphaeum* dates from the Farnese era (16C).

The traces of walls and columns and apses on the terrace behind the *triclinium* may mark the site of the libraries of the Imperial palace.

★**Sale sotterranee (Underground rooms)** ⊘ – These rooms are all that remained of houses from the Republican era and of Nero's constructions when they were buried under Domitian's building projects.

- Beneath the Basilica, a rectangular room: the paintings with which it was decorated are conserved in a room (**3**) east of the Antiquarium; they probably date from the Augustan era and depict the cult of Isis.
- Beneath the lararium, the **Griffin House** (Casa dei Grifi), sometimes also erroneously called "Catilina's house": it was built in the 2C BC (walls composed of irregular-sized stones mixed with mortar), altered in the 1C BC (walls composed of regular stone blocks arranged in a diamond pattern) and then altered again by Nero; many of the paintings have been removed to the Antiquarium for safe-keeping; one room contains a stucco relief of two griffins face to face.
- Beneath the peristyle: a circular chamber containing a well which communicates with another room by a passage. The discovery of this complex early this century caused quite a stir among archeologists who thought they had found the *Mundus*. At the time of the founding of Rome the *Mundus* was a well into which a handful of earth was thrown by each new immigrant who, through this symbolic gesture, became a citizen of the new city. In fact it is probably only a silo for water or grain.

★★**Domus Augustana** – This is not Augustus' own private house but the official Imperial residence. The rooms are arranged around two peristyles *(peristilium)*; one is very much lower than the other. At the centre of the upper peristyle (**4**), marked by an umbrella pine, is the base of a construction which was reached by a bridge from the edge of the surrounding basin. Around the sides are various living rooms.

The rooms on the south side of the upper peristyle overlook the lower peristyle. The central basin (**5**) which is composed of a pattern of compartments was designed to collect rain water. The palace itself faces the Circus Maximus from behind a concave façade.

Even in ruins the Domus Augustana gives an impression of grandeur and luxury owing to its sophisticated design, its soaring walls and the daring of some of the vaulting.

★**Stadio (Stadium)** – This was one of Domitian's projects. It looks like a gigantic trough (some 145m - 159yds long) surrounded by a two-storey portico. Some say it was designed to stage private games and spectacles for the emperor; others say it was a garden or an athletics ground. The small oval track (**6**) at the southern end dates from the 6C and is the work of Theodoric, the Ostrogoth, who occupied the Palatine at that period. The huge recess (**7**) in the centre of the long east side may have been reserved for the emperor.

On the east side of the Stadium are the ruins of a bathhouse attributed to Septimius Severus but probably built by Maxentius.

Antiquarium – *Same times as the Roman Forum.*

This museum is housed in a building which once belonged to the Convent of the Visitation, between the Domus Augustana and the Domus Flavia and contains articles and fragments found on the Palatine, although many pieces of sculpture have been removed to the National Roman Museum *(see PORTA PIA).*

In the room to the left of the entrance hall:

- the paintings (3C) which come from the Public Heralds' House (**Casa degli Araldi pubblici**) *(not open)* which is situated beside Via dei Cerchi: note the expressions on the faces;
- a fine painting *(left of the door)* from the Augustan era of Apollo with his lyre: beside him is the "Omphalos", a sacred stone laced with ribbons, which fell from the sky to land at Delphi and was thought by the Greeks to be the centre of the earth;
- a unique exhibit *(left arm of the room)*, which was found in the **Paedagogium** (the Imperial Pages' School): an immature hand has drawn Christ on the cross with an ass's head and a figure at the foot of the cross; written in Greek beneath is "Alexamenos adores his god"; perhaps it was drawn by a Roman to mock a Christian colleague.

In the inner section of the entrance hall: an altar to an unknown god; a money lender, C Sestius Calvinus, dedicated it in 1C BC without knowing whether to a god or a goddess.

In the room on the left: incomplete statue of Diana, very gracefully dressed.

Tempio di Apollo (Temple of Apollo) – For many years this temple was thought to be dedicated to Jupiter but it is probably the one mentioned by Suetonius: Augustus built a temple to Apollo "in a corner of his house on the Palatine which had been struck by lightning and which, according to the omens, Apollo was claiming for himself". The temple is fenced off; the podium and a column of the *pronaos* are recognisable.

★★Casa di Livia (Livia's House) ⊙ – This house which is named after Augustus' wife was probably where the Emperor himself lived. The diamond pattern on the walls and the style of the décor date the building to the end of the Republic. The wall paintings which had already deteriorated somewhat were detached and erected just in front of the walls to which they belonged; this means they can be appreciated in their original setting. The names given to the various rooms do not necessarily correspond to their use. On either side of the centre room (*tablinum* - study) are two narrow rooms (wings) where wax images of the family ancestors were kept or which, in more modest houses, were used as storerooms.

Left wing – The lower part of the wall is decorated to look like marble; above are panels showing people and griffins face to face.

Tablinum – On the righthand wall: a central panel, surrounded by architectural motifs, shows Io, Argos' daughter; Zeus fell in love with her and turned her into a heifer to protect her from the fury of his wife, Hera, who was nevertheless suspicious and set Argus, who had 100 eyes, to watch over the animal. The painting shows Hermes who was sent by Zeus to rescue Io.

On the lefthand wall: lead pipes engraved with the name IVLIAE AV (Julia Augusta). The archeologists who discovered this inscription in 1869 thought that it referred to Augustus' wife, the Empress, and attributed the house to Livia.

The rear wall depicts Galatea fleeing from Polyphemus.

Right wing – The decorations on the lefthand wall, although damaged by the opening of the door, are still fresh: simulated columns flanking beautiful garlands of fruit and leaves from which hang baskets, and sticks, horned animal heads, lyres and other representations of nature. Above on a yellow ground is a frieze showing people at work in the open air.

Cisterne (Cisterns) (8) – They date from the 6C BC; one is shaped like a beehive while the other is uncovered.

Scala di Caco (Cacus' Steps) – This was one of the three original approaches to the Palatine. The steps are named after a local villain, Cacus, who is linked in legend to Hercules. When Hercules was returning to the Argos with the cattle stolen from Geryon, he halted on the banks of the Tiber; Cacus, an evil three-headed monster who breathed fire from his three mouths, took the opportunity to steal three animals; he made them walk backwards to avoid detection but Hercules was not fooled and he killed Cacus.

Capanne del villagio di Romolo (Cabins from Romulus' village) (9) – Together with the Forum cemetery these huts are some of the earliest traces of the city (8C - 7C BC). The modern roof which covers them creates a real reliquary. Three huts have been discovered, oval or rectangular and sunk in the ground. The ring of holes held the posts which supported the walls and the roof. The gap in the south side (facing the Tiber) marks the doorway and is flanked by smaller post holes which indicate the possibility of a porch. The ditch surrounding each emplacement was probably to drain off the rain water from the roof.

Tempio di Cibele (Temple of Cybele) – Cybele, the great goddess of Phrygia (also called the Mother of the gods, the Great Mother or Magna Mater) was the personification of the powers of nature. Her cult was introduced into Rome late in the 3C or early in the 2C BC. In 204 BC at the height of the Second Punic War a hail of stones fell on Rome. The priests appealed to the gods and the Senate was obliged to send for the **"black stone"** symbol of the goddess Cybele, from Pessinus in Asia Minor. The temple on the Palatine was inaugurated in 191 and then rebuilt by Augustus after several fires. Today only the base of the *cella* walls remains in the shade of a group of holm oaks.

The goddess' statue (2C) has been placed under an arch (**10**) of Tiberius' palace.

Each year from 4 to 20 April a festival took place in front of the temple: the Megalesia which consisted of theatrical presentations and circus acts and had been founded in 204 in honour of Cybele. Terence's comedy "Andria" was played for the first time during the festival in 168 BC; but on that occasion the audience preferred the tightrope walkers, perhaps because Terence did not have Plautus' biting wit "nor his coarse jokes, his broad humour, his puns, his quips..."

Domus Tiberiana – The arches facing Cybele's Temple belonged to the rear façade of Tiberius' palace. Only a few traces of this huge rectangular building are visible since Cardinal Farnese's gardens cover the greater part of it.

The main façade of the palace faced the Forum. Caligula extended the building as far as Via Nova; Trajan and Hadrian added the ranges overlooking Clivus Victoriae.

Cryptoporticus – This is a network of passages, partially underground, which probably linked the various Imperial buildings which occupied the hill. It dates from Nero's reign although the arm linking up with Domitian's Domus Flavia must have been added later.

The stuccoes which decorated the vaulting in the section of the passage near Livia's house have been removed to the Antiquarium and replaced by copies.

The oval basin (**11**) on the left of the steps leading up to the Farnese gardens was a fish tank in the southeast corner of Tiberius' palace.

Orti Farnesiani (Farnese Gardens) – The gardens were laid out in the middle of the 16C by Cardinal Alexander Farnese, Paul III's nephew. The entrance, set in a semicircle at the level of the Forum (which was higher then than now), gave access to a series of terraces rising up the north face of the Palatine. On the flat top of the hill, over the ruins of Tiberius's palace, stretched the Farnese's magnificent botanical garden, one of the richest in the world at that time. The northwest corner of the gardens gives an excellent **view**★★ of the Forum, the Tabularium, the Senatorial Palace, the monument to Victor Emmanuel II, the domes of the Church of St Luke and St Martina and of the two churches next to Trajan's Column, the Militia Tower etc. In the northeast corner of the gardens are two buildings (reconstructed) which formed a complex comprising two aviaries above a nymphaeum. From the terrace there is a pleasant **view**★★, particularly at sunset, of the Basilica of Maxentius, the belfry of Santa Francesca Romana and the upper storeys of the Colosseum.

Below the aviaries there used to be a monumental gate marking the entrance to the gardens. It was begun by Vignola and completed by Girolamo Rainaldi but taken down in 1882. It now stands on the east side of Via di S Gregorio *(see plan under COLOSSEO)*.

Leave the Palatine by Clivus Palatinus, turning right into Via Sacra at Titus' Arch to visit the other monuments which belong to the Forum but are accessible only from outside the gates.

★**Tempio di Venere e Roma (Temple of Venus and Rome)** – The temple was built between 121 and 136 AD by Hadrian, completed by Antoninus Pius and restored by Maxentius, on the site of the vestibule to Nero's Golden House. It was the largest temple in Rome (110m - 361ft by 53m - 174ft) and designed in the Greek style with steps on all sides (the majority of Roman temples had only one flight of steps leading up to the *pronaos*). It was surrounded by a colonnade and uniquely comprised two cellae with apses back to back. One was dedicated to the goddess Rome and faced the Forum; the other was dedicated to Venus and faced the Colosseum.

The plans for the temple were drawn by Hadrian who was keen on architecture. He also designed two gigantic seated figures to be set in niches which were disproportionately small. Trajan's brilliant architect, Apollodorus of Damascus, commented that "if the figures tried to stand they would bump their heads on the vault". He had already poured scorn on the Emperor's rather peculiar taste for painting pumpkins. It was too much; Hadrian had the architect silenced once and for all.

The part of the temple which faces the Forum has been incorporated in the Church of Santa Francesca Romana and the adjoining convent of Olivetan monks. An idea of the temple's appearance is given by a few columns which were re-erected in 1935; the position of the missing parts is marked by bushes of privet, box and oleander.

Santa Francesca Romana – In 8C an oratory dedicated to St Peter and St Paul was built in the western half of the Temple of Venus and Rome by Pope Paul I. In the following century it replaced the Church of Santa Maria Antiqua in the Forum and was called Santa Maria Nova. The church was placed under the patronage of Santa Francesca Romana (St Frances of Rome) when she was canonized in 1608. The 12C Romanesque **belltower**★ is one of the most elegant in Rome.

The façade by Carlo Lombardi (1615) is characteristic of the Counter-Reformation. The use of a single order of flat pilasters resting on a high portico lends it a certain solemnity. Inside there is a beautiful 17C coffered ceiling.

Apsidal mosaic – The Virgin and Child are enthroned between St Peter and St Andrew, St James and St John. The mosaic dates from c1160 at a period when mosaic art was marked by a certain eclecticism: the vivid colours of the ancient art together with the rigidity of the figures typical of Byzantine art.

Right transept – Two stones are preserved behind a grating; they are supposed to bear the print of St Peter's knees. He prayed at length to God to prevent Simon Magus from flying and Simon crashed to earth near the church. The *Acts of the Apostles* (VIII, 9-25) tell the story of the sorcerer who practised in Samaria and who wanted to acquire spiritual powers from the Apostles for money. He is the source of the word simony.

There is also a monument (16C) to Gregory XI, the last French pope, who brought the Holy See back to Rome from Avignon in 1377. The central low relief shows St Peter entering Rome; the flanking statues are Faith and Prudence.

Crypt – Opposite the remains of St Frances of Rome is a marble low relief showing the saint and an angel (17C work by one of Bernini's pupils).

Sacristy – Beautiful painting of Santa Maria Nova showing a Virgin and Child which art historians date to the 5C or 8C.

Take Via dei Fori Imperiali.

Santi Cosma e Damiano (Basilica of St Cosmas and St Damian) – The basilica was dedicated in 526 by Pope Felix IV to two saints of Arabian origin, Cosmas and Damian, twin brothers whose help was invoked to cure illness. The church was established in the Temple of Romulus and in an adjacent room which had been the library of Vespasian's Forum; it was the first Christian church to occupy a pagan building in the Roman Forum. When the relics of the two saints were discovered in the 16C the popes began to alter the original church. In the 17C Clement VIII reduced the width of the nave by creating side chapels which cut off the outer edges of the mosaic on the chancel arch. The floor was raised and a doorway was opened in the west wall and a plaster arcade was added in front of the apse.

★**Ceiling** – Beautiful 17C coffered ceiling showing the triumph of St Cosmas and St Damian *(centre)* and *(at each end)* the coat of arms with the bees of Cardinal Francesco Barberini, who promoted the greater part of the 17C alterations.

★**Mosaics** – Those on the chancel arch date from the late 7C and show the Lamb of God surrounded by seven candelabra and four angels. The angels on the left and right, symbolizing the Evangelists, St Luke and St John, have survived the 17C alterations. The lamb and the throne were restored in 1936.

The mosaics in the apse date from the 6C. In the centre is the figure of Christ against a sunset sky. At his sides are the apostles Peter and Paul presenting St Cosmas and St Damian, dressed in brown. On the left is Pope Felix IV offering a model of his church while on the right is St Theodore dressed in a handsome chlamys (short mantle) like a Byzantine courtier. Below, partially screened by the Baroque altar (1637) is the Paschal Lamb surrounded by 12 beautiful angels representing the apostles and the Church.

Southeast chapel – *Facing the entrance.* Above the altar is a curious fresco showing the living Christ on the cross, a work in the Byzantine style, repainted in the 17C.

Neighbouring sights are described in the followng chapters: CAMPIDOGLIO – CAPI-TOLINO; COLOSSEO – CELIO; FORI IMPERIALI; PIAZZA VENEZIA.

GIANICOLO ★

Tour 2 hours

One of the oldest legends in Roman mythology maintains that the **Janiculum** Hill (Monte Gianicolo) was the site of the city founded by the god Janus, whence its name, who had several children, one of whom, Tiber, gave his name to the river.

For many years the Janiculum was a country district. It was not until the 17C that Urban VIII constructed a defensive wall with bastions on the line of the present-day Viale delle Mura Aurelie and Viale delle Mura Gianicolensi.

For grown-ups...

An open-air summer festival of improvised dance, drama, music and entertainment is held at the **Anfiteatro della Quercia del Tasso** in Passeggiata del Gianicolo.

and for children...

Carlo Piantadosi, the last active puppeteer in Rome, enacts his shows at the **Teatrino di marionette** in Piazzale del Gianicolo daily between 3pm and 8pm and additionally between 10am and 1pm on Sundays.

From Mucius Scaevola to Garibaldi – The Janiculum seems to have inspired many of the heroic acts, legendary or true, which have shaped the history of Rome.

The oldest goes back to the 6C BC when the town had broken free of the Etruscan kings and was being besieged by Lars Porsena. Mucius, a young Roman noble, infiltrated the enemy camp on the Janiculum in order to kill their chief. Unfortunately he made a mistake and killed one of the chief's aides; he was immediately arrested. To prove to Lars Porsena that life was of little account to a Roman defending his country, he put his right hand on a burning brasier. Porsena was so struck by such bravery that he let him go. Mucius was henceforth nicknamed Scaevola, left-handed.

In his footsteps came Cloelia, a young woman who, according to Livy, showed a courage "without precedent among women". Held hostage in Porsena's camp, she escaped with her companions and made them swim the Tiber to reach Rome.

In 1849 the Janiculum was the scene of one of the battles in the struggle for Italian unity. Garibaldi defended it valiantly in the name of the Roman Republic against the French troops commanded by General Oudinot; on 4th July the papal government was re-established after a month of bloody combat, particularly in the Villa Pamphili.

MAJOR SITES

Porta Settimiana – This was one of the gates in the Aurelian wall (Mura Aureliane); it was repaired by Alexander VI (1492-1503) and reinforced with merlons.

Palazzo Corsini ⊙ – The palace was built in the 15C by the Riario, nephews of Sixtus IV, and passed in the 18C to Cardinal Corsini, nephew of Clement XII, who had it rebuilt by Ferdinando Fuga. Now it houses an art gallery and the **Accademia dei Lincei**, a learned society of scholars and men of letters.

Galleria nazionale di pittura (National Art Gallery) – Part of **Room II** is devoted to Tuscan Primitive paintings including an admirable *Triptych* by Fra Angelico *(left of the entrance)* showing the *Last Judgement*, the *Ascension and Pentecost*. This painter, who experienced the silence of the cloister, expressed his deep faith by painting serene and saintly faces (central panel of the *Last Judgement*) and a Christ which inspires adoration (right panel of the *Ascension*). The room also contains a *Portrait of Philip II* by Titian. The stiff posture and death-like complexion are striking. Opposite is the painting by Rubens of *St Sebastian being ministered to by Angels*.

In **Room III** *St John the Baptist* by Caravaggio, which is in fact the portrait of a young man, is hung next to works by painters influenced by the master of tenebrism; these include, *Judith and Holophernes* by the Flemish artist Gerard Seghers and *Herodias* by Simon Vouet. **Room VI** contains canvases by 17C artists who tried to recreate the rich colours of Venetian painters a century earlier. The best examples *(left of the entrance)* are the *Triumph of Ovid* by Nicolas Poussin and the *Portrait of a Gentleman* by Andrea Sacchi *(in the far corner)*.

Villa Doria Pamphili

French interlude

On 31 August 1797 the Ambassador of the Directory, Joseph Bonaparte, accompanied by the young General Léonard Duphot, settled in the Palazzo Corsini. On 28 December a riot broke out in front of the palace led by a few revolutionaries who called for the intervention of the French against the papal government. Shots were fired and General Duphot was killed.

On 10 February 1798 General Berthier besieged Rome and drove out Pius VI who died in exile in Valence in France. Until 29 September 1799 Rome took its cue from the French Republic.

Room VII is dedicated to the Emilian school. It also displays some paintings by Guido Reni, including *Salome and the head of John the Baptist*, and the *Head of Christ crowned with Thorns* by Guercino.

In **Room VIII** are hung works of the Naples Baroque School including battle scenes by Rosa di Salvatore (1615-1673) as well as a large canvas – *Venus discovering the lifeless Adonis* – by the Spanish painter Ribera who settled in Naples in 1616 in the service of the Duke of Osuna.

★★**Villa Farnesina** ⊙ – The villa in its garden setting was built from 1508-11 for Agostino Chigi (1465-1520) the great banker. Known as the Magnificent, he entertained in sumptuous style, including Pope Leo X among his guests.

The villa is designed as a suburban house with two projecting wings. For the construction and the décor he commissioned the best Renaissance artists: Baldassarre Peruzzi, architect and painter, Raphael with his usual following of Giulio Romano, Francesco Penni, Giovanni da Udine, Sebastiano del Piombo, Sodoma. The friendship linking all these men is enshrined in the Farnesina Villa: Agostino Chigi was Raphael's most ardent patron and Leo X had a sincere affection for him. None of them saw the sack of the city which brought the Roman Renaissance to an end. Raphael died aged 37 on Good Friday 1520; a few days later came Chigi's death; the following year Leo X succumbed to a 'slight fever'.

Later in the 16C the villa was sold to Cardinal Alessandro Farnese and assumed the name of its new owner.

Gallery in the Villa Farnesina

Tour – The collection of paintings to be seen in this house is one of the gems of the Renaissance. On the ceiling of the **gallery** along the garden front is a fresco, depicting the legend of Cupid and Psyche (in the centre *The Council of the Gods* and *The Marriage of Cupid and Psyche*), painted by Raphael assisted by Giulio Romano, Francesco Penni and Giovanni da Udine. Finished in 1520 these paintings contain elements which were to become characteristic of the Mannerist style (a series of scenes as in a tapestry framed by garlands).

At the eastern end of the gallery is the **Galatea** room (1511) where Nereus' sea-maiden has been painted by Raphael riding in a shell drawn by dolphins *(right of the entrance)*. The monstrous Polyphemus as well as the scenes from Ovid's *Metamorphoses (in the lunettes)* are by Sebastiano del Piombo. The Constellations on the ceiling are the work of Baldasarre Peruzzi. The young man's head painted in grisaille *(left of the entrance)* is probably by Sebastiano del Piombo but tradition attributes it to Michelangelo who wanted to show Raphael that his figures were too small.

On the **first floor** the **salon** is decorated with landscapes in *trompe-l'œil* by Peruzzi and his assistants; views of Rome are revealed between the painted columns.

In the next room, formerly a bedroom, the **Marriage of Roxana and Alexander** is by Sodoma (1477-1549). Dismissed from his work in the Vatican by Julius II in favour of Raphael, Sodoma was commissioned by Agostino Chigi to decorate this room, probably in 1509. In a Renaissance setting Alexander extends the crown to Roxana against a cloud of cherubs. The merit of this pleasant painting lies in the beauty of the figures and the harmony and balance of the composition.

These qualities are lacking in the other scenes: Alexander and Darius' mother, Vulcan and three little angels *(on either side of the chimney piece)*, the battle scene. To the left of the entrance are Alexander and Bucephalus (late 16C).

Gabinetto nazionale delle Strampe ⊙ – The Villa Farnesina presently accommodates the Istituto nazionale per la Grafica, a body which was founded in 1975 as a collective archive of prints and drawings from the 15C-19C. Highlights include Baroque works of the Roman and Florentine Schools. The reference section includes photographic material and computer databases.

On the south side the Palazzo Corsini a street of the same name leads to the Orto Botanico.

Orto Botanico (Botanic Garden) – This garden (c12ha - 30 acres) contains over 3500 cultivated species and eight glasshouses ($1800m^2$ - 19 380sq ft); it provides a pleasant place of relaxation among the luxuriant vegetation of the Janiculum.

Return to the Porta Settimiana and turn right into Via Garibaldi; beyond the junction with Via G Mameli, take the second steps on the right which lead to San Pietro in Montorio.

★San Pietro in Montorio – This church, which has a commanding view of Rome, was built in Sixtus IV's reign at the end of the 15C by Ferdinand II of Spain and dedicated to St Peter who, according to a 15C legend, was crucified on the site.

The simple façade is typical of the Renaissance as is the interior, which consists of a nave flanked by apsidal chapels. The chancel was damaged in the siege of 1849 and has been restored.

Several Renaissance works have survived, particularly the **Flagellation★** *(first chapel on the right)*, a fresco by Sebastiano del Piombo, clearly influenced by the monumental art of Michelangelo.

The ceiling in the next chapel was painted by Baldassarre Peruzzi (1481-1536). The pale fresco of the Virgin, by Pomarancio (1552-1626), and the two transept chapels were added at the Counter-Reformation. In the righthand chapel the allegorical figures on the tombs and the cherubs on the balustrade are by Bartolomeo Ammanati, a pupil of Michelangelo. Beatrice Cenci *(see Index)* is buried beneath the high altar.

The fourth chapel on the left with its multitude of statues is typical of the Counter-Reformation.

Bernini designed the second chapel on the left in the Baroque period; his pupils were responsible for the sculptures.

★Il "tempietto" – *Access from outside the church through the iron gates on the right, from inside the church through the fourth chapel on the right.*

This charming miniature temple was one of Bramante's first works on his arrival in Rome in 1499. Despite its small scale the construction has all the grandeur and rigorous conformity of a Classical building. Perfectly proportioned, it is surrounded by a portico supported on Doric columns and surmounted by a dome.

Behind the building in a little chapel is a small cavity said to have held St Peter's cross.

Bramante's Tempietto

★★★View of Rome – *From the open space in front of the church.*

The view extends from Monte Mario *(left)* and Castel Sant'Angelo right across the city with its various roofs and domes: to the right of the monument to Victor Emmanuel II and the Capitol are the arches of the Basilica of Maxentius in the Forum; further right again beyond the green expanse of the Palatine is the façade of St John Lateran spiked with statues.

Return to Via Garibaldi.

On the left is a **monument (A)** set up in 1941 to those who died to ensure that Rome was not excluded when Italy was unified.

Fontana Paola (Pauline Fountain) – This fountain was commissioned by Pope Paul V; its shape – a commemorative arch – shows the nascent taste for Baroque pomp.

Either make a detour uphill to Porta San Pancrazio and the road of the same name which leads to the Villa Doria Pamphili (1 km - 1/2mile - 3/4 hr on foot Return) or turn right into Passeggiata del Gianicolo.

Villa Doria Pamphili – A vast public park surrounds a 17C country house *(casino)* which is decorated with statues and low relief sculptures and set among terraces.

PASSEGGIATA DEL GIANICOLO (JANICULUM WALK)

This road winds along the crest of the hill beneath the umbrella pines; it is lined by busts of Garibaldi's men and has some of the finest **views★★★** of Rome.

Monumento a Giuseppe Garibaldi (Giuseppe Garibaldi Monument) – In Emilio Gallori's grandiose work (1895) the hero is shown on horseback, gazing towards the Vatican, the object of his revolutionary struggles.

From here there is a **view** of Rome from Villa Medici to St John Lateran; in the distance are the Alban Hills. The cannon is fired daily at midday from below the parapet.

Monumento ad Anita Garibaldi (Anita Garibaldi Monument) – Garibaldi's wife is shown as an amazon as she appeared at her husband's side. After the 1849 retreat they tried to reach Venice which was fighting the Austrians but Anita fell ill and died near Ravenna. This monument was erected in 1932.

Further on near the lighthouse there is a fine **view** over the whole of the city of Rome.

Further on go down the steps on the right which cuts off the hairpin bend of the Passeggiata.

The old tree stump (**B**) is all that remains of the oak tree beneath which Tasso *(see below)* used to sit and reflect on all his misfortunes *(inscription)*.

View of Rome – *From the square in front of the Ospedale del Bambino Gesù (Hospital of the Infant Jesus).* To the left is the drum of Castel Sant'Angelo surmounted by its angel and the white mass of the Law Courts; just below the Janiculum across the river is the dome of San Giovanni dei Fiorentini; in the background on the edge of the park is the Villa Medici with its two towers and the dome of San Carlo al Corso; slightly to the right are the two belfries of the Trinità dei Monti; then the Quirinal Palace behind the shallow dome of the Pantheon; next, nearer the river, is the high dome of Sant'Andrea delle Valle with the lower dome of the Gesù Church behind it; in the background is the Militia Tower; before it rise the monument to Victor Emmanuel II and the flat façade of Santa Maria d'Aracoeli.

Sant'Onofrio ⊘ – This church has retained the appearance and atmosphere of a hermitage which it received from its founder, a monk of the order of the Hermits of St Jerome, in 1434. It was here that Tasso (1544-1595) came to die, pursued to the end, even to madness, by his religious doubts; his poem *The Liberation of Jerusalem* is a masterpiece of Italian Renaissance poetry. Chateaubriand too would have liked to finish his days here; on the outside wall of the church overlooking the river is a long quotation from his *Memories from Beyond the Grave.* On the right of the main door beneath the arcade are frescoes by Domenichino illustrating the life of St Jerome (1605). The attractive frescoes in the **apse★** were probably painted by Baldassarro Peruzzi assisted by Pinturicchio.

The graceful cloisters were built in the 15C.

Neighbouring sights are described in the following chapters: CASTEL SANT'ANGELO; TRASTEVERE; VATICANO – SAN PIETRO.

ISOLA TIBERINA – TORRE ARGENTINA★★

Tour 2 hours

From Tiber Island to Torre Argentina the walk passes through the old Jewish district with its synagogue to the Portico of Octavius, once a great monument but now reduced to an insignificant ruin. Torre Argentina takes its name from the residence of a 16C papal official, who named his house after his native city, Strasbourg (Argentoratum in Latin). Within this district lies the Area Sacra (Sacred Precinct), a large archeological site dating from the Republican period.

★ISOLA TIBERINA

This peaceful spot was the subject of many legends connected with the origins of Rome. The island is said to have been created by silt piling up on the crops of the Tarquins thrown into the Tiber when the last king of this line, Tarquin

Necessary sustenance...

For a flavour of Jewish Rome honed through the generations, head for the **Forno del Ghetto** at via Portico d'Ottavia 1. This baker specialises in ricotta-cheesecake, almond delicacies and marzipan, and the most delicious tarts.

the Proud, was driven out of Rome in the 6C BC. It it also said that the island's shape is that of the boat which brought Aesculapius, the god of Medicine, from Epidauros in Greece. To stress the resemblance the southern point of the island has been paved with slabs of travertine round an obelisk, set up like a mast. Downstream from Ponte Fabricio and below the Church of San Bartolomeo are pieces of travertine which faced the bow of the "ship" *(see below)*. Aesculapius arrived in Rome in 293 BC in the form of a serpent. The boat had scarcely come alongside when the serpent disembarked and hid on the island; the Romans interpreted this as the serpent's desire to have a temple built on that spot. The sanctuary was built on the site now occupied by St Bartholomew's Church. The hospital of the Brothers of St John of God (*Fatebenefratelli* - literally do-good-brothers) continues the island's medical tradition.

San Bartolomeo (St Bartholomew's Church) – Its Baroque façade and the Romanesque belltower (12C) rise from the centre of the island. Inside the building, at the centre of the great staircase, is a well (*c*12m - 39ft deep) surmounted by an ancient column carved with 12C saintly figures. One of the cannon balls fired during the French siege in 1849 is lodged in the wall *(left)* of the Lady Chapel at the back of the church. South of Ponte Fabricio, near the church, are the remains of travertine which faced the bow of the "ship" (**A**) *(see above)*.

According to tradition it was in the hospital attached to this church that Rahere, courtier to Henry I of England, recovered from an attack of malaria, usually fatal in those days. He had vowed, if he was spared, to found a priory and a hospital and on his return Henry granted land in Smithfield in London where the church and the hospital still stand (*see* Michelin Green Guide: LONDON).

From the square take the steps (right) which lead to the bank of the Tiber. Downstream of the island, in the middle of the river, are the remains of Ponte Rotto.

Ponte Rotto – In origin this bridge (the Broken Bridge) goes back to the Pons Aemilius which was built here towards the middle of the 2C BC. It had already collapsed twice when Pope Gregory XII rebuilt it in about 1575. It collapsed again in 1598. Only one arch remains to challenge the Tiber; poets have been attracted by the strange spectacle of a single span stranded in midstream cut off from the roar of the traffic.

Horatius Cocles and the Pons Sublicius – Downstream from the Ponte Rotto and its modern neighbour, the Palatine Bridge, was the Pons Sublicius, the first to span the Tiber, which was built to foster relations between the Latins on the Palatine and the Etruscans on the right bank.

Each year on 14 May human figures made of willow were offered to the river to appease it. The bridge was made of wood and the law forbade any iron to be used in its repair: it had to be easy to dismantle in the event of relations between the two peoples deteriorating. This happened when the last Etruscan king, Tarquin the Proud, was driven out of Rome in the 6C BC. Livy gives a good description; the Etruscans marched on Rome under the banner of Lars Porsenna; Horatius Cocles was guarding the bridge. While his men were dismantling the bridge, he held back the enemy single-handed: "withering the Etruscan leaders with his look, he challenged them one by one or taunted them." Finally the bridge was breached. Horatius jumped into the Tiber and rejoined his men. He was treated as a hero: he was granted land, his statue was put up in the Comitium and "every citizen set aside part of his own income to be given to Horatius".

The incident is also well known through Lord Macaulay's stirring ballad *Horatius* from his *Lays of Ancient Rome*.

Ponte Cestio (Pons Cestius) – It links Tiber Island to the Trastevere district. Its origins go back to 1C BC; it was partially rebuilt in 19C. To the left there is a view of the belltower of Santa Maria in Cosmedin and to the right of the Janiculum Hill with its lighthouse.

Cross to the north side of the island.

Ponte Fabricio

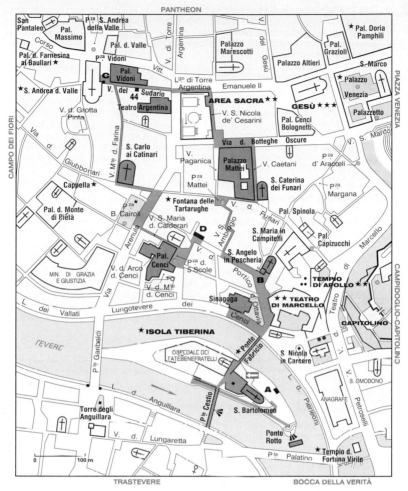

★Ponte Fabricio (Pons Fabricius) – It is sometimes also known as the Bridge of Four Heads on account of the Hermes with four heads set at the far end. It is the only Roman bridge to survive intact from the Classical period. Above the arches is an inscription stating that the bridge was built in 62 BC by the Consul Fabricius. It links the left bank with Tiber Island.

Cross the bridge.

From Isola Tiberina to Torre Argentina

Ghetto – The Jews who formerly lived in Trastevere moved to the left bank of the Tiber in the 13C. Pope Paul IV (1555-59) had the area enclosed within a wall thus creating the Roman ghetto. The wall ran from Ponte Fabricio along Via del Portico d'Ottavia returning to the riverbank along Via del Progresso. The gates were opened at dawn and closed in the evening on the 4 000 inhabitants (in 1656). The ghetto ended in 1848; the walls were taken down and the houses demolished in 1888.

Sinagoga (Synagogue) – The synagogue, inaugurated in 1904, occupies part of the old ghetto. It was designed by Costa and Armanni in the Assyrian-Babylonian style. The great dome is visible from all over Rome.

Museo di Arte Ebraica (Hebrew Museum) ⊘ – Souvenirs of the Jewish community in Rome together with an exhibition of liturgical articles.

Take Via Portico di Ottavia.

Portico di Ottavia (Portico of Octavia) (**B**) – This was one of the richest monuments in Rome. It was vast, extending back as far as the present Piazza di Campitelli and the Church of Santa Caterina dei Funari.
All that now remains is part of the entrance porch *(propylaea)* which faces the Tiber. The remaining Corinthian columns supporting sections of the entablature belonged to a portico built by Septimius Severus (193-211).

The original portico had been built in the 2C BC by Cecilius Metellus, who defeated the Macedonians, as an enclosure for two temples dedicated to Juno and Jupiter respectively. Augustus rebuilt the portico, which he dedicated to his sister Octavia, and included two public libraries, one Latin and one Greek, as well as an assembly hall where the Senate sometimes met.

Sant'Angelo in Pescheria – Nowadays the *propylaea* of Octavia's Portico serves only as a monumental entrance to the little Church of Sant'Angelo in Pescheria (founded in the 8C).

The name, like those of the neighbouring streets, recalls the **fish market** which occupied the Antique ruins in the 12C. The activity surrounding the stalls set out on the huge paving stones in front of the church and in Via di Sant'Angelo in Pescheria made this one of the most picturesque corners of Rome.

On the right of the portico is a stone bearing a Latin inscription which says that fish above a certain length went to the Conservators of Rome. This privilege was abolished in 1798.

West of the church turn right into Via Sant'Ambrogio to reach Piazza Mattei.

★**Fontana delle Tartarughe (Turtle Fountain)** – This is a late Renaissance work (1581-84) full of grace and charm by Taddeo Landini probably from a design by Giacomo della Porta. Local legend tells how Duke Mattei, the owner of the neighbouring palace and an inveterate gambler, lost his fortune in one night. His prospective father-in-law advised him to look for another fiancée. To prove that a Mattei, even when ruined, could achieve wonders, he had the fountain built in one night.

Palazzo Mattei – Five palaces were built by the Mattei in the 16C and 17C; they occupy the confined space bordered by Piazza Mattei, Via dei Funari, Via Caetani, Via delle Botteghe Oscure and Via Paganica. Carlo Maderno (1598-1611) was the architect of the palace with two entrances *(31 Via dei Funari or 32 Via Caetani)*. The decoration of the courtyards (statues, busts and low reliefs) shows the taste for antiquities which was then the fashion.

Santa Caterina ai Funari – *Closed*. This church has a very graceful façade, which was built from 1500 to 1564; the shallow pilasters are typical of the Renaissance but the many garlands indicate an attempt at the decorative effects typical of the Counter-Reformation. Unusual belltower.

> ### Via delle Botteghe Oscure
>
> This street was famous in the Middle Ages for its dimly lit shops which had probably been set up in the ruins of Balbus' Theatre. The street was widened in 1935 as part of a government plan for renovation.

In Via Caetani a commemorative bronze plaque marks the spot where the body of the statesman Aldo Moro was found on 9 May 1978, 54 days after he had been kidnapped by Red Brigade terrorists.

At the north end of Via Caetani turn left into Via delle Botteghe Oscure.

★★AREA SACRA DEL LARGO ARGENTINA
(LARGO ARGENTINA SACRED PRECINCT)

This is the name given to a group of ruins excavated between 1926 and 1929 in the Largo Argentina. The remains, which date from the days of the ancient Roman Republic, are among the oldest found in Rome. This marshy ground on the banks of the Tiber near the Campus Martius was often flooded. The necessary work of draining and embanking meant raising the ground level and modifying the buildings on the site. Traces of five building levels from the 5C BC to the beginning of the Empire have been revealed by the archeologists. In antiquity this large precinct was at the heart of a busy district: to the southeast stood the theatre built by Balbus in Augustus' reign, to the west Pompey's theatre and Curia, to the north the rear façade of Agrippa's baths and the Saepta *(plan Rome during the Empire)*.

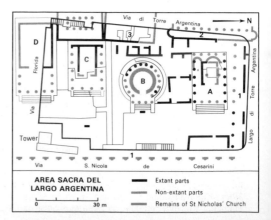

AREA SACRA DEL LARGO ARGENTINA

0   30 m

Extant parts
Non-extant parts
Remains of St Nicholas' Church

Tour – *The best overall view is from the east side (Via S Nicola de' Cesarini).* The Sacred Precinct consists primarily of four temples, including a round one, all facing east on to a square paved in travertine in the Imperial period. As it is not known to which gods the temples were dedicated, they are known as temples A, B, C and D.

Temple C – This is the oldest temple. Excavation of the podium has revealed the presence of blocks of tufa similar to those used in the construction of the Servian Wall (Mura Serviane); the original building therefore dates back to the 6C or 5C BC. The plan is that of the early Roman temples which followed the Etruscan model: a triple *cella* (containing three shrines), a fairly high podium without columns at the rear. In the Imperial period the *cella* was rebuilt at a higher level, the columns and the podium were faced with stucco and the floor was covered with mosaics.

The tower and portico in the southeast corner of the site, which were preserved during the excavations in 1932, were originally part of a group of medieval houses, built in the 12C near the Church of San Salvatore which stood in front of Temple C.

Temple A – The first building on this site dates from the 4C or 3C BC. The present remains of a temple surrounded by columns date from the 2C or 1C BC.

By the 12C the ground was level with the top of the podium; Temple A was converted into a church dedicated to St Nicholas, with a nave and south aisle both ending in an apse.

Temple B – This circular building dates from the 2C BC and may have been dedicated to Juno (a statue which is probably a representation of this goddess was found in the temple). The podium of tufa was covered by one of peperine which was in turn covered in stucco. The *cella* was enlarged and the surrounding columns were linked by tufa walls. The floor was raised and re-covered in mosaic.

Temple D – The greater part of this temple lies beneath the road (Via Florida).

The north and east sides of the precinct were bounded by a portico (**1**). The high wall (**2**) on the west side behind Temple A belonged to a public lavatory. The drainage trough is still visible. Further south several large blocks (**3**) have been identified as the remains of the podium of Pompey's Curia where, in 44 BC, Julius Caesar was assassinated during the Ides of March.

From Area Sacra to Palazzo Cenci

Teatro Argentina (Argentina Theatre) – The first performance of the Barber of Seville took place here in 1816 and was one of the most resounding failures in the annals of opera. It is said that Pauline Borghese *(qv)* was behind it: she had wanted to help the tenor who was a friend of hers to avenge himself on Rossini who had refused to alter the score.

Go west along Via del Sudario.

Palazzo Vidoni – *Nos 10-16.* The decision to build a palace here was taken by the Caffarelli, a rich Roman family, in 1500 and Raphael was asked to design it. One of his pupils, Lorenzo Lotto, supervised its construction. The robust elegance of the palace was altered in the 18C and 19C when the façade was enlarged and re-sited to face the Corso Vittorio Emanuele II and the top storey was added.

Tradition would have it that Charles V lodged here in 1536. In 1853 the Bishop of Perugia, the future Leo XIII, lived on the ground floor. Later the building became the offices of the Fascist Party.

Casa del Burcardo (Johannes Burckard's House) ☉ – *No 44.* There used to be a tower on the site where Burckard, the papal Master of Ceremonies, built his house in 1503. He called it Torre Argentina after the Latin name (Argentoratum) for Strasbourg, his home town. The house, which has been restored, is in the Gothic and Renaissance style. It contains a library and a collection of masks, theatrical costumes, play bills etc. connected with the theatre.

Turn right into Piazza Vidoni.

Statua dell'Abate Luigi (**C**) – This statue of a Roman in a toga is one of the famous 'talking' statues which exchanged comments with Pasquino, Madam Lucrezia and Marforio.

Take Via Monte della Farina south as far as Piazza B Cairoli.

San Carlo ai Catinari – The grandiose but rather heavy façade of this church was erected from 1635 to 1638. It is in the style of the Counter-Reformation.

The **interior★**, which is shaped like a Greek cross, is dominated by a handsome coffered dome. The artists who painted Sant'Andrea della Valle are to be found here too: Domenichino painted the Cardinal Virtues on the pendentives of the dome; in the apse Lanfranco accomplished his last work (1647), the Apotheosis of St Charles Borromeo; above the high altar is St Charles Borromeo leading a procession in Milan to ward off the plague by Pietro da Cortona (1650); the 17C St Cecilia's Chapel *(right of the chancel)* is verging on the rococo with its strained effects at perspective and its broken lines and animated stucco figures.

On the east side of Piazza B Cairoli turn left into Via S Maria dei Calderari; turn right into Piazza delle Cinque Scole.

The arch and two columns on the left are the remains of a 1C building.

An 'angelic parricide'

The scandal broke on 9 September 1598. In those days a bold man could get away with almost anything. The head of the rich Cenci family was Francesco Cenci, whose father had been Pius V's treasurer. A cruel and perverted man, Francesco was eventually murdered at the instigation of his daughter Beatrice with the support of her brother Giacomo and Francesco's wife Lucrezia. Pope Clement VIII sentenced them to death despite public opinion which supported the plea of self-defence. The scandal, in which incest, opium and crime were all involved, set Rome in a ferment. The guilty parties were beheaded on 11 September 1599 in Piazza di Ponte Sant'Angelo. Each year on 11 September a mass is celebrated in St Thomas' Church in Piazzetta di Monte Cenci for the soul of Beatrice Cenci.

Palazzo Cenci – The narrow streets which surround the palace repeat like variations on a theme the name of the great family which hit the scandal headlines in the 16C: Via dell'Arco de Cenci, Vicolo dei Cenci, Piazza de' Cenci, Via Beatrice Cenci, Via del Monte dei Cenci. The palace itself stands on a slight rise (Monte Cenci) formed by the rubble from ancient buildings (perhaps the Circus Flaminius).

At the north end of the square turn right into Via del Portico d'Ottavia.

Lorenzo Manili's house (**D**) (nos 1, 1b and 2) was built in 1468 with shops on the ground floor. It is decorated with low reliefs and has the proprietor's name written up in Latin and Greek. Above the name is an inscription praising the owner for contributing to making the city beautiful.

Neighbouring sights are described in the following chapters: BOCCA DELLA VERITÀ; CAMPIDOGLIO-CAPITOLINO; CAMPO DEI FIORI; PANTHEON; TRASTEVERE.

MONTECITORIO★★

The walk covers the northern part of the Campus Martius which was mostly reserved for the colossal tombs belonging to the Imperial families and the funeral pyres *(ustrina)* where the bodies were burnt, whereas the southern part was more elegant and contained theatres, porticoes, amphitheatres and sports facilities.

Like the other districts of the city through which the pilgrims passed on their way to the Vatican, this one was raised out of its medieval misery under Sixtus IV (1471-84). In his 13 years on the papal throne he changed the face of Rome, using the money from the sale of indulgences to pay for his projects. Early in the 16C Leo X cleared the way for Via Leonina (now Via di Ripetta) to run straight from the Porta del Popolo, through which foreigners from the north entered the city, to the Mausoleum of Augustus.

Some of the streets around St Augustine's Church and Via Scrofa have not changed much since the Renaissance while the palaces in Piazza Colonna and Piazza di Montecitorio have, since 1870, become banks or newspaper offices or department stores. At the same period the old river port of the Ripetta was destroyed. It had been built in 1706, a set of curving riverside steps, of which Piranesi has left some attractive engravings; it was one of the most famous 'views' in Rome.

A quick drink and a nibble...

At the centre of town is the winebar **Achilli al Parlamento** *(via dei Prefetti 15)* which serves a broad range of wines and spirits accompanied by cocktail-eats and canapés for which they have become famed.

TOUR *30min.*

Piazza di Montecitorio – In the square stands a 6C BC Egyptian obelisk, re-erected in 1792 by Pius VI and surmounted by a bronze ball bearing his coat of arms. The obelisk, which was brought back from Heliopolis by Augustus in 10C BC, served as the pointer for a gigantic solar clock marked out on the ground, more or less on the site of the Church of San Lorenzo in Lucina.

Palazzo di Montecitorio ⊙ – It stands on the site of the funeral pyres belonging to the Antonine family for the cremation of their dead. It was begun by Bernini in 1650, taken over by one of his pupils and completed in 1697 by Carlo Fontana. Little remains of Bernini's Baroque fantasies: the rustic effect, reminiscent of

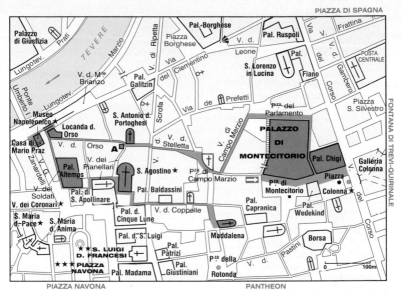

rockeries, of the rough-hewn stones framing some of the windows and the impression of enhanced size conveyed by the slightly convex façade which is surmounted by a clock tower. Since 1870 the palace has housed the Chamber of Deputies. The square is therefore full of comings and goings and solemn greetings; even the cafés with their regular patrons keep the same hours as the Montecitorio. To the rear (Piazza del Parlamento) the building was extended and provided with a majestic new façade (1903-25).

Take Via in Aquiro to Piazza Capranica and then Via delle Colonelle to reach the heart of papal Rome.

★Piazza Colonna – It is one of the most crowded places in Rome, being at the junction of the two main shopping streets (Via del Corso and Via del Tritone).

The **column★** at the centre of the square was probably erected between 176 and 193 in honour of **Marcus Aurelius** (161-80), who preferred philosophy to war but was forced to campaign on the banks of the Danube. He died at the front of the plague. His victories were short-lived and did not contain the barbarian thrust. Just as Trajan's Column illustrated that emperor's exploits against the Dacians, so Marcus Aurelius' column depicts the significant episodes in his wars with low relief carvings arranged in a spiral. The carving was done by a group of sculptors and even the designs were probably the work of several artists. In order to make the work more visible the scenes are larger and in higher relief than those on Trajan's column but the quality of the craftsmanship has suffered.

The overall appearance is spoiled by the lack of entasis two thirds of the way up the shaft which would have avoided the impression of concavity.

In 1589 Pope Sixtus V had the statue of the Emperor on the top of the column replaced with a statue of St Paul. He also restored the base and added an inscription wrongly attributing the column to Antoninus Pius, Marcus Aurelius' predecessor.

Palazzo Chigi – The building was begun in 1562 to designs by Giacomo della Porta; it was continued by Carlo Maderno according to the severe concepts of the Counter-Reformation; it was completed in 1630 in the Baroque era. In 1659 it was bought by Pope Alexander VII for his family, after whom it is named. Since 1917, when it was acquired by the State, the Palazzo Chigi has been associated with politics: Ministry of Foreign Affairs after the First World War, in the Fascist period it housed the Head of the Government; now it belongs to the Presidency of the Council of Ministers.

Take the street between Palazzo di Montecitorio and Palazzo Chigi; turn left into Piazza del Parlamento and left again into Via di Campo Marzio.

The street is lined with many luxury shops but in the reign of Octavius-Augustus a vast area of the Campus Martius was occupied by an enormous **solar clock** (160m × 60m - 525ft × 197ft). Some pieces of travertine paving, marked with bronze insets representing the signs of the zodiac, are still to be found beneath Via di Campo Marzio.

Bear right into Via di Stelletta, right into Via della Scrofa and immediately left into Via dei Portoghesi.

These charming and quiet streets are still the workplace of several artisans.

Torre della scimmia (Monkey Tower) (A) – The building on the corner of Via dei Portoghesi and Via dei Pianellari incorporates a 15C tower. It has been immortalised by the American novelist, Nathaniel Hawthorne (1804-64), with the following story.

The family living in the house owned a very facetious monkey. One day it climbed to the top of the tower carrying the new-born baby of the family. The father was terrified, not knowing what to do and fearful that the animal would let its precious burden fall. After praying to the Virgin for her to intercede he decided to whistle to the monkey to bring it back. The monkey came down by the drainpipe holding the child in its arms and they both returned safe and sound. Since then at the top of the tower a little light burns continuously before an image of the Virgin.

Sant'Antonio dei Portoghesi ⊙ – The Portuguese national church, which was built in the 17C, has an attractive Rococo façade; the interior is gorgeously decorated with gold, stucco, marble and paintings. The first chapel on the right contains a funeral monument by Canova (1806-08). In the first chapel on the left above the altar is a fine painting by Antoniazzo Romano (15C) depicting the Virgin between St Francis and St Anthony.

Continue west along Via dell'Orso.

Locanda dell'Orso (Bear Inn) – From the Middle Ages to the Renaissance, Via dell'Orso and Via Monte Brianzo consisted almost entirely of inns. The hostelry at the sign of the Bear was set up in a fine 15C building *(restored)*. It was here that Montaigne stayed for two days on his arrival in Rome in November 1580.

Either take Via dei Soldati or the steps in Via di Monte Brianzo.

★**Museo Napoleonico (Napoleon Museum)** ⊙ – The museum was founded in 1927 by Giuseppe Primoli, a descendant of Lucien Bonaparte, and contains many souvenirs of the Napoleonic presence in Rome. Lucien lived in the Via dei Condotti, Pauline had her villa near to the Porta Pia, while Napoleon's mother died in her palace in the Via del Corso.

The museum displays a collection of portraits of the emperor and his family, as well as mementoes, furnishings and personal effects. Rooms I and II are dedicated to the Premier Empire: notable exhibits include a red damasc suite of furniture by Jacob from Napoleon's apartment in St-Cloud, on the outskirts of Paris. Rooms IV and V are devoted to Napoleon's son who was declared King of Rome at his birth in 1811. Room VI, which is devoted to Pauline, Napoleon's sister, contains a couch similar to that featured in her portrait by Canova.

Casa di Mario Praz ⊙ – *Entrance in Via Zanardelli.* This is the house of Mario Praz (d 1982), a renowned Anglicist and essayist who earned great recognition for his study of English 19C literature. A passionate collector, he accumulated an infinite number of knick-knacks, pictures, sculpture, Neo-Classical furniture and objets d'art which he crammed into every corner of his house. Of particular note is the rare collection of 17C-19C wax models (effigies, portraits, busts, religious and mythological compositions) from England, Germany, France and Italy. In the study is a fine early-19C maple bookcase inlaid with mahogany intarsia.

Palazzo Altemps ⊙ – The palace was begun in about 1480 to Girolamo Riario, Sixtus IV's nephew. In 1568 it was acquired by Cardinal Marco Sittico Altemps who had it rebuilt by Martino Longhi the Elder. In 1725 it was the residence of Cardinal de Polignac, the French Ambassador. It now belongs to the Holy See.

Take Via dei Pianellari to reach Piazza Sant'Agostino.

★**Sant'Agostino** ⊙ – The church, which is dedicated to St Augustine of Hippo, was built between 1479 and 1483 owing to the generosity of Cardinal d'Estouteville, Archbishop of Rouen in France.

The broad travertine façade, with its rose-windows, was one of the first to be built in Rome according to the concepts of the Renaissance. The two orders are linked by large loose scrolls; the powerful moulding adds character to their ornamental effect.

The interior, which was decorated according to contemporary taste by Luigi Vanvitelli in 1760, has been cluttered by 19C additions which rob it of its soaring elegance, now only faintly perceptible in the nave.

The surviving features of the Renaissance building are the Latin cross plan with apsidal chapels in the transept and side aisles and the dome, one of the earliest of its type in Rome, which rises directly above the transept crossing without a drum. The church contains several fine works of art: near the main door is the much-loved **Madonna del Parto★** (1521) by **Jacopo Sansovino**; he took great interest in Antique sculpture (filmy draperies and proud bearing) during his visits to Rome and was also influenced by the vigour of Michelangelo's work.

On the altar in the right-hand transept chapel is a painting by Guercino (1591-1666). The side panels are illustrations of scenes from the life of St Augustine by Lanfranco (1582-1647).

The third pillar on the left in the nave bears a fresco painting by Raphael (1512) of the **Prophet Isaiah★**, which owes much to Michelangelo's work in the Sistine Chapel. The first chapel on the left contains the **Madonna of the Pilgrims★★★** (1605) by Caravaggio: the artist's contemporaries did not always recognise the force of his art, which was opposed to Mannerism and was a major influence in the development of painting. They criticised him for his rugged pilgrims, inspired by ordinary people, and for the ugliness of the man's feet. Even the Virgin, for all her gentleness, is nursing her bonny baby in a very realistic manner.

Take Via delle Coppelle east and turn right into Piazza della Maddalena.

Santa Maria Maddalena – The church, which is dedicated to St Mary Magdalene, stands on the site of a 15C oratory and hospice which were occupied in 1586 by St Camillus of Lellis, the founder of the Ministers of the Sick, a nursing order.

The church was rebuilt in the 17C by Carlo Fontana who was succeeded by followers of Bernini.

The façade was erected later in 1735 by Giuseppe Sardi; his contorted lines and abundant decoration are an exaggeration of Borromini's style.

The **interior★** is a rare example of the Rococo in Rome. The elaborate plan, also suggesting Borromini's influence, gives the church a majestic appearance despite its small size: an elliptical nave with recesses for altars set at an angle and a short transept covered by a dome. The rich decoration in stucco, gold and marble and the frescoes on the dome and in the apse which is bathed in a clear light, lend the church the charm of an old-fashioned drawing-room.

The relics of St Camillus are venerated at the altar in the south transept beneath the Glory of St Camillus painted by Sebastian Conca. In the passage south of the chancel is a 15C wooden statue of Mary Magdalene. The sumptuous organ dates from the 18C as do the attractive furnishings in the Sacristy.

Neighbouring sights are described in the following chapters: FONTANA DI TREVI – QUIRINALE; PANTHEON; PIAZZA NAVONA; PIAZZA DI SPAGNA.

MONTE MARIO

The modern districts bordering the Tiber to the north and northwest of Rome are not particularly interesting for walking so the sights are described in alphabetical order. To reach them, consult the adjacent plan and Plan of Rome.

Foro Italico – The huge sports centre was created by the Fascist government (1929-37). Once the seat of the Academy of Physical Education, it is now occupied by the Italian National Olympic Committee (CONI). There are tennis courts, a fencing school and swimming pool but the most important facilities are the Olympic Stadium and the Marble Stadium (stadio dei Marmi). The opening ceremony of the 1960 Olympic Games was held in the former (capacity: 100 000 spectators); the latter (capacity: 10 000 spectators) is decorated with 60 statues of athletes and groups of wrestlers in bronze (on the podium).

> ### A special evening...
>
> Why not make for **Lo Zodiaco** *(Viale Parco Mellini 90)* at nightfall: from here there is a fine view over the rooftops and it is a wonder to watch Rome assume her starry mantle while savouring some scrumptious ice-cream or sipping a glass of prosecco (sparkling dry white wine).

The road from the Piazza L de Bosis with its great obelisk to the Piazzale del Foro Italico is paved with mosaics bearing inscriptions to the glory of the 'Duce'.

Monte Mario – The natural beauty of this little hill makes it a popular place among Romans for taking a walk. It offers a fairly extensive **view★** of the Tiber and Rome which is particularly interesting at night when the city monuments are floodlit.

Monumento a Matteotti – This elegant monument in bronze gilt was designed by Torio Vivarelli and erected by the Tiber in 1974. Its symbol – a young shoot bursting from the earth – commemorates the Socialist MP Giacomo Matteotti who was assassinated in June 1924 for denouncing the illegality of the Fascist regime.

Palazzetto dello Sport – This concave structure was designed by Annibale Vitellozzi and Pier Luigi Nervi for the 1960 Olympics. It is composed of prefabricated concrete sections supported on a ring of distinctive piers which gives the impression of a lightweight construction.

Parco di Villa Glori – The steep slopes of this pleasant public park are dedicated to the memory of those who died for their country: one of the Cairoli brothers fell in combat here.

Ponte Milvio o Molle (Milvian Bridge) – There has been a bridge here since the 2C BC; it has frequently been restored and rebuilt, particularly in the 15C and 19C when it was enlarged and a fortified gate was added.

It was near here that the famous battle took place on 28 October 312 between Constantine and Maxentius, rival pretenders to the Imperial throne. On the eve of the battle, Constantine had a vision which resulted in his victory: Christ appeared to him and told him to mark his soldiers' shields with a Christian symbol – the alternative legend that a cross appeared in the sky with the words "You will conquer in this sign" is less reliable. Certain historians consider this to be the date of Constantine's conversion to Christianity.

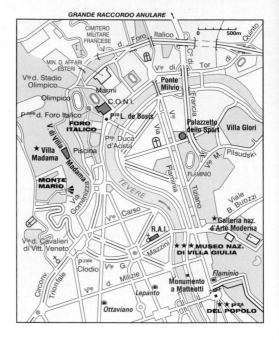

RAI (Palazzo della Radio e della Televisione) – The Radio and TV Centre is one of the many successful modern constructions in Rome. It is distinguished by a magnificent statue of a rearing horse in bronze by Francesco Messina and situated in the new district which has grown up around the Piazza Mazzini.

★**Villa Madama** ⊘ – *Walk up Via di Villa Madama.* This Renaissance villa, which has an enchanting **position**★ on the slopes of Monte Mario, was restored in 1925 to be used by the government for the entertainment of foreign visitors. It was built in 1515 by Cardinal Giulio de' Medici, the future Clement VII, to plans by Raphael and completed by Sangallo the Younger. Like the Palazzo Madama it passed to Madam Margaret of Austria and was named after her. The main entrance is set in the centre of the semicircular south front. The north front contains a magnificent deep loggia decorated with stucco work and grotesques by Giovanni da Udine and Giulio Romano, Raphael's pupils, overlooking a beautiful formal garden (9ha - 22 acres).

The walks proposed in this guide enable the visitor to discover the art treasures in the museums and the sites that played a historical role.

To find their location use the two Maps of Principal Sights For a stay of 3 or more days, consult the Sightseeing Programmes in the Practical Information at the end of the guide

PANTHEON ★★★

Tour 3 hours

This walk covers the ancient Mars' Field (Campus Martius) at the heart of Baroque Rome. The dark narrow streets provide a kaleidoscope of human activity: the hurrying tourist, the long-established trader who observes the passing crowds from the back of his little shop, men and women of the church, busy or meditative or strolling along Via dei Cestari past the shops which specialise in religious garb.

Every visitor to Rome gravitates towards the Pantheon: seeking peace and quiet after the noise and bustle of the Corso or looking for one of the many small restaurants *(trattorie)* in the area.

For that real Italian coffee...

Pop into the **Bar Sant'Eustachio** on the piazza *(no 82)* and order a *'gran caffè speciale'* – the secret of its goodness is jealously guarded by its creator.

...for an iced coffee

Caffè Tazza d'Oro in via degli Orfani *(no 84)* serves a mean coffee ice with lashings of whipped cream.

Historical Notes – For many years the **Campus Martius** was merely a marshy plain used for drilling the soldiery or conducting a census of the citizenry. In the 2C BC however, under the influence of the urban planning they observed in their new provinces in Greece, Macedonia and Pergamum, the Romans began to divide up the area into lots. In the eastern half, between the Pantheon and the present Corso, Caesar erected the *Saepta*, an enclosure for the assemblies which elected the tribunes of the people *(comitia tributa)* bordered on the south side by the *diribitorium* where the votes were counted and on the east and west by two porticos: the Meleager and the Argonauts. In about 43 BC two Egyptian temples dedicated to Isis and Serapis were built beside the *Saepta (see INTRODUCTION – plan Rome during the Empire)*.

Each Imperial dynasty felt honour-bound to leave its mark on the Campus Martius. Augustus' son-in-law, Agrippa, built the Pantheon and, between 25 and 19 BC, the first public baths in Rome. Domitian was responsible for a temple to Minerva and a portico to the deified Flavians. Under the Antonines a temple to the deified Hadrian was built. Alexander Severus, the last of the Severans, rebuilt Nero's baths.

In the 4C the Christians held sway. The Bishop of Rome, henceforward in control of the Caesars' capital, constructed Christian buildings often on the ruins of pagan monuments.

During the medieval struggle between the Ghibelline (Empire) and the Guelf (Papacy) Rome was peppered with towers and became *Roma Turrita*. Near the Pantheon stood the Crescenzi fortress which gave its name to the adjoining street: Salita dei Crescenzi. A tower was built nearby by the Sinibaldi. Then came the Renaissance and the Papacy was triumphant. The higher clerics and the wealthy citizens bought up whole blocks of hovels and replaced them with unostentatious but luxurious palaces.

Time seems to have stood still here since the Baroque age cast its veil of illusion over the buildings.

Piazza della Rotondo – This square, surrounding the Pantheon, is typically Roman. At the centre is a fountain designed in 1578 by G Della Porta; in 1711 it was surmounted by an obelisk by Clement XI. Like the one in the Piazza della Minerva, the obelisk came from the Temple of Isis and rests on a base decorated with dolphins and the papal coat of arms.

The **Albergo del Sole** (Sun Inn), at no 63, dates from the 15C. It is one of the oldest inns in the city; its guests have included both Ludovico Ariosto, the poet (1474-1533) and Pietro Mascagni, the musician (1863-1945).

★★★PANTHEON ⊙

Note: The building is a church and should be treated as such.

Originally the Pantheon was a temple, built by Agrippa, the great town planner, in 27 BC; it was dedicated to all the gods and faced south. In AD 80 it was damaged by fire and restored by Domitian. Then Hadrian (117-38) rebuilt it and gave it its present orientation to the north. It was closed in the 4C by the first Christian emperors together with all other places of pagan worship, sacked by the barbarians in 410 but saved from destruction by Pope Boniface IV who received it as a gift in 608 from Phocas *(see FORO ROMANO)*, the Emperor in Byzantium. It was then converted into a church dedicated to St Mary *ad martyres*.

Interior of the Pantheon

Until 756, when the Papal States came into being, Rome was subject to Byzantium. The only Eastern emperor to visit the Christian capital was Constantinus II in 356 when the Pantheon was despoiled of its bronze tiles for the embellishment of Constantinople. It was restored early in the Renaissance and then Urban VIII removed the nails and bronze plates which covered the beams of the porch roof and had them made into the magnificent baldaquin now in St Peter's. Pasquino responded with a neat pun on the Pope's family name: *Quod non fecerunt Barbari, fecerunt Barberini* (what the barbarians did not do, the Barberini have done). During Alexander VII's reign (1655-67) the porch was 'improved' by the addition of two belfries. Bernini was the architect responsible; immediately Pasquino talked about "Bernini's ass' ears". They were removed in 1883.

Exterior – The Pantheon is a compact building comprising the main circular chamber and a pillared porch *(pronaos)* beneath a pediment. The porch cornice bears two inscriptions: one concerns the original building by Agrippa and below, the other, scarcely visible, mentions restorations carried out by Septimius Severus and Caracalla.

From the side street, Via della Rotonda, the powerful relieving arches are visible set into the massive walls (6.20m - over 20ft thick). At the rear of the building are an apse, some hollow niches and sculpted fragments; they belonged to the Neptune basilica which stood between the Pantheon and Agrippa's baths *(map Rome during the Empire)*.

★★★**Interior** – The entrance is under the porch which is supported on 16 monolithic granite columns, all original except for the three on the left which were replaced owing to weakness under Urban VIII and Alexander VII; the papal emblems (the Barberini bees and the Chigi stars) can be seen on the capitals.

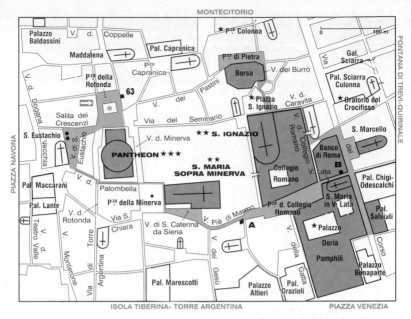

The bronze doors which date from the Empire were restored under Pius IV (16C). The harmony and grandeur of the interior have an immediate impact. The proportions are striking; the diameter of the building is equal to its overall height (43.30m - 142ft). The **antique dome**★★★ is an incredibly bold feature; its weight is distributed via relieving arches incorporated in the walls on to the eight piers of masonry which alternate with the deep recesses. At the centre of the coffered ceiling is an enormous round opening through which the interior is lit.

A series of superb monolithic columns punctuate alternate round and rectangular recesses. The piers between the recesses are decorated with shrines with alternating triangular or rounded pediments to which later Renaissance architects turned for inspiration in designing palazzo windows.

The upper stage between the cornice and the base of the dome was redesigned in the 18C with the present series of panels and blind windows. A section above the third chapel on the west side has been returned to the original décor.

The recesses have been converted into chapels: in the first to the west of the entrance is an attractive Annunciation attributed to Melozzo da Forlì. The next chapel contains the tomb of Victor Emmanuel II (1820-78), the first King of unified Italy.

Between the fifth and sixth chapels is the tomb of Raphael, who died aged 37 in 1520, composed of a fine Antique sarcophagus. On the upper edge is an inscription by Cardinal Pietro Bembo, poet and Humanist (1470-1547) which Alexander Pope translated without acknowledgement for another epitaph:

> *"Living, great nature feared he might outvie*
> *Her works; and dying fears herself to die."*

ENVIRONS

On the west side of the Pantheon *(via Salita dei Crescenzi and Via di S Eustachio)* is the site where the Crescenzi fortress stood in the Middle Ages. Nearby a tower was erected by the Sinibaldi family. Two ancient columns, once part of the Baths of Alexander Severus, have been re-erected at the junction of the two streets.

Go southeast along Via della Palombella to Piazza della Minerva.

Piazza della Minerva – It was Bernini's idea to embellish this charming square with an obelisk supported on an elephant's back. The obelisk is Egyptian and dates from the 6C BC; it was once part of the nearby Temple of Isis. The fantastic marble elephant, affectionately called the chick of Minerva, was sculpted by one of Bernini's pupils, Ercole Ferrata (1667).

★★**Santa Maria sopra Minerva** – The church was founded in the 8C near the ruins of a temple to Minerva built by Domitian and has undergone many alterations. In 1280 it was rebuilt in the Gothic style and then modified towards the middle of the 15C. The façade was constructed in the 17C; it is rectangular and very plain with the original 15C doorways.

Six plaques *(right)* mark the heights reached by the flood waters of the Tiber between 1598 and 1870.

The construction of the side chapels began in the 15C, the chancel was rebuilt in the 17C and the pillars were covered in grey marble in the 19C. The broad nave and aisles with heavy intersecting rib vaulting can give the illusion of a Gothic church.

The **works of art**★ in the Church of Santa Maria sopra Minerva place it in the first rank of the 'museum churches' of Rome.

Just inside the central door is the Renaissance tomb (**1**) of Diotisalvi Neroni who died in 1482 after being exiled from Florence for plotting against Piero de' Medici; by the side door is the tomb (**2**) of Virginia Pucci-Ridolfi adorned with a beautiful female bust; the two holy water stoops (**3**) date from 1588.

South aisle – In the fifth chapel (**4**) the painting by Antoniazzo Romano on the subject of the Annunciation recalls the beneficence of Cardinal Juan de Torquemada who provided poor girls with dowries. This work against a gold background is typical of the style of this late-15C painter which is marked with a certain religious conventionality.

The sixth chapel (**5**) was designed late in the 16C by Giacomo della Porta and Carlo Maderno. In the spirit of the Counter-Reformation the extravagance of the marble is tempered with a certain severity. The tombs of Clement VIII's parents are by Giacomo della Porta and Nicolas Cordier (a French sculptor who spent almost all his life in Rome).

The next chapel (**6**) contains one of Andrea Bregno's most famous works *(right):* the restrained and delicate decoration on the tomb of Cardinal Coca who died in 1477.

In the last chapel before the transept (**7**) is a beautiful 15C wooden crucifix.

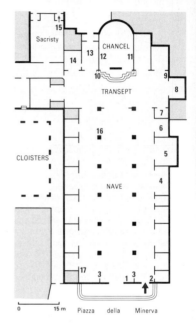

South transept – The Carafa chapel (**8**), which has a finely carved marble altar rail, was built and decorated between 1489 and 1493 with **frescoes**★ by **Filippino Lippi**: above the altar in a typical late-Renaissance frame is an Annunciation in which Thomas Aquinas presents Cardinal Oliviero Carafa to the Virgin. The expressive faces, the slender figures and the deeply pleated garments are characteristic of Filippino Lippi's art.

The rest of the wall is taken up with an Assumption in fine colours. The righthand wall shows scenes from the life of Thomas Aquinas.

On the left of the Carafa chapel is an example of the Italian Gothic style; the tomb of Guillaume Durand (**9**), Bishop of Mende in France who died in 1296.

Chancel – The heavy and inexpressive statue of Christ (**10**) was commissioned by a Roman nobleman from Michelangelo. The artist, having returned to Florence in 1520, started on the statue but then sent it to Rome where it was finished by his pupils. The gilded bronze drapery was added later.

The funeral monuments of the Medici popes, Clement VII (**11**) and Leo V (**12**), modelled on commemorative arches, are the work of Antonio da Sangallo (1483-1546); contemporary taste preferred architectural to decorative features in funerary art.

North transept – The first chapel (**13**) contains many fine **tombs**★: in the Gothic style *(right)*; dating from the 15C *(on either side of the rear door)*; in the Baroque style *(above the door and on the right)*; the tomb with the dead man resting on his elbow *(left)* is by Giacomo della Porta (late 16C).

Let into the floor is the tomb of Fra (the Blessed) Angelico, Giovanni da Fiesole, the Dominican painter who died in 1455.

In the next chapel (**14**) is a 15C tomb composed of an Antique sarcophagus *(Hercules and the lion)*.

St Catherine of Siena's Chapel (15) – It was built in the 17C using the walls of the room in which the saint died (1380) in the neighbouring Dominican convent.

North aisle – Monument to Venerable Sister Maria Raggi (**16**): flowing garments, an ecstatic expression and lively cherubs exemplify the art of Bernini (1643). The Renaissance tomb of Francesco Tornabuoni (**17**), who died in 1480, is one of Mino da Fiesole's most successful works owing to its fine decorative carving.

Walk westwards along Via Piè di Marmo.

The street is named after the enormous stone **foot** (**A**) which probably belonged to a Roman statue although no one knows how it came to be in its present position.

The **Roman College** (Collegio Romano), formerly the Jesuit College, was founded in 1583 by Gregory XIII who strove to re-establish the primacy of Rome after the Council of Trent. At the corner of Via della Gatta there is a charming Madonna beneath a canopy so typical of Rome.

★**Palazzo Doria Pamphili** – This palazzo, one of the largest in Rome, was begun in the 15C and gradually enlarged by the succession of noble families which owned it. First acquired by the della Rovere family, it then passed to Pope Julius II's nephew, the Duke of Urbino. Clement VIII, a member of the Aldobrandini family, then bought it for his nephew. Finally Donna Olimpia, Clement VIII's niece and heir, married Camillo Pamphili whose family was later allied with that of the Dorias.

The façade facing the Corso is an imposing 18C construction in the Baroque style whereas the front looking into Via del Plebiscito dates from 1643. The palazzo extends the whole length of Via della Gatta behind a 19C façade and round two sides of Piazza del Collegio Romano.

Since 1966 part of the palazzo has housed the Anglican Centre in Rome, a tangible outcome of the formal visit paid by Archbishop Michael Ramsey to Pope Paul VI in that year, where students of any age, particularly Roman Catholics, who wish to learn about the Anglican Communion, can consult the library of Anglican authorities, books of reference and history.

★★**Galleria Doria Pamphili** ◎ – *Time: 1 hour. Entrance at 1a Piazza del Collegio Romano (first floor).* The Gallery houses a fine collection of paintings and sculpture. Some of the more outstanding are mentioned below. The numbers used in the text correspond with those in the gallery.

First gallery – *Portrait of a young man* (**15**) is by Jacopo Tintoretto (1518-94). The portrait of two people (**23**) is attributed to Raphael. *Herodias* (**29**) is an early work by Titian. This gallery also houses three of the most famous paintings by **Caravaggio** (1573-1610) – moving away from Mannerist stylisation towards Realism, this painter's bold compositions, dramatic light effects and heightened perspective influenced many subsequent artists working in Rome.

Mary Magdalene (**40**) is simply painted as a despairing young woman without any reference to the New Testament story; the bottle of perfume and jewellery at her side are particularly clear. In the **Flight into Egypt**★★★ (**42**) the Virgin asleep with her child is shown in a similar attitude to that of Mary Magdalene; the scene on the left of the composition is unusually romantic for Caravaggio. **John the Baptist as a child** (**44**) recalls the painting hanging in the Conservators' Palace; Caravaggio had probably seen the nude figures painted by Michelangelo in the Sistine Chapel or by the Carracci brothers in the Great Gallery in Farnese Palace.

At the far end of this gallery is a **bust of Olimpia Maidalchini Pamphili**★★ by **Algardi**. She is said to have pestered and hounded her brother-in-law, Giovanni Battista Pamphili, until he attained the papal throne as Innocent X. Algardi who was an accomplished portraitist knew precisely how to express the energy and ambition of Donna Olimpia, as she was called by the Romans; she is shown in the distinctive headdress which she alone wore.

Several steps lead down into the Aldobrandini salon which is hung with some fine 16C Brussels tapestries illustrating the Battle of Lepanto (7 October 1571), and *Erminia finding Tancred wounded* (**77**) by Guercino.

Second gallery – *St Sebastian* (**135**) is by Ludovico Carracci (1555-1619) who together with his cousins, Agostino and Annibale, had Caravaggio as a pupil. The bronze and porphyry bust of Innocent X is by Algardi.

In the four rooms which open on the right can be seen *(3rd room)* a fine portrait of *Agatha van Schoonhoven* (**279**) painted in 1523 by Jan van Scorel, a painter from Utrecht, who was in Rome when his compatriot Adrian VI became Pope. In the next room is a *Portrait of a Franciscan* (**291**) by Rubens, *Earthly Paradise* by 'Velvet' Breughel and the unusual *Battle in the Bay of Naples* (**317**) by Breughel the Elder. At the end there is an octagonal room showing works by Flemish artists.

Third gallery – Decorated in the 18C style with mirrors and gilding, it ends in an alcove containing the **Portrait of Innocent X**★★★, a masterpiece by **Velazquez**, painted in 1650 during his second visit to Rome; the painter has succeeded in painting an official portrait quite lacking in nobility. Here also is a bust of Innocent X by Bernini, a very expressive interpretation of the Pope's authoritative personality.

Fourth gallery – It is dominated by two **works**★★ (**359** and **362**) by **Annibale Carracci**. They are semi-circular in shape and were part of a series painted from 1603 to 1604 for the palace chapel. In *Flight into Egypt* (**359**) the gentle but realistic landscape takes up almost all the picture presaging a taste which was to develop throughout the 17C. At the end of the gallery is an early version of Bernini's bust of Innocent X.

★**Appartamenti privati** (Private Apartments) – These are the rooms inhabited from the 16C to 18C by the families who owned the palace. In the Wintergarden are a small sleigh used in the 18C and a fine sedan chair, painted and gilded (18C). The Andrea Doria room bears the name of the most famous member of the Genoese Doria family; a mercenary *(condottiere)*, he commanded the French fleet for François I before being employed by Charles V. The 16C Brussels tapestries depicting the Battle of Lepanto are part of the same series as those in the Aldobrandini salon.

The smoking room, which is decorated in 19C English style, contains a 15C Tuscan polyptych.

The frieze in the dining room depicts the various properties belonging to the Doria Pamphili family (19C).

In the Green Drawing Room there is a graceful *Annunciation* by the Florentine Filippo Lippi (1406-69), Botticelli's master. A large 15C Tournai tapestry illustrates the medieval legend of Alexander the Great.

The tour continues with a suite of reception rooms starting with the Ballroom; its walls were lined with silk in the 20C and contains a beautiful table decorated with hard stone marquetry and supported on a 17C gilded wooden base in the shape of four dolphins.

The walls of the Yellow Drawing Room are hung with tapestry panels made at the Gobelins factory in Paris for Louis XV. In the Small Red Drawing Room hangs a portrait of James Edward Stuart, the Old Pretender, by A S Belle.

The tour ends in the Chapel which is decorated in *trompe-l'œil* (18C).

Take Via Lata between Santa Maria in Via Lata and Palazzo del Banco di Roma.

Fontana del Facchino (Porter's Fountain) (**B**) – Tucked against the wall *(right)* is an amusing little fountain composed of a porter *(facchino)* holding a barrel with water issuing from the bung hole into a basin. According to legend the sculptor took as his model a Renaissance water-carrier with a reputation for drunkenness, who is thus obliged to make do with water for the rest of time.

Turn right into via del Corso.

Santa Maria in Via Lata (Church of St Mary in Via Lata) – The façade of the church is of particular interest. Built between 1658 and 1662 by Pietro Cortona, it marks the transition in Baroque art to the period when detached columns, no longer an integral part of the walls, took on an essential role. Set out along two storeys, the columns seem to support the whole building and create remarkable effects of light and shade.

Palazzo Salviati – It was built by the Duke of Nevers, Cardinal Mazarin's nephew, in the 17C to house the French Academy.

San Marcello – The **Church of St Marcellus** was founded in the 4C on the site of a *titulus*, a private house used as a place of Christian worship.

The church was burned down in 1519 and completely rebuilt in the 16C and 17C. In 1683 Carlo Fontana designed the slightly concave Baroque façade. The palms linking the two storeys are typical of the Baroque style which delighted in the unusual. The empty frame above the entrance has never received its intended sculpture.

The single nave with side chapels, typical of the Renaissance, was designed by Jacopo Sansovino (1486-1570) in 16C. The late-16C coffered ceiling is richly decorated in gold, blue and red.

Works of art from the Renaissance to the Baroque period are to be found here. To the left of the entrance is the tomb of Cardinal Giovanni Michiel, who was poisoned on Alexander VI's orders in 1503. Below it is the tomb of his nephew, Bishop Antonio Orso, who died in 1511. The work was begun in 1520 by Andrea Sansovino and finished in 1527 by his pupil Jacopo Sansovino. The books at the base recall the Bishop's bequest of several works to the convent of St Marcellus.

In the fourth chapel on the right is a fine 15C wooden crucifix. The realistic figure of Christ in agony gave rise to a lugubrious legend: the sculptor was so obsessed with the desire to depict the suffering as realistically as possible that he killed a poor fellow who happened to be passing that way and studied the death throes to inspire his own carving. When the church burned down in 1519 it is said that the crucifix was recovered intact in the ruins. The frescoes in the vault are by Perin del Vaga, one of Raphael's pupils. In the base of the altar is a 3C Roman stele which was decorated with incrustations of marble in the 12C to serve as a reliquary.

The fourth chapel on the left contains busts of the noble family of the Frangipani; the three on the right were carved by Algardi in 1625.

Walk back to Via Lata.

Palazzo del Banco di Roma (Bank of Rome) – The palazzo was built between 1714 and 1722 for the Carolis, and converted early in the 20C. From 1769 to 1794 it was the residence of Cardinal de Bernis, the French Ambassador, who gave splendid receptions and called it "the French hostelry at the crossroads of Europe"; it was also the residence of Chateaubriand, Ambassador of Charles X.

Turn left and right into Via del Collegio Romano and left into Via del Caravita to reach Piazza Sant'Ignazio.

★**Piazza Sant'Ignazio** – The square is best observed from the steps of the church. It was designed in imitation of a theatre set, in ochre and stone, and has an unusual charm with curved façades on the street corners where people make their entrances and exits like actors on a stage.

★★Sant'Ignazio – The church, which is dedicated to the founder of the Jesuit Order and of the Roman College, the first free school, is typical of the Counter-Reformation and was begun in 1626 to the plans of a Jesuit, Orazio Grassi. It stands within the precincts of the Roman College and served for many years as the college chapel.

Orazio Grassi also designed the high façade; the two superimposed orders linked by scrolls produce a solemn and austere ensemble.

★★Central ceiling fresco – For the best effect stand on the disc in the centre of the nave. The fresco is the work of **Andrea Pozzo** (1684). A Jesuit, he chose a subject dear to the Counter-Reformation which exalted the saints in the face of Protestantism. Here St Ignatius is bathed by a divine light which is reflected on the four corners of the world shown allegorically. Pozzo used his knowledge of three-dimensional perspective to create the *trompe-l'œil* effect. Against an architectural background he has arranged an animated crowd of figures.

Apsidal fresco – Also the work of Andrea Pozzo, it glorifies the miracles worked by St Ignatius' intercession.

Transept – Above the crossing rises a 'cupola' in *trompe-l'œil* painted by Andrea Pozzo. Between 1696 and 1702 he wrote a treatise entitled *Perspectiva pictorum et architectorum* which had considerable influence on painters and architects in the 18C.

The altar at the end of the right transept is dedicated to St Luigi Gonzaga. Above the lapis lazuli urn containing the saint's relics and between the beautiful green marble columns wreathed in fronds of bronze is an admirable 'marble picture' carved by **Pierre Legros,** a French student at the French Academy (1629-1714), who collaborated with Andrea Pozzo in most of his works. The Director of the Academy however did not appreciate one of his students working to the glory of the Roman Jesuits rather than the king of France, so Pierre Legros had to leave the Academy.

Opposite in the left transept is a corresponding altar in honour of St John Berchmans. The high relief sculpture of the Annunciation is the work of Filippo Valle. Both altars boast bold interpretations by Andrea Pozzo of the pediments so dear to Borromini.

Take Via dei Burrò.

Via dei Burrò owes its name to the administrative offices established in the area by Napoleon Bonaparte.

Piazza di Pietra – The south side of this colourful square is occupied by a building which now houses the Stock Exchange but in the 18C was the Customs House where any visitor to Rome was obliged to present himself.

Incorporated in the present building are eleven beautiful marble columns of the Corinthian order which belonged to a **temple** which stood here in antiquity. It was erected in honour of the deified **Hadrian** by his adopted son Antoninus Pius and consecrated in AD 145. The grandeur of the ancient columns contrasts with the intimate character of the square.

Neighbouring sights are described in the following chapters: FONTANA DI TREVI-QUIRINALE; ISOLA TIBERINA-TORRE ARGENTINA; MONTECITORIO, PIAZZA NAVONA; PIAZZA VENEZIA.

PIAZZA NAVONA ★★★

Tour 2 $\frac{1}{2}$ hours

In Antiquity the district bordered by Corso Vittorio Emanuele II (opened in the late 19C), Corso del Rinascimento (1936-39) and Via Zanardelli (c1906), was part of the Campus Martius which had been the admiration of the Greek geographer Strabo when he visited Rome in about 7 BC, for being covered with grass throughout the year. Domitian (AD 81-96) built a large stadium and an Odeon where poetry readings and musical concerts were given (approximately on the site of the Palazzo Massimo and Piazza di San Pantaleo). Except for the outline of Domitian's stadium which is preserved in the shape of the Piazza Navona, no traces of ancient Rome have survived here.

The network of picturesque lanes and streets between the Piazza Navona and the Tiber recalls the splendour of the Papal era in the heart of Renaissance Rome.

As early as the beginning of the 16C cardinals, ambassadors, papal officials, wealthy bankers and distinguished courtesans took up residence here. Around them intellectual life flourished: booksellers, engravers and miniaturists settled around the Piazza Navona and Piazza Pasquino and to this day there are still numerous craftsmen to be found in the area. The recommended walk passes many 15C and 16C palaces and also offers many pleasant surprises to the curious visitor prepared to turn into the courtyards off the main square. The rusticated façades with their plain rectangular windows and somewhat austere pediments often conceal some fine Renaissance architecture: beautiful balconies and colonnades, cornices with antique motifs, coats of arms, walls decorated with *grisaille,* friezes and medallions.

★★★PIAZZA NAVONA

This is perhaps the place which most effectively characterises the true spirit of the Eternal City where tourists can gain an altogether unique image of the contrasting facets of Rome. Set apart from the noise and smell of the traffic, Piazza Navona seems to be permanently on holiday: the balloon-seller has his pitch beside a caricaturist who sketches his customer with a few deft strokes of charcoal; a dear old body lovingly feeds the pigeons next to a trade-unionist exhorting his comrades; tourists and locals come to savour a *tartuffo* on the terrace of the *Tre Scalini*.

The long and narrow shape of the square is due to **Domitian**: in AD 86 he had a **stadium** built on this site and immediately instituted a series of games in the Greek style. Unlike the games in the amphitheatre where the gladiators confronted one another with violence, these games were contests of wit and physical fitness; the speaking, poetry and musical competitions were held in the Odeon while running, wrestling, and discus and javelin throwing took place in the stadium.

Domitian's stadium was stripped of its marbles in 356 by Constantinus II on a visit to Rome and by the 5C it was in ruins.

It came to life again during the Renaissance when it developed into one of the most beautiful sights in Rome under the popes. In 1477 the market from the foot of the Capitol was moved here and other attractions were added to bring in the

Piazza Navona

crowds, such as the *Cuccagna*, a greased pole which strong men tried to climb, or puppet shows. In the mid-17C the square was partially flooded to accommodate water games at the weekend in summer. Since 1869 it is only at Christmas and Epiphany that market stalls appear in Piazza Navona for the fair of the *Befana*, a kindly old witch who brings toys for the children.

The Fountains – There are three fountains in the square.

★★★**Fontana dei Fiumi** – The **Fountain of the Rivers**, which occupies the centre of the square, was created by Bernini for Pope Innocent X who wanted to provide worthy surroundings for his residence, the Palazzo Pamphili. The brilliant Baroque architect contrived a pile of rockwork hollowed out into grottoes on top of which he erected an obelisk; the rigidity and symmetry of the latter contrasts strikingly with the fluid

A. Lo Giudice

Fountain detail

lines of the base; the wind seems to tear at the trees and the marble statues seem to gesticulate. They were carved from the master's designs by some of his pupils and represent four rivers symbolizing the four quarters of the world: the Danube for Europe, the Nile for Africa (the veiled head indicated that the source was unknown), the Ganges for Asia and the Plate for America. The obelisk, a Roman work dating from Domitian's reign, was recovered by Innocent X from the Via Appia where it lay. The fountain was completed in 1651. To illustrate the rivalry between Bernini and Borromini, who designed the façade of St Agnes' Church, a Roman legend explains that the statues of the Nile and the Plate, their arms raised in a defensive gesture, are trying to protect themselves from the façade which is about to collapse. In fact the façade was built several years after the fountain.

A. Froissardey/EXPLORER

Fontana del Moro (**A**) – The **Fountain of the Moor** was built at the end of the 16C. In 1653 at Innocent X's request it was renovated by Bernini, who designed the central figure of the Moor while one of his pupils was responsible for the vigorous way in which it was interpreted. The statues on the tritons and those on the edge of the basin date from the 19C.

Fontana del Nettuno (**B**) – The **Fountain of Neptune** was moved to Piazza Navona at the end of the 16C. The statue of Neptune at the centre and those around it date from the 19C.

★★**Sant'Agnese in Agone** ⊙ – According to tradition a small oratory was built in the 8C on the site where St Agnes was thought to have been martyred. In 1652 Pope Innocent X commissioned Girolamo Rainaldi and his son Carlo to rebuild the church as a family chapel attached to his palace. From 1653 to 1657 Borromini took charge of the work. The church was completed at the end of the century by a group of architects. Borromini was responsible for part of the dome and for the façade which demonstrates his taste for contrasting convex and concave lines, particularly in the campaniles.

The **interior**★ is captivating: the deep recesses in the pillars supporting the dome transform the Greek cross plan into an octagon. The altars are adorned with beautiful 'marble pictures' by Bernini's pupils. The decorations in stucco, gilt and painting are far from the spirit of Borromini's sober interiors and were added at the end of the century.

Palazzo Pamphili – This was the Pamphili residence; it was enlarged between 1644 and 1650 by Girolamo Rainaldi when Giovanni Battista Pamphili became Pope Innocent X.

ENVIRONS

At the north end of the Piazza take Via Agonale.

The remains of **Domitian's Stadium** can be seen in Via di Tor Sanguigna, adjacent to the piazza.

Santa Maria dell'Anima – *As the main entrance is usually closed, enter by the side door in Via della Pace and start with the interior.* This is the church of German-speaking Roman Catholics. There had been a pilgrim hostel on the site since 1386 when the present building was begun in 1500. It was restored in the 19C.

Interior – Designed as a "hall church", where the nave and aisles are all of the same height, the plan is rather unusual for Rome which has almost no Gothic architecture. The decoration dates from the 19C.

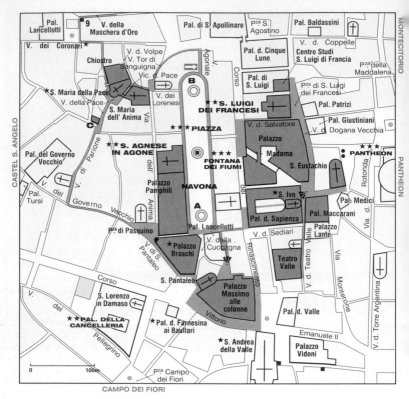

CAMPO DEI FIORI

There are several works by pupils or lesser artists imitating the styles of the great masters. There is a painting (1618) *(first chapel on the right)* by Carlo Saraceni, a follower of Caravaggio. A *Pietà* (1532) *(fourth chapel)* by Nanni di Baccio Bigi is a clumsy imitation of Michelangelo. Above the high altar there is a *Holy Family with Saints* by Giulio Romano, one of Raphael's assistants, and by the third pillar on the left in the nave lies the tomb of Ferdinand van der Eydem by Duquesnoy (1594-1643) who worked with Bernini.

The **façade** in Via dell'Anima was designed by Giuliano da Sangallo and built in 1511. Its flatness, which gives it the appearance of a screen, belongs to the Renaissance period. The pediment above the central door contains a sculpture of the Virgin between two figures, each representing a soul (*anima* in Italian), which is a copy of a painting which gave the church its name. The original is kept in the Sacristy *(apply to the Sacristan)*. To the right of the façade there is a view of the belltower which is capped by a slim cone faced with multicoloured ceramics (1516-18).

★**Santa Maria della Pace** ⊙ – There was already a small church on this site in the 12C. Sixtus IV had it rebuilt in 1480. In the Baroque era it changed in appearance when Alexander VII (1655-67) invited Pietro da Cortona to design a new **façade**. He created a pleasing combination of constrasting effects: a semi-circular porch with six columns beneath a double pediment – a curved one within a triangular one – flanked by two concave wings. To provide a suitable setting for his work the architect designed a charming square lined with elegant colour-washed façades.

Cloisters – *Entrance at no 5 Vicolo Arco della Pace*. They were built in 1504 and were one of Bramante's earliest Roman works. The handsome proportions give an air of great simplicity. The columns on the ground floor are complemented by those on the first floor which alternate with smaller columns placed centrally over the lower arches.

Interior – The 15C plan in very unusual; it comprises a short rectangular nave and an octagonal domed section. The arch of the first chapel on the right in the nave was decorated by Raphael in 1514; he painted the four **Sibyls**★ inspired by the angels no doubt after seeing Michelangelo's Sibyls in the Sistine chapel. His skill in turning an awkward surface to good account is to be admired. The prophets were painted by one of his pupils. The first chapel on the left is decorated with elegant frescoes by Baldassarre Peruzzi (1481-1536) who also worked on the Farnesina. The very rich decoration on the arch leading into the second chapel on the right is typical of the high Renaissance.

In the octagonal section over the high altar is an image of the Virgin which is supposed to have bled when struck by a stone in 1480; Sixtus IV had the church rebuilt to house the miraculous image. In the chapel on the left of the choir is a 15C wooden crucifix and in the next a fine painting by Sermoneta, one of the first Mannerists to imitate Raphael.

Between the chuches turn into Vicolo della Pace which leads into Via della Pace.

The **Caffè della Pace** (**C**), which has been in Via della Pace since 1800, has retained its 1900 interior décor. It is a pleasant place from which to admire the Church of Santa Maria della Pace.

Take Via dei Coronari; turn left into Piazza Lancellotti to find Via della Maschera d'Oro.

Via della Maschera d'Oro – No 9 on the corner of Vicolo di San Simeone is a small palace which shows how secular architecture developed in the 16C as a result of Sixtus IV's essays in town planning.

At this period the streets of Rome were lined by charming façades engraved and painted with monochrome frescoes. **Polidoro da Caravaggio** and **Maturino da Firenze** were the masters of this technique. The wall was first given a rough rendering blackened with smoke and then covered with a coat of plaster. The artist then engraved mythological scenes or motifs taken from Antique art so as to reveal the dark undercoat. These decorations were extremely fragile and have almost all disappeared.

Return to Via della Pace before continuing south along Via di Parione; turn left into Via del Governo Vecchio to reach Piazza di Pasquino.

Piazza di Pasquino – The statue of **Pasquino**, which was probably part of a 3C BC group, was found in the Piazza Navona in the 15C. It was in such a pitiable state that no collector wanted it, and so it was placed on the corner against the building which occupied that site before the Palazzo Braschi, and there it stayed. People called it Pasquino after a local tailor with a very caustic tongue and used it as their mouthpiece. During the night satirical or even libellous comments, criticising morals and politics and expressing popular claims, sometimes in Roman dialect, were secretly hung on Pasquino. The following day the 'Pasquinades' spread through Rome as far as the doors of the papal officials; some were even carried to the ears of foreign sovereigns and started more than one diplomatic incident. The draconian laws sentencing the perpetrators of these libels to death were rarely applied; or if they were the prisoner was immediately pardoned.

Pasquino was the most loquacious of the Roman 'talking statues'.

Take Via di S Pantaleo.

★**Palazzo Braschi** ⊙ – It is named after the family of Pope Pius VI who had it built in the late 18C for his nephews. It was the last papal family palace to be built in Rome. The neo-Classical style then in vogue was used for the ponderous façades which dominate the surrounding streets: Via della Cuccagna, Via di Pasquino and Via di San Pantaleo.

★**Museo di Roma** – Rome since the Middle Ages is the subject of the museum housed in the Palazzo Braschi.

The colossal staircase with its antique granite columns and decorative stucco is by Cosimo Morelli who designed the palace.

In the third room are three anonymous paintings depicting the jousts held in the 16C and 17C in the Belvedere courtyard in the Vatican, Piazza Navona and on the Testaccio. In the fifth room are **frescoes**★ from demolished buildings; the sixth room contains chiaroscuro decorations by Polidoro da Caravaggio and Maturino da Firenze (16C); the delicate frescoes in the next room showing Apollo and the nine Muses belong to the 16C Umbrian School and come from a papal residence. In the ninth room are various anonymous paintings illustrating the bustle of the old market near the Capitoline in the 17C and the pageantry of the Corpus Christi processions in St Peter's Square. The next room is hung with 18C Gobelins tapestries. The subjects, children in a garden, are taken from the paintings of Charles le Brun (1619-90) for the Aurora Pavilion in the Parc de Sceaux near Paris. From the windows there is a fine view of Piazza Navona.

In the first room on the second floor hang three huge canvases on Greek mythological themes by Gavin Hamilton (1723-98), a Scottish painter who settled in Rome in 1755 and spent most of his working life in Italy. Also on the second floor are the famous **watercolours**★ in the series "Lost Rome" *(Roma sparita)*. The sixth room contains fragments of mosaic from the old St Peter's Basilica (late 12C - early 13C). On the ground floor *(entrance in northeast corner of the courtyard)* is the papal train built for Pius IX in 1858 at Clichy in Paris. It consists of an open-sided coach, upholstered in damask, containing two long sofas and a throne, which is linked to a closed coach by an open platform where the Pope could stand in full view of the crowds; the third coach is fitted out as a small chapel.

Palazzo Massimo alle Colonne – The palace, which belongs to the Massimo, o of the oldest families in Rome, comprises three separate buildings. The one on right of the **Church of San Pantaleo** (designed by Valadier in 1806) is known as

Pyrrhus Palace because of a statue which was kept there. The Palazzo Massimo *colonne (facing on to Corso Vittorio Emanuele II)* is screened by a fine curved portico Doric columns, designed (1532-36) by Baldassarre Peruzzi. The original windows of the upper storeys of the façade heralds the Mannerist style. The oldest part of the palazzo is on the north side *(access from Corso Vittorio Emanuele II via a narrow lane into Piazza de'Massimi)* and is known as the "illustrated palace" owing to the grisailles painted on the façade c1523 by some of Daniele da Volterra's pupils.

The column standing in Piazza de'Massimi may have been part of the **Odeon** of Domitian. From the north end of the Piazza there is a view of the Fountain of the Rivers in Piazza Navona.

Turn right and then left into Corso del Rinascimento.

Palazzo della Sapienza – Until 1935 it was occupied by Rome University. Now it houses among other things the archives of the Papal States from the 9C to 19C. The simple façade, begun in 1575 to a design by Giacomo della Porta and coloured burnt umber, gives no hint of the elegance of the inner courtyard, which is surrounded on three sides by a two-storey portico.

★ **Sant' Ivo alla Sapienza** ⊙ – Equally unexpected is the audacity of Borromini's façade for St Ivo's Church which closes the fourth side of the courtyard. Just as Bernini aimed at extensiveness so Borromini tried to confine his ideas within a restricted space, using such exaggeratedly curved lines that his architecture was termed perverse and contrary. An amazing variety of curves is used in this building: in the many-faceted drum, in the convex line of the dome and the concave buttresses, in the spiral surmounting the lantern.

The interior, very high and light, is a constant interplay of concave and convex surfaces, a foretaste of the Rococo style; it incorporates the bee from the Barberini coat of arms.

Exit by the side door (under the arcade on the right) into Via del Teatro Valle.

In this street, where basket-makers still work at their craft, stands the **Teatro Valle** with its 19C décor.

Return up the street to Piazza S Eustachio.

From the piazza there is a splendid view of the spiral dome of St Ivo's Church. On the south side stands the **Palazzo Maccarani** (1521), an austere building in the Renaissance style by Jules Romain; it incorporates one of the most popular cafés in Rome, the Caffè S Eustachio.

The early 18C façade of the Church of **Sant'Eustachio** is screened by a portico; the head of a deer bearing a cross between its antlers recalls the vision which St Eustace experienced in the hunting field while he was still a Roman general and which led to his conversion.

Take Via della Dogana Vecchia to Piazza S Luigi dei Francesi.

★★**San Luigi dei Francesi** ⊙ – The first stone of this building was laid in 1518 by Cardinal Giulio de' Medici, the future Pope Clement VII. After very slow progress between 1524 and 1580 the church was completed in 1589 partly with the aid of subsidies from France given by Henri II, Henri III and Catherine de' Medici and was consecrated as the national church of the French in Rome and dedicated to St Louis.

The façade, which bears the salamander of François I of France, was probably designed by Giacomo della Porta between 1580 and 1584. Its elegant lines accord well with Piazza di San Luigi dei Francesi. The prominent columns hint at the flamboyance of the Baroque style.

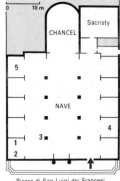

Piazza di San Luigi dei Francesi

The interior, consisting of a nave, side aisles and lateral chapels, was embellished in the Baroque period and in the 18C with marbles, paintings, gilding and stucco work.

The vault was decorated in 1754 by Natoire *(Death and Glory of Saint Louis)*; beneath it many Frenchmen have been laid to rest: Cardinal de Bernis (**1**) who lived in style in the Palazzo del Banco di Roma, Pauline de Beaumont (**2**), Chateaubriand's romantic friend: the Pope turned a blind eye to their illegal liaison and Chateaubriand, then the French Ambassador, commissioned her memorial; Claude Gellée, also known as Lorraine, who captured the Roman light so marvellously in his paintings, has a memorial here (**3**) although he was buried in the Trinità dei Monti.

★**Frescoes by Domenichino** – *In the chapel of St Cecilia (**4**); restoration in progress.* The frescoes, which were executed in 1614, tell the story of St Cecilia. Domenichini, who had arrived in Rome in 1602, resisted the exuberance of the Baroque and strove rather after balance and clarity of texture in his art. On the right – *St Cecilia* *distributing her own wealth;* on the left – *The Death of St Cecilia;* on the ceiling – *An Angel crowns the saint and her husband Valeriano; Cecilia refuses to carry out sacrifices to pagan gods; St Cecilia in Glory.*

★★★**Caravaggio's paintings** – In St Matthew's chapel (**5**) are three paintings depicting St Matthew's life. The vault is by Cavaliere d'Arpino whose Mannerist style so exasperated Caravaggio.

Above the altar: *St Matthew and the Angel:* the artist's delight in contradiction is expressed here in the rather acrobatic posture of the old man writing his Gospel at the angel's dictation.

– On the left: *the Calling of St Matthew:* in a dark room five men seated at a table are distracted from their occupation by the entrance of Christ accompanied by St Peter; His pointing finger singles out Matthew seated beside an old man in spectacles who is counting out the money; the shaft of light striking the wall and illuminating the faces is typical of Caravaggio's art; the young man with a feather in his cap watching with a slightly scornful air is a familiar figure in Caravaggio's paintings.

– On the right: *the Martyrdom of St Matthew:* the naked figure *(centre)* and the gesture of the young

Detail of *The Calling of St Matthew* by Caravaggio

boy *(right)* are in the academic style. The definition of the forms by the interplay of light and shade is typical of Caravaggio's style.

Take Via Salvatore; turn left into Corso del Rinascimento.

Palazzo Madama – *Not open to the public.* It was built by the Medici in the 16C. In the days of Cardinal Giovanni de' Medici, the future Leo X, a succession of banquets and literary gatherings was held here. Later Pope Clement VII made it the residence of his great niece, Catherine de' Medici. When she became the Queen of France she renounced her Medici possessions and the palace passed to Alessandro de' Medici, whose wife, Madama Margherita d'Austria (1522-86) gave the palace its name. Since 1870 when Rome became the capital of Italy the Senate has occupied the building.

The Baroque façade in the Corso del Rinascimento was built c1642.

At the southern end of the street rises the façade of Sant'Andrea delle Valle *(see CAMPO DEI FIORI).*

Neighbouring sights are described in the following chapters: CAMPO DEI FIORI; CASTEL SANT'ANGELO; MONTECITORIO; PANTHEON.

PIAZZA DEL POPOLO ★★

Tour 2 hours

This walk incorporates some of the famous Roman streets – Via del Corso, Via Margutta and Via del Babuino – before reaching the Pincian Hill, a luxuriant park with a splendid view of the city. For a longer circuit, this walk may be extended to include the Mausoleum of Augustus, the Aris Pacis Augustae, Piazza di Spagna and the latter section of the Trident *(see PIAZZA DI SPAGNA).*

In the days of the 'Grand Tour' before the railway came to Rome, English travellers usually approached from the north down the Via Flaminia and entered the city through the Porta del Popolo. They took lodgings in the neighbouring streets between Piazza del Popolo and Piazza di Spagna (Spanish Square) so that the district came to be known as the English Ghetto.

This district also recalls the numerous French interventions in Italian affairs in the 18C and 19C. In 1798 General Berthier marched on Rome and deposed Pope Pius VI, establishing a Republic; in 1800 Pope Pius VII was elected by the Venice conclave and regained possession of the Papal States; after the Concordat of 1801 had re-established religious peace in France, Pius VII crowned Napoleon Emperor in Notre-Dame Cathedral in Paris on 2 December 1804; but the Emperor decided on a continental blockade: all the European sovereigns obeyed except Pius VII; on 2 February 1809

If in need of a pint

The decidedly British Victoria House pub extends a warm welcome to all – providing an altogether different atmosphere from the bustle of more Roman establishments.

General Miollis breached the walls of Rome at the Porta del Popolo with a force of 8 000 men; finally on 17 May 1809 Napoleon recorded that "the Papal States are reunited to the French Empire". This action led to a complete breach and excommunication followed by five years of French government while the Romans hurled continuous insults at the accomplices of the man whom they called the Antichrist.

★★PIAZZA DEL POPOLO

The square was laid out by **Giuseppe Valadier** (1762-1839), the favourite architect and town planner of Pius VI and Pius VII. In an effort to open up Rome, he made Piazza del Popolo one of the largest squares in the city. He retained the Porta del Popolo, the central obelisk and the twin churches flanking the Via del Corso, and opened out the space into two semicircles adorned with fountains and allegorical neo-Classical statues. The east side of the square was linked to the Pincio gardens above by a series of monumental arcaded terraces screened by trees and shrubs.

On 18 December 1813 a guillotine was set up in the square by the French government to deter the gangs of thugs who roamed the streets.

★**Porta del Popolo** – This gateway in the 3C Aurelian wall stands more or less on the site of the ancient *Porta Flaminia*. The exterior façade was built between 1562 and 1565 by Pius IV who wanted to impress visitors arriving from the north with an entrance worthy of the splendour of his capital. The Medici arms are the dominant feature. When Queen Christina of Sweden, newly converted to Roman Catholicism, arrived in 1655 the internal façade was decorated by Bernini with two scrolls supporting a garland beneath the star of the Chigi coat of arms which belonged to the then Pope, Alexander VII. On 24 May 1814 Pius VII, liberated by Napoleon, was given a delirious welcome.

Obelisk – It was brought from Heliopolis in Lower Egypt in the reign of Augustus and set up in the Circus Maximus. It was Sixtus V and his architect, Domenico Fontana, who raised it in the centre of Piazza del Popolo in 1589. The basins and marble lions at the base were added by Valadier at Leo XII's request in 1823.

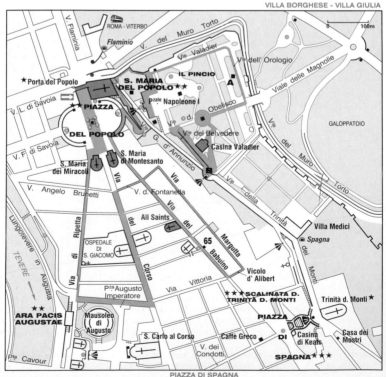

PIAZZA DI SPAGNA

Twin churches – From the obelisk one can appreciate the impact of good town planning on the south side of the square; Carlo Rainaldi designed the two churches to provide a background to the obelisk and a theatrical entrance to Via del Corso. Their apparent similarity is created by the fact that the sides of the drums facing the square have the same dimensions. In fact the church on the left is eliptical in plan beneath a twelve-sided dome and the church on the right is circular in plan with an octagonal dome and occupies a broader site. The domes were covered with slates by Leo XII in 1825.

Santa Maria di Montesanto ⊙ was the first of the twin churches to be built – from 1662 to 1667 by Carlo Rainaldi and from 1671 to 1675 by Bernini. **Santa Maria dei Miracoli** ⊙, meanwhile, was begun by Carlo Rainaldi and completed (1677-79) by Carlo Fontana.

★★**Santa Maria del Popolo** – Despite its simple exterior, the church contains **art treasures**★ worthy of a museum.

The building which was commissioned by Sixtus IV in 1472 and finished in 1477 is one of the first examples of the Renaissance style in Rome; its façade rises, almost devoid of ornament, to a triangular pediment; the plainness is relieved by typical Renaissance features: shallow pilasters and simple scrolls linking the lower and upper stages of the façade (the elaborate curves are Baroque additions).

The **interior** abounds in Renaissance features. The Latin cross plan is used in preference to a basilical one. The nave, which has groined vaulting, is flanked by two aisles lined by side chapels. The usual columns and walls of a basilical church have been replaced by massive square pillars composed of engaged columns.

During the Baroque period stucco statues were added above the arches of the nave by Bernini.

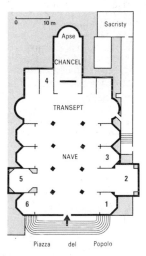

Piazza del Popolo

Della Rovere Chapel (1) – The chapel rail shows the coat of arms of the Della Rovere family to which Pope Sixtus IV belonged. Above the altar is the **fresco**★ depicting the *Adoration of the Child* by the Umbrian painter **Pinturicchio** (1454-1513). The face of the Virgin is a typical expression of serene gentleness, while the scene is animated with incidental detail: a grazing goat, a lamb suckling its mother and a watchful ox.

On the left is the tomb of two members of the Della Rovere family; the decorative motifs were carved by Andrea Bregno late in the 15C; the oval medallion of the Virgin, its simple lines expressing a harmony of strength and gentleness, is by Mino da Fiesole, who worked at the Papal court from 1473 to 1480.

Cybo Chapel (2) – The Baroque chapel was designed by Carlo Fontana (1682-87) on a Greek cross plan beneath a dome.

Basso della Rovere Chapel (3) – The tomb of Giovanni Basso della Rovere (15C) on the righthand wall is by a pupil of Andrea Bregno and the frescoes above the altar and on the lefthand wall are by the Pinturicchio school.

Transept – The chapels opening off the east side of the transept and the apses at either end are characteristic of the Renaissance. The Baroque style is represented by the cherubs supporting the picture frames above the transept altars.

The dome above the crossing was probably the first Renaissance dome to be produced in Rome.

The chancel arch is decorated with gilded stucco low reliefs, one *(right)* showing Pope Paschal II (1099-1118) chopping down a walnut tree. According to legend the church was built on the site of the tomb of the terrible Nero which was marked by a walnut tree. The population which went in fear and trembling of Nero's ghost appealed to Paschal II who felled the tree, threw Nero's remains into the Tiber and erected a chapel, which under Sixtus IV became Santa Maria del Popolo.

Apse and Chancel – *Go round behind the high altar.* The apse was extended by Bramante for Julius II (1503-13). The ceiling fresco is by Pinturicchio. The stained glass in predominantly neutral tones picked out with flashes of brilliant colour is the only old glass in Rome; it is the work of a Frenchman, Guillaume de Marcillat (16C). The two **tombs**★, carved in about 1505 by **Andrea Sansovino**, are elegant works of art in which the influence of Classical architecture (commemorative arches) mingles with the decorative style of 15C Florence.

★★★**Caravaggio's Paintings** – *In the Cerasi Chapel* (**4**). Two pictures, painted in 1601, illustrate two scenes from Holy Scripture.

In the *Conversion of St Paul (right)*, as in all Caravaggio's works, light is the dominant feature. The effect of the divine light illuminating St Paul on the road to Damascus should have been sublime but it falls first of all on the horse, which is out of proportion, before touching the foreshortened figure of the saint.

The *Crucifixion of St Peter (left)* illustrates Caravaggio's taste for creating a diagonal axis. The treatment of the subject avoids all reference to the sublime: three brawny men whose faces are hidden are raising a cross bearing a man of rugged but noble mien. Above the altar is *The Assumption of the Virgin* by **Annibale Carracci.**

★**Chigi Chapel (5)** – The design was entrusted to Raphael in 1513 by his champion, Agostino Chigi, banker, patron and consort of princes and popes. The dome mosaic, from a drawing by Raphael, dates from the Renaissance as do the figures of Jonah (after Raphael) and the prophet Elijah in their niches and the altarpiece, a Nativity in muted tones by Sebastiano del Piombo.

In the Baroque period Bernini was commissioned by Fabio Chigi, the future Alexander VII; he faced the base of the pyramid-shaped tomb of Agostino and Sigismondo Chigi with green marble, carved the figures of Daniel, the lion, Habakkuk and the angel, which seem to burst from their niches, and inserted in the floor a winged skeleton with the Chigi coat of arms.

In the last chapel (**6**) is a recumbent figure in bronze of Bishop Girolamo Foscari sculpted by Vecchietta in the 15C.

IL TRIDENTE (THE TRIDENT)

To Romans this name means the three streets which diverge from Piazza del Popolo like the three prongs of a trident – Via di Ripetta, Via del Corso and Via del Babuino.

Via di Ripetta – This street follows the course of an ancient Roman street which ran beside the Tiber. Originally it was called Via Leonina, as it was remodelled in 1515 by Leo X; some sources state that the cost of the work was financed by a brothel tax. This street, which is quite unlike the other two prongs of the trident, contains a multitude of shops and boutiques.

Turn left into Piazza Augusto Imperatore and left again into Via del Corso.

Via del Corso – Following the route of the ancient Via Flaminia the modern street runs in a straight line (1500m - 1640yds) from Piazza del Popolo to Piazza Venezia. Its medieval name was Via Lata but now it is called after the famous horse races organised by Pope Paul II in the 15C. It is lined by handsome Renaissance palaces. Nowadays the 'Corso' is the main street of central Rome; its fashionable shops and cafés attract the crowds. The German poet Goethe, beloved to students

---

At the heart of the festivities

Throughout the years, the Corso has been the place where fashionable Romans made their appearance. In the 18C it was good form for a lady to be seen there with her *sigisbeo*, a faithful admirer. The *sigisbeo* became so firmly fixed in local custom that the Church tolerated the practice, and clauses permitting a wife to have one or more admirers were included in marriage contracts.

During the **Carnival** in February processions and mascarades proceeded along the Corso. The high point of the festivities was reached when the horse racing began. Each evening in the week leading up to Ash Wednesday the grooms led the horses round the course. Dickens described the race vividly "Down the whole length of the Corso they fly like the wind: riderless, with shining ornaments upon their backs and twisted in their plaited manes; and with heavy little balls stuck full of spikes dangling at their sides to goad them on. The jingling of these trappings and the rattling of their hoofs upon the hard stones, the dash and fury of their speed along the echoing street; nay, the very cannon that are fired – these noises are nothing to the roaring of the multitude: their shouts: the clapping of their hands. But it is soon over – almost instantaneously. More cannon shake the town. The horses have plunged into the carpets hung across the street to stop them."

On the last evening of the Carnival the *Moccoli* (wax tapers) appeared; everyone carried a lighted candle in his hand and tried to put out his neighbour's flame. The scene on 9 February 1788 was described by the German poet Goethe, who spent two years in Rome at no 18 Via del Corso: "The idiots made another great din on Monday and Tuesday, particularly Tuesday evening when the craze for *Moccoli* was at its height."

Only in 1809 did the Romans boycott the Carnival in protest against the French government. Pasquino, the famous talking statue which presides over his own square west of Piazza Navona, observed mockingly: "The bear may dance under the rod but not men."

of the Antique on the Grand Tour. In his *Italian Journey*, he describes the carnival at some length to *'provide those who are planning to visit Rome with a general introduction to its overcrowded and torrential merriment... Unlike the religious festivals in Rome, the Carnival does not dazzle the eye: there are no fireworks, no illuminations, no brilliant processions. All that happens is that, at a given signal, everyone has leave to be as mad and foolish as he likes, and almost everything, except fisticuffs and stabbing is permissible.'*

This area is traditionally where foreigners gather. Indeed before the railways extended to Rome, most travellers arrived in Rome southwards down the via Cassia, crossing the Tiber over the Ponte Molle or the Ponte Milvio to enter the city through the Popolo Gate only to find accommodation nearby.

Turn right into Via della Fontanella and second right into Via Margutta.

Via Margutta – This street in the artistic heart of Rome is named after a famous little 15C theatre where they performed parodies of chivalrous epic poems such as Luigi Pulci's comedy *Morgante* with its two heroes, Morgante and Margutta.

The houses in Via Margutta, often decorated with balconies and courtyard gardens, are occupied on the ground floor by art galleries. In June and October this peaceful backwater comes to life for the Via Margutta Exhibition — *Fiera di Via Margutta* – when artists exhibit their work in the street.

Via Margutta leads into **Vicolo d'Alibert** which in the 18C contained the *Teatro delle dame;* here for the first time women sang on stage in the Papal States. Formerly the female roles in opera had been sung by *castrati*.

Turn right into Vicolo d'Alibert and right again into Via del Babuino.

Via del Babuino – The street was opened by Clement VII for Jubilee Year in 1525. Its present name was given to it by popular usage when the statue of a Silenus was discovered in such a hideous state that the Romans compared it to a baboon. The statue is now to be found next to the fountain on the corner by St Athanasius' Church (S Atanasio).

Today the street is known for its antique shops often situated in the 17C and 18C palazzi.

Chiesa Anglicana (All Saints Anglican Church) ⊙ – The church, which is now a protected building, was designed by **G E Street** in the early 1880s shortly before his death. It is built in the English Gothic style of specially-made bricks with a distinctive white travertine spire erected in 1937. The spacious interior is enriched by a variety of coloured marbles from different

Rome from the Pincian Hill

parts of Italy: white and green Carrara, red Perugia, black Verona, yellow Siena and white Como. The pulpit designed in 1891 by A E Street, the architect's son, is reminiscent of the early Christian basilicas. Above the high altar hang seven lamps bought in Venice by a former Hon Asst Chaplain out of money given him by the congregation "to be spent on himself". The stained glass, depicting various saints and commemorating people connected with the church, is English, as is also the organ, a large and complex instrument, originally made in Huddersfield and presented in 1894, which has been used by famous guest organists for recitals and master classes.

A medieval legend tells of the Pincio walnut tree, growing from the bones of Nero, was haunted by demons which manifested themselves as black crows nestling in the branches. The very existence of these buried remains became the ultimate nightmare of the Roman people who claimed to have seen a ghost of the Emperor prowling restlessly racked by the torments of the netherworld.

The first Anglican services, for which papal permission was sought and granted, were held in Rome in 1816. After several years in hired rooms the congregation found a more permanent base in 1824 in the granary chapel outside the Porta del Popolo, until the building was demolished in a road-widening scheme in 1882.

From Piazza del Popolo climb up the Pincian Hill by the steps which lead to Piazzale Napoleone I.

IL PINCIO (PINCIAN HILL)

The Pinci family, who had a garden here in the 4C, have left their name to this little hill which is still covered by a garden, one of the pleasantest in Rome. The Pincio was laid out in its present style during the Napoleonic occupation (1809-14) according to the designs of **Giuseppe Valadier.** The avenues are shaded by magnificent umbrella pines, palm trees and evergreen oaks. The statues of Italian patriots were added by Giuseppe Mazzini (1805-72).

From the terrace of Piazzale Napoleone I there is a magnificent **view**★★★ particularly at dusk when the golden glow so typical of Rome is at its best. Below the terrace is Piazza del Popolo with the domes of the twin churches marking the beginning of the Corso. Opposite are the buildings of the Vatican grouped round the dome of St Peter's next to the green slopes of the Janiculum; just in front stand Castel Sant'Angelo and the white bulk of the Law Courts. The line of the Corso is marked by the domes of San Carlo, San Giovanni dei Fiorentini, Sant'Andrea delle Valle, the Pantheon (shallow) and the Gesù Church ending with the monument to Victor Emmanuel II.

The water clock (**A**) in Viale dell'Orologio was built in 1867 by a Dominican monk, Giovan Battista Embriago and presented to the Universal Exhibition in Paris (1889).

Half way along Viale dell'Obelisco which leads to the gardens of the Villa Borghese stands an obelisk which was set up here in 1822 by Pius VII after being found near the Porta Maggiore in the 16C; it was originally erected by the Emperor Hadrian in memory of his young friend Antinoüs.

From the Casina Valadier in Viale del Belvedere there is a magnificent **view** of the roofs of the city.

The **Cairoli Monument** (**B**), commemorates two brothers, Enrico and Giovanni, Italian patriots, who fought beside Garibaldi against the papal troops and died in 1867 in the bloody struggles which marked the long road to Italian unity.

From the monument there is an extensive view of the city of Rome.

Neighbouring sights are described in the following chapters: PIAZZA DI SPAGNA; VILLA BORGHESE – VILLA GIULIA.

Help us in our constant task of keeping up-to-date
Please send us your comments and suggestions

Michelin Tyre PLC
Tourism Department
Edward Hyde Building
38 Clarendon Road
Watford WD1 1SX
Tel : 01923 415164/5/6
Fax : 01923 415250

PIAZZA DI SPAGNA★★★

Tour 2 ½ hours

The walk covers the district south of the area within the "Trident", the three streets leading south from the Piazza del Popolo. Via del Babuino emerges into the very lively Spanish Square at the foot of the famous Spanish Steps – which lead up to the Church of Trinità dei Monti – and the busy rows of flower sellers sheltering from the heat under their colourful umbrellas. At certain times of the year the steps are completely covered in flowers – azaleas in April – and offer a feast for the eye. Via del Corso, lined with elegant shop windows, is one of the busiest streets in Rome. Via di Ripetta, near the river, leads to one of Rome's most famous monuments – Augustus' Altar of Peace – an immense altar which the Senate had built to celebrate the peace brought about by Augustus throughout the whole of the Roman Empire. These three streets are linked by Via dei Condotti, one of Rome's most elegant thoroughfares, which offers a truly magnificent view of the Spanish Steps.

★★★PIAZZA DI SPAGNA (SPANISH SQUARE)

The square is famous throughout the world and the steps are a favourite meeting place for young Romans.

Shaped like two triangles joined at their points, **Spanish Square** got its name in the 17C when the Spanish Ambassador to the Holy See took up residence in the **Palazzo di Spagna.** Thereupon the area bounded by Via dei Condotti, Via del Corso and Via della Mercede became Spanish territory and any foreigner crossing the boundaries at night often disappeared, having been impressed into the Spanish army. The French however, who owned the land around the convent of the Trinità dei Monti, claimed the right to pass through the square. They named part of it "French Square" and set out to rival the Spanish by giving ever more sumptuous entertainments. In 1681 the Spanish celebrated the birthday of their Queen, Marie-Louise, by transforming the square with a variety of paste-board decorations. In 1685 it was the turn of the French; to celebrate the Revocation of the Edict of Nantes they covered the whole hillside with candelabras and decorated the church to look like a wayside altar from which they set off fireworks which lit up the whole town.

In the 18C it became very popular among the English on the Grand Tour. In 1820 Henry Matthews set down his first impressions in his diary:

"We were soon in the Piazza di Spagna, the focus of fashion and the general resort of the English. Some travellers have compared it to Grosvenor Square but the Piazza di Spagna is little more than an irregular open space, a little less nasty than the other piazzas in Rome because the habits of the people are in some measure restrained by the presence of the English... The English swarm everywhere. We found all the inns full. It seemed like a country town in England at an assizes."

★**Fontana della Barcaccia (Boat Fountain)** – *At the foot of the steps.* It was designed by Bernini's father, Pietro (1627-29) for Pope Urban VIII. The boat, which is decorated at either end with the suns and bees of the Barberini coat of arms, seems to be letting in water. The sculptor is supposed to have conceived the idea from seeing a boat stranded in Spanish Square by the flood waters of the Tiber.

Casina di Keats (Keats' House) ⊙ – *26 Piazza di Spagna.* The house on the right at the foot of the Spanish steps where Keats died of tuberculosis in February 1821 was purchased in 1903 by the Keats-Shelley Memorial Association. The rooms which Keats occupied on the first floor now contain a collection of manuscripts, letters, mementoes and documents on the lives not only of Keats but also of Shelley, Byron and Leigh Hunt, together with a library of 10 000 volumes. In the entrance hall on the ground floor hang portraits of Keats and his contemporaries by English artists of the period.

★★★**Scalinata della Trinità dei Monti (Spanish Steps)** – Built between 1723 to 1726 by de Sanctis in accordance with designs by Specchi (a pupil of C Fontana), the steps show the Baroque taste for perspective and *trompe-l'œil*.

Construction was preceded by fierce diplomatic struggles between the Holy See and France which are recalled in the eagles from the Conti coat of arms for Innocent XIII and the Lily of France. The idea of a flight of steps linking Spanish Square with the Church of the Trinità dei Monti had first been proposed in the 17C. The French Ambassador even contributed 10 000 écus towards the cost, while Cardinal Mazarin proposed to make the steps a symbol of the greatness of the French monarchy in Rome. A grandiose design was prepared dominated by an equestrian statue of Louis XIV. The idea of a king's statue in the Papal City! Alexander VII objected. Neither the Cardinal's death in 1661 nor the Pope's death in 1669 ended the quarrel. It was not finally settled until Innocent XIII (1721-24) agreed to the French architect and the French abandoned the statue of Louis XIV. De Sanctis designed three successive flights of steps, some broader, some narrower, some divided, exaggerating the effect of height and creating a graceful and majestic décor.

From the upper terrace there is an excellent view of the city.

Spanish Steps

In the square in front of the Church of the Trinità dei Monti stands an imitation Egyptian obelisk transported from Sallust's gardens near the Salaria Gate by Pius VI.

★**Trinità dei Monti** ⊙ – The church – Holy Trinity on the Hill – was founded in 1495 by Charles VIII at the request of St Francis of Paola for the Minims who lived in the neighbouring convent. The building rose slowly during the 16C. It was severely damaged by French revolutionaries and completely rebuilt in 1816 by the architect Mazois assisted by several students from the Villa Medici. It is now French property and the convent is occupied by the Ladies of the Sacred Heart.

Façade – An elegant stairway, built in 1587 by Domenico Fontana, leads up to the façade which is surmounted by two belfries, erected in 1588 by the Duc de Joyeuse and modelled on those designed by Giacomo della Porta for St Athanasius in Via del Babuino. In 1613 a clock was added to tell the time in the "French manner".

Interior – *Apply in advance for guided tour:* ☎ *06 79 22 45, 06 79 41 79.* The single nave flanked by intercommunicating chapels is reminiscent of the Gothic churches in the south of France. It is quite possible that it was designed by an architect from the southwest of that country (the windows which formerly decorated the chancel were sent for by Cardinal Briçonnet from Narbonne). The decorative latticework in the transept vaults, the oldest part of the church, is typical of late-Gothic art. The side chapels are decorated with Mannerist paintings. The third on the right contains a fresco of the *Assumption* by Daniele da Volterra. The figure in red on the right of the picture is a portrait of Michelangelo; his assistants were responsible for the paintings on the side walls: the *Massacre of the Innocents (left)* and the *Presentation in the Temple (right)*.

★**Deposition from the Cross** – *Second chapel on the left.* This fresco (1541), which has been much restored, is a masterpiece by **Daniele da Volterra** who was a great admirer of Michelangelo. See how skilfully he has arranged his composition around the pale body of Jesus.

Take Viale della Trinità dei Monti.

On the right is a **bust of Chateaubriand** (**A**), better known as a writer, who was the French Ambassador in Rome from 1828 to 1829.

Villa Medici

Villa Medici – The villa, which now houses the French Academy (Accademia di Francia), was built c1570 for Cardinal Ricci di Montepulciano and passed to Cardinal Ferdinando de' Medici in 1576. In the 1C BC the site was covered by the gardens of Lucullus. There is a fine view of Rome from the terrace opposite the entrance.

The fountain, which was installed in 1587 by Cardinal Ferdinando de' Medici, is the one which Corot painted. Legend has it that the ball in the centre of the basin is a cannon ball fired at the Villa from Castel Sant'Angelo by Queen Christina of Sweden who adored practical jokes. She wanted to wake up the master of the house to invite him to join a hunting party.

French Academy – It was founded by Colbert under Louis XIV in 1666 and occupied various buildings in Rome before moving to the Villa Medici in 1803. Its previous home, the Palazzo Salviati, had been closed, sacked and burned during the Revolution. Originally the pupils were chosen by competition, the Prix de Rome; the first batch comprised six painters, four sculptors and two architects. After 1803 the field was widened to include engravers and musicians. The struggle for Italian unity and the Second World War forced the Academy to move to Florence, then Nice and finally Fontainebleau before returning to the Villa Medici in 1946. Since then new areas of study have been admitted: literature, cinema, history and restoration of art. There are now about 25 students, chosen by the Ministry of Culture on the recommendation of specialists, and they study for one or two years.

From Trinità del Monti to Ara Pacis

Casa dei Mostri (Monsters' House) – *At the beginning of Via Gregoriana (no 30).* The door and windows are framed by curious carved monsters with gaping mouths.

In the 17C and 18C **Via Gregoriana** and its neighbour Via Sistina usually provided lodgings for the wealthier visitors to Rome.

Continue along Via Gregoriana to the junction with Via Crispi.

★**Galleria comunale d'Arte moderna e contemporanea** – *Temporarily housed in the Carmelite convent at 24 Via Crispi.* The **Gallery of Modern and Contemporary Art** accommodates a collection of paintings and sculptures from the early half of the 20C. Of particular note are Rodin's *Bust of a woman* and Balla's allegory of **Doubt**, a beautiful portrait of his wife. On the 2nd floor is Amedeo Bocchi's huge canvas entitled *In the Park* painted in vivid, almost violent colours. There are also works by Sartorio, Trombadori, Casorati, Morandi, Guttoso *(Self-portrait).*

Palazzo di Propaganda Fide – This imposing building, the property of the Holy See, houses the Congregation for the Evangelisation of Peoples, which originated in the institution of the Congregation for the Propagation of the Faith by Gregory XV in 1622. It was Urban VIII (1623-44) who began construction of the building by inviting his protégé, Bernini, to design the façade overlooking Spanish Square. The result is unexpectedly sober for this brilliant Baroque architect. On Innocent X's accession Bernini fell into disgrace. The new pope wished to give his reign a new look and he turned to Borromini – the only architect able to compete with Bernini – whom he commissioned to design the façade overlooking Via di Propaganda. With Borromini a touch of fantasy was introduced: in the cornices and in the elaborate pediments over the windows.

Within the palazzo *(on the left of the door in Via di Propaganda no 1/c)* is another building (1666) by Borromini, the tiny Church of the **Re Magi** (Three Wise Men) ⊙.

Sant'Andrea delle Fratte – St Andrew's Church, which originated in the 12C, stands in Via di Capo Le Case (end of the houses) which in the Middle Ages was the northeastern limit of the city. Its name recalls the thickets *(fratte)* which used to abound in the vicinity. Early in the 17C the rebuilding of the church was begun; the work was completed by Borromini. From higher up the street there is a view of the **campanile**★ and the **dome**★ which he treated as precious objects, abandoning the traditional form and giving full expression to the eccentric products of his fertile imagination: the dome, which would normally soar into the sky, is imprisoned in a space circumscribed by convex and concave surfaces. The façade is 19C.

Inside at the entrance to the chancel are two statues of **angels**★ presenting the Instruments of the Passion. When Bernini sculpted them in 1669, his art was very close to the extreme delicacy characteristic of the Rococo period. They were designed to accompany the other statues commissioned by Clement IX for the Sant' Angelo Bridge but the Pope found them too beautiful to be exposed to the elements. They remained with Bernini's family until 1729 when they were placed in the church.

Take Via della Mercede.

Piazza San Silvestro is dominated by the façade of the Central Post Office which was established in the 19C in the monastery of the Church of San Silvestro in Capite. Every bus route and taxi fare seems to end in this square, which with its church and the post office, its café and its newspaper stall, is an excellent place for observing the Roman way of life.

Turn right into Via del Gambero and left into Via Frattina to reach Piazza S Lorenzo in Lucina.

San Lorenzo in Lucina – The **Church of St Lawrence** was built in the 12C on the site of a 4C *titulus (see* INTRODUCTION: Christian Rome), the house of a woman called Lucina. The belltower, the porch and the two lions flanking the door date from the medieval period. Inside is a monument *(against the pillar between the 2nd and 3rd chapels on the right)* erected by Chateaubriand, the French Ambassador, to commemorate Nicolas Poussin who spent many years in Rome. The fourth chapel on the right contains a bust *(back left-hand corner)* of Dr Gabriele Fonseca, by Bernini, a late and rather theatrical work (1668).

Take Via del Leone which leads into Largo Fontanella Borghese.

From the piazza there is an interesting view of the Church of Trinità dei Monti.

Palazzo Borghese (Borghese Palace) – The palace was built at the end of the 16C and the façade overlooking Piazza Borghese demonstrates the dignity and austerity of the Counter-Reformation. The palace was acquired by Cardinal Camillo Borghese who became Pope in 1605 as Paul V. The courtyard *(entrance in Largo della Fontanella di Borghese)* with its loggias, statues, fountains and rockeries is a beautiful evocation of the luxurious life of the noble families in the 17C.

Paul V gave the palace to his brothers who commissioned Flaminio Ponzio, the architect (1560-1613), to extend it towards the Tiber. He it was who designed the picturesque front in Via di Ripetta which used to overlook the Ripetta riverside port.

In **Piazza Borghese** there is a most attractive antiques market **(Mercato dell' Antiquariato)** specialising in antique books and prints. Wandering round the stalls, the collector might even be able to find prints from as early as 1600. It is open all year round and offers an excellent excuse for a welcome break during sight-seeing.

Take Via di Ripetta north as far as Piazza Augusto Imperatore.

Beside Ponte Cavour (Cavour Bridge) stands a small kiosk (**B**) selling the famous *grattachecche* made of fruit syrup poured over crushed ice.

Botticella Fountain (**C**) – It was built in 1774 at the expense of the Ripetta watermen's association. There is a fine view of the apse and dome of San Carlo al Corso *(see below).*

Mausoleo di Augusto – The ruins of the **Mausoleum of Augustus** are now surrounded by the modern buildings of Piazza Augusto Imperatore which was laid out in 1940.

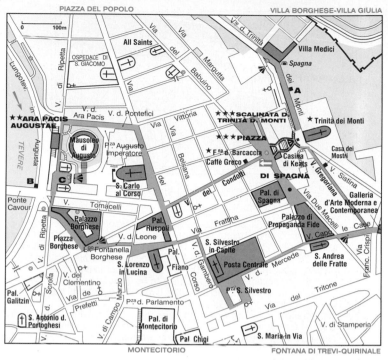

Augustus' Mausoleum was one of the most sacred monuments in Antiquity. It was built between 28 and 23 BC and, like Hadrian's mausoleum, the Castel Sant'Angelo, it took the form of an Etruscan tumulus tomb. On a rectangular base stood a cylindrical section surmounted by a conical hillock of earth *(tumulus)* planted with cypress trees. On the south side flanking the entrance stood two obelisks, Roman imitations of Egyptian models, which now stand in Piazza dell' Esquilino and Piazza del Quirinale. The funeral chamber in the middle of the mausoleum was reserved for the Emperor; round it was a series of chambers for the other members of the Julio-Claudian family.

In the Middle Ages the mausoleum was converted into a fortress by the Colonna family; Gregory IX (1227-41) dismantled it and stripped it of its blocks of travertine; in 1936 the concert hall which it then contained was closed and the remains were restored.

★★ARA PACIS AUGUSTAE (ALTAR OF AUGUSTUS) ⊘

Housed in a modern building between the Mausoleum of Augustus and Lungotevere in Augusta.

The monumental altar was erected by the Senate and inaugurated in 9 BC in honour of the Peace which Augustus established throughout the Roman world and in the capital where the concentration of power in one person put an end to 20 years of civil war. The Ara Pacis originally stood in the Campus Martius beside the Via Flaminia (now Via del Corso) about where the Palazzo Fiano stands today. In 1970, to celebrate Rome's centenary as the capital of modern Italy, the monument was opened to the public. It had been reconstructed from excavated fragments assembled from various museums and modern reproductions of the pieces which were missing entirely. The altar was the major work of the Augustan 'golden age' and marks the apogee of Roman art. It consists of the altar itself standing within a marble enclosure decorated with low relief carvings. There were two entrances to the enclosure in opposite walls: the entrance facing the Campus Martius was the main one used by the Pontifex Maximus and his suite of priests and Vestals; the rear entrance was used by the *camilli*, who were the priests' young assistants, by the men who performed the sacrifice and by the animals to be sacrificed.

External decoration of the enclosure – On the outside of the enclosure the lower part is decorated with scrolls of acanthus leaves and swans, a faithful representation carved with great skill and variety. Two panels ·flank the main entrance: Aeneas making a sacrifice *(right)* and Faustulus the shepherd finding Romulus and Remus *(left – a few fragments)*. These two scenes illustrate the legendary founding of Rome and glorify Augustus who claimed to be descended from Aeneas.

Imperial Procession on the Ara Pacis

The east side facing Via di Ripetta shows a procession of people including the Emperor and his family, some of whom have been identified: at the head Augustus (incomplete figure); Agrippa, his son-in-law, is probably the tall figure following the four priests *(flamines)* and a sacrificer (the symbolic axe on his shoulder); Antonia has turned to speak to her husband Drusus, Augustus' grandson. The human touch is not omitted: the young couple is cautioned to be quiet by an old woman standing between them with a finger to her lips. The two children behind Drusus are shown with natural simplicity.

The rear entrance is flanked by two panels: the personification of Rome Triumphant *(right* – mostly missing) seated on a pile of weapons, dominating the world; the personification of the Fruitful Earth *(left)* accompanied by two figures symbolizing Wind and Water. The latter scene is full of the realism characteristic of Roman art: a sheep is grazing at the goddess' feet while the two children play on her lap. Both scenes reflect the glory of Augustus, author of the Roman peace and token of the earth's fertility. The side facing the river shows a procession composed of members of the various priestly colleges.

The procession shown on the Ara Pacis represents the procession which took place on inauguration day.

Internal decoration – The lower half is decorated with broad vertical flutes which represent the temporary wooden palissade which surrounded the altar on the day of its consecration; the upper half is covered with garlands of fruit and flowers and the heads of the cattle which were sacrificed on that day; the vessels between the garlands were used for pouring a liquid on to the altar. The altar itself, which is flanked by winged lions, is decorated with a frieze of clear-cut small figures.

On the outside of the modern building facing Via di Ripetta is a reproduction of the *Res Gestae*, the text drawn up by Augustus of the acts accomplished in his reign; it also contained his Will. The original, which has been lost, was engraved on bronze plaques at the entrance to his mausoleum but a copy of it was found in the Temple of Augustus in Ankara (formerly Ancyra in Asia Minor).

East of the Mausoleum turn right into Via del Corso.

To Via dei Condotti

San Carlo al Corso – *Open daily, 0700 to 1230 and 1700 to 1900.* In 1471 the Lombard community in Rome was given a small church in the Corso by Sixtus IV. They rebuilt it and dedicated it to St Ambrose who was Bishop of Milan in the 4C. In 1610 they wanted to enlarge the building in honour of Charles Borromeo, Archbishop of Milan, who had just been canonised. The full name of the church is therefore Sant'Ambrogio e San Carlo al Corso. Construction began in 1612. The majestic interior is in the shape of a Latin cross with an ambulatory, a rarity in Rome, more usually found in northern churches. The heart of St Charles Borromeo now rests in the chapel behind the high altar. The **dome★** is the work of Pietro da Cortona (1668). The *Apotheosis of St Ambrose and St Charles*, on the high altar, is one of the best works of Carlo Maratta (1685-90), restored in the 19C. The handsomely carved 15C tabernacle on the pillar to the left probably comes from St Ambrose' sanctuary.

Palazzo Ruspoli ⊙ – This 16C palace is now a bank. After the downfall of Napoleon, in 1825 it became the refuge of Hortense de Beauharnais, ex-Queen of Holland, under the name of the Duchess of St Leu. "A flirt and a gossip, sentimental and romantic, Hortense was a pretty woman with forget-me-not eyes" (M Andrieux). Her salon became the centre of attraction for every pleasure-loving member of society. Her son, Prince Charles Louis Napoleon, the future Napoleon III, brought this sumptuous life to an end when he was implicated in a scheme to declare a republic in Rome and was expelled from the Papal States together with the Duchess of St Leu.

Throughout the year temporary exhibitions are held in the palazzo *(No 418/A Via del Corso)*.

Turn left into Via dei Condotti

Via dei Condotti – The street is named after the conduits *(condotti)* which brought water to Agrippa's baths in 19 BC.

It was in this street in 1760 that a Greek opened the famous **caffè Greco**, a meeting place for artists and men of letters: Goethe, Berlioz, Wagner, Leopardi, d'Annunzio. Here Elizabeth Barrett Browning, who lived in Via Bocca di Leone, was introduced to Hans Andersen, who lived above. Tennyson, Thackeray and Keats' friend, Joseph Severn lodged in the house opposite.

The room at the back of the café, called the Omnibus owing to its narrow width, is still hung with portraits of famous people. One can imagine its elegance and the unpopularity of Pope Leo XII when on 24 March 1824 he forbade his subjects to enter the café. The door was to remain locked and the owner was restricted to serving his customers through an opening in the window. The penalty was three months in the galleys.

Neighbouring sights are described in the following chapters: FONTANA DI TREVI – QUIRINALE; MONTECITORIO; PIAZZA DEL POPOLO; VILLA BORGHESE – VILLA GIULIA.

PIAZZA VENEZIA★★

Tour 1 $\frac{1}{2}$ hours

Rome's principal thoroughfares all converge on Piazza Venezia but traffic is regularly stilled by now infamous bottlenecks. The square's close proximity to the parliament buildings means that it is often targeted by picketing strikers and rallying demonstrators. Given its position and its imposing 19C monuments to the glory of Victor Emmanuel, it is also a convenient meeting point for strangers to the city at a loss to find their bearings.

The modern pedestrian trying to reach the other side of the square may be consoled to learn from Juvenal that conditions were worse in 1C: "Hurry as we may, we are blocked by a surging crowd in front, and by a dense mass of people pressing in on us from behind: one man digs an elbow into me, another a hard sedan-pole; one bangs a beam, another a wine cask against my head. My legs are bespattered with mud; soon huge feet trample on me from every side and a soldier plants his hobnails firmly on my toe. If that load of marble overturns on to the crowd, what is left of their bodies? Who can identify the limbs, who the bones? The poor men's crushed corpses wholly disappear, just like their souls."

★**Piazza Venezia** – Formerly the square was much more compact than today. The south side – going towards the Victor Emmanuel II Monument – was closed by the smaller Palazzetto Venezia, a building in harmony with the tower of the more famous Palazzo Venezia. In 1911, however, while work on the Victor Emmanuel II Monument was in progress, the palazzetto was "moved" to its present position at the far end of Piazza San Marco. Although this change allows a better view of the Victor Emmanuel II Monument, it has undoubtedly spoiled the balance of a Renaissance square.

Behind the Palazzo Venezia stands the beautiful Gesù Church, the main Jesuit church in Rome.

Walk to the Victor Emmanuel II Monument.

From here there is a typical Roman view including the domes of the churches of Santa Maria di Loreto and Santissimo Nome di Maria, as well as a group of umbrella pine trees around Trajan's column.

MONUMENTO A VITTORIO EMANUELE II (VITTORIANO)

This huge monument by **Giuseppe Sacconi**, which was begun in 1885 and inaugurated in 1911, was erected in honour of **King Victor Emmanuel II** who achieved the unification of Italy in 1870 with Rome as the capital city. The dazzling white marble clashes with the warm tones of the Roman townscape and the grandiloquent style strikes a jarring note. It is nicknamed the wedding cake.

A very broad flight of steps, flanked by two allegorical groups in bronze gilt representing *Thought* and *Action*, leads up to the *Altar to the Nation;* the steps divide before meeting at an equestrian statue of Victor Emmanuel; they then divide again and lead up to the concave portico which is surmounted by two bronze quadrigas bearing statues of winged victory. The foot of the stairway is flanked by two fountains representing the *Tyrrhenian Sea (right)* and the *Adriatic (left)*.

Victor Emmanuel II Monument

Tomba di Caio Publicio Bibula (Tomb of G Publicius Bibulus) – The travertine and brick remains of the tomb of Bibulus, who died 2 000 years ago, are of major archeological interest: as burials were forbidden within the precincts of the city, the position of this tomb shows that in the 1C BC the city boundary skirted the Capitoline Hill and the Via Flaminia, the trunk road to the north, began at this point.

Altare della Patria (National Shrine) (A) – At the foot of the statue of Rome is the tomb of the Unknown Soldier constantly guarded by two sentries. Since 1921 the tomb has contained the remains of a soldier who died in the 1915-18 war.

Statue equestre di Vittorio Emanuele II (B) – The **equestrian statue of Victor Emmanuel II** by **Enrico Chiaradia** was unveiled on 4 June 1911 in the presence of the King and some veteran Garibaldi troops before a crowd gathered in Piazza Venezia. A contemporary chronicler recorded that 50 tonnes of bronze had been used to cast the monument in a foundry in Trastevere and that His Majesty's moustaches were 1m - 3ft long.

Portico – *Temporarily closed*. There is a unique **view**★★ of the city from the portico.
From the west terrace in the foreground are Santa Maria d'Aracoeli and the Capitol. Beyond the Tiber rise the Janiculum, the dome of St Peter's, the Vatican and Castel Sant'Angelo. Then again on this side of the river are the domes for which Rome is famous: Sant'Andrea della Valle, the Gesù Church and the shallow curve of the Pantheon.
From the centre of the terrace: immediately below is Piazza Venezia linked to Piazza del Popolo by the straight line of Via del Corso. At the beginning of this street on the left is the **Palazzo Bonaparte**; built in 1660, it later came into the possession of Napoleon's mother who lived there after her son's fall from power taking great pleasure, so it is said, in watching what was going on in the street below from behind the shutters of the first floor balcony. She died there in 1836.
From the east terrace: the whole extent of the Imperial Fora (built by Caesar, Augustus, Trajan etc). In the distance, slightly to the left of the Colosseum, are the statues on the pediment of St John Lateran. To the right of the Colosseum is the Basilica of Maxentius, the belltower and façade of Santa Francesca Romana; in the foreground is the dome of the Church of St Luke and St Martina.

★PALAZZO VENEZIA

With this building which extends from the Piazza Venezia to Via del Plebiscito and Via degli Astalli, the Renaissance made a timid debut into civil architecture.

Historical Note – When Pietro Barbo was made a cardinal by his uncle Eugenius IV, he took a small house near the Capitol. He prided himself on doing everything with great show and in 1455 he began to build a palace worthy of his rank. When he became Pope in 1464, as **Paul II** he continued his project on a larger scale. Like the majority of the Renaissance popes, Paul II was both a military chief concerned with defence and a lover of the arts; but he was not very fond of the Humanists. His quarrels with Platina, legal draughtsman at the Vatican Chancery, are recorded in the Papal annals: Platina, who was dismissed for sedition, threatened to incite the princes to call a council against the Pope and he formed his friends into an academy which held well publicised meetings in the catacombs. Paul II imprisoned his opponent and talked of chopping off his head; Platina finally got off with milder corporal punishment and the dissolution of his academy.

In 1471 the Pope died before his house was finished. His nephew completed it. It was later altered several times: under Sixtus IV (1471-84) a smaller palace *(palazzetto)* was added opening on to a garden surrounded by a portico. Several popes lived in this agreeable residence from Alexander VI to Clement VIII early in the 17C. On his way to the conquest of the Kingdom of Naples, Charles VIII of France stayed in the house in 1494 and 1495.

Under Paul III (1534-49) a covered passage was built linking the Papal Palace with the Aracoeli Convent on the Capitol where the popes liked to spend the summer. It was Pius IV who gave the palace its present name in 1564 when he allowed the ambassadors of the Republic of Venice to lodge in part of the building. Following the Treaty of Campoformio between Austria and Napoleon in 1797, the Republic of Venice ceased to exist and almost all its property (including the Palazzo Venezia) reverted to Austria.

By order of Napoleon in 1806 it became the seat of the French administration, and was again at the forefront of Roman history in 1910 when the Italian government decided to lay out a huge square in front of the monument to King Victor Emmanuel II; Paul III's covered passage was demolished; the *palazzetto* which stood at the foot of the tower in the southeast angle was pulled down and immediately put up again where it stands today on the corner of Piazza di San Marco and Via degli Astalli. At the same time the **Palazzo delle Assicurazioni Generali di Venezia** was built on the other side of the square in imitation of the Palazzo Venezia.

Mussolini set up his office on the first floor of the palace. Now the Palazzo Venezia is one of the most prestigious buildings in the capital housing a museum and the library of the Institute of Art and Archeology. It was restored several times in the 18C and 19C and again from 1924 to 1936.

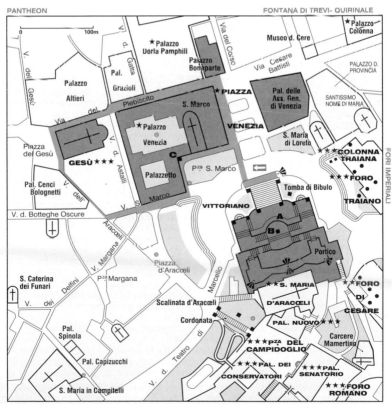

Exterior – The crenellations on the façade overlooking Piazza Venezia and the huge tower in the southeast corner show how the severe style of the fortified houses of the Middle Ages persisted. The mullion windows, the doors on to the square and in Via del Plebiscito and above all the attractive façade of St Mark's Basilica are pleasing manifestations of the Renaissance.

Statue of Madama Lucrezia (C) – It stands in Piazza di San Marco in the angle where the Palazzo Venezia and the *palazzetto* join and may have belonged to the Temple of Isis which stood on the Campus Martius.

It was one of the four talking statues of Rome, the others being Pasquino, Marforio and the Abate Luigi – Madama Lucrezia's favourite.

Interior – *Access from Piazza di San Marco; entrance beside the statue of Madama Lucrezia.* The unsophisticated outward appearance of Roman Renaissance palaces gives no hint of the elegant décor often to be found within.

Courtyard – At the centre is a flourishing garden, partially flanked on two sides by an elegant but incomplete portico by Giuliano da Maiano (1432-90). The east side is formed by St Mark's Basilica, which stands within the palace beneath its medieval belfry. The attractive fountain dates from the 18C: Venice, the lion of St Mark at its feet, is throwing a ring into the sea, a symbol of the marriage between the Serenissima and the sea.

Museo di Palazzo Venezia (Palazzo Venezia Museum) ⊙ – *First Floor.* The first rooms, devoted to Medieval art, contain some very fine 17C objects including some from the collection of Athanasius Kircher, a Jesuit priest. Particularly interesting are the antique ceramics which include some 14C pieces from Orvieto **(Room IV). Room V** displays a fine Byzantine enamel **Christ Pantocrator★★** from the second-half of the 13C, a very finely carved ivory **Byzantine Triptych★★** from the 10C and a small bronze head sculpted by Nicola Pisano in 1248. In **Room VI** there are some paintings on wood by primitive artists from Florence and Siena belonging to the **Sterbini Collection★★. Room VII** houses the 14C "Orsini" cross, made of embossed silver in the Abruzzi, and the painted ceiling taken from the Palazzo Altoviti (1533) with its central figure, Ceres, framed by medallions depicting the agricultural labours of the year. The wings of the museum display ceramics, porcelain and a large collection of small bronzes from the 15C to 17C. Next comes a collection of terracotta objects. The picture gallery shows many paintings.

Paul II's suite of rooms (overlooking Piazza Venezia and Via del Plebiscito) comprises the Royal Room where ambassadors waited to be received by the Pope; the Battle Room (from the Battles of the First World War) which is the former Consistory Room where the Pope brought the Cardinals together in assembly; and the Map Room which owes its name to the map of the world which was displayed there in the 15C. The architectural features painted on the walls by Mantegna have been extensively restored in the 20C. From the balcony Mussolini used to address the crowds gathered in Piazza Venezia.

Basilica di San Marco (St Mark's Basilica) – Founded by Pope Mark in 336 and dedicated to St Mark the Evangelist this basilica was rebuilt by Gregory IV in the 9C. Excavations beneath it have uncovered traces of an earlier 4C building and of the 9C crypt where Gregory IV caused the relics of Abdon and Sennen, Persian martyrs, to be deposited.

In the 12C a belfry was added and then in 1455 the church was rebuilt and incorporated in the Palazzo Venezia by Cardinal Pietro Barbo. In the 17C and 18C further restoration and alterations took place.

The **façade★** overlooking Piazza San Marco is attributed to Giuliano da Maiano or Leon-Battista Alberti: the double row of arches, in which the upper ones are carried on slimmer supports, lends elegance to this charming Renaissance composition.

In the porch, among the various fragments, are the medieval stone surround of a well and the tombstone *(right)* of Vanozza Caetani, mother of Pope Alexander VI's children, Caesar and Lucrezia Borgia *(see CAMPO DEI FIORI)*.

The sumptuous **interior★** is a typical Roman example of the overlapping of styles down the centuries. The medieval basilica plan of a nave and two aisles remains. In the 15C the elegant coffered ceiling was added with the arms of Paul II and clerestories were inserted in the nave above the alternate panels of stucco and 18C paintings which illustrate the legend of Abdon and Sennen.

The mosaic in the apse was commissioned in the 9C by Gregory IV. To the right of Christ among a group of saints is the Pope offering his church; on his head is a square nimbus showing that he was still alive.

Below are 12 sheep, representing the Apostles, advancing towards the Lamb, symbol of Christ, over a flowered meadow.

The chancel arch shows a bust of the Saviour, the Evangelists and St Peter and St Paul. In the sacristy is a charming 15C tabernacle carved by Mino da Fiesole in collaboration with Giovanni Dalmata; it stood originally on the high altar but was moved in the 18C.

Go round the outside of the Palazzo clockwise; from Via San Marco turn right into Via dell'Aracoeli to reach Piazza del Gesù.

★★★IL GESÙ (GESÙ CHURCH)

The salient features of Piazza del Gesù are the church and the wind. According to a Roman legend it has been so since the Devil asked the wind to wait for him while he went into the church. He never came out and the wind has been waiting ever since.

This building is the main Jesuit church in Rome. The Society of Jesus was founded in 1540 by Ignatius Loyola, a Spaniard. After the Council of Trent the Society became the prime mover in the Counter-Reformation which sought to rebut the ideas put forward by Martin Luther and Calvin. In 1568 the decision was taken to build a church in the centre of Rome. Cardinal Alexander Farnese undertook to provide the funds and insisted on his choice of architect: Vignola. The Vicar General of the Society engaged his own Jesuit architect, Father Giovanni Tristano, to see that the demands of the Jesuit rule were met.

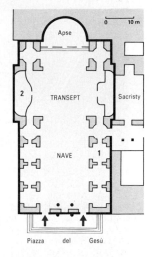

Piazza   del   Gesù

Façade – The design chosen in 1575 was by Giacomo **della Porta**. Very solemn and severe, it became a model for a transitional style, half-way between Renaissance and Baroque art, long known as the 'Jesuit style'. Art historians no longer use the expression since the Jesuits neither invented nor promoted a new style of architecture; at the most Rome gave practical advice on the construction of the Society's churches abroad.

The façade consists of two superimposed orders linked by powerful scrolls and has a double pediment, one curved and one triangular. These are the features which later became characteristic of Baroque architecture: several engaged columns are used instead of the flat pilasters of the Renaissance; projecting features and effects of light and shade are more pronounced. The height and width of the façade to some extent mask the dome which is seen to best advantage from above.

Interior – Compared with the purity of Gothic or the austerity of Romanesque, the richness of the décor is astonishing. A distinction must be made between the architecture of the building, a fairly plain product of the Counter-Reformation, and the ornate decoration which was added a century later in the Baroque period when the Papacy was triumphant.

The majestic Latin cross **plan** was ideal for the Society's main purpose: preaching – which enabled the congregation to understand the ceremonies which they attended. In the single broad nave, unobstructed and well lit, the worshippers could concentrate on the celebrant and read the prayers with him. Special attention was paid to the acoustics to give resonance to the canticles, which were essential to the worship of God.

The **decoration** inspired by the Counter-Reformation was intended to reinforce the conclusions of the Council of Trent: for example, the third chapel on the right (**1**) which is decorated with angels and the Virgin interceding for the souls in Purgatory, illustrates ideas which were contested by the Reformers. The 17C Baroque decoration expresses the victory of the Roman Church: against the Turks at Lepanto in 1571; against Protestantism renounced by Henri IV, King of France, in 1593.

The abundance of polychrome marble, paintings, sculptures, bronzes, stuccowork and gilding which covers every inch of space is overwhelming.

★★**Baciccia Frescoes** – In 1672, through the good offices of Bernini, Giovanni Battista Gaulli, called "Il Baciccia", was commissioned to do the paintings in the Jesuit Church. *The Triumph of the Name of Jesus*, which he painting on the nave ceiling, was certainly his masterpiece and entitled him to be considered as the main exponent of Baroque decoration. The work, which was completed in 1679, combines the technique of composition with the exuberance of *trompe-l'œil*; the eye moves without check from the painted surface to the sculptures by Antonio Raggi. The Damned, who spill over the edge in a tumult of plunging bodies, do not break the unity of the composition imparted by the rays of divine light. He also painted the *Adoration of the Lamb* in the apse and the *Assumption on the dome*.

★★★**Chapel of St Ignatius Loyola** (**2**) – This chapel, where the remains of St Ignatius rest in a beautiful urn, was built by **Andrea Pozzo**, a Jesuit, between 1696 and 1700. Behind a bronze rail embellished with cherubs bearing torches, stands the altar bearing a statue of the Saint in marble and silver. The original statue, which was the work of Pierre Legros, a Frenchman, was of solid silver but was melted down by Pius VI to pay the taxes imposed by Napoleon under the Treaty of Tolentino (1797).

Ignatius Loyola's Chapel in the Gesù Church

Andrea Pozzo used precious stones and metals with which he achieved impressive colour combinations: four columns faced with lapis lazuli rest on green marble bases adorned with low reliefs in bronze gilt. Above, among the figures of the Trinity, is a child supporting a terrestrial globe in lapis lazuli.

On the sides of the altar, two groups of allegorical statues illustrate the work carried on by the Jesuits. On the left *Faith triumphing over Idolatry* by Giovanni Théodon and on the right *Religion vanquishing Heresy* by Pierre Legros, a pupil of Andrea Pozzo.

In the building to the right of the church are the rooms where St Ignatius lived and died ⊙ *(access 45 Piazza del Gesù)*. The ceiling and walls of the flanking passage are decorated all over in *trompe-l'œil* paintings by Andrea Pozzo (17C).

Take Via del Plebiscito east as far as Piazza Venezia.

Palazzo Bonaparte – This 17C palazzo of modest appearance became the property of Napoleon's mother and she took up residence in 1815 when the Empire fell. Without rancour Pius VII granted asylum to all the exiled members of the Imperial family. Lucian, Jerome and Louis, the ex-King of the Netherlands, formed the old lady's circle in the palace. From the enclosed balcony on the first floor she liked to see what was going on in the street below. On 8 February 1836, attended by her son Jérome and Cardinal Fesch, she died. She was buried quietly in the nearby church, Santa Maria in Via Lata, while the Carnival was in full swing.

Neighbouring sights are described in the following chapters: CAMPIDOGLIO – CAPITOLINO; FONTANA DE TREVI – QUIRINALE; FORI IMPERIALI; PANTHEON.

PIRAMIDE CESTIA – TESTACCIO ★

Tour 90min

The walk begins beside the great white pyramid, which is the Mausoleum of Caius Cestius, and continues on the north side of this monument before entering the Testaccio district which centres on the hill of the same name.

Respite from the heat of summer

In the shaded garden of the **Café du Parc** off Via della Piramide Cestia, sit back and enjoy a *cremolato* at which this particular establishment excels. These are the famous unctuous Roman ice-creams served in chilled glasses that are so much creamier than the delicate fruit sorbets.

From Piramide Cestia to San Saba

★**Piramide di Caio Cestio (Mausoleum of Caius Cestius)** – Caius Cestius, Praetor and Tribune of the people, who died in 12 BC, devised the most original mausoleum in Rome. The marble-covered pyramid testifies to the grandeur of the Augustan era when a simple citizen could erect a tomb worthy of a Pharaoh. Nowadays the white silhouette is one of the most famous sights in Rome.

★**Porta San Paolo (St Paul's Gate)** – This gate is an interesting example of the alterations that have been made to the Aurelian Wall (Mura Aureliane) (270-75); in Aurelian's day the gate consisted of two arches flanked by two semi-circular towers on the outside. Maxentius (306-12) raised the towers, extended them towards the inside and linked them to an inner gate also consisting of two arches. Honorius, Emperor in the West (395-423), replaced the two outer arches with the present single arch and added the crenellations to the towers. The gate has been restored on subsequent occasions, particularly in the 15C and 18C.
Known in Antiquity as the Porta Ostiensis, the gate opened into Via Ostiense which led to St Paul's Basilica from which the gate took its present name in the Middle Ages.

Via Ostiensis – The road dates from the 4C BC; it was one of the most important commercial arteries in Antiquity. Starting in the Forum Boarium, it followed the line of Lungotevere Aventino and Via della Marmorata, passed through the wall by a gate situated slightly to the west of the Porta Ostiensis and then more or less followed the route of the present Via Ostiense as far as Ostia, thus linking the salt marshes of the Tiber estuary to Rome.
The road continued to be used in the Christian era since it led to the site of St Paul's martyrdom (Tre Fontane) and to his tomb in St Paul's Basilica.
Take Viale della Piramide Cestia, turn right up the steps in Via Baccio Pontelli and then left into Via Annia Faustina.
The San Saba district occupies one of the peaks of the Aventine; its elegant mansions interspersed with open spaces, dating from early this century, have made it a model of town planning for many years.

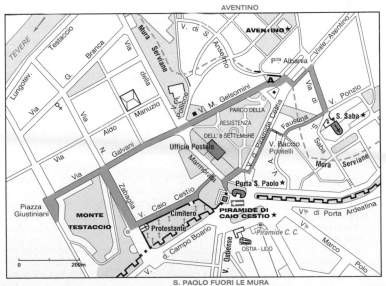

S. PAOLO FUORI LE MURA

175

★San Saba – The church is dedicated to St Sabas, who founded a monastery, called the Great Lavra, in Palestine in the 5C. Two hundred years later its monks were dispersed by the Persians and then by the Arabs; many of them took refuge in Rome in a building inhabited a century earlier by St Sylvia, the mother of St Gregory the Great. Towards the end of the 10C the monks from the East constructed the present church on top of their smaller 7C oratory. Over the centuries the building was subject to various alterations but was restored from 1911. Excavations below floor level have revealed traces of the early oratory and of a building from the Imperial era which may have been the headquarters of a fire brigade formed by Augustus.

A flight of steps and a porch lead into a courtyard.

Façade – The portico is contemporary with the church but the columns have been replaced with thick pillars. In the 15C a single storey surmounted by a loggia was built on top of the portico by Cardinal Piccolomini, nephew of Pius II; later the floor of the loggia was lowered, the original windows were filled in and replaced by the five existing openings. The belltower on the left dates from the 11C.

The main door was attractively decorated in 1205 by one of the Cosmati at the invitation of the Cluniac monks who had succeeded the original community.

Interior – The basilica plan, with a nave and two aisles each ending in an apse, has been conserved. The lack of uniformity between the pillars (bases, shafts and capitals) is typical of medieval buildings in which material from a variety of sources was used. An unusual feature is the additional aisle on the east side of the church; it probably linked the church to the monastery of the Eastern monks. It was the Cluniac monks who rebuilt the convent in a new position in the 13C thus exposing the additional aisle on the exterior of the church; it contains vestiges of 13C paintings.

The paving was part of the refurbishment carried out by the Cosmati, as is a section of chancel screen, now placed against the wall in the west (right) aisle. In the frieze at the top of the right-hand central pillar is a small sculpted head with black stones for eyes; both it and its inscription are an enigma.

During the Counter-Reformation (16C) the paintings in the apse were executed for Gregory XIII; the paintings above the episcopal throne date from the 14C.

The Annunciation above the apse dates from the 15C.

Take Via di S Saba down into Piazza Albania.

In Piazza Albania, at the beginning of Via Sant'Anselmo, are the remains of the **Servian Wall** (Mura Serviane) (**A**), which was built round Rome by Servius Tullius from the 6C BC; this stretch of the wall was probably rebuilt in the 1C BC.

Take Via M Gelsomini and Via Galvani as far as Piazza Giustiniani.

TESTACCIO

This district, with its more down-to-earth atmosphere, grew out of an area which had been abandoned for 1500 years and was then included in the development plans of 1873 and 1883 as a district for working-class people, organised according to the general town-planning principles current in Roman times.

The main attraction is the **Monte Testaccio** (some 35m - 115ft high). It takes its name from the amphorae (*testae* in Latin) which, either unusable or broken in the food shops in the immediate vicinity or in the port of Ripa Grande (very little evidence remains of any of these), were reduced to potsherds (*cocci* in Italian) and piled up here. It is therefore also called "Monte dei Cocci". Excavations have uncovered several "grottoes" some of which revealed what appeared to be Roman restaurants and night spots.

> **After dinner but before going dancing...**
>
> Why not stop at the **Libreria Testaccio** in Piazza Santa Maria Liberatrice *(no 23/26)* open late into the night, to browse through the shelves of Italian literature and rows of reference material, or to link up on the internet and mail a message home...

Return to the previous crossroads; turn right into Via N Zabaglia and left into Via Caio Cestio.

Cimitero Protestante – It is also known locally as the Testaccio Cemetery which is a better name as it is in fact a cemetery for non-Roman Catholics, both foreign and Italian, and includes the graves of members of the Orthodox Church. Between the neat box hedges in the shade of pines and cypress trees many famous people are buried: at the eastern end of the gravel path – John Keats and his faithful friend Joseph Severn, Axel Munthe the author of *San Michele;* at the foot of the last tower in the Aurelian Wall – Shelley's tombstone on which Byron had some verses of Shakespeare engraved; half-way down the slope in the main cemetery between two tall cypress trees – a tombstone bearing a bronze medallion which marks the grave of Goethe's son who died in Rome in 1830 (the son's name is not given).

Continue along Via Caio Cestio; turn left into Via della Marmorata.

On the left is the **Post Office** (Ufficio Postale) of the Aventine district, a good example of Italian rationalist architecture, designed by the architects A Libera and M De Renzi, who adhered to the rules of the Modern Movement which formed the debate on architecture between the two World Wars.

Neighbouring sights are described in the following chapters: AVENTINO; SAN PAOLO FUORI LE MURA.

PORTA PIA ★

Tour 1 hour

The district north of the Porta Pia contains **Via dei Villini**, an example of early 20C town planning. It is worth strolling along this road to admire the two types of dwellings defined in a new development plan prepared in 1909: the *palazzino*, a 4- or 5-storey block of flats for letting, and the *villino*, a smart little house with its own garden. Beneath this district lie the Catacombs of St Nicomedes.

The road ends in Piazza Galeno, opposite **Villino Ximenes**, an unusual little house, built for himself by Ettore Ximenes (1855-1926), sculptor, painter and illustrator, who designed many official buildings in Rome and abroad.

PORTA PIA TO PIAZZA DELLA REPUBBLICA

Porta Pia – The outside façade of the gate, facing down Via Nomentana, is the work of Benedetto Vespignani (1808-82), who with Giuseppe Valadier, was very active during the 19C. The other **façade ★**, facing down Via XX Settembre, is spectacular, the last architectural design by Michelangelo. It was erected between 1561 and 1564 at the request of Pope Pius IV. At the centre are six balls, the device of the Medici family. The curious white motif, which appears several times, is said to be a barber's basin wrapped in a fringed towel, a reminder to Pius IV that one of his ancestors was a barber.

Via XX Settembre – The street is named after the date – 20 September 1870 – when Italian troops entered the Papal capital. It replaced the old Strada Pia and was the first street to be developed in the post-1870 town planning. It was designed to link the Ministries and to reflect the grandeur of the city's new status. It was therefore lined with pompous buildings in imitation of the Renaissance and Baroque styles.

Near the Porta Pia *(left)* is a very modern building by Sir Basil Spence which houses the **British Embassy** (Ambasciata del Regno Unito).

20 September 1870

That day was the culmination of the Risorgimento. The united Kingdom of Italy had been in existence since 1861. Cavour had declared in Parliament: "I assert that Rome, and Rome only, ought to be the capital of Italy". On 20 September 1870 Italian troops entered Rome through a breach in the Aurelian wall. The site of the breach, in Corso d'Italia, on the left on leaving the Porta Pia, is marked by a column surmounted by a representation of Victory.

Villa Paolina ⊙ – *Seat of the French Ambassador to the Holy See.* The villa is named after Napoleon's sister Pauline, who in 1803 married Prince Camillo Borghese, great nephew of Pope Paul V. She took up residence after the fall of the Empire since her husband, whom she had abandoned a few years earlier, had banished her from the family property. She spent long periods in the house until her death in 1825.

Museo numismatico della Zecca italiana (Currency Museum) ⊙ – *On the ground floor of the Treasury building.* The Treasury building dates from 1877. The Numismatic Museum displays the currencies of every country in the world including coins issued by the Popes from the 15C. There is also a fine collection of wax impressions (about 400) by Benedetto Pistrucci (1784-1855) who was chief engraver to the Bank of England for 40 years: heads of George IV, Victoria, Duke of Wellington, Napoleon during the 100 days, Pauline Borghese.

Turn left into Via Pastrengo and right towards Piazza della Repubblica.

Piazza della Repubblica – Despite the heavy traffic the circus is one of the better post-1870 examples of town planning.

It is sometimes called Piazza dell'Esedra on account of the semicircle formed by the two palaces which flank the southwest side. They were designed in 1896 by Gaetano Koch to trace the line of the exedra in the southwest wall of the baths of Diocletian. The porticoed buildings are reminiscent of the architecture of Turin; the unified Kingdom of Italy, with Rome as its capital, had as its king Victor Emmanuel II, head of the House of Savoy, who lived in Turin.

The Naiad Fountain at the centre of the circus dates from 1885.

The southwest side of the Piazza opens into **Via Nazionale**, a street which links the mainline railway station, **Stazione Termini**, with Piazza Venezia, in the city centre. It is lined with shops which attract both tourists and Romans. Halfway down is the **Palazzo delle Esposizioni** which houses art exhibitions of international reputation. Near the south end is the **Teatro Eliseo.**

TERME DI DIOCLEZIANO (BATHS OF DIOCLETIAN)

The few extant rooms and the bold vaulting are evidence of the original splendour of the building which now houses the Church of St Mary of the Angels and the National Roman Museum.

In the 4C there were some 900 bath houses in Rome but the largest (13ha - 32 acres) and most beautiful were the Baths of the Emperor Diocletian. Building took ten years from 295 to 305 under the direction of Maximian acting for Diocletian who lived in Nicomedia in Asia Minor until he moved to Split after his abdication in 305; he never visited Rome.

As well as the suite of rooms, each at a different temperature, in the bath house itself, which could accommodate up to 3 000 people simultaneously, there were libraries, concert halls, gardens with fountains playing, galleries for the exhibition of sculpture and paintings and exercise rooms.

The baths were abandoned in 538 when the aqueducts were destroyed by the Ostrogoths under Witigis. Michelangelo was commissioned by Pius IV (1559-65) to convert the ruins into a church and Sixtus V (1585-90) removed a great deal of material from the site for his many building projects.

★★Santa Maria degli Angeli ⊘

This prestigious church which is dedicated to **St Mary of the Angels** is often used for official religious services.

According to tradition the Baths of Diocletian were built by 40 000 Christians condemned to forced labour; in 1561 Pius IV decided to convert the ruined baths into a church and a charterhouse.

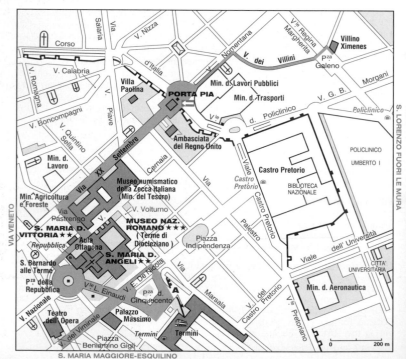

S. MARIA MAGGIORE-ESQUILINO

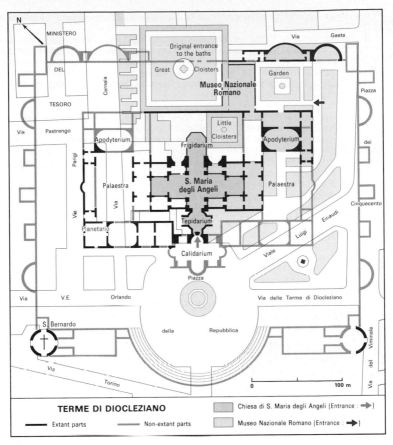

TERME DI DIOCLEZIANO

—— Extant parts —— Non-extant parts

Chiesa di S. Maria degli Angeli (Entrance : ➡)

Museo Nazionale Romano (Entrance : ➡)

Michelangelo, by then 86 years old, was put in charge. His design, which closely followed the architecture of the original baths, was continually altered after he and the Pope had died within a year of one another (1564 and 1565 respectively) so that by 1749 the church was a jumble of dissociated features and Vanvitelli, the Neopolitan, was commissioned to reintroduce a degree of uniformity.

The outer façade which he designed was demolished in the early 20C revealing the unusual unadorned curved wall of the *caldarium* of the original baths.

The interior, which is designed to the Greek cross plan, was extensively remodelled by Vanvitelli.

Vestibule – This was the *tepidarium* of the baths. On the left is the tomb (1) of the Neapolitan poet and painter **Salvatore Rosa** who died in 1673; on the right the tomb (2) of **Carlo Maratta** (1625-1713) who designed it himself.

Between the vestibule and the transept the statue of **St Bruno** (3 - *right*), founder of the Carthusian order, is by the French sculptor Houdon (1741-1827) who spent 14 years in Rome (1764-78), staying originally at the French Academy. The niche opposite once contained a plaster statue by the same artist of John the Baptist. Unfortunately it was broken by the Sacristan, re-made to a smaller size and placed in the Borghese Gallery.

On either side of the entrance to the transept are two **stoops**; the one on the right is 18C Baroque (4), the other is a modern copy (5).

S. MARIA DEGLI ANGELI

179

★Transept – This part of the church gives the best idea of the solemn magnitude of the ancient building.

It occupies the central hall of the baths with its eight monolithic granite columns. To create a uniform effect, Vanvitelli copied the columns in painted masonry, adding four more in the two recesses leading to the vestibule and the chancel. In addition to the present entrance, Michelangelo had intended two more, one at each end of the transept but eventually two chapels were created instead and painted in *trompe-l'œil* with architectural effects.

The transept is a virtual picture gallery, particularly of 18C works. The majority of them come from St Peter's where they were replaced by mosaics. Here in St Mary's Vanvitelli arranged them to cover the wall spaces between the pillars.

Of particular significance is the painting depicting **St Basil celebrating mass before Emperor Valens** (**6**) by the French painter Subleyras (1699-1749) who settled in Rome in 1728; the Emperor, overwhelmed by the dignity of the ceremony, has fainted; his uniform and background are treated in the Classical manner.

The Fall of Simon Magus (**7**) by Pompeo Batoni (1708-86) is typical of this artist's work with its fine colours and effects of contrasting light and shade.

The Virgin with St Bruno's and other saints (**8**) is a gentle and luminous work by Giovanni Odazzi (1663-1731), a pupil of Baciccia; he continued to work in the Baroque Mannerist style.

The south transept contains the **tombs** of three First World War heroes: Marshal Armando Diaz (**9**) who won the Battle of Vittorio Veneto in 1918; Admiral Paolo Thaon di Revel (**10**), commander-in-chief of the allied forces in the Adriatic 1917-18; Vittorio Emanuele Orlando (**11**), Minister of State.

Running across the floor from the south transept to the chancel is a meridian (**12**). Between 1702 and 1846 the clocks of Rome were regulated by it. Nowadays midday is announced by the firing of a cannon on the Janiculum.

Chancel – Like the transept the chancel is generously decorated with paintings, the most notable being **The Martyrdom of St Sebastian** (**13**) by Domenichino (1581-1641), and **The Baptism of Jesus** (**14**) by Carlo Maratta; note the affectation of the figures of Christ and John the Baptist.

Behind the high altar is a much venerated picture (**15**) showing the Virgin surrounded by adoring angels. It was commissioned in 1543 from a Venetian artist by Antonio del Duca, a Sicilian priest, who had a vision in which he saw a cloud of angels rising from the Baths of Diocletian. From then on he never stopped demanding the construction of a church on the site of the baths; eventually Pius IV acceded to his request.

War memorial – To the southeast of the church on the south side of Viale Luigi Einaudi stands a monument to the memory of 500 Italians who died at Dorgali in Eritrea in 1887; this was an incident in the wars of Italy's colonial expansion. The obelisk sur-mounting the monument comes from the Temple of Isis in the Campus Martius.

Stazione Termini – In Piazza dei Cinquecento stands the main **railway station**. The present building was begun before the Second World War to replace the old station which had been built when the railway first arrived in Rome during the reign of Pope Pius IX (1846-78). Interrupted during the war, work on the new station began again in 1947 and was completd to mark the Holy Year in 1950. The roof with its undulating lines is considered one of the most significant examples of architecture of this period. In the station forecourt are imposing remains of a wall (**A**) built round the city after the Gauls invaded in the 4C BC.

This district of Rome developed after 1870 as the city assumed its new role as the capital of Italy. The government of the newly-unified Italy installed their soldiers in the Castro Pretorio, formerly the barracks of the Emperor's personal bodyguard – the Pretorian Guard founded by Augustus.

In Via D de Nicola (no 79) is the entrance to the museo Nazionale Romano.

Museo Nazionale Romano (National Roman Museum) ⊙

Pending the eventual transfer of all collections from the National Roman Museum to Palazzo Massimo, artefacts are scattered in different places: besides the Palazzo Massimo, a number of important objects are on permanent display in the Aula Ottagona and the Ludovisi Boncompagni Collections are housed in the Palazzo Altemps.

The museum is housed in part of the Baths of Diocletian and in the Charterhouse which, like the Church of Santa Maria degli Angeli, dates from the 16C. It was inaugurated in 1889 and has continually made new acquisitions, in particular the Ludovisi collection in 1901; it is one of the great museums of Greek and Roman antiquities. Owing to the acquisition of the paintings from the Villa Farnesina and the frescoes from Livia's Villa at Prima Porta it now closely rivals the Archeological Museum of Naples for Classical painting.

TERME DI DIOCLEZIANO

Garden – In Diocletian's day there was already a garden here. Set among the cypresses and pink and white oleanders is a collection of archeological fragments. The huge vase in the centre once adorned the villa of a rich Roman citizen (there is a similar vase in the courtyard of St Cecilia's Church in Trastevere).

On the northeast side of the garden is what must have been a luxurious room, panelled with marble and paved with mosaic; the curved inner wall decorated with columns faced a screen wall pierced with niches in which stood statues.

At present most of the rooms are closed; only Room 1 and the Great Cloisters are open.

The door with glass panels leads to the galleries.

Room 1 – In this room are displayed two 2C **Roman copies**★★ of the original bronze statue of the **Discobolos by Myron** (5C BC).

The discobolos of the **Casa Lancellotti**, named after its former owner, was considered to be an excellent copy. The artist has chosen to represent the moment where the athlete has already grasped the discus in his right hand and is flexing the muscles of his whole body prior to the throw. The impassive expression, devoid of any sign of physcial effort, is characteristic of Greek works from the Classical period. The hair and the veins in the arms are sculpted in great detail.

The other replica is the Discobolos of Castel Porziano, named after the estate where it was found in 1906; it is less complete and less well executed.

Follow through to the Great Cloisters.

On leaving turn right into the Great Cloisters of the Charterhouse.

Chiostro Maggiore – The Great Cloisters are sometimes attributed to Michelangelo although he died in 1564 aged 89 and the cloisters were completed in 1565, if one believes the date inscribed on the corner pillar near the entrance. At the centre is a pleasant garden containing sculpted fragments and many inscriptions. In the northeast walk particularly sarcophagi are on display. At the north end of the walk is a very fine mosaic in vivid colours representing the banks of the Nile. It was found in a vineyard on the Aventine and is typical of the exotic and picturesque art which was in fashion in the 1C and 2C.

The huge pieces of sculpture, the animal heads, which rear up above the bushes, probably come from Trajan's Forum.

On leaving the Baths of Diocletian, turn right towards Palazzo Massimo.

PALAZZO MASSIMO ⊙

The fabulous collection of Greek and Roman antiquities of the National Roman Museum is now permanently housed in the former Collegio Massimo. Here, pieces are displayed in a few rooms arranged around the inner courtyard, divided into bays with glass.

The first floor of the palace, presently in a state of reorganisation, will accommodate Augustan works from the Farnesina and 1C frescoes from Livia's villa at Prima Porta (north of Rome).

Ground floor – Cross an un-numbered room dominated by a statue of Minerva dating from the 1C BC, made of pink alabaster, basalt and Luni marble.

Rooms are numbered with Roman numerals; works are arranged thematically.

Rooms I-II: Image and celebration – From the era of Sulla to the age of Augustus.
Among the portraits of high ranking officials and statesmen (magistrates and generals), is a fine statue of a Roman mercenary discovered at Tivoli. In the corridor, besides the portrait busts, note the 2C BC mosaic showing the abduction of Hylas (a favourite page-boy of Heracles abducted by water nymphs) and the statue of a Roman emperor.

Room III: The Imperial ideal – The Julio-Claudian Emperors.
During the reigns of the Julio-Claudian dynasty (from Augustus to Nero), Roman citizens were happy to be represented by effigies displaying the traits and style of the Imperial family. The cycle of Mentana makes this particularly evident.

Room IV: Metals and currency – Permanent display from the numismatic collection.
Coins chart the evolution of time.

Room V: Augustus – Ambition to rule.
The room with the three arches is the only one to give directly on to the inner courtyard and therefore is one of the best lit. It encloses the **statue of Augustus**★★★. The Emperor is shown at about the age of 50, dressed in the High Priest's toga. The face is treated with simple realism, perhaps with a little flattery: age does not seem to have wrought any change since the Emperor was portrayed at the time of

the Battle of Actium when he was 32 years old: this earlier statue preserved in the Capitoline Museum, together with this later one displayed here, convey the solemn majesty and authority of Augustus. No better psychological study could be made of the Emperor.

The frescoes, from a columbarium on the Esquiline *(see SANTA MARIA – ESQUILINO)* depict scenes from Ilium and the foundation of Rome. The fine altar, bearing the date AD 124 and dedicated to Mars and Venus, was discovered at Ostia.

In the passage-way is a large mosaic illustrating a cat and ducks.

Room VI: *In the process of installation.*

Before proceeding to Room VII note the two male heads: one represents Alexander the Great, the other Philip V of Macedonia.

Room VII: Power and the fine art of sculpture – Hellenistic originals.

The statues here assembled would once have graced the gardens of the historian Sallust (86-35BC). These Greek originals were imported to Rome following the conquest of Southern Italy.

This room accommodates the famous **Ludovisi Throne★★★**, a strange monument suggesting a throne for a cult statue which was found in the Villa Ludovisi in 1887. It is an original Greek sculpture from the early Classical period (5C BC). The high quality of the decorative low relief carving make it a masterpiece of Antique art.

The main panel shows a young woman being assisted by two attendant young women who shield her body with a veil. Acheologists have interpreted this scene as the birth of Aphrodite (Venus), goddess of Love, who emerged from the sea foam, accompanied by the Seasons whose feet brush the pebbles of the shore. The very light, delicate mantle gently envelops the lower half of the goddess's body, its rippling folds echoing the curves of the tunic about her neck. The artist has endowed the face of Aphrodite with joyful serenity. The side panels are ornamented with scenes associated with the cult of Aphrodite: a naked woman plays the flute while another, fully clothed, burns incense – these figures are often regarded as embodiments of sensuality (the courtesan) and modesty (the wife).

Another splendid example of Antique sculpture is the **Daughter of Niobe**, an original Greek work (mid-5C BC) which would probably have adorned the pediment of a temple. The statue represents an episode in Greek mythology: Niobe was mother of seven sons and seven daughters, and was scornful of Leto who had borne only one of each, Artemis and Apollo. To avenge their mother, they set about killing all Niobe's fourteen children with arrows (Niobe wept for them until she turned to stone from which her tears continued to flow). This statue shows a young woman attempting to withdraw the arrow that will kill her and was one of the first representations of the naked female figure in Greek art after the cycladic statues from the third millenium BC.

The 4C BC **Pedagogue** represents the minder of one of Niobe's young children responsible for accompanying them to school. Note also the graceful and elegant headless **Peplophorus** or peplum carrier (woven outer robe or shawl).

Room VIII: Power and art – Figurative forms.

This room is dedicated to a series of works from the neo-Attic period, inspired and modelled upon Hellenistic figurative art.

Other than the statues of divinities (Athena, Aphrodite and a muse), note the various ornamental garden pieces – a base bearing dancing Maenads (mad women, followers of Dionysus), an altar carved with Muses and Maenads. Between these two works is a large fountain bowl (1C BC) supported on a single twisted column wreathed with Tritons (mermen) and Nereids (sea maidens) and a tripod with animal feet – this dates from the early years of the Empire.

The same decorative iconography is evident in the low relief illustrating a procession of Nymphs (personifications of natural elements – rivers, trees, mountains) or Hesperides (Daughters of Evening), the frieze showing Nike (Victory) leading a bull, and above, the band of decoration around the bases of figures of Apollo.

First floor: *In the process of installation.* The **stuccoes and paintings★★★** were found in a building of the Augustan era near the Villa Farnesina. The stuccoes, which decorated the ceilings, are marvellously delicate, typical of the second and third styles *(see* INTRODUCTION – Roman art: Painting).

The beautiful collection of 1C **frescoes★★★** comes from the villa at which Livia, wife of Augustus, lived at Prima Porta (north of Rome). The room is painted to represent an orchard: around the four walls runs a band of fruit trees, flowers and birds. Perspective is heightened by the skilful use of chiaroscuro as muted fresco colours are used to suggest depth and relief, making this cycle of frescoes a masterpiece of Roman painting.

Leave the Palazzo Massimo and continue in the direction of Piazza della Repubblica, walking along the Bath gardens and before Santa Maria degli Angeli. The Aula Ottagona is a little further beyond.

AULA OTTAGONA (BATHS OF DIOCLETIAN PLANETARIUM) ⊘

Painted to resemble a planetarium, this wonderful domed octagonal room houses several more prize examples of **Classical sculpture★★★**.

Museo Nazionale Romano

Pugilist resting

– **Pugilist resting:** this superb figure cast in bronze is an original from the Hellenistic period. Typical is the realism which characterises Greek works of the 3C BC: this fighter is no longer the ideally handsome hero represented by the Classical artists but a man overwhelmed with fatigue. The figure was found in 1884 at the same time as the *Youth leaning on his spear.* Not only are these statues rare examples of supreme craftsmanship, they are also in the most remarkable condition.

– **Venus of Cyrene:** this fabulous statue is made from Parian marble which has the consistency of ivory. It was discovered during the excavations of the baths at Cyrene in Libya. Venus is engaged in twisting up her hair while still rising from the sea. The figure is a copy of a Greek original typical of the female divinities produced by Praxiteles. In order to stabilise the statue the sculptor has devised a draped garment falling over a dolphin which has a fish in its mouth.

– **Venus Anadyomene:** Venus emerging from the waves, tying up her hair.

– **Hercules:** fine example of an athletic figure in motion.

– **Lycean Apollo** and head of **Aesculapius** (who was invoked against pestilence).

Set into the central part of the floor is a glass panel revealing the excavated foundations of the building.

In Piazza Beniamino Gigli, south of Piazza della Repubblica, is the **Teatro dell'Opera**, a theatre begun by A Sfondrini and completed in 1880; the façade is the work of M Piacentini, who restored and enlarged part of the building in 1926.

Neighbouring sights are described in the following chapters: S LORENZO FUORI LE MURA; S MARIA MAGGIORE – ESQUILINO; VIA VENETO.

SAN GIOVANNI IN LATERANO★★★

Tour 3 hours

The name is taken from the Laterani family who owned a wealthy property which was confiscated by Nero and restored by Septimius Severus. Excavations in Via dell'Amba Aradam (beneath the INPS building) have revealed traces of a house identified as belonging to the Laterani. It was combined with a neighbouring property in the 4C and may have been the residence of Fausta, Maxentius' sister and Constantine's wife, who in 313 lent her house to Pope Melchiades so that he could hold a council of bishops, one of the first official manifestations of Christianity.

Beneath the St John Lateran Hospital are traces of a building which has been identified as the house of the Annii, Marcus Aurelius' family; the remains of the base of a statue were found in a peristyle; it may have carried the statue of the Emperor which now stands in the Capitoline Museum.

The walk begins at **St John's Gate** (Porta San Giovanni) which was made in the 16C in the Aurelian Wall (Mura Aureliane) which was built around Rome in the 3C and is very well preserved at this point.

Lost luggage in transit...

The market which runs the length of **Via Sannio** (from 10am to 1pm) sells discounted clothing and footwear: end-of-line, second-hand, samples at rock-bottom prices. Good to know in emergencies or to resolve the problem posed by an invitation to a fancy-dress party.

Outside the gate in Via Sannio a busy clothing market takes place each morning.
The **monument to St Francis of Assisi** (**A**) is a reminder that the Saint and his companions came to the Lateran one day in 1210 to have their rule approved by Innocent III.

From Piazza di Porta San Giovanni bear left towards the basilica.

There is a marked contrast between the noisy square which is a busy road junction and the calm solemnity diffused by the east front of the basilica.

★★★ BASILICA DI SAN GIOVANNI IN LATERANO (ST JOHN LATERAN) ⊙

This basilica was the first church to be dedicated to the Holy Redeemer; it symbolized the triumph of Christianity over paganism and thus deserved its title of 'Mother and Head of all the churches in the City and the world'. It is the cathedral of Rome. The dedication to St John came later.

Constantine's Basilica – On 28 October 312, after defeating Maxentius in battle, Constantine made a triumphal entry into Rome and immediately forbade the persecution of the Christians. In 314 Pope Sylvester I took up residence in the Lateran (a group of buildings comprising a palace, a basilica and a baptistry); the palace became the official papal residence from the 5C until the papacy departed to Avignon in France.

Before starting St Peter's in the Vatican, Constantine built the Lateran basilica on the site of Maxentius' bodyguards' barracks. He thus asserted his victory by destroying one of the signs of his enemy's greatness and by stressing his intention of giving the Christians his approval.

After being laid waste by the barbarians in the 5C, damaged by an earth tremor in 896 and destroyed by fire in 1308, the basilica was rebuilt in the Baroque era and in the 18C. In all over 20 popes contributed to its rebuilding, restoration and embellishment, from Leo the Great (440-61) to Leo XIII (1878-1903).

A strange trial – The trial took place in 896 in the Lateran. The accused was the corpse of Pope Formosus, dressed in his papal vestments; his enemies had not forgiven him for having bestowed the Emperor's crown on the 'Barbarian' Arnoul, last of the Carolingians.

He was set up opposite his judge, Pope Stephen VI, declared unworthy and a perjuror, and finally thrown into the Tiber.

Stephen VI was in his turn punished and strangled in prison.

Lateran Councils – Some of the most decisive councils in the history of the Church took place in the Lateran. In **1123** the Diet of Worms was confirmed putting an end to the Investiture Controversy. The council of **1139** condemned **Arnold of Brescia**, a canon, who challenged episcopal authority and preached in favour of a return to the poverty of the early church; he founded a free commune in Rome and drove out Eugenius III.

Pediment of St John Lateran

In **1179** Alexander III called for a crusade against the Albigensian (Cathar) heresy. Following the Council in **1215**, which was attended by 400 bishops and 800 abbots and at which every court in Europe was represented, it was laid down that the faithful must go to confession once a year and take communion at Easter. Innocent III decided to put an end to the Albigensian heresy and launched a crusade in the Languedoc. In **1512** Julius II opened the fifth Lateran Council by asserting the supremacy of the Church of Rome.

Exterior

The well-balanced 18C **façade** is the major work of Alessandro Galilei (1691-1736), one of the architects who used the Baroque style in Rome. He had a masterly touch in contrasting the clear lines of the columns with the dark cavities behind them. On the roof, the gigantic figures of the saints surrounding Christ and St John the Baptist and St John the Evangelist seem to be preaching to the heavens. The **huge statue of Constantine**, the first Christian Emperor (**1**) in the porch comes from the Imperial baths on the Quirinal. Since 1656 the **central entrance** (**2**) has been fitted with the doors from the Curia in the Roman Forum; in 1660 they were enlarged by the addition of a border decorated with the stars on the arms of the reigning Pope, Alexander VII.

Interior

It is hard to envisage the basilical plan of Constantine's building. The central nave and four aisles of today are those of a Baroque church, sometimes considered cold and severe on account of its grandiose dimensions and pale stuccoes. In fact it is a very old building dressed in 17C taste.

Nave and aisles – This part of the church was designed by the great Baroque architect Borromini; his plan included a dome. Just as Urban VIII had commissioned Bernini to complete St Peter's, so his successor Innocent X in his desire to mark his reign in a prestigious manner invited Borromini in about 1650 to refurbish St John Lateran. Whereas Bernini knew exactly how to adapt Baroque art to earlier styles of construction, Borromini was unable to give free rein to his genius as Innocent III asked him to retain the existing ceiling. The ceiling seems to crush the pillars in the nave which replace the ancient columns and were designed to support a dome; the prominent niches faced with dark marble spoil the effect of the low relief sculptures and the oval medallions above them.

★★**Ceiling** – It was begun by Pius IV in 1562; his arms are in the centre. It was completed in 1567 by Pius V, whose arms are near the chancel. In the 18C it was restored by Pius VI who added his arms near the main door. The original design was by a group of Michelangelo's pupils.

★**Statues of the Apostles** (**3**) – They are in the late Baroque style by some of Bernini's followers. Borromini created twelve huge recesses in the pillars of the nave to receive them. The columns of green flecked marble, which Borromini shortened and re-employed, originally separated the nave and aisles in the ancient basilica. Above each recess he placed the dove from the arms of Innocent X. The low relief sculptures *(above)*, executed under the direction of Algardi, depict stories from the Old and New Testaments. The Prophets in the oval medallions

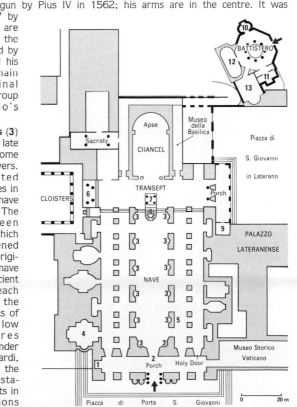

(top) were painted in the 18C. This decoration replaced the 15C frescoes painted by Pisanello and Gentile da Fabriano for Martin V and Eugenius IV.

★**Corsini Chapel (4)** – Alessandro Galilei, who designed the east front, was also responsible for this chapel which is built on the Greek cross plan beneath a dome. The red porphyry coffer *(left)* beneath Clement XII's tomb came from the Pantheon. The allegorical statues are fine 18C work. The fragment of heavily restored **fresco (5)**, attributed to Giotto, shows Boniface VIII announcing the Jubilee Year in 1300.

Transept – *Closed temporarily.* The nave is as bare of ornament as the transept is adorned with frescoes, marble and gilding. It was renovated in about 1595 by Clement VIII with Giacomo della Porta as architect. It is a good example of Mannerist decoration: the great wall frescoes resemble a theatrical décor and were painted principally by Cesare Nebbia, Pomarancio and Cavaliere d'Arpino who, in the *Ascension (end of left transept)* imitated the *Transfiguration* by Raphael (Vatican Gallery).

The elaborate marble decoration includes high relief angels, placed in small niches, which do not show the liberty of movement which characterises Baroque art. The ostentatious **ceiling★★** bearing the arms of Clement VIII is rich in colour and gilding and was designed by Taddeo Landini (late 16C).

The pediment in the **Chapel of the Holy Sacrament (6)** is supported by four beautiful antique **columns★** in gilded bronze, the only ones of this kind in Rome. Legend has it that in the 1C BC they belonged to the Temple of Jupiter on the Capitol.

The 14C **baldaquin (7)** was repainted at the Renaissance. At the top are kept some relics of the heads of St Peter and St Paul placed in silver reliquaries, partly paid for by Charles V of France (repaired in the 18C). In the 19C Pius IX had the high altar faced in marble. During this work it became apparent that the wooden altar contained some much older planks, one of which very probably belonged to the altar at which Pope Sylvester I officiated (314-35).

The confessio **(8)**, created in the 9C, contains the tomb of Martin V, the first pope to reign after the Great Schism. His tomb is the work of Donatello's brother.

Apse – The apse of Constantine's basilica was rebuilt in the 5C and again in the 13C but was not substantially altered until the 19C when Leo XIII moved it back in order to extend the chancel. The ogival windows and particularly the **mosaic** in the top of the apse were retained. This mosaic had already been restored in the 13C by **Jacopo Torriti** who took several features from the original model: the representation of the Cross, celestial Jerusalem with the palm and the phoenix, symbols of the Resurrection *(beneath the cross)* and the Jordan full of fishes, birds and boats, which forms the base of his composition. To these he added the Virgin and Nicholas IV kneeling, St Peter and St Paul *(left)*, St Andrew and the two St Johns *(right)*. He also included two smaller figures: St Francis of Assisi *(left)* – Torriti was a Franciscan monk – and St Anthony of Padua *(right)*.

The mosaic is dominated by the figure of Christ; the first representation of Christ in the apse dates from the 4C. Not long before, paganism was still the State religion so that, when Pope Sylvester consecrated the basilica, the appearance of such an image was considered miraculous by the faithful. In his desire to perpetuate the 'miracle' Jacopo Torriti managed to transfer the ancient figure to his own composition. During the 19C alterations this original figure was broken and replaced by a copy.

Museo della Basilica – *Right of the chancel.* The Basilica Museum displays the treasures of the basilica – gold chalices and reliquaries. The **station cross** (cabinet V) is in silver gilt (12C).

★**Chiostro** ⊙ – This charming 13C cloister is one of the most remarkable by the Vassalletti (father and son). Their art, like that of the Cosmati, consisted of cutting and assembling fragments of antique marble. The twisted columns with varied capitals, the mosaic frieze and the delicate carving of the cornice make this a poetic place where one would like to linger. A fine 9C well has been placed in the middle of the garden.

Leave the basilica by the right transept.

In the **porch** is a bronze statue of Henri IV of France **(9)** by Nicolas Cordier (1567-1612) in recognition of the King's gift to the Lateran Chapter of the Abbey of Clairac in Agenais. In memory of France's beneficence to the Lateran the President of the French Republic belongs as of right to the Lateran Chapter (a mass is said for France on 13 December).

The **façade of the north transept** is so majestic it could be the main front; it was built by Domenico Fontana in 1586.

Visitors are requested not to walk about in churches during services.

★BATTISTERO (BAPTISTERY) ⏱

Like the basilica the baptistery was built by Constantine. In the 4C every Christian was baptised there; nowadays it is used for the ceremonies of Holy Saturday. It was rebuilt in the 5C by Sixtus III who set up the eight porphyry columns in the centre and had verses appropriate to baptism inscribed on the octagonal entablature. The upper colonnade and the lantern are 16C additions. Various popes built the adjoining chapels and Urban VIII gave it its present appearance when he added the wall frescoes in the 17C.

Chapels – *Ask the keeper to open the doors.* The **Chapels of St John the Baptist** (**10**) and **St John the Evangelist** (**11**) were built by Pope Hilary (461-68). While legate to Pope Leo the Great, Hilary was sent to the Council of Ephesus to argue against a heresy. During the hearing there was a disturbance and Hilary took refuge on the tomb of St John the Evangelist where he made a vow to build a chapel to the Baptist and the Evangelist.

The Chapel of St John the Baptist has kept its original door which is made of an alloy of silver, bronze and gold and is very heavy; it makes a very special sound when it swings on its hinges.

The Chapel of St John the Evangelist was given a new bronze door in the 12C. The ceiling is covered with a beautiful 5C mosaic (delicate colours on a gold ground).

Chapel of St Rufina and St Secunda (**12**) – In 12C the original narthex which was the entrance to the Baptistry was converted into a chapel; it is rectangular in shape with an apse at either end, one of which is decorated with a fine 5C mosaic.

Chapel of St Venantius (**13**) – Built in the 7C by John IV, it is decorated with mosaics in the Byzantine style (slim slightly stiff figures) and has a fine cedar ceiling.

PALAZZO LATERANENSE (LATERAN PALACE)

When Gregory XI returned to Rome in 1377 after the popes' period in Avignon, he found that the palace had been gutted by fire and he was obliged to install his household in the Vatican.

The present building was constructed in 1586 by Domenico Fontana during the reign of Sixtus V. The Lateran Treaty *(see VATICANO - SAN PIETRO)* was signed here in 1929. The palace is now the headquarters of the Diocese of Rome (Vicariate), with the Pope at its head, in his capacity as Bishop of Rome, and of the Vatican Historical Museum.

Museo Storico Vaticano (Vatican Historical Museum) ⏱ – *Entrance by the main portico.* – The museum comprises two parts – the **Papal Apartment** and the **Historical Museum.** The apartment contains ten rooms, each decorated with frescoes by late

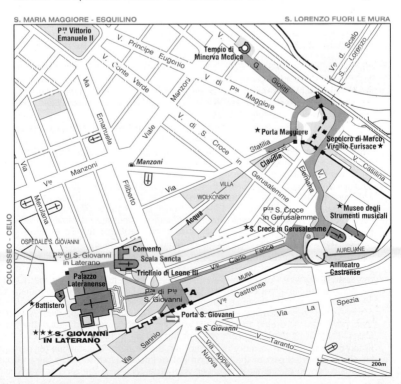

16C artists. It was in the last salon, called the Conciliation Room, that the Lateran Treaty was signed in 1929 by Cardinal P Gaspari and Mussolini. The Historical Museum consists of three sections devoted to the history of the papacy, to papal ceremony and to the papal guard respectively.

In **Piazza di San Giovanni in Laterano** stands a fine Egyptian obelisk made of granite, the tallest in Rome. It dates from the 15C BC and was brought to Rome in the 4C by Constantinus II to adorn the Circus Maximus at the foot of the Palatine where it was found in 1587. It was repaired and re-erected in its present position by Domenico Fontana at Sixtus V's behest.

Traces of the medieval palace – In the Middle Ages the papal palace extended from its present site as far as Via Domenico Fontana. Two features from this building, the *triclinium* of Leo III and the Scala sancta, have been reconstructed on the east side of the square.

Triclinium of Leo III – This Pope (795-816) built two rooms in the palace. All that remains of the *triclinium* (dining room) is an apse decorated with a mosaic, repaired in the 18C. It celebrates the alliance of Leo III with Charlemagne: the Emperor re-instated the Pope on his throne and the Pope crowned the Emperor in St Peter's in the Vatican.

Scala Sancta ⊙ – Sixtus V (1585-90) demolished what remained of the medieval palace with two exceptions: the stairs, which according to tradition came from Pontius Pilate's palace and had been used by Christ, and the private chapel of the popes, which was re-sited not far from its original position in a building specially designed by Domenico Fontana to incorporate the famous steps, which are climbed by the faithful on their knees. There are other stairs on either side for those who prefer to go up on foot.

At the top is the popes' chapel, known as the **Holy of Holies**★★ *(Sancta Sanctorum)*, by analogy with the Temple in Jerusalem, because of the precious relics it contained. It is always closed and can be seen only through heavy grills decorated with fine Cosmati work. Above the altar is the famous icon of Christ called the *Acheiropoeton*, which means it was not made by human hand: St Luke began it and it was completed by an angel; it arrived in Rome miraculously from Constantinople in the 8C. The ancient bronze door with its impressive locks which gives access to the Popes' Chapel can be seen from St Lawrence's chapel *(right)*.

PORTA MAGGIORE DISTRICT

Take Viale Carlo Felice as far as Piazza S Croce in Gerusalemme.

In Antiquity the district to the east of the Esquiline was a suburb of Rome, well wooded and covered with tombs which stretched for miles along the Praenestina Way and the Labicana Way (now Via Casilina). From Augustus' reign (31 BC to AD 14) onwards the cemeteries gradually gave way to huge gardens laid out by rich Romans. Under the Empire these sumptuous properties, designed by skilful landscape gardeners with temples and avenues lined with works of art, were absorbed into the Imperial estates either by confiscation or by legacy (members of the patrician class often willed their property to the Emperor). This practice restricted development to the east and aggravated the problem of lack of space in the city centre which was becoming overcrowded with huge prestigious buildings. In the 3C the district was enclosed by the Aurelian wall (Mura Aureliane). It remained untouched by the building projects of the popes in the Renaissance and Baroque periods and was not developed until the 19C when Rome had become the capital of Italy.

★**Museo degli Strumenti Musicali** ⊙ – The charming **Museum of Musical Instruments** displays a variety of instruments dating from Antiquity to the 19C. Antique whistles, horns and handbells are succeeded by exotic instruments such as beautiful inlaid mandolins; tambourines and ocarinas evoke provincial folk dances. Every sort of instrument is here: mechanical, portable, military, religious and domestic, adorned with fine paintings or inlaid with mother-of-pearl and ivory.

The sumptuous exhibits of the museum include a pianoforte made in 1722 by Bartolomeo Cristofori, one of the instrument's inventors *(Room 5)*; the 17C Barberini harp *(Room 13)*, which bears the name of the famous family to which it belonged and is decorated with magnificent gilt carvings; a rare example of a vertical clavecin (17C) with a pretty painted lid *(Room 15)*.

★**Santa Croce in Gerusalemme** ⊙ – In this church, originally known simply as Jerusalem, the legend of the Holy Cross is closely linked with history. Here stood the **Sessorium** where Constantine's mother, Helen, lived; it was built in the 3C and remained an Imperial palace until the 6C. In the 4C Helen went on a pilgrimage to Jerusalem as was the custom at that time. She returned in 329 bearing a fragment of the True Cross which she kept in the palace. The same year she died. A legend then developed according to which it was she herself who had found the True Cross. The cult of the Holy Cross was not introduced to Rome until the 7C.

History of the church – In memory of his mother, the Emperor Constantine (or perhaps his sons) converted part of the Sessorian Palace into a church to house the precious relic. It consisted of one large chamber with an apse where the services were held and of a smaller room (the present St Helen's Chapel) where the relic was kept. In the 12C Pope Lucius II (1144-45) divided the larger chamber into three and built a campanile without altering the outside walls. He raised the level of the floor in the church but not in the chapel, perhaps because according to tradition the floor of the chapel was composed of soil brought back from Calvary. The chapel was isolated from the church and had a separate entrance until the Renaissance when it was linked to the church by two stairways one on each side of the apse. The church acquired its present appearance in the 18C.

Tour – The 12C campanile is flanked by a lively façade and oval vestibule in the 18C style consistent with the principles dear to Borromini.

The nave vault was re-fashioned in the 18C; the impressive baldaquin over the altar is of the same period. The apse has conserved the mark of the Renaissance; it is decorated with an attractive fresco by Antoniazzo Romano (late 15C) illustrating the legend of the Discovery of the Cross by St Helen.

Capella di Sant'Elena *(access by one of the sets of steps beside the chancel)*. The chapel is decorated with beautiful **mosaics★**, designed by Baldassarre Peruzzi and, perhaps, by Melozzo da Forlì. The statue above the altar is a Roman work originally representing Juno but converted into St Helen.

Cappelle della Croce e delle Reliquie (Chapel of the Holy Cross and Relics Chapel) *(access by steps to the right of the left aisle)*. The relics of the Passion kept in the Chapel of the Holy Cross attract large numbers of pilgrims. In the first chapel they venerate the arm of the cross of the good robber crucified next to Christ *(at the beginning of the flight of steps opposite the entrance)*. In the Relics Chapel a glass case behind the altar displays fragments of the True Cross; the "heading" on the Cross, ie the inscription it bore; two thorns from the Crown; St Thomas' finger; some fragments from the Flagellation stake, from the grotto in Bethlehem and the Holy Sepulchre; a nail from the Cross.

On leaving the church bear left through the opening in the Aurelian Wall.

Anfiteatro Castrense – Its name comes from the Latin word *'castrum'* which in the 4C meant an Imperial residence. This amphitheatre, like the Sessorian Palace *(see above)*, was probably part of the imperial properties in this district. It seems to have been of great importance since the Aurelian Wall made a detour in order to enclose it. It was built entirely of red brick and dated from the end of the Severan dynasty (3C); it originally consisted of three storeys, of which only the first is well preserved.

Take Via Eleniana to Porta Maggiore.

★Porta Maggiore – The gate was built in the 1C AD to carry the Claudian aqueduct across the Praenestina Way and the Labicana Way where it entered the city. The use of huge roughly-hewn blocks of travertine (even for the supports) is an innovation typical of the Claudian era. The upper section which carried the water channels is inscribed with details of the work ordered by Claudius and also the restoration work ordered by Vespasian (AD 71) and Titus (AD 81).

In the 3C the gate was incorporated in the Aurelian Wall (Mura Aureliane). When Honorius (395-423) restored the fortifications a bastion was added on the outside; its demolition in the 19C revealed the tomb of Marcus Vergilius Eurysaces *(see below)*.

★Sepolcro di Eurisace (Tomb of Marcus Vergilius Eurysaces) Eurysaces was a baker who lived in Rome at the end of the Republic. As supplier to the army he probably grew rich during the civil wars of this period and built an enormous tomb in travertine (dating from c30 BC) designed to commemorate his trade.

The cylindrical motifs, some vertical and some horizontal, recall the receptacles in which the flour was kept. The inscription identifies the owner of the tomb. The low relief frieze round the top illustrates the different steps in breadmaking.

Go west along Via Statilia.

On the left among the trees are the elegant arches of the Claudian aqueduct.

Acqua Claudia (Claudian Aqueduct) – Aqueducts are without doubt the most remarkable public works in Roman architecture. This one, which was begun by Caligula in AD 38 and completed by Claudius in AD 52, is the most impressive. Starting in the mountains near Subiaco it reached Rome after 68km - 42 miles of which 15km - 9 miles were above ground. From Porta Maggiore, Nero (AD 54-68) built a branch channel, traces of which remain in the gardens of Villa Wolkonsky, in Piazza della Navicella and at the eastern end of Via di San Paolo della Croce (Dolabella's Arch). This aqueduct was extended by Domitian as far as the Palatine to supply his palace with water.

Turn left into Via G. Giolitti.

Tempio di Minerva Medica – The beautiful circular temple (4C) was originally covered by a dome and was probably a *nymphaeum* in one of the patrician gardens.

Neighbouring sights are described in the following chapters: COLOSSEO – CELIO; SAN LORENZO FUORI LE MURA; SANTA MARIA MAGGIORE – ESQUILINO.

SAN LORENZO FUORI LE MURA ★

Tour 1 hour

The major point of interest on this walk is the Basilica of San Lorenzo fuori le Mura which, since the earliest days of Christianity has been the goal of countless pilgrims. The building has been remodelled several times over the centuries and consists of two distinct churches built at an interval of 700 years, which reflect the changes introduced by different popes. This district also includes the University Campus, a remarkable architectural complex dating from the 1930s.

★★SAN LORENZO FUORI LE MURA (ST LAWRENCE WITHOUT THE WALLS)

The church is also known as San Lorenzo al Verano since it is built on land that belonged to a certain Lucius Verus in Antiquity. To the north ran the Via Tiburtina, lined, like other roads on the outskirts of Rome, with pagan tombs and then with underground Christian cemeteries, the catacombs. One of them contains the grave of St Lawrence who was martyred in 258 under the Emperor Valerian soon after Pope Sixtus II was put to death. According to legend Lawrence was roasted on a grill and was highly venerated in the Middle Ages.

As pilgrims to the tomb of St Lawrence became more and more numerous the Emperor Constantine had a sanctuary built (330). By the 6C it was in such a poor state of repair that Pope **Pelagius II** (579-90) had it rebuilt.

It was probably enlarged in the 8C but underwent major alterations in the 13C under Pope **Honorius III** (1216-27): the apse of Pelagius' church was demolished, the church was extended westwards and its orientation reversed. The original nave was raised and became the chancel of the new church.

Later Baroque additions were removed by Pius IX in 1855; he also revealed the original nave while retaining Honorius' chancel.

On 19th July 1943 a bomb fell on the church; the roof, the upper part of the walls and the porch were destroyed. Repair work was put in hand immediately with the aim of restoring the church to its 13C appearance.

Façade

The very elegant porch, which dates from the time of Honorius (13C), was reconstructed after the 1943 bomb damage using some of the original material. Above the architrave which is supported on simple columns is a beautiful mosaic frieze in vivid colours. Above this is a cornice delicately carved with flowers, fruit and acanthus leaves punctuated with lion-head gargoyles. This fine example of medieval decorative sculpture is attributed to the Vassalletti, a family who worked in marble with the Cosmati from early in the 12C to late in the 13C.

The belltower *(right)* was erected in the 12C, probably at the same time as the cloisters. Its restoration in the 14C may have been due to damage caused by an earthquake or a fire.

Under the portico there is a rare example of a sarcophagus (**1**) with a sloping canopy which probably stood over a tomb in the floor of a church. The work is probably 11C.

Next to it is a 4C sarcophagus (**2**) with a likeness of the occupant in a medallion. The concise decoration depicts scenes from the Old and New Testaments.

The **'harvest' sarcophagus ★** (**3** – *left*) is quite remarkable. It is shaped like a funeral bier and decorated with vine leaves, bunches of grapes gathered by Cupids, birds and animals, very varied and lively. It was carved in the 5C or 6C; the clear-cut relief and the large smooth surfaces are characteristic of the Middle Ages.

Two modern works honour Pope Pius XII (**4**) and Alcide de Gasperi (**5**), President of the Council from 1945 to 1953, in recognition of their assistance in the work of restoration following the bomb damage.

The two lions (**6**) on either side of the main door are Romanesque.

Interior

The two distinct parts of the church are immediately apparent, divided by the triumphal arch and built on two different axes, one for the church built by Honorius III (13C) and one for the church built by Pelagius II (6C).

Church built by Honorius III – The funerary monument (**7** – *right of entrance*) of Guglielmo Fischi (1256), nephew of Pope Innocent IV, was reconstructed in 1943. Beneath a small temple resembling a 13C baldaquin is a 3C sarcophagus decorated with a marriage scene.

Honorius' church comprises a nave and two aisles separated by beautiful Antique granite columns of varying diameters. The Ionic capitals, like those in the porch, date from the Middle Ages and are attributed to the Vassalletti. They show with what happy results the medieval marble workers adapted their technique to ancient columns.

The lighting of the nave has hardly changed since the 13C. After 1943 the ceilling was rebuilt exactly as it had been in the 19C when Vespignani, who was working for Pius IX, had inserted a wooden coffered ceiling beneath the open roof frame.

The floor, which was damaged by the bomb, is bright with the colours of the 13C Cosmati work.

The two **ambones**★ are not identical. They are Cosmati work: a combination of white marble, porphyry and serpentine encrusted, with multicoloured insets gleaming with touches of gold. The one on the right (**8**) was used for reading the Gospel and was more sumptuously decorated (early 13C) than the one on the left (**9**) which was used for reading the Epistle and has the simple elegance of late-13C Cosmati work.

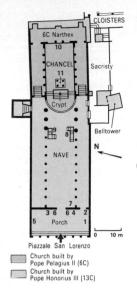

Piazzale San Lorenzo

▨ Church built by
Pope Pelagius II (6C)

▨ Church built by
Pope Honorius III (13C)

Church built by Pelagius II – The central section containing the high altar has been raised and is approached by two sets of steps. Its original orientation with the apse projecting west of the present chancel arch was reversed so that it could serve as the chancel of Honorius' church, as it does today. Pelagius' church comprised a nave and two aisles. From the raised nave only the tops of the ancient fluted columns are visible, supporting a magnificent sculpted architrave composed of disparate fragments which once belonged to a frieze or a door lintel. Over the aisles are galleries *(matrones)* for the women; the arcades rest on fine slim columns, their capitals decorated with leaves (6C).

The chancel arch which opened into the apse of Pelagius' church is decorated with a late 6C mosaic. At the centre is Christ, his hand raised in blessing. On his right are St Peter and St Lawrence and Pope Pelagius II offering his church to the Saviour. On his left are St Paul, St Stephen and St Hippolytus.

The bishop's **throne**★ (**10**) at the east end of the chancel is by the Cosmati (1254). The whiteness of the marble contrasts with the vivid colours and the gold inlays to create a fine decorative effect. The elegance of the throne is enhanced by the fine craftsmanship of the screen which closes off the choir.

The **baldaquin** (**11**) over the high altar is supported by four porphyry columns. The last two sections of the columns were repaired in 1862. This is Cosmati work (1148) and Is signed by the four sons of Paolo, the oldest of the group. It is one of the earliest examples of this sort of miniature temple with columns supporting an architrave.

Beneath the high altar in the **crypt** are the remains of St Lawrence, St Stephen and St Justin.

It was during some work commissioned by Pope Pius IX in the 19C that the lower part of the 6C church and the narthex were discovered. There are two sets of steps leading down, one on each side of the chancel *(if the gates are closed, enquire in the Sacristy).*

The narthex is decorated with modern mosaics by craftsmen of the Venice School and contains the **tomb of Pius IX** (1846-78).

Cloisters – *Entrance through the Sacristy in the south aisle or from the outside on the right of the belltower.* The 12C cloisters with their archaic charm formed part of the fortified convent which was like a citadel in the Middle Ages. St Lawrence's Basilica, being outside the walls of Rome, was easy prey for thieves and looters. The cloister walk contains many inscriptions from the neighbouring catacombs.

CITTÀ UNIVERSITARIA (UNIVERSITY CAMPUS)

In 1935 the University of Rome, which had suffered cramped conditions in the Palazzo della Sapienza (Palace of Wisdom) was transferred to the new University Campus near the Municipal Clinic *(Policlinico Umberto I)* built in 1890. The campus includes many buildings designed by the leading architects of Rome at that time, who worked on developing a collection of buildings reflecting the various thematic possibilities of modern architecture.

The overall design was awarded to **Marcello Piacentini** who, having become the major exponent of large-scale building projects (he had also overseen the plans for Rome's EUR), was inclined to apply the rules so dear to the "Twenties", as can be seen in the Rectorate and the vast entrance area. The overall impression is, however, one of balance and shows no excess of grandeur for its own sake. The final effect was the work of various architects, some of whom were members of the rationalist movement, whose inclinations differed somewhat from those of the academics. One of the most important of the rationalists was Giuseppe Pagano, whose style can clearly be seen in the Institute of Physics.

The architects who collaborated on the project were: Pietro Aschieri – Institute of Chemistry; Giò Ponti – Institute of Mathematics; Giovanni Michelucci – Institute of Mineralogy and Institute of Physiology; Giuseppe Capponi – Institute of Botany.
All the faculties are not, however, located on the University Campus itself but are spread all over Rome. In recent years, in fact, separate premises, known as University II, were set up at Tor Vergata.

Neighbouring sights are described in the following chapters: CATACOMBE DI PRIS-CILLA; PORTA PIA; SAN GIOVANNI IN LATERANO.

SAN PAOLO FUORI LE MURA★★

Tour: allow about 1 hour for San Paolo fuori le Mura and 45min for the Tre Fontane (excluding travelling time)
Access: by underground or by bus (see Plan of Rome); by car (see Plan of Rome in Michelin Red Guide Italia).

This walk describes two sites situated outside the Aurelian Wall *(Mura Aureliane)* linked by the history of St Paul; the Basilica of St Paul Without the Walls contains his tomb and the demesne of Tre Fontane, a few kilometres away, was the site of his martyrdom.

An extraordinary market

The **Emmaus Community** provides shelter and assistance to the homeless and unemployed. One initiative they have taken to raise money is to collect bric-a-brac from householders, restore it in their workshops and sell it on at a market on Tuesdays, Thursdays and Saturdays (from 2pm to 6pm) held in the forecourt before the church.

Saint Paul – Paul was a Jew called Saul, who was born early in the 1C AD at Tarsus in Cilicia in Asia Minor (southeast Turkey, not far from Adana). At first he persecuted Christ's disciples; then on his way from Jerusalem to Damascus one day, he was blinded by a light, fell from his horse and heard Jesus's voice saying: "Saul, Saul, why persecutest thou me?" This event precipitated his conversion: he changed his name from Saul to Paul and became the chief agent in preaching Christianity to the Gentiles. His very active life as an apostle contrasted with his mean physique. According to an apocryphal account dating from mid-2C, he was a pale little man, bald but bearded, with a hooked nose and knock-knees; he made long missionary journeys throughout Syria, Cyprus, Asia Minor, Macedonia and Greece.
Accused by the Jewish community of Caesarea in Palestine he demanded to be brought before the Emperor Nero (Paul was a Roman citizen). This is why he set out for Rome in about AD 60. He landed in Pozzuoli and from there travelled to Rome where he was welcomed by the Christians. Two years later he appeared before the Imperial court and was acquitted.
The date of Paul's martyrdom is not known for certain. Like Peter he may have been a victim of the persecution of the Christians organised by Nero after the terrible fire in AD 64 which destroyed the greater part of Rome. When the rumour began to spread that Nero himself had started the fire to clear the land for his Golden House, he quickly found someone to take the blame. Innumerable Christians died a variety of deaths. Tacitus writes: "Mockery was added to their suffering; covered with the skins of beasts, they were torn by dogs and perished; or were nailed to crosses; or were doomed to the flames to serve as human torches as daylight waned. Nero threw open his garden for the spectacle..."
As a Roman citizen, St Paul was sentenced to be beheaded.

★★BASILICA DI SAN PAOLO FUORI LE MURA
(BASILICA OF ST PAUL WITHOUT THE WALLS) ⊘

Together with St Peter's in the Vatican, St John Lateran and St Mary Major, St Paul Without the Walls is one of the major basilicas in Rome. Its historical significance attracts visitors from all over the world. Pilgrims to the tomb of the Apostle to the Gentiles are united by a common spirit of veneration.
St Paul's body was buried beside the Via Ostiensis which was lined with tombs as were all the major roads leading out of Rome. A small shrine *(memoria)* was erected over his grave. In the 4C the Emperor Constantine undertook to build a basilica over the tomb, as he had done for St Peter's tomb. This first basilica was consecrated by Pope Sylvester I in 324. It was smaller than St Peter's Basilica and faced the Via Ostiensis. The Apostle's tomb was enclosed by the apse on the spot where the high altar now stands. By 386 it had become such a popular place of

pilgrimage that three emperors – Valentinian II, Theodosius I and his son Arcadius – decided to enlarge the building. It could not be extended across the road (because of the rising ground) and since the Apostle's tomb could not be moved the orientation was reversed, with the apse on the Via Ostiensis and the façade facing the Tiber so that the tomb occupied a central position at the head of the nave.

The new basilica was magnificent; it was larger than the contemporary basilica of St Peter in the Vatican. The huge project was not completed until 395 in the reign of the Emperor Honorius. For the next 14 centuries the basilica was maintained with great care and attention.

When the building was sacked by the Lombards in the 8C and by the Saracens in the 9C, the damage was immediately repaired. John VIII (872-82) had a defensive wall built enclosing both the basilica and the community which had grown up around it; this came to be known as 'Johannipolis' after the Pope.

The greatest artists were employed to embellish the basilica: from Pietro Cavallini and Arnolfo di Cambio to Carlo Maderno.

When therefore on the night of 15 to 16 July 1823 fire broke out in the roof and almost totally destroyed the basilica, it was a great catastrophe.

Reconstruction began immediately and it was decided not to preserve the undamaged parts which had survived. Thus the nave and aisles were rebuilt in their entirety although the south side of the basilica had not been touched by the flames; the apse and transepts were extensively restored.

Although St Paul's basilica is now adorned with gleaming marble and vivid colours, it still follows the original plan and manifests the grandeur of the early Christian basilicas in Rome.

Tour

To appreciate the vast size of the building, enter by the main door from Viale di S Paolo.

The west front is preceded by a huge courtyard surrounded by covered arcades *(quadriporticus)* which was built early in the 20C.

The statues of St Paul (**1**) and St Luke (**2**) are 19C. The mosaics now on the pediment replaced those done in the 14C by Pietro Cavallini.

The central portal (**3**), which replaced the 11C original, is flanked on either side by statues of St Peter and St Paul and has two magnificent bronze and silver doors depicting scenes from the lives of the two saints.

★★★**Interior** – No visitor can fail to be impressed by the multitude of columns – 80 granite monoliths – which divide the nave and four aisles.

The gold and white coffered **ceiling** bears the arms of Pope Pius IX (1846-78) who consecrated the new basilica.

At the west end of the inner south aisle is the Holy Door, an 11C bronze door, made in Constantinople for Gregory VII (1073-85).

During the reconstruction every alternate window in the **nave** was suppressed; the daylight is filtered by a screen of alabaster.

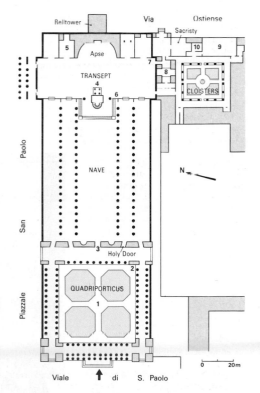

The medallion portraits of the popes painted in the 5C have been replaced by mosaic roundels showing the long line of succession from St Peter to John Paul II.

In the long **side walls** windows and recesses alternate. The recesses contain statues of the Apostles sculpted by various 19C and 20C artists.

Two gigantic granite columns support the **chancel arch** above which are two inscriptions recalling the construction of the basilica by Theodosius and Honorius and its embellishment by Galla Placidia, Theodosius' daughter, who was responsible for the 5C mosaic, which was reconstructed after being badly damaged in the fire. It shows Christ flanked by two angels and the 24 elders of the Apocalypse; above are the symbols of the Evangelists; below are St Peter and St Paul. On the reverse side of the arch, fragments of the original mosaic have been re-employed.

The **Ciborium**★★★ (**4**) is a Gothic work by Arnolfo di Cambio (1285). It is supported on four fine porphyry columns with gilded capitals.

Detail and proportion are delicately blended: the many decorative figures are executed with great skill, from the pairs of angels supporting the pierced rose-window on each of the four pediments to the animals on the vault.

The side facing the nave shows Abbot Bartolomeo, who commissioned the baldaquin, offering it to St Paul.

Beneath the baldaquin is the high altar; the table is 1.37m - 4 1/2ft above a 4C marble plaque engraved with the name of Paul, Apostle and Martyr. The plaque marks the position of Paul's grave and has never been moved.

The mosaic in the **apse** dates from the 13C and is the work of Venetian artists commissioned by Pope Honorius III; it is in the characteristic style of the Venetians who even at that time still followed Byzantine models: the little figure at Christ's feet represents Pope Honorius in all humility. The whole work was restored in the 19C.

The ceiling of the broad **transept** is richly decorated with the arms of St Paul (an arm and a sword) and the arms of successive popes from 1800 to 1846 (Pius VII who died a few days after the fire in 1823, Leo XII, Pius VIII, Gregory XVI). The altars which face one another from the far ends of the transept are symmetrical and decorated with lapis lazuli and malachite.

To the left of the apse is the **Chapel of the Holy Sacrament**★ (**5**), the work of Carlo Maderno (1629), which contains a 14C wooden crucifix, a statue of St Bridget kneeling by Stefano Maderno (c1576-1636) and a wooden statue of St Paul dating from the 14C.

The Paschal **candlestick**★★ (**6**) by Nicolà di Angelo and Pietro Vassalletto (12C) is a remarkable piece of Romanesque art. The base is decorated with monsters while on the shaft are decorative motifs, scenes from the life of Jesus (note the expressions of the squat figures), tendrils and more monsters supporting the candle socket.

The **stoop** (**7**) is a charming piece of sculpture by Pietro Galli (1804-77) showing a child threatening a terrified demon with holy water.

The **baptistry** (**8**), rebuilt in 1930, is an elegant chamber in the shape of a Greek cross, incorporating four ancient columns.

★**Cloisters** ⊙ – These probably formed part of the work done by a member of the Vassalletto family (13C) who, like the Cosmati, was skilled in marble incrustation work. The north gallery (backing on to the church) is particularly fine.

The great variety among the columns, their marble incrustation picked out in gold and the exquisite workmanship of the mosaic frieze above the arcades make the cloisters a charming composition.

The galleries contain numerous archeological specimens, some of which come from the old basilica.

Picture gallery (**9**) – The gallery displays not only 13C to 19C pictures but also a series of engravings showing the basilica, particularly in its ruined state after the fire in 1823; the *St Paul Bible*, a 9C illustrated manuscript; a reproduction of the slab over St Paul's tomb; several papal portraits from the series painted in the nave in the 5C for Leo the Great.

Chapel of Relics (**10**) – Among the precious articles housed here is a beautiful 15C reliquary cross in silver gilt.

J.-P. Langeland/DIAF

Cloisters of San Paolo Fuori le Mura

★ABBAZIA DELLE TRE FONTANE (THREE FOUNTAINS ABBEY)

From Via Laurentina a drive leads to Three Fountains Abbey.

The place known in Antiquity as *Ad Aquas Salvias* is where St Paul was beheaded. Legend has added an epilogue: the Apostle's head bounced three times and from the ground spouted three fountains.

Pilgrims have been coming here since the Middle Ages. Many oratories were built; one of them, still decorated with traces of 9C painting, is now the entrance gateway. Surrounded by green hillsides and the scent of eucalyptus trees is a group of buildings: a Trappist monastery, a convent of the Little Sisters of Jesus and three churches.

Santa Maria "Scala coeli" – Cistercian monks settled here in 1140. The history of the church is connected with one of St Bernard's ecstatic visions: while celebrating mass in the crypt he had a vision of the souls in Purgatory ascending into Heaven, released by his intercession.

The present church, which was restored in 1925, was built in 1583 by Giacomo della Porta to an octagonal plan beneath a shallow dome. In the left-hand chapel there is an attractive 16C mosaic above a painting of St Bernard's vision.

Behind the altar in the crypt is a room supposed to be where St Paul waited before his execution.

Santi Vincenzo e Anastasio – The church, which is dedicated to **St Vincent** and **St Anastasius**, is the abbey church of the Trappist monks who have occupied the neighbouring monastery since 1868. The origins of the church go back to the 7C when Pope Honorius I (625-38) built a convent to house some oriental monks (as at St Sabas).

The church, which was rebuilt in brick in the 13C, is austere in appearance with its unusually high elevation and its solid pillars which still bear traces of paintings of the Apostles executed by some of Raphael's pupils.

San Paolo alle Tre Fontane – The Church of **St Paul at the Three Fountains** was designed in the 16C by Giacomo della Porta to replace two chapels built on the spot where, according to legend, the fountains had spouted from the earth. Excavations beneath the church in the 19C uncovered traces of a small building which in the 7C marked the site of Paul's martyrdom; some tombs were also discovered belonging to a Christian cemetery dating back to the 4C and beyond. The statues of St Peter and St Paul on the façade are by Nicolas Cordier. The ancient mosaics set into the floor come from Ostia. The sites of the three fountains are marked by three shrines set at different levels.

We came across the Colosseum at twilight. Once one has seen it, everything else seems small. It is so huge that the mind cannot retain its image; one remembers it smaller than it is, so that every time one returns to it, one is astounded by its size.

Goethe: Italian Journey. Rome, 11 November 1786

SANTA MARIA MAGGIORE – ESQUILINO★★★

Tour 3 hours

The **Esquiline**, one of the seven hills of Rome, has been inhabited since the 8C BC. It is an uneven plateau with three peaks which the Romans named the **Oppius**, now covered by the Parco Oppio, the **Fagutalis**, which overlooks the Imperial Fora, and the **Cispius**, now crowned by Santa Maria Maggiore.

Long used as a burial ground for poor people, the Esquiline was one of the most sinister parts of Rome. Augustus gave it a new face. He divided the city into fourteen districts, one of which was the Esquiline; he arranged for part of it to be given to his friend Maecenas who built a magnificent villa surrounded by gardens. In the course of time the district came to be coveted by the Emperors themselves and after a series of confiscations it was added to the Imperial domain. After the fire in AD 64 had cleared the ground, Nero built his Golden House on the Oppius.

Piazza di Santa Maria Maggiore – The fluted column which stands at the centre is the sole survivor of the eight columns which graced the Basilica of Maxentius in the Forum. It was brought here in 1614 on the initiative of Pope Paul V and set up on its base by the architect Carlo Maderno and crowned with a statue of the Virgin.

A tip for culture vultures...

Orbis *(Piazza Esquilino 37)* is an agency providing tickets to concert and theatrical venues in the city. It is a good place to pick-up last minute returns.

***BASILICA DI SANTA MARIA MAGGIORE (ST MARY MAJOR) ⊘

It is one of the four Roman basilicas which bear the title 'major' (the others are St John Lateran, St Paul Without the Walls and St Peter's in the Vatican) and enjoys the privilege of extraterritoriality conferred by the Lateran Treaty in 1929. The basilica was built by Sixtus III (432-40) in honour of Mary one year after the Council of Ephesus at which Nestorius, the Patriarch of Constantinople, had claimed that Mary was not the Mother of God.

Subsequent popes have left their mark; in their desire to contribute to the glory of the Virgin they made numerous alterations. The portico was rebuilt in the 12C by Eugenius III, in the 16C by Gregory XIII and again in the 18C by Benedict XIV. The campanile, the highest in Rome, was added in 1377 by Gregory XI. In the 17C and 18C under Clement X and Clement XI the apse was remodelled. The main façade was given its present appearance in the 18C under Benedict XIV by Ferdinando Fuga (1743-50).

Façade

The portico and loggia are sandwiched between two identical wings although more than a century elapsed between the construction of the one on the right (1605) and the one on the left (1721-43). Like the majority of architects in the first half of the 18C, **Ferdinando Fuga** had a taste for Classical forms but also adopted certain elements from the Baroque art of Borromini. The façade is enlivened by sculptures, the broken lines of the pediments and the interplay of the openings in the portico and the arcade of the loggia.

In the portico stands a statue of Philip IV of Spain (**1**), a benefactor of the basilica; it is by a pupil of Algardi (1692). The loggia from which the Pope used to give his blessing *Urbi et Orbi* was added to the original façade which still retains its early-14C mosaic decoration restored in the 19C.

★**Loggia Mosaics** ⊘ – *Access by the steps on the left of the porch.*

The upper part – Christ, angels, the evangelistic symbols, the Virgin and the saints – is the work of **Filippo Rusuti** (late 13C), who took over from Pietro Cavallini.

Below are four scenes illustrating the **legend of the basilica** which was built here late in the 4C by Pope Liberius; the Virgin appeared in a dream to a Giovanni Patrizio, a rich man, and to Pope Liberius, inviting them to build a church in her honour; the site for the sanctuary was to be marked by a fall of snow on the morrow. When the Pope and Patrizio consulted one another they were astonished to find that in spite of the time of year (5 August 356) there had been a snow fall on the Esquiline. The Pope drew up a plan of the church; Patrizio financed the construction. The graceful lines, richly apparelled figures and fine deep perspectives link these scenes with the Florentine style of Cimabue and Giotto.

Santa Maria Maggiore

***Interior

It too has undergone many alterations: at the end of the 13C Nicholas IV (1288-92) extended the chancel and in the middle of the 15C Cardinal Guillaume d'Estouteville, archpriest of the Basilica, covered the aisles with vaulting in keeping with Renaissance taste. Despite that, the interior of this basilica with its almost perfect proportions and two rows of Ionic columns is a remarkable example of early Christian architecture; brilliant with colour, it is at its most spectacular on Sundays and feast days.

***Mosaics – Those in the nave, on the chancel arch and in the apse are beyond compare.

Nave – Dating from the 5C they consist of a series of panels above the entablature which is decorated with a fine frieze of interlacing. They are some of the oldest Christian mosaics in Rome, together with those in Santa Pudenziana, Santa Costanza and the Lateran Baptistry. They are examples of an art which had rediscovered a taste for vivid narrative after accepting the rigidity of the late Empire.

The scenes are taken from the Old Testament with Abraham, Jacob, Moses and Joshua in the leading roles. On the left-hand side of the nave, beginning at the chancel end, are incidents from Genesis:

2) Melchizedek comes to meet Abraham.

3) Abraham's dream near the Mamré oak.

4) The separation of Abraham and Lot.

Next comes the arch opened up in the 17C during the construction of the Pauline chapel which entailed the destruction of the mosaics at this point. Then:

5) Isaac blesses Jacob. Esau returns from hunting.

The next panel is a painting.

6) Rachel tells Laban of the arrival of Jacob, his nephew. Laban and Jacob embrace.

7) Jacob agrees to serve Laban for seven years and to receive Rachel as his wife.

8) Jacob reproaches Laban for giving him Leah, his elder daughter, in marriage. Jacob marries Rachel.

9) Jacob asks Laban for the speckled and spotted sheep. The division of the flock.

10) God tells Jacob to leave. Jacob announces his departure to the women.

Next between two painted panels:

11) The meeting of the two brothers, Jacob and Esau.

12) Hamor and his son Shechem ask Jacob for the hand of his daughter Dinah, whose brothers are angry.

13) Dinah's brothers insist that the men among Hamor's people be circumcised. Hamor and Shechem explain the situation to their people.

The last three panels on this side are painted.

On the right-hand side of the nave, starting at the chancel end, there is first a painted panel and then:

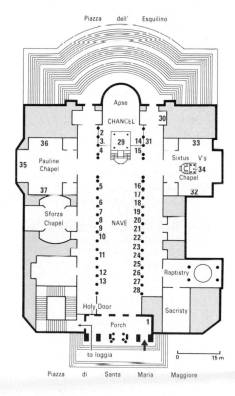

14) Pharaoh's daughter receives Moses. He discusses with the Egyptian doctors.

15) Moses marries Zipporah. God appears in the burning bush.

Then comes the arch opened up during the construction of Sixtus V's Chapel which takes the place of the mosaics (1741-50).

16) The passage of the Red Sea.

17) Moses and the people of Israel. The miracle of quails.

18) The salt sea of Mara. The people of Israel reproach Moses who, after praying to God, touches the water with a rod sent by God and makes it fresh. The meeting of Moses and Amalek.

19) The battle against the people of Amalek and Moses praying on the hillside.

20) The return of the chiefs of the tribes who had gone to explore the Promised Land. The stoning of Moses, Joshua and Caleb.

21) The tablets of Law are handed down. The death of Moses. The transport of the Ark.

22) The passage of the Jordan. Joshua sends spies to Jericho.

23) The angel of God (the captain of the Lord's host) appears to Joshua. The harlot Rahab helps the spies to scale the walls of Jericho. The return of the spies.

24) The besieging of Jericho. The procession of the Ark to the sound of trumpets.

25) The taking of Ai. Joshua before God and among the soldiers.

26) Joshua fights the Amorites. Hail of stones on Israel's enemies.

27) The sun and moon stand still upon Gibeon.

28) Joshua punishes the rebel kings.

The last three panels are paintings.

Chancel arch – It dates from the 5C and has the liveliness of the first Christian mosaics. It is divided into four horizontal bands. Probably later than the mosaics in the nave, it shows Byzantine influence:
– In the Annunciation scene *(top row left)* where Mary is dressed like an oriental empress;
– In the Epiphany scene *(second row left)*, presented as a sumptuous court reception, where the Child Jesus is sitting on a throne decorated with precious stones. The cities of Jerusalem and Bethlehem *(two lower rows)* with sheep representing the Apostles appear in almost every mosaic from this date.

Apse – This dazzling composition comprises elements taken from a 5C mosaic, which was transformed at the end of the 13C by **Jacopo Torriti** when Nicolas IV rebuilt the apse. All the figures are the work of Torriti since the earlier mosaic consisted only of birds, foliage and scrolls. The main subject of the composition is the *Crowning of the Virgin*, surrounded by groups of angels and a procession of saints. Kneeling before them are Nicolas IV and Cardinal Colonna.

The four 15C sculptured panels lower down come from the altar of Sixtus IV.

Baldaquin (29) – It was designed by Fuga and is supported on porphyry columns wreathed in fronds of bronze. Unfortunately it hides some of the mosaic.

Beneath the baldaquin is the **Confessio** where Pope Pius IX (1846-78) is shown at prayer, resplendent in bronze gilt, marble and frescoes (19C); fragments thought to belong to Jesus's crib are venerated here.

★**Ceiling** – The coffers were decorated with the first gold to come from Peru which was offered to Pope Alexander VI, a Spaniard (1492-1503), by Ferdinand and Isabella of Spain. The Pope continued the work begun by Calixtus III (1455-58) in constructing this ceiling which is decorated with the arms of the Borgia family to which the two Popes belonged. The roses at the centre of the coffers are 1m - 3 1/4ft in diameter. Vasari, a 16C art historian and author of *'Lives of Italian Artists'*, attributes this work to Giuliano da Sangallo (1445-1516).

Floor – The 12C Cosmati work was radically restored by Ferdinando Fuga in the 18C.

Right aisle – The tomb of Cardinal Consalvo Rodriguez (**30**) (late 13C) is typically Gothic (a recumbent figure under a trilobed arch, flanked by angels beneath a mosaic of the Virgin). In the floor is the tombstone (**31**) of the family of Bernini *(qv)*.

Sixtus V's Chapel – The chapel is named after Sixtus V who during his five year reign (1585-90) turned Rome into a huge building site with his restorations, conversions and new constructions. His favourite architect was Domenico Fontana, to whom he therefore entrusted the design of this chapel. It is almost a church in itself. Designed on the Greek cross plan beneath a dome painted with frescoes, it is resplendent with gilding, stucco and marble. In the right and left arms of the cross are the monumental tombs of Popes Sixtus V (**32**) and Pius V (**33**) decorated with low relief sculptures illustrating the great events of their reigns.

Beneath the high altar (**34**) in 1590 Domenico Fontana set up the Oratory of the Crib which had held the relics of the grotto in Bethlehem since the 7C.

Baptistry – It is the work of the Baroque architect Flaminio Ponzio. The beautiful porphyry font was decorated in the 19C by Giuseppe Valadier. The high relief of the Assumption on the altar is by Pietro Bernini, father of Gian Lorenzo.

Left aisle – It contains in particular two beautiful chapels.

Sforza Chapel – Its highly original architectural style is by Giacomo della Porta, probably from designs by Michelangelo.

Pauline Chapel – It is also called the Borghese Chapel after the family name of Pope Paul V who commissioned it in 1611 from Flaminio Ponzio. It is identical in plan to Sixtus V's Chapel but with even more sumptuous decoration. In 1612 Cigoli painted the dome without first sub-dividing it with ribs; he was the first to follow this course and the result was not perfect. When, some ten years later, Lanfranco (who also worked on the Pauline Chapel) painted the dome of Sant'Andrea della Valle using the same process, he achieved a masterpiece. The main altar (   ) is incomparably rich, like a jewel, set with jasper, lapis-lazuli, agate and amethyst.

The altarpiece is of a Virgin and Child in the Byzantine style. She may have been painted in the 12C after a 9C Byzantine original. She is greatly venerated among the faithful and has even been attributed to St Luke. She is surrounded by a 'glory' of angels in gilded bronze, a feature very popular with Baroque artists. Above the altarpiece is a sculpted panel by Stefano Maderno illustrating the legend of the tracing of the basilica's plan *(see above)*. As in Sixtus V's Chapel the right and left arms of the cross contain papal tombs: Clement VIII (   ) and Paul V (   ).

Leave the church by the door at the end of the aisle to the right of the choir.

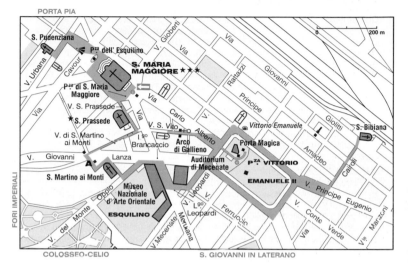

ENVIRONS

Piazza dell' Esquilino – From here there is a fine **view★★** of the apse of Santa Maria Maggiore. When the Pauline and Sistine chapels were added beneath their domes they looked like two separate buildings. Clement IX (1667-69) therefore commissioned Bernini to integrate them with the basilica by altering the apsidal end of the church. Bernini conceived a grandiose design but the excessive cost prevented it from being carried into effect. The following pope, Clement X, therefore gave the work to Carlo Rainaldi.

The Egyptian obelisk at the centre of the square comes from the mausoleum of Augustus. Sixtus V ordered it to be moved and set up by Domenico Fontana, a specialist in such matters.

Turn left into Via Urbana.

Santa Pudenziana ⊙ - The church, dedicated to St Pudens or the Roman virgin St Potentiana, is one of the oldest in Rome. Legend tells how Senator Pudens, who lived in a house on this site, welcomed Peter under his roof. In the 2C a bath house stood on the site. Late in the 4C a church *(ecclesia pudentiana)* was established in the baths. The similarity between the girl's name Pudentiana and the adjective derived from Pudens turned Pudentiana into the daughter of Pudens. Pudentiana, like her sister Praxedes, was not martyred but both are shown with the martyrs whose bodies they prepared for burial.

The façade was repaired in the 19C. The belltower dates from the 12C as does the elegant doorway, with its fluted columns and its sculpted frieze inset with five medallions. The interior shows the signs of many changes: in the 8C the aisles were added. In 1589 the dome was built and the chancel altered so that several figures in the fine 4C **mosaic★** were lost. It is one of the oldest examples of a Christian mosaic in Rome (together with those in the nave of Santa Maria Maggiore in Santa Costanza and the baptistry of St John Lateran. The way in which Christ is represented, the brilliant colours and the lively figures show the persistence of Roman qualities in Christian mosaic art before it was influenced by Byzantium and its stylised forms.

The Caetani Chapel in the left aisle, richly decorated with marble and stucco, was built by Francesco da Volterra during the Counter-Reformation (late 16C) and completed by Carlo Maderno early in the 17C.

Excavations ⊙ – Excavations carried out under the church have uncovered the remains of Pudens' house, mosaics and baths which partly covered it at the end of the 2C, as well as of the Roman road built in the 3C. A 6C fresco depicts St Peter with the sisters St Pudentiana and St Praxedes.

Return to Piazza di Santa Maria Maggiore and beyond the church bear right into Via Santa Prassede.

★**Santa Prassede** ◷ – *Entrance in the right aisle.* The brick façade with the main doors giving on to a small courtyard can be seen through the entrance arch *(closed)* which opens into Via di San Martino ai Monti beneath a loggia supported on two columns.

The church is an old *titulus*, ie a private house where Christian services were held in Antiquity. The present building was put up by Paschal I in 822.

It was built to the basilical plan, the nave and aisles separated by two rows of columns directly supporting the architrave. It was altered in the 13C by the addition of three transverse arches in the nave, decorated with frescoes in late 16C-17C and a coffered ceiling in the 19C.

★**Chancel mosaics** – They date from the 9C, the reign of Paschal I, and show the influence of Byzantine traditionalism and then of Carolingian art. Colour is paramount and no longer used in half tones. In this respect it is interesting to compare the apsidal mosaic here with the one in the Church of St Cosmas and St Damian which is three centuries earlier and inspired the iconography of the later one: against a background of sky quite lacking in depth, the figure of Christ is flanked by St Peter and St Paul presenting Praxedes and Pudentiana. The other two figures are St Zenon and Pope Paschal I offering his church (his square halo showing that he was alive at the time). The two palms represent the Old and New Testaments and the Phoenix on the one on the left symbolizes the Resurrection.

The chancel arch shows *(upper part)* the arrival of the Elect in the Celestial City of Jerusalem with groups of the Blessed *(lower part)* (spoiled in the 16C by the balconies).

★★**Cappella di San Zenone** – *Right aisle.* St Zenon's Chapel was built between 817 and 824 by Pope Paschal I. The doorway is made up of various elements taken from earlier buildings: two black granite columns, the entablature, the column bases decorated with an interlaced pattern, the marble urn in the arch over the entrance. Above this are several portrait medallions arranged in two arcs, one centred on Christ surrounded by the Apostles and the other on the Virgin and Child surrounded by various saints. The two portraits in the rectangular panels at the bottom of the arrangement are much later than the 9C.

The interior is covered in mosaics with a gold background *(time switch):* on the central vault Christ, in strict Byzantine style, is supported by four angels; above the opening to the left of the altar is the Virgin accompanied by two saints and the mother of Paschal I, Theodora Episcopa, with a blue halo; the mosaic above the opening to the right of the altar was spoiled in the 13C when an oratory was built to house a fragment of the scourging column. This relic is greatly venerated by pilgrims especially during Holy Week.

Take Via di San Martino ai Monti.

The street leads into a square. The two **Cappocci towers** (**A**), despite extensive restoration, still evoke the power of the noble families in the Middle Ages.

The apse of the Church of San Martino ai Monti dates from the 9C *(see below).*

San Martino ai Monti ◷ – This venerable church was founded in the 5C and dedicated to St Martin by Pope Symmachus (498-514) next to a *titulus* existing in the 3C in the house of Equitius *(the underground remains can be visited: ask in the Sacristy).* As Pope Sylvester (314-35) was revered in the *Titulus Equitii*, when Pope Sergius II rebuilt the church in the 9C, he dedicated it to both St Martin and St Sylvester.

The church was completely transformed in the 17C. The interior was divided into a nave and two aisles by two rows of marble columns with capitals which date from the time of Symmachus (set on their bases in the 17C). In the aisles Gaspard Dughet, Poussin's brother-in-law, painted frescoes of Roman landscapes and the story of the Prophet Elijah. At either end of the left aisle are views of the interiors of the old basilicas of St Peter in the Vatican and of St John Lateran (before the intervention of Borromini) by Filippo Gagliardi (17C).

On leaving the church, turn left into Largo Brancaccio and then right into Via Merulana.

Museo nazionale d'Arte orientale ◷ – Accommodated on the *piano nobile* of **Palazzo Brancaccio** is the National Collection of Oriental Art. On the right before going upstairs, is the nymphaeum designed by Francesco Gai who was also charged with the interior decoration of the palace.

The museum charts the history of the Orient starting with the Near and Middle East, particularly Iran. The first section of the exhibition is particularly interesting, it illustrates through artefacts from Shahr-i-Sokta daily life in the third to the second millenia BC: social organisation, pottery, tools, the working of semi-precious stones. The neighbouring rooms are dedicated to areas of Western Iran: note the intricate zoomorphic figures in bronze from Luristan.

Two further sections are given over to exhibits from the Far East, notably Tibet and Nepal (votive sculptures, paintings and ornately carved, inlaid wooden window frames), Gandhara and finally China (vases, bronze statuettes, mirrors, masks, enamel-decorated porcelain).

Auditorium di Mecenate ⊙ – The **Auditorium of Maecenas**, part of the luxurious Villa of Maecenas (early 1C) which was surrounded by large gardens, was discovered in 1874. Steps lead down to a vestibule and a large hall with a tiered exedra. The underground structure with its drainage system and fresco decoration of gardens and landscapes was probably a nymphaeum originally but Maecenas used it as an auditorium where he entertained his learned friends.

Take Via Leopardi which leads into Piazza Vittorio Emanuele II.

Piazza 'Vittorio' – The square is usually thronged with people attending the large market held there. It was laid out in the late 19C by Gaetano Koch and other architects with arcades at street level, as in Turin.
In the north corner of the square are the ruins of a huge 3C fountain which was adorned with the 'Trophies of Marius'. The adjacent **Magic Gate** (Porta Magica) continues to excite speculation; the signs inscribed round the doorway (bricked up) have never been deciphered.

From the northwest side take Via Carlo Alberto, bear left into Via di S Vito.

Arco di Gallieno – The **Arch of Gallienus** was erected in 262 in honour of the Emperor Gallienus (253-68) who was assassinated by some Illyrian officers. It stands on the site of the Esquiline Gate (Porta Esquilina) in the Servian wall *(plan Rome during the Empire)*. Traces of this wall, which was probably started in the 6C BC and several times repaired, can be seen in Via Carlo Alberto (next to the Church of St Vito e Modesto).

Santa Bibiana – The church was rebuilt in the 17C and was one of Bernini's first architectural projects. His **statue★** of St Bibiana (or Viviana) *(inside above the altar)* is also one of his early works; note the pictorial effect of the left hand gathering up the folds of the garment.

Return to Piazza Vittorio and take Via Cairoli.

Neighbouring sights are described in the following chapters: COLOSSEO – CELIO; FORI IMPERIALI; PORTA PIA; SAN GIOVANNI IN LATERANO.

Beware of the fact that many museums close during the afternoon and that most churches are closed during the afternoon siesta...
... opening times and charges of sites marked ⊙ are listed in the Practical Information section at the end of the guide.

TERME DI CARACALLA ★★

Tour: about 3 hours including the Baths (1 hour) – 2,5 km starting from Piazza di Porta Capena

This walk is centred on the Old Appian Way which, between the Porta Capena and the Porta San Sebastiano, is called Via delle Terme di Caracalla and Via di Porta San Sebastiano. The road is pleasantly shaded by trees and bordered by parks and gardens which lend a rural touch.
The **Porta Capena** is a gate in the defensive wall built by Servius Tullius in the 6C BC which was rebuilt at the end of the 4C BC after its weakness had been made apparent by the invading Gauls. It was here, according to Livy, that in the reign of Tullus Hostilius (672-40 BC) the last of the Horatii, who had defeated the Curiatii of Alba, slew his sister with his sword because she had dared to weep for her fiancé, one of the Curiatii: "Let that be the fate of any Roman who mourns the enemy."
An **obelisk** *(obelisco)*, brought back from Axum, a religious town in Ethiopia, in 1937, marks the beginning of Via delle Terme di Caracalla, which is flanked by umbrella pines and flowering laurels.

Take Via di Terme di Caracalla and bear right into Via Guido Baccelli.

On the right stands the building of the FAO (Food and Agriculture Organisation), an agency of the United Nations, which employs over 3000 people of all nationalities. It studies food production, control of plant and animal diseases and experimentation with new strains.

Santa Balbina ⊙ – In 1927 the church underwent a thorough restoration which returned it to its medieval simplicity. It was probably a 4C house converted to a place of worship. A pitched roof covers a single nave punctuated by recessed chapels and lit by high barred windows.

On the right of the entrance is Cardinal Surdi's **tomb**★, bearing a recumbent Gothic figure and decorated with multicoloured marble inlay in the Cosmati style (1295). In the fourth chapel on the right the low relief showing Mary and John the Baptist standing by the Cross is a fine sculpture by Mino del Reame (15C); it came from the Medieval church of St Peter in the Vatican.

The third chapel contains the remains of some 13C frescoes.

The *Schola Cantorum* where the choristers stood has been reconstructed in front of the high altar.

Behind the high altar is the **episcopal chair**★, a fine piece of Cosmati work (13C). The frescoes in the apse are 17C.

Beyond the church turn left into Via Antonina and then sharp right.

★★★ TERME DI CARACALLA (BATHS OF CARACALLA) ⊙

Four sets of baths had already been built – by Agrippa, by Nero on the Campus Martius, by Titus near the Golden House and by Trajan on the Aventine – when the Emperor Antoninus Caracalla began (AD 212) the largest baths that Rome had ever seen (11ha - 25 acres); Diocletian's Baths were to be more extensive. They were finished by Elagabalus and Alexander Severus (AD 222-35), the last two emperors of the Severan dynasty.

The sober exterior concealed a contrastingly rich interior: floors paved with marble and mosaic, walls covered with mosaic and gilded stucco work; the white marble capitals and cornices contrasting with the multicoloured marble, porphyry and granite of the columns. The huge building, with its massive walls and bold vaulting (30m - 98ft high) was much admired; it offered facilities for 1600 bathers. The Romans used the baths daily, early in the afternoon at the end of a day's work. The poorest people were not excluded, although they had fewer slaves than the

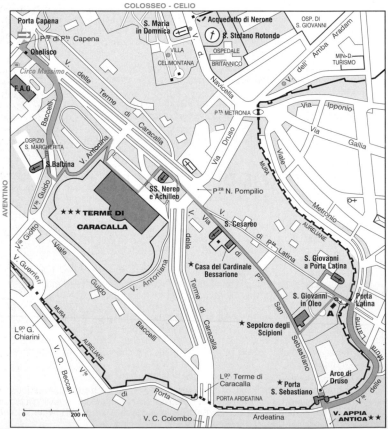

COLOSSEO - CELIO

APPIA ANTICA

rich to assist them with their ablutions. Baths were an important element in Roman life; they offered facilities for keeping fit through bathing and physical exercise as well as libraries for the cultivation of the mind; they were also however places of assignation and by Caracalla's time the Romans were already denouncing the notorious manners of such establishments.

Caracalla's Baths were in use until 537 when the Goths under Witigis damaged the aqueducts which supplied water to Rome. Shelley's poem Prometheus Unbound "was chiefly written upon the mountainous ruins of the Baths of Caracalla".

Excavations in the 16C, 19C and 20C have uncovered magnificent statues, vases and mosaics and also a **mithraeum** (temple of Mithras) ⊘ in the northeast corner.

Baths of Caracalla

Plan – The baths consisted of a central block enclosed by a wall with gateways opening into Via Nova which runs at the foot of the Aventine parallel with the Appian Way. The southwest side of the enclosure was almost entirely taken up with water tanks screened by an amphitheatre, on either side of which were two pavilions containing the libraries. The bays in the southeast and northwest sides were probably gymnasiums. The principal rooms *(caldarium, tepidarium, frigidarium)* were at the heart of the central block; symmetrically arranged on either side were the secondary rooms (changing rooms, gymnasiums, steam baths). On entering the building the bathers separated, some to one side, some to the other, only to meet again in the main rooms.

Tour – After passing the chambers *(right)*, which were perhaps used for meetings, one enters *(left)* the central block. Immediately on the right is an oval room *(laconicum)*, where the temperature was kept constantly high for use as a turkish bath. This leads to the gymnasium *(palaestra)* where there are still some mosaic fragments to be seen on the floor and walls. In the changing room *(apodyterium)* a fair amount of the mosaic floor is still intact. Next comes the swimming pool *(natatio)*; the fresco *(right)* has a religious theme and was added in the Middle Ages. The tour returns to the starting-point symmetrically via the second changing room and the second gymnasium which has fine mosaics.

The Romans followed the routine prescribed by their doctors. From the changing rooms (traces of fine mosaics on the floor) they went into the gymnasiums where they indulged in various forms of exercise; it is such a setting that Petronius described in his *Satyricon* when Encolpius and his friends meet the rich Trimalchio, a "bald old man... who played ball with his long-haired slaves...".

Perspiring after the exercise, the bather went on into an oval room heated to a very high temperature *(laconicum)*; the heat induced greater perspiration. The heating system was very efficient; hot air from huge stoves in the basement circulated beneath the floors, which were supported on little brick pillars, and spread into ducts in the walls.

Next the bather passed into the *caldarium* for a very hot bath after which he scraped his skin to remove all impurities. The *caldarium* was a huge circular room (34m - 112ft in diameter), covered by a dome; some of the supporting pillars can still be seen. Bathers from both sides of the building met in the *caldarium*. From here they went on into the *tepidarium* for a cooler bath before plunging into the bracing water of the cold bath *(frigidarium)*.

They could then take a swim in the open-air swimming pool *(natatio)*. *(In summer, operas are performed in the ruins of the caldarium; for this reason the caldarium and tepidarium are closed to the public.)*

After bathing Trimalchio, who followed the latest fashion, went off in his litter to carouse. Less wealthy or more serious Romans stayed to talk to their friends, to walk in the gardens or to read in the libraries until the baths closed. The following day they would all be back again.

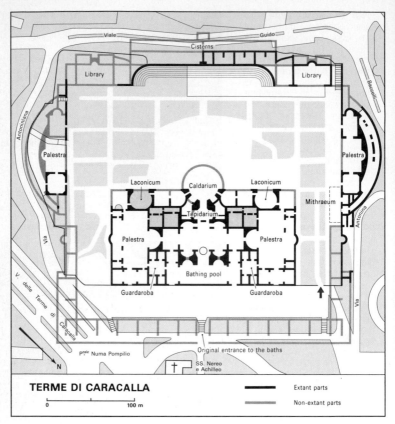

TERME DI CARACALLA

Extant parts
Non-extant parts

0   100 m

To the Porta San Sebastiano

The second part of this walk goes from the church of St Nereus and St Achilleus along Via di Porta San Sebastiano, which is bordered by buildings of historical and architectural interest set in rural surroundings.

Santi Nereo e Achilleo ⊙ – There was a little church here in the 4C called *Titulus Fasciolae*. Its presence on this site is explained by the legend of the bandage *(fasciola)* which had been bound round St Peter's leg to cover the sores caused by the chains which had held him in the Mamertine prison; when Peter fled from Rome in fear of the fate which awaited him there, the bandage fell from his leg on this spot which was venerated as a place of worship. A little further on along the Appian Way came St Peter's meeting with Christ and his question "Domine, quo vadis?" *(see APPIA ANTICA).*

The church was completely rebuilt by Leo III (795-816) and later restored by Sixtus IV (1471-84). In 1596 the incumbent appointed to the church was Clement VIII's confessor, Cardinal Baronius, who had a great devotion to St Nereus and St Achilleus. He had their relics transferred from Domitilla's Catacombs and converted the church into a handsome sanctuary for them. He retained the basilical plan, with its pitched roof and the octagonal pillars dating from the 15C restoration which divided the nave and aisles. He transferred the high altar from the crypt of St Paul Without the Walls, decorated it with Cosmati work and crowned it with an attractive baldaquin.

The left-hand reading desk *(ambo)* stands on a porphyry base which came from the Baths of Caracalla. Baronius commissioned Pomarancio to paint the walls but the mosaic on the chancel arch dates from the reign of Leo III and shows Byzantine influence. The mosaic has been much restored and is eclipsed by the painting in the apse. On the back of the bishop's throne, which is adorned with beautiful Medieval lions, Baronius had engraved a passage from the sermon given by St Gregory over the martyrs' tomb.

From Piazzale Numa Pompilio take Via di Porta San Sebastiano.

San Cesareo ⊙ – Little is known of the church's history before 1600 when Clement VIII entrusted its restoration to Cardinal Baronius. The latter followed contemporary taste in the coffered ceiling bearing the arms of Clement VIII and in the paintings by Cavaliere d'Arpino on the upper walls of the nave. Elsewhere he tried to reproduce the decoration of a medieval church: the marble facing on the chancel screen, the pulpit, the altar and the bishop's throne were composed of rich Cosmati fragments; the apse and chancel arch are decorated with mosaics from drawings by Cavaliere d'Arpino.

There is some Renaissance work: the two angels drawing back the curtains before the confessio *(below the altar)* and the pretty little fresco of the Madonna and Child *(above the throne).*

Beneath the church is the floor of a 2C bath house *(apply to the Sacristan)* paved with a marine mosaic in black and white.

★**Casa del Cardinale Bessarione (Cardinal Bessarion's House)** ⊙ – This handsome house, surrounded by gardens and furnished with fine Renaissance pieces, belonged to Cardinal John Bessarion, the Humanist scholar (c1402-72). In 1439 he attended the Council of Florence and was one of the authors of the union between the Greek and Roman Churches. Pope Nicholas V, who started the Vatican library, invited him to translate Aristotle.

★**Sepolcro degli Scipioni (Scipio Family Tomb)** ⊙ – *9 Via di Porta S Sebastiano.* Before the construction of the Aurelian Wall (Mura Aureliane) this site was beyond the town boundary and could therefore, according to Roman custom, be used as a burial ground.

The Scipios belonged to one of the greatest patrician families which died out at the end of the Republic. As members of the Cornelia clan *(gens)* the men all bore the name Cornelius Scipio, preceded by their own individual name (often abbreviated to an initial letter) and sometimes followed by a nickname.

The Scipio family tomb was discovered in 1614 and restored in 1926. The funeral inscriptions constitute a remarkable document of the Republican period and of the infancy of Latin literature. Their concentration

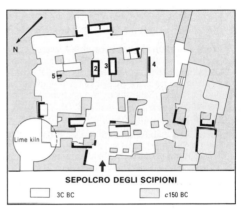

SEPOLCRO DEGLI SCIPIONI

☐ 3C BC ▨ c150 BC

on the dead man's public spiritedness and his moral rectitude reveal the mentality of those days when Roman civilization was being forged.

The tomb is hollowed out of a low hill. It consists of passages roughly arranged in a square. The sarcophagi, carved from a single block of stone or composed of separate panels assembled together, are placed in the passages or in recesses made in the walls. The tomb was probably full by the middle of the 2C BC so that an annexe *(to the right of the original square)* was excavated. It was at this period that the entrance façade was constructed in the northwest corner.

Tour – The first person to be buried here was L Cornelius Scipio Barbatus; Consul in 298 BC he fought against the Etruscans. His sarcophagus (**1**) – the original is in the Pius-Clementine museum in the Vatican – bears a description of his exploits.

Of his son's sarcophagus (**2**), only a few fragments and the inscription remain. Opposite is a fine inscription (**3**) dedicated to a young man of the Scipio family who died at the age of 20; his courage made up for his lack of years.

In the next passage lay Scipio Africanus' son, P Cornelius Scipio (**4**); as Augur in 190 BC he interpreted the auspices; he was also a Priest of Jupiter *(Flamen Dialis)*, one of the highest religious offices. In all about 30 people were buried in the tomb

The inscription (**5**) to be found in a small recess in the later part of the tomb refers to the burial of a member of the Cornelius Lentulus family which inherited the tomb during the Empire and buried some of its dead there.

In the northwest corner of the tomb a lime kiln was constructed in the Middle Ages for converting marble fragments into chalk.

Columbarium ⊙ – *Below ground in front of the Scipio tomb.* The *columbarium* was a type of communal tomb which became popular at the beginning of the Empire. It consisted of a chamber fitted with rows of recesses in which the cinerary urns were placed. The wealthy families built them for the ashes of their slaves and freedmen.

Nearby are the remains of a three-storey house which was built in the 3C on top of the Scipio tomb without regard for the site's venerable connections.

Columbarium of Pomponius Hylas (**A**) ⊘ – Part way down the ancient stair which leads into the chamber is a recess decorated with a mosaic which contained the urns of one C Pomponius Hylas and his wife. The *columbarium* itself is decorated with stucco work and fine paintings and probably dates from the Julio-Claudian period (AD 31-68).

San Giovanni in Oleo – *Key available from the Rector of S Giovanni a Porta Latina.* This small octagonal temple was built in the Renaissance style in 1509 by Benoit Adam, a Frenchman and member of the Rota (Roman Catholic ecclesiastical court); over the door he placed his arms and his motto *"Au plaisir de Dieu"* (at God's pleasure). The oratory commemorates an event in the martyrdom of St John the Evangelist, which took place during the reign of Domitian; St John was supposed to have emerged unscathed from a cauldron of boiling oil.

San Giovanni a Porta Latina ⊘ – The Church of **St John at the Latin Gate** occupies a charming **site★**; the peaceful forecourt, flanked by the campanile, is decorated by a Medieval well and shaded by a cedar tree.
The beautifully simple interior is decorated with 12C frescoes; although much damaged, they are a fine example of Romanesque painting.

Porta Latina (Latin Gate) – This gate in the Aurelian Wall *(Mura Aureliane)* was restored by Honorius (5C) and again by Belisarius (6C). The key stone bears a Greek cross on the town side and the Chi Rho on the outside.
Turn right outside the gate into Viale delle Mura Latine which skirts the city wall.

★Mura Aureliane – Work on these walls was initiated under the Emperor Aurelian in the 3C as the existing walls could no longer contain the expanding city. Punctuated by a series of towers, remains of which are still in evidence today, this wall is a compelling piece of Roman civil engineering, notably between The Porta Latina and Porta San Sebastiano *(the section in the opposite direction to Porta Metronia is nonetheless interesting, and may be seen from Bus no 218).*
Access up on to the wall itself is from Porta San Sebastiano.

★Porta San Sebastiano (St Sebastian Gate) – The gate is without doubt the most spectacular of the gates of Rome with its base of tall marble blocks supporting crenelated towers. It is the ancient Porta Appia which Aurelian (AD 271-275) constructed when he built his defensive wall; it has been strengthened several times particularly by the Emperor Honorius who carried out fortifying work along the full length of the wall between 401 and 402 in the face of invasion by the Goths.

Museo delle Mura (Wall Museum) ⊘ – The museum, which is housed within the gate, consists of five rooms displaying documents and models which show how the wall has changed from Antiquity to the present day. It is possible to walk along part of the wall westwards as far as Via Christoforo Colombo.

Arco di Druso (Arch of Drusus) – The arch dates from the 2C AD and was not therefore raised in honour of Drusus (39-38BC), the younger brother of the Emperor Tiberius. It was used by Caracalla (AD 211-17) to support the aqueduct which supplied water to his baths.

Neighbouring sights are described in the following chapters: APPIA ANTICA; AVENTINO; COLOSSEO – CELIO.

TRASTEVERE★★

Starting point Piazza Sonnino

Trastevere (from *trans Tiberim* meaning over the Tiber) was not originally part of Rome; it was the beginning of Etruscan territory.
From the time of the Republic it was inhabited mainly by Jews and Syrians and was incorporated into Rome by Augustus as the fourteenth administrative district. Not far from the present San Cosimato hospital, Augustus created a *naumachia*, a vast pool where naval warfare spectacles were mounted; there were temples dotted here and there but Trastevere was above all a popular district inhabited by artisans and small traders attracted by the proximity of the docks to the south of Tiber Island.
Few public buildings were situated here but rather utilitarian services such as a 2C fire station near Via dei Genovesi of which traces were discovered in the 19C. Among the religious buildings is a Syrian sanctuary, traces of which were found under the Villa Sciarra near Via Emilio Dandolo.
In the 3C the whole of Trastevere was enclosed by the **Aurelian wall** (Mura Aureliane) pierced by three gateways: the Porta Settimiana to the north, the Porta Aurelia (now Porta S. Pancrazio) *(see plan under* GIANICOLO) to the west and to the south the Porta Portuensis (further south than the present Porta Portese).
In the Middle Ages however some powerful Roman families had palaces in Trastevere and the tradition persisted under the Renaissance and into the 18C *(see* GIANICOLO).

Fruit stall in Trastevere

Trastevere has never lost its popular character. Throughout the centuries the inhabitants have kept their reputation of stout fellows ready to lend their strength and courage to a revolutionary cause. The district has sometimes been decried but Stendhal thought it superb; it was, he said, "full of energy".

Poets who celebrated Rome in the local dialect have always found a response there. The exploits of the Trasteverians, who defied the inhabitants of the Santa Maria Maggiore district with catapults, have been the subject of several sonnets in Roman folklore. Even nowadays the cafés of Trastevere re-enact the comic efforts of Meo Patacca in his dogged defence of his district against Marco Pepe.

While waiting for a pizza...

The Romans are unlikely to forego the traditional *entrée* at a pizzeria. **Bruschetta** consists of toasted bread rubbed with raw garlic, sprinkled with salt, drizzled with delicious olive oil and in some cases topped with freshly chopped tomatoes, basil or capers. **Fritto misto alla romana** will comprise a number of different seasonal delicacies (courgette flowers stuffed with mozzarella and anchovies, fillets of salted cod, stuffed giant green Ascoli olives, potato croquettes) dipped in batter and deep-fried. **Supplì** – a particularly local speciality – consist of rice (sometimes flavoured with tomato sauce) compacted around mozzarella which melts into unctuousness when fried.

All along the noisy Viale di Trastevere, the side streets are packed with stalls and costers' barrows beneath the benign watch of Madonnas lit up by small lanterns.

On summer evenings the quiet squares are transformed by happy family groups eating out in the open air; a charming aspect of the Roman way of life.

On Sundays the **Porta Portese** and the neighbouring streets become a huge **flea market** where the pickpockets have a field day; even if one does not pick up a great bargain, it is well worth going to see the spectacle.

TOUR *3 hours*

Torre degli Anguillara (Anguillara Tower) – The 13C tower, attached to a small palace of the same name, recalls one of the most powerful Roman families. Whether as warriors, magistrates, outlaws, forgers or clerics, the Anguillara were at the forefront of events from the Middle Ages to the Renaissance.

The palace, built in the 15C, underwent major restoration in the 19C and now houses the Institute for Dante Studies.

San Crisogono – The Church of **St Chrysogonus,** which dates from the 5C, bears witness to the many and various changes which have taken place in it over the centuries.

The **belfry,** which was erected in the 12C when the church was almost entirely rebuilt, was altered in the 16C by the addition of a spire.

The **façade** is the work of Giovanni Battista Soria who was put in charge of the refurbishment of the building in the 17C by Cardinal Scipione Borghese, a nephew of the Pope and incumbent of the church at the time.

★**Interior** – Only the basilical plan of a nave and two aisles has survived from the 12C; the floor is 13C work by Roman marble masons. The overall effect – half Mannerist, half Baroque – was acquired in the 17C from G B Soria who retained the ancient pillars refashioning their capitals in stucco, opened up great windows in the nave to let in more light and installed a fine coffered ceiling of complex design, showing the arms of Cardinal Borghese. Two monolithic porphyry columns support the chancel arch. The baldaquin is also the work of Soria. The fine wood carving in the chancel dates from 1863. The mosaic in the apse, showing the Virgin and Child with St James and St Chrysogonus, comes from the Cavallini school (late 13C).

Underground church ⊘ – *Access from the Sacristy by an awkward iron stair.*
6m - 20ft below floor level archeologists have discovered traces of the 5C building which was altered by Gregory III in the 8C and then abandoned in the 12C when the present church was built.
Here is the lower part of the apse (probably partially 5C) below which Gregory III hollowed out a confessio in the 8C; it is similar in design to the confessio in St Peter's in the Vatican (6C) and follows the curve of the apse before drawing in on each side into a horse-shoe shape, thus creating a semicircular corridor; it is divided in two by a straight passage at the end of which (towards the nave) is a relic chamber. This passage and the apse still bear traces of 8C painting. There are 10C paintings on the walls of the semicircular corridor.
The baptistry (left), now divided into two by a wall, was used for the baptism of early Christians.

From Piazza Sonnino take Via della Lungaretta, Piazza in Piscinula, Via dei Salumi and Via dei Vascellari to reach Piazza Santa Cecilia.

★**Santa Cecilia** ⊘ – A sanctuary dedicated to St Cecilia existed in a private house on this site in the 5C. Pope Paschal I (817-24) replaced it with a church which was much altered in the 16C, 18C and 19C.
The church is preceded by a courtyard planted with flowerbeds around a large Antique vase. A fine 12C campanile flanks the façade which was remodelled in the 18C but the 12C porch with its ancient columns and mosaic frieze was preserved.
The interior has lost its overall medieval appearance although it still retains the **mosaic** with which the apse was adorned by Paschal I in the 9C: the Byzantine influence absorbed by Roman workers in mosaic in earlier centuries is evident in the way the figures are presented: on Christ's right – St Paul, St Agatha and Pascal I with a square halo since he was still alive; on the left – St Peter, St Valerian and St Cecilia; the lively postures and the beautiful colours are also typically Roman.

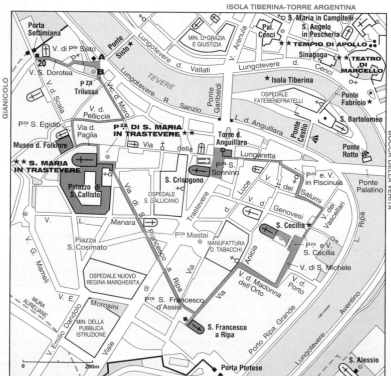

The **baldaquin** (**1**) over the high altar is by Arnolfo di Cambio (1293); it is eight years later than a similar work by the same artist for St Paul Without the Walls and shows a growing heaviness of style and the influence of Classical works; in the left back corner is an equestrian statue of a saint reminiscent of the statue of Marcus Aurelius which is now in the Capitoline Museum *(qv)*.

★**St Cecilia's Statue** – *Below the altar.* This fine sculpture by Stefano Maderno (1599) recalls the history and legend of St Cecilia. Paschal I (817-24) who was desperately searching all the Christian cemeteries for the remains of St Cecilia, was guided by a dream. He found the Saint's corpse lying beside her husband St Valerian in a catacomb on the Old Appian Way. He had them transferred immediately to a place beneath the altar. Seven centuries later, during the reign of Clement VIII, Cardinal Sfondrati undertook alterations to the chancel; during the work the sarcophagi came to light and St Cecilia's body was discovered in the posture in which Maderno has represented it.

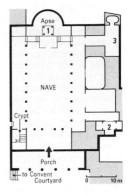

The Cardinal also wanted to restore the little room (**2**) venerated as the site of St Cecilia's martyrdom. This work disclosed several pipes against the wall which are thought to have served to raise the temperature in the room in which Cecilia was condemned to suffocate; she was saved by a miraculous dew only to be beheaded so inefficiently that she lingered in agony for three days. The Cardinal commissioned Guido Reni to paint the Decapitation of the Saint; the picture stands on the altar.

Cardinal Rampolla's Tomb (**3**) – This dramatic exercise in perspective (1929) commemorates the Cardinal whose generosity made it possible to open up the crypt.

Crypt ⊙ – The crypt was created from 1899 to 1901 in the Byzantine style. The excavations uncovered the remains of several ancient houses among which was the first sanctuary dedicated to St Cecilia. Also visible is a room containing seven grain silos and another in which are exhibited sarcophagi and inscriptions: a low relief representing Minerva (2C BC) in a little recess and a column also from the Republican period.
Behind the grating in the confessio *(beneath the apse)* are several sarcophagi including those of St Cecilia and St Valerian.

★★★**The Last Judgement by Pietro Cavallini** ⊙ – This masterpiece of Roman Medieval painting by Pietro Cavallini (c1293) was formerly on the inside wall of the façade of the church but was badly damaged in the 16C. All that remains is the figure of Christ in Judgement surrounded by angels with magnificent outspread wings, flanked by Mary and John the Baptist, hands raised beseechingly; below are the Apostles and angels blowing trumpets.
Note the perfect distribution of light and shade, the individual expression on each face and the subtle harmony of the colours.

Take Via di San Michele.

San Michele a Ripa ⊙ – Since 1992 the church houses the collection of paintings known as the **Quadreria della Galleria Borghese** whilst the Villa Borghese undergoes major refurbishment.

San Francesco a Ripa – The Church of St Francis was rebuilt in 1682 to replace the earlier church of the Franciscan order. The fourth chapel in the left-hand aisle contains a **statue of Blessed Ludovica Albertoni**★★ by Bernini; she was a member of the Franciscan Tertiaries (1474-1533) and is buried beneath the altar. Bernini shows her suffering and in this, one of his later works (1674), the marble perfectly expresses the final agony of a Saintly life.

Take Via di S. Francesco a Ripa to reach Piazza Santa Maria in Trastevere.

The **Piazza Santa Maria in Trastevere**★★ is probably the most charming corner of Trastevere and full of local colour. The fountain at the centre was remodelled by Bernini in 1659.
On the left is the fine 17C façade of the **Palazzo di San Callisto**.

★★**Basilica di Santa Maria in Trastevere (Basilica of St Mary in Trastevere)** – It was on this spot in 38 BC that a fountain of oil *(fons olei)* flowed for a whole day. Christians later interpreted this as a sign of the grace which Christ would spread throughout the world. Pope Calixtus (217-22) is said to have built the first sanctuary but it was the energetic Pope Julius I (337-52), a keen builder, who constructed a proper basilica. The building was altered in the 9C by Gregory V to provide a crypt in which he laid the saintly remains of Calixtus, Pope Cornelius and Calepodius.
The present basilica dates from the 12C; it was built about 1140 during a brief period of calm in the troubled reign of Innocent II who was beset by the anti-popes, Anacletus II and Victor IV. Despite St Bernard's assistance, when Innocent II died, Rome was in the hands of revolutionaries who had proclaimed a Republic. His successors restored and embellished the church on many occasions right up to the 19C.

Façade – The belfry is 12C; a small recess at the top is decorated with a mosaic of the Virgin and Child to whom the basilica is dedicated. The Virgin and Child are also celebrated in the mosaic on the façade (12C-13C) which shows a procession of women approaching from both sides.

The statues of the saints on the balustrade over the porch were erected from the 17C to 18C. The re-opening of the three windows in the façade and the addition of the paintings took place under Pius IX in the 19C.

The porch, which was restored early in the 18C, shelters several fragments, some from the buildings which preceded the present one. Two 15C frescoes (**1**) (rather damaged) depict the Annunciation. The door frames are made of friezes dating from the time of the Empire.

Interior – The basilical plan of Pope Innocent II's 12C church is still visible. As in all medieval Roman buildings, the columns dividing the nave from the aisles were taken from ancient monuments; all are crowned with their Classical capitals in either the Ionic or the Corinthian orders; the figures of some Egyptian divinities were removed in the 19C by Pope Pius IX.

The cornice is composed of an assortment of ancient fragments.

The ceiling (17C) bears a beautiful painting by Domenichino of the *Assumption of the Virgin (ask the Sacristan to turn on the lights)*.

★★★**Chancel mosaics** – The mosaics on the chancel arch (the Prophets Isaiah and Jeremiah and the symbols of the Evangelists) date from the 12C; so do those in the half-dome of the apse: to the right of Christ and the Virgin are St Callixtus, St Lawrence and Pope Innocent II offering his church to Mary; on the left are St Peter, St Cornelius, St Julius and St Calepodius. During the Romanesque period mosaic art was still influenced by the Byzantine style: the Virgin is adorned with gold like an empress, the group of figures betrays a certain oriental rigidity and loses some of its expressive force in the multitude of detail (the Virgin's dress). At the top is a representation of Paradise with the hand of God placing a crown on Christ's head; at the bottom are lambs, symbols of the Apostles, coming from the cities of Jerusalem and Bethlehem and facing the Lamb of God.

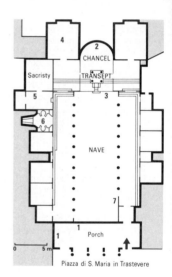

Piazza di S. Maria in Trastevere

The mosaics between the windows and at the base of the chancel arch are a masterpiece by **Pietro Cavallini** (late 13C) representing scenes from the life of the Virgin (her birth, the Annunciation, the Nativity, the Epiphany, the Presentation in the Temple and the Dormition). The medallion above the throne shows the Virgin and Child between St Peter and St Paul with Cardinal Stefaneschi, who commissioned the work, on a smaller scale.

The bishop's throne (**2**) standing in the apse is made of marble (12C).

An inscription (**3**) before the chancel marks the site of the oil fountain.

Altemps Chapel (4) – The stucco and frescoes of this chapel are in the style of the Counter-Reformation which developed after the Council of Trent (late 16C).

Transept – The fine coffered ceiling is late 16C work. The central low relief in gilded and painted wood illustrates the Assumption.

The **Sacristy** lobby contains two very fine old mosaics (**5**).

The **Avila Chapel** (**6**) with its dome is the exuberant creation of Antonio Gherardi (late 17C); the *trompe-l'œil* has been used to create a Baroque effect.

Among the treasures of this church is the charming tabernacle (**7**) by Mino da Fiesole (late 15C).

On leaving the church turn left into Via delle Paglia and right into Piazza S Egidio.

Museo del Folklore (Folk Museum) ⊘ – The museum occupies what was once the Convent of St Egidius in Trastevere. There are many artefacts (watercolours, prints and ceramics) which tell the story of life and popular dress in 18C and 19C Rome. As well as the various display cases showing scenes from everyday life, there is a reconstrucion of the room where the Poet Trilussa worked.

Take Via Pelliccia and Vicolo di Moro to reach Piazza Trilussa.

The narrow streets leading to the square contain a charm quite foreign to the bustle of a capital city.

The Piazza Trilussa commemorates Carlo Alberto Salustri who wrote poetry in the Roman dialect under the pseudonym **Trilussa** (1871-1950); in his racy and mildly satirical style he highlights the popular spirit of the Roman people describing their lives in a long and colourful story. A monument (**A**) was set up in his honour in 1954.

Nearby is a colossal fountain (**B**) installed by Paul V in 1612 at the beginning of the Via Giulia and transferred here in the 19C when the Tiber embankments were built.

Opposite is the **Sistine Bridge** (ponte Sisto) named after Sixtus IV (1471-84) who had it built (modernised in the 19C).

Take Via di Ponte Sisto and then Via S. Dorotea.

According to local tradition the house before the corner (no 20) with the charmingly decorated window on the second floor was the home of **La Fornarina**, Raphael's mistress, whom he immortalised in his famous painting now in the National Museum of Antique Art in Palazzo Barberini.

Neighbouring sights are described in the following chapters: BOCCA DELLA VERITÀ; GIANICOLO; ISOLA TIBERINA – TORRE ARGENTINA.

Trastevere

VATICANO – SAN PIETRO ★★★

Tour 2 half days

Planning a visit

Allow at least one entire day to visit the Vatican. Given that certain departments of the Musei Vaticani are opened to the public in rotation at differing times it is worth planning a visit around the advice given by the museum services on ☎ 69 88 33 33.

Beware that visitors who are deemed to be inappropriately dressed may be refused access to the basilica: this includes shorts, mini-skirts, sleeveless shirts and bare shoulders.

Vatican bus services

A bus shuttles visitors between Piazza San Pietro and the Vatican Museums. From February to December these depart from the Ufficio Informazioni Pellegrini e Turisti every 30mins between 8.45am and 12.45pm. 2000 L. ☎ 69 88 44 66.

Papal audiences

When in residence at the Vatican the Holy Father gives a **public audience** once a week (hour and place to be checked in advance). Audiences may be granted at short notice over the telephone but to ensure against disappointment it is worth writing one to two weeks in advance to the Prefettura della Casa Pontificata, Città del Vaticano, 00120 Rome. ☎ 69 88 32 73. To arrange group attendences numbers of attendees and provenance should be given.

It may be helpful to have a letter of recommendation from one's local parish priest, although this is not essential.

The Pope will also publicly bestow his benediction over crowds gathered in St Peter's Square at the **Sunday Angelus** (midday).

VATICAN STATE

The decision to create **Via della Conciliazione** was taken in 1936 and this wide thoroughfare was opened in 1950, Jubilee Year. The façades of the buildings flanking the southern end bear the arms of Pius XII *(right)* and of Rome *(left)*. Two rows of street lamps in the shape of obelisks line the broad road which leads directly to St Peter's Basilica.

Once in St Peter's Square the visitor has left Italy and is in the Vatican State. The Vatican City, which lies to the north of the Janiculum Hill and is bounded on three sides by the wall overlooking the Viale Vaticano and on the east by the curved colonnade in St Peter's Square, is the largest part of the Papal State. It comprises St Peter's Basilica, the Vatican palaces and the beautiful gardens surrounding the various administrative offices of the Papal State.

Historical Notes

Although the **Ager Vaticanus** lay outside the boundary of Ancient Rome, it was nonetheless well known in Antiquity. In the days of the Empire Caligula chose it as the site of a circus, which was embellished by Nero and used by him for the massacre of the first Roman martyrs; their number may have included St Peter. Hadrian built his mausoleum, the present Castel Sant'Angelo, in the gardens belonging to the Domitii. The history of the Vatican took on a new significance when the Emperor Constantine built a basilica there over St Peter's tomb, which is now St Peter's Basilica.

Bishop of Rome – From the first days of Christianity, the bishop was Christ's representative on earth. The Bishop of Rome maintained that his See in the traditional capital of the Empire had been founded by the Apostles, Peter and Paul, and therefore claimed first place in the ecclesiastical hierarchy. The expression "the Apostolic See" appeared for the first time in the 4C during the reign of Pope Damasus. Gradually the name "Pope", derived from the vulgar Latin *papa* meaning father, which had been used for all bishops, was reserved for the Bishop of Rome alone.

Gift of Quiersy-sur-Oise – In 752, the Lombards occupied Ravenna and the Imperial territory between the river Po, the Apennines and the Adriatic. In Rome the King of the Lombards Astolphe demanded a tribute of one gold piece per head. When the intervention of Constantine V, the Emperor in Byzantium (to whom Rome was in principle subject), proved useless, Pope Stephen II approached the Carolingian dynasty. In 756 at Quiersy-sur-Oise Pepin the Short, King of the Franks, undertook to restore the occupied territory not to the Emperor in Byzantium but to the "Republic of the Holy Church of God", that is to the Pope. This led to the creation of the Papal States and to the temporal power of the Pope.

"Leonine City" – On 23 August 846 the Saracens invaded Rome, pillaging the Basilicas of St Peter and St Paul. In the following year therefore Leo IV energetically set to work to raise a defensive wall round the Vatican district, which was known as the Borgo. The wall was restored in the 15C by Nicholas V, reinforced with bastions by Sangallo the Younger under Paul III in the 16C and extended by Pius IV in 1564 to Santo Spirito Gate.

Lateran Treaty – The unification of Italy (1820-70) would have been incomplete without the inclusion of the Papal States in the new Kingdom. On 20 September 1870 the troops of King Victor Emmanuel II entered Rome and proclaimed the city the capital of the Kingdom. On 2 May 1871 the Italian Parliament passed the **Law of the Guarantees** to show that it did not wish to subjugate the Papacy. The Pope was to retain the Vatican City and to receive an annual allowance. Pius IX excommunicated the authors of the Act and shut himself up in the Vatican declaring that he was a prisoner. His successors maintained this stance and the Roman Question was not resolved until 1929 when the **Lateran Treaty** was signed on 11 February by Cardinal Gaspari, representing the Holy See, and Mussolini, the head of the Italian Government.

The terms included a political agreement recognising the Pope as sovereign of the Vatican State which comprised the Vatican City itself and a number of other properties which enjoy the privilege of extraterritoriality: the four major basilicas (St John Lateran, St Peter's in the Vatican, St Paul Without the Walls, St Mary Major), the Roman Curia, colleges and seminaries and the Villa at Castel Gandolfo; in all 44 ha - 109 acres and just under 1 000 inhabitants. The Treaty also included a financial indemnity and a religious settlement granting the Church a privileged position in Italy in respect of schooling and marriage. The Republican constitution of 1947 established a new relationship between the Roman church and the Italian State on the basis of the Lateran Treaty. Another agreement modifying the 1929 Lateran Treaty was signed on 18 February 1984 by the President of the Council and the Vatican Secretary of State. Although the smallest state in physical size, the Vatican spreads the spiritual influence of the Roman Church throughout the world through the person of the Pope.

The Pope, supreme head of the Roman Church

The Pope is also called the Roman Pontiff, the Sovereign Pontiff, the Vicar of Christ, Holy Father, His Holiness. Sometimes he calls himself *Servus servorum Dei*, the Servant of the Servants of God. In his mission as Pastor to the Church founded by Jesus Christ, he is assisted by the Sacred College of Cardinals and by the Roman Curia.

College of Cardinals – In 1586 Sixtus V fixed their number at 70; it was increased to 85 by John XXIII in 1960. In 1970 there were 145 cardinals; 128 in 1984. A cardinal's dress consists of a scarlet cape (a short hooded cloak) worn over a linen rochet (a surplice with narrow sleeves). The cardinals are the Pope's closest advisers; it is they, assembled in "conclave", who elect the Pope.

Conclave – This is the name of the secret meeting at which a new pope is elected. This method of election was established by **Gregory X** (1271-76) whose own election lasted nearly three years. He imposed very strict regulations involving confinement and secrecy and requiring the election to be held within 10 days of the death of the previous pope in a palace from which the cardinals would not be released until the new pope had been elected. He added that if after three days no vote had been held the cardinals would be reduced to one meal a day for five days and then to bread and water. Nowadays the cardinals meet in conclave in the Sistine Chapel and absolute secrecy is maintained. A vote is held twice a day and after each inconclusive vote the papers are burned so as to produce dark smoke. A majority of two thirds plus one is required for an election to be valid; then a plume of clear smoke appears above the Vatican. The senior cardinal appears at the window in the façade of St Peter's from which papal blessings are given and announces the election in the Latin formula: *Annuntio vobis gaudium magnum: habemus papam* (I announce to you with great joy: we have a pope...). The new pope then gives his first blessing to the world.

Roman Curia – The Curia consists of a group of bodies, the dicasteries, which, together with the Pope, administer the Holy See. Each dicastery has a cardinal at its head. Since the reform instituted in 1967 by Paul VI, the Curia has consisted of two supreme bodies presided over by the Cardinal Secretary of State. One is the **Secretariat**

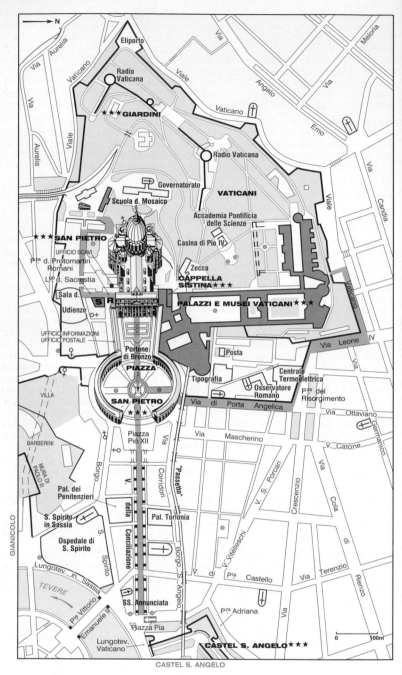

CASTEL S. ANGELO

of State which carries into effect the decisions taken by the Pope; in the Pope's immediate entourage the Secretary of State periodically assembles the cardinals who are heads of dicasteries into a sort of cabinet under his presidency. The other is the Council for the Public Affairs of the Church which deals with diplomatic relations with foreign governments.

Questions of doctrine, the organisation of the churches and the administration of the papal household are dealt with by congregations (the equivalent of civil ministries), secretariats, councils, commissions, committees and offices.

There are also three courts contained in the Curia. The Tribunal of the Apostolic Signatura is a final court of appeal for ecclesiastical disputes and an administrative tribunal concerned with protecting the law. The Roman Rota is a court of appeal and of first instance which deals in particular with the annulment of marriages. The Apostolic Penitentiary judges matters of conscience.

Councils – Within the Roman Church there are two rites (oriental and Latin); all the constituent churches belong to one or the other and are grouped into dioceses under the direction of **bishops.** The spiritual authority of a bishop is symbolized by his crozier, his pectoral cross, his ring and his mitre. His dress is no different from that of a cardinal except that it is purple. The episcopal college, consisting of about 4000 bishops spread throughout the world, is presided over by the Pope who calls them together in an **Ecumenical Council** to discuss the life of the Church. There have been 21 Councils in 20 centuries, the last being the Second Vatican Council (the First which took place in St Peter's Basilica was held in 1869-70). The Second assembled in 1962 under John XXIII and was disbanded three years later by Paul VI.

Holy Year – According to the Law of Moses one year in 50 should be devoted to God and to rest. Boniface VIII revived this tradition in 1300 when he proclaimed the first Jubilee or Holy Year. Clement VI (1342-52) fixed the frequency of Jubilees at every 50 years; Paul II (1464-71) reduced it to 25 years. The most recent Holy Years were 1950, 1975 and exceptionally 1983, announced by Pope John Paul II. The beginning of a Holy Year is marked with great solemnity by the opening of the Holy Door in each of the four major basilicas. Pilgrims who visit Rome during Holy Year and visit certain basilicas are granted exceptional grace.

Papal Audiences – The audiences are held in St Peter's Square in summer and in winter either in St Peter's Basilica or in the huge modern hall designed by Pier Luigi Nervi under Paul VI. During the ceremony the Pope gives his blessing and preaches on the great questions of the Church and humanity. His homily is delivered in Italian and then translated into English, French, German, Spanish and Polish. Official groups of pilgrims are greeted by name in the appropriate language.

The Pope, head of State

The Pope is the Sovereign of the Vatican State and in this capacity wields the full range of legislative, executive and judicial power. He is assisted in the internal administration of the Vatican by a **Pontifical Commission** composed of cardinals and a lay member. Beneath the commission is the **Administration (Governatorato)** which since 1969 has been assisted by a **Council of State** and is composed of offices and directorates employing lay staff.

The Vatican State has a yellow flag, bearing the tiara and the crossed keys, and a hymn, the Pontifical March composed by Gounod.

The armed regiments were disbanded by Paul VI in 1970; only the Swiss Guards have been retained, dressed in their picturesque yellow, red and blue uniforms which are supposed to have been designed by Michelangelo.

The Vatican issues its own stamps, mints its own coins which are valid currency in Italy, operates a post office and has a railway station linked to the national rail network.

Cultural, scientific and artistic activity – The **Apostolic Vatican Library** ranks very high; it was founded by papal bull in 1475 and contains over 60 000 volumes of manuscripts, 100 000 autographs, 800 000 prints, 100 000 engravings and maps and a collection of coins including an important section consisting of Roman money from the Republican era.

The **Secret Archives**, composed of documents dating from the 13C, have been open to the public for consultation since 1881 and are of worldwide importance in historical research.

The **Pontifical Academy of Science** was founded in 1936 by Pius XI and consists of 70 Academicians chosen by the Pope from among scholars throughout the world.

The **Fabric of St Peter** is the body of architects and specialists in charge of the conservation of St Peter's Basilica. The mosaic workshop is annexed to it.

The Vatican has a printing works which produces texts in almost all languages; there is also a daily newspaper, the Osservatore Romano, and a weekly paper, the Osservatore della Domenica which is published in several languages. The Vatican Radio transmits programmes in 40 different languages. Press conferences take place in the press room of the Holy See.

The number of masterpieces in the Vatican is so great that a
rigorous selection of the outstanding items has had to be made;
for a more detailed description of the exhibits
consult the Guide to the Vatican City
and the Guide to the Vatican Museums published by
Monumenti, Musei e Gallerie Pontificie.

★★★BASILICA DI SAN PIETRO (ST PETER'S BASILICA) ⊙

The basilica, which is the largest of all Christian places of worship, reflects many centuries of Christian history.

The building of St Peter's Basilica is linked to the martyrdom of Peter (cAD 64). After a huge fire which destroyed the greater part of Rome and for which the Emperor Nero held the Christians responsible, he ordered many of them to be executed. Simon, called Peter by Jesus, was probably among the condemned. According to the law, he was simply a Jewish fisherman, a native of Capernaum in Galilee, sentenced therefore to the appalling punishment of crucifixion in Nero's Circus at the foot of the Vatican Hill. So as to distinguish his own death from Jesus', Peter humbly begged to be crucified upside down.

Constantine's Basilica – Following his conversion to Christianity, Constantine built a sanctuary in 324 over the tomb of St Peter, who had been chosen by Christ as his chief Apostle. In 326 Pope Sylvester I consecrated the building which was completed some 25 years later. The basilica had a nave, four aisles and a narrow transept; the apsidal wall stood just behind the present papal altar. The entrance was through an *atrium* which was graced with a fountain decorated with the beautiful pine cone *(la Pigna)* which can now be seen in a courtyard of the Vatican Palace. The façade gleamed with mosaics. The *confessio* (a crypt containing the tomb of a martyr) was not completely underground; an opening at floor level gave access to the tomb. At the end of the 6C Pope Gregory the Great raised the chancel; beneath it the confessio took the form of a corridor following the curve of the apse and contained a chapel called *ad caput*.

For more than a century the basilica was pillaged by barbarians: Alaric in 410 and Totila in 546. In 846 it was raided by the Saracens. Its prestige however remained intact. Imperial coronations were held there in solemn state. On Christmas Day AD 800 Leo III crowned Charlemagne King of the Romans. 75 years later it was the turn of his grandson, Charles the Bald, during the pontificate of John VIII, the first soldier pope and the first to be assassinated. Arnoul, the last of the Carolingians, became Pope Formosus on 22 February 896. John XII, who lived like a Mohammedan prince, surrounded by slaves and eunuchs, crowned Otho I on 2 February 962 and then conspired against him. His intrigues brought the papacy under the control of the German Emperor for over a century.

After 1 000 years, despite frequent restoration and embellishment, St Peter's Basilica was in a parlous state.

St Peter's Basilica

1452, Nicholas V intervenes – B Rossellino was appointed by the Pope to restore the basilica. While retaining the dimensions of Contantine's building, Rossellino proposed a cruciform plan with a dome and a new choir. The Pope died in 1455 and the project was abandoned. For the next 50 years his successors were content to shore up the existing building.

1503, Julius II, an energetic pope – His plan for renovation was radical. His architects were Bramante, who had arrived in Rome in 1499, and Giuliano da Sangallo. The chosen design was Bramante's: a Greek cruciform plan with jutting apses beneath cupolas and over the crossing a central dome similar to the Pantheon dome. On 18 April 1506 the first stone was laid at the base of a pillar; a temporary chancel had been provided and a large part of the apse and transept demolished, causing Bramante to be nicknamed the "Destructive Maestro". Sometimes a young man came to watch the work. His name was Michelangelo. Julius II had commissioned him to design his tomb which was to be placed at the heart of the new basilica. Michelangelo admired Bramante's plan but disapproved of his administration. Having at first been regarded as an intruder, he came to be hated by Bramante. Believing himself to be in danger, Michelangelo retreated to Florence but returned to Rome after violently denouncing the Pope and Rome where, so he wrote, "they turn chalices into swords and helmets".

Julius II died in 1513 and Bramante in 1514. For the next 30 years the design of the building was the subject of interminable discussion. Raphael and Giuliano da Sangallo suggested going back to a Latin cruciform plan. Baldassare Peruzzi drew up another plan based on Bramante's design. Antonio da Sangallo, Giuliano's nephew, wanted to keep the Greek cross plan while adding a bay in the form of a porch with two towers flanking the façade and altering the dome; he died in 1546.

From Michelangelo to Bernini – In 1547 Paul III appointed Michelangelo, then 72 and chief architect to the Vatican, to put an end to all the discussion. "To deviate from Bramante's design is to deviate from the truth", declared the Master. He therefore returned to the Greek cruciform plan, simplified so as to accentuate its circular base; the circle, the sign of Infinity, glorifying the Resurrection. The dome was no longer the shallow dome of the Pantheon but reached high into the sky. His Intransigence in carrying out his ideas exasperated his detractors. He worked on St Peter's, surrounded by intrigues, refusing any payment, doing all for the glory of God and the honour of St Peter. When he died in 1564, the apse and

A. Gaël

transepts were complete and the dome had risen as far as the top of the drum. It was completed in 1593 by Giacomo della Porta assisted by Domenico Fontana, who may have been inspired to raise the dome even higher by one of the Master's alternative designs.

In 1606 **Paul V** (1605-21) finally settled for the Latin cruciform plan; it was more suitable for high ceremony and preaching, and thus more in accordance with the preoccupations of the Counter-Reformation. The new basilica was to cover all the area occupied by the original church, whereas Michelangelo's plan had not extended so far east. The façade was entrusted to Carlo Maderno. The new basilica was consecrated by Urban VIII.

The final phase in St Peter's architectural history was directed by Bernini who took over on Maderno's death in 1629. He turned what would have been a fine example of Renaissance architecture into a sumptuous Baroque monument.

In all, from Bramante to Bernini, the building of St Peter's encompassed 120 years, the reigns of 20 popes and the work of ten architects.

Exterior

★★★**Piazza San Pietro (St Peter's Square)** – The square, which was intended to isolate the basilica without creating a barrier in front of it, acts in fact as a sort of vestibule. The gentle curves of the colonnades like two arcs of a circle framing the rectangular space are a gesture of welcome extended to the pilgrims of the world.

The square was begun by **Bernini** in 1656 under Pope Alexander VII and completed in 1667. By flanking the façade with a broader and lower colonnade, the architect aimed to minimise the width and accentuate the height of the basilica. To create the effect of surprise so dear to Baroque artists, the colonnade was designed to enclose the square and mask the façade so that the basilica was hidden from view until the visitor stood in the entrance between the arms of the colonnade. Bernini's intention was not fully realised: the triumphal arch planned to link the two arms was not built and Via della Conciliazione gives a distant view of the basilica. Two belfries were planned but the foundations proved too weak to carry the additional weight. At its widest point the square measures 196m - 643ft across. The **colonnade** is formed by rows of columns, four deep, surmounted by statues and the arms of Alexander VII: a remarkably sober and solemn composition.

At the centre of the square stands an **obelisk**, a granite monolith, carved in the 1C BC in Heliopolis for Caius Cornelius Gallus, the Roman Prefect in Egypt. It was brought to Rome in AD 37 by Caligula who had it set up in his circus (left of the basilica). It was still there when **Sixtus V** decided to erect it in St Peter's Square. It was the first obelisk to be moved by this Pope who was responsible for re-siting several others. His official architect was **Domenico Fontana**. The work took four months and gave birth to an appropriate legend. The obelisk was to be re-erected on 10 September 1585; 800 men and 75 horses were required to raise the 350 tonnes of granite to its full height (25.5m - 84ft). After giving his blessing the Pope enjoined absolute silence on pain of death and to make sure his order was clearly understood he set up a gallows in the square. The work began but the ropes chafed on the granite and threatened to give way under the friction. Then one of the workers cried out *Acqua alle funi* (water for the ropes) and the Pope congratulated him for disobeying the order. A relic of the True Cross is preserved at the top of the obelisk.

The two fountains are attributed to Carlo Maderno *(right)* and Bernini *(left)*. Between them and the obelisk are two discs set into the paving to mark the focal points of the two ellipses enclosing the square; from these points the colonnades appear to consist of only one row of columns. This perspective is achieved by increasing the diameter of the columns from the inner to the outer row and placing them an equal distance from one another.

East Front – A majestic flight of steps, designed by Bernini, leads up to the east front. On either side stand statues of St Peter and St Paul (19C). The east front, which was begun by **Carlo Maderno** in 1607 and completed in 1614, was the object of spirited comment; owing to its dimensions (45m - 147ft high and 115m - 377ft wide), it masks the dome. It is from the balcony beneath the pediment that the Pope gives his blessing *urbi et orbi* (to the city and to the world). The entablature carried Paul V's dedication. The horizontal pediment above it is crowned by statues of Christ, John the Baptist and 11 Apostles (excluding Peter). The clocks at either end are the work of Giuseppe Valadier (19C).

Porch – It was designed by **Carlo Maderno**. On the left behind a grill stands an equestrian statue of Charlemagne (**1**) (18C). The Door of Death (**2**) with sober sculptures on its bronze panels is by **Giacomo Manzù** (1964); low down on the right in the left-hand section is a low relief figure of John XXIII. The bronze door (**3**) was sculpted in 1445 by Antonio Averulino, known as **Il Filarete**. The true artistic spirit of the Renaissance is seen in the juxtaposition of religious scenes (in the six panels), episodes from the life of Eugenius IV (in the spaces below the panels) and mythological figures, animals and portraits of contemporary personalities (in the frieze surrounding the panels). In the two central panels strange inscriptions in Arab characters appear around the figures of St Peter and St Paul and in their haloes. To the right is the Holy Door: only the Pope may open and close this door to mark the beginning and end of a Holy Year.

The "Navicella" mosaic (**4**) by Giotto dates from 1300. It originally adorned the *atrium* of Constantine's basilica but has been restored and re-sited many times since.

At the north end of the porch in the vestibule of the Scala Regia *(closed to the public)* stands a statue of Constantine (**5**), the first Christian Emperor, by Bernini (1670).

Interior

Here everything is so well proportioned that the scale, though large, is not over-whelming. The seemingly life-size angels supporting the holy water stoops (**6**) are in fact enormous. St Peter's Basilica, with its 450 statues, 500 columns and 50 altars, and its reputed capacity to hold 60 000 people, is a record of the history of Christianity and art in Rome.

Nave – The overall length of the church, including the porch, is about 211m - 692ft. Comparisons can be made with the length of other world-famous churches by means of marks set in the floor. When Charlemagne received the Emperor's crown from the Pope on Christmas Day AD 800 he knelt on the porphyry disc (**7**) now let into the pavement of the nave, although in the original church it was placed before the high altar.

Pietà Chapel (**8**) – Here is **Michelangelo's** masterpiece, the **Pietà★★★** which he sculpted in 1499-1500 at the age of 25. The execution of the profoundly human figures is perfect, revealing an amazing creative power. The group was commissioned by a French cardinal in 1498 and immediately hailed as the work of a genius. Even so Michelangelo already had enemies who started a rumour that the work was not his. He therefore added his signature across the Virgin's sash the only piece of his work to be so marked.

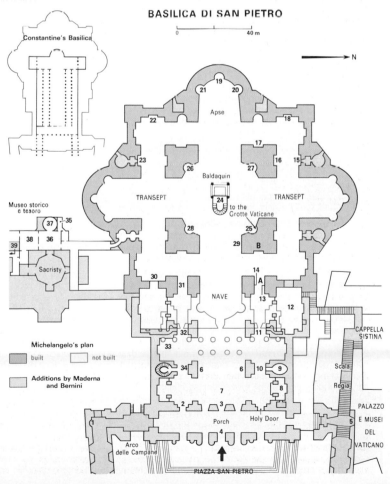

BASILICA DI SAN PIETRO

Crucifix Chapel (or Chapel of Relics) (9) – Bernini designed the elliptical chapel which contains a fine wooden crucifix attributed to Pietro Cavallini (early 14C).

Queen Christina of Sweden's Monument (10) – In 1654 Queen Christina abdicated her throne; she was converted to Roman Catholicism and came to live in Rome the following year. She is buried in the 'grottoes' *(see below)*. Her monument was executed by G Theodon from designs by Carlo Fontana (18C).

Countess Mathilda of Tuscany's Monument (11) – She was the first woman to be buried in the basilica. At the time of the Investiture Controversy it was she who received the Emperor Henry IV when he submitted to Gregory VII at Canossa (1077). This incident is represented in the low relief carving on the sarcophagus. The monument was designed by Bernini assisted by several of his pupils (1635).

Chapel of the Blessed Sacrament (12) – The wrought-iron screen at the entrance is by Borromini. The high altarpiece representing the Trinity is one of the few paintings of St Peter by Pietro da Cortona (most pictures are mosaics). On the altar, the tabernacle, which is similar to the *tempietto* of San Pietro in Montorio, and the kneeling angels are by Bernini (1675) (the angel on the right is by a pupil).

Bernini brings unity to the Basilica – The passage (**A**) marks the line between Maderno's later and Michelangelo's earlier work. Bernini's task was to create a harmonised whole. The first problem was the junction of the nave with the eastern wall of Michelangelo's square plan. As this wall supports the oblique thrust of the weight of the dome, it could not be pierced to create a wide monumental doorway similar to the entrance doors in the nave. Bernini's solution was to erect two columns, like those flanking the doorways in the nave, and to fill the space below the arch and the pediment with a shield supported by two angels. The second problem was the pier (**B**) which could not be pierced as it supports the dome. He erected two columns and an arch of identical size to those in the passage. The visitor approaching along the north aisle of the church receives an impression of depth accentuated by the two narrow arches.

★**Gregory XIII's Monument (13)** – The low relief carving on the white marble sarcophagus (1723) illustrates the reform of the calendar which the Pope instituted in 1582. The Gregorian calendar has now been adopted world-wide.

Gregory XIV's Monument (14) – According to legend the monument was despoiled to meet the expense of the Pope's illness which had to be treated with a mixture of gold and precious stones. The plaster sarcophagus was not faced with marble until 1842.

★★★**Clement XIII's Monument (15)** – The fine neo-Classical design by Canova dates from 1792. The lack of emotion for which Canova's art is often criticised here contributes to the purity of line; the balance of the whole is however upset by the statue on the left which represents the Triumph of Religion.

Pictures in mosaic – It was in the 16C that famous pictures began to be copied in mosaic. In the spirit of the Counter-Reformation the Church hoped thus to make its glories more intelligible to the faithful. This practice was further developed when Benedict XIII founded a mosaic school in 1727. These mosaics therefore have immense religious significance. They illustrate the power of St Peter; his walking on the water (**16**) and his raising of Tabitha (**17**); they celebrate the martyrs, popes, saints and angels challenged by the Reformation.

St Michael's or **St Petronilla's Chapel (18)** – The mosaic illustrates St Petronilla's martyrdom after a painting by Guercino. St Petronilla, whose relics lie beneath the altar, was venerated in St Peter's from 8C. Pepin the Short built a chapel to her in which Michelangelo's *Pietà* was to have stood.

Apse – The dominant feature is '**St Peter's Chair**'★★★ (**19**), an extraordinary work designed by **Bernini** to contain the remains of an ancient episcopal chair said to have been used by St Peter; these remains, which date from the 4C, are encased in a throne, decorated with ivory, which was given to John VIII by Charles the Bold at his coronation in 875. Bernini's throne is made of sculpted bronze apparently supported by the four great doctors of the Church (measuring between 4.50m and 5.50m - 15ft and 18ft). Above is a gilded stucco "gloria", veiled in clouds and a host of cherubs. Silhouetted against a sun-like central opening, which lets in the light, is the dove of the Holy Ghost (its wing span is 1.75m - just under 6ft). This work, completed in 1666 when Bernini was in his 70s, is a crowning example of his astounding art, full of movement and light.

★★★**Urban VIII's Monument (20)** – This work by **Bernini**, commissioned in 1628 and finished in 1647, is considered to be the masterpiece of 17C funerary art. His hand raised majestically in blessing, the Pope sits enthroned above the sarcophagus, surrounded by statues of Justice and Charity, while Death inscribes his name.

★★★**Paul III's Monument (21)** – **Guglielmo Della Porta** (1500?-77), a follower of Michelangelo, conceived a grandiose project: the monument was to be surrounded by eight allegorical statues and placed in the centre of the chancel. Michelangelo objected and asked for the number of statues to be reduced to four. When Bernini altered the apse in 1628 he reduced the number to two; the other two statues are in the Farnese Palace.

St Leo the Great's Altar (**22**) – The **altarpiece** is a 'picture in marble' by **Algardi** of the Pope halting Attila at the gates of Rome. This type of sculpture, which resembles a picture owing to the vivid effects it creates, is characteristic of Baroque art.

★★Alexander VII's Monument (**23**) – **Bernini** completed this monument in 1678, two years before his death. He was anxious that he himself should sculpt the head of the Pope who was his protector.

The Pope kneels among allegorical statues, the work of pupils who, in their effort to imitate their master, have somewhat exaggerated the effect of movement. Even Bernini's own art gives way to excess here (Death is represented by a skeleton draped in mottled marble beckoning the Pope).

★★★Baldaquin – **Bernini's** canopy, begun in 1624, was unveiled by Urban VIII in 1633. Despite the weight of the bronze and its great height (29m - 95ft - the height of the Farnese Palace), it has captured the light-weight effect of an original baldaquin, usually made of wood and cloth, to be carried in processions. As the eye is caught by the wreathed columns, the valance seems to stir. The bees (on the columns and valance) are from the arms of the Barberini family to which Urban VIII belonged. The work attracted much criticism, first because the bronze had been taken from the Pantheon and also because it was thought to be too theatrical and in bad taste. The high altar below the baldaquin, where only the Pope may celebrate mass, stands over the confessio (**24**), designed by Maderno, which contains St Peter's tomb.

Piers of the Crossing – They were begun by Bramante and completed by Michelangelo; they stand at the crossing of the transepts. Their austerity did not please Baroque taste and in 1629 Bernini faced them in marble and created recesses at the base in which he placed four statues (5m - 16ft high). Above them he designed balcony chapels for the exhibition of relics and re-used the wreathed columns from the baldaquin of the 4C church which had inspired his own canopy.

Bernini's Baldaquin in St Peter's

Each statue represents the relics deposited in the basilica: a fragment of the spear (St Longinus – **25** – by Bernini commemorates the soldier who pierced Jesus' side with his spear, which has become a symbol of Pity); the napkin bearing the Holy Image (St Veronica – **26** – wiped Jesus' face on the road to Calvary); a fragment of the True Cross (St Helena – **27** – brought the remains of the Cross to Rome); St Andrew's head (St Andrew – **28**). The last three statues are by Bernini's collaborators: Francesco Mochi, Andrea Bolgi and François Duquesnoy.

★★★**Dome** – Bramante's design was for a dome resembling the one on the Pantheon but **Michelangelo** made it larger and raised it higher. He himself carried out the work up to the lantern; it was finished in 1593 by **Giacomo Della Porta** and **Domenico Fontana.** It is the largest dome in Rome; the whole building seems to have been designed to support it, a symbol of God's perfection.

The pendentives carry four mosaic medallions (8m - 26ft across) representing the Evangelists. Above in Latin are Christ's words to Peter: "Thou art Peter and upon this rock I will build my church; and I will give unto thee the keys of the Kingdom of Heaven." The interior of the dome is decorated with figures of the Popes and the Doctors of the Church; seated are Christ, Mary, Joseph, John the Baptist and the Apostles; above them are angels. The figure on the ceiling of the lantern is God the Father.

★★**Statue of St Peter** (**29**) – This 13C bronze by Arnolfo di Cambio is greatly venerated. Countless pilgrims have kissed its foot. It is said to have been made out of the bronze statue of Jupiter on the Capitol.

Pius VII's Tomb (**30**) – Pius VII died in 1823 after bearing the brunt of the Napoleonic storm. His tomb was designed by Thorwaldsen, a Dane.

Leo XI's Monument (**31**) – **Algardi** was responsible for the white marble monument (1642-44). The low relief sculpture on the sarcophagus illustrates Henri IV's conversion to Roman Catholicism; the King is being received by the future Pope who was then Clement VIII's legate.

★★★**Innocent VIII's Monument** (**32**) – This is a Renaissance work by Antonio del Pollaiuolo (1431-98), one of the few monuments to be preserved from the earlier church. The tomb is designed in typical 15C style against a wall.

When the monument was re-erected in 1621 the two figures were reversed; originally the recumbent figure was above the Pope, signifying the supreme power of death. An error has crept into the epitaph which says that the Pope 'lived' (vixit) rather than reigned for eight years, ten months and 25 days.

John XXIII's Monument (**33**) – The low relief sculpture on the right of the Chapel of the Presentation is by a contemporary artist, Emilio Greco.

Stuart Monument (**34**) – **Canova** designed this work (1817-19) to the glory of the last members of the Scottish Royal family: James Edward, Charles Edward and Henry Benedict, who are buried in the crypt (see below). The monument was commissioned by the Prince Regent and paid for by George III. The **angels**★ in low relief were much admired by Stendhal who also remarked that "George IV, in keeping with his reputation as the most accomplished gentleman in the three kingdoms, wished to honour the ashes of the unhappy princes whom he would have sent to the scaffold had they fallen into his hands alive."

★**Museo Storico e Tesoro** ⊙ – The Treasury has been pillaged on many occasions – by the Saracens in 846, during the sack of Rome in 1527, by Bonaparte under the Treaty of Tolentino in 1797 – but it has always been built up again and today contains gifts from many countries.

In **Room I** (**35**) are two mementoes of the 4C basilica: the 'Holy Column' which is identical to those re-used by Bernini in the balcony chapels in the piers supporting the dome, and the gilded metal cockerel (9C), which Leo IV had placed on top of the basilica.

Room II (**36**) displays a fine dalmatic said to have belonged to Charlemagne; it is in fact a Byzantine-style liturgical vestment dating from the 10C at the earliest. This room also contains a copy of the wooden and ivory chair contained in Bernini's throne and a 6C Papal cross.

The beautiful tabernacle in the **Benefactors' Chapel** (**37**) is attributed to Donatello, the Renaissance master artist from Florence. The plaster mould of Michelangelo's *Pietà* proved valuable when the original was damaged in 1972 and had to be repaired.

Room III (**38**) contains the **tomb of Sixtus IV**★★★ (1493) by A Pollaiolo. The accuracy of the portraiture and the delicacy of its execution make it a true masterpiece of bronze sculpture portraiture and delicate craftsmanship. Several rooms, glittering with gold and silver ware and liturgical objects, including a terracotta version of Bernini's angel before it was cast in bronze for the Chapel of the Blessed Sacrament, lead into the **gallery** (**39**) displaying the tiara of silver and gold and precious stones with which St Peter's statue is crowned on ceremonial occasions. **Junius Bassus' sarcophagus**★★★ (4C) was found beneath the basilica and is a remarkable example of Christian funerary sculpture, richly decorated with biblical scenes; on the sides are children gathering the harvest, a symbol of the souls saved by the Eucharist.

Detail of the tomb of Sixtus IV by Antonio Pollaiolo

"Grotte" Vaticane ⊙ – *Access in the northeast pier supporting the dome*. The grottoes embrace the area beneath the basilica containing the papal tombs and parts of the earlier basilica. They consist of a semicircular section which follows the line of Constantine's apse, with the Ad Caput Chapel *(see below)* on the eastern side, and three aisles projecting eastwards.

In the centre of the apsidal passage are Pius XII's tomb *(west)* and the Ad Caput Chapel *(east)*.

The low relief sculptures by Antonio Pollaiuolo (15C) on the inner wall of the passage illustrate the lives of St Peter and St Paul.

Among the tombs in the aisles are those of Pope John XXIII, Christina of Sweden, Benedict XV and Hadrian IV, born Nicholas Breakspear, the only English Pope.

★Salita alla cupola (Ascent to the Dome) ⊙ – *Access from the exterior to the right of the basilica*. From an internal gallery at the base of the dome visitors can best appreciate the vast dimensions of the basilica, the prodigious height of the dome as well as its decorations. Two people, diametrically opposite one another and facing the wall, can hold a conversation in a low voice. A stairway inside the drum climbs up to a terrace surrounding the lantern at 120m - 394ft above St Peter's Square. The **view★★★** is magnificent: the geometric precision of the square, a model of architectural town planning; the Vatican City, including an interesting aspect of the gardens, the palaces, the museums, and the fortress-like Sistine Chapel; and the whole city of Rome from the Janiculum to Monte Mario.

On the way down a broad terrace at the foot of the dome affords a **view** of the domes of the transept and aisles. There is also an extensive view of the city from the east balustrade, which is surmounted by huge statues of Christ, St John the Baptist and the Apostles (excluding St Peter).

★★Necropoli Vaticana (Vatican Necropolis) ⊙ – *Guided tour only*. The excavations, carried out between 1939 and 1950 on the orders of Pope Pius XII, revealed a pagan necropolis completely infilled with earth by Constantine to form a foundation for the original ancient basilica in which was found the tomb of St Peter. After crossing one of the foundation walls in Constantine's basilica, the necropolis is reached. Two rows of tombs (dating from the 1C to early 4C) separated by a path are arranged on a slope parallel with the axis of the main nave and run from east to west. The entrance to one of the tombs bears an inscription recording the occupant's wish to be buried "in Vaticano ad circum" alluding to Nero's circus where St Peter may have perished. In another tomb, that of the Julian family, are the oldest known Christian mosaics. These show "Christ as the Sun" on a horse-drawn chariot and the two stories of Jonah and the fisherman.

Return in the direction of the apse of the present basilica.

Set in the east side of the so-called "Red Wall" *(Muro Rosso)* is the recess (2C) known as the "Trophy of Gaius" *(Trofeo di Gaio)*; beneath is the **tomb of St Peter**. It was the presence of the Trophy in that location, apparently marking the site of the apostle's tomb, that made Constantine decide to build the basilica on top of the necropolis with the floor on the same level as the Trophy. The Emperor then enclosed the tomb and trophy in marble and the whole structure was given the name of the "Constantine Memorial".

The position of St Peter's tomb has aroused lively controversy among historians, archeologists and theologians. Until the Vatican excavations were made, his tomb was thought to be in St Sebastian's Catacombs. According to M Carcopino, the

Saint's relics have had a hazardous existence. Fearing desecration during the Valerian persecution, the Christians may have moved them in 258 to St Sebastian's Catacombs which did not then belong to the Church and were therefore unlikely to attract attention from the authorities. Not until 336, when Christians were again entitled to practise their religion, would the relics have been returned to their original resting place in the Vatican.

★**Cappella Clementina (Clementine Chapel)** – This is the **Ad Caput Chapel** (at the head of St Peter). It stands behind the shrine very close to the Apostle's tomb. Some bones, found in one of the walls which in the 3C bordered the shrine to the north, are displayed by the guide; they may be the bones of St Peter.

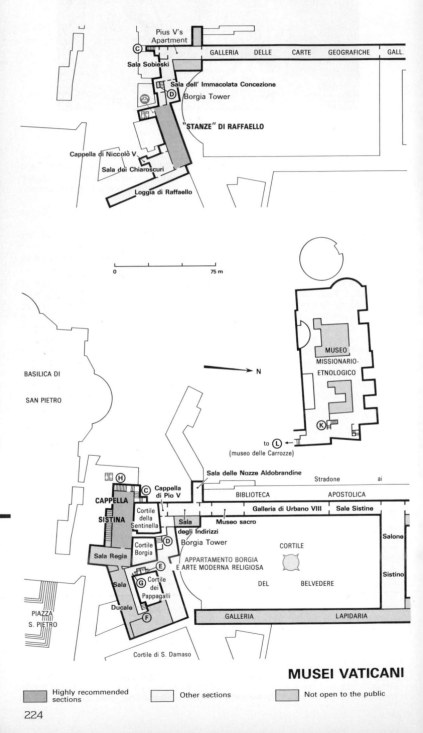

MUSEI VATICANI

Highly recommended sections	Other sections	Not open to the public

★★★ MUSEI VATICANI (VATICAN MUSEUMS) ⊘

Entrance in Viale Vaticano; from Piazza Risorgimento take Via Leone IV and turn left.

The museums are housed in part of the palaces built by the popes from the 13C onwards.

Palaces – It was probably during the reign of Pope Symmachus (498-514) that some buildings were erected to the north of St Peter's Basilica. Nicholas III (1277-80) intended to replace them with a fortress and towers but his project was only partially realised. Upon their return from Avignon in 1377 the popes gave up living in the Lateran Palace, which had been destroyed by fire, and settled in the Vatican.

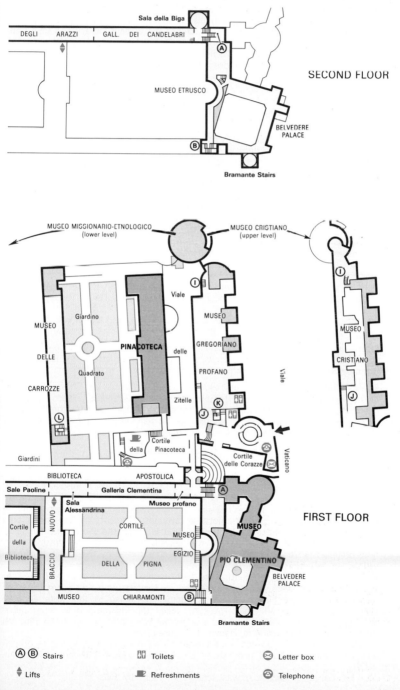

Ⓐ Ⓑ Stairs   ⛛ Toilets   ✉ Letter box

⬍ Lifts   ☕ Refreshments   ☎ Telephone

Nicholas V (1447-55) decided to enlarge the accommodation. Around the Parrot Court *(Cortile del Pappagallo)* he constructed a palace incorporating the 13C buildings. He kept the fortress-like exterior but the interior was sumptuously decorated. The chapel by Fra Angelico can still be seen. Almost all the popes have altered or enlarged Nicholas V's palace.

Sixtus IV (1471-84) established a library on the ground floor of the north wing (now a conference room used by the Pope) and built the Sistine Chapel to the west. About 300m - 984ft north of Nicholas V's palace, **Innocent VIII** (1484-92) built a summer residence, the Belvedere Palace. From 1493 to 1494 **Alexander VI** added the Borgia Tower *(Torre Borgia)* to Nicholas V's palace and created his own apartments above Sixtus IV's library.

Pope **Julius II** (1503-13) commissioned Bramante to link Nicholas V's and Innocent VIII's palaces by two long narrow galleries, thus creating the Belvedere Court *(Cortile del Belvedere)*, a huge rectangular courtyard, which provided a setting for grandiose spectacles and was later divided into the present Library and Pine Cone Courts *(Cortile della Biblioteca e Cortile della Pigna)*. He lived above Alexander VI's apartments in the rooms which Nicholas V had had painted by Piero della Francesca, Benedetto Bonfigli and Andrea del Castagno and had them redecorated by Raphael. The façade of the palace was too austere for his taste so he had another built consisting of three loggias, one above another. The second floor loggia was decorated by Raphael.

Paul III (1534-49) strengthened the foundations and restored the southwest wing of the early palace.

Pius IV (1559-65) commissioned Pirro Ligorio to alter the Belvedere Court. To the north (on the Belvedere Palace side) the architect constructed a large semicircular niche before which was erected the Pigna, a huge pine cone, which had adorned the fountain in the *atrium* of Constantine's basilica *(see above)*. The design is based on Classical architecture, particularly Domitian's Stadium on the Palatine Hill. To the south, backing on to Nicholas V's palace, he created a semicircular façade one storey high with a central niche. Later the Belvedere Court was divided by two transverse galleries: between 1587 and 1588 during the reign of Sixtus V, Domenico Fontana built the Papal Library (Sistine Rooms); later, between 1806 and 1823 Pius VII built the New Wing *(Braccio Nuovo)*.

The Belvedere Court was thus divided into three separate courts: the Belvedere Court *(Cortile del Belvedere)*, the Library Court *(della Biblioteca)*, the Pine Cone Court *(della Pigna)*.

During the Baroque period the only addition to the Vatican Palace was the Scala Regia *(not open)*, a monumental stairway constructed by Bernini between 1633 and 1666. From the Great Bronze Door *(Portone di bronzo)* which is the main entrance to the palace *(plan above)* a long corridor along the north side of St Peter's Square leads to the foot of the *Scala Regia* (Royal Stairway).

Papal Court – By providing his nephews with ecclesiastical titles and benefices and surrounding himself with rich cardinals, artists and men of letters, Sixtus IV (1471-84) created a virtual court like that of a secular prince.

Pope's Apartments – The 16C buildings surrounding Sixtus V's Court *(Cortile di Sisto V) (plan above)* contain the present Papal apartments. Heads of State, diplomats and other important people enter the Vatican City by the Bell Arch *(Arco delle Campane)*. Papal receptions are held in the Pope's private library, a large room between Sixtus V's Court *(Cortile di Sisto V)* and Majordomo Court *(Cortile del Maggiordomo)*.

In the summer the Pope moves to Castel Gandolfo, a property 120km - 75 miles southeast of Rome.

Museums – Their origins go back to 1503 when Julius II displayed a few Classical works of art in the Belvedere Court. His successors continued to collect Greek and Roman, paleo-Christian and Christian antiquities. After acquiring a number of antiques with the lottery revenues, Clement XIV created a new museum, which was enlarged by Pius VI and is called the Pio-Clementino after the two popes. The rooms joining the Belvedere Palace to the West Gallery, now occupied by the Apostolic Library, were constructed by the architect Simonetti as an extension.

Following the Treaty of Tolentino in 1797 many works of art were sent to Paris. Those that were left were arranged by Canova, who had been appointed Inspector General of Fine Arts and Antiquities belonging to the State and the Church by Pope Pius VII, in a museum, called the Chiaramonti Museum (after the Pope's family name). When the lost works were returned in 1816 Pius VII built the New Wing *(Braccio Nuovo)* to house them.

In 1837 Gregory XVI opened an Etruscan Museum to house the results of private excavations of burial grounds in Etruria; an Egyptian museum followed in 1839.

The Art Gallery *(Pinacoteca)* was opened in 1932 by Pius XI.

1970 saw the inauguration of a very modern building to house the Antique and Christian Art Collections formerly in the Lateran Palace.

The Missionary collections were transferred from the Lateran in 1973, the same year as the creation of the History Museum and the Museum of Modern Religious Art.

For the interest and diversity of their treasures the Vatican museums rank among the best in the world.

TOUR Entrance in Viale Vaticano

3 hours for the ★★★ highly recommended sections; 1 day for all the galleries.

The present entrance hall was opened in 1932. A spiral ramp with a sculpted bronze balustrade leads up to the ticket offices from which the museums are reached either through

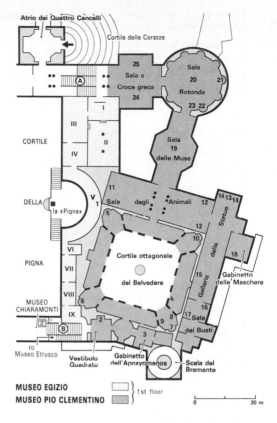

the Cortile delle Corazze (Cuirasses) or through the Atrio dei Quattro Cancelli (Atrium of the Four Gates) and Simonetti's 18C staircases (**A** on the plan)

Visitors must follow the official one-way tour, which has options at various points and is liable to variation; see plan below.

The official tour starts with the Egyptian and Chiaromonti Museums (see below). The visit of the Pio-Clementino Museum begins in the Square Vestibule.

Museo Egizio (Egyptian Museum)

Founded by Pope Gregory XVI, it was laid out in 1839 by Father Ungarelli, one of the first Italian Egyptologists to take an interest in Champollion's work. The collection includes antiquities acquired by the popes in 18C and statues found in Rome and its environs; these were brought back from Egypt during the Empire or are Roman copies of 1-2C works.

Room I contains inscriptions including documents from the Old Kingdom (c2650 BC) to the 6C AD: throne of the bust-less statue of Pharaoh Ramses II (19th dynasty; c1250BC).

Room II is devoted to Ancient Egyptian funerary art: the mummy of a woman (c1000 BC) with henna-dyed hair; sarcophagi in painted wood and stone; canopic vases (organs extracted from the body were mummified separately and kept in these vases) and various amulets.

Room III displays reproductions of the sculptures which decorate the Canopus in Hadrian's Villa at Tivoli. The main theme is the re-awakening, represented by twin busts on a lotus flower, of Osiris-Apis, also known as Serapis, a deity introduced in the 4C by Ptolemy. At the end of the passage stood a colossal bust of Isis-Sothis-Demeter, the goddess protecting the sources of the Nile; from it gushed a waterfall which symbolized the flooding of the Nile. Statues of Antinous deified under the name of Osirantinoos complete the decoration in the room.

In the **hemicycle (V)** are Egyptian statues discovered in Rome and its environs: the fine Pharaoh's head of the 11th dynasty (c2100 BC) exemplifies the art of the Middle Kingdom. The colossal statue of Queen Thuya (**1**), Ramses II's mother (19th dynasty, c1250 BC) illustrates the art of the New Kingdom. The pink granite statues are Egyptian-style representations of the Greek King of Egypt Ptolemy Philadelphus (283-246 BC), his sisters Arsinoe and Philotera.

Museo Chiaramonti e Galleria Lapidaria
(Chiaramonti Museum and Lapidary Gallery)

The **Chiaramonti Museum**, set up by Pius VII whose family name was Chiaramonti, has generally kept the appearance given to it by Canova in 1807. It contains Roman copies of Greek works, portraits, funerary monuments: one low relief bearing a millstone, donkey, baskets etc. obviously commemorates a miller *(on the right, Row X)*.

The **Lapidary Gallery** houses over 3000 pagan and Christian inscriptions *(open to specialists on request)*.

From the Chiaramonti Museum the tour proceeds to the New Wing.

Braccio Nuovo **(New Wing)** (Roman antiquities) *plan see above*

The "**Doryphoros**" *(3rd recess on the left of the entrance)* depicts a spearbearer. It is a copy of a bronze original by Polyclitus (440 BC). In all probability the original was the model (the Kanon) which demonstrated Polyclitus' theories about proportions in sculpture. The **statue of Augustus★★** *(4th recess on the right)*, known as "from the Prima Porta" because of where it was found, is a fine example of official Roman art. The decoration of the Emperor's breastplate is an extraordinarily precise illustration of the King of the Parthians returning the standards lost by Crassus in 53 BC. *The Nile (il Nilo) (in the central hemicycle)* is a 1C Roman work inspired perhaps by a Greek original from the Hellenistic period. It depicts the river-god surrounded by 16 children, a symbol of the 16 cubits by which the river must rise in order to flood the plain and make it fertile. The gilded bronze peacocks may have come from Hadrian's mausoleum. The **statue of Demosthenes** *(last recess on the left of the entrance)* is a Roman copy of a Greek bronze (3CBC).

Return to the entrance of the Chiaramonti Museum and go into the Pio-Clementino Museum.

★★★Museo Pio-Clementino **(Pius-Clementine Museum)**
(Greek and Roman antiquities)

The museum is housed in the Belvedere Palace and the rooms added by Simonetti in 18C.

Vestibolo Quadrato (Square Vestibule) – This is the atrium of the former Clementino Museum. The sobriety of early Roman art shows in the **sarcophagus of Scipio Barbatus** (**2**), carved in peperine (3C BC). Its shape is inspired by the Greek models which the Romans discovered after the capture of Rhegium in 270 BC.

Gabinetto dell'Apoxyomenos – The **Apoxyomenos★★★** (**3**) is the name given to the statue of an athlete scraping his skin with a strigil after taking exercise. It is a 1C AD Roman copy of a Greek original by Lysippus (4C BC). In the weary body the artist reveals the living human being rather than an idealistic image as in the Classical period.

Scala del Bramante – Bramante's noble spiral stairway, which was used by men on horseback, was designed early in the 16C during the alterations ordered by Julius II.

★Cortile ottagonale del Belvedere (Belvedere Octagonal Court) – The internal courtyard of the Belvedere Palace, originally on a square plan and planted with orange trees, acquired its octagonal outline when Simonetti added a portico in the 18C.

★★★**Laocoön** (**5**) – One morning in January 1506 the architect Giuliano da Sangallo rushed up to Michelangelo inviting him to come and see an extraordinary sculpture which was being unearthed in Nero's Golden House. This was the work of a group of artists from Rhodes (1C BC) representing the death of Laocoön, priest of Apollo, who had incurred the god's anger and, together with his two sons, was crushed to death by serpents. In this composition Hellenistic art attains an intense realism; in an attempt to show the extremes of suffering it achieved an exaggerated style which earned the description "Greek Baroque".

The Laocoön

P. Roy/EXPLORER

★★★**Apollo** (**6**) – The statue was placed in the Belvedere Court by Julius II in 1503. It is probably copied from a 4C BC Greek original by a Roman sculptor who has captured the serenity of the Greek gods. The figure may have held a bow in the left hand and an arrow in the right.

Works by Canova (1757-1822) – Pope Pius VII bought these three neo-Classical statues from Canova to make up for the loss of certain works removed under the terms of the Treaty of Tolentino: **Perseus**★★ (**7**) who conquered Medusa, and the boxers Kreugas (**8**) and Damozenos (**9**) who met in fierce combat at Nemea in Argolis.

★★★**Hermes** (**10**) – This 2C AD Roman work, inspired by an original Greek bronze, represents Zeus' son, the messenger of the gods.

Ara Casali – Under the north portico sits the 3C altar presented by the Casali family to Pope Pius VI. On the front is carved a scene with Venus and Mars, while the back shows Romulus and Remus.

Sala degli Animali (Room of the Animals) – Various animal sculptures, heavily restored in the 18C. The statue of **Meleager**★ (**11**) is a 2C Roman copy of a bronze sculpture by Skopas, a Greek artist (4C BC). Beside Meleager is the head of the boar which caused his death at Diana's behest.

The fine mosaics of the pavement are Roman. A crab made of green porphyry, a rare stone, is displayed in a show case (**12**).

Galleria delle Statue (Statue Gallery) – This part of the Belvedere Palace was converted into a gallery in the 18C.

★**Sleeping Ariadne** (**13**) – A Roman copy of a Greek original illustrating the characteristic taste for unusual poses and elaborate draperies of the Hellenistic period (2C BC). On waking, Ariadne will be married to Dionysius and carried away to Olympus.

Candelabra (**14**) – These fine examples of 2C Roman decorative work come from Hadrian's Villa at Tivoli.

★**Apollo Sauroktonos** (**15**) – This statue of Apollo about to kill a lizard is a Roman copy of a work by Praxiteles, a Greek artist of the 4C BC. An expert in feminine models he made the young god very graceful.

Sala dei Busti (Room of the Busts) – The three rooms of this gallery are divided by fine marble columns. The **busts of Cato and Portia**★ (**16**), a husband and wife group intended for a tomb (1C BC) are in the typically austere style of the Republican era.

The numerous Imperial portraits include a particularly expressive bust of Julius Caesar (**17**).

Gabinetto delle Maschere (Cabinet of the Masks) – It owes its name to the mosaic of masks (2C) removed from Hadrian's Villa and let into the floor. The **Venus of Cnidos**★★ (**18**) is a Roman copy of Praxiteles' statue for the sanctuary at Cnidos in Asia Minor (4C BC) which was famous both for its artistic merits and for being the first representation of a goddess in the nude. The Greeks, versed in the legend of Actaeon who was killed for watching a goddess bathing, were shocked.

Return to the Room of the Animals.

Sala delle Muse (Room of the Muses) – It owes its name to the statues of the Muses which, together with statues of Greek philosophers, are arranged around the room.

★★★**Belvedere Torso** (**19**) – Like the statue of the Pugilist *(in the National Roman Museum),* this is the masterly work of the Athenian Apollonius, Nestor's son, who lived in Rome in the 1C BC. The expressive torso, which was part of a statue of Hercules seated, was much admired by Michelangelo.

★**Sala rotonda (Round Room)** – This fine room by Simonetti (1780) was inspired by the Pantheon. The monolithic porphyry **basin** (**20**) may have come from Nero's Golden House. The **statue of Hercules** (**21**) in gilded bronze dates from the late 2C. **Antinoüs** (**22**), the young favourite of the Emperor Hadrian, drowned in the Nile in 130. After his death the Emperor raised him under the name Osirantinoos to the ranks of the gods. He bears the attributes of Dionysius and the Egyptian god Osiris (on his head is the Uraeus, a serpent which formed part of the headdress of the Pharaohs). The **bust of Jupiter**★ (**23**) is a Roman copy of a Greek original dating from the 4C BC.

Sala a Croce Greca (Greek Cross Room) – Two large porphyry **sarcophagi**★ have pride of place. The one belonging to St Helena (**24**), the Emperor Constantine's mother, dates from the early 4C and is heavily sculptured with conquering Roman cavalry and barbarian prisoners, an inappropriate theme for such a holy woman. This suggests that the sarcophagus was originally intended for her husband, Constantinus Chlorus, or her son Constantine, who may have had it made before moving his court to Constantinople. The other is the sarcophagus of Constantia (**25**), Constantine's daughter, and dates from the middle of the 4C.

Climb the Simonetti stairs (Ⓐ*) to the second floor.*

★Museo Etrusco (Etruscan Museum)

Founded in 1837 by Gregory XVI, this museum houses objects found in Southern Etruria. In Room I are displayed the oldest artefacts (9C-8C BC cinerary urns in the form of a house). Room II accommodates the two-horse chariots used by high-born members of 8C BC society. A variety of exquisite Greek black and red-figure vases found in several tombs provide some indication of the considerable wealth of the dead.

Items retrieved from the **Regolini-Galassi tomb** (named after the archbishop and the general who discovered it in 1836), south of Cerveteri are particularly fine.

In the showcases along the wall on the right of the entrances are displayed the items found in the tomb; belonging to the woman were the bronze throne and jewellery; the incomparable golden **clasp★★**, decorated with lions and ducks in the round and dating from the 7C BC, shows the perfection attained by the Etruscans in such work; the incised pectoral medallion lay on the woman's breast surrounded by golden leaves (fragments) sewn on to her dress. The man lay on the bronze couch; the two horse chariot *(biga)* would also have been his.

The little inkstand in *bucchero* is inscribed with an alphabet and a syllabary *(penultimate showcase facing the windows near the door to Room III)*. The **Bronze Room (III)** houses the **Mars★★** found at Todi, a rare example of a large bronze statue from the late 5C BC. The style of the work is akin to the rigour of Classical Greek works. The oval cist *(last case to the right of the Mars)*, a toilette receptacle, is attractively decorated with the Battle of the Amazons; fantastic figures adorn the handle.

The hemicycle and the adjoining rooms contain many Greek, Etruscan and Italiot vases from the 6C to 3C BC.

In the hemicycle, note the striking large black-figure **amphora★★** *(second middle glass case to the left of the entrance)* painted by Exekias. In perfect condition, this object is a rare example of the master's artistry. It illustrates Achilles playing draughts with Ajax.

Sala della Biga (Biga Room)

The **two-horse chariot★★** *(biga)* after which the hall is named is 1C Roman. It was reconstituted in the 18C when the body of the chariot was recovered from St Mark's Basilica where it had served as an episcopal throne.

Galleria degli Candelabri (Candelabra Gallery)

The loggia was transformed into a gallery in 1785 by Pius VI. It is subdivided by arches and pillars flanked by 2C marble candelabra and houses antiquities.

Galleria degli Arazzi (Tapestry Gallery)

The tapestries were hung by Gregory XVI in 1838. Facing the windows: the New School series, commissioned by Leo X in the early 16C, was woven by Pieter van Aelst's workshops in Brussels from cartoons by Raphael's pupils. On the window side: the life of Cardinal Maffeo Barberini, later Pope Urban VIII (Barberini workshop, Rome-17C).

★Galleria delle carte geografiche (Map Gallery)

The ceiling is richly decorated with stucco work and paintings by a group of 18C Mannerists: 80 scenes from the lives of the saints closely associated with the maps below. The extraordinary maps on the walls were painted from 1580 to 1583 from cartoons by Fr Ignazio Danzi who explained that he had divided Italy in two down the line of the Apennines: the one side bathed by the Ligurian and Tyrrhenian seas, the other bordered by the Alps and the Adriatic. The 40 maps are supplemented by town plans, a map of the region round Avignon (once a Papal possession) and two maps of Corfu and Malta. The 16C cartography is fantastically embellished with inscriptions, ships and turbulent seas.

Sala Sobieski e Sala dell'Immacolata Concezione (Sobieski and Immaculate Conception Rooms)

In the former hangs a 19C painting by Jan Mateiko of John III Sobieski, King of Poland, repulsing the Turks at the Siege of Vienna (1683). The 19C frescoes in the latter illustrate the dogma of the Immaculate Conception pronounced by Pius IX in 1854; an elaborate showcase displays richly decorated books on the same theme.

★★★Stanze di Raffaello (Raphael Rooms)

During part of the year in order to avoid overcrowding there is one-way access from the Room of the Immaculate Conception via an external terrace. The visit of the Raphael Rooms then starts in the Hall of Constantine. The rest of the year the tour is in the opposite direction.

These rooms had been built during the reign of Nicholas V (1447-55) and decorated with frescoes by Piero della Francesca among others, except the Hall of Constantine which was part of the 13C wing of the Papal Palace. On becoming

Pope in 1503, Julius II arranged to have them redecorated for his own use by a group of artists which included Sodoma and Perugino. In 1508 on Bramante's recommendation he sent for a young painter from Urbino. Charmed by Raphael's youthful grace, he entrusted the whole of the decoration to him; the other painters were dismissed and their work effaced. The frescoes in what came to be known as the "Raphael Stanze" are among the masterpieces of the Renaissance. They were damaged by the troops of Charles V during the sack of Rome in 1527 but have been restored.

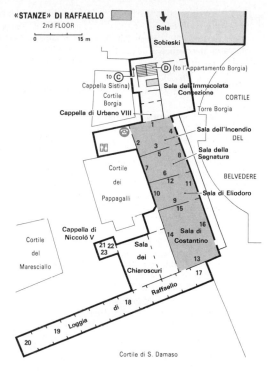

«STANZE» DI RAFFAELLO
2nd FLOOR

Sala dell'Incendio del Borgo (Room of the Borgo Fire) (1514-17) — This was the last room to be painted by Raphael. The immedi ate success of his work and the large number of commissions that followed led him to speed up his work. From 1515 he worked with a group of assistants. In this room he only designed the frescoes and some of the cartoons which were completed by his assistants. The ceiling frescoes are by Perugino.

To glorify the reign of Leo X, Julius II's successor, who had confirmed Raphael in his appointment, the artist painted the life of the Pope and of his predecessors Leo III and Leo IV. In the fresco of the **Coronation of Charlemagne** (1) the Emperor is portrayed as François I of France and Leo II as Leo X (who signed the Concordat of Bologna with François I in 1516).

The Borgo Fire (2) — According to the "Liber Pontificalis" a fire which broke out in 847 in the area near St Peter's (the Borgo) was quenched by Pope Leo IV with the sign of the cross. Inspired, like all Renaissance artists by Antiquity, Raphael painted the colonnade of the Temple of Mars Ultor on the left; the old man supported by a youth recalls Virgil (Aeneas fleeing from Troy, carrying his father Anchises, his son Ascanius at his side, while his wife Creusa follows behind).

Parnassus by Raphael

In the background is the Loggia of Benedictions of Constantine's basilica as it was in Raphael's lifetime.

Battle of Ostia (**3**) – Here Leo X is again represented in the guise of Leo IV who defeated the Saracens at the battle of Ostia in 849.

Oath of Leo III (**4**) – According to the medieval account, when Leo III sought to clear himself of a libel in St Peter's itself, a voice rang out declaring "It is for God not men to judge bishops" (Latin inscription to the right of the window). Leo III is portrayed as Leo X.

Sala della Segnatura (Signature Room) (1508-11) – This room was used as a library, a study and for signing papal bulls. It was the first room painted by Raphael. The decorative theme, probably proposed by a court scholar versed in neo-Platonic philosophy, illustrates the three great principles of the human spirit: Truth, Goodness and Beauty.

The medallions on the ceiling and wall paintings illustrate closely linked subjects. Above the Triumph of Religion *(Dispute over the Blessed Sacrament)* is shown the allegory of Theology and, above that, Philosophy *(School of Athens)*. They represent the two aspects of Truth – the supernatural and the rational. Above the fresco representing canon and civil law and the cardinal virtues is the allegory of Justice. These represent Goodness. The allegory of Poetry, representing Beauty, crowns *Parnassus*. Smaller paintings in the corners underline the significance of the allegories: *Adam and Eve* in which a woman imparts motion to the universe; the *Judgement of Solomon, Apollo and Marsyas*.

Part of the ceiling decoration is attributed to Sodoma and the octagonal area to Bramantino (*c*1465-1530).

Dispute over the Blessed Sacrament (**5**) – This name is wrongly attributed to the fresco illustrating the Glorification of Religion: at the top surrounding the Trinity appears the Church victorious with Mary, St John the Baptist, the Apostles, Prophets and Patriarchs, martyrs and angels.

On earth, grouped round the altar, stand the Doctors of the Church, the Popes and the faithful including Dante *(right)*, crowned with laurel, Savonarola, Sixtus IV, Fra Angelico, Gregory the Great with the features of Julius II. The lines converge on the Host, the incarnation of Christ, linking the Church on Earth and the Church in Heaven.

The School of Athens (**6**) – Beneath the vaults of a Classical building designed by Bramante stands a crowd of philosophers. In the centre are the Greeks, Plato and Aristotle, representing the two main streams of Classical thought: idealism and materialism. Plato's raised finger indicates the realm of ideas, Aristotle's open hand indicates that without the material world ideas would have no existence. Raphael has given Plato the face of Leonardo da Vinci.

On the left, Socrates, in a tunic, is speaking to his pupil Alcibiades. The cynic Diogenes is lounging contemptuously on the steps before a disapproving follower. Epicurus, in a laurel wreath, is giving a dissertation on pleasure, while Euclid, who resembles Bramante, is tracing geometric figures on a slate. In the right-hand corner Raphael has included himself in a black beret standing next to another painter, Sodoma, in a tunic and white beret.

In the foreground is the solitary figure of Heraclitus, his head resting in his left hand; he has the facial features of Michelangelo, who was at that time decorating the Sistine Chapel. Raphael added this figure when the fresco was almost finished in noble homage to this rival.

The Cardinal and Theological Virtues (**7**) – Above the window are Strength (oak branch, emblem of the Della Rovere family to which Julius II belonged), Prudence and Temperance, Faith, Hope and Charity (as cupids). On the right Raimond de Pennafort hands Gregory IX (1234) the body of rules which make up canon law (Decretals); on the left Justinian approves the "Pandects", a collection of Roman jurisprudence, comprising civil law. Gregory IX is a portrait of Julius II. Beside him stand Cardinal Giovanni de' Medici (future Leo X) and Alessandro Farnese (future Paul III).

The "Parnassus" (**8**) – Around Apollo and the nine Muses are grouped the great poets, starting with Homer and Virgil.

Sala di Eliodoro (Heliodorus Room) (1512-1514) – This was the suite's private antechamber and it was decorated by Raphael after the Signature Room. The theme is the divine protection of the Church.

Expulsion of Heliodorus from the Temple (**9**) – The biblical subject, taken from the Book of Maccabees (Heliodorus, intent on stealing the temple treasure, is expelled by the angels), was probably chosen by Julius II himself, whose own policy was to expel usurpers from Papal property. He appears on the left in the Papal Chair. It is an excellent portrait revealing the authority of the Pope who fought alongside his own soldiers and one day broke his cane across Michelangelo's back. This fresco is exceptional for Raphael in the vigour and movement of the figures (Heliodorus, the three angels and a person flattening himself against a pillar).

Miracle of the Bolsena Mass (10) – The miracle, celebrated today as the feast of Corpus Christi, took place in 1263 when a priest, who doubted the doctrine of the real presence, saw blood on the host at the moment of consecration while celebrating mass in Bolsena. Julius II is kneeling before the priest. The Pope, his suite and the Swiss guards are among Raphael's masterpieces.

The composition is masterly. The problem of the round lunette with its off-centre window is accommodated by the asymmetric positioning of the stairs on either side of the altar and by the lively treatment of the crowd on the left where the painting is most restricted.

St Peter delivered from prison (11) – According to the Acts of the Apostles, while in prison in Rome, Peter dreamt that an angel set him free and on waking found that he was free. One notable element in the composition is the use of various light sources: the moon, the guard's torch, the angel. This painting is a masterpiece in the painting of light, anticipating the work of Caravaggio and Rembrandt by more than a century.

St Leo the Great repulsing Attila (12) – On learning of the Huns' approach, Leo I went to meet them and, aided by the appearance of St Peter and St Paul armed with swords, he repulsed Attila.

Raphael has moved the event to the gates of Rome which is indicated by the Colosseum, a basilica and an aqueduct. The calm comportment of the Pope and his suite contrasts with the disorder of the barbarian hordes. The painting was not finished when Julius II died in 1513. Raphael therefore substituted a portrait of Leo X although he already appeared in the picture as Cardinal Giovanni de Medici *(left)* wearing the *cappa magna* (a long hooded cloak).

A large part of the painting *(right)* was executed by Raphael's pupils.

Sala di Constantino (Hall of Constantine) (1517-1525) – In 1520 Raphael died. The painting of this room, intended for receptions, which had been begun during Leo X's reign, was finished in Clement VII's by a group of Raphael's followers led by Giulio Romano and Francesco Penni. This was the beginning of Mannerism; overwhelmed by the legacy of Raphael and Michelangelo, artists began to abandon national idealism in favour of exaggerated form and contorted movement.

The apparition of the Cross (13) and the Battle of the Milvian Bridge (14) – These two works are by Giulio Romano. Constantine's victory over Maxentius at the Milvian Bridge in 312 suffers from exaggeration.

The Baptism of Constantine (15) – Francesco Penni was the artist. Pope Sylvester who baptised Constantine is shown with the features of Clement VII and in the baptistry of the basilica of St John Lateran.

Constantine's Donation (16) – Giulio Romano and Francesco Penni collaborated on this scene which is set inside the old St Peter's and shows the Emperor Constantine (306-37) giving Rome to the Pope and thus founding the temporal power of the Papacy. In his Divine Comedy Dante spoke out vehemently against the gift: "Ah, Constantine, what evil was spawned not by your conversion but by that gift which the first rich pope accepted from you."

The vault – The old beamed ceiling was replaced at the end of the 16C.

★★Loggia di Raffaello (Raphael's Loggia)

Open to specialists only. Access via the Hall of Constantine. On the second floor of the galleried building.

At the beginning of the 16C, before the construction of St Damasus' Court *(Cortile di San Damaso)* and the buildings on its north, south and east sides, the façade of the 13C palace looked out over Rome. Julius II (1503-13) decided to give it a new look. He engaged Bramante to design three superimposed loggias. Work began in 1508 and when Bramante died in 1514 only the first tier had been built. Julius II's successor, Leo X, appointed Raphael to take over.

The loggia takes the form of a vaulted corridor, richly decorated (probably between 1517 and 1519). The walls and arches are adorned with stuccoes and 'grotesques' inspired by Classical models which Raphael and his friends had found in Nero's Golden House. Various artists collaborated with Raphael: Francesco Penni and Giulio Romano, Giovanni da Udine and Perin del Vaga. Their work abounds with fantastic invention: garlands of fruit and flowers, animals, reproductions of famous statues, people, scenes from contemporary life.

The loggia is divided into 13 bays; the vault of each being decorated with four paintings, representing scenes from the Old Testament except in the first bay **(17)** which has scenes from the New Testament. The loggia is sometimes called "Raphael's Bible". These charmingly fresh paintings include *Moses in the Bullrushes* **(18)**; *Building Noah's Ark* **(19)**; *Creation of the Animals* **(20)**.

★★Sala dei Chiaroscuri e cappella di Niccolò V (Chiaroscuro Rooms and Nicholas V's Chapel)

The rooms owe their name to the monochrome paintings of saints and apostles executed from Raphael's cartoons by his followers (1517). The paintings were restored in the late 16C.

★★**Cappella di Niccolò V (Nicholas V's Chapel)** – The chapel is one of the oldest parts of the Vatican Palace. It probably formed part of a tower which was absorbed into the first papal palace in the 13C. Nicholas V converted it into a chapel and had it decorated by **Fra Angelico** (1447-51), a Dominican monk and master of Florentine art. He was assisted by Benozzo Gozzoli, also from Florence.

In the angles are the Doctors of the Church; the Evangelists are on the ceiling. The two-tier wall paintings illustrate the lives of St Stephen and St Lawrence *(upper tier)* and were extensively restored in the 18C and 19C.

Life of St Stephen – *Upper level.* On the right (**21**) are two legendary episodes in the saint's life: St Stephen being ordained deacon *(left)* by St Peter (whose figure shows great nobility); St Stephen distributing alms *(right)*. Above the entrance door (**22**): St Stephen preaching in a square in Florence *(left)* and St Stephen addressing the Council *(right)*. On the left (**23**): the Stoning of St Stephen.

Life of St Lawrence – *Lower level.* Sixtus II, resembling Nicholas V, ordaining St Lawrence as deacon (**21**) whose face shows that saintly expression which only Fra Angelico could impart. Above the door (**22**): St Lawrence receiving the treasure of the Church from Sixtus II and distributing alms to the poor. The portrayal of a blind man *(right)* is exceptional in the idealised art of the Renaissance. On the left (**23**): the Roman Emperor Decius pointing to the instruments of torture; the martyrdom of St Lawrence.

On leaving Nicholas V's chapel, return to the first Raphael Room (Borgo Fire). Pass through Urban VIII's Chapel and turn right down the stairs to the Borgia Apartment.

★Appartamento Borgia (Borgia Apartment)

These rooms, which formed the suite of Alexander VI, the Borgia Pope from Spain, now house examples of modern art. They are decorated (end of 1492 to 1494) with paintings by **Pinturicchio**, full of pleasant fantasy.

The first, known as the **Sybilline Room (I)**, is painted with figures of Sybils and Prophets.

In the **Creed Room (III)** the Prophets and Apostles carry scrolls bearing the articles of the Creed.

Next is the **Liberal Arts Room (IV)**, probably used by Alexander VI as a study. It is decorated with allegories of the Liberal Arts, i.e. the seven subjects taught in the universities in the Middle Ages. On the ceiling are the arms of the Borgias.

The **Saints' Room (V)** was probably painted by Pinturicchio himself whereas in the other rooms he was assisted by many of his pupils. The legendary lives of the saints are combined with mythology, a common practice in the Renaissance period. Facing the window is one of Pinturicchio's best works, St Catherine of Alexandria arguing with the philosophers, against his usual landscape of delicate trees, rocks and hills. In the centre is the Arch of Constantine. Before the Emperor St Catherine expounds her arguments in defence of the Christian faith. The vault is painted with mythological scenes.

The **Mysteries of the Faith Room (VI)** depicts the principal mysteries in the lives of Jesus and his mother. On the wall framing the entrance: the Resurrection; on the left: very fine portrait of Alexander VI, in rapt adoration.

The **Pontiffs' Room (VII)** was used for official meetings. The ceiling, which collapsed in 1500 narrowly missing Alexander VI, was reconstructed in the reign of Leo X and is decorated with stucco ornaments and 'grotesques' by Perin del Vaga and Giovanni da Udine. At one time the room was hung with portraits of the popes, hence its name. Nowadays only the dedications remain.

★★**Collezione d'Arte Moderna Religiosa** – This very rich collection of modern religious art brings together some 500 paintings and sculptures, given by artists and collectors. The greatest artists in the world are represented here. On the upper floor the Chapel of Peace by Giacomo Manzù (Room XIV) leads into a room devoted to Rouault (Room XV), followed by a series of smaller rooms revealing traces of the 13C palace and containing works by Chagall, Gauguin, Utrillo, Odilon Redon, Braque, Klee, Kandinsky, Moore, Morandi, De Pisis etc.

Downstairs in rooms partially beneath the Sistine Chapel gleams stained glass by Fernand Leger, Jacques Villon, George Meistermann. There are several canvases by Ben Shahn, J. Levine, Bernard Buffet, Yugoslavian Naive paintings, sculptures by Marini, Lipchitz and Mirko, Picasso ceramics and Bazaine tapestries.

At the inauguration on 23 June 1973 Paul VI declared "Even in our arid secularised world there is still a prodigious capacity for expressing beyond the truly human what is religious, divine, Christian."

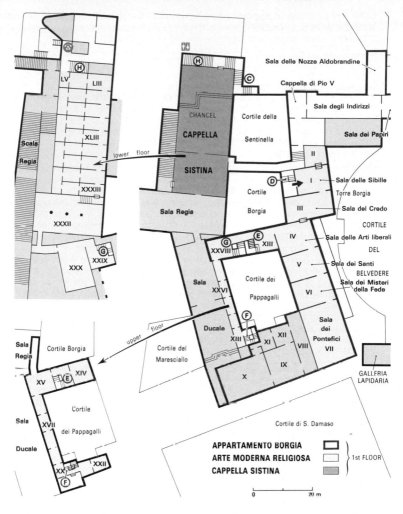

★★★ Capella Sistina (Sistine Chapel) (Stairs H)

It is named after Pope Sixtus IV for whom it was built from 1477 to 1480. As well as being the papal palace chapel, it seems to have served a defensive role in view of the surviving external crenellations.

The long chamber has a barrel vault flattened by small lateral vaults and is lit by 12 windows. **Sixtus IV** sent for painters from Umbria and Florence to decorate the walls. His nephew **Julius II** (1503-13) commissioned Michelangelo to redecorate the ceiling (originally it depicted a starry sky). Twenty years later the artist was again engaged by **Clement VII** and **Paul III** to paint the wall behind the altar. The chapel is not only the setting for the most solemn ceremonies of the Holy See, where the cardinals meet in conclave but also a masterpiece of Renaissance art; its dimensions – 40.23m - 132ft long, 13.41m - 44ft wide and 20.70m - 68ft high – are exactly the same as those given in the Bible for Solomon's Temple and the decorations too are charged with spiritual meaning.

Restoration of the Sistine Chapel – This vast undertaking, which was carried out by Italian experts and financed by Japanese patrons, took 18 years to complete of which 12 (1980-92) were spent on Michelangelo's frescoes. Most of the restoration work consisted in cleaning the frescoes, darkened by dust and candle smoke, with a mixture of bicarbonate of soda and ammonium. After 500 years Michelangelo's original colours ranging from bright orange, clear pink, pale green to brilliant yellow and turquoise, sparkle gloriously.

Side walls – In the decoration of the walls (1481-83) Sixtus IV wanted to perpetuate the decorative tradition of the early Christian basilicas. The lowest section represents the curtains which were hung between the columns of the old basilicas. Between the windows are portraits of the early popes from St Peter to Marcellus I (308-09). The figures of Christ and the first three popes were obliterated when the Last Judgement was painted above the altar. The paintings half-way up the walls depict parallel scenes in the lives of Moses and of Jesus, showing the human condition before and after the coming of the Messiah.

Life of Moses – *(South wall from the Last Judgement)* The first fresco *(Moses in the Bullrushes)* was covered up by the *Last Judgement. Moses in Egypt* (**I**) by **Perugino** is followed by *Moses' Youth* (**II**) by **Botticelli**; the two female figures of Jethro's daughters show the more lyrical side of the artist's style. These are followed by the *Crossing the Red Sea* (**III**) and *The Giving of the Tablets of the Law on Mount Sinai* (**IV**) by **Cosimo Rosselli**. In *The Punishment of Korah, Dathan and Abiram* (**V**) for denying Moses' and Aaron's authority over the Jewish people, Botticelli set the scene against a background of Roman monuments – Constantine's Arch and the Palatine Septizonium *(see FORO ROMANO-PALATINO). The Testament and Death of Moses* (**VI**) is by **Luca Signorelli**.

Life of Christ – *(North wall from the Last Judgement)* The first fresco, the *Nativity*, disappeared under **Michelangelo's** *Last Judgement*. The series begins with the *Baptism of Jesus* (**VII**) by **Perugino** and **Pinturicchio** featuring many members of Sixtus IV's court. The next panel, *The Temptation of Christ* and *The Healing of the Leper* (**VIII**), directly faces the papal throne; here **Botticelli** has given greater weight to the healing scene in deference to Sixtus IV who had written a theological treatise on the subject; he also painted the Temple in Jerusalem to look like the Santo Spirito Hospital which the Pope had had reconstructed. The small scenes at the foot of the painting represent the *Temptation of Christ (left to right)* in a thicket, on a pinnacle of the temple and on a high mountain. The next painting is an illustration of *The calling of St Peter and St Andrew* (**IX**) by **Ghirlandaio**. In *The Sermon on the Mount* and *The Healing of the Leper* (**X**), **Cosimo Rosselli** assisted by **Piero di Cosimo** made one of the first attempts to paint a sunset. The *Delivery of the Keys to St Peter* (**XI**) is a masterpiece by **Perugino**; the Arch of Constantine appears twice flanking the Temple in Jerusalem which is drawn by the artist according to his imagination. The final panel is *The Last Supper* (**XII**) by Cosimo Rosselli in which Judas is shown face to face with Jesus, apart from the other Apostles.

Ceiling – When Julius II abandoned his project for a funerary sculpture, Michelangelo returned unhappily to Florence. In 1508 he was recalled to Rome by the Pope who asked him to paint the 12 Apostles on the ceiling of the Sistine Chapel. He had barely started, as he later recorded, when he realised the work was going badly; the Pope then gave him a free hand and instead of the blue star-spangled vault (some 520m^2 - 660sq ft) he created a masterpiece filled with powerful movement. The animated figures compose an epic of the creation of the world and the history of the human race.

Julius II came regularly to ask Michelangelo when he would finish; from the top of the scaffolding came the regular reply "when I can".

On 14 August 1511, bursting with impatience, the Pope insisted on seeing the fresco; he was overwhelmed. About a year later it was finished.

From the Creation to the Flood – *Starting from the altar.*

1) *God divides the light from the darkness.*
2) *Creation of the sun, the moon and plant life.*
3) *God divides the waters from the earth and creates living creatures in the seas.*
4) *Creation of Adam.*
5) *Creation of Eve.*
6) *Original sin and expulsion from the Garden of Eden.*
7) *Noah's sacrifice:* contrary to biblical chronology this scene precedes the Flood. Michelangelo may have wanted to give more space to the Flood scene or to stress Noah's loyalty to God thus justifying his being saved in the Ark.
8) *The Flood:* this was the first scene to be painted. Some of the figures are too small in proportion to their surroundings.

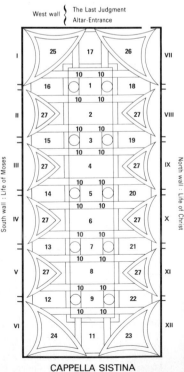

CAPPELLA SISTINA

9) *Noah's Drunkenness:* the whole series could have terminated with the Flood; by including the last scene where Noah is scorned by his son, Michelangelo pessimistically reminds us that life on earth began again under a bad omen.

The "Ignudi" (10) – These are the figures which Michelangelo painted at each corner of the central panels. These remarkable figures, which glorify the human body, are modelled on Classical sculptures and influenced many Renaissance and Mannerist artists.

Prophets and Sibyls – There is great variety in these twelve portraits: *Zacharias* (**11**), the old man with a beard; *Joel* (**12**), the critic; the *Erythraean Sibyl* (**13**), not knowing where to begin her study; *Ezekiel* (**14**), in earnest debate; the *Persian Sibyl* (**15**), shortsighted and bowed with old age; *Jeremiah* (**16**) in his melancholy; *Jonah* (**17**), symbol of Christ's Resurrection, ejected from the whale in a movement recalled by Baroque artists; the *Libyan Sibyl* (**18**), her study completed, descending from her throne with gracefulness; *Daniel* (**19**), inspired by a new idea; the *Cumaean Sibyl* (**20**), a muscle-bound giant apparently puzzled by what she is reading; *Isaiah* (**21**), troubled by an angel; the young *Delphic Sibyl* (**22**).

Bible Stories – At the centre of these four scenes are the heroes of the Jewish people – David, Judith, Esther, Moses – in whom Christ reaffirmed the promise of His coming foretold by the Prophets: *Judith and Holophernes* (**23**), *David and Goliath* (**24**), *the Punishment of Haman* (**25**), *the Brazen Serpent* (**26**).

Jesus' Forefathers (27) – Their names *(above the windows)* correspond to the scenes painted in the triangular sections. There the Jewish families wait for their deliverance.

The Last Judgement – Twenty years after painting the ceiling, Michelangelo was sent for by Clement VII in 1534 to complete the decoration of the Chapel. The Pope, who had seen Rome sacked by Charles V's troops in 1527, wanted the Last Judgement to deliver its message boldly from above the altar as a warning to the unfaithful. Paul III took up his predecessor's idea and work began in 1535. The 15C frescoes were obliterated as well as two panels in the series depicting Jesus' ancestors. When the fresco was unveiled on 31 October 1541, people were amazed and dumbfounded. Stamped with the mark of violence and anger, this striking work, with its mass of naked bodies writhing in a baleful light, is an expression of misfortune: Rome had been sacked in 1527; Luther's doctrine was dividing the Western Church. In the 16C and 18C the fresco was touched up. The austerity of the Counter-Reformation moved Pius IV to have the naked figures clothed by Daniele da Volterra; in all about 30 figures were clothed.

This fresco introduced a new style in the history of art which led to the Baroque. The composition follows a strict scheme: the elect are welcomed on high by the angels *(left)* while the damned tumble headlong into hell *(right)*.

At the bottom *(left)* the dead slowly awake; in vain the devils try to restrain them. Up above the elect seem drawn by the movement of Christ's right hand. Beside the terrifying figure of Christ the Judge, the Virgin turns away from the horrific spectacle. Around them are the Saints, bearing the instruments of their martyrdoms: St Andrew with his cross beside the Virgin, beneath them St Lawrence and his gridiron, St Bartholomew with his skin (in its folds appears the distorted face of Michelangelo).

In his boat Charon waits for the damned whom he throws into the river of Hell. Minos, the Master of Hell, his body wreathed by a snake *(in the corner)* resembles Biagio da Cesena, the Master of Ceremonies at the Papal Court; the latter was shocked that such a work could appear in so venerable a place and complained to the Pope, Paul III, who retorted that he did not have the power to rescue someone from Hell.

The fresco as a whole is dominated by angels bearing the Cross, the Crown of Thorns, the Column and the other instruments of the Passion.

Pavement and Choir Screen – The chapel was paved in the 15C in the Cosmati style. The delicate choir screen and the choristers' gallery are by Mino da Fiesole (15C).

★Biblioteca Apostolica (Vatican Library) (Precious objects)

Cappella di San Pio V (Pius V's Chapel) – On display are the Treasures of the Sancta Sanctorum, the private chapel of the popes in the Lateran Palace.

Sala degli Indirizzi (Room of the Addresses) – Secular items from the Roman and early-Christian era are exhibited together with religious items from the Middle Ages to the present day.

Sala delle Nozze Aldobrandine (Aldobrandini Marriage Room) – A fresco from the Augustan period depicting wedding preparations (centre wall) is named after its first owner, Cardinal Pietro Aldobrandini.

Museo Sacro (Sacred Museum) – It was founded in 1756 by Benedict XIV for early-Christian antiquities.

239

Sale Sistine (Sistine Rooms) – Beyond the Gallery of Urban VIII with its instruments of astronomy and mappa mundi are the Sistine Rooms, created by Sixtus V (1585-90) to hold archives.

★**Salone Sistina (Sistine Salon)** – *Used for temporary exhibitions.* The Salon was built in 1587 by Sixtus V and was the reading room of the Vatican Library. The Mannerist decoration by C Nebbia shows episodes of Sixtus V's papacy, the history of books, the Councils of the Church and the inventors of the alphabet *(on the pillars)*. It contains 17C cupboards painted in the 19C.

The Vatican Library is followed by the Pauline Rooms, created by Paul V (1605-21). Next come the Alexandrine room, created by Alexander VIII (1690), and the **Clementine Gallery**, commissioned by Clement XII. Next is the **Profane Museum** which was founded in 1767 by Clement XIII (Etruscan, Roman and Medieval artefacts).

★★★Pinacoteca (Picture Gallery) ⊙

Italian Primitives (I) – The **Last Judgement** (**1**) painted on wood in 12C is an excellent painting of the Roman School and is very similar to Byzantine art.

Giotto and his School (II) – The **Stefaneschi Triptych** (**2**) is named after the Cardinal who commissioned it and was executed by Giotto, no doubt with the assistance of his pupils, in 1315. It was intended originally for the high altar of Constantine's basilica.

Florentines' School: Fra Angelico and his pupil Benozzo Gozzoli, Filippo Lippi (III) – These artists are among the great 15C painters. Fra Angelico's (1400-55) slightly old-fashioned style, which links him to the Middle Ages, nonetheless expresses his deep religious feeling, as the small painting of the **Virgin and Child with saints and angels** (**3**) demonstrates; the two **scenes from the Life of St Nicholas of Bari** (**4**) come from an altarpiece predella. The **Coronation of the Virgin** (**5**) is by Filippo Lippi (1406-69) and **St Thomas receiving the Virgin's girdle** (**6**) is by Benozzo Gozzoli (1420-97).

Melozzo da Forlì (1438-94) (IV) – The graceful **Musical Angels** (**7**) with their bright colours, elegant curls and delicate features are remarkable. They are fragments of a fresco depicting the Ascension of Christ painted on the apse ceiling of the Basilica of the Holy Apostles (Santi Apostoli). The fresco (transferred to canvas) of **Sixtus IV and Platina the Librarian** (**8**) adorned the Pope's library. The cardinal is a portrait of Sixtus IV's nephew Giuliano della Rovere, later Julius II.

Polyptychs (VI) – The *Virgin and Child* (**9**) is by **Carlo Crivelli** (1430-93), a Venetian. While the Florentines were experimenting with line, the Venetians were taking an interest in colour. In addition Crivelli had a marked taste for gold decoration (very beautiful painted fabrics).

15C Umbrian School (VII) – The *Virgin and Child* (**10**) by **Perugino** and the *Coronation of the Virgin* (**11**) by **Pinturicchio** illustrate the clear and poetic style of the Umbrian artists.

★★★Room VIII: Raphael (1483-1520)

– The artistic development of the painter of the *Stanze* is illustrated by three works. The **Coronation of the Virgin** (**12**), painted in 1503 has a youthful freshness and shows the influence of Perugino. The **Madonna of Foligno** (**13**) was painted in 1511-12 while Raphael was in Rome at the height of his glory; the fine portrait of Sigismondo dei Conti, on his knees, which dominates the picture, the exquisite pose of the Virgin and the luminosity surrounding her are the work of a master. The beautiful **Transfiguration** (**14**), with its dramatic contrasts in chiaroscuro, was intended for Narbonne Cathedral in France and was completed by Raphael shortly before he died in 1520.

Room IX – With his **St Jerome**★★ (**15**) Leonardo da Vinci (1452-1519) shows his mastery of anatomy, expression and light. The picture was put together after being discovered in two pieces, one in an antique shop and the other at a shoemaker's.

The **Pietà** (**16**) by the Venetian **Giovanni Bellini** (1429-*c*1516) combines accurate drawing and deep inspiration with fine tonality.

Room X – In his **Madonna of San Nicola dei Frari** (**17**) Titian uses the marvellous colours of the Venetian painters. The

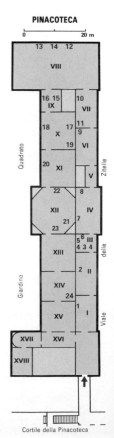

PINACOTECA

0   20 m

Cortile della Pinacoteca

Coronation of the Virgin (18), by Giulio Romano *(upper part)* and Francesco Penni *(lower part)*, two artists who often finished off Raphael's work, shows the Mannerist style.

In Veronese's **Sant'Elena (19)** the saint is depicted in an unusual position, her hand supporting her head.

Mannerists (XI) – The works include *Rest on the Flight into Egypt* (**20**) by **Frederico Barocci** (1528-1612), as delicate and luminous as a pastel.

Caravaggio and his followers (XII) – The **Descent from the Cross★★ (21)** by **Caravaggio** (1573-1610) clearly expresses the painter's reaction to Mannerist sentimentality. His characters, even in the most religious scenes, are drawn from life. The firmness of his line and the way the light falls further emphasise his realism (note how Nicodemus and St John hold the body of the dead Christ). Mary Magdalen, her head bowed, is a truly remarkable figure. Caravaggio had a great influence on the French painter **Valentin** (1594-1632) – *Martyrdom of St Processus and St Martinian* (**22**). **Guido Reni** (1575-1642) was also inspired – **Crucifixion of St Peter (23)**.

Rooms XIII-XIV – These rooms contain works from the 17C and 18C, particularly by **Pietro da Cortona**, the great Baroque artist. Note the portrait of Clement IX (**24**) by Carlo Maratta (1625-1713). There is also a model for St Peter's dome.

Room XV – Sir Thomas Lawrence's portrait of George IV of England was a gift from the King to Pius VII.

★Musei Gregoriano Profano e Cristiano

A fine modern building begun in 1963 houses the **Profane** and **Christian museums** which were opened to the public in 1970. They contain the collections comprising the museum of Antique art assembled by Gregory XVI (1831-46) and the museum of Christian art founded in 1854 by Pius IX, formerly kept in the Lateran Palace.

Gregorian Profane Museum

It is divided into four sections: copies of sculpture from the Imperial period (1C BC to 3C AD); 1C and 2C Roman sculpture; sarcophagi; 2C and 3C Roman sculpture. The modern materials – metal, concrete and wood – provide an ideal setting for the exhibits which can be viewed from all sides.

Imperial period copies – The **basalt head** (**1**) is a fine copy of a Greek original linked to the art of Polyclitus (5C BC). **Sophocles** (**2**), the Athenian tragic poet, is represented by a large statue of noble mien with a headband to show he is a priest of

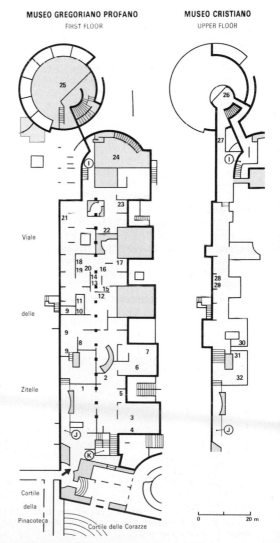

MUSEO GREGORIANO PROFANO
FIRST FLOOR

MUSEO CRISTIANO
UPPER FLOOR

Amynos, a healer. The beautiful **mosaic** (**3**) on the ground is decorated with fantastic designs. There are several **herms** (**4**), their head and shoulders springing from a pillar. The **relief of Medea and the daughters of Pelias** (**5**) is a 1C BC Roman copy of a late 5C BC Greek original; despite being damaged it illustrates the story of the deception of Pelias' daughters by Medea with great elegance. There is a **headless statue** (**6**), probably inspired by a 5C original, and also the **"Chiaramonti" Niobe** (**7**), a copy of a statue which was part of a group representing the death of Niobe and her daughters.

Roman sculpture (1 and early 2C) – The low relief of the **Vicomagistrates' altar** (**8**) is a particularly fine 1C sculpture which probably decorated the lower part of an altar. It shows a procession of people leading animals to the temple for the sacrifice; following the four Vicomagistrates (street magistrats) are the assistants bearing statues of the Lares (the gods of the household and the highways). The narrative style of the sculpture and its naturalism make it a truly Roman work.

There is a fine collection of **urns and funerary altars** (**9**), dating from the 1C, which come from the Via Appia in particular, and also the **base of a column** (**10**) from the Basilica Julia in the Roman Forum, a fine example of Roman decorative art.

Among the major pieces in the section are the **Cancelleria Relief★**, so called because they were discovered beneath the Palazzo Cancelleria in the Campus Martius. Classical in style, they illustrate two events in the life of the Emperor Vespasian and his son Domitian. One sculpture (**11**) shows Vespasian's arrival in Rome after his election to the Imperial throne; the Emperor makes a noble figure in his toga on the right. His son Domitian greets him. Between them is the genius of the Roman people, bearing the horn of plenty, with one foot resting on a milestone, showing that the meeting is taking place at the limit of the *pomerium* (the sacred boundary of Rome). The other sculpture (**12**) shows Domitian's departure on a campaign. When the Senate banned memorials of Domitian, his head was replaced by that of his successor, Nerva.

The **Haterii tomb sculptures** are the remains of a family tomb from the end of the 1C. They represent the popular taste in Roman art which developed parallel with the official style (realism and detailed precision to the detriment of the overall effect). The family concerned was probably that of Haterius Tychicus, constructor of public buildings; two low reliefs in particular allude to the building trade: one (**13**) represents the monuments of Ancient Rome (the unfinished Colosseum is easily recognisable); the other (**14**) shows a huge funerary monument in the form of a temple; appearing above the building are the scenes which took place inside the tomb; the detailed treatment lacks proportion: to the left of the scenes the sculptor has placed a crane. The portraits are particularly realistic: a woman in a recess with wavy hair (**15**) is executed with great skill; likewise the little pillar wreathed in finely modelled roses (**16**) is exquisite.

There are several fine **decorative sculptures**: two pillars ornamented with foliated scrolls (**17**) and fragments of 2C friezes (**18, 19, 20**).

Sarcophagi – Many are illustrated with mythical subjects. The fragment of the "philosopher's" sarcophagus (**21**) shows a group of scholars: the faces are so realistic that they seem like portraits; they date from about AD 270.

Roman sculpture (2 and 3C) – The **porphyry torso** (**22**) probably belonged to an Imperial statue (2C). The statue of a **young woman arrayed like Omphale** (**23**) (Queen of Lydia who assumed Hercules' attributes) is typical of the 3C style which aimed at immortalising the subject in such a disguise.

★**Mosaics from the Baths of Caracalla** – *Visible from the Christian Museum*. They (**24** and **25**) date from the 3C and show the figures of athletes, gladiators and their trainers; their brutality is evidence of the Roman taste for violent spectacles.

Christian Museum *(up Staircase I)*

Statue of the Good Shepherd (**26**) – It is heavily restored and probably dates from the 3C. The Christian artist has taken the pagan image of a shepherd offering his finest animal to the gods or of Hermes leading the dead into the next world but here the figure is suffused with the meaning of the new religion and illustrates the parable of the lost sheep saved by the good shepherd: "When he hath found it, he layeth it on his shoulders, rejoicing."

Sarcophagi – The Christian sarcophagi are similar to the pagan ones in their decoration: figures in relief in a continuous band; the sides divided into panels separated by arcades; strigils and central medallion.

The first Christian artists decorated the sarcophagi with garlands, baskets and putti, using the pagan motifs to which they added the symbolic themes of sheep – Christ's flock, vine branches – symbol of union with God through the Eucharist, etc. From the middle of the 3C scenes and figures were added to the symbols, as for example on the **side of a sarcophagus found in St Lawrence Without the Walls** (**27**) which shows Christ and the Apostles as well as sheep representing the Christian flock.

In the 4C new subjects appear: on a **covered sarcophagus found in St Calixtus' Catacombs** (**28**) and also on a **sarcophagus with two bands of decoration** (**29**) are two scenes often shown together: Peter's arrest and Moses striking water from the rock *(on the right-hand side of the former and in the lower section of the latter).*

On a 4C **sarcophagus found in St Lawrence Without the Walls** (**30**) are various scenes including: Adam and Eve receiving a grain of wheat and a sheep from God *(upper section left of the central medallion)*, symbols of the labour to which they were condemned after their fall from grace.

On another 4C **sarcophagus from St Paul Without the Walls** (**31**) the cross is placed in the centre as a sign of triumph while the Christian monogram is surrounded with a crown of laurel.

Note also the **moulding of the sarcophagus of Junius Bassus** (**32**).

Museo missionario-etnologico (Missionary-Ethnological Museum) ⊘
Take stairs **Ⓚ**.

It was founded in 1927 by Pius XI and first housed in the Lateran Palace but moved into ultra-modern premises in the Vatican during Paul VI's reign.

It comprises a large collection of articles illustrating the great world religions (Buddhism, Hinduism, Islam) and Christian artefacts designed in the ethnic style of the local artists from every continent except Europe.

Museo delle Carrozze (Carriage Museum) ⊘
Take stair **Ⓛ**.

The museum, which was opened in 1973 in the reign of Paul VI in an underground chamber, displays popes' and cardinals' carriages and the first papal motor vehicle.

Vatican Gardens

*VATICAN CITY AND GARDENS ⊘

The Bell Arch *(Arco delle Campane)* (**R**) leads into the Piazza dei Protomartiri Romani, which is situated more or less in the centre of the Circus of Caligula and Nero where many early Christians were martyred; a black stone with a white border set in the ground marks the former site of the obelisk which is now in St Peter's Square. On the left is the German and Dutch burial ground (**S**) which, according to a pious legend, consists of earth brought from Jerusalem. Next, on the left, comes the church dedicated to St Stephen where Charlemagne spent the night before being crowned in 800. After the **Mosaic School** *(Scuola del Mosaico)* are the various buildings from which the Vatican State is administered. There are fine views of the Leonine City. The tour finishes with a view of the dome of St Peter's, designed by Michelangelo, rising majestically above the magnificent **gardens★★★**; the fountains and statues are gifts from various countries. Pius IV's 'Casina' is a charming 16C building decorated with paintings and stucco work.

Neighbouring sights are described in the following chapters: CASTEL SANT'ANGELO; GIANICOLO.

VIA VENETO ★

Tour 2 ½ hours

A good idea...

The tiny shop **Florilegio** at 32 Via Quattro Fontane makes up the most marvellous floral bouquets and arrangements with paper flowers. What better way to convey a lasting thank-you.

Porta Pinciana – The gateway in the wall which Aurelian built around Rome in the 3C was fortified in the 6C by Belisarius, the Emperor Justinian's great general, who strove to regain the Western territories of the Roman Empire. He captured Rome in 537 and expelled the Ostrogoths and Pope Silverius.

Via Vittorio Veneto – This street, which was created after 1879, bears the name of the commune of the Veneto which in 1866 adopted the name of King Victor Emmanuel II (Vittorio Emanuele) and in 1918 was the scene of the battle in which the Austro-Hungarian army was beaten by Italian troops. The Via Veneto, as it is often called, runs through the heart of the beautiful **Ludovisi district**, which was divided into building lots in 1883 when Prince Ludovisi sold up his magnificent 17C property. Its luxury hotels, boutiques and elegant cafés have made it a meeting-place for the smart set – rich tourists and those who like the sophisticated life.

Turn right into Via Lazio, left into Via Aurora and right again into Via Lombardia.

★**Casino dell'Aurora** ⊘ – The Aurora Casino is the only extant building of the Ludovisi estate. Just as Cardinal Scipione Borghese, Paul V's nephew, had his casino decorated by Guido Reni, so Cardinal Ludovico Ludovisi, Gregory XV's nephew, invited Guercino to decorate his. Both artists, who were pupils of the Carracci, chose the subject of Aurora.

Return along Via Lombardia and turn right into Via Vittorio Veneto.

Palazzo Margherita – It was designed by G Koch in 1886 and was the residence of Margaret of Savoy, King Humbert I's wife; it is now the Embassy of the United States of America.

Santa Maria della Concezione
⊘ – The church was built in 1624 in the austere style imposed by the Counter-Reformation. In the pavement at the entrance to the chancel lies the tombstone of Cardinal Antonio Barberini, who founded the church, with the inscription *Hic jacet pulvis, cinis et nihil* (Here lie dust, ashes and nothing).
Below the church *(access on the right of the front steps)* there is a most unusual gallery curiously 'decorated' with the bones and skulls of Capuchin friars.

Fontana delle Api – The fountain, which incorporates the **bees** *(api)* from the Barberini coat of arms, is the work of Bernini (1644).

Turn into Piazza Barberini.

★**Fontana del Tritone** – Bernini's **Triton Fountain** (*c*1642) is a happy example of Roman Baroque. The composition – four dolphins supporting an open scallop shell in which sits a triton blowing into a conch – demonstrates the powerful and lively qualities of his art. The Barberini bees on the coat of arms recall that a Barberini, Urban VIII, was then Pope.

S. Grandadam/EXPLORER

Triton Fountain in Piazza Barberini

★★PALAZZO BARBERINI (BARBERINI PALACE)

Entrance no 13 Via delle Quattro Fontane

In 1623 Cardinal Maffeo Barberini became Pope Urban VIII and decided to build a Baroque palace to house his family. Work began in 1627 under Carlo Maderno; the palace was completed from 1629 to 1633 by Borromini and Bernini.

The main façade, which is framed by two wings, in the style of a Roman country villa, is the work of Bernini. By super-imposing three tiers of attached columns and shallow pilasters to frame two floors of huge windows (slightly splayed on the upper storey) over an open porch at ground level, he created a sense of the dignity and solemnity appropriate to the Barberini family.

Borromini has left his mark in the two small curiously pedimented upper windows in the intermediate sections linking the wings to the central block of the palace.

The windows in the rear façade were decorated by Borromini who also designed the oval spiral staircase at the right-hand *(south)* end of the front porch.

★★**Gallery Nazionale d'Arte Antica** ⊘ – The monumental staircase *(left end of the porch)* was designed by Bernini. The first floor is devoted to works from the 13C to 16C.

Restoration in progress in part of the second floor.

Room I – *Virgin and Child* (**1**) by the master of the **Palazzo Venezia** from the elegant drawing in which can be seen the influence of the great 14C Sienese painter Simone Martini. A *Crucifix* (**2**) by Bonaventura **Berlinghieri** who came from Lombardy, died in 1243 and painted several similar works with the detailed application of a calligrapher.

VILLA BORGHESE-VILLA GIULIA

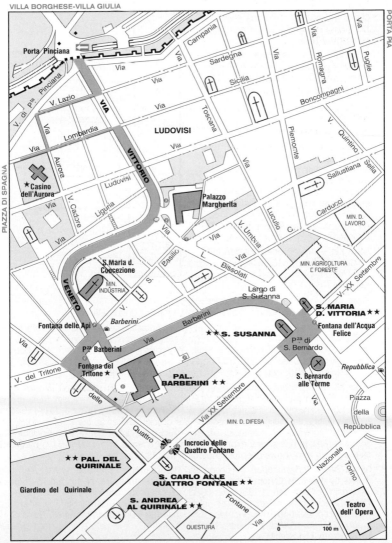

FONTANA DI TREVI-QUIRINALE

Room II – *Virgin and Child* (**3**) and *Annunciation* (**4**) by **Filippo Lippi** (1437). The architectural elements such as windows and columns which Lippi introduced into his paintings were a novelty in early Italian art.

Room III – *Adoring Angels* (**5**), a beautiful painting by **Gentile da Fabriano**; the *Magdalen* (**6**) by **Piero di Cosimo**.

Room IV – *Virgin and Child with Saints* (**7**) and *St Sebastian* (**8**) by **Antoniazzo Romano**, chief exponent of the firm style being used in Latium at the end of the 15C; *St Nicolò da Tolentino* (**9**) by **Perugino**.

Room V – *The Holy Family* (**10**) by **Andrea del Sarto**.

Room VI – *La Fornarina*★★★ (**11**) by **Raphael** is a painting of his beautiful mistress. The authorship of this work, painted during the year Raphael died, was the subject of much argument. It was attributed to a pupil of Raphael, then to Sebastiano del Piombo. Next to it are three paintings by **Sodoma** (1477-1549): *The Three Fates* (**12**), *The Rape of the Sabines* (**13**) and *The Mystical Marriage of St Catherine* (**14**). Sodoma was a great admirer of Raphael's flowing lines and was his friend and collaborator in Rome. The *Portrait of Stefano Colonna* (**15**) (1546) is by **Bronzino** and is typical of this refined artist and portrait painter who endeavoured to present his subjects in a suitably noble pose rather than bring out their more ordinary characteristics.

Room VII – The fine ceiling by Andrea Sacchi shows *Divine Wisdom*. The room also contains *Christ and the Woman taken in Adultery* (**16**) by **Tintoretto** and two small paintings by **El Greco**: *Nativity* (**17**) and *the Baptism of Christ* (**18**), and a *Venus and Adonis* (**19**) by **Titian**.

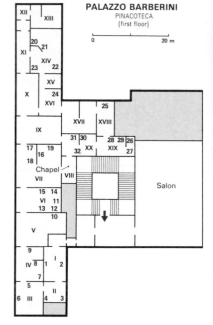

PALAZZO BARBERINI
PINACOTECA
(first floor)

0   20 m

Room XIV – The **Narcissus**★ (**20**) and *Judith and Holofernes* (**21**) illustrate the novel style of **Caravaggio** (1573-1610) who was a contemporary of Guido Reni and Guercino. Dispensing with background, he painted his figures in close-up to stress a detail (Narcissus' knee). Although Caravaggio's unruly way of living prevented him from having any pupils, his powerful style had considerable influence on the painters of his day as is evident from *St Gregory* (**22**) with his splendid red cloak by **Saraceni** and *Christ Turning the Money-changers out of the Temple* (**23**) by **Valentin de Boulogne**.

Room XVI – Among the rare foreign artists influenced by Caravaggio was the Flemish painter, van Honthorst (**24**).

Room XVIII – The **Portrait of Beatrice Cenci**★ (**25**) by **Guido Reni** (1575-1642) is a work of great dellicacy.

Room XIX – This room is devoted to Baroque painters. The *Portrait of Bernini*★ (**26**) by **Baciccia** (1639-1709) is one of the rare surviving portraits by this artist who was famous mainly for his decorative skill. Two other Baroque masters are **Pietro da Cortona** with his *Guardian Angel* (**27**) and **G L Bernini** with his two paintings *David with the Head of Goliath* (**28**) and the *Portrait of Urban VIII* (**29**).

Room XX – This room displays several anamorphoses (**30**) (distorted images to be viewed from a particular angle or in a curved mirror so as to regain their proper shape); they are by 17C French painters. The **Portrait of Henry VIII**★★★ (**31**) (1540) is by **Hans Holbein the Younger,** who became the official painter at the English court and produced portraits of members of the court with impartiality and psychological analysis. Next to it is a very expressive **Portrait of Erasmus**★★★ (**32**) (1517) by **Quentin Metsys** which also shows deep psychological insight into this subject.

★★★**Central Salon** – *Restoration in progress*. The ceiling is the best work ever produced by **Pietro da Cortona** who showed the true measure of his talent here. It was painted between 1633 and 1639 to celebrate the glory of the Barberini family whose coat of arms (bees in a crown of laurel) is carried by allegorical figures representing the Virtues. On the left Divine Providence, holding a sceptre, reigns from the clouds. Note how skilfully the painter has used *grisaille* to separate the scenes.

The walls of the salon are hung with cartoons by Baroque painters (Andrea Sacchi, Lanfranco, Bernini) for the mosaics for one of the small cupolas in St Peter's in the Vatican and for tapestries produced in the Barberini factory (17C).

Second floor – Here are displayed 17C and 18C paintings. These include studies by **Andrea Pozzo** commissioned for churches or palaces in Rome; paintings by **Angelika Kauffmann** (1741-1807) who was a friend of Goethe, and portraits by **Pompeo Batoni** (1708-87). The melodramatic quality of **Alessandro Magnasco** (1667-1749), known as **Il Lissandrino**, is exemplified by *Demons tempting Monks and Hermits at Prayer.*

The corner room with its elegant white marble fireplace is decorated with neo-Classical grisaille paintings.

The landscapes or *vedute* in Italian (literally meaning view or vista) date from an era when foreign travellers collected topographical pictures to take home: these include works by the Dutch painter **Gaspar Van Wittel** (1653-1736) known as Vanvitelli, the Frenchman **Hubert Robert** (1733-1808) who excelled at depicting ruins, **Luca Carlevarijs** (1665-1731) who painted views of Venice, the Venetians **Canaletto** (1697-1768) and **Francesco Guardi** (1712-1793)...

On the second floor of the south wing of the palazzo is a suite of seven low-ceilinged rooms with an echo – painted at the end of the 18C in a neo-Baroque style.

Return to Piazza Barberini in order to turn down Via Barberini.

★★SANTA SUSANNA ⊙

A Christian sanctuary was probably established here in the 4C in the house of Pope Caius where St Susanna was thought to have been martyred. Rebuilt by Leo III in the 9C and restored at the end of the 15C by Sixtus IV, the church assumed its present appearance in the late 16C.

★★Façade – This beautifully proportioned masterpiece was designed by Carlo Maderno and finished in 1603. It is derived from the Counter-Reformation style typified by the façade of the Gesù Church but the use of semi-engaged columns and the effect of perspective, created by recesses and pediments which relieve the austerity, give it an individual distinction.

The two storeys are harmoniously linked by the repetition of the two super-imposed pediments and the elegant lateral scrolls.

Interior – The decoration is typical of the Roman Mannerist style (late 15C): the walls of the nave are covered with paintings made to look like tapestries and executed by Baldassarre Croce (1558-1628); they illustrate the biblical story of Susanna. The scenes in the chancel depict the history of St Susanna and of other martyrs whose relics are kept in the church; they were painted by Cesare Nebbia (1536-1614) and Paris Nogari (1558-1628). The wreathed columns framing the paintings in the nave were probably added in the 17C after Bernini had designed the baldaquin in St Peter's (1624).

★★SANTA MARIA DELLA VITTORIA ⊙

Carlo Maderno was commissioned to design the church in 1608. The original dedication was to St Paul but this was changed in 1622 to St Mary of the Victory after an image of the Virgin, whose miraculous intervention had delivered the Battle of the White Mountain near Prague (1620) to the Catholics, had been carried to the church with great pomp.

Façade – Although the façade was built some 20 years after that of Santa Susanna, between 1624 and 1626, it is not so daring; with its flat pilasters in place of columns, it is closer to the Counter-Reformation style. It was designed by Giovanni Battista Soria for Cardinal Scipione Borghese.

★★★Interior – Maderno's plan is based on the Gesù Church; a nave, a broad shallow transept and a dome over the crossing. The simple lines of the design enhance the elegant decoration of the cornice; during the 17C a very rich Baroque décor was applied throughout; the vault, originally white and coffered, and the dome were painted with *trompe-l'œil* frescoes of the Virgin triumphing against heresy and entering into Heaven; the walls were faced with multicoloured marble, their warm tones mingling with the gilded stucco and the white cherubs. The decoration of the organ is by one of Bernini's pupils.

The apse was entirely rebuilt after being destroyed in 1833 by a fire in which the sacred image of the Virgin disappeared.

The Baroque decoration culminates in the **Cornaro Chapel** *(left transept)* which was designed by **Bernini** in 1652 to resemble a theatre: eight members of the Cornaro family, as if in boxes at the theatre, gaze at the **Ecstasy of St Theresa of Avila★★★**. Marble has never been made to look so supple nor to express so accurately the texture of rough cloth (the Carmelite habit), the light veiling in the angel's garment and the delicacy of the flesh. This presentation of divine love must be appreciated in conjunction with St Theresa's own description of her ecstasy when God sent his seraph to pierce her heart with an arrow: "The pain was so sharp that I cried aloud but at the same time I experienced such delight that I wished it would last for ever."

The chapel in the right transept was created late in the 17C to complement the Cornaro Chapel.

The paintings in the chapels include the *Life of St Francis* by Domenichino *(2nd chapel on the right)* and the *Trinity* by Guercino *(3rd chapel on the left)*.

ADDITIONAL SIGHTS

Fontana dell'Acqua Felice – This huge fountain was designed in 1587 by Domenico Fontana. It is supplied by an aqueduct built by Sixtus V which runs from near Colonna on the Via Casilina and bears the Pope's Christian name: Felice Peretti.

It is dominated by the colossal statue of Moses; it was sculpted by Prospero Bresciano who was no doubt inspired by Michelangelo's *Moses;* his disappointment was so great when he saw the finished work that he died.

San Bernardo alle Terme – St Bernard's Church was created late in the 16C in a rotunda, formerly the southwest corner of Diocletian's baths. The handsome coffered dome, similar to the one in the Pantheon, lends dignity to the interior.

Neighbouring sights are described in the following chapters: FONTANA DI TREVI – QUIRINALE; PIAZZA DI SPAGNA; PORTA PIA; VILLA BORGHESE – VILLA GIULIA.

For information on the main historical events consult the table and notes in the **Introduction**

VILLA BORGHESE – VILLA GIULIA★★

This walk explores Rome's largest public park, which borders on the elegant Parioli district and contains two museums, an art gallery and various national academies of art – notably the **British Academy** (Scuola Britannica d'Arte) for students taking courses in history, the arts and classics – in a setting of lakes and lawns and groves of trees.

When Cardinal Camillo Borghese acceded to the papal throne in 1605 he made generous gifts to his family. To his nephew Scipione Caffarelli he gave his name. On becoming a cardinal Scipione Borghese started to build a private house, a little palace *(palazzina)* set in magnificent gardens. Two men were employed on the plans: the architect Vasanzio and the landscape gardener Domenico Savino da Montepulciano.

The section of the Aurelian Wall *(Mura Aureliane)* from the Porta del Popolo to the Porta Pinciana, which marks the southwest boundary of the Villa Borghese, follows such an irregular line that the Romans call it the crooked wall **(Muro Torto)** and tell many legends about it. When the Goths led by Witigis besieged Rome in the 6C, they failed to take advantage of a breach in the Muro Torto and the Romans concluded that the area must be protected by St Peter. Imagination ran riot in the Middle Ages when the vicinity was used as a cemetery where people denied a Christian burial were interred.

TOUR $\frac{1}{2}$ *day including visits to the museums*

Via Flaminia – This modern artery follows the line of the ancient Flaminian Way which was constructed in 220 BC by the Consul Flaminius who died in the battle of Lake Trasimene against Hannibal. It ran almost straight from the city centre along Via del Corso to Rimini on the Adriatic (314km - 195 miles).

Films for little people...

Merry-go-rounds, a miniature train and pony rides provide recreation for small children in the park itself: an alternative on rainy days is the **Cinema dei Piccoli** *(Viale della Pineta 15)* nearby which screens Disney films and cartoons between 3pm and 8pm for its young audience.

Palazzina di Pio IV – The little palace was built by Pius IV (1559-65) who offered it to his nephew Cardinal Charles Borromeo. The slightly concave façade exhibits the mannered style typical of late Renaissance works. Since 1929 the building has housed the Italian Government Embassy to the Holy See.

Sant'Andrea – St Andrew's Church was built in the 16C by Vignola for Julius III. It is an unusual little building, with a clear-cut silhouette, stressed by heavy dentilated cornices, an elliptical dome resting on a solid base and plain brick walls.

★★★MUSEO NAZIONALE DI VILLA GIULIA
(VILLA GIULIA NATIONAL MUSEUM)

The museum is devoted to **Etruscan civilization.** The exceptional interest of the collection is enhanced by its charming situation in Julius III's country villa.

★**Villa Giulia** – Julius III's reign (1550-55) was contemporary with the Council of Trent but the Pope did not therefore lose his taste for the cultivated life of a Renaissance prince. In 1551 he invited Vignola to design a summer villa for him. The plain and sober façade is typical of Vignola who also studied and wrote about architectural theory. The first courtyard is framed by a semicircular portico with tunnel vaulting.

Beyond in the main courtyard is a charming Mannerist construction designed by Bartolomeo Ammannati who collaborated on the Villa Giulia from 1552: a little loggia, perfectly proportioned, opens on to horse-shoe steps descending to a *nymphaeum* adorned with caryatids, rockeries and false grottoes. Several pieces of Roman sculpture are on display.

In the past the public was permitted to enjoy the tranquillity of this villa and to gather the fruit and flowers. When the poet Joachim du Bellay was visiting Rome as secretary to his cousin the French ambassador Jean du Bellay, he disapproved severely of the Pope for leading a life of pleasure to the detriment of affairs of state. When Julius III raised a young man of 17, who led a troop of performing monkeys, to be a Cardinal, du Bellay did not omit to poke fun at the new Jupiter and his Ganymede.

The courtyard is laid out in pleasant gardens bordered by the modern galleries of the museum. To the right of the *nymphaeum* an Etruscan temple has been reconstructed.

Etruscans – No one knows where they originated but they arrived in the Italian peninsula towards the end of the 8C BC and settled between the Arno and the Tiber (an area covering Tuscany and parts of Umbria and Latium). More advanced than their neighbours, they governed Rome from the end of the 7C BC and established a veritable 'empire' stretching from Corsica to the shores of the Adriatic and from Capua to Bologna. Decline set in at the end of the 6C BC and Rome, now free of their domination, began to expand and attacked their cities; in the 1C BC the Etruscans became Roman citizens.

Traces of Etruscan civilization have mostly disappeared; some however have survived in their tombs which contained objects, once the property of the dead person, from which it is possible to deduce the character of their society. Until the 18C Etruscan art was thought to be a derivative of Greek art without any aesthetic value. The re-evaluation of the canons of Greek art, the elegant stylization of Etruscan works and their expressive quality have aroused a very lively interest in Etruscan art which has an unusual affinity with modern forms.

Ground Floor

Italic civilizations – *Room 2.* The Italic civilizations at the time of the Etruscans' appearance are represented by funeral urns shaped like huts, such as the Latins built, and clay urns characteristic of the Villanovan civilization, which is named after the village of Villanova near Bologna and developed around the year 1000 BC in the Po valley, Tuscany and the north of Latium where the Etruscans later settled.

Etruscan tomb – *Beneath room 5.* This is a reconstruction of a tomb dating from the 6C BC, with two funeral chambers, similar to the tomb found in the necropolis at Cerveteri to the northwest of Rome.

Bisenzio Tombs – *Room 6.* Among the objects found in the tombs in this city are two small pieces of bronze (**1**) which illustrate early Etruscan art (late 8C to early 7C BC): a miniature chariot and a covered vessel decorated with figures in the round. These objects were used for domestic decoration before being buried beside their owners.

★★★**Veii (Veio) Sculptures** – *Room 7.* The statue of a goddess with a child (**2**), which probably represents Apollo and his mother Leto, and the statue of Apollo (**3**) were sculpted at the end of the 6C BC when Etruscan art was at its zenith. Set up as they were originally on the roof ridge of a temple, they give an idea of how they would have looked silhouetted against the sky. They are made of terracotta and are strikingly realistic and animated.

The other sculptures include a fine head of Hermes (**4**) and several antefixae in the shape of Gorgon heads which masked the ends of the roof beams and the painted pediments (**5**). These sculptures all come from the same temple and may be the work of Vulca, the only Etruscan sculptor known by name; his reputation was such that the King of Rome sent for him in 509 BC to do the statues for the Temple of Jupiter on the Capitol.

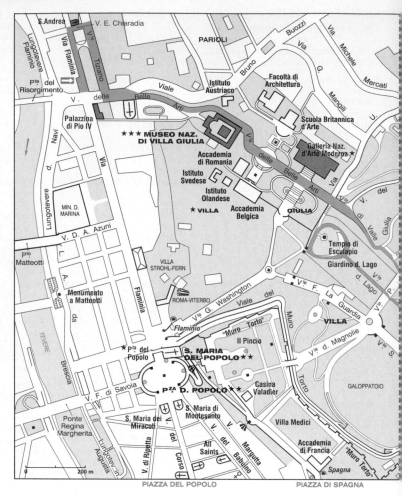

PIAZZA DEL POPOLO PIAZZA DI SPAGNA

★★★**Terracotta sarcophagus** (**6**) – *Room 9*. This is one of the masterpieces of Etruscan terracotta sculpture. It dates from the end of the 6C and comes from Cerveteri. It expresses the Etruscan belief in the afterlife. The husband and wife, reclining as if at a banquet, seem to be pursuing their life in the beyond. The artist has given the figures individual faces as if they were portraits.

First floor

The rooms in the north gallery of the museum are chiefly devoted to small **bronze objects**★, both useful and decorative. Bronze was one of the main Etruscan exports which contributed largely to their wealth; they fashioned it with great creative skill: rudimentary **clasps** dating from the 8C to 6C BC, **mirrors** very finely etched on the back with elegant scenes from family life or mythology, statuettes with astonishingly modern forms. The Etruscans' liking for bronze is explained by the rich copper deposits in Etruria and the island of Elba which belonged to them. The tin may have been imported from Great Britain or from the neighbouring islands.

Room 15 contains the famous **Chigi wine pitcher**★★ (**7**) which

Etruscan terracotta sarcophagus
(Museo Nazionale di Villa Giulia)

Da una foto Gab. Fot. Naz.

250

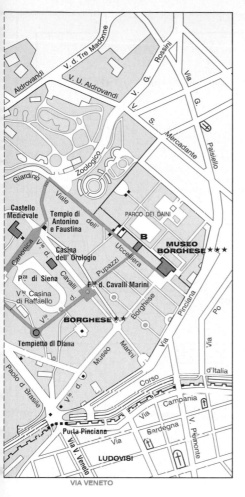

VIA VENETO

was found at Veii (Veio); it is one of the most beautiful examples of Greek art from the middle of the 7C BC. This is the proto-Corinthian period when the ceramics produced in Corinth, an important port on the sea routes to the East, were decorated with subjects treated in miniature in bands of delicate silhouettes. On the upper part two groups of warriors marching into battle against one another can still be seen. The incision work shows each detail clearly. The lower part is covered with figures and hunting scenes.

The same display cabinet shows two *bucchero* **vases★** dating from the 6C BC (*bucchero* is a sort of clay); the technique for producing this particular type of Etruscan ceramic, which is black, is not well understood.

One of the vases bears the Etruscan alphabet, the other a long inscription. The Etruscan alphabet has been deciphered but the meaning of their language is still unknown.

★ **Castellani Collection** – *Room 19. Reorganisation in progress.* The collection traces the evolution of Greek and Etruscan ceramics from the 8C BC to the Roman era. The Etruscans imported a considerable amount of Greek pottery, so much in fact that it could be said that the finest Greek vases have been found in Etruscan tombs.

The numbering in the text follows the order in which the exhibits are described; owing to the reorganisation, it does not correspond with the numbers on the display cabinets.

Case 2 – The elongated vases, which date from the 7C and 6C BC and come from eastern Greece, are imitations of Egyptian alabaster vessels. They were used by athletes for the perfumed oil with which they massaged their bodies; hence the flat lip.

There are several *bucchero* vases dating from the 7C and 6C BC.

Case 3 – The two water pitchers which date from between 530 and 520 belong to the Caere *hydriae*, so called because this type of water pot was found in a necropolis in Cerveteri (ancient Caere). The decoration of picturesque mythological scenes includes the Abduction of Europa by Zeus on one and on the other Hercules in his lion skin leading Cerberus against Eurystheus who is hiding in a large jar in terror.

Case 4 – Beautiful wine bowl made in Sparta in about 570 (*stile laconico*) and decorated with lotus flowers, an Eastern motif.

Cases 5 to 7 – From 540 to 530 BC Attic ceramic art was transformed by the change from black to red figure technique. Henceforth artists signed their work; two amphorae (Case 5) are signed by Nicosthenes. Case 8 contains two vases by Cleophrades; one is decorated with a very realistic painting of Hercules and the Nemean lion.

Cases 8 to 10 – From the beginning of the 5C to about 480 BC the red figure technique made Athens the capital of Attic vase painting. Articles produced during this period can be identified by the fact that the face is shown in profile while the eye is drawn full face. The quality of the work is remarkable; the detail within the outline of the body and garments is done with a fine brush.

Case 9 – Here the style is different. At the end of the 4C BC Hellenistic production experimented with other techniques, not only in Athens but in Magna Graecia (southern Italy) and Apulia: the artist has decorated the black varnished surface of the vases with flowers, fronds and elaborate decorations painted in white, yellow and dark red. The ceramics from Egnatia in Apulia belong to this period.

The raised decoration on some pieces is the result of a desire to produce a cheap imitation of metal vessels.

★**Castellani Collection of Jewellery** – *Closed during reorganisation.* This stunning collection of over a thousand pieces assembled by the Castellani family of jewellers consists of Antique jewellery dating from the 8C BC to 7C AD, of copies or of arrangements of Antique jewels.

Rooms I to IV – They contain Etruscan pieces found during the excavations at Cerveteri, Veio, Vulci etc.

At the far end of the semicircular corridor two flights of steps lead down to the first floor of the south wing of the museum.

Tombs from Capena and the Faliscan region – *Rooms 24 to 28.* A showcase (**8**) in **Room 25** contains a plate decorated with an elephant accompanied by its calf and guided by some archers perched on the ele-

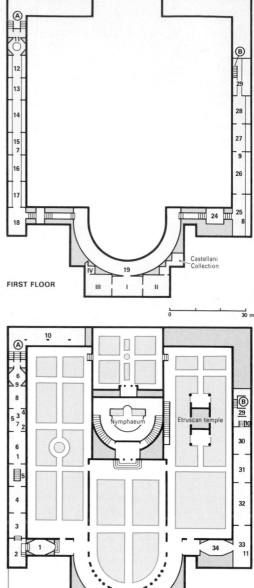

FIRST FLOOR

Castellani Collection

0   30 m

Nymphaeum

Etruscan temple

Portico

GROUND FLOOR

Piazzale   di   Villa   Giulia

MUSEO NAZIONALE DI VILLA GIULIA

phant's back in a sort of tower. This example of the ceramic art of Egnatia was found at Capena (an Etruscan town north of Rome) and dates from the early 3C BC. It is evidence of the impression made on the Etruscans by the elephants in Pyrrhus' army which appeared in 280BC during the war between Rome and Tarentum.

The exhibits in **Room 26** are drawn in particular from Falerii Veteres, the capital of the Faliscans (who were attached to the Confederation of Etruscan Cities); the site is now occupied by Città Castellana. The city was always in a state of rebellion and was finally destroyed in 241 BC.

The wine bowl (**9**) dates from about the middle of the 4C BC; it shows Aurora and Cephalus in their chariot and Peleus abducting Thetis; round the neck a deer and a bull are being attacked by griffins.

Ground floor

★Temples of Falerii Veteres – *Room 29, split level.* The architecture of these buildings is known to us from plans left by Vitruvius, a Roman architect and theorist (1C BC). The room contains partial reconstructions of pediments, examples of *antefixae* and *acroteria* (decorative elements, often in terracotta, which beginning in the 4C were placed on the peak and at either end of the pediments). The **bust of Apollo★** (**10**) shows late-Greek Classical influence.

'Barberini' and 'Bernardini' Tombs – *Room 33.* These rich tombs, situated near Palestrina (Ancient Praeneste) contained mid-7C BC articles, including carved **ivory pieces** – the result of trading relations between the Etruscans and Phoenicians.
The Etruscans were expert goldsmiths and worked in this metal from the 7C BC using the filigre technique; they perfected the granulation technique, splitting the gold into granules only a few tenths of a millimetre in diameter. The **jewellery** on display includes some beautiful brooches decorated with small figures in the round.

★★★Ficoroni Cists (**11**) – The cists were marriage coffers; they were also sometimes used for toilet or religious articles. Some magnificent examples were produced by the Etruscans between the 4C and 2C BC. Their manufacture was a speciality of Praeneste where the largest known example, called the Ficoroni cist after its owner, was found in the 18C. It stands on feline feet which are attached to the body by carved plaques; it is decorated with fine engravings of the Argonauts arriving among the Bebryces, with Pollux tying King Amycos to a tree. On the lid are hunting scenes and three statues in the round – the central figure is Dionysius.
Continue along Viale delle Belle Arti.

British School (**Scuola Britannica d'Arte**) – *Not open to the public.* It was founded in 1901 as a School of Archeology analogous to the one in Athens. The present Classical-style building was designed by **Sir Edwin Lutyens** in 1912 on the site of the British Pavilion at the International Exhibition of Fine Arts held in Rome in 1911. In this year the school was reconstituted with scholarships funded by the Royal Commissioners of the Great Exhibition of 1851. It has since been enlarged to provide studios and accommodation for the staff and 24 resident post-graduate students in various fields: painting, sculpture, art history, architecture, archeology (Classical and Medieval) and Classical studies (history and letters).
By the steps is a statue of the Danish sculptor Thorwaldsen (1770-1844), who worked in Rome from 1797 to 1838, receiving many honours and commissions.

★GALLERIA NAZIONALE D'ARTE MODERNA
(NATIONAL GALLERY OF MODERN ART) ◷

The 1911 building houses the national collection of 19C and 20C painting and sculpture; it also accommodates temporary exhibitions and a good library.
After passing through the barrier in the entrance hall, bear left.

Entrance corridor and Spadini room – These pieces in mixed media are by Galileo Chini, an exponent of the Italian Liberty style. Together they explore the subject of spring.
The museum is in the process of being reorganised. Some works are accommodated on a temporary basis, others are awaiting to be displayed.

Room I – The **Giacomo Balla** (1871-1958) donation. Of particular note are three of the four panels that make up the *Polittico dei Viventi (Polyptych of the Living): The Beggar* and *The Sick* verge on the monochrome while *The Mad Woman* is a riot of colour – illustrating the painter's detailed study of light.

Room II – Light, colour, movement and speed were the principal concerns of **Futurism**. By 1910, a year after Filippo Marinetti (1876-1944) had published its manifesto, the group's cohesion was apparent in the works of such artists as Balla *(Dynamic demonstration + velocity)* and **Umberto Boccioni** (1882-1916) *(Horse + rider + building).*

I Lampi by L Russolo

Galleria Nazionale d'Arte Moderna, Roma.ALINARI-GIRAUDON

253

Room III – Dedicated to **Giorgio de Chirico** (b1888): represented are some early works *(The Mother)*, his return to Classicism in the 1920s and examples of his metaphysical phase *(Hector and Andromache)*. Besides pieces by **Giorgio Morandi** (1890-1964) there is a Dada composition by Duchamp which characteristically desecrates the concept of Art.

Glass Room – Sculptures from the 1920s and 1930s including works by Arturo Martini and Marino Marini.

Central Room – Dedicated to Italian painting from the 1920s and 1930s, the distinctive feature of which was a return to the classical Italian tradition set by the early primitives and developed by masters before the Renaissance in the 15C. The principal protagonists being **Carrà** *(Horses)*, **De Chirico**, **Mario Sironi** *(Solitude)* – an artist associated with Fascism – **Guidi** *(Street Car)*, **Trombadori** *(Female Nude)*, **Felice Casorati** whose paintings *(Apples)* tend towards a palette of icy-cold colours, **Rosai** and Morandi, represented here by a selection of landscapes. The members of the so-called **Scuola Romana** or Roman School reacted against this archaic stylisation which they considered overtly optimistic. Instead they (Mafai, Scipione, Pirandello) developed a more nervously expressive and restless mannerism which was to influence the sculptors Mazzacurati, Mirko Basaldella and Leoncillo.

Room IV – **Filippo de Pisis** used Impressionist techniques to infuse his perception of reality with magic and mystery: in his *Quai de Tournelles* figures are reduced to patches of colour which, on occasion merge with their inanimate surroundings of houses, trees and street.

Room V – Painting in Rome during the 1930s and 1940s.

Room VI – **Abstraction** including **Kandinsky's** *Angular Line* and the **Turin Six** who aspired to a more European vision looking to new movements emerging in France notably at the hands of the Impressionists, Cézanne and Matisse.

Up the stairs.

Upper Room – This is dominated by the **Guttuso** gift *(Crucifixion)* and Italian works post-1945 which seek to interpret new figurative experiences in reaction to international avant-garde ideas. The reaction of Dorazio, Perilli, Accardi and Consagra (some of whose sculptures are on display in the garden) was to re-evaluate the actual creative process and the tendency of the artist to assume pre-eminence in his work. Others meanwhile such as Vedova, Birolli, Corpora, Leoncillo, Franchina explored a different approach towards figurative realism or pure abstraction. With the advent of the 1950s, the *Origine* group (Capogrossi, Colla) discarded more traditional techniques in favour of experimenting with different materials. By 1960 the break with tradition was completed: the artist **Fontana** was free to pierce, tear or split the canvas and use whatever materials he so desired.

The section to the left of the main entrance is dedicated to painting from the 19C and early 20C.

After Neo-Classical works by Canova *(Hercules and Lica)* come pieces from the Romantic Age and the likes of **Francesco Hayez** *(Sicilian Vespers)*. Paintings of the **Neapolitan School** by Toma *(Luisa Sanfelice in prison)*, Mancini and Morelli show an uncanny sympathy with the French landscape painters of the Barbizon School.

On the floor above are displayed the works from the late 19C and early 20C. Alongside works of Italian origin are works by foreign artists which exemplify new international trends: *The Three Ages* by **Klimt**, the *Portrait* by **Boldini** bears a striking resemblance to Manet and Cézanne, **Monet's** *Waterlilies*, Van Gogh's *Portrait of the Gardener* and *l'Arlésienne*, or Rodin's *Age of Bronze*.

The Pointillistes and later the Divisionists practised a special technique juxtaposing primary colours with their complementary colour to obtain a heightened, intense luminosity. The leading Italian exponent of this technique was **Giovanni Segantini** *(Mountain huts in the Snow, Alla Stanga)*.

★★WALK IN THE BORGHESE GARDENS

This walk wanders through a romantic landscape of lakes, trees and flower gardens set with imitation Antique sculpture.

Take Viale di Valle Giulia and then the first path on the right which leads to Viale Pietro Canonica; turn left.

The little **castle** *(castello medioevale)*, an imitation of a Medieval fortress, used to be the house and studio of the sculptor Pietro Canonica (1869-1959).

The **Temple of Antoninus and Faustina** was built in the late 18C.

Continue along the path as far as Viale dell'Uccelliera; turn right.

The building topped by a wrought-iron cage (**B**) is a 17C aviary. The Viale dell' Uccelliera (Aviary Avenue) leads to the Borghese Gallery *(see below)*.

The walk continues after the Borghese Gallery.

★★★MUSEO BORGHESE (BORGHESE MUSEUM AND GALLERY) ⊙

The museum is currently being refurbished. The picture collection (Quadreria) is presently on display in the Church of San Michele a Ripa (see TRASTEVERE).

This little palace *(palazzina)* was designed in 1613 by a Dutchman, Jan van Santen (called Vasanzio in Italian), for Cardinal Scipione Borghese. It is a delightful example of a rich prelate's house.

In the late 18C during the restoration of the gardens organised by Prince Marcantonio, the southwest façade (the present front entrance) was considered too ornate and stripped of some of its decoration and the steps were altered. Early this century the balustrade bounding the forecourt (but not the statues which were classed as works of art) was acquired by Lord Astor and removed to Cliveden.

Between 1801 and 1809 the Borghese collection was greatly depleted; Prince Camillo, Pauline Bonaparte's husband, sold over 200 sculptures which went to swell the collection in the Louvre in Paris. In 1891 the paintings which had hung in the Borghese Palace were moved to the *palazzina*; this led to the official distinction between the 'Borghese Museum' comprising the collection of sculpture on the ground floor and the 'Borghese Gallery' comprising the paintings on the first floor. Its silvan setting in the Borghese Gardens, its elegant late-18C décor and its outstanding collections make this museum-cum-gallery one of the most agreeable in Rome.

The **main hall** is decorated with Antique statues (originals and copies), paintings and reliefs and provides a good idea of neo-Classical taste. The pieces of 3C mosaic, set into the floor, were discovered on a property belonging to the Borghese family near Tusculum.

Ground floor

Room I – The **statue of Pauline Bonaparte★★★** as Venus by Canova dominates the room. Enthusiasm for the artist together with the celebrity of the model, the 'idol of high society', meant that the sculpture was accepted as a masterpiece.

Room VIII – This room is dedicated to works by Raphael and his follower Giulio Romano.

★★★**Opere del Bernini (Bernini Rooms)** – The artist was 21 when he sculpted **David** *(Room II)*. Whereas Michelangelo, working during the Renaissance, chose to present the calm and victorious hero, Bernini has captured the moment of most intense effort: the movement of the body in action and the facial expression make the statue a masterpiece of Baroque sculpture.

In his **Apollo and Daphne** *(Room III)* Bernini shows the metamorphosis of Daphne from nymph to laurel bush coinciding with Apollo's attempt to seize her and thus embodies the intentions of Baroque art in an incomparably graceful composition.

The **Rape of Proserpina** *(Room IV)* is one of Bernini's youthful works, probably done in collaboration with his father, Pietro Bernini. Although the statue of Pluto, God of the Underworld, shows traces of the Academic style, the supple modelling of Proserpina foreshadows Bernini's works of genius.The sumptuous room in which the sculpture is displayed is called the Emperors' Room owing to the 18 busts sculpted in porphyry and alabaster in the 17C.

The group of **Aeneas carrying Anchises** *(Room VI)*, in which the figures are rather stiff with set expressions, was for a long time attributed to Bernini alone but his father's collaboration is now recognised. **Truth**, holding a sun in her hand, is a fairly emphatic work which Bernini began in 1645; when he fell from grace on Innocent X's accession to the papal throne he intended to recommend himself with a representation of "Truth being unveiled by Time"; the second statue was never executed.

First floor

Closed for restoration (access through Room IV).

Room IX – The *Crucifixion with St Jerome and St Christopher* (**1**) by **Pinturicchio** (1454-1513) reflects the artist's liking for miniatures which characterised the art of the 15C Primitives. The *Portrait of a Man* (**2**) by **Raphael** (1483-1520), a work of admirable vigour, still shows signs of 15C art: full-face presentation, indistinguishable background. The portrait of a *Lady with a Unicorn* (**3**), spoiled by being changed into a St Catherine but restored in 1935, is a fine example of the nobility of Raphael's art: the delicacy of the necklace and pendant.

The attribution of the *Virgin and Child with St John and Angels* (**4**) to **Botticelli** is disputed; the painting is thought to be too sentimental.

In the *Virgin and Child with St John the Baptist* (**5**) by **Lorenzo di Credi** (1459-1537) and in the *Holy Family* (**6**) by **Fra Bartolomeo** (1475-1527) the influence of Leonardo da Vinci and the Renaissance is quite marked: in the delicacy of the Virgin's expression in the one and in the indistinct outline of the background landscape in the other.

The **Deposition★★★** (**7**) by **Raphael** was painted while the artist was still in Florence.

Room X – In his painting of the *Virgin and Child with St John the Baptist* (**8**) **Andrea del Sarto** (1486-1531) was influenced by Michelangelo's drawing and by Leonardo da Vinci's *sfumato* technique. *Venus* (**9**) by **Lucas Cranach** (1472-1553) is one of the rare works by a Northern artist in Cardinal Borghese's collection. The *Portrait of a Man* (**10**) by **Dürer** shows remarkable psychological insight.

Room XI – The *Holy Conversation (Virgin and Child with saints)* (**11**) and the *Portrait of a Man* (**12**) are fines examples of the very varied work of the Venetian **Lorenzo Lotto** (*c*1480-1556).
The *Holy Conversation* (**13**) by **Palma the Elder** (1480-1528) is remarkable for its colours and for the keenly observed portrait of the pious woman *(left side of the painting)*. *Tobias and the Angel* (**14**) by **Girolamo Savoldo** (1480-1548) presages Baroque painting in the powerful figures and the bold effects of light.

Room XIII – The panels of the door are painted with attractive 18C landscapes. The low relief **Crucifixion**★ (**15**) is by Guglielmo della Porta, modelled in wax on a slate base framed in ebony set with precious stones.

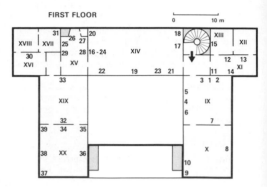

FIRST FLOOR

0   10 m

Room XIV – After the insipid Mannerist style, two currents brought about the transition to Baroque painting. In Bologna a style based on tradition developed around the Carracci which **Domenichino** (1581-1641) helped to propagate; his painting of **Diana the huntress**★★★ (**16**) demonstrates the Bologna expertise very well (the detail of the trees and the bird hit by arrows).

In contrast to the "teachers" in Bologna **Caravaggio** (1573-1610) drew his inspiration from nature. His figures sprang out from the canvas with dazzling effects of light and he brought about a veritable revolution in painting.

The **Madonna dei Palafrenieri**★★★ (**17**), showing the Virgin, Jesus and St Anne, had been intended for an altar in St Peter's Basilica but the realism of the three characters was too great for it to hang there. St Anne was compared by the art critic Bernard Berenson to a *ciociara*, ie a pleasant woman from the hills between Rome and Cassino. Three other admirable works by Caravaggio are a sorrowful *David showing Goliath's head* (**18**), a sad *St John the Baptist* (**19**) and *St Jerome* (**20**).

This room also contains some fine **sculptures by Bernini** two busts of Cardinal Scipione Borghese; the second (**21**) was executed because there was a vein in the marble in the first one (**22**) on the Cardinal's forehead. *Young Jupiter with the goat Amalthea* (**23**) was probably the artist's first work (*c*1615). Sixty years later in 1673 he made a terracotta model for an equestrian statue of Louis XIV (**24**) for Versailles; after all sorts of intrigues the commission went to Girardon; Bernini altered his statue to represent Marcus Curtius.

Room XV – **Bernini** was not only a renowned sculptor but also a brilliant painter. One of his por-

Rape of Proserpina by Bernini (Museo Borghese)

traits (**25**) bears comparison with Velazquez. A *Self-portrait* (**26**) and *Portrait of a Man* (**27**) who has been identified as the painter's younger brother, are noteworthy.

The *Portrait of Monsignor Merlini* (**28**) by **Andrea Sacchi** (1559-1661) shows a restraint quite unusual in the Baroque period. The *Deposition* (**29**) by **Rubens** was painted early in the 17C during the artist's visit to Rome.

Room XVI – Most of the works are by **Jacopo Bassano** (1516-1592); he enjoyed painting country scenes and interiors which he used even in his religious works (*Last Supper* – **30**); he was a Venetian and used exceptional colour effects.

Room XVII – Late Renaissance works including a painting of *St Stephen Martyr* (**31**) in the soft style of **Francesco Francia** (1450-1517).

Room XIX – The outstanding painting here is **Danaë★★★** (**32**) by **Correggio** (*c*1489-1534) which illustrates the myth of Zeus visiting Danaë as a shower of gold. The use of oils has produced very subtle colour tones. Contemporary with Bassano and Correggio, **Dosso Dossi** (*c*1489-1542) demonstrates his great talent as a colourist in *Circe the Sorceress* (**33**).

Room XX – The **Portrait of a man★★★** (**34**) by **Antonello de Messina** (1430-79), with its powerfully expressive look, its precision (garment folds) and the delicate modelling of the face, is a masterpiece. In the *Virgin and Child* (**35**) by the Venetian **Giovanni Bellini** (*c*1429-1516) the firm line of the figures is bathed in a beautiful luminosity.

Sacred and Profane Love★★★ (**36**) by **Titian** (*c*1490-1576) shows the young artist's search for an ideal of beauty. When he painted *The Education of Love* (**37**) at 88 his art had been utterly renewed. As well as Titian in 16C Venice there was **Veronese**; *St John the Baptist preaching* (**38**) and *St Anthony of Padua preaching to the fish* (**39**) (when the citizens of Rimini had refused to listen to him) demonstrate Veronese's attraction to the narrative picture.

Take Viale dei Pupazzi to continue the walk in the gardens.

The **Sea horse Fountain** was commissioned in 1791 by Prince Marcantonio Borghese who renovated the gardens.

The **Piazza di Siena** further on is named after the native town of the Borghese. Set among umbrella pines, it is sometimes used for international equestrian events. On the northeast side stands the **Casina dell' Orologio,** built in the late 18C.

Viale dei Pupazzi leads to the **Temple of Diana,** modelled on an ancient building. From there an avenue runs north to the **Lake Garden** *(Giardino del Lago),* one of the most popular corners of the park; it was created by the architect, Asprucci, who worked on the enlargement of the Borghese Gardens at the end of 18C; the waters of the lake reflect the columns of the little Temple of Aesculapius, another imitation of an ancient building.

Neighbouring sights are described in the following chapters: PIAZZA DEL POPOLO; PIAZZA DI SPAGNA; VIA VENETO.

B. Lipnitzki/EXPLORER

La Bocca della Verità (Santa Maria in Cosmedin)

On the outskirts of Rome there are several quiet spots among gardens and woodland where it is pleasant to retreat in summer. The gardens of the Villa d'Este at Tivoli (in the photograph) are one of the favourite places in which to escape from the oppressive heat and traffic of the capital.

Gardens of the Villa d'Este

Excursions
from
Rome

Lago di BRACCIANO★★

Michelin Map no 430, P 18, fold 25, 39km - 24 miles northwest of Rome
By bus (ACOTRAL): departure from Via Lepanto.
By train (FS): departure from Ostiense, Termini or Tiburtina Stations.

By car: take S2 Via Cassia, direction Viterbo; after crossing the Gran Raccordo Anulare (Rome ring road) and passing through Giustiniana, bear left towards Bracciano-Anguillare; after about 7.5km - 5 miles in Osteria Nuova bear right into Via Anguillarese to Anguillara-Sabazia.

Bracciano Lake

Bracciano lake is of volcanic origin, like the lakes at Castelli Romani, and occupies a series of craters in the Sabatini Mountains (Monti Sabatini) (northeast). It is more or less circular and is the eighth largest lake in Italy (57.5 km^2 - 22sq miles; 160m - 525ft at its deepest point; 164m - 538ft above sea-level). It produces a fairly rich variety of fish including pike, eel, carp and a local fish called *latterino*. The Ancient Romans called it *Lacus Sabatini* and it has always played an important part in supplying the city of Rome with water. In 109 Trajan built an aqueduct (30km - 19 miles long) to carry water to the district of Trastevere; it terminated on the Janiculum. It was destroyed and restored several times. When Paul V restored it in 1609, he gave it his own name and also commissioned the Pauline Fountain (Fontana Paulina) on the Janiculum so that the water from Bracciano should emerge in Rome against a spectacular and dramatic background. In ancient times Rome was connected to Bracciano by the Via Clodia (also Claudia) which then went on into Lower Etruria. Today the part of the Bracciano road near the lake ostensibly follows the route taken by the old road.

LAKE TOUR *36km - 22 miles*

★**Anguillara-Sabazia** – The village is set on a rocky promontory (185m - 607ft above sea level). Access to this charming medieval town is through an impressive 16C gate decorated with a clock. Opposite is Via Umberto I which climbs to the top of the village. Immediately after the gate is a small belvedere *(left)* which has a fountain with eels in it. Right at the end of Via Umberto I is a flight of steps *(left)* leading to the 18C Collegiate Church of the Assumption (Collegiata dell'Assunta): from the small square there is a magnificent view across the lake. Narrow but enchanting streets lead down to the lake and there is a good view of the old town from the shore.

On leaving the town turn left immediately after the public garden into Via Trevignanese.

Trevignano Romano – This characteristic village has developed round an outcrop of basalt beside the lake. The medieval town with its fishermen's cottages extends along the lake shore like a fish bone and climbs up the hill which is crowned by the ruins of the Orsini Rock (Rocca degli Orsini). From Via Umberto I *(right)* the road climbs to the Church of the Assumption where there are some interesting frescoes inspired by the school of Raphael. Beyond the clocktower in Piazza Vittorio Emanuele III is the Town Hall *(right)* with its 16C door.

Take Via IV Novembre to Bracciano.

★**Bracciano** – All the main streets converge on Piazza 1° Maggio. On the right is the Town Hall in Piazzetta IV Novembre. To the left Via Umberto I leads to Piazza Mazzini, where there is a splendid view of the cylindrical towers of the impressive **Orsini-Odescalchi Castle** (Castello Orsini-Oderscalchi).

★★★**Castello Orsini-Odescalchi** ⊘ – The castle was originally built around the Medieval Rock of the Prefects of Vico who governed till the 13C. It passed to the Orsini family in 1419 but it was not until 1470 that Napoleone Orsini added to the original which then began to take on all the appearances and functions of a palace. In 1696 the palace was acquired by the Odescalchis, whence it passed in 1803 to the Torlonia family, before reverting in 1848 to the Odescalchis who are still the owners to-day.

Six impressive cylindrical but somewhat irregular towers mark the outer limits of the castle which was built almost entirely of lava rock on top of volcanic tufa. There are two walls surrounding the monument and the old medieval township. Beyond the ticket office there is an open space; on the left can be seen the old armaments store; on the right there is a door decorated with roses, the Orsini family's coat of arms.

★**Interior** – The tour passes through the second north tower to a lobby with a well and a stone arcade. A spiral staircase leads up to the first rooms on the main floor. **Room I** (library): It is also called the papal room since Pope Sixtus V stayed there in 1481 when fleeing from the plague in Rome. The ceilling was painted by Taddeo Zuccari. As in all the rooms, the furnishings are of a later date. **Room II** *(closed):* little study adjoining the library. **Room III**: interesting orignal coffered ceiling with beams painted in the 15C (all the ceilings on this floor are original). **Room IV**: large triptych from the Umbrian School (15C) depicting the *Annunciation* (the central panel is missing). **Room V**: numerous hunting trophies; the large painting *(left)*, previously in the porch leading to the central courtyard, is attributed to Antoniazzo Romano; a little balcony looks out over the lake. **Room VII**: a bust of *Paolo Giordano II Orsini* by Bernini and a bust of *Isabella de Medici* by one of Bernini's pupils. **Room IX**: the last room on this floor leading via a spiral staircase to the second floor. **Room XIII**: also called the Arms' Room; display of arms and suits of armour from the 15C to 17C. **Room XV**: a very beautiful 16C Sicilian wrought iron bed. **Room XVII**: room leading to a loggia with a magnificent view of the old rock

The tour continues with the **Sentry Walk** (cammino di ronda) connecting the magnificent towers of the castle. From here there is a glorious view over the town and the lake. Steps then lead down to the **Central Courtyard**★ (Cortile Centrale) which seems to revert, as if by magic, to the era when chivalry was not fabulous but real. Double doors lead to a very fine external staircase made of lava rock. After a brief visit to the kitchens, the tour ends, in the entrance hall.

Return to Piazza Mazzini and turn left into Via della Collegiata.

In the square beyond the archway is **St Stephen's Church** which in ancient times was actually inside the Rock of the Prefects. The walk continues along the narrow and picturesque streets of the old town.

Take Via Agostino Fausti and then Via Braccianese to return to Rome.

Consult the index to find reference to any sight described in this guide (church, museum, palace, archeological site, historical person, artist...)

CASTELLI ROMANI ★★

Michelin Map no 430, 919-20

Castelli Romani, "Roman fortresses", is the name given in the Middle Ages to the region southeast of Rome. While anarchy reigned in Rome, the noble families sought refuge in the outlying villages building themselves castles. Thirteen villages were fortified in this way: Frascati, Grottaferrata, Marino, Castel Gandolfo, Albano, Ariccia, Genzano, Nemi, Rocca di Papa, Rocca Priora, Monte Compatri, Monte Porzio Catone, Colonna.

Nowadays the Romans readily leave the capital for the 'Castelli' where they find fresh air, extensive views, clear skies and little country inns with pleasant arbours.

Historical and geographical notes – The 'Castelli' are situated in the **Alban Hills** *(Colli Albani)* which are volcanic in origin. They form a circle, the circumference of which is the edge of an immense burnt-out crater, pockmarked with secondary craters which have now turned into lakes.

Meadows and sweet chestnut trees spread up the hillsides, while the lower slopes are covered with olive groves and vineyards which produce the famous Castelli wine. In the valleys the volcanic soil is particularly suited to the cultivation of early vegetables. The history of the Alban Hills is linked to that of Rome. Cicero, the Emperors Tiberius, Nero and Galba had country houses there and Cato the Censor was born near Camaldoli in 234 BC.

★★EXCURSION FROM ROME

122km (76 miles) – 1day – local map below

From Rome take via Tuscolana S 215 (exit (21) on Michelin Map 430). After crossing the Gran Raccordo Anulare (Rome ring road) continue to Frascati.

On the outskirts of Rome the route passes **Cinecittà** the Italian equivalent of Hollywood.

★**Frascati** – This was the favourite resort of the affluent and insouciant youth of Ancient Rome. From the main square, Piazza G Marconi, there is an extensive view downhill as far as Rome and uphill to the terraces of the Villa Aldobrandini.

Frascati has gained a reputation for its white wine and for its 16C and 17C villas, particularly the **Villa Aldobrandini★** ⊘ set high on the hillside above its terraces, clipped avenues, fountains and rockeries.

From Piazza G Marconi take the road to Monte Porzio Catone.

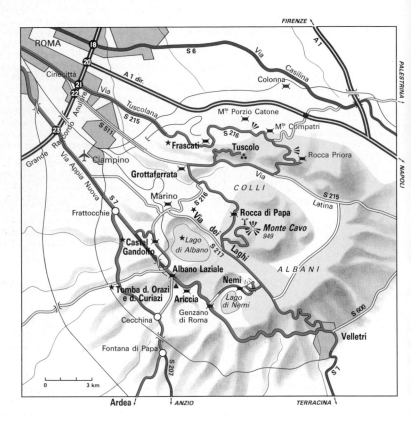

The road offers a good view of **Monte Compatri** and **Monte Porzio Catone** as it climbs up to **Rocca Priora** which clings to the northern rim of the huge crater in the Alban Hills.

Continue downhill; turn right into Via Latina; after 4km (2.5 miles) turn right to Tuscolo (no sign) into a winding road leading to the ruins.

Tuscolo – It was in his villa in ancient Tusculum that Cicero set his series of philosophical treatises known as the Tusculanes.

The city was once the fief of the Counts of Tusculum; from the 10C to 12C this powerful family owned most of the Castelli and extended its power as far as Rome, also providing several of the popes. Tusculum was completely destroyed in 1191 in an engagement with the Romans and was never rebuilt. A few traces survive: up the slope to the left near the large cross which is now half hidden in the trees on what was once the citadel, are the ruins of a small theatre with the remains of a water cistern at the back.

Return downhill; turn right into Via Latina. In Grottaferrata take Corso del Popolo (main street).

Grottaferrata – In 1004 a monastery was founded by Greek monks in the ruins of a Roman villa, which had perhaps been owned by Marcus Tullius Cicero himself.

★**Abbazia** – The **abbey** is situated at the end of the main street. It looks like a fortress and is surrounded by ramparts and a moat which were added in the 15C by order of Cardinal Giuliano della Rovere, later to become Pope Julius II. The abbey is served by monks of the Eastern rite. In the courtyard of the castle there is a bronze statue of St Nilus and the entrance *(left)* to the monastery and the abbey museum.

Museo ⊙ – The large doorway opens to a beautiful courtyard flanked by the church of St Mary of Grottaferrata and the Sangallo doorway. The **museum** is housed in the rooms previously occupied by the Cardinals commendatory. On display are Roman and Greek finds and paintings of scenes from the Old Testament which had been in the central nave in the church. One of the rooms is decorated with frescoes done by Francesco da Siena in 1547.

★**Santa Maria di Grottaferrata** ⊙ – *2nd castle terrace*. In the narthex *(on the left)* is an attractive marble font (10C). The doorway into the church is in the Byzantine style decorated with representations of animals and leaves; the carved wooden doors are 11C; above them is an 11C mosaic. The interior was remodelled in the 18C but the chancel arch is still decorated with a late 12C mosaic representing the Apostles at Whitsuntide. St Nilus' chapel *(right)* has a 17C coffered ceiling and is adorned with frescoes (1608-10) painted by Domenichino. In the right aisle is the *cripta ferrata*, a room in the Roman villa which was converted to a place of Christian worship in the 5C and which has given its name to the church and the village.

On leaving the church turn left into Viale San Nilo; after the traffic lights, turn right into Via Roma to Rocca di Papa.

Rocca di Papa – The village fans out on a picturesque **site**★ on the slopes of Monte Cavo facing the Alban lakes and hills. It lies at the heart of hunting country and is a favourite spot among those who appreciate hare and rabbit dishes *(coniglio alla cacciatora)*.

Before reaching Via dei Laghi, turn left to Monte Cavo surmouted by TV masts.

Monte Cavo ⊙ – Alt 949m - 3 114ft. On the way up there are glimpses of huge stones which paved the ancient Sacred Way leading to the Temple of Jupiter on the top of Monte Cavo. Here in the 5C BC the representatives of the cities of the Latin League, including Rome, used to meet. In the 4C BC, however, Rome defeated the other cities in the League and embarked on her conquest of the peninsula.

The site of the Temple of Jupiter is now abandoned but at one time it was occupied by a convent, which was later converted into a hotel. From the square there is a fine **view**★ of the Apennines, the Castelli Romani, Lake Albano and Lake Nemi, Rome and the surrounding countryside.

Return downhill; turn left and left again into S 217, Via dei Laghi.

★**Via dei Laghi** – This is a beautiful road winding between oak and sweet chestnut woods.

After 3.5km - 5.5 miles turn right to Nemi.

Nemi – The village occupies a charming **site**★★ in a natural amphitheatre on the steep slopes of a crater now filled by Lake Nemi. One tower of the Ruspoli Castle still stands, the only trace of the medieval *castello*. In June delicious wild strawberries are served in Nemi.

Drive through the town towards the lake.

Lago di Nemi (Lake Nemi) – The road down to the lake passes through fields of daisies, poppies and strawberries. The lake is called Diana's mirror because the sacred wood next to the Temple of Diana is reflected in it. In 1929 the level of the water was lowered by 9m - 30ft so that two boats from the reign of Caligula (AD 37-41) could be recovered. They were burned during the war and only a few charred remains are housed in the museum ⊙.

Continue on Via dei Laghi to Velletri.

Velletri – The town has been prominently involved in Italian history: it resisted Joachim Murat, was captured by Fra Diavolo the Calabrian brigand chief, was fought over by the troops of Garibaldi and Naples and was damaged by bombardments during the Second World War. It is now a prosperous modern town on the south-facing slope of a crater in the Alban Hills at the centre of a wine-producing region.

The imposing 14C **Torre del Trivio** rises from the main square, Piazza Cairoli.

From Velletri drive to Ariccia.

Ariccia – The main square, with its two fountains, was given its present appearance in 1664 by Bernini: the palace on the right *(north side)* of the road became the property of the Chigi banking family in the 17C; the **Church of the Assumption** on the left *(south side)* is elegantly flanked by two porticoes (the circular interior, capped by a dome, is worth a visit).

In culinary matters Ariccia is known for its roast suckling pig *(porchetta)*.

On the outskirts of Ariccia stop.

★**Tomba degli Orazi e dei Curiazi** (Tomb of the Horatii and the Curiatii) – *At the entrance to the Albano, on the left, over a wall and below the level of the road.* The tomb which dates only from the last days of the Republic *(see below)* is made of huge blocks of peperine, with truncated cones at the corners.

Albano Laziale – The town probably derives its name from Domitian's villa, Villa Albana.

Take Via Cavour, turn right into Via A Saffi, turn left into Via della Rotonda.

★**Santa Maria della Rotonda** – This church is a converted *nymphaeum* belonging to Domitian's villa. It has been restored to its original brick appearance. Bold Romanesque belltower (13C).

Return to Via Cavour; turn into Via A de Gasperi.

Porta Pretoria – *At the lower end of Via A. Saffi in Via Alcide de Gasperi.* These ruins were once the entrance gate to a fortress built by Septimius Severus (193-211).

★**Villa communale** – *Piazza Mazzini.* The huge public garden contains traces of a villa which belonged to Pompey (106-48 BC).

Continue to Castel Gandolfo.

★**Castel Gandolfo** – On the edge of a crater now filled by Lake Albano stands Castel Gandolfo, famous worldwide as the summer residence of the pope.

Alba Longa – The site of Ancient Alba Longa has been identified as that of Castel Gandolfo. It was the oldest town in Latium founded, according to legend, *c*1150 BC. Its rivalry with Rome led to the famous battle between the Horatii and the Curiatii. Tired of fighting a costly war, the two cities decided to settle their differences by single combat between three Roman brothers, the Horatii, and three Alban brothers, the Curiatii. At the first encounter two of the Horatii were killed, the three Curiatii were wounded; the last of the Horatii pretended to take flight in order to separate his adversaries and then turning, defeated them one by one. On returning to Rome, Horatius met his sister Camilla at the Capena Gate mourning her lover, one of the Curiatii, and cursing Rome, the "sole object of her resentment". He killed her, was put on trial but acquitted.

Papal Villa – *Not open.* The entrance is in the main square. The Holy See acquired the 'Castello' Gandolfo at the end of 16C. In 1628 Urban VIII commissioned Maderno to design a villa on the site of Domitian's earlier villa (81-96 AD) which had extended as far as Albano Laziale. The Vatican observatory *(Specola Vaticana)* was established here in Pius XI's reign.

★**Lake Albano** – There is a good **view**★ of its enclosed site from a terrace at the entrance to the village; there is a road down to the lakeside.

From Castel Gandolfo continue north; turn right into S 7, Via Appia Nuova.
In Frattochie EITHER continue north on S 7 to return to Rome OR make a detour south (30km - 19 miles) to visit the Manzù Collection in Ardea.
From Frattocchie take S 207 south (direction Anzio) via Pavona, south of Cecchina, bear right into the road to Ardea.

Ardea – The town stands on land which once belonged to the Rutuli of which it was the capital city. According to legend, the death of Turnus, King of the Rutuli, who was defeated by Aeneas, and the founding of Lavinium, in which Aeneas was involved, marked the decline of Ardea and the birth of the myth in Rome. The town stands on a tufa rock. At some spots the remains of the city walls in the form of square blocks of tufa can still be seen.

The Museum is situated 100m - 100yds after the junction with Via Laurentina, on the left going towards Rome.

★★**Museo della Raccolta Manzù** (Manzù Collection) ⊙ – The museum was the idea of the artist's wife and a group of his friends. It was inaugurated in 1969, given to the State in 1979, and opened to the public in 1981. Most of the work belongs to the artist's mature period (1950-1970) when he reworked some of the themes of his earlier years. Although there are only a few works from that earlier period, they are very important. Altogether there are 462 works in the collection including sculpture, drawings, engravings and jewellery. The museum also puts on temporary exhibitions on other subjects.

Take Via Laurentina, S 148, to return to Rome.

Mint and peppermint are used a good deal in Roman cooking, with vegetables, fish, in salads and soups. Anyone who has walked among the ghostly ruins of Ostia Antica will remember the haunting scent of the wild mint which rises from the ground, for one cannot help treading it underfoot.
Elizabeth David: Italian Food

OSTIA ANTICA★★

Michelin Map no 430, Q 18.
24km - 15 miles southwest of Rome

Access – *by car: by Via del Mare (see town plan in the Michelin Red Guide "Italia"; by underground (Metro Line B), direction Laurentina as far as Magliana and then by train to Ostia Antica; by aquabus, see Practical Information.*

The long grey sandy beach at **Ostia Lido** is the nearest to Rome and the most popular.

★★OSTIA ANTICA (OLD OSTIA)

There is nothing to see of the medieval village of Ostia except the 15C **castle** built by Cardinal Giuliano della Rovere (Julius II) to protect Rome from attack by sea.

The main interest of a visit to Ostia Antica lies in the vast area of ruins which once constituted the principal port of Rome.

Historical Notes

Ostia, at the mouth of the Tiber, takes its name from the Latin word *ostium* meaning mouth. According to Virgil, Aeneas disembarked here. Livy says that it was Ancus Martius (640-616 BC), the fourth King of Rome after Romulus, who 'extended his dominion to the sea, founded Ostia at the mouth of the Tiber and established salt pans all around'. Archeologists, however, place the founding of Ostia in the 4C BC while also admitting that an earlier village of salt extractors may have existed. Ostia's development has reflected that of Rome: it was a military port when Rome embarked on her conquest of the Mediterranean shores and a commercial port when the victorious city established an organised system of trade.

Military port – Roman control of the mouth of the Tiber, set at *c*335 BC, corresponds with her expansion in the Mediterranean; several years earlier (in 338 BC) the Romans had won their first naval victory at Antium. During the war against Pyrrhus (278 BC) the fleet sent by Carthage to assist the Romans docked in Ostia. During the Punic Wars (264-41 and 218-01) Ostia served as an arsenal; Scipio's army embarked here for Spain (217 BC) to prevent reinforcements reaching Hannibal who had already crossed the Alps and defeated Flaminius at Lake Trasimeno; two years later about 30 ships set sail from Ostia for Tarentum which was planning an alliance with Hannibal; in 211 BC Publius Cornelius Scipio (known as Scipio Africanus Major) took ship for Spain in order to avenge the defeat of his ancestors; barely 25 years old and exceptionally invested with proconsular power, he covered himself with glory.

Commercial port – At first there was simply a castle *(castrum)* to protect the port from pirates but by the 1C BC Ostia had become a real town. In 79 BC Sulla built a rampart round three sides using the Tiber to protect the fourth side. The last bend in the river was then further east than it is now so that the river flowed in a straight course along the north side of the town *(plan below)*. Rome imported food from her numerous overseas provinces. A cargo of wheat from Sardinia was unloaded in Ostia as early as 212 BC. It was essential that the cargoes should be protected. The efforts of Pompey in 67 BC and of Agrippa from 63 to 12 BC had rid the sea of pirates. Only the problem of entering port remained: frequent strong winds restricted access to the summer months and the adjacent coastline consisted of dunes, lagoons and shallows. As a result the merchant ships usually docked in the Neapolitan ports and the goods had to be carried overland to the capital.

Claudian Harbour – In Antiquity the shoreline ran parallel to the west side of the excavated site *(plan below)*. Claudius' engineers avoided the mouth of the Tiber itself because of the presence of a sand bar created by the currents. Instead they sited the harbour on the right bank of the river, north of the town of Ostia and the Fiumicino branch of the Tiber (roughly corresponding to the site of the Leonardo da Vinci international airport). The harbour covered about 70ha - 173 acres and was protected by two incurving breakwaters, with an artificial island in the harbour entrance between the ends of the breakwaters. Since the entrance faced northwest the harbour was sheltered from the strongest winds such as the *Libeccio* (from the southwest) and the *Scirocco* (from the southeast).

Trajan's Harbour – When the Claudian harbour became too small, Trajan (98-117) built a second harbour inland. It was hexagonal in shape, covered 30ha - 74 acres and was lined with docks and warehouses. It was joined to the Claudian harbour by a broad channel and to the Tiber by a canal *(Fossa Trajana)*.

Decline and excavation of Ostia Antica and the Isola Sacra – Like Rome, Ostia began to decline in the 4C. The harbours silted up, the alluvium deposited by the Tiber extended the shoreline seawards and malaria depopulated the town. Ostia suffered the fate of all Roman ruins and was pillaged for its materials. Regular excavations have been undertaken since 1909; the western sectors of the town were excavated from 1938 to 1942.

Between the town and the harbour the **necropolis of Trajan's Harbour** was discovered on the Sacred Island *(Isola Sacra)* which had been created by digging the Fiumicino channel; since the days of Antiquity the land has advanced several miles towards the sea.

Life in Ostia – Ostia was a very busy commercial town and under the Empire its population rose to 100 000. Its main streets were lined with shops; administrative buildings clustered round the forum; warehouses and industrial premises were concentrated near the Tiber; the residential districts extended towards the seashore.

It was a cosmopolitan town, which welcomed a variety of foreign religions; several of their places of worship have been discovered: the oriental cults of the Great Mother (Cybele), of Isis and Serapis, of Jupiter Dolichenus and particularly of Mithras.

Christianity too had its adherents; Minucius Felix, a Christian writer, chose the sea baths at Ostia during the harvest holiday as the setting for his conversation with Octavius Januarius, another Christian, and Caecilius, a pagan whom they were trying to convert.

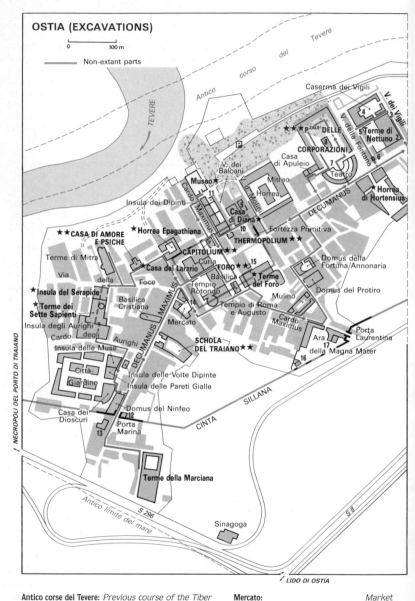

Antico corse del Tevere:	*Previous course of the Tiber*
Antico limite del mare:	*Previous coastline*
Basilica cristiana:	*Christian basilica*
Casa:	*House*
Caserma del Vigili:	*Firemen's barracks*
Cinta Sillana:	*Sulla's Wall*
Città giardino:	*Garden suburb*
Curia:	*Curia*
Foro:	*Forum*
Fortezza primitiva:	*Early fortress*
Mercato:	*Market*
Mulino:	*Mill*
Museo:	*Museum*
Necropoli del Porto di Traiano:	*Necropolis of Trajan's Port*
Porta:	*Gate*
Sinagoga:	*Synagogue*
Teatro:	*Theatre*
Tempio Rotondo:	*Circular Temple*
Terme:	*Baths*

In 387 St Augustine's mother, Monica, died in Ostia on her way home to Africa.

Ostia dwelling-houses – Their discovery has added to our knowledge of the houses of the lower-paid in the ancient world.

The most common dwelling in this densely populated town was the **insula**, a block of flats to let, several storeys high; the wealthier citizen lived in a **domus**, a detached house with a courtyard and garden.

All the buildings were of brick and probably unrendered. Some have elegant entrances framed by a triangular pediment resting on two pillars. Here and there a porch or a balcony adds interest to the street front. Sometimes the brickwork is finished with a decorative effect. **Opus reticulatum** is the technique most frequently used: small squares of dark tufa and lighter limestone are laid on edge to form a diaper pattern; this technique was practised from the 1C BC to 2C AD; after the 1C AD the corners were sometimes reinforced with courses of brick. Another technique used in Ostia, particularly in the 2C AD, is **opus testaceum**: pyramid-shaped bricks are laid very regularly on their sides – point inwards, flat bottom outwards; to strengthen the structure, courses of ordinary rectangular bricks were inserted every so often between the bands of triangular patterning.

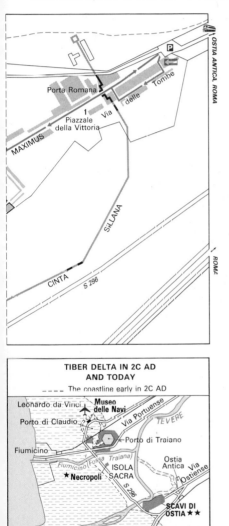

Tour of the excavations (SCAVI) ⊙

A tour of this extensive ruined site is shaded by parasol pines and cypresses. On the left inside the entrance but outside the town limits is **Via delle Tombe** reserved for burials of various types: sarcophagus, *columbarium* or chapel.

Porta Romana (Rome Gate) – This was the main entrance to the town and led into the **Decumanus Maximus**, the east-west axis of all Roman towns; in Ostia it was paved with large slabs and lined with porticoed buildings and warehouses *(horrea)*. From the outer side of the gate the broad and busy Via Ostiense carried traffic to Rome.

Piazzale della Vittoria – The small square took its name from a **statue of Minerva Victoria** (1C) (**1**), a copy of an original Greek work. The statue probably adorned the town gate.

Terme di Nettuno (Neptune Baths) – This 2C building has a terrace *(steps up from main street)* with a view of the fine **mosaics**★★ which depict the marriage of Neptune and Amphitrite (**2**).

Via dei Vigili – The construction of this street in the 2C meant the demolition of earlier buildings which contained a **mosaic**★ (**3**) showing the heads of figures symbolizing the Winds and four Provinces (Sicily, Egypt, Africa, Spain). At the end of the street stand the firemen's barracks *(caserna dei vigili)* built in the 2C; on the far side of the courtyard is the *Augusteum* (for the cult of the Emperor) (**4**); the floor mosaic shows a bull being sacrificed.

Take Via della Palestra.

Via della Fontana – This well-preserved street still contains its public fountain (**5**). On the corner with the Decumanus Maximus stood Fortunatus' tavern; the mosaic floor bears the inscription: *"Dicit Fortunatus: Vinum cratera quot sitis bibe"* (Fortunatus says: Drink wine from the bowl to quench your thirst) (**6**).

Turn left into Via della Palestra which leads into Via della Fontana.

★**Horrea di Hortensius (Hortensius' Warehouses)** – These grand 1C warehouses (horrea), built round a pillared courtyard and lined with shops, are a striking example of *opus reticulatum*. On the right of the entrance is a small shrine dedicated to Hortensius (floor mosaic).

Teatro (Theatre) – Ostia was probably provided with a theatre under Augustus. It has been much restored. The three fine masks (**7**) come from the stage.

★★★**Piazzale delle Corporazioni** – Under the portico in the square were the offices of the 70 trading corporations; set into the mosaic pavement are their emblems showing in which commodity they traded and their country of origin: grain assessors, caulkers, rope-makers, ship-builders and fitters, from Alexandria, Arles, Narbonne, Carthage etc.

The **temple** (**8**) in the centre of the square (only the podium and two columns remain) is sometimes attributed to Ceres and sometimes to the *Annona Augusta*, i.e. the Imperial corn supply which was worshipped like a god (Ostia was a centre for the *Annona*, the office responsible for organising the distribution of corn among the people of Rome.

Casa di Apuleio (Apuleius' House) – A house with a pillared *atrium* and mosaic floors.

Mitreo delle Sette Sfere (Seven Spheres Mithraeum) – This is one of the best preserved of the many temples dedicated to Mithras which have been found in Ostia. One can still see the two benches for the initiates and a relief showing the sacrifice of the bull.

Return to the Decumanus Maximus; turn right into Via dei Molini.

Via dei Molini – The street is named after some mill stones which were found in one of the buildings (**9**). Opposite are the ruins of several warehouses (horrea) where goods were stored.

Return to the beginning of the block and turn right into Via di Diana.

Piazza dei Lari (**10**) – In the square (left) there is an altar dedicated to the Lares. Here also are traces of a primitive fortress (castrum) made of huge blocks of tufa.

Return to the beginning of the street and turn right into Via di Diana.

★**Casa di Diana (Diana's House)** – Facing on to the square is a striking example of an *insula* (block of flats) with rooms and passages arranged round an internal courtyard; note the fine corbel in the side street (Via dei Balconi).

★★**Thermopolium** – This was a bar, as is implied by its name which is of Greek origin and means "sale of hot drinks". The building had a marble counter, shelving and paintings of the fruit and vegetables on sale within.

Turn right into Via dei Dipinti.

Insula dei Dipinti – Block containing several dwellings grouped round a garden; fine mosaics on the wall.

At the end of the Via dei Dipinti on the right an oil store (**11**) was found with huge jars half buried in the ground.

★**Museo** – The museum displays the articles found at Ostia in a clear and well-lit presentation. **Rooms I** to **IV** are devoted to crafts illustrated by low reliefs and to the oriental religious cults which flourished in Ostia owing to its overseas contacts. The Mithras group about to sacrifice the bull (**Rooms III**) is a clear indication of the strength of this cult which had some 15 shrines in Ostia.

Room VIII contains a fine 1C BC statue of a Hercules by Cartilius Poplicola as well as a series of **portraits★**, especially of the Antonines; the quality of expression and the fine detail indicate the high standard of 2C Roman portraiture.

Room IX displays some sarcophagi (2C-3C) found in the city's burial ground.

Room X shows portraits of the last Emperors.

Room XI and **XII** contain examples of the rich interior decoration found in Ostia: walls covered with mosaics (opus sectile), paintings and frescoes from the 1C to 4C.

Take the Via del Capitolium which opens into Cardo Maximus.

Cardo Maximus – This important street, at right angles to the Decumanus, kinks left to skirt the temple known as the **Capitolium.**

Pass the Capitolium and enter the Forum.

★★**Capitolium and Forum** – The **Capitolium** was the largest temple in Ostia, built in the 2C and dedicated to the Capitoline trio – Jupiter, Juno and Minerva. Although the marble facing is missing from the walls, the brick remains are impressive, as are the steps leading up to the *pronaos*; in front of the steps is a partial reconstruction of the altar.

The **forum** was enlarged in the 2C; the few pillars still standing belonged to the surrounding portico. At the far end stands the **Temple of Rome and Augustus** (1C), a grandiose building once faced with marble, which indicates the loyalty of Ostia, the first Roman colony, to the government in Rome.

As in all Roman towns, the forum in Ostia had a **basilica**, a covered building where the citizens could meet, and a senate house **(curia)** where the municipal council met.

Return to Decumanus Maximus.

Tempio Rotondo (Circular Temple) – It was built beside the basilica and was probably dedicated to the cult of the Emperors in the 3C.

★**Casa del Larario (House with Lararium)** – The building consists of shops ranged around an internal court. The recess decorated in attractive red and ochre bricks housed the statues of the Lares.

Continue along the Decumanus Maximus; turn right into Via Epagathiana.

★**Horrea Epagathiana (Epagathus' Warehouses)** – This huge complex of warehouses built near the Tiber in the 2C has a fine doorway with columns and a pediment. It belonged to two rich freedmen - Epagathus and Epaphroditus.

★★**Casa di Amore e Psiche (House of Cupid and Psyche)** – Like most of the buildings facing the seashore, this was a private house (4C); fine remains of mosaic and marble floors and of a *nymphaeum* decorated with niches, arcades and columns.

Turn left into Via del Tempio di Ercole, right into Via della Foce and right again into Via delle Terme di Mitra.

Terme di Mitra (Baths of Mithras) – An arcade leads into the 2C building. Inside is a flight of steps descending to the underground hypocaust (heating system) and traces of a *frigidarium* (pool and columns with Corinthian capitals). Traces of floor mosaics.

Return to Via della Foce and walk through the Insula del Serapide.

Forum and Capitolium in Ostia

★**Insula del Serapide (Serapis Insula)** – The two blocks of dwellings were built in the 2C with porticoes round a courtyard and a bath house in between. Traces of stucco work on a doorway.

★**Terme dei Sette Sapienti (Seven Sages' Baths)** – There is a mosaic floor in the large circular room and one room is roofed with a dome decorated with mosaics on a white ground.

Insula degli Aurighi (Charioteers' Insula) – At the centre of this block of dwellings is an attractive court with a portico; some rooms still have traces of paintings.

Turn left into Cardo degli Aurighi and right into Via delle Volte Dipinti.

Insula delle Volte Dipinte; Insula delle Muse; Insula delle Pareti Gialle – *Open only to specialists; apply to the Soprintendenza di Ostia.* 2C residential houses with traces of mosaics and paintings.

Città-Giardino (Garden Suburb) – *Right*. Example of a 2C residential complex with blocks of dwellings surrounded by gardens and fountains (remains of several fountains, one containing mosaic).

Casa dei Dioscuri (Dioscuri House) – It was built in the 4C in one of the garden suburb blocks. The rooms are paved with beautiful multi-coloured mosaics, one of which shows the Dioscuri.

Domus del Ninfeo (House with Nymphaeum) – Incorporated in the 4C into a 2C building; one of the rooms is screened by three arches supported on slim columns with capitals.

Return to the Decumanus Maximus and turn right.

Porta Marina (Marine Gate) – This gate in Sulla's walls gave access to the seashore. A few huge blocks of tufa remain. Inside the gate *(left)* was the tavern of Alexander Helix (**12**) and outside *(right)* a tomb (**13**).
The Decumanus came to an end outside the gate in a large colonnaded square.

Turn left into Via Cartilio Poplicola and walk to the end.

Terme della Marciana (Marciana Baths) – Behind the massive pilasters of the *frigidarium* apse, a beautiful **mosaic★** shows athletes in the pose characteristic of the various sports with trophies and equipment on a table in the centre.
From the baths there is a distant view of the columns and capitals of the synagogue built in the 1C.

Return to the Porta Marina and walk back along the Decumanus Maximus.

★★Schola del Traiano – *Right*. This impressive 2C to 3C building was the headquarters of a guild of merchants. On the left of the entrance is a plaster copy of a statue of Trajan which was found in the building, hence its name. Next comes a court with a rectangular central basin surrounded by brick columns. The basin was altered when more rooms were built on the far side of the court in the 3C. The central room, preceded by two columns, contains a fine mosaic floor. During excavations a 2C house was discovered on the east side of the court furnished with a *nymphaeum* (paintings and mosaics) and a peristyle.

Basilica Cristiana (Christian Basilica) – *Left*. In this 4C Christian building, a row of columns separates the aisles which end in apses; an inscription on the architrave of a colonnade marks the entrance to what has been identified as the baptistry.

Mercato (Market) – There were two fishmongers' shops (**14**) on either side of an alley which led to a pillared podium standing on the west side of the market square. On the third pillar on the left it says in Latin: "Read and know that there is a lot of gossiping in the market."

Turn right into Via del Pomerio, then left into Via del Tempio Rotondo and continue past the Tempio di Roma e Augusto (left) and Cardo Maximus (right).

★Terme del Foro (Forum Baths) – The largest baths in Ostia showing the heating ducts in the walls. Adjacent to the north side of the baths is a public lavatory (**15**).

Turn left into Cardo Maximus.

Mulino (Mill) – On the left of the Cardo Maximus are several millstones beneath a pergola.

Ara della Magna Mater (Altar of the Great Earth Mother) – This sacred enclosure contains the remains of a temple dedicated to Cybele (the Great Mother – *Magna Mater*) (**16**). The Sanctuary of Attis (**17**) has a statue of the goddess in the apse and two fauns flanking the entrance.
The Cardo Maximus ends at the Laurentina Gate **Porta Laurentina** in Sulla's wall (**Cinta Sillana**).

Turn left into Via Semita dei Cippi.

The **Domus del Protiro** *(right; closed for restoration)* is an exception in Ostia in that it has a marble pediment above the door.

Domus della Fortuna Annonaria – *Closed for restoration.*
3C to 4C house with a well in the garden and mosaic floors; one of the rooms has three arches opening on to the garden.

Take Via del Mitreo dei Serpenti to return to the Decumanus Maximus.

★NECROPOLI DEL PORTO DI TRAIANO (TRAJAN'S PORT NECROPOLIS)

5km - 2.5 miles from the excavations. Access by car: by S 296 (direction Leonardo da Vinci Airport at Fiumicino); right turn into Via Cima Cristallo; entrance to the necropolis on the left of the access road.
Access by bus no 02 (every 15min) from the bus-stop on the panoramic road Guido Calza, in front of Ostia Antica station, to the corner of Via Cima Cristallo; return journey in the direction Ostia Lido.
Open on request. ☎ 06 56 50 022.

Isolated and silent the necropolis is an impressive place, studded with umbrella pines, cypresses and laurels. The inhabitants of Trajan's harbour buried their dead here from the 2C to 4C. Ostia had its own graveyards outside the town.

There are tombs of every sort. The simplest are marked by an amphora buried in the ground or by several amphorae arranged in an oval or by a row of tiles set up to form a ridge. Other tombs built of brick comprise one or more chambers where the sarcophagi were placed. Sometimes there is a court in front of the chambers fitted out as a *columbarium* (with recesses for the cinerary urns) which the owner made available to his household.

The majority of the tombs have a low door beneath a lintel resting directly on the uprights; the inscription gave the name of the dead person with sometimes a low relief sculpture depicting his occupation in life.

MUSEO DELLE NAVI (SHIP MUSEUM) ⊘ in Fiumicino

Access: from Ostia Antica by bus no 02 towards Fiumicino Paese; from Rome by underground (metro) from Roma Ostiense station to Leonardo da Vinci Airport and then by train.

The maritime museum, a modern building on the site of Claudius' Harbour *(see above)*, houses the Roman remains which were uncovered during the building of the airport in the late 50s. On display are the hulls of five **vessels:** two large and one small shallow draft cargo barges, drawn by oxen, for transporting goods from the port up the Tiber to Rome; a sea-going sailing boat; a fishing boat, propelled by oars, with a central wooden keep for live fish; and smaller articles: pottery, fishing floats, rope, nails, wooden pegs, needles, money. There are two electronic wall **panels** which show, at the touch of a button, the pattern of imports in the Roman Empire from the 1C to 4C AD and the position of all the Roman boats which have been excavated. A low relief sculpture *(copy)* shows the boat which transported Caligula's obelisk, now in St Peter's Square. The boat was sunk deliberately to provide a foundation for the lighthouse at the harbour mouth; the lighthouse stood 50m - 164ft high and the light could be seen up to 30km - 18 miles out to sea.

Northwest of the museum are remains of the harbour quay where the lighthouse stood; northeast was the customs house; other related buildings have been excavated to the southeast *(across the road)*.

PALESTRINA ★

Michelin map no 430, Q20. 42 km – southeast of Rome.
By car from Rome by Via Prenestina; bus from Rebibbia (Metro Line B).

Ancient Praeneste, like modern Palestrina, was built on the southern slopes of Monte Ginestro, an outcrop in the chain of Prenestini hills. The main attractions of this little town consist of the fabulous views it enjoys, its medieval quality and the remains of the famous Temple of Fortune (Fortuna Primigenia).

Praeneste rose to its full glory during the 8C and 7C BC; it was besieged subsequently through the centuries because of its strategic position. Under the rule of Rome from the 4C BC, the town became a favourite country retreat in Imperial times for dignitaries and nobles alike. The cult of Fortune lasted well into the 4C AD when the temple was abandoned and its site became encroached upon by the medieval city.

The superb 8C necropolis, together with the Barberini and Bernardini tombs in which fabulous funerary ornaments were found (now displayed at the Museo Nazionale di Villa Giulia) are a lasting testament to Palestrina's illustrious past.

★**Tempio della Fortuna Primigenia** – This temple was once a grandiose sanctuary dedicated to the goddess Fortune. Built during the 2C-1C BC, it stands as one of the most important examples of Roman architecture based upon Hellenistic archetypes in Italy. The complex would have occupied most of the area now covered by the town; it comprised a series of terraces linked by a system of ramps and stairways aligned one above the other. A large basilica-shaped room, two lateral buildings, a natural cave and an apse paved with the famous Nile Mosaic (now in the local archeological museum – Museo archeologico prenestino) survive from the lower sanctuary that was accommodated on the site of the old forum, on the second level of the temple. The upper sanctuary was located on the fourth terrace of the temple complex where Piazza della Cortina is now situated. On this platform that once was graced with steps arranged in semicircles, was built the Palazzo Colonna (11C) – later known as the Palazzo Barberini (1640). Here, behind the elegant façade ornamented with three Barberini bees (the family crest) is housed the local archeological museum.

Park the car at the bottom of the steps. The ticket office is on the right of the building. The entrance to the museum is at the top of the stairs up to the Terrazza degli Emicicli.

Museo archeologico prenestino ⊘ – The collection comprises important finds recovered from various necropoli excavated nearby and a series of artefacts relating to the Barberini family.

In the room to the right of the entrance are displayed cists (stone receptacles); bronze mirrors; wooden, ivory and clay toilet articles placed alongside the dead person in their sarcophagus or limestone urns. The room on the left houses sculpture: note the large marble Hellenistic head dating from the 2C BC – possibly a fragment of a larger statue of the divinity Fortune. Also on the ground floor is a collection of inscribed or carved stones.

The most interesting rooms are on the top floor: the **Nile Mosaic**★★ depicts Egypt with the Nile in flood. This is the largest known mosaic from the Hellenistic era. Opposite is a detailed scale-model of the Temple of Fortune complete with its superimposed Classical orders of columns rising from the Doric through the Ionic to the Corinthian.

On leaving the museum, cross the street and walk down the flights of steps to marvel at the succession of terraces which still evoke the magnificent splendour and elaborate design of this ancient site.

Follow the one-way road system into town by means of the Via Anicia.

Town centre – Many buildings in the old town include stones from the former city walls. The main square, Piazza Regina Margherita, replaces the old forum.

The 11C duomo, flanked by a Romanesque bell tower, was constructed among the ruins of a rectangular Roman temple (note the remains of the enclosure inside the church). It is dedicated to St Agapito, the patron saint of the town.

At the centre of the piazza is a statue of **Giovanni Pierluigi da Palestrina** (1524-1594), the renowned composer of polyphonic religious music.

TIVOLI★★★

Michelin map no 430, Q 20. 31km - 19 miles east of Rome.
Access by coach from Rebibbia (Metro Line B); by car from Rome
by Via Tiburtina

Tivoli is a small town on the lower slopes of the chalky Apennines (Monti Simbruini) where the river Aniene plunges in cascades into the Roman plain before joining the Tiber. Its main commercial enterprises are the travertine quarries, paper mills, hydro-electric power stations and chemical industries.

A Greek seer and a Roman sibyl – Tivoli, Tibur in Antiquity, is said to have been founded earlier than Rome by Tiburtus, grandson of the Greek seer Amphiaraos whom Zeus caused to be swallowed up in the earth outside Thebes. Tibur came under Roman control in the 4C BC and became a holiday resort under the Empire.

Several centuries later, according to a medieval legend, two great prophecies were made by a sibyl. When Augustus asked her whether there would be anyone greater than he, she sent him a vision of the Virgin and Child on the Capitol in Rome and added that on the Child's birthday a spring of oil would bubble up from the ground; this is supposed to have taken place in Trastevere.

The Tivoli Rebellion or the downfall of an emperor and a pope – In 1001 Tivoli rebelled against the German Emperor Otho III, who was in Italy with Pope Sylvester II. The Romans who had no love for their neighbours in Tivoli, made common cause with the Emperor. The Pope intervened and the Emperor spared the town and the rebels but, when the Pope and the Emperor returned to Rome, the Romans reproached them for their leniency; both had to flee the mob. The following year Otho died and Sylvester the year after. Tivoli retained its independence until 1816 when it was attached to the Papal States.

★★★VILLA ADRIANA (HADRIAN'S VILLA) ⊘

By coach: 4.5km (3 miles) before reaching Tivoli, get off the coach at the stop (fermata) called "Bivio Villa Adriana". 1.5km - 1 mile on foot from the turning to the excavations. By car: follow the signs.

The perimeter (5km - 3 miles) enclosed an estate consisting of vast gardens adorned with works of art, an Imperial palace, baths, libraries and theatres. It was probably the richest building project in Antiquity and was designed entirely by Hadrian. He had visited every part of the Roman empire and it was on his return from the Oriental provinces in AD 126 that he began work on his villa. He was very knowledgeable about art and architecture and tried to recreate the works and sites he had visited during his travels. In 134 the villa was almost finished; Hadrian was 58. Ill and griefstricken at the death of his young favourite Antinoüs, he died in Baiae in 138. His remains were buried in his huge mausoleum in Rome. The Emperors who succeeded him probably continued to come to Tivoli. It was here that Zenobia, Queen of Palmyra, ended her days as Aurelian's prisoner.

Then the villa fell into ruin. From the 15C to 19C the site was explored; over 300 works were recovered which now enrich museums and private collections in Rome, London, Berlin, Dresden, Stockholm and St Petersburg. Since 1870 the site has belonged to the Italian Government which has organised its excavation. The vegetation has been cleared from the ruins revealing magnificent vaults, columns, stucco work and mosaics.

The present entrance is probably not the one used in Hadrian's day. The design of the villa is so unusual that archeologists have not been able to identify the buildings or their uses with any certainty. Before exploring the site it is advisable to study a model of the villa which is displayed in a room next to the bar.

★★**Pecile** – The **Poikile** was the name of a portico in Athens which Hadrian wished to reproduce. Only the north wall remains through which the visitor enters the excavation site itself. Notice the lattice-work effect created by small blocks of tufa set on their edges to form a diaper pattern; Hadrian's Villa is one of the last examples of this technique which fell into disuse in the 2C. The horizontal grooves in the wall

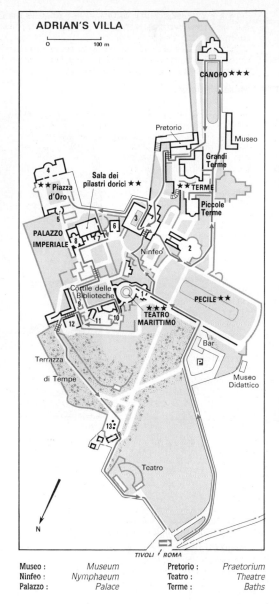

ADRIAN'S VILLA

Museo :	*Museum*
Ninfeo :	*Nymphaeum*
Palazzo :	*Palace*

Pretorio :	*Praetorium*
Teatro :	*Theatre*
Terme :	*Baths*

were filled with bricks which disappeared when the villa was plundered for its materials, in particular for the Villa d'Este in Tivoli.

The Poikile was built in the shape of a large rectangle with slightly curved ends and lined with a portico; it was sited so that one side was always in the shade.

The apsidal chamber called the **philosophers' room** (**1**) was perhaps a reading room.

★★★**Teatro Marittimo** – The **Maritime theatre** is a circular construction consisting of a portico and a central building surrounded by a canal which was spanned by small swing bridges. It was obviously an ideal retreat for the misanthropic Hadrian.

Walk south towards the Ninfeo and climb the steps.

The ruins look down on a *nymphaeum*, which can be reached by part of the **cryptoporticus,** a network of underground passages which made it possible to walk from one end of the site to the other without returning to above ground level.

Walk through the Cryptoporticus (right).

Ninfeo – The *nymphaeum*, the flat area enclosed between sections of high wall was originally thought to be a stadium. The building *(west)* was composed of three semicircular rooms around a courtyard (**2**).

★★Terme – The **Baths** consist of the Small Baths and the Great Baths. They both show the high architectural standards attained in the villa: rectangular rooms with concave walls, octagonal rooms with alternate concave and convex walls, circular rooms with recesses alternating with doors. The most impressive room is in the Great Baths; it has an apse and the remains of some superb vaulting.

The tall building, called the **Praetorium** (Pretorio), was probably a storehouse.

Museo (Museum) – *Closed for restoration*. The **museum** contains the results of the most recent excavations: Roman copies of the Amazon by Phidias and Polyclitus; copies of the Caryatids from the Erechtheion on the Acropolis in Athens. These statues adorned the sides of the Canopus.

There are more ruins belonging to the villa to the west of the museum in a large olive grove but it is private property.

★★★Canopo (Canopus) – It was his visit to Egypt that gave Hadrian the idea of constructing a souvenir of the town of Canope with its famous Temple of Serapis. The route to Canope from Alexandria consisted of a canal lined with temples and gardens. Hadrian had part of his estate landscaped to look like the Egyptian site and completed the effect with a canal down the centre and a copy of the Temple of Serapis at the southern end. He combined the cult of Serapis with the cult of

Hadrian's Villa – Canopus

Antinoüs, his young favourite who had been drowned in the Nile.

On leaving the Canopus bear right between the Grandi Terme and the Praetorio, climb to the upper level and continue towards the Ninfeo before bearing right.

The path circumscribes a large **fish pond** surrounded by a portico (Quadriportico con peschiera) (**3**).

Return to the Pretorio and the Grandi Terme and walk as far as the ruins overlooking the Ninfeo and bear right.

Palazzo Imperiale – The **Imperial Palace** complex extended from the Piazza d'Oro to the Libraries.

★★Piazza d'Oro – The rectangular area was surrounded by a double portico; the Piazza was an aesthetic caprice serving no useful purpose. On the far side are traces of an octagonal chamber (**4**): each of the eight sides, which are alternatively concave and convex, was preceded by a small portico (one of which has been reconstructed). On the opposite side is a chamber (**5**) covered by a dome and flanked by two smaller chambers: the one on the left contains traces of a fine black and white mosaic pavement.

★★Sala dei pilastri dorici – The **Doric Pillared Hall** takes its name from the surrounding portico which was composed of pilasters with Doric bases and capitals supporting a Doric architrave (partial reconstruction in one corner). Opposite stood the **firemen's barracks** *(caserma dei vigili)* (**6**).

Adjoining the Pillared Hall *(north side)* is a huge section of curved wall which may have been part of a summer **dining room** *(triclinio estivo)* (**7**); the oval basins further east mark the site of a **nymphaeum** *(ninfeo di palazzo)* (**8**). These buildings overlook a courtyard which is separated by a *cryptoporticus* from the **library court**; the east side of the latter court is composed of a complex of ten rooms ranged down both sides of a corridor; this was an infirmary (**9**); each of the rooms held three beds; the **floor★** is paved with fine mosaics. The library courtyard offers a pleasant **view★** over the countryside.

Biblioteche – The ruins of the **library buildings** are on the north side of the courtyard; according to custom there was both a Greek library (**10**) and a Latin library (**11**).

Next to the libraries *(east side)* is a group of rooms paved with mosaic which belonged to a **dining room** *(triclinio imperiale)* (**12**).

Terrazza di Tempe – A grove of trees hangs on the slope above a valley which Hadrian called his **Vale of Tempe** after the Greek beauty spot in Thessaly. The path runs through the trees past a **circular temple** (**13**) (reconstructed) which contained a statue of the goddess Venus and was thus attributed to her. Further along *(left)* is the site of a **theatre**.

Proceed to Tivoli (town plan in the Michelin Red Guide Italia (hotels and restaurants).

Piazza Garibaldi is dominated by the **Rocca Pia**, a fortress built by Pius II (1458-64).

***VILLA D'ESTE

In 1550 Cardinal Ippolito II d'Este, who had been raised to great honours by François I of France but had fallen into disgrace when the King's son Henri II succeeded to the throne, decided to retire to Tivoli, where he immediately began to convert the former Benedictine convent into a pleasant country seat. The Neapolitan architect, Pirro Ligorio, was invited to prepare plans.

The simple architecture of the villa contrasts with the elaborate gardens (3ha - 7.5 acres) which descend in a series of terraces on the western slope of the hill. The statues, pools and fountains enhance the natural beauty with all the grace of the Mannerist style. Many distinguished guests visited the Villa, including Pius IV and Gregory XII and after the Cardinal's death, Paul IV, Paul V, Pius IX and writers and artists: Benvenuto Cellini, Titian and Tasso, and Liszt.

In 1759 when the avenues were overgrown with brambles and the fountains silent, Fragonard and Hubert Robert, who were staying at the French Academy in Rome, came to spend the summer in Tivoli with their patron the Abbé de Saint Non; there is scarcely a corner of the gardens where they did not set up their easels nor a perspective that escaped their brushes.

Santa Maria Maggiore – This is the old Abbey Church of St Mary Major belonging to the Benedictine convent. It has an attractive Gothic façade and a 17C belltower. The interior contains two 15C triptychs *(in the chancel)* above the one on the left is a painting of the Virgin by Jacopo Torriti, who also worked in mosaic at the end of the 13C.

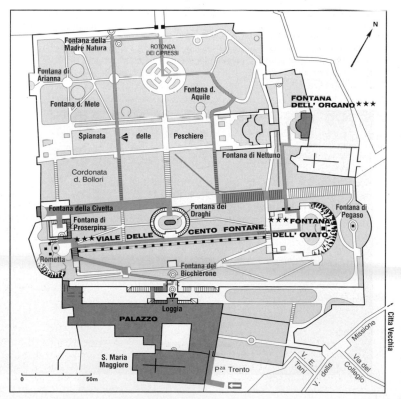

★★★ Villa and Gardens ⊘ – The **Old Apartment** *(Vecchio Appartamento)* on the first floor of the Villa now holds temporary exhibitions.

Descend to the floor below.

Sala grande – The **central Salon** is decorated in the Mannerist style by pupils of Girolamo Muziano and Federico Zuccari. The fountain which is decorated with mosaics faces a wall panel showing the gardens in the 16C. On the ceiling is a fresco of the *Banquet of the Gods.* From the Salon loggia is a lovely **view★** over the gardens and Tivoli.

Leading out of this room is a series of four rooms in the west wing. The mythological paintings in the first room are attributed to Muziano and Luigi Karcher: the Labours of Hercules surround a fresco of the *Synod of the Gods (ceiling).* Federico Zuccari and his school painted the allegorical frescoes in the next room, known as the Philosophers' Hall, and also the frescoes in the third room called the *Glory of Este.* In the Hall of the Hunt Tempesta's frescoes show hunting trophies and scenes of hunts in the country around Tivoli.

From the balcony of the Central Hall there is a pleasant **view★** of the gardens and Tivoli itself.

Double flights of steps lead down to the upper garden walk.

Fontana del Bicchierone – The fountain, which is often attributed to Bernini, consists of a huge moss-covered **beaker** from which water overflows into a shell-shaped basin.

La "Rometta" – This fountain, known as **"mini Rome"** is an attempt by the Cardinal to reproduce some of the most famous monuments of Classical Rome: a pool bearing a boat (Tiber Island) surmounted by an obelisk; higher up next to some artificial ruins an allegorical statue of Rome and the she-wolf.

★★★ Viale delle Cento Fontane – The **Avenue of a Hundred Fountains** is one of the most charming spots in the gardens. One side of the straight walk is lined by fountains of water spouting from small boats, obelisks, animal heads, eagles and lilies which recall the Este coat of arms.

★★★ Fontana dell'Ovato – The **Oval Fountain** is dominated by the statue of the Sibyl, which is flanked by allegorical figures of rivers. Round the edge of the basin, half-covered in moss, are statues of naiads pouring the water of the river Aniene from their water pots. An attractive ceramic decoration adorns the front rim of the oval basin.

★★★ Fontana dell'Organo – The **Organ Fountain** used to play music on a water-powered organ concealed in the upper part of the fountain. This ingenious mechanism was invented by a Frenchman, Claude Venard, in the 16C. After seeing and hearing the fountain Montaigne, the French writer and philosopher, wrote in his journal that "the organ music is made by water falling into a cave with such power that the air is forced out through the organ pipes while another stream of water turns a toothed wheel which operates the keyboard; one can also hear the distorted sound of trumpets."

Oval Fountain, Villa d'Este

Spianata delle Peschiere – The three basins were **fishponds** which supplied the Cardinal's table on fast days. There is a fine **view**★★ of the water spouts and the Organ Fountain.

Fontana della Madre Natura – The **Fountain of Mother Nature** is decorated with a statue of Diana of Ephesus, goddess of Fertility.
The gate in the wall *(right)*, overlooking the valley below, is the main entrance to the villa.

Fontana dei Draghi – The **Dragon Fountain** was created in honour of Pope Gregory XIII who visited the villa in September 1572 shortly before the Cardinal's death; the dragons recall the coat of arms of the Buoncompagni family to which the Pope belonged.

Fontana della Civetta – The **Owl Fountain** is more commonly known as the **Bird Fountain** on account of the hydraulic mechanism, originally concealed in a recess, which used to produce bird song; periodically an owl appeared and uttered a mournful screech. Several times restored, the fountain is now silent.

Fontana di Proserpina – *(left)* The **Fountain of Proserpina** *(restored)* recalls the mythological figure who was abducted by Pluto.
It is possible to walk down to the Villa Gregoriana through the streets of the old town (città vecchia).
The town is agreeably lively and some traces of the past still remain.
The **cathedral**, rebuilt in the 17C and flanked by a 12C Romanesque campanile, contains a fine group of carved wooden figures depicting the **Deposition**★ (13C).

★VILLA GREGORIANA ⊙

A tangle of paths winds down the steeply wooded slopes to the river Aniene where it cascades through the ravine.
Take the path downhill from the entrance and bear right to the **Great Waterfall**★★ *(Grande Cascata)*.
There is a terrace overlooking the waterfall from above. Take the path which zigzags down to a viewpoint near the foot of the fall *(Veduta inferiore della Cascata)* where the river plunges into the ravine throwing up a fine spray.
Return to the last junction and take the path marked *Grotte di Nettuno e Sirena, cascata Bernine* which starts with a short flight of steps and winds down into the valley bottom to the **Siren's Cave** where the Aniene plunges out of sight into a cavern with a great roar.
Return to the sign marked *Grotto di Nettuno e Tempio di Vesta* and take the path leading up the opposite side of the valley. Ignoring the righthand turning to *Tempio di Vesta e Sibilla*, bear left towards *Grotta di Nettuno*. After the tunnelled section bear left downhill. In **Neptune's Cave** the water bursts from the rock face which has been eroded into eerie configurations.
Return to the beginning of the tunnelled section but bear left up the path which climbs the slope overlooking the ravine and its many little waterfalls.
Next to the park gates which lead into the town stand the ruins of two temples.

Tempio della Sibilla — *Access through to Sibilla Restaurant.* The **Temple of the Sybil** is also known as the **Temple of Vesta** as shrines dedicated to this goddess were usually round. This elegant Corinthian structure dates from the late Republic. Next to it stands a contemporary building in the Ionic style, also supposed by some to be dedicated to the Sibyl. Both temples were built of travertine.

MICHELIN GUIDES

The Red Guides (hotels and restaurants)
Benelux – Deutschland – Espana Portugal – Europe – France – Great Britain and Ireland – Italia – Switzerland

The Green Guides (fine art, historic monuments, scenic routes)
Austria – Belgium and Luxembourg – Brussels – Canada – California – Chicago – England: The West Country – Europe – France – Germany – Great Britain – Greece – Ireland – Italy – London – Mexico – Netherlands – New England – New York City – Paris – Portugal – Quebec – Rome – Scotland – Spain – Switzerland – Scandinavia-Finland – Tuscany – Venice – Wales – Washington DC
and the collection of regional guides to France

Practical
Information

Before departure

Passport – Visitors travelling to Italy must be in possession of a valid national passport. Citizens of other European Union countries only need a national identity card. In case of loss or theft report to the embassy or consulate and the local police.

Visas – Entry visas are required by Australian, New Zealand, Canadian and US citizens (if their intended stay exceeds three months). Apply to the Italian Consulate (visa issued same day; delay if submitted by mail). US citizens may find the booklet **Your Trip Abroad** (US$1.25) useful for information on visa requirements, customs regulations, medical care, etc. when travelling in Europe – available from the Superintendent of Documents, PO Box 371954, Pittsburgh, PA 15250-7954, ☎ *(202) 512-1800*.

Customs – **A Guide for Travellers** outlines British customs regulations and duty-free allowances; it is available from the HM Customs Office (UK) ☎ 0181 346 1144 or 0171 620 1313. The US Customs Service, PO Box 7407, Washington, DC 20044, ☎ (202) 927-5580, offers a free publication **Know Before You Go** for US citizens.

Health – As the UK is a member of the European Union, British subjects should obtain **medical form E111** from the Ministry of Social Security, Newcastle-upon-Tyne, before leaving home.
Separate travel and medical insurance is highly recommended – check with your local travel agent before departure.

Disabled travellers – Many Roman historic monuments do not have modern lifts or wheelchair facilities. For detailed information contact **RADAR** (Royal Association for Disability and Rehabilitation) 12 City Forum, 250 City Road, London EC1V 8AF ☎ 0171 250 3222
Associazione Italiana per l'Assistenza agli Spastici (**AIAS**) via Cipro 4/H, 00136 Rome ☎ (06) 38 96 04 or AIAS Milano via San Barnaba 29, 20122 Milano ☎ 02 55 01 75 64; Fax 02 55 01 48 70.

When to go – Located 28km – 16 miles from the coast, Rome enjoys a mild Mediterranean climate: bright and crisp in winter, hot in summer. The most temperate months being May and June, September and October.

Italian State Tourist Board – The **Ente Nazionale Italiano per il Turismo** (ENIT) has offices abroad and in Italy – for local tourist information services see below:

> 1 Princes Street, London W1R 8AY ☎ 0171 408 1254, Fax 0171 493 6695 *(Open Mondays to Fridays, 9am to 5pm)*.
> Suite 1565, 630 Fifth Avenue, New York, NY 10111; ☎ 245 4822.
> Suite 550, 12400 Wilshire Boulevard, Los Angeles, California 90025; ☎ 820 0098.
> Suite 1914, 1 Place Ville Marie, Montreal, Quebec; ☎ 866 7667/8/9.

Arrival

By air – Rome is served by two airports: Leonardo da Vinci Airport at Fiumicino *(26km – 16 miles southwest of Rome)* and Ciampino Airport *(15km – 10 miles southeast of Rome)*.

Fiumicino handles national and international scheduled flights. It is linked to the centre of Rome by train: services to Roma-Termini (EX) (L 13000) depart hourly (every 30min at peak times) between 7.50am to 10.05pm from the airport; between 7am and 9.15pm from Roma-Termini; journey time 25min. Roma Termini is served by both metro lines. FM1 Fiumicino-Fara Sabina services run trains every 20min (except on public holidays) to Trastevere, Ostiense (CZ) Tuscolana and Tiburtina (L 7000); journey time between 40min and 75min; services operate from the airport between 6.15am and 8.15pm (0.15am to Tiburtina only) and between 6am to 11pm from Tiburtina.

Ciampino handles charter flights (details from travel agencies) and is linked by bus to the Metro line A station Anagnina.

Alitalia
> 27 Piccadilly, London W1 ☎ 0181 745 8200, Fax 0171 602 5584
> Norwich Union House, 60/63 Dawson Street, Dublin 2, ☎ 01 677 5171
> Via Bissolati 13, Rome, ☎ (06) 46881, 65645

Aer Lingus
> 41 Upper O'Connell Street, Dublin 1 ☎ 01 844 4747
> 223 Regent Street, London W1 ☎ 0181 899 4747

British Airways
> 156 Regent Street, London W1 ☎ 0171 434 4700
> Via Bissolati 54, Rome, ☎ (06) 479 991

By train – The mainline national and international trains arrive at **Stazione Termini** (EX) or **Tiburtina** (FV). Termini is on both Metro lines (A – Ottaviano-Anagnina and B – Laurentina-Rebibbia) and the bus station in the forecourt serves almost all the bus routes in Rome.

Special concessions (less 30%) are available to rail-users in Italy under the age of 26 and senior citizens over the age of 65 (men) or 60 (women) on presentation of an inter-rail card. Children aged between four and twelve travel half-price. Unlimited travel concessions are also available to foreigners in Italy: check for details.

Timetables are available at the Italian Tourist Office in London and from newsstands in Italy.

For tickets, prices and concessions apply to:

Italian State Railways, CIT Marco Polo House, 3-5 Lansdowne Road, Croydon, Surrey ☏ 0181 686 0677; Fax 0181 686 0328.

Ultima Travel, 424 Chester Road, Little Sutton, South Wirral L66 3RB ☏ 0151 339 6171; Fax 0151 339 1919.

Wasteels Travel (adjacent to Platform 2 at Victoria Station), 121 Wilton Road, London SW1V 1JT. ☏ 0171 834 7066, Fax 0171 630 7628.

Local trains – Services from places north of Rome arrive at Piazzale Flaminio station (BV). The line from Ostia Lido stops at Magliana station which is linked to Termini station by the underground (Line B – direction Rebibbia).

By coach – Coach services from Victoria Coach Station, London are organised by Eurolines, 52 Grosvenor Gardens, London SW1W 0AU, ☏ 0171 730 8235 or through National Express Offices and agents.

By car – Nationals of the European Union require a valid **national driving licence**. Nationals of non-EU countries should obtain an **international driving licence** (obtainable in the US from the American Automobile Association, cost for members: US$10, for non-members US$22). Other documents required include the vehicle's current **log book** and a **green card** for insurance.

All-night service stations – Fuel may be purchased from service stations dotted along the GRA ring road, along the Lungotevere Ripa, in Piazzale della Radio and at 504 Via Salaria.

Maps – Michelin Map no 970 Europe (1/3 000 000), no 988 Italy (1/1 000 000) and no 430 Central Italy (1/400 000) will make route planning easier.

On the outer edge of the city is the **Grande Raccordo Annulare** (GRA), a multi-lane ring road from which all the motorways (A1 to Florence and Bologna to the north, to Naples in the south; A12 to Fiumicino, Civitavecchia and the west coast; A24 east to Aquilla and the Adriatic) and main roads *(strada statale)* radiate.

The **Tangenziale Est** links the Stadio Olimpico to the Piazza San Giovanni in Laterano via such eastern quarters as Nomentano, Tiburtino, Prenestino.

Remember!

Traffic drives on the right.
The **minimum driving age** is 18 years.
Seat belts must be worn at the front and back of the vehicle. Drivers must wear **shoes**, carry spare lights and a **red triangle** to be displayed in case of a breakdown or accident.
Emergency **road-rescue** services are offered by ACI (Automobile Club Italiano) ☏ 116.
Motorways (*autostrade* – subject to tolls) and dual carriageways (*superstrade*) are indicated by green signs; ordinary roads by blue signs; tourist sights by yellow signs.
Italian **motorway tolls** can be paid with money or with the **Viacard**, a magnetic card with a value of L 90 000 or L 50 000 which is sold in Italy at the beginning of the motorways, in Autogrill restaurants and in the offices of ACI (Automobile Club Italiano), Via Marsala 8, 00185 Rome, ☏ (06) 4477.
The following **speed restrictions** operate:
50kmph in built-up areas
90-110kmph on open country roads
90 (600cc) – 130kmph (excess of 1000cc) on motorways depending on engine capacity.
Fuel is sold as *super* (4 star), *senza piombo* (unleaded 95 octane), *super plus* or *Euro plus* (unleaded 98 octane) or *gazolio* (diesel).
Petrol (US: Gas) stations are usually open between 7am and 7pm. Many close at lunchtime (12.30pm to 3pm), Sundays and public holidays and many refuse payment by credit card.

Places to stay

Hotels – The Michelin Red Guide **Italia** and the Michelin Red Guide **Europe**, which are revised each year, recommend a large selection of establishments together with their type, location, price, amenities and level of comfort.

Places marked with red symbols provide a particularly pleasant and restful stay.

The organisation Hotel Reservation, a **telematic hotel reservation service** *(Open 7am to 10pm.* ☎ (06) 69 91 000. No charge), has desks at Fiumicino Leonardo da Vinci Airport and at Termini Railway Station (platform 10).

Budget accommodation – The central organisation for **Youth Hostels** in Italy is the AIG (Associazione Italiana Alberghi per la gioventù), Viale delle Olimpiadi 61, Roma (near Foro Italico) ☎ (06) 32 36 279 and (06) 32 36 267, Fax (06) 32 42 613.

AIG Head Office, Via Cavour 44; ☎ (06) 48 71 152.

Youth Hostels Association, Trevelyan House, 8 St Stephen's Hill, St Albans, Herts AL1 2DY

American Youth Hostel Inc, National Offices, P O Box 37613, Washington DC 20013-7613

Student accommodation is available to students visiting on holiday as well as on courses; information from Casa dello Studente in Rome.

The **Salvation Army** offers accommodation to young people at Esercito della Salvezza, Via degli Apuli 3942; ☎ (06) 44 65 236 or (06) 44 67 482 (AIG card not necessary).

Young women may stay at the **YWCA**, Via Balbo 4; ☎ (06) 48 80 460 or (06) 48 83 917 and at Protezione della giovane, Via Urbana 158; ☎ (06) 48 81 489 or (06) 48 80 056 (AIG card not necessary).

Convents – Convents offer accommodation at a reasonable price but close their doors at 10.30pm. A list of convents is available from Peregrinatio ad Petris Aedem, Piazza Pio Dodicesimo 4 (Vatican City); ☎ (06) 69 88 48 96, Fax (06) 69 88 56 17; the centre will make a reservation at a particular convent.

Camping – Most sites are on the north side of Rome; there is one on the west side and several outside the city in Ostia, Castel di Guido, Acilia etc.

Information available from:

EPT, Via Parigi 5, Rome; ☎ (06) 48 89 92 00;

Touring Club Italiano, Corso Italia 10, 20122 Milano, ☎ 02 85 261;

Centro Internazionale Prentotazioni, Federcampeggio, Casella Postale 23, 50041 Calenzano (Firenze), Italy, ☎ 055 88 23 91, Fax 055 88 25 918;

Camping and Caravanning Club, Greenfields House, Westwood Way, Coventry CV4 8JH, ☎ 01203 694 995.

All roads lead to Rome...

Most of the ancient Roman roads retain their names:

the **Via Aurelia** (S1) was built by the Romans to undermine the maritime monopoly of the Ligurian tribes north of Pisa by providing a landward means of transport along the coast.

Via Cassia (S2) was the main route north across Tuscany taken by Caesar's marching armies, it was later the main pilgrimmage route south from the Alps.

Via Flaminia (S3) runs inland to Terni, across Umbria to Fano on the east coast, it was probably used by Justinian at the Fall of the Roman Empire to reach Ravenna.

Via Salaria (S4) via Rieti and Ascoli to the coast was used to transport salt *(sale)* to Rome; later, cured meats and regional delicacies (wine and truffles) were requesitioned by the Vatican from the papal states that included the Marche.

Via Tiburtina Valeria (S5) allowed Imperial noblemen and senators to reach their country villas in and around Tivoli, the popes to retreat to the Castelli Romani, and Roman conquerors to reach the coast from where they would sail for Split (latter day Yugoslavia).

Via Casilina (S6) runs southwards to Naples as does the **Via Appia** (S7).

Public transport

Bus, tram and underground – Public transport services are organised by **ATAC** (Azienda Tramvie e Autobus del Comune di Roma). City route plans are on sale in bookshops and kiosks; the plan *Rete dei Trasporti Urbani di Roma*, published by ATAC, is sold (L 1 000) at the information kiosk in Piazza dei Cinquecento (**DX**).

Tickets should be purchased before the beginning of the journey and punched in the machine in the bus and on the underground to be validated.

Different types of ticket *(biglietto)* are sold at newspaper kiosks or in tobacconists' shops: those bearing the name **Metrebus** may be used on all means of transport – bus, tram, metro and overground FS *(Ferrovie Statali)* trains in second class except on services Roma Termini – Fiumicino aeroporto and Ponte Galliera – Fiumicino aeroporto. Individual tickets may also be acquired from machines at metro stations and end-of-line bus stops.

– a BIT ticket costing L 1 500 is valid for a journey up to 75 minutes on various lines from its time of validation.
– a BIG ticket, costing L 6 000 is valid 24 hours from its time of validation.
– a CIS pass costing L 24 000 is valid for a month.
– a different type of pass costing L 50 000 is also available.

Bus and trams stops are indicated by a sign *Fermata;* request stop = *fermata richiesta*. The entrance door *(salita)* is at the back of the bus and the exit *(uscita)* in the middle.

Buses operate from 5.30am to 12 midnight. The following established routes are amongst the most useful – for additional lines see below:

– **64** Termini Station (**EX**), Via Nazionale (**DX**), Piazza Venezia (**CX**), near the Gesù Church, Largo di Torre Argentina, Corso Vittorio Emanuele II (**BX**), Vatican (**AVX**) – however, beware of pickpockets, notably at rush hour.
– **85** Colosseum (**DY**), Imperial Fora, Piazza Venezia (**CX**), Via del Corso (**CVX**).
– **118** Via Appia Antica, Baths of Caracalla (**DZ**), Colosseum (**DY**), St John Lateran (**EY**).
– **218** Piazza San Giovanni in Laterano (**EY**) south to Via Ardeatina (passing the north end of the Old Appian Way);
– **319** from Termini Station (**EX**) north to Villa Ada (Priscilla Catacombs).

Trams operate from 5am to 9pm. There are 8 lines; the following routes are amongst the most useful to tourists:

– **13** Piazza Preneste, Trastevere (**BY**), Piazza San Giovanni di Dio – operating in tandem with the 30b.
– **14** from the east side of the city to Termini Station (**EX**).
– **19** from Piazza dei Gerani to Piazza del Risorgimento (near the Vatican – **AV**), crossing the city west-east and passing near the Villa Borghese (**CDUX**) and through to the Piazza di Porta Maggiore.
– **30b** from Piazzale Ostiense (Piramide de G Cestius – **CZ**) to Piazza Thorwaldsen, passing near the Galleria d'Arte Moderna and Villa Borghese (**CDUV**) and through the city centre past the Colosseum (**DY**), St John Lateran (**EY**) and Piazza Porta Maggiore (**EFXY**).

Metro (underground) trains operate from 5.30am to 11.30pm; the section Termini-Rebibbia runs until 9pm weekdays and 11pm weekends and holidays. There are two lines.

Line A runs from Ottaviano (**AV**) to Via Anagnina: Flaminio (Piazza del Popolo – **BCV**), Spagna (Piazza di Spagna – **CV**), Barberini (Piazza Barberini – **DV**), Termini (Termini Station – **EX**), S Giovanni (St John Lateran – **EY**) and Cinecittà.

Line B runs from Laurentina to Rebibbia via EUR: EUR Fermi (EUR district), S Paolo (Basilica of St Paul Without the Walls), Piramide (Mausoleum of G Cestius – **CZ**), Circo Massimo (near the Circus Maximus and the Baths of Caracalla – **DZ**), Colosseo (Colosseum – **DY**), Cavour (Piazza Cavour) and Termini (Termini Station – **EX**).

Taxi – To call a taxi dial 3570, 4994, 6645, 4157. Fixed starting charge: L 4 500 rising L 200 every 50 seconds. Extra charges apply for luggage, night service (between 10pm and 7am), Sundays and holidays. It is advisable to negotiate a fixed price before setting out on journeys outside the town to the airports etc.

Car – Not advised as access to the city centre is very difficult and parking severely restricted; many streets are reserved for pedestrians, taxis, buses and local residents. The historic centre is delineated as blue zone *(fascia blu)* from which private cars are excluded between 6am and 7.30pm (also Fridays and Saturdays, from 10pm to 2am).

There are two large underground **car parks** in central Rome: Villa Borghese, near the Porta Pinciana (CV) and Parking Ludovisi, 60 Via Ludovisi (CV). Other ACI car parks are scattered at random around town.

Disabled people using their own vehicle must display the orange badge; further information from Radar, 25 Mortimer Street, London W1M 8AB, ☎ 0171 637 5400.

Scooter – A scooter *(motorino)* may be hired from the third level of the underground parking at Villa Borghese (between 9am and 7pm), from Via di Porta Castello, a stone's throw from St Peter's, from Via Filippo Turati near Termini and from Via della Purificazione by Piazza Barberini.

Bicycle – Bicycles can be hired at several places in the city centre: Piazza di Spagna, near the entrance to the metro (CV); Piazza del Popolo, on the corner of the street containing Café Rossetti (BV) *(Open in summer, 6am to 1am, in winter Sunday mornings only)*; Piazza San Lorenzo in Lucina, in Via del Corso (CV) *(Open March to October, 10am to 6pm [2am in summer])*; Villa Borghese underground car park, sector III (CV).

Carriage – A more Romantic view of Rome is to be had from an open horse-drawn carriage (*carozzella* or *botticella* in Roman dialect) which can be hailed for 30min or longer from St Peter's Square (AVX), the Colosseum (DY), Piazza Venezia (CX), Piazza di Spagna (CV), Piazza Navona (BX), Trevi Fountain (CX), Via Veneto (DV) and Villa Borghese (CDUV).

Waterbus – Two services operate on the River Tiber:
Ponte Duca d'Aosta to Isola Tiberina (CY) with one stop en route *(Operates May to October, 8am to 8pm (12midnight in August), every 25min)*.
Ponte Marconi downstream to Ostia – ideal introduction to the excavations of the Roman port *(Departs at 9.30am and arrives 11.15am; departs from Ostia at 2.30pm, arrives at 4.15pm)*. ☎ (06) 68 93 033.

Air – For a bird's eye view of the city in a Cessna or B66, contact the dell'Urbe airport at Via Salaria 825 ☎ (06) 81 20 290 or 81 20 297. 30min flights available Saturdays and Sundays 9am to 1pm, 2pm to 4pm. ☎ (06) 88 63 012 for flight times. Approximate cost L 70 000 to L 80 000 per person.

Roman carriage

Sightseeing

Tourist information – Three municipal information offices provide details of cultural events such as concerts, recitals, exhibitions and tourist information. These are located in Via Nazionale opposite the Palazzo delle Esposizioni, on the Largo Corrado Ricci in front of the Imperial Fora, on the Largo Goldoni between the Via del Corso and the Via dei Condotti. Offices are open Tuesday to Saturday 10am to 6pm and Sunday 10am to 1pm. Information, updated daily, is provided in Italian and English.

Italian State Tourist Board – The Ente Nazionale Italiano per il Turismo (ENIT) has offices at home and abroad (see above 'Before departure'). Their headquarters in Rome are at Via Marghera 2, Rome ☎ (06) 49 71 222.

Provincial Tourist Board – The Ente Provinciale per il Turismo (ETP) has several offices in Rome, which provide brochures, maps and hotel lists free of charge:

    Rome, Via Parigi 5 (DV 27), ☎ (06) 48 89 92 00;
    Rome, Termini Station (Platform 4), ☎ (06) 48 71 270, 48 24 078.
    Leonardo da Vinci Airport, ☎ (06) 65 95 44 71, 65 01 02 55.
    Bracciano, Via Claudia 58, ☎ (06) 99 86 771;
    Castel Gandolfo, Piazza della Libertà, ☎ (06) 93 60 340;
    Tivoli, Largo Garibaldi, ☎ 0774 33 12 94.

Internet – Those with access to the Internet may find additional information listed on http://www.comune.roma.it/.

Bus tours – Public services have implemented a number of new routes that allow visitors to discover the historical centre from the comfort of a bus:
– **110** departs from Termini at 2.30pm and wanders through the city for 3 hours. Tickets costing L 15 000 are available 30min before departure from Piazza Cinquecento opposite the mainline station.
– **Minibus 119** is a standard route which operates a scheduled service through town Monday to Saturday (suspended after 3pm and on Sundays).

Guided tours – Travel agents and the ATAC offices in Piazza del Cinquecento (DX) provide details of organised guided tours in foreign languages. For independent group visits contact the Sindacato Nazionale CISL, Guide Turistiche, Rampa Mignatelli 12 ☎ (06) 67 89 842.

Museums and monuments – Most museums are closed all day Mondays; on other days most close at 2pm and the ticket offices at 1.30pm.
Ancient monuments, archeological sites and public parks (Roman Forum, Colosseum etc) close about one hour before sunset according to the following timetable:
    9am to 6pm, mid-April to 1 September
    9am to 5.30pm, 2 September to last day of summertime
    9am to 4.30pm, first day of wintertime to 30 September
    9am to 4pm, 1st to 31 October
    9am to 3pm, 1 November to mid January
    9am to 3.30pm, mid January to mid February
    9am to 4pm, mid February to mid March
    9am to 4.30pm, mid March to last day of wintertime
    9am to 5.30pm, first day of summertime to mid April.

Churches – The major basilicas (St Peter's, St John Lateran, St Paul without the Walls, St Mary Major) are open from 7am to 6pm but most churches are closed between 12 noon and 2pm; exceptions are marked with the ⊙ in the Sights Section and listed with their times and charges in the Practical Information Section.
Visitors should be appropriately dressed: long trousers for men; no bare shoulders or very short skirts for women; those who do not observe this convention may be refused entry by the Verger or others in authority.
As many of the works of art are positioned high up, it is a good idea to take binoculars. Small change is needed for the light switches.

Church services – Roman Catholic mass in **Latin** is celebrated on Sundays at: St Peter's in the Vatican; St John Lateran; Santa Maria Maggiore; San Silvestro; St Stanislas, Via delle Botteghe Oscure 15.
Roman Catholic services in **English** are held on Sundays at San Silvestro, Piazza San Silvestro 1; San Tommaso di Canterbury, Via di Monserrato 45; Santa Susanna, Via XX Settembre 14; St Patrick's Church, Via Boncompagni 31.
Anglican services at All Saints' Church, Via del Babuino 153B; St Paul's Church, Via Nazionale. Methodist services at Piazza Ponte Sant'Angelo; Via Firenze 38.
Presbyterian services at St Andrew's Church, Via XX Settembre 7.
Baptist services at Rome Baptist Church, Piazza S Lorenzo in Lucina 35.

WHAT TO SEE

With such a profusion of sights to see in Rome it may be useful to plan a visit in the time available around individual personal interests. Otherwise, most of the three-star sights are highlighted in yellow-ochre boxes on the Principal Sights map in the opening pages of this guide.

Three days in Rome

Day 1 – Roman Forum★★★ and Palatine★★★ (starred sights only). **Imperial Fora★★★**, **Colosseum★★★**, **Arch of Constantine★★★**, San Pietro in Vincoli★ (Michelangelo's *Moses*★★★). **Santa Maria Maggiore★★★**. Stroll and dinner in or around Via Veneto.

Day 2 – Castel Sant'Angelo★★★, the Vatican★★★ and its museums (restricting visit to principal masterpieces), St Peter's Basilica★★★ and Square★★★. Stroll through the old quarters in the loop of the Tiber to **Piazza Navona★★★**. Lunch. **San Luigi dei Francesi★★** (paintings★★★ by Caravaggio), **Pantheon★★★**. Dinner in Trastevere.

Day 3 – Capitoline Hill★★★ (only recommended items in the museums), **Piazza Venezia★** and the Monument to Victor Emanuel II, the **Gesù★★★**, **Trevi Fountain★★★**, **Piazza di Spagna★★★**, **Spanish Steps★★★**, **Trinità dei Monti★**, **Piazza del Popolo★★** with its twin churches, notably **Santa Maria del Popolo★★** (paintings★★★ by Caravaggio); an amble through the pedestrianised section of Via del Corso and Via dei Condotti to be dazzled by the elegant window displays.

Seven days in Rome

Day 1 – **Piazza Venezia★** dominated by the Monument to Victor Emanuel II. The **Capitoline Hill★★★** including **Santa Maria degli Aracoeli★★**, **Piazza del Campidoglio★★★**, **Conservator's Palace Museum★★★**, **Capitoline Museum★★**, **Theatre of Marcellus★★**, **Temple of Apollo★★**, **Roman Forum★★★** and the **Palatine★★★**. Evening in the Via Veneto.

Day 2 – **Ara Pacis★★** and the Mausoleum of Augustus. **Piazza Colonna★**. The **Pantheon ★★★** and its environs including **Sant'Ignazio★★**, **Galleria Doria Pamphili★★**, **Santa Maria sopra Minerva★★**. **Piazza Navona★★★** and neighbouring churches such as **Santa Maria della Pace★** and **San Luigi dei Francesi★★**; **Palazzo della Cancelleria★★**; **Campo dei Fiori★**, **Palazzo Farnese★★**. Dinner in some informal trattoria in the old quarter nestling in the loop of the Tiber.

Day 3 – **Castel Sant'Angelo★★★**, **Vatican Museums★★★**, **St Peter's Basilica★★★** and **Square★★★**. Stroll around the **Janiculum** to enjoy the glorious views★★★ over Rome and on to **St Pietro in Montorio★** (Bramante's Tempietto★) and the **Villa Farnesina★★** beyond. In the evening, have dinner in Trastevere followed by a short walk around the area to soak up the atmosphere.

Day 4 – **Imperial Fora★★★**, **San Pietro in Vincoli★** (Michelangelo's *Moses*★★★), **San Clemente★★**, **St John Lateran★★★**. The **Baths of Caracalla★★★**, **Porta San Sebastiano★**, **Via Appia Antica★★** and its **Catacombs★★★** as far as the **Tomb of Cecilia Metella★**.

Day 5 – Day out at **Tivoli★★★** *(31km outside Rome)* to visit Hadrian's Villa★★★, the Villa d'Este★★★, and the Villa Gregoriana★.

Day 6 – The **Gesù Church★★★**, **Largo Argentina Sacred Precinct★★** *(Area Sacra del Largo Argentina)*, **Isola Tiberina★**. Then continue into the area of the **Bocca della Verità★★**, this includes Santa Maria in Cosmedin★, Temple of Vesta★, Temple of Human Fortune★. The **Aventine★** encompasses such historic monuments as the Circus Maximus, and the Church of Santa Sabina★★, Piazza dei Cavalieri di Malta while beyond stands **Piramide Cestia**, otherwise known as the Mausoleum of Caius Cestius★, Porta San Paolo and the **Basilica of St Paul Without the Walls★★** *(San Paolo fuori le Mura)*. Evening in the popular district of Testaccio.

Day 7 – The itinerary under the section for **Villa Borghese – Villa Giulia** includes the **National Etruscan Museum★★★** and the **National Gallery of Modern Art★**. The view★★★ from the Piazzale Napoleone I on the Pincian Hill is worthy of a detour. **Piazza del Popolo★★** with its twin churches notably **Santa Maria del Popolo★★** (paintings★★★ by Caravaggio). In the afternoon, an excursion to Ostia Antica or EUR is recommended – this contrasts well with the architecture and history of central Rome. Access is by underground Line B, direction Laurentina, stop at Magliana for Ostia or EUR Fermi for EUR.

Day 8 – Do not miss, however, **Santa Maria Maggiore★★★**, the **National Roman Museum★★★**, **Santa Maria degli Angeli★★**, **Santa Maria della Vittoria★★**, Bernini's **Triton Fountain★**, **Palazzo Barberini★★** and its fabulous collection of paintings★★, **San Carlo alle Quattro Fontane★★**, **San Andrea al Quirinale★★**, the famous **Trevi Fountain★★★**, **Piazza di Spagna★★★** graced with the **Spanish Steps★★★** leading up to **Trinità dei Monti★**. The streets around this area are lined with beautifully dressed shop windows displaying alluring selections of exquisitely tailored clothes and luxury goods.

I have been here now for seven days and am gradually beginning to get a general view of the city. We walk about a good deal, I study the layout of Ancient Rome and Modern Rome, look at ruins and buildings and visit this villa or that. The most important monuments I take very slowly; I do nothing except look, go away, and come back and look again. Only in Rome can one educate oneself for Rome.

Goethe: Italian Journey. Rome, 5 November 1786

Food and drink

Roman specialities – Roman citizens take their food extremely seriously. Tradition has it that the best delicacies were imported to the city from all the surrounding regions almost as a duty to government officials or to the Church.

Antepasti – Seasonal variations of vegetables are all wonderful: look out for *puntarelle* (salad flavoured with garlic and anchovies) and *carciofi alla giudia* (artichoke hearts fried in olive oil and served with garlic and parsley), *melanzane* (grilled, fried or baked aubergine or egg-plant), *zucchini* (baby courgettes), *cippolle agro-dolce* (sweet and sour onions), *frutta di mare* (mixed fish appetiser of squid marinated in lemon juice and olive oil)...

Pasta – Pasta comes in many shapes and sizes, selected according to the sauce it is designed to compliment:

> *Cannelloni* are broad tubes filled with a meat, spinach or other sauce.
> *Farfalle* are the butterfly-shaped pasta.
> *Fettuccine* and *tagliatelle* consist of long flat ribbons of pasta of different widths.
> *Fusilli* are spiral-shaped pasta.
> *Gnocchi alla romana* is a dish of pasta baked in the oven with butter and cheese.
> *Ravioli* are little cushions filled with minced meat or spinach and ricotta cheese (especially delicate if prepared *'al burro e salvia'* – with melted butter flavoured with sage).
> *Tortellini* are small parcels of pasta filled with meat or cheese; these are often served in a home-made broth or with tomato sauce *(sugo)*.

Primi – Typical main course dishes – often served without vegetables – include the following:

> *Saltimbocca*, veal escalope rolled around a slice of ham and sage and baked in a butter and marsala sauce.
> *Abbacchio*, tender and delicious suckling lamb grilled on a spit with herbs *(scottadito)* or chasseur *(alla cacciatora)*.
> *Trippa* (tripe), *coda alla vaccinara* (ox tail), and *pagliata* (lamb offal) are also long-standing favourites among the working people.
> *Baccalà* (salt cod) together with all sorts of fresh fish are common and to be recommended.
> *Ricotta*, *caciocavallo*, *pecorino* are among the many cheeses to be found.

Wine and water – The most renown local wines are the crisp flavoured dry whites from the Castelli Romani: Frascati, Marino, Velletri and Colli Albani. The reds tend to be from Tuscany (Chianti, Brunello di Montalcino), the Abbruzo, Umbria or Sicily (Barolo). Wine may be ordered from a wine list or as a house table wine *(vino della casa, in caraffa)* in quantities of a half litre *(mezzo litro)* or a quarter litre *(un quartino)*.
Mineral water *(acqua minerale)* may be ordered still *(naturale, liscio)* or fizzy *(gassata, frizzante)*. Tap water, which in Rome is perfectly safe to drink, is requested by asking for *acqua dal robinetto*.

Restaurants – The finest restaurants are listed in the **Michelin Red Guide ITALIA** – stars (from 1 to 3) indicate restaurants where the cooking is of a particularly high quality. More informal establishments are listed in the main text. Rome is provided with a huge number of restaurants but Trastevere is particularly well known for its *trattorie* and *pizzerie* and Testaccio for its *osterie* where one can enjoy typical Roman cooking.

Café Greco

Cafés and bars – The most famous cafés include the **Caffè Greco** in Via dei Condotti (CV), **Antico Caffè della Pace** in Via della Pace, **Danieli** in Via Veneto, **Bar Tre Scalini** in Piazza Navona and **Caffè Rossetti** in Piazza del Popolo.

Note that it is usual to pay a cashier before being served by the barman. If drinks or snacks are to be served by a waiter to a table outside on the pavement, prices will be considerably inflated – so beware! It is not acceptable, however, to be served at the bar before wandering out to a table in the sunshine...

Favourite drinks – Chilled beer *(birra)* is served in bottles or on draught *(alla spina)*. Common non-alcoholic alternatives include freshly pressed orange juice *(spremuta di arance)* and 'lemon soda' – a fizzy bitter lemon drink with real fruit pulp.

Snacks and sandwiches – Large loaf bread tends not to be salted – ideally designed if topped with cured ham, mortadella or salty cheese and served with artichoke hearts, anchovies or tiny mushrooms *'sott'olio'* (lightly cooked and kept in oil). Tidy square slices may be spread with a thin smear of mayonnaise and filled with ham cooked / cured *(prosciutto cotto / crudo)*, fresh cheese like stracchino or mozzarella, tomatoes, egg, tuna fish *(tonno)* spinach or rucola salad; these, cut into triangles are known as *tramezzini*.

Other scrummy snacks include *schiacciata*, a crisp pizza base sprinkled with salt, rosemary and olive oil; the standard slice of pizza; *panino* – a long or round roll filled with cheese or ham; *supplì alla Romana*, deep-fried rice croquettes (plain or flavoured with tomato) stuffed with melted, therefore elasticated mozzarella cheese.

Italian coffee

Espresso – very short, sharp, black and very strong

Caffè lungo / caffè americano – a short, strong espresso with added hot water

Caffè corretto – an espresso with added brandy or 'grappa' (fire-water!)

Caffè macchiato – an espresso with a dash of (cold) milk

Cappuccino or *cappuccio* – an espresso topped with hot fluffy milk and powdered chocolate

Caffè latte – a glass of hot milk flavoured with an espresso coffee

---

Ice-creams – The fame of Italian ice-cream *(gelato)* is of long date and best bought from a gelateria. The range of flavours is endless: **Straciatella** – plain with chocolate chips. **Gianduia** – smooth chocolate and hazelnut (wicked!). **Bacio** – milk chocolate. **Fior di latte** or **panna** – plain milk or cream. **Crema** – vanilla enriched with egg. **Cioccolato** – chocolate. **Nocciola** – hazelnut...
Frutta di bosco – fruit of the forest (blueberries, blackberries – delicious!). **Limone** – lemon sorbet. **Fragola** – strawberry. **Pistacchio** – violent green colour. **Pesca** – peach. **Albicocca** – apricot. **Lampone** – raspberry...

G. del Magro/SIPA PRESS

Shopping

Luxury goods – Italians are renowned for their refined tastes in art, elegant clothes and exquisite leather goods. Bargains, however, are difficult to find.

Fashion – Expensive clothes, jewellery, etc are to be found in Via dei Condotti (**CV**) and the neighbouring streets (Via Borgognona, Via Bocca di Leone) or in Via Veneto (**DV**). Younger fashion is sold through shops and boutiques around Via del Corso (**CVX**), Via Nazionale (**DX**), Via del Tritone (**CVX**) and Via Cola di Rienzo (**BV**).

Note

Italian sizes differ from other Continental European sizes. For women a British 12 in clothes corresponds to an Italian size 44; a British 5 in shoes corresponds to an Italian size 38.

For men a British 40 in clothes corresponds to an Italian size 50, a British 15 in collar size to an Italian size 38, and a British size 8 in shoes corresponds to an Italian size 42.

Shopping precincts and malls – As it is impossible to list them all, here are a selection, most also have a choice of refreshment facilities:

Cinecittà Due – *Viale Palmiro Togliatti 2*, on the corner of Via Tuscolana (Metro: Cinecittà). Open Monday to Saturday from 9am to 8pm. 2hr free parking.

I Granai – Via Tazio Nuvolari 100 (Metro: Ardeatino). Over 130 separate businesses open from 10am to 8pm. Panorama supermarket open Tuesday to Saturday 9am to 9pm, Monday afternoon only. Free parking.

Tiburtina Shopping Center 30 – Via Tiburtina 515-543 (Metro: Tiburtino; Bus routes 9, 11, 163, 448, 492, 495). Open daily between 9am and 7.30pm. Facilities include shops, a bar, restaurant, travel agency, MacDonald's and a tanning centre.

Centro Euclid – Via Flaminia at junction for the Cassia 8.2km out of Rome (Bus routes 033, 034, 035, 039). Open Tuesday to Sunday from 10am to 8pm.

Art and antiques – Antique shops line Via del Babuino (**CV**); art galleries run parallel in Via Margutta (**CV**). Other bric-a-brac and second-hand shops are to be found in Via dei Coronari (**BX**). The best place to browse through second-hand goods is the flea market held on Sunday mornings at Porta Portese (**BY**) – see below for other markets.

For books and engravings check out the **Mercato dell'antiquariato di Fontanella Borghese** in Piazza Borghese (**BCV**) held 9am to 5pm (7pm Saturdays and Sundays).

Markets – Fresh produce and end of line goods sold at factory prices feature in the various markets which promise to attract eloquent salesmen and chattering housewives.

Porta Portese – *Sunday mornings from dawn until 2pm*. This flea market has operated since the end of the Second World War. Stalls selling general bric-a-brac, end-of-line and second-hand clothes, old photographic equipment, books and records extend down Via Portuense.

Campo dei Fiori Market

Campo dei Fiori – *Daily until noon.* This was once one of Rome's most important market squares. Now only a small collection of stalls set up around the statue of Giordano Bruno.

Piazza Vittori Emanuele – *Daily until noon.* The fresh produce here is reputed to be the best value: fish, (horse) meat, exotic spices.

Viale Parioli – Sparkling trinkets, clothes, hardware and knick-knacks are to be found among the fresh produce. A covered flower market in Via Trionfale operates between 10.30am and 4pm.

Piazza Alessandria – *Monday to Saturday, until noon.* Fine Art Nouveau building sheltering stalls of fresh produce.

Underground – Parking Ludovisi, Via Crispi 96. *Open 3pm to 10pm Saturday, 10.30am to 7.30pm Sunday.* Entrance fee. Large underground area at the heart of the old city. Goods of all kinds: old and new, bric-a-brac, collectables and valuable antiques.

Bancarelle dell'usato di Ponte Milvio – Piazzale Ponte Milvio. *Monday to Saturday until noon.* Clothing – American army surplus on Mondays, Wednesdays and Saturdays.

Bancarella di Compact Disc – Via dei Baullari. *Monday to Saturday 9.30am to 7.30pm.* Classical music exchange and mart.

Bancarelle di Scarpe a Testaccio – Piazza di Testaccio. *Monday to Saturday until noon.* Shoes: factory seconds at bargain prices.

Late night opening – Most shops close around 7.30pm in winter and 8pm in summer. First and last edition **newspapers** are sold throughout the night at news-stands in Piazza di Spagna, Piazza del Cinquecento, Piazza Cavour, Via Nomentana 587 and Piazza Sonnino.

Bookshops: Mel Bookstore in Via Nazionale (until 10pm). **Rinascita** at Via delle Botteghe Oscure 1/2 (open until 12midnight). **Invito alla Lettura** in Corso Emanuele II (open until 2am). **Farenheit** at Piazza dei Fiori 451 (open until 11pm).

As morning breaks over Rome after a night out on the tiles, or simply wandering through the peaceful streets at night under the stars, certain bakeries sell *cornetti* fresh from the oven on their way to the bars. Unmarked by any ensign, these bakeries may be sought out in Trastevere (Vicolo del Cinque) and Testaccio (Via Volta). Among the bars that stay open late are **Quelli della Notte** (Via Leone IV 48, in the Prati quarter), which is particularly renowned for its nutella-filled *cornetti*, and **Bambu's Bar** (Viale Parioli 79) which sells a variety of *fagottini* (stuffed parcels).

Videos

Beware! Pre-recorded Italian **videos** tend to be recorded on the PAL system.

Entertainment

News, views and reviews – **Il Messaggero** is Rome's most popular broadsheet newspaper. It carries information and notices on lectures, conferences, exhibitions and the theatre. Every Thursday it publishes a supplement entitled *Metro* to rival the weekly pocket guide to what's on in Rome entitled **Roma c'è**, which was founded in 1995. Information includes details of nightclubs, restaurants, shopping promotions, films screened at the cinema and such like.

The other national broadsheet widely read in Rome, **La Repubblica**, also produces a supplement on a Thursday. *Trovaroma* reviews all that is new from one week to the next.

Theatre – A broad selection of theatres provide a complete range of drama and entertainment to satisfy all tastes, assuming an understanding of the language. The more traditional productions are put on in the historical centre. The more classical establishments include:

Teatro di Roma *Largo Argentina 52* ☎ (06) 68 80 46 01

Teatro Valle *Via del Teatro Valle 23/A* ☎ (06) 68 80 37 94 and her sister theatre **Teatro Quirino** *Via M Minghetti 1* ☎ (06) 67 94 585. Both of these are affiliated to the ETI (Ente Teatrale Italiano).

Teatro Sistino *Via Sistina 129.* This often hosts shows and musicals imported from abroad.

Among the more avant-garde are:

Colosseo Ridotto *Via Capo d'Africa 5/A* ☎ (06) 70 04 932.

Dei Cocci *Via Galvani 69* ☎ (06) 57 83 502.

Dei Satiri *Via di Grottapina 19* ☎ (06) 68 71 639.

Dell'Orologio *Via dei Filippini 17/A* ☎ (06) 68 30 87 35.

Light-hearted – Several places host cabaret evenings and variety performances. The most typical being **Alfellini** *Via F Carletti 5* ☎ (06) 57 57 570 and **Farno Tardi** *Via G Libetta 13* ☎ (06) 57 44 319.

Opera, ballet and the classical repertoire – The principal venues include:
Teatro dell'Opera *Piazza Beniamino Gigli* ☎ (06) 48 16 01.
Teatro Brancaccio *Via Merulana 244* ☎ (06) 48 74 563.
Teatro Olimpico *Piazza G da Fabriano 17* ☎ (06) 32 34 890.
Auditorium dell'Accademia Nazionale di Santa Cecilia *Via della Concellazione 4* ☎ (06) 68 80 10 44.

Cinema – Prices vary according to the days of the week from L 10 000 (L 8 000 on Wednesdays) to L 12 000 at weekends.
Besides the **Pasquino** in Trastevere which only shows films in English, the Azzurro Scipioni, Libirinto, Cinema dei Piccoli Sera also show films in their original language with sub-titles.

Did you know?

The Eternal city celebrates her birthday on 21 April: on this day are organised a whole host of activities including concerts, special events for children, free guided tours of the municipal museums, the floodlighting of major monuments. In 1997, Rome reached the grand old age of 2750 years!

Parks and gardens

Rome may to some appear completely chaotic and devoid of trees and flowers, but this is not the complete picture for there are many 'green' spaces where her citizens take the air.

Just as the gardens of the **Villa Borghese** are famous, so there are a number that remain unknown. These more remote, secluded gardens are scattered throughout the city, open from sunrise to sunset.

The **Roseto comunale** on the Aventine Hill consists of a rose garden open exclusively when the plants are in bloom (end April to end June). Prizes are awarded annually to new varieties, and the prize-giving ceremony attracts great crowds.

Ornamented with statues, fountains and antiquities, the gardens of the **Villa Sciarra** (in the Monteverde Vecchio quarter) have recovered their intended Baroque splendour. Renowned for its collection of plants, the park also accommodates the library of the Italian Institute for Germanic studies (Istituto Italiano di Studi Germanici).

Villa Celimontana (Celio quarter) is one of the few Roman parks to possess a skating rink. This park is also favoured by smiling young newly-weds, who go there to have their photographs taken amongst the trees.

The gardens of the **Villa Ada** (Salario quarter) are graced with an artificial lake and an ornamental Classical temple, together with a children's play area.

Villa Torlona (Nomenatano district) is the former residence of the Mussolini family. This is the only park to remain open to the public until midnight (although a section of the gardens of the Villa Borghese do remain accessible throughout the night).

At **Villa Giori** (Parioli district) a large section of the grounds are planted with olive trees. Once a favourite place for children to go pony and donkey riding, all but a few animals have now gone.

Villa Doria Pamphili (Aurelia district) is regarded as the green lung of the western part of the city. There, come late afternoon, the paths are pounded by joggers and the verges are populated by kite flyers. Scattered among the greenery, glasshouses and 18C pond are a number of follies: a reduced Villa Corsini, a few arches from the Paolo Aqueduct, the Bel Respiro pavilion, an old villa.

MICHELIN GREEN GUIDES

Art and Architecture
History
Geography
Ancient monuments
Scenic routes
Touring programmes
Plans of towns and buildings
A selection of guides for holidays at home and abroad

Further reading

People

Stories of Rome – Livy, translated by R Nicholls (1982)
The Caesars – Allan Massie (1983, 1988)
The Twelve Caesars - Suetonius translated by Robert Graves (1978)
The Italians – Luigi Barzini (Penguin 1964)
Romans, their Lives and Times – Michael Sheridan (Weidenfeld and Nicholson 1994)
Rome, the Biography of a City – Christopher Hibbert (Penguin 1995)
The English Road to Rome – Brian Barefoot (Images Publishing [Malvern] 1985)
The Enchanted Ground – Americans in Italy 1760-1900 – E Amfitheatrof (Little, Brow & Co. Boston and Toronto)
The New Italians – Charles Richards (1994)

History

A History of Italy – Stuart Woolf (Routledge 1979, 1991)
A Traveller's History of Italy – Valerio Lintner (Windrush Press, Gloucestershire 1989, 1993)
The Etruscans – M Grant (Weidenfeld & Nicholson)
Roman Society – D Dudley (Pelican)
The Romans – K Christ (Chatto & Windus, The Hogarth Press [translated from German])
Rome: Its People, Life and Customs – U E Paoli (Longman [translated from Italian])
The Popes and the Papacy in the Early Middle Ages – J Richards (Routledge & Kegan Paul)
Renaissance Rome: A Portrait of a Society – P Partner (University of California Press)
The World of the Italian Renaissance – E R Chamberlin (George Allen & Unwin)
The Counter Reformation – A G Dickens (Thames & Hudson)
The Risorgimento and the Unification of Italy – D Beales (Longman)
Italy in the Age of the Risorgimento – H Hearder (Longman History of Art)
The Pope and the Duce – P C Kent (Macmillan)
The Power of Rome in the Twentieth Century – A Rhodes (Sidgwick & Jackson)

Art and Architecture

Roman Building – Jean Pierre Adam (Batsford 1994)
Roman Art and Architecture – Sir Mortimer Wheeler (Thames & Hudson)
A Handbook of Roman Art – M Henig (Phaidon)
Roman Imperial Architecture – J B Ward Perkings (Pelican History of Art)
Lives of the Artists – G Vasari (Penguin Classics)
The Italian Painters of the Renaissance – B Berenson (Phaidon)
Guide to Rome Baroque – A Blunt (Granada)

Useful Guides

Guide to the Vatican Museums; Guide to the Vatican City (Monumenti, Musei e Gallerie Pontificie)
The Companion Guide to Rome – Georgina Masson (Collins)
A Traveller in Rome – H V Morton (Methuen)
The Waters of Rome – H V Morton (Methuen)

Commentaries and fiction

The Path to Rome – Hilaire Belloc
Pictures from Italy – Charles Dickens (1846, 1989)
Italian Journey – Wolfgang Goethe (1788, 1970)
Italian Hours and *Daisy Miller* – Henry James (1987 and 1880, 1986)
The Voyeur – Alberto Moravia (1985, 1991)
Enderby – Anthony Burgess (1973, 1982)
The Child of Pleasure – Gabriele D'Annunzio (1889, 1991)

Si fueris Romae, Romano vivito more;
Si fueris alibi, vivito sicut ibi.

When in Rome, live as the Romans do;
when elsewhere, live as they live elsewhere.
Advice to St Augustine from St Ambrose

Films

1945   Roma, città aperta – Roberto Rosselini
1948   Ladri di biciclette (Bicycle thieves) – Vittorio De Sica
1949   Domenica d'agosto – Emmer
1953   Roman Holiday – William Wyler
1958   Poveri ma belli – Dino Risi
1960   La Dolce Vita – Federico Fellini
1960   Era notte a Roma – Roberto Rossellini
1960   Fantasmi a Roma – Antonio Pietrangeli
1961   L'oro di Roma – Lizzani
1969   Satyricon – Federico Fellini
1970   Nell'anno del Signore – Luigi Magni
1971   Fellini-Roma – Federico Fellini
1974   Ci siamo tanto amati – Ettore Scola
1977   Una giornata particolare – Ettore Scola
1977   In nome del papa re – Luigi Magni
1985   La Storia – Luigi Comencini
1987   The Belly of an architect – Peter Greenaway
1994   Caro diario (Dear Diary) – Gianni Moretti

Practical tips
(listed alphabetically)

Electricity – The voltage is 220ac, 50 cycles per second; the sockets are for two-pin plugs. It is therefore advisable to take an adaptor for hairdryers, shavers, computers, etc.

Embassies and Consulates:
Australia – Via Alessandria 215, 00198 Rome; ☎ (06) 83 27 21.
Canada – Via G B Rossi 27, 00161 Rome; ☎ (06) 44 59 81.
Ireland – Largo Nazareno 3, Rome; ☎ (06) 67 82 541, Fax (06) 67 92 354.
UK – Via XX Settembre 80a, Rome; ☎ (06) 48 25 441, 48 25 551, Fax (06) 48 73 324.
USA – Via Veneto 119a, 00187 Rome; ☎ (06) 46 741.

Money – The unit of currency is the **lira** which is issued in notes (L 100000, L 50000, L 20000, L 10000, L 5000, L 2000 and L 1000) and in coins (L 500, L 200, L 100, L 50).

Banks – Banks are usually open Monday to Friday, 8.30am to 1.30pm and 3pm to 4pm but closed on Saturdays, Sundays and public holidays. Most hotels will change travellers' cheques. Money can be changed in post offices (except travellers' cheques), money-changing bureaux and at railway stations and airports. Commission is always charged.

Eurocard – Eurocheques are widely accepted, although the value guaranteed is restricted – it is advisable to check on these rules prior to departure. Money withdrawn from Bancomat machines with a PIN incurs a lesser commission than from a withdrawal transacted over the counter at a bank.

Credit cards – Payment by credit card is widespread in shops, hotels and restaurants and also some petrol stations. The Michelin Red Guide **Italia** and the Michelin Red Guide **Europe** indicate which credit cards are accepted at hotels and restaurants. Money may also be withdrawn from a bank but may incur interest pending repayment.

Pharmacies – These are identified by a red and white cross. When closed each will advertise the names of the pharmacy on duty and a list of doctors on call. There is a 24-hour service at the pharmacy near the Termini station **(Farmacia della Stazione)**.

Postal services – In Italy post offices are open from 8.30am to 2pm (12noon Saturdays and the last day of the month). Letters sent **poste restante** (fermo posta) can be collected from the central post office in Piazza San Silvestro. Stamps are sold in post offices and tobacconists. The rates are: postcards L 750, letters L 850.

Public holidays – A working day is un giorno feriale; giorni festivi include Saturdays, Sundays and the following public holidays:
    January: 1 (New Year) and 6 (Epiphany)
    Easter: Sunday and Monday (lunedì dell'Angelo)
    April: 25 (St Mark's day and liberation in 1945)
    May: 1 (Festa dei Lavoratori)
    June: 29 (the feast of St Peter and St Paul, patron saints of Rome)
    August: 15 (The Assumption – Ferragosto)
    November: 1 (All Saints - Tutti i Santi)
    December: 8 (Immaculate Conception), 25 and 26 (Christmas and St Steven's day).

Telecommunications – The telephone service is organised by TELECOM ITALIA (formerly SIP). Each office has public booths where the customer pays for units used *(scatti)* at the counter after the call.

Reduced rates operate after 6.30pm and even less between 10pm and 8am.

Phone cards – These are sold in denominations of L 5 000, L 10 000 or L 15 000 *(schede da cinque, dieci, quindici mila lire)* and supplied by CIT offices and post offices as well as tobacconists (sign bearing a white T on a black background).

Public phones – Orange phones in the street or in bars may be operated by phone cards, coins or L 200 brass tokens – to make a call: lift the receiver, insert payment, await dialling signal, punch in the required number and wait for a response.

Telephoning – For calls within Rome, dial the correspondent's number.

For calls to places outside Rome, dial the code for the town or district beginning with a 0 followed by the correspondent's number.

For international calls dial 00 +

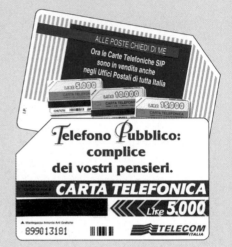

> 61 for Australia
> 1 for Canada
> 64 for New Zealand
> 44 for the UK
> 1 for the USA

If calling from outside Rome, the international code for Italy is 39, the code for Rome is 6.

Useful numbers:

113	general emergency services (equivalent of British 999)
12	directory enquiries
15	assisted operator service (reverse charge calling)
176	information in foreign languages

Time – The time in Italy is usually the same as the rest of mainland Europe (one hour ahead of the United Kingdom) and changes during the last weekend in March and September between summer time *(ora solare)* and winter time *(ora legale)*.

Tobacconists – Besides cigarettes and tobacco, *tabacchi* sell postcards and stamps, confectionery, phonecards, public transport tickets, lottery tickets and such like. Those at 11 Via del Corso and 275 Viale Trastevere stay open all night.

Roman type

The first printing types were based upon the national or local handwriting. Roman type developed from the *litera umanistica*, the conscious revival of the old Roman capital and the Carolingian minuscule which the Humanist scholars of the Italian Renaissance considered more appropriate for the transcription of recently discovered Classical manuscripts than the everyday forms of Gothic handwriting. It was first used in 1465.

Help us in our constant task of keeping up-to-date
Please send us your comments and suggestions

Michelin Tyre PLC
Tourism Department
Edward Hyde Building
38 Clarendon Road
Watford WD1 1SX
Tel : 01923 415164/5/6
Fax : 01923 415250

Traditional feast days and holidays

A detailed calendar of events can be obtained from the Vatican Information Office (Ufficio Informazioni Pellegrini e Turisti) and from local Tourist Information offices (ETP).

January

New Year is celebrated with a banquet dinner *(il cenone)* complete with lentils for luck and financial fortune. People rally in Piazza Navona for celebrations of goodwill at midnight.

6 January – Festival of the *Befana*: the last of the Twelve Days of Christmas; market stalls overflow with presents and sweets (candy coal) to the great delight of the children.

21 January – In the Church of Sant'Agnese Fuori le Mura, the saint's feast day is celebrated with the benediction of two lambs before being presented to the Benedictines of Santa Cecilia who use the wool to weave the *palium* which each new archbishop receives from the Pope.

March

9 March – The Blessing of automobiles near the Church of Santa Francesca Romana, patron saint of drivers.

19 March – In the Trionvale district on the feast of St Joseph stalls sell typical *bignè*, a sort of doughnut, and *frittelle*, a sort of choux pastry, made specially for the occasion.

St Peter's Square at Easter

M. Siragusa/CONTRASTO-REA

Easter

Good Friday – Stations of the Cross by night between the Colosseum and the Palatine Hill.

Easter Sunday – At midday in St Peter's Square the Pope gives his blessing *Urbi et Orbi*.

April

To mark the arrival of Spring the steps of Trinità dei Monti are decked with blooming azaleas, a dazzling sight.

21 April – Solemn ceremony on the Capitoline Hill to commemorate the anniversary of the founding of the Eternal City (753 BC).

May

International equestrian competition in Piazza di Siena (*see* Villa Borghese).
Open air art exhibition in Via Margutta.
Antiques Fair in Via dei Coronari.
Roses in bloom in the municipal rose gardens at Roseto di Roma (*see* Parks and gardens).

June

23 and 24 June – On the feast of St John, in the district bearing his name, there is great rejoicing: popular games and spectacles; snails in broth and roast pork.

29 June – Service in St Peter's Basilica on the feast of St Peter and St Paul, the most solemn of the religious festivals in Rome.

June-July

Tevere-Expo: exhibition of Italian and international crafts on the banks of the Tiber.
15 to 30 July – Fiesta de Noantri: popular festival in the streets of Trastevere.

July to August

Roman Summer: throughout the City musical concerts and various spectacles *(see also* Terme di Caracalla*)*.
5 August – Commemoration in the Basilica of Santa Maria Maggiore of the miraculous fall of snow which led to the construction of the church: a shower of white flower petals is released in the Pauline Chapel.

December

8 December – Celebration of the doctrine of the Immaculate Conception in Piazza di Spagna in the presence of the Pope.
Advent – At Christmas, the Holy Child (Santo Bambino) is solemnly put on show in the Church of Santa Maria d'Aracoeli.
In Via Giulia every year there is an exhibition of over 50 nativity scenes; there are beautiful cribs in the following churches: SS Cosma e Damiano, Santa Maria in Via, San Alessio, Basilica dei Santi Apostoli, San Marcello, the Gesù Church, Santa Maria d'Aracoeli, Santa Maria del Popolo, Santa Maria Maggiore (13C crib).
Midnight mass is celebrated with particular solemnity in Santa Maria Maggiore and in Santa Maria d'Aracoeli. In St Peter's Square the Pope's blessing *Urbi et Orbi* is bestowed.
Throughout the Christmas period red carpets are laid in the streets and in front of the shops.

Rome – St Peter's Square

Pocket-size binoculars are most useful when visiting the major basilicas for viewing the exquisite details of painted ceilings or mosaic friezes

Admission times and charges

The visiting times marked in the text with the **clock-face** symbol⊙ indicate the normal hours of opening and closing. These are listed here in the same order as they appear in the main text.

Admission times and charges are liable to alteration without prior notice and so the information given here should merely serve as a guideline. *Where up-to-date information has been withheld, times and charges from the previous edition have been listed in italics.*

Please note that museums, churches or other monument may be closed without prior notice or may refuse admittance during private functions, religious services or special occasions; they may also stop issuing tickets up to an hour before the actual closing time.

When **guided tours** are indicated, the departure time for the last tour of the morning or afternoon will once again be prior to the given closing time.

Most tours are conducted by Italian speaking guides but in some cases the term 'guided tour' may cover group visiting with recorded commentaries. Some of the larger and more frequented museums and monuments offer guided tours in other languages. Enquire at the ticket desk or book stalls.

The **admission prices** indicated are for single adults benefiting from no special concession; reductions for children, students, the over 60s and parties should be requested on site and be endorsed with proof of ID. In some cases, admission is free (notably Wednesdays, Sundays and public holidays).

For nationals of European Union member countries, State-run or City of Rome-run museums provide free admission to visitors under 18 and over 60 – with proof of identification.

During National Heritage Week (sometime in December) access to a great number of sights is free of charge.

Churches and chapels are usually open from 8am to 12noon and from 2pm to dusk. Notices outside a number of churches formally request visitors to dress in a manner deemed appropriate to entering a place of worship – this excludes sleeveless and low-cut tops, short miniskirts or skimpy shorts and bare feet.

Visitors are not admitted during services and so tourists should avoid visiting at that time. As it is the norm for all churches to be open daily, only exceptional conditions are here listed. Although no fee is charged, donations towards maintenance and upkeep are welcome.

IMPORTANT WARNING

If intending to visit a particular monument or see a specific artefact it is important to ring in advance and check opening times. Many Roman monuments may be closed at short notice for holidays or staff shortages. There is a risk of lengthy periods of closure – sometimes running into years – if restoration work is being undertaken.

Telephone numbers are given here with the (06) prefix code for Rome: this is only necessary if calls are made from outside the city. If calling from overseas, dial 00 39 6 + number.

APPIA ANTICA

Catacombe di San Callisto – Same times and charges apply as for the Domitilla Catacombs . Closed Wednesdays. ☎ (06) 51 36 725.

Catacombe di Domitilla – Guided tour (1hr) daily from 8.30am to 12noon and from 2.30pm to 5pm (5.30pm in summer). Closed Tuesdays and from late December to late January. 8 000 L. ☎ (06) 51 10 342.

Fosse Ardeatine – Open from 9am to 4.45pm (6.30pm in summer).

Catacombe di San Sebastiano – Same times and charges apply as for the Domitilla Catacombs . Closed Thursdays. ☎ (06) 78 87 035.

Mausoleo di Quirino e «Domus Petriœ» - Open to specialists only.

Circo di Massenzio e Tomba di Romolo – Open Tuesday to Saturday from 9am to 5.30pm (7pm in summer) and Sundays from 9am to 1.30pm all year round. Closed Mondays, 1 January, 1 May and at Christmas. 3 750 L. ☎ (06) 78 01 324.

Tomba di Cecilia Metella – Open Monday to Saturday from 9am to one hour before sunset, and Sundays from 9am to 1pm. Closed 1 January, 1 May and at Christmas. No charge.

AVENTINO

Santa Prisca: Santuario di Mitra – *Closed for restoration.* ☎ *(06) 69 90 110 or 67 90 333.*

BOCCA DELLA VERITÀ

Santa Maria in Cosmedin – Open from 9am to 1pm, and from 3pm to 5pm in summer.

Oratorio di San Giovanni Decollato – Guided tour by prior arrangement only (apply 15 days in advance to Governatore dell'Arciconfraternità di San Giovanni Decollato, Via San Giovanni Decollato 22): Mondays, Wednesdays and Fridays between 10.30am and 12noon. ☎ (06) 67 91 890.

CAMPIDOGLIO – CAPITOLINO

Santa Maria d'Aracoeli – Open daily. Guided tour 9am to 12noon, 3.30pm to 5.30pm. ☎ (06) 67 98 155.

Museo del Palazzo dei Conservatori – Open Tuesday to Saturday from 9am to 7pm (2pm on Sundays). Closed Mondays, 1 January, 1 May and at Christmas. 10 000 L; no charge last Sunday of the month, 15 December and during National Heritage Week. ☎ (06) 67 10 20 71.

Braccio nuovo – Access temporarily restricted to specialists.

Museo nuovo – Closed for restoration.

Museo Capitolino – Same times and charges apply as for the Museo del Palazzo dei Conservatori. ☎ (06) 67 10 20 71.

San Nicola in Carcere: Excavations – *Guided tour Monday to Saturday from 9am to 12noon.* ☎ *(06) 68 69 972.*

Santa Maria in Campitelli – Open daily from 9am to 12noon, from 4pm to 7.30pm. ☎ (06) 68 80 39 78.

CAMPO DEI FIORI

Palazzo della Cancelleria – *Open by appointment only (Amministrazione del Patrimonio della Sede Apostolica, Città del Vaticano). Closed Saturday, Sunday, public holidays, throughout July and August.* ☎ *(06) 69 88 47 67.*

Museo Baracco – Open Tuesday to Saturday from 9am to 7pm; Sunday and holidays from 9am to 1pm. Closed Mondays, 1 January, 1 May and at Christmas. 3 750 L. ☎ (06) 68 80 68 48.

Sant'Andrea della Valle – Open daily from 7.30am to 12noon, 4.30pm to 7pm.

Cappella del Monte di Pietà – Open only on written application 20 days in advance to Banca di Roma, Servizio Affari generali, via M Minghetti 17, 00187 ROMA. ☎ (06) 51 721.

Galleria Spada – Open Tuesday to Saturday from 9am to 7pm, Sunday from 9am to 1pm. Closed Monday, 1 January, 1 May and at Christmas.
Guide tour available on Sundays at 11am. 4 000 L. ☎ (06) 68 61 158.

San Tommaso di Canterbury – Open during term-time (October to mid-June) – ring at Porter's Lodge, 45 Via di Monserrato.

CASTEL SANT'ANGELO

Castel Sant'Angelo – Open daily from 9am to 2pm. Last admission one hour before closing time. Closed 1 January, 1 May and at Christmas. 8 000 L. ☎ (06) 68 75 036.

Oratorio dei Filippini – *To arrange a visit ring* ☎ *(06) 68 80 26 62.*

CATACOMBE DI PRISCILLA

San Agnese fuori le Mura - Open daily from 7am to 12noon, 4pm to 7.30pm. **Catacombs** - Guided tour (15min) daily from 9am to 12noon, 4pm to 6pm. Closed Monday afternoons, Sunday mornings and public holidays. 8 000 L.

Mausoleo di Santa Costanza – Guided tour from 9am to 12noon, 4pm to 6pm. Closed Sunday mornings and Monday afternoons. ☎ (06) 86 20 54 56.

Catacombe di Priscilla – Guided tour (40min) Tuesday to Sunday from 8.30am to 12noon, 2.30pm to 5pm (5.30pm in summer). Closed Mondays, throughout January, Easter, 15 August and at Christmas. 8 000 L; no charge 26 January. ☎ (06) 86 20 62 72.

COLOSSEO – CELIO

Colosseo – Open daily from 9am to one hour before sunset (1pm Wednesdays, Sundays and public holidays). Closed 1 January, 1 May and at Christmas. 8 000 L; no charge 21 April and during National Heritage Week. ☎ (06) 70 04 261.

San Pietro in Vincoli – Open daily from 9.30am to 12.30pm, 3.30pm to 6pm (7pm during the summer). ☏ (06) 48 82 865.

Domus Aurea – *Due to recent subsidence, visits have been suspended while reinforcement work is undertaken.*

San Clemente: Lower Basilica – *Open daily from 9am (10am Sunday and public holidays) to 12.30pm, 3.30pm to 6pm. 2 000 L.* ☏ *(06) 70 45 10 18.*

Santo Stefano Rotondo – Closed on Sundays.

Santa Maria in Domnica – *Open daily from 8am to 12noon, 4pm to 6pm.*

Santi Giovanni e Paolo – *Open daily from 8am to 11.30am and from 3.30pm to 6pm.*

San Gregorio Magno – Open daily from 9am to 1pm, 4pm to 7pm.
The chapels painted by Guido Reni and Domenichino may only be visited by prior arrangement with an official from the Sovrintendenza alle Belle Arti. ☏ (06) 70 08 227.

Museo Luigi Pigorini – ♿ (50%). *Open daily from 9am to 7pm (1pm Sundays. Closed 1 January, 1 May. 6 000 L, no charge under-18s and over-60s, and during National Heritage Week. Guided tour (1hr).* ☏ *(06) 59 23 057 / 59 10 702.*

Museo dell'Alto Medioevo – Open daily from 9am to 2pm (1pm Sundays); last admission 30min before closing time. Closed 1 May. 4 000 L; no charge during National Heritage Week. ☏ (06) 59 25 806.

Museo della Civiltà Romana – Open Tuesday to Saturday from 9am to 7pm, Sunday from 9am to 1.30pm. Closed Mondays, 1 January, 1 May and at Christmas. 5 000 L; no charge the last Sunday in the month. ☏ (06) 59 26 041.

Museo delle Arti e Tradizioni popolari – ♿. Open daily from 9am to 2pm (1pm Sundays). Closed 1 January, 1 May and at Christmas. 4 000 L. Guided tours available on Sundays. ☏ (06) 59 10 709.

FONTANA DI TREVI – QUIRINALE

Museo nazionale delle Paste alimentari – Open daily from 9.30am to 12.30pm, 4pm to 7pm (except Saturdays). 12 000 L. ☏ (06) 69 91 119.

Palazzo del Quirinale – Authorised access the second and fourth Sundays of each month. Closed throughout July and August. No charge. ☏ (06) 46 991 (ask for the Ufficio Visite).

Sant'Andrea al Quirinale – Open daily except Tuesdays from 8am to 12noon, 4pm to 7pm except in August when opening times are restricted from 10am to 12noon. ☏ (06) 47 44 801.

San Carlo alle Quattro Fontane – *Open from 9am to 12.30pm, 4pm to 6pm (except Saturday afternoon). Closed Sundays.*

Palazzo Pallavicini: Casino – *Open the first day of each month from 10am to 5pm.*

San Silvestro al Quirinale – *Open from 9am to 12noon and by appointment during the afternoon. Entrance at 10 via 24 Maggio.* ☏ *(06) 67 90 240.*

Galleria di Palazzo Colonna – Open Saturdays only from 9am to 1pm. Closed public holidays and throughout August. 10 000 L. ☏ (06) 67 94 362.

Museo delle Cere – *Open daily from 9am to 9pm. 5 000 L.*

Basilica dei SS Dodici Apostoli – Open by appointment (apply at least one week in advance). ☏ (06) 69 95 71.

Oratorio del Crocifisso – Open daily from 7am to 12noon, 4pm to 6.30pm (7.30pm in summer).

Galleria dell'Accademia di San Luca – Open Mondays, Wednesdays and Fridays and the last Sunday of the month from 10am to 1pm (last admission at 12.30pm). Closed Tuesdays, Thursdays, Saturdays, public holidays, throughout July and August. No charge. ☏ (06) 67 98 850.

FORI IMPERIALI

Carcere Mamertino – Open daily from 9am to 12noon, 2.30pm to 5pm (6pm in summer). Donation. ☏ (06) 67 92 902.

Mercati Traianei – Open Tuesday to Sunday from 9am to 6.30pm (1pm Sundays) in summer and to one hour before sunset in winter. Closed Monday and public holidays. 3 750 L; no charge the last Sunday of the month and during National Heritage Week. ☏ (06) 67 90 048.

Casa dei Cavalieri di Rodi - *Open Tuesdays and Thursdays from 9am to 1pm by prior appointment, apply in writing to the Sovrintendenza, Ripartizione X, piazza Campitelli 1, 00186 ROMA.*

San Lorenzo in Panisperna – *For access, ring at the convent.*

FORO ROMANO – PALATINO

Foro Romano – Open daily from 9am to two hours before sunset (1pm Sundays and public holidays. Closed 1 January, 1 May and at Christmas. 12 000 L; no charge on 21 April and during National Heritage Week. ☎ (06) 69 90 110.

Santa Maria Antiqua – Open to specialists only and then only on prior application in writing (at least one week) to the Soprintendenza archeologica di Roma, piazza Santa Maria Nova 53, 00186 ROMA. ☎ (06) 69 90 110.

Palatino – *Same conditions apply as to the Foro Romano.*

Underground Rooms – *By prior application only.*

Casa di Livia - *Closed during restoration.*

GIANICOLO

Palazzo Corsini: Galleria nazionale di Pittura – Open from July to December Tuesday to Friday from 9am to 7pm, Saturday from 9am to 2pm, Sunday from 9am to 1pm. Open the rest of the year Tuesday to Saturday from 9am to 2pm and on Sunday from 9am to 1pm. Last admission 30min before closing. Closed Mondays, 1 January, 1 May and at Christmas. 8 000 L; no charge during National Heritage Week. ☎ (06) 68 80 23 23.

Villa Farnesina – Open Monday to Saturday from 9am to 1pm. Closed Sunday and public holidays. No charge. ☎ (06) 68 38 831.

Gabinetto nazionale delle Stampe – Open Monday to Saturday from 9am to 1pm (although specialists only on Monday). Closed Sunday and public holidays. ☎ (06) 69 98 02 42.

Orto Botanico – Open Monday to Saturday from 9am to 5.30pm (6.30pm during summer). Closed Sunday and public holidays. 4 000 L. ☎ (06) 68 64 193.

Sant'Onofrio – *Open Sundays from 9am to 1pm except during August.*

ISOLA TIBERINA – TORRE ARGENTINA

Museo di Arte ebraica – Open Sunday to Friday from mid-September to mid-June from 9.30am to 1.30pm, and from 2pm to 5pm (2pm Fridays and 12.30pm Sundays) and from mid-June to mid-September from 9.30am to 6pm (2pm Fridays and 12.30pm Sundays). Closed Saturdays and Jewish holidays. 8 000 L. ☎ (06) 68 75 051.

Casa del Burcardo – The Theatre museum is presently undergoing restoration. The **Library** is open Monday to Friday from 9am to 1.30pm (5.30pm Thursdays). Closed throughout August. ☎ (06) 68 80 67 55.

MONTECITORIO

Palazzo di Montecitorio – Guided tours (30min) of the Chamber of Deputies (Camera dei Deputati) the first Sunday of each month between 10am and 4.30pm (groups of 50 people maximum). No charge. ☎ (06) 67 601.

Sant'Antonio dei Portoghesi – Open Monday to Friday from 8.30am to 1pm and from 3pm to 6pm, Saturday mornings only, Sunday between 3.30pm to 6.30pm from early October to late June. ☎ (06) 68 80 24 96.

Museo Napoleonico – Open Tuesday to Saturday from 9am to 7pm, Sundays and public holidays from 9am to 1.30pm. Closed Mondays, 1 January, 1 May and at Christmas. 3 750 L; no charge the last Sunday of the month. Guided tours (1hr). ☎ (06) 68 80 62 86.

Casa di Mario Praz – Guided tour (1hr) daily between 9am and 1pm, 2.30pm and 6.30pm. Closed Monday mornings and some public holidays. 4 000 L. ☎ (06) 68 61 089.

Palazzo Altemps – Open on special authorisation only: ring ☎ (06) 68 33 759.

Sant'Agostino – Open daily from 8.30am to 12noon, from 4.30pm to 6.30pm.

Santa Maria Maddalena – Open by request; apply one week in advance. ☎ (06) 67 97 796.

MONTE MARIO

Villa Madama – Open Monday to Saturday from 9am to 2pm on written request from the Ministero degli Affari Esteri, Cerimoniale diplomatico della Repubblica, Servizio Segreteria. ☎ (06) 36 91 42 84.

PANTHEON

Pantheon – Open Monday to Saturday from 9am to 4.30pm (sunset from April to October), Sunday from 9am to 1pm. Closed 1 January, 1 May and at Christmas. No charge. ☎ (06) 68 30 02 30.

Galleria Doria Pamphili – ♿ (80%). Open Fridays to Tuesdays from 10am to 1pm. Closed Wednesdays, Thursdays, 1 January, at Easter, 1 May, from mid to late August and at Christmas. 12 000 L. ☎ (06) 67 97 323.

PIAZZA NAVONA

Sant'Agnese in Agone – *Open Monday to Saturday from 5pm to 7pm. Sundays and public holidays from 10am to 1pm.*

Santa Maria della Pace – Closed during restoration until end 1996.

Palazzo Braschi: Museo di Roma – Closed during restoration.

Sant'Ivo alla Sapienza – *Open Sunday from 9am to 12noon. During the week by prior arrangement from 9am to 2pm in writing (or fax) from the Rettore di Sant'Ivo alla Sapienza, Corso Rinascimento 40, 00186 ROMA.* ☎ *(06) 68 64 987; Fax: 69 88 64 35.*

San Luigi dei Francesi – Open daily except Thursday afternoons. ☎ (06) 68 82 271.

PIAZZA DEL POPOLO

Santa Maria di Montesanto – *Open April to September, Monday to Saturday from 5pm to 8pm (4pm to 7pm in winter), Sunday from 11am to 1.30pm.*

Santa Maria dei Miracoli – *Open daily 8am to 1pm and from 5pm to 7.30pm.*

Chiesa Anglicana di All Saints – *Open from 8.30am to 12noon. Closed usually on Thursdays.*

PIAZZA DI SPAGNA

Casina di Keats – *Open Monday to Friday 9am to 1pm and from 3pm to 6pm from May to September (2.30pm to 5.30pm from October to April). Closed Saturdays, Sundays, 29 June, second and third weeks in August, a week over Christmas and all public holidays. 5 000 L; no charge for children under the age of 10.* ☎ *(06) 67 84 235.*

Trinità dei Monti – Open daily from 10am to 12.30pm, and from 4pm to 6pm. Best avoided Saturdays when the church is likely to be crowded.

Villa Medici – Temporary exhibitions only, check press for details.

Galleria comunale d'Arte moderna e contemporanea – Open Tuesday to Sunday from 9am to 6.30pm (1pm Sundays). Closed Monday. 10 000 L. ☎ (06) 47 42 843.

Palazzo di Propaganda Fide: Chiesa dei Re Magi – *On written application from the Superiori della Congregazione di Propaganda Fide, Piazza di Spagna 40, 00187 ROMA.*

Ara Pacis Augustae – Open Tuesday to Sunday from 9am to 6pm (1pm Sundays and public holidays). Closed Mondays, 1 January, 1 May and at Christmas. 3 750 L; no charge last Sunday of each month. ☎ (06) 68 80 68 48 (Barracco Museum).

Palazzo Ruspoli – *Open for temporary exhibitions only from 10am to 9pm.* ☎ *(06) 68 32 17 / 68 32 19.*

PIAZZA VENEZIA

Museo di Palazzo Venezia – &. Open Tuesday to Sunday from 9am to 2pm (1pm Sundays and public holidays). Closed Monday, 1 January, 1 May and at Christmas. 8 000 L. The monument rooms are used for temporary exhibitions. ☎ (06) 69 99 43 19.

Chiesa del Gesù: Lodgings of St Ignacius of Loyola – Open Monday to Saturday from 4pm to 6pm and Sunday from 10am to 12noon. These times may change during the summer: ring for details ☎ (06) 67 95 131.

PORTA PIA

Villa Paolina – Access to groups only by prior arrangement at least 15 days in advance. Write to Monsieur l'Ambassadeur, Ambassade de France près le Saint-Siège, via Piave 23, 00187 ROMA. ☎ (06) 48 83 841.

Museo numismatico della Zecca italiana – open daily from 9am to 12noon. Closed public holidays and throughout August. No charge. ☎ (06) 47 61 33 17.

Santa Maria degli Angeli – Open from 9am to 12noon, 4pm to 6pm. ☎ (06) 48 80 812.

Museo nazionale romano – & (50%). Open Tuesday to Sunday from 9am to 2pm (1pm Sundays). Closed Monday, 1 January, 1 May and at Christmas. 12 000 L. ☎ (06) 48 80 530 / 48 90 350.

SAN GIOVANNI IN LATERANO

Basilica di San Giovanni in Laterano: Basilica – Open daily from 7am to 6pm. ☎ (06) 69 88 64 33.

Museo della Basilica – *Open from 9am to 1pm, from 2pm to 5pm (3pm to 6pm in summer). 2 000 L.*

Chiostro – *2 000 L shared ticket with museum.*

Battistero – *Open from 9am to 1pm, 3pm to 5pm (4pm to 6pm in summer).*

Museo Storico Vaticano – *Open each first Sunday of the month from 8.45am to 1.45pm (last admission at 1pm). Guided tour (1hr) on Tuesdays, Thursdays, and Saturdays at 9.30am, 10.45am, 12noon. 6 000 L.*

Scala Sancta e Sancta Sanctorum – Open from 6.15am to 12.15pm, 3pm to 6.30pm (7pm in summer).

Museo degli Strumenti Musicali – Open Tuesday to Saturday from 9am to 2pm (7pm Tuesday and Friday), Sunday and public holidays from 9am to 1pm. Closed Monday, 1 January, 1 May and at Christmas. 4 000 L; no charge during National Heritage Week. ☎ (06) 70 14 796.

Santa Croce in Gerusalemme – *Open from 6am to 12.30pm, 3.30pm to 7.30pm or apply in writing one week in advance to Ufficio Parrochiale, Piazza S Croce in Gerusalemme 12. ☎ (06) 70 14 769.*

SAN PAOLO FUORI LE MURA

San Paolo fuori le Mura – Open Monday to Saturday from 7.30am to 6.30pm, Sunday from 1pm to 4pm. ☎ (06) 54 10 341.

Cloisters – *Closed between 1pm and 3pm.*

SANTA MARIA MAGGIORE – ESQUILINO

Basilica di Santa Maria Maggiore – *Open daily from 7am to 6.45pm, services permitting.*

Loggia Mosaics: *4 000 L – tickets on sale from the souvenir shop at the entrance.* ☎ *(06) 48 81 094.*

Santa Pudenziana – *Open from 8am to 12noon, 3pm to 6pm. If the church is closed ring the bell to the left of the entrance.*

Excavations – Presently closed. ☎ (06) 48 14 622 (Sacristy).

Santa Prassede – Open from 7.30am to 12noon, 4pm to 6.30pm. ☎ (06) 48 82 456.

San Martino ai Monti – *Guided tour between 9am and 12noon, 4pm and 5pm on written application two weeks in advance to Ufficio parrocchiale di San Martino ai Monti, Via Monte Oppio 28, 00184 ROMA.*

Museo nazionale d'Arte orientale – Open Tuesday to Friday from 9am to 2pm (5pm Tuesday and Thursday). Closed Monday. 8 000 L. ☎ (06) 48 74 415.

Auditorium di Mecenate – Open Monday to Saturday 9am to 5pm (7pm in summer), Sunday from 9am to 1pm. 3 750 L; no charge last Sunday of the month. ☎ (06) 48 73 262.

TERME DI CARACALLA

Santa Balbina – Open from 7am to 5.30pm (access through the garden). ☎ (06) 57 80 207.

Terme di Caracalla – Open Monday to Saturday from 9am to two hours before sunset (2pm Mondays), Sunday and public holidays from 9am to 1pm. Last admission one hour before closing time. Closed 1 January, 1 May and at Christmas. 8 000 L; no charge during National Heritage Week. ☎ (06) 57 58 626.

Mithraeum – *Apply in writing to the Sovrintendenza Archeologica, 52 Piazza S Maria della Nova, ROMA.*

Santi Nereo e Achilleo – *Open Saturday to Thursday late April to October from 10am to 12noon, 4pm to 6pm. Closed Friday and from November to late March.* ☎ *(06) 57 57 996.*

San Cesaro – *To gain access, ring at the Porter's Lodge, 4 Via di Porta S. Sebastiano. Donation.*

Casa del Cardinale Bessarione – *Closed during restoration.*

Sepolcro degli Scipioni – *Closed pending restoration.*

Colombarium – *Closed during restoration.*

Colombarium de Pomponius Hylas – Open on written application to the Comune di Roma, X Ripartizione, Ufficio Monumenti antichi e scavi, Via del Portico d'Ottavia 29, 00186 ROMA. ☎ (06) 67 10 34 30 / 70 47 52 84 (Museo delle Mura di Roma).

San Giovanni a Porta Latina – Open daily although it may be advisable to check with Don Franco Costaraoss. ☎ (06) 70 49 17 77.

Porta San Sebastiano: Museo delle Mura - *Open Tuesday and Thursday from 9am to 1.30pm, Saturday from 4pm to 7pm, Sunday and public holidays from 9am to 1pm. Closed Monday. 3 750 L.*

TRASTEVERE

San Crisogono: underground church – Open daily from 7am to 11am, 4pm to 7pm (Sundays and public holidays from 8am to 1.30pm, 4pm to 7pm) – except during services. 2 000 L.

Santa Cecilia – Open daily from 10am to 11.45am and from 4pm to 5pm.

Crypt – Same times apply. Visiting suspended during services. 2 000 L.

Last Judgement by Pietro Cavallini – *Open Tuesday and Thursday between 10am and 11.30am. Donation.*

Quadreria Borghese a San Michele a Ripa – Open Tuesday to Sunday from 9am to 7pm (1pm Sunday and public holidays). Closed Monday. Guided tour Sunday at 10.30am, by theme at 11.45am. 4 000 L.

Museo del Folklore – Open Tuesday to Sunday from 9am to 6.30pm (1.30pm Sundays and public holidays). Closed Monday, 1 January, 1 May and at Christmas. 3 750 L. ☎ (06) 58 16 563.

VATICANO – SAN PIETRO

Basilica di San Pietro – Open from 7am to 6pm (7pm during summer) services permitting.

Museo storico e tesoro – Open from 9am to 5.30pm (6.30pm April to September) Closed at Easter and Christmas. 5 000 L. ☎ (06) 69 88 18 40.

Grotte vaticane – Open from 8am to 5pm (6pm in summer). Closed Wednesday and during services.

Ascent to the Dome – Access from 8am to 5pm (6pm in summer April to September) suspended during services. 6 000 L by lift; 5 000 L by stairs.

Necropoli vaticana – Closed Sunday and during Catholic holidays. Guided tour only (90min) on long-term written application to the Delegato della Fabbrica di San Pietro, Ufficio scavi, 00120 Città del Vaticano (offices open to public Monday to Saturday between 9am and 7pm). ☎ (06) 69 88 53 18. 10 000 L. No children under the age of 14.

Musei Vaticani – ♿. Open daily from 8.45am to 1.45pm (4.45pm from April to mid June and during September and October except Saturdays and last Sunday of the month). Last admission 45min before closing time. Closed all Sunday except the last one of the month, 1 and 6 January, 11 February, 19 March, Easter Sunday and Monday, 1 May, Ascension Day, Corpus Christi, 29 June, 15 and 16 (or 14) August, 1 and 8 November, 25 and 26 December. 15 000 L; no charge last Sunday of the month. Four different guide tours (lasting 90min to 5hr). Audioguides in 6 languages. 4 itineraries disabled visitors. Wheelchairs available on request. ☎ (06) 69 88 33 33.

Cappella Sistina – No photography.

Pinacoteca – *Closes at 1pm.*

Museo missionario etnografico – *Open Wednesday and Saturday from 8.45am to 1.45pm.*

Museo delle Carrozze – *Closed during restoration.*

Vatican City and Gardens – Guided tour (2hr) daily excepting Wednesday, Sunday and public holidays at 10am (in January, February, November and December on Saturdays only) on prior application from the l'Ufficio informazioni. Closed Wednesday, Sunday and same holidays as the Vatican Museums. 16 000 L. ☎ (06) 69 88 44 66 or 69 88 48 66.

VIA VENETO

Casino dell'Aurora – Open Friday from 11am to 12noon on written application 20 days in advance to the Amministrazione Boncompagni Ludovisi, Via Lombardia 46, 00187 ROMA. 10 000 L. ☎ (06) 48 39 42.

Santa Maria della Concezione – *Open daily from 7am to 12noon and from 4pm to 7.30pm.* **Gallery** – *same times as the church. Donation.*

Galleria Nazionale di Arte Antica – Open daily except Monday from 9am to 7pm (1pm on Sunday and public holidays). Closed Monday, 1 January, 1 May. 8 000 L. ☎ (06) 48 14 591.

Santa Susanna: National American Church – Open daily from 9am to 12noon, from 4pm to 7pm except Sunday afternoon. Services in English at 6pm weekdays, 9am and 10.30am on Sunday. ☎ (06) 48 82 748.

Santa Maria della Vittoria – Open from 6.30am to 12noon, 4.30pm to 7.30pm. ☎ (06) 48 26 190.

VILLA BORGHESE – VILLA GIULIA

Museo nazionale di Villa Giulia – Open daily except Monday from 9am to 7pm (1pm Sunday and public holidays). Closed Monday, 1 January, 1 May and at Christmas. Guided tour. 8 000 L.

VILLA BORGHESE - VILLA GIULIA

Galleria nazionale d'arte Moderna – *Open daily except Monday from 9am to 7pm 1pm Sunday and public holidays. Closed Monday, 1 January and 1 May. 8 000 L; no charge for under-18s and over-60s. Note that a large section of the museum is undergoing refurbishment.* ☎ *(06) 32 24 151.*

Museo Borghese – Partially closed during refurbishment. While the entrance to the museum is from the rear of the building, a tour of the collection begins with rooms on the ground floor. Open daily except Monday from 9am to 7pm (1pm Sunday and public holidays). Closed Monday. 4 000 L. Note that a large section of the museum is closed for refurbishment. While work continues 8 000 L. ☎ (06) 85 48 577.

Excursions from Rome

BRACCIANO

Castello Orsini-Odescalchi – Open daily except Monday from 10am (9am in summer) to 12noon and from 3pm to 5pm (6pm in summer). Guided tour (1hr) every hour on Tuesdays, Wednesdays and Fridays; every 30min on Thursdays and Saturdays, every 20min on Sundays and public holidays. Closed Monday except during August, 1 January and at Christmas. 11 000 L. ☎ (06) 99 80 43 49.

CASTELLI ROMANI

Frascati: Villa Aldobrandini – Open Monday to Friday from 9am to 1pm by arrangement with A A S T Del Tuscolo, Piazza Marconi 1 ☎ (06) 94 20 331 (the same day if required).

Grottaferrata: Museo – Open daily except Monday from 8.30am to 12noon (10am on Sunday) and from 4.30pm to 6pm. Closed Monday. No charge. ☎ (06) 94 59 309.

Santa Maria di Grottaferrata – Open daily except Monday from 9am to 12noon, 4.30pm to 6pm. ☎ (06) 94 59 309.

Monte Cavo – *Road toll 2 000 L.*

Nemi: Museo – Open from 9am to 2pm (7pm in summer). Closed certain public holidays. 4 000 L. ☎ (06) 94 59 309.

Ardea: Museo della Raccolta Manzù – Open from 9am (2pm on Monday) to 7pm. Closed 1 January, 1 May and at Christmas. 4 000 L. ☎ (06) 91 35 022.

OSTIA ANTICA

Excavations – *Open from 9am to 7pm in summer (April to September); 9am to 6pm during March and October; 9am to 5pm the rest of the year. Last admission one hour before closing time. Closed 1 January, 1 May and at Christmas. 8 000 L.*

Necropoli del porto di Traiano – Open from 9am to 6pm. No charge. ☎ (06) 65 83 888.

Fiumincino: Museo delle Navi – Open daily from 9am to 1pm and from 2pm to 5pm Tuesday and Thursday only. Closed 1 January, 1 May and at Christmas. 4 000 L. ☎ (06) 50 10 089.

PALESTRINA

Museo archeologico prenestino – Open daily from 9am to 2pm (12noon Sundays and public holidays). 4 000 L. ☎ (06) 95 58 100.

TIVOLI

Villa Adriana – ♿ (40%). Open daily from 9am to one hour before sunset. Closed 1 January, 1 May and at Christmas. 8 000 L. ☎ (0774) 53 02 03.

Villa d'Este – Open from 9am to 6.45pm from April to October, from 9am to 4.30pm the rest of the year. 8 000 L. ☎ (0774) 22 070.

Villa Gregoriana – Open from 10am to one hour before sunset. 2 500 L. ☎ (0774) 33 45 22.

Glossary

BASIC VOCABULARY

si / no – yes / no
per favore – please
grazie – thank you
buongiorno – good morning
buona sera – good afternoon
buona notte – good night
arrivederci – goodbye
scusi – excuse me
piccolo / un po – small / a little
grande – large or big
meno – less

molto – much
più – more
basta! – enough
quando? – when?
perche? – why
con / senza – with / without
l'aeroporto – the airport
la stazione – the station
un biglietto – a ticket
una schede per il telefono – a telephone card

NUMBERS AND NUMERALS

1	– uno	11	– undici	30	– trenta
2	– due	12	– dodici	40	– quaranta
3	– tre	13	– tredici	50	– cinquanta
4	– quattro	14	– quattordici	60	– sessanta
5	– cinque	15	– quindici	70	– settanta
6	– sei	16	– sedici	80	– ottanta
7	– sette	17	– diciassette	90	– novanta
8	– otto	18	– diciotto	100	– cento
9	– nove	19	– dicianove	1 000	– mille
10	– dieci	20	– venti	2 000	– due mila...

TIME, DAYS OF THE WEEK AND SEASONS

1.00 – l'una
1.15 – una e un quarto   one fifteen
1.30 – un ora e mezzo – one thirty
1.45 – l'una quaranta cinque – one forty-five
mattina – morning
pomeriggio – afternoon
sera – evening
ieri – yesterday
oggi – today
domani – tomorrow
una settimana – a week

Lunedì – Monday
Martedì – Tuesday
Mercoledì   Wednesday
Giovedì – Thursday
Venerdì – Friday
Sabato – Saturday
Domenica – Sunday
inverno – winter
primavera – spring
estate – summer
autunno – autumn/fall

SIGHTSEEING AND ORIENTATION

si puo visitare? – can one visit?
chiuso / aperto – closed / open
destra / sinistra   right / left
nord / sud – north / south
est / ovest – east / west
la strada per ...? – the road for ...?
una vista – a view
al primo piano – on the first floor
tirare – pull
spingere – push
bussare – ring (the bell)
i luci – lights

le scale – stairs
l'ascensore – lift
i bagni per uomo / donna – WC facilities men's / ladies
una camera singola / doppia / matrimoniale – a single room, with twin beds, double bed
con doccia / con bagno – with shower / bath
un giorno / una notte – one day / night

FOOD AND DRINK

un piatto – a plate
un coltello – a knife
una forchetta – a fork
un cucchiaio – a spoon
il cibo – food
un piatto vegetariano – a vegetarian dish
un bicchiere – a glass
acqua minerale (gassata) – (fizzy) mineral water
vino rosso / bianco – red / white wine
una birra (alla spina) – a beer (draught)
carne – meat
manzo / vitello – beef / veal
maiale – pork

agnello – lamb
prosciutto cotto (crudo) – ham cooked (cured)
pollo – chicken
pesce – fish (pesca – peach)
uova – eggs (uva – grapes)
verdura – green vegetables
burro – butter
formaggio – cheese
un dolce – a dessert
frutta – fruit
zucchero – sugar
sale / pepe – salt / pepper
olio / aceto – oil / vinegar

SHOPPING

un negozzio – a shop
la posta – a post office
francobolli – stamps
macellaio – a butcher's
pharmacia – a chemist's
sciropo per la tosse – cough mixture
pastille per la gola – throat pastilles
cerotto – sticking plaster
scottato dal sole – sun burn

mal di pancia – stomachache
mal di testa – headache
punture di zanzara / ape / vespa –
mosquito bites / bee- / wasp-sting
il panificio – a baker's
pane (integrale) – bread (wholemeal)
un supermercato – a supermarket
il giornale – the newspaper
pesce vendolo – a fishmonger

URBAN SITES

la città – the town
una chiesa – a church
il duomo – the cathedral
una cappella – a chapel
il chiostro – the cloister
la navata – the nave
il coro – the choir or chancel
il transetto – the transept
la cripta – the crypt
un palazzo – a town house or mansion
una casa – a house
un castello – a castle
un monastero / convento – an abbey /
monastery
un cortile – a courtyard

un museo – a museum
una torre – a tower
un campanile – a belfry
una piazza – a square
un giardino – a garden
un parco – a park
una via / strada – a street / road
un ponte – a bridge
un cimitero – a cemetery
gli scavi – archeological excavations
la barca – the boat
il motoscaffo – motor boat
pericolo – danger
vietato – prohibited or forbidden

NATURAL SITES

il fiume – the river
un lago – a lake
un belvedere – a viewpoint

un bosco – a wood
la spiaggia – the beach
il mare – the sea

ON THE ROAD

l'autostrada – a motorway/highway
la patente – driving licence
un garage – a garage (for repairs)
nel parcheggio – in the car-park
benzina – petrol/gas

una gomma – a tyre
i luci – headlights
il parabrezza – the windscreen
il motore – the engine

USEFUL PHRASES

Parla l'inglese? – Do you speak English?
Non capisco. – I do not understand.
Parla piano per favore. – Please speak slowly.
Dove sono i bagni? – Where are the toilets?
Dove....? – Where's ....?
A che ora parte il treno / l'autobus / l'aereo ...? – At what time does the train /
bus / plane leave?
A che ora arriva il treno ? – At what time does the train arrive?
Quanto costa? – What does it cost?
Dove posso comprare un giornale inglese? – Where can I buy an English news-
paper?
Dove posso cambiare i miei soldi? – Where can I change my money?
Entra! – Come in!
Posso pagare con una carta di credito? – May I pay with a credit card?

Hurry! We burn
For Rome so near us, for the phoenix moment
When we have thrown off this traveller's trance
And mother-naked and ageless-ancient
Wake in her warm nest of renaissance.

Cecil Day-Lewis: Flight to Italy

Index

Cicero — *Names of famous people or events*

Colosseum — Names of places, buildings, monuments and streets

Page number in bold type — Chapter headings

Note: certain sights are listed collectively for easy reference: Arco (arch); Basilica; Casa; Catacombs; Churches, chapels and oratories; Circus; Column; Domus; Fontana (fountains); Forum; Lago (lake); Mausoleum; Museums and art galleries; Palazzo; Piazza; Ponte (bridge); Terme (baths), etc.

Notes

MANUFACTURE FRANÇAISE DES PNEUMATIQUES MICHELIN

Société en commandite par actions au capital de 2 000 000 000 de francs

Place des Carmes-Déchaux - 63 Clermont-Ferrand (France)

R.C.S. Clermont-Fd B 855 200 507

© Michelin et Cie, Propriétaires-Éditeurs 1997

Dépôt légal Septembre 1997 – ISBN 2-06-153902-5 – ISSN 0763-1383

No part of this publication may be reproduced in any form without the prior permission of the publisher.

Printed in the EU 08-1997/1

Photocomposition : A.P.S., Tours

Impression et brochage KAPP, LAHURE, JOMBART, Évreux

Cover illustration by Bernard DUMAS

Michelin Red Guides

Benelux • Deutschland •
España/Portugal • Europe • France •
Great Britain and Ireland • Ireland •
Italia • London • Paris • Portugal •
Suisse, Schweiz, Svizzera

MICHELIN

Travel *with* Michelin

Maps, Plans & Atlases

With Michelin's cartographic expertise you are guaranteed easy-to-read, comprehensive travel and tourist information. And you can also be confident that you'll have detailed and accurate mapping, updated annually to make this collection the best travel companion for any motorist.

Red Guides

Each of these 12 titles, revised annually, offer a range of carefully selected hotels and restaurants rated according to comfort; From the friendly farmhouse to the luxury hotel, there is something to suit everyone.
Titles: Benelux, Deutschland, España/Portugal, Europe, France, Great Britain & Ireland, Ireland, Italia, London, Paris, Portugal, Suisse.

Green Guides

With over 160 titles covering Europe and North America, Michelin Green Guides offer independent travellers a cultural insight into a city, region or country, with all the information you need to enjoy your visit.
Each guide includes recommended main sights with detailed descriptions and colour photographs, accurate plans, suggested routes and essential practical information.

In Your Pocket Guides

These handy pocket-sized guides are designed for short breaks and are available to destinations all over the world. Drawing on Michelin's acclaimed expertise in this field, they offer essential cultural and practical information in an easy-to-read, colourfully illustrated format, to help the reader make the most of any visit.
Titles available in English, 'In Your Pocket" and French, "Escapade".

Michelin Route planner on the Internet

With Michelin's new website all you have to do is type in your start and finish points and your route is planned for you in a matter of seconds, with travel time, distances, road numbers, and tolls, for any destination in Europe
http://www.michelin-travel.com

Michelin
Green Guide
Collection

France

USA

MICHELIN